D0622973

Stanny

STANNY

The Gilded Life
OF
Stanford White

PAUL R. BAKER

THE FREE PRESS
A Division of Macmillan, Inc.
NEW YORK

Collier Macmillan Publishers
LONDON

The Free Press
A Division of Macmillan, Inc.
866 Third Avenue, New York, N.Y. 10022

Collier Macmillan Canada, Inc.

Printed in the United States of America

printing number
1   2   3   4   5   6   7   8   9   10

Library of Congress Cataloging-in-Publication Data

Baker, Paul R.
Stanny: the gilded life of Stanford White/Paul R. Baker.
p.   cm.
Includes index.
ISBN 0–02–901781–5
1. White, Stanford, 1853–1906.   2. Architects—United States—
Biography.   I. Title.
NA737.W5B27   1989
720′.92—dc20
[B]   89–11781
                                                CIP

FOR

Alice Elizabeth Baker

Contents

Contents

Introduction

For some reason, newspaper reporters and his business correspondents all too often could not get his first name right. In the public press and in private letters from people who did not know him personally—and even from a few who did—Stanford White, the American architect, was not infrequently misnamed "Sanford," "Standford," "Sandford," or "Stamford," and on occasion even "Standard" or "Stanfield." He resented such carelessness and frequently dashed off an irritated reply to correct the offender. His mother called him "Stannie" as a child. Many of his friends called him "Stan." A few friends had nicknames for him, such as "Bianco." But to his closest friends as an adult he was usually "Stanny," a slightly matured version of his mother's endearment. White liked that name and its hint of warm affection.

To countless friends, White reciprocated that affection. His range of friendships was vast, and his capacity for friendship was remarkable. He cherished friendships and worked tirelessly and indulgently to maintain and strengthen them. Time and again, others commented on his ability to weave bonds of loyalty and affection. He was, his friend Royal Cortissoz wrote, "a very prince of friends."

To his partners, Charles F. McKim and William Rutherford Mead, in the prestigious architectural firm of McKim, Mead & White, Stanny was not only a close friend but also a talented colleague. White was involved in countless major architectural projects, and he and his partners contributed more to the crafting of the physical character of turn-of-the-century New York than anyone else. In his own designs, White's emphasis on decorative beauty was surely the most striking aspect. Much of his work was truly an architecture of sensuality. Gifted himself as a painter, White brought to his building designs a fine sensitivity for color and texture and for the play of light on surfaces. Suitability of forms, appropriateness of scale, and harmonizing of proportions and relationships were important for him, but even more so was ornamental detail that would both elaborate architectural motifs and delight the beholder's eye. His rich building designs were a striking artistic contribution to America's Age of Elegance.

White, though, was involved in much more besides creating buildings. He was one of the most important interior decorators of the time, setting standards for others to emulate; he was a designer, as well, of countless fine objects, from jewelry and book covers to statue pedestals and picture frames. For a quarter of a century, White was at the center of the New York art community, helping painters, decorators, sculptors, and other artists obtain commissions, purchasing their works, supporting the allied arts in his architectural undertakings, bringing European treasures to America, and serving as an art dealer. He was a major promoter of art in America. More than anyone else at the turn of the century, he was tastemaker for his age.

While still a young man, White became a well-known public figure, called upon several times to help decorate New York and to assist in creating civic extravaganzas for public occasions. At Madison Square Garden, which he designed, he became a producer of public entertainments, a showman and an impresario. An indefatigable collector of paintings and art objects, he created for himself one of the better-known and most opulent homes in New York. He joined all the important gentlemen's clubs in the city and became a central figure in high society. A connoisseur of fine food and drink, of theatrical entertainments, and of shows of all sorts, White savored the pleasures of his city to the fullest. A family man, in many ways devoted to his wife and son, he nonetheless carried on a secret life of pleasure-seeking and philandering, surrounded by a small group of companions. Beneath White's gilded exterior was a life of compulsive behavior and indulgent sensuality, a life that grew increasingly out of control.

Although his name is probably the most widely known of all American architects, next to that of Frank Lloyd Wright, Stanford White is popularly remembered today more for the manner of his death than for specific architectural accomplishments or other achievements. White lost his life, ironically, in the pleasure garden that he himself had created on the roof of Madison Square Garden, the victim of bullets fired by a crazed playboy, who was obsessed by White's intimate involvement with his wife several years earlier.

Perhaps as much as anyone could, Stanny personified the nature, the very essence, of New York City in the late Gilded Age and at the turn of the century. His many activities, his personal code of values, and his life were unique, and yet a telling of what he was and what he wanted and what he accomplished relates to much beyond the man himself. White's life reveals a great deal about the possibilities of Gilded Age urban American life, its opportunities and its promises, but also about its dangers and its tragedies.

1

"A Thorough-bred Man of the World"

~

Pride was widely evident among New Yorkers in 1853, the year of Stanford White's birth: The great Crystal Palace, erected at Sixth Avenue south of Forty-second Street, was opened that year for the Exhibition of the Industry of all Nations. This was the earliest international fair held in the United States and the American response to the London Exhibition of 1851, the first major world's fair of the nineteenth century. Visitors crowded into the large iron-and-glass structure in New York to inspect American machinery, manufactured goods, agricultural products, and works of art, and to marvel at the spectacular "greenhouse" design of the Crystal Palace itself. Compared with later American fairs, the New York Exhibition was small, yet it signaled that the United States was prepared to seek international recognition for its economic and technological achievements and that New York City was ready to proclaim itself a world-class urban center.[1]

Directly across Forty-second Street from the Crystal Palace, the Latting Observatory, an imposing iron-and-timber tower, was also erected as a public attraction for the 1853 fair. Here, paying customers could take that new device, a steam-powered elevator, to two upper landings for views by telescope of the city spread out before them. From the tower the panorama, especially to the south, was spectacular. In the foreground, directly below, was the imposing Crystal Palace, its dome rising 150 feet and the corners decorated by flag-topped minarets. Adjacent to the east, bordering on Fifth Avenue, was the massive Croton Distributing Reservoir. Beyond, the streets and buildings of the lower part of Manhattan Island, where nearly 675,000 New Yorkers made their homes, stretched

1

out in the distance. Church steeples here and there punctuated the mass of three- to five-story buildings, while the edges of the island, along the East River, the upper harbor, and the Hudson, were outlined by the countless masts of ships and vessels.

Below the observation tower, along Sixth Avenue, the viewer could see omnibuses drawn by horse teams along double tracks, bringing visitors to the Crystal Palace. To the east, Fifth Avenue, straight and broad, extended southward to the green expanse of Washington Square, the Gothic towers of the University Building and the South Dutch Reformed Church rising beside it. Northeast of Washington Square, the spectator could glimpse Union Square and the waters gushing from the large fountain there, and, just beyond, thrusting skyward, the tall, light-colored stone steeple of the newly erected Grace Church, the most fashionable place of worship in the city and a masterpiece of Gothic Revival design. The line of Broadway cut south from Union Square to the island's southern tip at the Battery. With a telescope, the viewer at the Latting Observatory might make out in the distance the cupola atop City Hall; the spire of Trinity Church, the highest in the city; possibly the dome of the Merchants Exchange on Wall Street; and, at the southern tip of the island, just offshore, Castle Garden, the circular former Castle Clinton fortification, now used as a civic hall.

At midcentury, New York was bustling, dynamic, exciting. Americans from farms and country towns and newly arrived immigrants from Europe crowded into the city in ever larger numbers. The most cosmopolitan center in the United States and in many ways the cultural capital of the country, New York had a concentration of playhouses, concert halls, art galleries, publishing houses, and hotels and restaurants surpassing any other American place. From Europe, musicians and dancers, actors and lecturers visited the city, attracting large audiences.

Commercial activity dominated New York life, however. In the business districts, the streets were crowded, noisy, and mostly dirty; they were jammed with wagons loaded with goods on their way from factories to warehouses or on to retail establishments. On the crowded sidewalks, women shoppers, their long skirts sweeping the ground, and prosperous merchants in long frock coats, tight-fitting trousers, and stovepipe hats rubbed elbows with raggedly dressed day laborers, cartmen, and newsboys. Broadway, the principal shopping thoroughfare, was lined below Canal Street with dry goods shops, many of them "commercial palaces," so called because of their design in the fashionable "palazzo style," with Italian Renaissance details.

To the north, at Forty-second Street, one repeated visitor to the Crystal Palace Exhibition was Richard Grant White, then in his early thirties and already gaining recognition in New York cultural life. White had been named to the jury on art for the Exhibition and was invited to prepare the illustrated catalogue for the art works displayed there. That same year he prepared a catalogue of the Thomas Jefferson Bryan Collection of European paintings, a group of some three hundred works exhibited in a gallery on lower Broadway. In the years that followed, Richard Grant White became widely known in New York as a journalist and cultural and social critic whose views were sharply expressed. Because of his writings, some men came to fear him, others held him in awe, and still others found him slightly ridiculous. Often highly critical of his fellow New Yorkers, White sought refuge from the abrasiveness of city life within his small family. He was devoted to his wife and two sons, especially to Stanford, the younger, who was born on November 9, 1853, and who grew in maturity to resemble his father physically. What Stanford White became as a person and accomplished in his own life was, to a considerable degree, due to the influence of his father.

Richard Grant White's features were aquiline, his hair, beard, and mustache reddish, and at 6 feet, 3 inches he towered over most other men. He was not easy to ignore either in person or in print. By his mid-twenties, already a familiar figure at the theater and the opera, he was publishing articles of music criticism. It was said that people recognized and stared at him in the busy streets of New York. He usually carried a book with him, and even in the horse cars he would sit reading, tall, erect and indifferent to those about him. Passengers would whisper to one another, "There's Mr. White!"[2]

Some years before the Crystal Palace Exhibition, an 1846 newspaper sketch on life in New York City portrayed the twenty-four-year-old White at Delmonico's restaurant, sitting "in an attitude of listless self-complacency," just finishing his breakfast. He was, the newspaper reported, "a tall, striking-looking man, with a ruddy beard and moustache, setting off a voluptuous and decidedly handsome mouth . . . evidently a thorough-bred man of the world—an epicure, an amateur, a dilettante, a gallant, a critic, almost a coxcomb." One might imagine that the young man had traveled widely; nonetheless, the sketch continued, his travels had been "only between book-covers. There are few operas he does not know—from the score; few pictures, statues, or churches he is not familiar with—by description; but he has in reality never been out of New York." At this time a newspaper music critic, Richard Grant White, the article concluded, was, "prejudice, vanity, obstinacy and all, a remarkable young man" who "wields an intellectual battle-axe between his thumb and forefingers."[3]

The young journalist's musical knowledge was extensive, his taste refined, and his opinions adamant. His first magazine essay, in the *American Whig Review* of June 1846, was one of the earliest critical accounts of Beethoven published in the United States and one of the first important essays on that composer in English. Music, one of Richard Grant White's biographers wrote, was always "the chief pleasure of his life."[4]

White's early articles of music criticism caught the eye of Henry J. Raymond, the managing editor of *The Morning Courier and New York Enquirer*, who invited him to become the music critic for that newspaper. Soon White was asked to provide drama, art, and literary criticism along with lead pieces for the journal. A series of articles he wrote on the question of copyright, an important issue for American writers, attracted widespread attention.

Although only a second-generation New Yorker, Richard Grant White had a long American lineage of which he was very proud, a feeling his son Stanford later came to share. That his roots were deeply planted in American soil undoubtedly gave Richard a secure sense of family position and a firm base from which to pass judgments on American society and culture. John White, the founder of the American family, had come to New England on the ship *Lion* in 1632, settling first in Cambridge, Massachusetts, and then in 1636 moving on to Connecticut to become an original proprietor of Hartford. Richard Grant White once boasted that he was "a Yankee of the Yankees," since his "forefathers sat for a hundred years consistently on the General Court" in Massachusetts Bay Colony.[5]

Among his forebears, it was his paternal grandfather, the Reverend Calvin White, whom Richard most admired. Born in Upper Middletown, Connecticut, in 1762, Calvin White took a degree at Yale College in 1786 and was later ordained as a Congregational minister. Subsequently he became a Presbyterian minister, later yet an Episcopalian clergyman, and finally, in 1821, his religious progression brought him into the Roman Catholic Church. A staunch Tory opposed to American independence, Calvin White deplored America's turn toward popular democracy. To the time of his death at the age of ninety in March 1853, just eight months before his great-grandson Stanford was born, he lived like "a displaced Englishman," feeling out of place in his egalitarian homeland. He was, Richard Grant White wrote, "a better scholar and a better gentleman than I can ever hope to be."[6]

The reverend divine's son, Richard Mansfield White, Richard's father and Stanford's grandfather, was more in tune with the times. Born in Bloomfield, New Jersey, in 1797, he was appointed as a young man to the West Point Corps of Cadets but resigned to enter business in New

York City. He prospered as a shipping and commission merchant in South Street and took a leading role in the establishment of Episcopal Sunday schools in New York City and Brooklyn. Richard Grant White, his eldest son, was born in New York City on May 23, 1822. The well-to-do businessman settled his family in a large house in Brooklyn, where the five children of the family were much indulged by their parents. His later position as secretary and financial manager of the Allaire Iron Works in New Jersey added to his fortune. In the mid-1840s, however, the apparently secure businessman unexpectedly saw his clipper ships driven out by steam-powered vessels and suffered a crushing financial setback. He was "hopelessly ruined." Richard Mansfield White died in poverty at the age of fifty-one on January 19, 1849. His son Richard would never get over the sudden loss of the family fortune and often bitterly lamented his unanticipated penurious condition.[7]

Richard Grant White became interested in music, especially opera, when he was very young. As he later wrote: "I can remember as a child, hardly knowing what the word opera meant, hearing the talk of my elders at the breakfast table about it, and wondering what it could be that excited so much enthusiasm." His first experience was a performance of Beethoven's *Fidelio,* sung at the Park Theatre. As a youth he became an accomplished violinist and cellist. He sang in a church choir and arranged musical programs, and tinkering with stringed instruments was his chief hobby throughout his life. He was "one of the earliest subscribers to the Philharmonic Society" and for twenty years did not miss any of its rehearsals or concerts.[8]

After completing the course of study at the Columbia College Grammar School, to which he traveled from Brooklyn each day by ferry, Richard began his advanced education at Bristol College in Pennsylvania, then transferred to the University of the City of New York (New York University) as a junior. An outstanding student, he was frequently asked to speak in public. In a talk before the Philomathian Society at the University, sixteen-year-old Richard denounced the "increasing spirit of gain" in American society, while in another oration he took the position that the structure of government in the United States was such that it could only lead to corruption. Upon graduation in the class of 1839, White was chosen class marshal. His commencement address dealt with what seemed to him the dominant spirit of enterprise and utilitarianism, which militated against a truly high civilization and true beauty in the country. The pervasive commercialism and materialism of Jacksonian America seemed to the youth completely inhospitable to the development of genteel manners and high literary and artistic achievements. Cultural refinement,

5

he believed, was lacking in America. Only through responsible public criticism, he suggested, could such refinement be seriously cultivated. In later years he followed his own advice, devoting the main energies of his life as a journalist-critic toward seeking that very goal.[9]

After graduation, White first turned to the study of medicine in the office of Dr. Alfred Post, a surgeon, who was a family friend. He spent hours in the dissecting room and served as a "senior walker" at the New York Hospital. White soon discovered, however, that medicine was not to his liking, and he gave it up to immerse himself in study of the law. In 1845 he was admitted to the bar. But the law, too, he realized, was not for him. When his father's financial reverses put the burden of support of two younger sisters on him, Richard took a position for a brief time in the New York Custom House and simultaneously began a journalistic career. By the midpoint of the nineteenth century, Richard was well established as a journalist and acquainted with many prominent literary figures. He soon became known as a scholar as well. Like his grandfather he was ill at ease in America and in many ways out of step with his times. He found much to criticize.

Soon after the 1846 newspaper sketch of Richard Grant White was published, he became acquainted with Alexina Black Mease through her married sister Fanny. Frances Elizabeth Mease Barrow, who became well known as "Aunt Fanny," a writer of popular children's books, aided Richard's courtship of her sister. They were daughters of Charles Bruton Mease from Charleston, South Carolina, and Sarah Graham Mease, whose father was a Scotsman. Although Alexina was not considered a beauty, her sparkling eyes and the amused expression around her mouth gave her a most attractive appearance. Alexina, or Nina, as she was known in the family, had been born on June 4, 1830, and was well educated for the time. She had considerable talent in versifying and shared Richard's interests in music, literature, and art. After Richard and Nina were engaged in 1849, Daniel Huntington painted their companion portraits, which reveal a stern, seemingly self-confident Richard and a pensive, sensitive Nina. They were married on October 16, 1850.[10]

The 1850s were happy years for the young couple, though sometimes difficult because of the frustrations for Richard of the unremitting hard work of Grub Street journalism and the burdens of a growing family with a small income. They had two sons: Richard Mansfield White (Richie or Dick to the family), born on Christmas day, 1851, was named for his paternal grandfather, while Stanford, two years younger, was named for David Stanford, a piano dealer and music-loving friend of the Whites, who was invited to be the baby's godfather. Richard's much younger sister, Augusta, or Gussie as she was called, came to live with her brother and his family. As he would later do with his own sons, Richard took a fatherly interest in his sister's intellectual development, often criticizing her spelling, proposing studies for her, and suggesting books for her to read.[11]

Richard was uncommonly devoted to his young wife; nonetheless, his early letters to her, like those he wrote to Gussie, were often preachy and even condescending. When Nina suggested to Richard that he should leave the uncomfortable country house he was visiting on a trip to Wakefield, New Hampshire, in July 1852, he responded bluntly that her suggestion "involved a want of consideration for the teachings of the golden rule of life which I have noticed before in my dear Nina & which puzzles me exceedingly in one of her truly kind heart & utterly unselfish spirit." He emphasized he could not think of giving any offense to his host.[12]

In another letter to his wife about the same time, Richard touched on the theme that became a leading complaint of his life—his poverty, contrasted to what his earlier expectations had been: "A few thousand dollars would do much toward making you & me happy, would it not, darling? I was rich enough when getting my education to fit me to enjoy money, & have been poor long enough to humble my spirit, & learn content, if not prudence." He then added patronizingly that "my dear Nina has one of those happily constituted minds which do not need discipline to teach them fore-thought & self-denial." In this same letter, Richard asked his wife to kiss Richie, the "dear little monkey . . . for his reputed father & tell him that I could not love him more if I really was his father"—a curious statement, perhaps giving voice to the new father's reluctance to enter upon the responsibilities of parenthood.[13]

To earn extra income, as his small family was enlarged, Richard tried public lecturing, joining the throng of writers who traveled about dispensing cultural enlightenment to Americans. His first endeavor, a talk on the painter Holbein, at Pittsburgh in the winter of 1856 turned out successfully, much to Richard's surprise. "I delivered it well, which I feared might not be the case, & cared nothing for my audience except to interest them—stopped spontaneously to talk to them two or three times,—got a hearty laugh out of them thrice & a couple of hearty rounds. Very well for a first effort, but might be much improved." The train to Pittsburgh had been delayed by snowdrifts, and he had just managed to make it to the lecture on time. Then another lament, which probably reflected a deeper unease in White's soul: "It seems to be my fortune to get through life by the skin of my teeth.'' He could not wait ''to get home to Nina & my boys.''[14]

In the early 1850s, Richard Grant White began preparing an annotated edition of the plays of Shakespeare, a work that along with his other books on the bard would make him one of the foremost Shakespeare scholars of the nineteenth century. Every day from half past seven in the morning until one o'clock in the afternoon and again each evening he devoted himself to his study of Shakespeare. He often worked at the Astor Library on Lafayette Street. Afternoons he spent on his editorial duties on the *Courier and Enquirer* and writing articles for other journals. Books were everywhere in the rented brownstone house that White and his family occupied at 173 East Thirteenth Street. The walls were lined with bookshelves, filled with double rows of volumes, and the large library table was always cluttered with books and working papers. Engravings of Italian Renaissance paintings, a bust of Shakespeare, and a portrait of Beethoven decorated the rooms. Visitors to the house were usually men involved in literature or the arts, though guests were few, since White felt that he could ill afford to entertain.[15]

Although caught up in the literary, artistic, and musical life of the rapidly enlarging city, Richard White believed himself misplaced in New York; he often mused that he would have been more at home among the literati of New England. On a visit to Cambridge, Massachusetts, in May 1857, when his earliest study of Shakespeare and the first annotated volume of the collected works had already been published, White was delighted to be well received there and to become acquainted with several famous writers. Henry Wadsworth Longfellow invited him to dinner; the historian Jared Sparks spent an evening with him; and James Russell Lowell came to call. ''Ah darling,'' Richard wrote Nina, ''they make more of me here than I deserve''—though it is doubtful that he really thought so. A return visit to Boston the following year brought ''countless invitations,'' including one from the mayor himself for a drive through the outskirts of the city. The drive unsettled Richard, however, for he found himself divided ''between delight and envy'' over the lovely country houses he saw in Roxbury and Brookline. Nonetheless, he was gratified again by his reception and by the opportunity to publish articles in Lowell's *Atlantic Monthly*.[16]

White prided himself on his English manner and appearance. People he met on his American journeys often mistook him for an Englishman, even on one occasion for a British officer. ''What pleases me in being taken for an 'Englishman,' '' he once wrote, ''is that it shows me I am free from many of these disagreeable peculiarities of which our British

8

cousins make test points." He sometimes asserted that he was "a misplaced Englishman" and that he had "made a mistake in being born too far west . . . living upon the remotest & most attenuated edge of Christendom; this revolving upon the extreme periphery of civilization, ready to be thrown off at any moment into the unknown regions of barbarism & the chaos of incompleteness, is a very unsatisfactory state of existence." America, alas, lacked the refining touches of traditional social forms and especially of a recognized cultivated upper class. American life, in contrast to European, seemed to him thin and unformed, often coarse and chaotic, views that the novelist Henry James would later develop with consummate artistry in much of his writing.[17]

In June 1858, in a dispute over money, White resigned from the *Courier and Enquirer.* His financial situation quickly became "precarious," and for a time he had to give up his labors on Shakespeare to provide for his pressing family expenses. He worked briefly as editor of the *Albion,* an Anglophile journal, and in the summer of 1860 he helped found and, surprisingly, invested in the *New York World,* which was established as a religious journal in reaction to the sensationalism of many New York newspapers. Considering his constant laments over his penurious state, one wonders just how White managed to purchase the stock, valued at $5,000, in the new venture; possibly some of the money came from a substantial advance on his Shakespeare edition. For a brief time White removed his family from New York to Ravenswood, Long Island, near Hell Gate, where the rent was only a third of the $750 annual sum he had previously paid. In 1861, when the *World* took over the older *Courier and Enquirer,* raising its circulation and taking on a secular perspective, White received no editorial voice. He abruptly terminated his connection with the *World.* It was clear that his personal relationships were often strained when matters did not go his way. A plan he was involved in at the time to establish a journal critical of the new Republican administration was not realized, and his career as a newspaper editor came to an end.[18]

The loss of his regular newspaper income led White to look for a salaried position, and he settled on becoming head clerk of the Revenue Cutter Office of the federal Custom House in New York, an administrative position he held for seventeen years. With a small but steady income, he continued his scholarly work on Shakespeare and turned out an avalanche of articles on questions of the day, most of them highly critical of American manners, which he found abrasive, and American values, which he deemed superficial.

Back in New York, living in a rented house at 186 East Tenth Street,

9

Richard decided to part with some of his library. For years, even though his financial resources were limited, he had been collecting books, spending far more than he could really afford; other books had come to him from the estates of his grandfather and father. In 1860 James Wynne, in *The Private Libraries of New York,* described White's collection as one of the most impressive private holdings in the city. It included rare works, first editions, and autographed copies, many with fine bindings. More than six hundred volumes were by or about Shakespeare, some five hundred fifty were poetry, and two hundred fifty concerned painting and the arts of design. A few were volumes of erotica. The 644 books offered at auction in late January 1861 brought White only about a thousand dollars. He was pleased, however, that what still remained were the best of his holdings.[19]

A few weeks later, on March 4, Abraham Lincoln assumed the presidency, and on April 12 the firing on Fort Sumter in South Carolina brought the outbreak of the Civil War. Despite his antagonism to some of the Republican financial policies, White gave his unswerving support to the Union cause in the Civil War, though Nina, with her family background in the South, may have had mixed loyalties. Richard was elected a second lieutenant of the New York Rifles, and for a time he regularly drilled with the group. In hopes of forwarding the Union position, White once wrote to Lincoln advising the president to order General McClellan, then entrenched before Richmond, to attack the rebels: "For once let us dare, and dare *today,* for days are precious." There is no evidence that Lincoln responded. In 1864, White was named secretary of the large Metropolitan Fair, held in New York City to raise funds for the Sanitary Commission, to provide support for the troops. He refused to accept a salary. George Templeton Strong, a diarist, who also drilled with the Rifles, worked closely with White on the commission and frequently invited him to his home. In his diary Strong characterized White as "a decorated, flamboyant gent . . . generally underrated and slighted, . . . but he is clearly a second-rate fellow." White, Strong wrote, had been "blackballed at the Century three or four years ago," perhaps, we may surmise, because he struck others around him as opinionated and arrogant. The Century Association would later be very important for his son Stanford.[20]

White's most significant Civil War contribution was a series of weekly letters supporting the Union cause, which he sent to *The Spectator* of London, beginning in the summer of 1863. The anonymous letters from "A Yankee" were aimed to help the British understand the Northern position in the war. They were widely reported and commented on both

10

in British journals and in Parliament, and several influential Englishmen judged that they had an impact on public opinion. The letters clearly revealed the author's considerable devotion to American democracy but also underlined his dismay at its deficiencies, somewhat in the same vein as James Fenimore Cooper's *American Democrat*. Most of the problems of the United States, the Yankee suggested, arose from the curse of slavery and from the tremendous influx of uneducated immigrants, who all too quickly gained a vote and a voice in government.[21]

At the close of the Civil War, White's discontent with American life grew deeper. Like Mark Twain and Charles Dudley Warner, whose novel christened the times the Gilded Age, Richard White was disturbed by the materialism, fraud, and dishonesty he saw about him in postwar America. In books and newspaper articles he voiced a bitter attack on his countrymen. A satirical treatment, in mock Biblical language, of Copperhead Democrats and the graft and chicanery of American institutions, in *The New Gospel of Peace* (1863 to 1866), struck a popular response, for the book with the articles reprinted sold more than 100,000 copies and made some $10,000 in royalties for the author. The financial success of this book, however, stood out in marked contrast to the limited sales of most of his works.[22]

Graft and corruption of Tweed Ring leaders in New York greatly concerned him. Two pamphlets, *The Chronicles of Gotham,* published in 1871 and 1872, again were written in Biblical language, with the names of prominent persons only slightly disguised. The graft in Gotham, White suggested, reflected the general attitudes of a crudely materialistic people corrupted by wealth: "For in Gotham if a man had great possessions he might do what was right in his own eyes, even if what was right in his own eyes would have been wrong in the eyes of other men, if he had not great possessions." The moral tone of the day was abysmal, and in this "Age of Burlesque," society sought "only to be amused."[23]

Letters to the editors of the *New York Times* and other newspapers were outlets for White's sharp criticisms of the manners and values of his fellow New Yorkers. One such letter reported on an encounter he had had in a street railway car with a "big, besotted fellow . . . one of our ruling classes," who was smoking a vile cigar and blowing smoke into the faces of the other passengers. When White remonstrated with this "ugly customer," the man loudly abused him and threatened to smash his face in. The conductor refused to interfere in the altercation, and a policeman told White that his only possible remedy was a civil suit. So much for manners in a public conveyance! New Yorkers seldom lived up to his standards.[24]

Several of his newspaper articles of those years dealt with the subject of the American language and stressed the importance of simplicity and common sense in the determination of correct usage for Americans. His 1870 book *Words and Their Uses,* derived from those articles, sold well and went into many editions. White craved serious scholarly recognition for his writings on language and literature, and indeed, it was said, he was twice offered a position as professor of English at the University of the City of New York but declined each time because he did not wish to tie himself to the routines of the classroom. His general public reputation, though, as reflected in Strong's view, was that of an opinionated, arrogant, self-admiring snob. Privately, his letters reveal he was often obsessed by doubts over his writings and dissatisfied with his own achievements.[25]

Although the household was patriarchal, dominated by the outspoken and self-questioning Richard, Alexina, quiet, self-effacing, and clever, was closer to her young sons than her husband was. She, like Richard, took great delight in the children. Her feelings were evidenced in poems, some of which she must have written in the late 1850s, though they were not published until 1879 as *Little-Folk Songs.* Two of the verses dealt directly with young Stanford and his activity and exuberance. In "My Boy Stannie," she characterized her son, in a Scottish dialect, as a "Wee busy mannie! / Aye trottin' roun' the garden lot, / Wi' Wheelbarrow, spade, and waterin'-pot / All bent and battered!" "Stannie's Hiding" pictured a mercurial "scalawag" always hiding from his mother: "Where is Stannie, where can he be? / Where is he hiding away from me?" (He was finally discovered "tucked under grandmamma's gown.") The mother's intense love for her sons permeates these verses, but a note of fear creeps in about the future, made explicit in the dedication: "Hope strives with dread / To see you stand forth men."[26]

Of the two boys, Richie, more temperamental and more troublesome than his brother, especially caused his parents concern. In an October 1858 letter to Nina, then away from the city visiting relatives, Richard announced "Good news for dear little Stannie. Stanford [the godfather] has conveyed to me fifty shares of stock as trustee for him. They are worth but $500 now, but will surely be worth $5000 ere long. So it will be always. Stannie, darling little soul, will have benefits showered upon him, but my poor boy Richie will have few real friends or efficient friends, except the father whose unhappy name he bears—& how efficient even his love can be is yet to be discovered."[27]

When Stanford, a lively red-haired lad, was six or seven years old, his parents entered him in the public Grammar School No. 35 at 74

West Thirteenth Street, which he and Richie attended for six years, walking there from their home on East Tenth Street. The school was a large one, with more than a thousand boys enrolled. Each morning the students assembled for prayers and Bible reading, conducted by the principal, Thomas Hunter, who subsequently took charge of the city college that bears his name. In later years, when he was questioned about this time, Stanford White could recall nothing of any particular interest about elementary school, possibly because he did not wish it generally known that in those early years he had had to attend public school classes. Indeed, in later published autobiographical sketches, he maintained that he "was educated in private schools and under tutors," in this case constructing a past for himself that related to the person he wished to be. The experiences of Stan and his brother at this school probably had an influence on their father's attitude toward public school education: In a series of articles in the 1880s, Richard White attacked the public school system for failing to teach fundamentals of education and, especially, to inculcate discipline.[28]

Although their grammar school education was unexceptional, Stanny and his brother were indulged by their parents, who bought them many books and sent them for long summer holidays to the home of their maternal aunt, Mrs. Laura Fellows, near Newburgh, some 50 miles north of New York City, and to paternal relatives in Orange, New Jersey. When Stanny was thirteen, he and Richie hiked more than 100 miles on a four-day trip in New Jersey. Already Stanny had shown marked talent as an artist. It was reported that he had begun to draw almost as soon as he could hold a pencil. Before he could spell his name, he painted a watercolor of a bird and a morning glory as a present for his father. By the time he was twelve he was making sensitive pencil and wash sketches of trees and river scenes, and depicting mills, barns, and old houses that had caught his eye. Julian Hawthorne, the son of Nathaniel Hawthorne, remembered the youth about this time as a "handsome little lad, fond of drawing fantastic houses on bits of paper" and "quick at arithmetic and algebra." Those early drawings and watercolors foreshadowed Stanny's principal avocation in years to come.[29]

In 1867 Richard and Nina moved from their East Tenth Street house in New York to the rural countryside of Bay Ridge in Brooklyn, near Fort Hamilton and The Narrows. Though Stanny was apparently a model pupil, Richie, before the move, had been having problems in school: He was, his father reported, considered "forgetful, mischievous, and troublesome," and had gotten into particular trouble for flashing light reflected from a mirror about a classroom. In Bay Ridge, Stanny kept his artistic interests secret from the boys of the neighborhood, perhaps for fear of ridicule; at least one young friend of that time later expressed surprise to learn of his artistic talent.[30]

Richard Grant White's pride in Stanny grew when the younger son showed ingenuity in carpentry and building. One September day in 1868, the father and his sons dug a drainage ditch near their Bay Ridge house; a covering was needed over the road so that vehicles could pass: "The contrivance by which we were enabled to accomplish this last was Stanny's, who was very quick & saw well what was needed, but, dear little soul," his father wrote, he "told it in such a head over heels way that I could not understand him. Tom Burns did & said that 'the youngest man of the lot was the wisest.' "[31]

The family remained at Bay Ridge for about two years. The Brooklyn home, however, was inconvenient for Richard and his work, and so they returned to Manhattan to take another house rental at 118 East Tenth Street, which would be the family residence for the 1870s. In Brooklyn and on their return to Manhattan, the boys may have attended private school classes or may have had tutorial instruction.

Soon after their move from Bay Ridge back to New York, Richard Grant White reluctantly decided once again to sell at auction a good part of his book collection, which now numbered more than 5,500 volumes. He supervised the preparation of a sale catalogue with 3,281 entries offered to the public in four auction sessions in October 1870. The *New York Times,* in an editorial taking note of the White auction, suggested that "such an opportunity for acquiring really valuable editions does not occur above a few times in one generation." The sale books included volumes on history, travel, art, poetry, drama, Shakespeare, and women, the latter category including works of erotica. But the auction brought only a small return to White, many of the volumes going for just a few pennies. In a subsequent front-page article, the *Times* expressed the view that "the biddings were too much in the hands of a few professional dealers," who worked in concert to keep prices down. Yet another disappointment for White.[32]

The fact that Richard Grant White, the collector of books on women and of erotica, was "unusually susceptible to beauty in women," as one biographer later put it, is evident from his frequent epistolary references to young ladies, even in letters to his wife. He obviously had an eye for female beauty and was sometimes disparaging if women did not measure up to his standards of appearance or appropriate female behavior. On a trip to Niagara Falls: "Twelve women at breakfast with me. All ugly, all ill dressed, all with bad figures, all talked through their noses." As for actresses, Richard found "no particular charm in their society except a certain freedom from restraint that makes intercourse with them easier than it is with purely domestic women." Actresses often tended to exhibit "the open-hearted freedom of a good fellow," their "womanly weaknesses and graces being . . . a little more pronounced" than was usual in women. One evening in New York, White befriended a young lady who had become separated from her mother, had lost her way on Broadway, and was very upset. The moment she realized where she was and regained her bearings, though, "she became sharp & self-reliant & independent"—which White did not like at all. As she regained her composure, he reported, "she disgusted me by her lack of womanly weakness & trust. . . . She was a regular 'American' woman, Confound them." White was most attracted by lovely young women who looked to him for guidance and protection.[33]

Besides Nina, who always played the subordinate role in their marriage, Richard found at least one other woman who satisfied his particular need for female companionship. According to his friend the author Julian Hawthorne, Richard Grant White had a mistress in New York, a woman of whom he was very proud. White once told Hawthorne, "among other sacred confidences, of a woman whom he had found and loved in New York, how beautiful in all ways she was, and she was English." In the early twentieth century a rumor circulated in the White family that for years Richard Grant White had actually maintained two separate households, indeed that he was a bigamist. A letter from White requesting advice for the education of a girl of an age to have been his daughter was taken as evidence of his "other family," as was his constant poverty over the years despite a prolific journalistic output with a steady income from the Custom House. White's "poverty," undoubtedly, was due at least in part to his large-scale collecting of rare books and musical instruments. Despite Richard's philandering—of which Stan as a young adult must have become aware—the father prized his regular family life, and his surviving letters, it must be emphasized, are permeated by feelings of great warmth toward his wife and his sons.[34]

A small volume that Richard White published in 1871 is curiously revelatory. *The Fall of Man* was a humorous gibe at the currents of evolutionary thought in the air since the publication of Charles Darwin's *Origin of Species* (1859) and *The Descent of Man* (1871). In this tale, dedicated to Darwin, the narrator relates the story of a visit he had recently made to Africa, where, after encountering Dr. Livingston, the explorer, at the source of the Nile River, he had been taken to a mass meeting of gorillas. There he heard a large and solemn male gorilla lecture on "the fall of man," a mournful tale of descent from "the glorious perfection of monkey-hood" to the degenerated condition of humanity. As the narrator stood listening, he suddenly found himself the object of "amorous attentions" from a large female gorilla, who with "a loathsome leer" advanced on him. As he turned to run away through the jungle, tree branches stripped off all his clothing except for his gun belt. Finally, to ward off her insistent advances, the naked narrator had no choice but to shoot her with his pistol.[35]

At that moment, in a striking revelation of sexual ambiguity, the protagonist discovered that "my enamored female was a male," and he had been "saved not from marriage but from death." The dying gorilla asked why the man had hurt him so and explained that he had only wanted to show the narrator some good coconut trees and talk things over with him. Then "drawing my ear down near his lips," the gorilla uttered his final words: " 'Don't go on supposing that every female that may look pleasantly and seek your society has selected you.' . . . He died, and I walked slowly on, musing upon my adventure, a more modest, if not a wiser man." Surely this note of admonition in the climactic passage of the book was more than just a humorous twist to this tale, with its extraordinary sexual innuendo. Two of Richard's readers were his teenage sons; what better way might there be to provide some fatherly, cautionary advice about possible dangers of casual involvements with women?[36]

At the time this volume was being written, White seemed increasingly dissatisfied with the life he was leading. He often expressed a longing to get away from the drudgery of his Custom House job and of churning out articles. "I am weary, so weary of this grind," he wrote Nina. "Sampson in the mill, with his blindness and without his strength." Perhaps, he suggested, he himself was to blame for his failure to attract the really large audience and gain the financial security he longed for. And he blamed himself for involving Nina in this life of unremitting toil. "My folly. Let's begin it all over again & do it better. . . . And you; Poor girl, what did you do it for? But my little woman *you* needn't go to worry. Stan's all right. Dick'll come right, dear good Dick; & as for me, perhaps after a little while even I'll come right."[37]

That Richard would feel that Stan, his artistically talented, well-behaved, and ingenious younger son, was "all right" is not surprising. The father adored the by now lanky, red-haired, good-looking boy and had great expectations for him. Others around Stan, too, found the lively, outgoing youth remarkably engaging. He was well liked. In 1870, Stan's life would take an important turn that would ultimately affect the entire White family.

2

"Mr. R."

R ichard Grant White's involvement with music and literature and his interest in painting and the decorative arts as well as the general cultural atmosphere of the Whites' home helped foster young Stanford's artistic talent. With no formal instruction in drawing or painting, Stanny as a boy already had demonstrated a remarkable artistic gift with an ability to create striking compositions and convey on paper a sense of outdoor atmosphere or a particular mood. He greatly enjoyed his art and eventually decided he wanted to follow a career as a painter. In post–Civil War America, however, the vocation of an artist seemed so uncertain that he did not even know how to prepare himself. Systematic art instruction was scarce, and American painters were largely self-taught. Stan went to the painter John La Farge, a friend of his father, for advice.

La Farge, who had struggled to make a living and achieve recognition during ten years' work as a painter, bluntly told young White to abandon his thoughts of a painting career. La Farge judged that Stanny had "some of the gifts of the painter" but, all in all, would do better and achieve more in architecture. "White's bent for building and decorating was decisive," he pronounced. To assist his son, now determined on a career in the arts, Richard Grant White, who years before had floundered about from one career to another, sought advice about the boy's choice of a profession and appropriate training from Frederick Law Olmsted, the well-known landscape designer. Olmsted, already famous for his work on the design for Central Park, came to the same conclusion as La Farge and took it upon himself to introduce the journalist to the architect Henry Hobson Richardson, then working from a small office at 6 Hanover Street, near the southern tip of Manhattan Island. Richardson talked with Stanny and was obviously impressed by his artistic ability. He agreed to take him into his office.[1]

17

In the late summer of 1870, when Stan entered Richardson's office, he was only sixteen years old. Very tall, rather thin, freckle-faced, and greenish gray-eyed, the red-haired youth already exhibited the ebullience and enthusiasm that later so characterized the mature man. His intelligence was lively, and, just as he had rapidly determined a solution to the problem of the drainage ditch as a young boy, he quickly grasped and worked out the problems he now faced in his work. His skill in drawing was soon expanded to include architecture and the arts of design. He had an almost instinctive feel for materials and their uses and quickly learned to deal constructively with issues of space, mass, and form. Although he had not had any advanced education, he was broadly culti- vated for his age, and he is not known ever to have expressed regrets that he entered professional training at so early an age, forgoing a college education. Associated with Richardson, he could absorb all the factors needed in the making of important, high-quality architecture.

At the time, the thirty-two-year-old Richardson had been practicing architecture in New York for just four years. One of the first Americans to study at the Ecole des Beaux-Arts in Paris, he had received formal academic training surpassed among American architects only by that of Richard Morris Hunt, who had preceded him to the Ecole and had returned in 1855 to take up practice in New York. Richardson's office was therefore a superb place for a talented youngster to learn the fundamentals of architectural practice. During his eight years with Richardson, Stanny learned a great deal.[2]

Young White's education in his new vocation was typical of the times. By the beginning of the 1870s young American men aspiring to an architectural career customarily began their training as apprentices in the office of an architect already working in the field. A very few Ameri- cans went to Paris to the Ecole des Beaux-Arts for systematic instruction and the congenial stimulation of an atelier under the guidance of a distin- guished senior practitioner. In New York City, Richard Morris Hunt had set up in 1857 an American atelier providing architectural instruction on the French model for a few select students, but it did not last long. The first specialized courses of architectural study were established at the Massachusetts Institute of Technology in 1868, the University of Illinois in 1870, and Cornell in 1871. In 1867, the American Institute of Architects, founded ten years earlier, had become a national association, working for higher standards of training, design, and construction, and for public recognition of the new profession.

Richardson at once provided his young assistant with a personal model of a successful creative artist. Well-educated and highly confident of his ability, Richardson was blessed with tremendous vitality and infectious enthusiasm. Here was an impressive older role model utterly different from Stanny's own supercritical, chronically dissatisfied, often pompous, self-questioning father. Just under 6 feet tall, with a full beard and moustache, "Mr. R.," as Stanny usually referred to him, enjoyed the pleasures of the table and was already showing the corpulence that later became disabling and grotesque. The architect's brilliant smile, his wit and humor, his slight stammer, and his cordiality all drew others to him. A legislator at Albany once said of Richardson that "he would charm a bird out of a bush." People wanted to please him.[3]

Richardson's background was considerably more cosmopolitan than young White's, and he had been brought up accustomed to a far more lavish style of living. The architect's Southern-born mother was a grand-daughter of the celebrated English scientist and theologian Joseph Priestley, and his father was a native of Bermuda. He had spent a comfortable childhood on the Priestley plantation in Louisiana and in New Orleans. He had hoped to enter the United States Military Academy to train as a civil engineer, but a speech impediment proved a barrier. After attending Tulane University for a year, he enrolled at Harvard, where he was accepted into the most select college clubs and enjoyed considerable social prominence. He graduated with the class of 1859, then traveled to France. Richardson was admitted to the Ecole des Beaux-Arts on his second try at the entrance examinations in 1860 and joined the atelier of Jules-Louis André. He came back to the United States briefly in 1861–62, then returned to Paris. The Civil War cut off funds from his family, however, and he could attend the Ecole for only a short time after his return. In October 1865 he arrived back in the United States, and in 1866 set up an architectural practice in New York, entering into partnership in 1867 with Charles Gambrill, who had previously been associated with George B. Post, both of them former pupils of Richard Morris Hunt. Richardson became the designing partner of the new firm, while Gambrill took charge of business matters.

When Stan came into the Gambrill & Richardson office, he no doubt worked first as a general helper and office assistant while receiving instruction in drawing. Architecture, White later counseled, "depends on draughtsmanship more than anything else, because it is in this way only that ideas can be expressed"; anyone going into architecture must, above all, "give as much of his time as possible to the study of free hand and mechanical drawing." For the young apprentice the most important direct influence in the office after Richardson himself was the head draftsman of the small firm, Charles Follen McKim.[4]

McKim, twenty-three years old that summer, was of medium height and blue-eyed, with a very high and prominent forehead and reddish hair, but already beginning to turn bald. As a beginning architect young McKim exhibited many of the personal qualities that characterized his later adult life. He always impressed acquaintances by his high-mindedness, his noble "idealistic spirit." His convictions about art and most other matters were firm, yet his manner was quiet, unassuming, deferential, and invariably polite, and he seemed to be able to bring others around to his viewpoints so effortlessly that he became known as "Charles the Charmer."

Like Richardson and Hunt, McKim had also studied in Paris at the Ecole des Beaux-Arts, where he had been associated with the atelier of Pierre-Gérôme-Honoré Daumet. Born on August 24, 1847, in Chester County, Pennsylvania, McKim had grown up in a household intensely devoted to the abolitionist cause. His father served as the publicity agent of the Pennsylvania Anti-Slavery Society and later as corresponding secretary of the American Freedmen's Relief Association, and his mother had been raised as an ardent antislavery Quaker. In the fall of 1866, Charles entered the Lawrence Scientific School at Harvard College, intending to become a mining engineer; for recreation at Harvard he played on the baseball team. He did not find the training he shortly came to want at Harvard, however, and left after only one year. In the summer of 1867 he spent a few weeks working in the architectural office of Russell Sturgis in New York and then went on to Paris and the Ecole, where he studied three years, working in Daumet's atelier. McKim visited England in the summer of 1869 and became well acquainted with Gothic Revival architecture there. He made a general European tour, including visits to Germany, Austria, and Italy. More than any other place in Europe, the city of Rome captivated him. Just before the outbreak of the Franco-Prussian War he returned to the United States, and soon after his arrival in late May 1870 he entered the office of Gambrill & Richardson as head draftsman, at a salary of eight dollars a week.[5]

Recently returned from travel in Europe and from the classes at the Ecole and the rigorous design projects of his atelier, McKim had a fund of architectural information and shrewd advice about tricks of the trade to impart to his enthusiastic young assistant. Stanny liked and respected the older draftsman, and McKim immediately recognized Stanny's artistic talent. It soon became apparent to those in the small office that though White had not received previous architectural training, he surpassed McKim in his drawing skill, especially in delineating room interiors with an impressionistic flair. McKim, by contrast, brought his well-organized, systematic design abilities to bear in creating tightly integrated and highly precise drawings.

On the projects undertaken by the firm, Richardson's technique of design was to provide a small and very rough sketch of his conception to the draftsmen and then, as the design developed, to make numerous suggestions so that eventually the final design was very much his own, even though he had drawn nothing beyond the original rough sketch. As this process went on, the assistants learned how to develop architectural ideas and realize in precise ways what were initially often inchoate ideas. They "learned to think for themselves, to design for themselves," one critic wrote. Richardson's method, as one of his chief assistants later said, "was not teaching but suggestion and inspiration. [He] had the faculty of drawing clever men to him and enthusing them." His men were devoted to him.[6]

Yet Richardson was always ready to modify plans in order to accommodate his clients. Like Hunt, who reportedly said that he would build a house upside down standing on its chimney if a client wanted it that way, Richardson once wrote: "I'll plan anything a man wants, from a cathedral to a chicken coop. That's the way I make my living." Yet, again like Hunt, he usually brought clients around to his ideas as to what was appropriate and most attractive for a building. To one client, Richardson was "the most versatile, interesting, ready, capable and confident of artists, the most genial and agreeable of companions."[7]

Richardson's earliest projects differed little from what other American architects at the time were doing in the English Victorian Gothic Revival and the French Second Empire styles, which, with the Italianate, dominated fashionable building design in the late 1860s and early 1870s. His first commission, Unity Church in Springfield, Massachusetts, was a handsome Gothic Revival structure, which the architect won in competition in 1866 and completed in 1869. Other church, domestic, and commercial building projects, along with a large high school in Worcester, Massachusetts, followed. Then, in July 1870, a major commission for the Brattle Square Church on Commonwealth Avenue in the new Back Bay section of Boston was awarded to the firm. Here, what became Richardson's characteristic style began taking shape, with round-arch windows and a triple round-arch arcade, the outer walls of rugged texture, quarry-faced stone. Dominating the church was a powerful 176-foot tower, its most distinctive feature a carved frieze of the Sacraments, with four angels at the corners blowing trumpets (leading to the popular name, "Church of the Holy Bean Blowers"). McKim came into the office just as the competition drawings for the Brattle Square Church had been completed, and the modifications after acceptance and the detailed working drawings surely came in large part from his hand.[8]

Two other substantial projects—the Buffalo State Hospital, a large insane asylum, and the Hampden County Courthouse in Springfield, Massachusetts—were soon in full progress in the office, and the great amount of detailed work necessary for them no doubt was the reason that young White was taken on in the small office. With those and some smaller projects, Stan in his first months with Richardson became well acquainted with the workings of a busy architectural office and could see how competitions were carried on, how projects were developed, and how designs were modified and implemented. Here in the small New York office was intense and practical architectural education, rather different from the formal, abstract training of the Ecole in Paris.[9]

The first house White worked on in Richardson's office was a large summer cottage for Frank Williams Andrews built overlooking the sea at Middletown, Rhode Island. Construction on the Andrews house was begun in July 1872 and completed in 1873. Influenced to some extent by the ideas of Norman Shaw, a prominent English architect instrumental in developing what became the popular Queen Anne style, Richardson arranged the principal rooms of the house about a large living hall from which the massive main staircase ascended. Although the Andrews house in the picturesque massing of the forms was similar to other cottages being built in the Newport area about the same time, the use of shingles on the upper exterior surfaces was innovative, an early step in the development of the American shingle style. The emphasis on surface texture in this house no doubt pleased young White. With his painterly instincts, he would develop this mode further.[10]

But Trinity Church in Boston gave Stanny his first chance to demonstrate his skill as a draftsman. Soon after the Reverend Phillips Brooks became rector of Trinity in 1869 a decision was made to build a large new church for the growing congregation in the newly opened Back Bay section of Boston. The competition for Trinity Church was an important one: Six architectural firms were invited on March 12, 1872, to submit designs. Richardson entrusted McKim with preparing the firm's competition drawings, which were rushed to completion by May 1. A month later, on June 1, the commission was awarded to Richardson. During the time that the designs were being considered by the selection committee, additional property was acquired by the church, and in June Richardson revised his prize-winning entry to accommodate it to the enlarged site. New plans were turned over to the church by April 1873, the same month that work began on the foundation piles.[11]

In June 1872, soon after the award of Trinity Church, however, McKim resigned from Gambrill & Richardson to set up his own architectural office. He moved into two small rooms adjoining his former employers, now at 57 Broadway, and continued to do occasional work for them. On McKim's departure, the Trinity Church drawings were placed in the charge of eighteen-year-old Stanford, a stunning achievement for a man of that age. In the coming months the Trinity Church design was revised with innumerable changes, so that almost nothing was left from McKim's competition drawings except the plans. White later asserted that he had "made every drawing for Trinity Church, Boston, with my own hands." That the senior architect would entrust this important project to the young draftsman is convincing evidence that Stan, by his work over the previous months, had established a firm basis for Richardson's confidence in him.[12]

Soon there were frequent trips for Stan from New York to Boston to meet with the Trinity Building Committee as well as tedious journeys to Buffalo to look after the work on the state asylum and to Springfield, where he superintended the Hampden County Courthouse work. In a letter to his mother in February 1873, Stan wrote that he had spent so much time with architectural committees that he felt he "had been standing on my head all week." While on the road he and Richardson rewarded themselves liberally with food and drink—Stanny, "unteetotal-like" with champagne for dinner, and Richardson, with "brandies, gins, wines and cigars" and boiled tripe, "which he still insists on calling the 'entrails of a Cow.' " Stan was often tired and uncomfortable on these trips. He wrote his mother time and again that he wanted nothing more than to be back at home or at his aunt's place in Newburgh, where he had spent holidays since early childhood. Sometimes his funds ran low. "Thursday, Buffalo": "Left Boston at 9 P.M. Tuesday, in the beastliest sleeping car it has been my lot to inhabit. If Mr. Richardson don't join me, I shall be in a state of bankruptcy." But there were holidays, too, and White's sketches of an old well near Woodstock, Vermont, and Black Rock at Lake George provide evidence of temporary release from his labors.[13]

In the office, Stan was closest to Charles Rutan, some two years older than he, who had come into the firm as an office boy before Stan arrived. Rutan would spend his entire career with Richardson and the successor firm after Richardson's death, becoming highly accomplished as a structural engineer. One observer in the early 1870s was struck by the "strong religious ideas" of White, the younger of these apprentice architects. Stan, like many young people in their late teens, for a time, it appears, became caught up in religious fervor, just as his great-grandfather had throughout his life. One day the two young men were sent out to take measurements of a church about to undergo alterations. "Entering by the Sacristy door they were obliged to pass before the altar. The church was unheated and Rutan without removing his coat or hat immediately set about taking the measurements." A few moments later, Rutan noticed Stan "still kneeling before the altar in prayer. His religious devotions finished, White launched forth in a strong criticism of Rutan's lack of faith, and the resulting controversy seriously affected the exactness of the measurements." Stan for a while, it was said, absolutely refused to take pay for work he had to do on Sundays. When Rutan tried to make White change his mind, "White replied hotly, 'To work on the Sabbath is to break one of the Ten Commandments and so I take no pay for it.'" After Richardson insisted that he accept his wages for Sunday work, Stan was said to have turned the money over to a religious society. Within a short time, however, young White's intense religiosity had vanished.[14]

Stan's brief spurt of religious intensity was no doubt largely eroded by the continuing interest and pleasures of his position with Richardson in the workaday world. The hours were long and the work load heavy, but the frequent travel, the fine food and drink, the consultations with well-to-do, socially prominent clients, and the use of costly materials for construction and decoration that became a regular part of his job introduced young White to a new world of high living much different from the genteel, penurious conditions of his childhood. His duties were varied, often fascinating and exciting, and he came to enjoy greatly the life-style associated with the work. Richardson lived well: The senior architect's accumulations of fine objects, his extravagant purchases of expensive clothing, his indulgence in rich food and drink—and his chronic indebtedness—made a strong impression on his young assistant.

By the time the final plans for Trinity Church were accepted, Richardson had decided to relocate in the Boston area in order to be closer to his most important commission. His partner, Charles Gambrill, remained in New York, while Richardson settled in 1874 in Brookline, close to Boston. Here, in his house on Cottage Street, he set up his studio-office. Stan continued to live with his parents and work in the New York office, where most of the drafting was done, though he frequently visited Brookline and traveled from one job to another. Just after the architect moved to Brookline, Stanny wrote to his "Darling Mama" that "We've been a whole week preparing for work, 'organizing' Mr. R. calls it—& nothing done." Then he added, "I am never away from home two days, but (strange as it may seem to you) I'm deuced impatient to get back again. . . . Mr. R. sends his regards."[15]

After they were settled, White found some compensation for being away from his own family, especially at Brookline: He had his own drafting table in the Brookline studio, and while there he became a temporary member of Richardson's extended family. The senior architect found enormous pleasure in the company of his six children, sometimes consulted them as to the placement of doors and windows in buildings under design, encouraged them to entertain clients, and lavished presents on them. Stanford liked Richardson's children, especially his daughter Julia, to whom he was particularly close; he often took her skating on a nearby pond in the winter, and casting, fishing, and bathing in the summer.[16]

In the Brookline studio, Stan devoted himself largely to Trinity Church. For the church project, the original Romanesque competition design included a very high Flemish-type tower "resembling the sections of a spy glass partly closed." But when Norcross Brothers, the contractors who were building the church, had completed the first stage of the tower, they cautioned that the pile foundations were not strong enough for the tower and the "excessive complications" they were supposed to carry. The design had to be changed. In its final form, Richardson returned to a tower concept he had created for a rejected Connecticut State Capitol project of February 1872, which looked back to the Torre del Gallo of the twelfth-century Old Cathedral of Salamanca in Spain. Lightening his earlier tower design by additional openings and reinforcing the upward thrust with elaborated dormer pediments on each of the four faces, as in the Salamanca prototype, Richardson—most likely with White's assistance—created what his early biographer, Mariana Griswold Van Rensselaer, called "the most beautiful feature of the whole." For Mrs. Van Rensselaer, the tower had "that felicity which we instinctively call artistic rightness." Stan executed an impressive drawing of the new design.[17]

As funds for the interior decoration of Trinity Church were made available, White became friendly with several artists he would be close to for many years. Richardson brought in John La Farge to take charge of the wall murals. Frank Millet, Kenyon Cox, and Francis Lathrop were among the artists employed to work on the church walls, as was Augustus Saint-Gaudens, whom Stanny had previously come to know in New York before the work on the Trinity project. As a painter himself, White was particularly drawn to those artists. With only five months until the consecration in February 1877, La Farge and his assistants faced a tremendous challenge, racing to complete their work. The roof had not yet been finished when they began in September 1876, and working conditions inside the church were hazardous.

Trinity Church was the turning point of Richardson's career. The massive, rugged-walled, Romanesque-style structure became the most widely acclaimed American building of the late nineteenth century. In an 1885 poll of architects, Trinity Church easily led the list of the ten best American buildings; indeed, five of Richardson's works stood among the top ten selected that year by American architects. A 1982 poll of architects who voted on the best American buildings constructed in the previous one hundred twenty-five years again placed Trinity Church among the top five choices. With Trinity Church, Richardson became one of the best-known architects of the day, much sought after; his personal Romanesque style became a significant influence on the architecture of his time. Stan could not have found himself at the feet of a better master.[18]

As the large and complex Trinity Church project evolved and Mr. R.'s reputation ascended, commissions poured into the office, and Stan was kept very busy. One of the more important projects Stan worked on was the William Watts Sherman house in Newport, Rhode Island. Already Newport was developing into the leading summer resort for wealthy and socially prominent Americans, and the town would later become the center for the most lavish and luxurious domestic buildings in the country. In Newport, White would later create some of his most interesting buildings, and this early work for Richardson marks the start of his involvement with rich and grand houses. Sherman was a well-to-do New York banker who had married the sister of George Peabody Wetmore, later governor of and senator from Rhode Island and the very wealthy owner of Chateau-sur-Mer, at that time the largest house in Newport. Drawings for the Sherman house were begun in 1874 for a site close to the Wetmore mansion. To White, now twenty years old, was given the responsibility for much of the design work for this house, which, with its textured exterior surfaces of stone, timbering, and variously shaped shingles, its projecting gable ends and medieval chimneys, and its free-flowing main floor arrangement, was a pioneer of the Queen Anne style in the United States. The first floor interior was dominated by the great living hall, into which the vestibule, the drawing room, the library, and the dining room all opened. In 1875, the *New York Sketch Book of Architecture* published a drawing of the living hall, most likely by White, whose painterly eye seems evident in the decorative approach of the illustration. Some years later, in 1879–81, White returned to work on the Sherman house and rebuilt the former drawing room into a new library, faced with dark green paneling, enlivened by various colonial motifs and by gilded tracings of plant forms.[19]

Early in 1876, Stanford was sent to Hartford, Connecticut, to supervise construction work on the Cheney Building, a block of offices and stores, with a rugged Romanesque, arched façade. There he encountered Glenn Brown, then a young clerk of the works for the project. White's "appearance and manner produced a lasting impression" on Brown, who years later recorded in his memoirs that Richardson's young assistant "came into the clerk's office, tall, lank, red-haired, freckle-faced . . . with interest and enthusiasm expressed in every feature and movement." Stan wanted to inspect the building, and after a rapid walk around the exterior he climbed up to the roof, soon returning, however, to ask for watercolors, paper, and a board, because the sunset was "so bully" that he wanted to capture it. Brown gave him the materials, and an hour or so later Stan "came back rejoicing over the beauties he had caught in a very effective sunset sketch. . . . His enthusiasm, quick grasp of the beauties of a commonplace scene, and his facility with his brush and pencil left a lasting impression upon my memory," Brown recorded.[20]

White's involvement with the Cheney Building in Hartford was the beginning of a long association with the Cheney family, textile manufacturers in South Manchester, Connecticut. It is likely that White did most of the work on a house projected for Rush Cheney, which appeared in a drawing published in the *New York Sketch-Book of Architecture* in September 1876, the large house echoing many of the stylistic features of the Sherman house and still in the Richardsonian mold but with more openness and delicacy of detailing. The same tendencies are found in the drawing that White signed of a house projected for James Cheney, a nephew of Rush Cheney, published in the *American Architect and Building News* on May 23, 1878. Although neither of those houses was erected, Stanford's professional and personal contacts with the Cheneys would continue for the rest of his life.[21]

An important project for the Richardson office at that time was the New York State Capitol, a structure demanding grandeur and dignity befitting a growing and prosperous state. The history of the Albany capitol building is complex. Construction was originally begun in 1867, but following countless complaints a state commission was set up in 1875 to review the work on the structure. The commission appointed an architectural advisory board comprising Richardson, the architect Leopold Eidlitz, and the landscape designer Frederick Law Olmsted. The advisory board advocated detailed alterations both in the design and in the general style of the capitol, including changing the exterior from

Renaissance to Romanesque. Eventually Richardson and Eidlitz were employed to continue the capitol work, following the revised plans. Along with exterior work, Richardson had to design the Senate and executive chambers, as well as the state library, the court of appeals room, and a grand staircase, while Eidlitz was employed on the Assembly chamber. Beginning in 1876, White worked closely with his boss, "making several suggestions for changing the Senate chamber," as Richardson wrote Olmsted. The two of them designed the Senate as a showplace of semiprecious stonework: a lower wall of Knoxville marble, arches of yellow Siena marble, railings of gray marble, and four massive columns of dark, red-brown granite were included in the rich treatment. The Senate chamber was ready for use in 1881.[22]

Increasingly, Richardson relied on his young and talented draftsman for decorative elements. Some of the most personal creations by White in 1877 and 1878 were carvings for the Ames Free Library in North Easton, Massachusetts, where Stanny's hand was particularly evident in the fireplace in the reading room, with a handsome low relief of vines and leaves forming an intricate arabesque on the overmantel. In Stan's drawings for the fireplace, the sinuous forms spring forward as if asking the viewer to touch and caress them. A medallion of Oliver Ames II created by Augustus Saint-Gaudens provided the focal point of the fireplace design.[23]

As Richardson became nationally recognized, young White could take pride in his connections with the figure who was acknowledged as one of the foremost of American architects. The years in Richardson's office gave Stan invaluable practical experience in working out specific problems of planning and design. Moreover, he learned how to deal with clients, to superintend construction, and, perhaps as important as anything else, to organize his own time and energies as he worked on the different stages of several ongoing projects. During those years of the 1870s, the young architect's own hand was becoming surer and the work he did, especially as seen in the Cheney houses, more fully his own. Richardson taught him artistic integrity and independence. Stanny was a very apt pupil.

He had begun work in Richardson's office as little more than a boy but was quickly thrust into a position of considerable responsibility and power in his work on major projects. As Stan trained for and began to practice his new vocation, he was brought into a new social realm as well as a business and an artistic one; he made many new friendships and acquaintances with both wealthy clients and creative artists. The job introduced him to a grand and rich vision of a life-style he had not experienced before. The world opened up widely for young White during those eight years as he moved into manhood.

And in those years of working closely with Mr. R., the tall young architect already impressed those about him by qualities of character and personality that would impress a much larger world later on. His commitment to his work, his passion to do his very best, and his concern for beauty were central to him. His energy and enthusiasm, tending toward unrestrained exuberance, for whatever he was involved with were readily apparent. And he wanted to be noticed: He craved recognition. Above all, he was intensely sociable, gathering friends about him, loyal to and considerate of them. Just as his occupation was becoming a profession, so too his sociability was apparently becoming almost a calling for him.

3

A Web of Friendships

While young White was gaining valuable professional experience under Richardson, he also kept up a busy social schedule as he forged a life increasingly independent of his parents. When not away from New York working on various projects for Richardson or spending a day or two at his aunt's place at Newburgh, he stayed with his parents at 118 East Tenth Street. But even while living at home, Stan was always on the go. In a letter to Nina, who was then away from the city, his father complained that he saw "little or nothing of [Stan]. When he isn't at the office, he is at Newburgh or on his way there or back; when he is in town he dont come to dinner half the time, & in the morning, he breakfasts generally before I do." Stan himself, in a chatty letter to his cousin Maggie White in Gambier, Ohio, while writing of his love of music—Beethoven's Pastorale Symphony and Seventh Symphony were his favorites—boasted of the hectic life he led, burning his candle not only at both ends but also in the middle.[1]

Now and then Stan spent an evening with his father, occasionally accompanying him to a play or a concert. Richard liked to have his sons join him for theatrical and musical performances (afterward, in the late evening, he often wrote newspaper reviews), but Stan was frequently "already engaged" and not available when Richard requested his company. At times Stan stayed at home when his father's string quartet played at the Whites' house. Richard Grant White, who was considered a good musician and owned several superb musical instruments, organized the quartet of string players in November 1875, with himself as cellist; thereafter the musicians met each Thursday evening in the dining room of the journalist's house to play together and forget "all the annoyances that came to them during the week." Stan's love of music remained a lifelong passion.[2]

31

When he was at home, Stan saw something of his brother Dick, who was also in and out of the house, but increasingly the two young men went their separate ways. Tall, red-haired, florid-faced, and, unlike Stan, slow-moving and taciturn, Dick White was a continuing worry to his parents. He had studied hydraulics with H. R. Worthington, the inventor of a hydraulic pump, but he just could not keep a job in the field. Moreover, he got into frequent scrapes. One day, after he refused to get off a train when his ticket was not honored, he was "ejected by personal violence from a railroad car." Then, in 1878, Dick got mixed up with "a nest of blackguards and sharpers" while working in Philadelphia. A controversy arose over the company records that were in Dick's care, and, unwisely, he made off with them. When his father interceded, Dick returned the records, but Richard Grant White, assertive and outwardly self-assured, had to go to Philadelphia to assist his twenty-six-year-old son, bringing his legal knowledge to the situation. Apparently, just by his towering presence, Richard intimidated one of the "rogues," who realized, Richard wrote his wife, that "if he attempted to trouble Dick he would have to fight with me." The matter ended peaceably, but a pattern was clearly set: Dick, would be involved in one disastrous scheme after another in the years to come. Moreover, it is apparent that Dick and Stan had long since fallen into family roles: Dick, the older and less favored, as the troublesome son, and Stan, the younger, favored and talented, as the good one.[3]

Stan's home life was altered for a few weeks in 1876, from August to late October, when Richard Grant White visited England for the first and only time. For years the journalist-scholar had passionately desired to experience for himself the land that he already knew so well from his Shakespearean studies. White was always delighted when people mistook him for an Englishman, and even before the trip it was said that "he knew more of England, literary and historical, and even geographical, biographical, and archaeological, than most men to the manner born." At last, in his mid-fifties, though his health was not good, White used a small sum of money he had accumulated to fit himself out with new clothing, including a fashionable, plum-colored waistcoat; packed up an elegant fitted traveling case; carried along his favorite cello; and set out for new adventures. Nina dutifully remained at home and kept house for her sons.[4]

Richard had a splendid time. As he had anticipated, he felt England to be his true home. He admired traditional social forms and deferential manners and was delighted by the treatment accorded him. He enjoyed being identified as "a swell" and having train porters escort him, as a matter of course, to the first-class carriages. In Hyde Park, London, he was astonished when an Indian "let fifty people pass him unnoticed" but gave White, "whom he had never seen before, a gracious salaam." Probably, he suggested with a certain pride, his face revealed something that people of the lower orders "liked to serve." Richard White, it seemed, always considered himself something of a "natural aristocrat," superior to most of those about him. That self-image, which must have made an impression on Stanford, undoubtedly gave strength to his opinions as a social critic but also may have led Richard to feel that some of the accepted standards of the time just did not apply to him.[5]

Richard Grant White was well received by the English gentry to whom he carried introductions, and at several country houses he enjoyed a luxurious life-style that contrasted markedly with his constricted existence at home. From Sevenoaks, Kent, Richard wrote Stan about some of the great estates he had visited. At the country seat of the Earl of Stanhope, he especially admired the 600-acre park "with yews in it under which the Canterbury pilgrims passed in Chaucer's time, & before, on their way to the shrine of Thomas a Becket." In England, White saw a good deal of the author Julian Hawthorne, who took him to Hampton Court and accompanied him on long walks in the rain. White was pleased to find himself described in print as "the most accomplished and the best bred man that America had sent to England within the memory of the present generation." The enjoyment of his visit was somewhat lessened, however, when his money ran short and he had to write home in haste, asking "to have all sent that could be easily spared."[6]

Alas for Richard, the time abroad flew by all too quickly. In an expression that Stan would make his own, Richard wrote that with all the visiting and sightseeing, he had been "so driven these last few days" he had not been able to report home what he had been doing. In response to a letter from both Dick and Stan, he expressed the wish that his sons had been able to visit England: "O, my boys, it ought to have been you, and particularly Stan, that came here," realizing how much his younger son might gain professionally by seeing at first hand the art and architecture of England. He lamented, too, that he had not made the journey to England twenty years earlier, for then the trip might have "borne some fruit" rather than being "a mere trip of pleasure—pleasure mingled with sadness."[7]

Yet the English visit was certainly rewarding to him and indeed bore "some fruit." The journey brought him not only an "entire change of air" and "an absolute freedom from work, & in part from anxiety, eating, drinking sleeping in a very large style, & with very great success,

& the succession of pleasant people & pleasant objects—all to my liking—with which I was brought into contact," but also a public sharing of his impressions. White's articles on the English scene, published in the *Atlantic Monthly*, were brought together in his genial book, *England Without and Within* (1881), which, one critic said, was "the best work on England by an American author since the appearance of Emerson's *English Traits* and Hawthorne's *Our Old Home.*" White's subsequent novel, *The Fate of Mansfield Humphreys* (1884), one of his favorite books, presented a roseate picture of an England favorable to pleasant living, contrasting sharply with a crude America, where life was far less satisfactory. For Stan, who was pleased at the success of these works, his father's trip provided a vicarious introduction to England and strengthened his own desire to visit Europe as soon as he could.[8]

As Stan's circle of friends expanded, he socialized mostly with other young architects and artists in the city, especially Charles Rutan, from Richardson's office, and George Fletcher Babb, and he was close for some years to Henry Casey, a friend who was hoping to apprentice in Richardson's office. Henry and his sister, Anais, were the children of family friends of Richard Grant White. Their French-born mother had died when Anais was eleven years old, and the girl had helped care for her younger brothers and sister. Henry, two years older than Stanny, unfortunately contracted tuberculosis while in his early twenties. He arranged to take a voyage around Cape Horn to San Francisco with the hope of staying the course of the disease, but by the time he got to California his condition had worsened greatly. He returned to the East almost at once. For some weeks, Stanny kept all-night vigils at Henry's bedside, helping Anais nurse her dying brother. Henry's lingering illness and death were an emotional jar for young White, as he experienced the death of someone close to him for the first time.[9]

It is possible that Stanford was romantically inclined toward Anais Casey, but evidence is lacking. We can be certain, however, about his interest in Sara Delano, who much later gained fame as the mother of the president of the United States. On weekend visits with his aunt in Newburgh, Stan came to know the wealthy Delano family, whose estate, Algonac, was just north of Newburgh. He was especially attentive to the tall, slim, gentle-mannered Sara, who was about a year younger than he. White's visits were recorded in the Delano family diary. Sara later recalled that he had come often and had impressed them by his shock of red hair, his great vitality, and his love of Beethoven's sonatas. Many admirers called on Sara, but young White, whose social position was well below that of the Delanos, may well have been the one her father referred to as "the red-haired trial," whom he did not care for and wished to discourage. From late in 1876 to midsummer 1877, Sara was sent away from Algonac on a trip to China, where her family had exporting interests. After her return, Stan called again to see her on September 16, 1877, but that was apparently his last visit. (According to one report, a member of the Delano family once said Sara Delano had loved only one man in her life, and that man was Stanford White.)[10]

Stanford also continued to socialize with Charley McKim, whose office was adjacent to that of Gambrill & Richardson and who still did occasional work for Richardson, and he became acquainted with William Rutherford Mead. McKim and Mead a few years later would become his closest business and artistic associates. In the fall of 1872, soon after McKim had set up for himself, Charley encountered Mead, who had just returned from a year of architectural study in Italy. Mead had stopped at 57 Broadway to call on the architect Russell Sturgis, in whose office he had previously studied and worked, and had learned that McKim was "very much in need of assistance" with both his own projects and his work for Richardson. It was soon arranged that Mead would help him out.

At the age of twenty-six, about a year older than McKim and more than seven years older than White, Mead was considered an extraordinarily handsome man, with a fair complexion, a dazzling smile, and penetrating dark blue eyes. His manner was quiet and low-keyed but authoritative. He had been born in Brattleboro, Vermont, on August 20, 1846; his father was a prominent lawyer, and his mother the sister of John Humphrey Noyes, the Oneida utopian. His brother, Larkin G. Mead, became a well-known sculptor, and a sister became the wife of the novelist William Dean Howells. Mead had attended Norwich University in Vermont for two years and had then gone on to Amherst College in Massachusetts, where he was active in fraternity life and college affairs but received low marks in deportment. He took a degree at Amherst in the class of 1867. Subsequently, he worked for an engineer in New York but left to study architecture with Sturgis as a paying pupil for two years, working under George Fletcher Babb in Sturgis's office. In 1871 he went to Florence to study at the Accademia di Belle Arti for about a year, followed by six months of general travel in Europe. Mead and McKim hit it off well and were soon associated in several projects. They jointly submitted a competition design in 1874 for a new city hall for Providence, Rhode Island, in a Queen Anne mode, but were unsuccessful. In 1874 Mead also set up an independent architectural office.[11]

In his own practice, McKim largely devoted himself to private houses on the New Jersey shore and in Newport, using colonial American elements along with the increasingly popular Queen Anne in several commissions. McKim also served as the working editor of a new architectural publication, *The New York Sketch Book of Architecture,* of which Richardson had been named nominal editor, and he used the periodical to reflect his own ideas on architecture. In its pages from January 1874 to December 1876, in an eclectic selection, McKim surveyed recent architectural work, including some of his own designs and drawings that White had done, and he also gratified his interest in older American structures by featuring some buildings from colonial times and the period of the early republic. The mid-1870s, around the time of the centennial of American independence, brought a widespread interest in the American past, which in architecture eventually led to a full-scale Colonial Revival movement.[12]

In October 1874, McKim largely removed himself from bachelor socializing when he was married to seventeen-year-old Annie Bigelow, the daughter of a New York cotton trader, whose family summered in Newport. With her olive skin and oval face, "pure Grecian, that might have matched a description of a heroine in Euripides," Annie was "exquisitely lovely." She came to New York in September, a month before the wedding, with her close friend and confidante Rose Wagner, to prepare an apartment for herself and Charley after the marriage. No doubt Stanford became acquainted with her at this time.[13]

The summer of 1875 brought a momentous encounter between Stan and the artist who would become his closest friend. One day, as he was climbing the stairs in the German Savings Bank building at Fourth Avenue and Fourteenth Street, he heard someone "bawl out" a theme from Beethoven's Seventh Symphony, one of his favorites, and the serenade from Mozart's *Don Giovanni.* When he investigated the source of the singing, Stan found himself in a small sculpture studio face to face with another redhead, whose well-defined features were dominated by a sloping brow, a prominent nose, and a jutting chin. Augustus Saint-Gaudens had learned the Beethoven from a French sculptor in New York and the Mozart from "a howling Frenchman in the Beaux-Arts who could shout even louder than [he]." The two young men immediately became friends, and soon their artistic and social lives were intertwined.[14]

Gus, at twenty-seven, was five and a half years older than Stan and had had far greater experience in the world. Born in Dublin, Ireland, on March 1, 1848, of an Irish mother and a French father, he had been brought to the United States when he was six months old. In New York City, his father set up a shoemaker's shop, where he crafted fine, fashionable footwear. When Gus was thirteen, he was apprenticed to a cameo maker who had emigrated from France, and about the same time he began evening drawing classes at the Cooper Institute. By then he was already committed to becoming a sculptor, and for two years he took classes at the National Academy of Design. He went off to Paris in 1867 and was admitted the following year to the Ecole des Beaux-Arts, where he spent nearly two years in the atelier of François Jouffroy, a prominent French sculptor. He worked in Rome the next two years, returning to New York briefly in 1872 to see his family, and then went back to his studio in Rome to work on his first projects, including a statue of Hiawatha.

Three years later Saint-Gaudens returned to make his home in New York and embark on an American career as a sculptor in a small studio in the German Savings Bank building. To remind himself of the sound of the fountains of his beloved Rome, Gus let the water run continuously in the studio wash basin, much to the annoyance of the building engineer, who barged in one day looking for the source of the water leak. Gus, Stan discovered, was the consummate artist. Even more than Richardson or McKim, Gus was passionately absorbed in his work. "He was full of enthusiasms and he wanted the world to enjoy his enthusiasms," it was said. His approach to art and to life generally was highly sensual; his basic impulse was not to analyze things but rather to enjoy them. He loved good times and was very fond of going out on the town and "whooping it up." As one friend said, he "craved excitement." But at the same time he was often reticent, almost shy, caring little for formal society, perhaps basically insecure in company because of his lack of a traditional education.[15]

Although Stan was considerably younger, less experienced, and less sophisticated than the well-traveled Gus, the two young men hit it off well. They began to see each other often and enjoyed evenings together on the town. Stan's exuberant personality, his sympathetic manner, and his passion for art endeared him to Gus. Stan soon took Gus to meet Richardson, who hired the sculptor in 1876 to work under John La Farge on the decorations for Trinity Church. Richardson developed a high regard for Gus's artistic judgment; he once remarked that the young sculptor "seemed to be able to pick out the best instinctively." La Farge also gave Gus commissions for an ornamental screen for St. Thomas Episcopal Church in New York and for a tomb in Newport.[16]

Stan and Gus soon combined their talents on two other projects. While still in Rome, Saint-Gaudens had become interested in sculpting a statue of Admiral David G. Farragut, the hero of the Civil War battles of New Orleans and Mobile Bay ("Damn the torpedoes, full speed ahead!"), who had died in September 1870. On his return to New York, Gus began a bust of Farragut in plaster. Through Edwin D. Morgan, a former governor and senator from New York, who had purchased his statue of Hiawatha in Rome, he was introduced to the publisher William Appleton, a member of the New York Farragut Monument Commission, which was arranging for a memorial. Although the commission members favored awarding the project to the better-known John Quincy Adams Ward, the established sculptor generously declined the work in favor of Saint-Gaudens. The Farragut statue commission was awarded to Gus in December 1876. A contract was signed the following spring, whereby the statue was to be completed in two years. White soon volunteered to help with the project and made a large pedestal drawing for his friend. Like other American architects at the time, White considered statues and their pedestals an important element of civic embellishment and was eager to be involved in the work, which might, as well, bring him some public recognition. A second joint endeavor was a tomb in Hartford, Connecticut, for the Edwin Morgan family, on which it was agreed that Stan would do the architectural work and Gus the sculpture.

Saint-Gaudens at the time was becoming increasingly irritated with the conservatism of the National Academy of Design, where he had studied earlier. Dominated by painters of the Hudson River School, who in their works usually highlighted the beauties of and moral values associated with American nature, the National Academy, some painters felt, was tied to the past. New art currents, focusing on portraiture, the human figure, and decorative effects, were being championed by Americans who had studied in Germany and France. With the magazine editor Richard Watson Gilder and his wife, Helena de Kay Gilder, a painter, whose studio home, a former carriage house at 103 East Fifteenth Street, was a meeting place for artists, Saint-Gaudens and a few others talked over the possibility of setting up an organization to promote the new cosmopolitan trends in art coming from Europe.

At midday on June 1, 1877, Saint-Gaudens came storming to the Gilders' front gate and loudly rang the bell. He was, Gilder wrote, "as mad as hops!" An Academy jury had just rejected a piece of his sculpture for an exhibit that was being prepared. Saint-Gaudens's anger precipitated the actual founding of a new art society: That evening Gus met with Helena Gilder and the painters Wyatt Eaton and Walter Shirlaw to form an organization for "advancing the interests of Art in America" to be called "The American Art Association." The name was soon changed to "The Society of American Artists," and the group was enlarged as new members joined, including Albert Pinkham Ryder, Louis C. Tiffany,

William Merritt Chase, J. Alden Weir, and Frank Duveneck, all of whom Stan came to know. Beginning in the spring of 1878, the Society held annual exhibitions, which continued for twenty-seven years, until eventually the Society was reunited with the Academy. In the pages of *Scribner's* and later the *Century*, Richard Watson Gilder championed the Society of American Artists and the new painting. Gilder subsequently would be closely associated with White in various civic art endeavors, and the architect later did work for the Gilders at their New York homes and at their summer cottage at Marion, Massachusetts.[17]

Almost immediately after his outburst, the sculptor ended his direct involvement with the new art movement, and Stanford, in effect, was abandoned by his best friend. On June 4, 1877, Saint-Gaudens was married in Boston to Augusta Homer, whom he had first met as an art student in Rome, and two days later the newlyweds sailed from New York for Europe. After a short visit in London, they settled in Paris, where Saint-Gaudens completed the St. Thomas Church commission; he spent part of the following winter in Rome, working on the Farragut commission. Back in Paris, Saint-Gaudens rented a small studio near the Arc de Triomphe and a short time later "an enormous studio" on the Left Bank that had once been a public ballroom, where he could work on the various commissions he had brought from the United States. He and Stan kept in close touch by letter.

Although the painters White knew best were now turning away from the nationalism of the Academy and incorporating new ideas from Europe in their works in a new cosmopolitanism, the architects he was closest to, by contrast, were, to some degree, turning away from the longtime direct influence of European styles and back to the colonial American past for inspiration. McKim's fascination with colonial American architecture, elements of which he incorporated both in alterations and in new work in the 1870s, was contagious. At some point in 1877, probably in midsummer, McKim, Mead, and White, along with William Bigelow, Annie McKim's older brother, toured New England to study colonial buildings. The four architects sketched and made measured drawings of colonial dwellings in Marblehead, Salem, Newburyport, and Portsmouth. Near Newburyport, they visited Ben Perley Poore, a journalist, whose house, Indian Head, had been in his family since the seventeenth century and was filled with a splendid collection of colonial furniture. There they stayed four days, delighted not only with their host and his rambling old house but also with his two lively and attractive daughters, who helped entertain the visitors.[18]

The following December, at a meeting of the New York chapter of the American Institute of Architects, McKim gave a talk on the need for knowledgeable understanding of the architectural work of the American past. *The American Architect and Building News,* he suggested, might be an appropriate vehicle to disseminate "antiquarian researches into American history as illustrated by our buildings"; by that means, "the architects of to-day could improve their practice by a study of those admirable touches of real art and honest workmanship which the colonial houses offered." An "Antiquarian Committee" of architects was organized to gather information so that "the line of investigation proposed in the paper" might be pursued. McKim's early designs, the New England excursion, and his Institute talk were important stimuli to what soon became a Colonial Revival movement in American building design.[19]

Late that same summer, 1877, Stan was pleased to learn that his three traveling companions had decided to associate themselves in a new architectural firm. McKim and Mead reached an agreement with William Bigelow, McKim's brother-in-law, forming a partnership as the firm of McKim, Mead & Bigelow, with a small office at 57 Broadway. Bigelow had studied in Paris at the Ecole des Beaux-Arts in 1873 and 1874, and was said to be "an amazing clever sketcher and free-hand draftsman." In December, the *American Architect* reported that the new firm was "postively busy." One of its most important commissions was a long, rambling, shingled country house for the banker Samuel Gray Ward at Lenox, Massachusetts; the Ward house had "such a quaint look," it was stated, "that but for a few Queen Anne fantasies, it might pass for an old Puritan homestead"; its shingled surfaces, many gables, small windows, and massive grouped chimneys recalled New England architecture of the seventeenth century. A Victorian-Gothic church rectory in Rye, New York, a colonial-inspired house covered by redwood shingles for the novelist William Dean Howells at Belmont, Massachusetts, and the large wine-red brick Tuckerman Building, later known as the Benedict Apartments, rising six stories with handsome bay windows, on the east side of Washington Square, were other projects the new firm undertook.[20]

Although his professional life was prospering, McKim's private affairs were in turmoil. Charley's marriage with Annie was not happy and soon deteriorated. In August 1877 Mrs. McKim left her husband, taking their two-year-old daughter with her, and returned to her family in Newport. Although she maintained that her departure had been mutually agreed to, McKim claimed that she had deserted him. He asserted that Rose Wagner, who lived with them and served as the baby's nurse, had "obtained undue influence over his wife" and had alienated her affections from him. Annie protested that Rose was not to blame. In May 1878 Annie McKim obtained a legal separation, and in July 1879 she filed for divorce in Rhode Island, charging neglect, cruelty, and "gross misbehavior and wickedness, repugnant to and in violation of the marriage contract," by her husband. She petitioned the court for sole custody of her daughter. McKim battled in court over the custody issue; he was eventually allotted a single visit of one hour a week, to take place in the home of a third party in Newport. For many years he saw nothing whatsoever of his daughter. McKim's distress over the failure of his marriage was deep and long lasting, but his return to single status brought him closer in friendship to White.[21]

The reasons for the collapse of McKim's marriage have always been obscure. James H. Morse, a New Yorker who knew all of the participants well, believed the breakup arose from incompatibility between the high-minded, exacting Annie, with Rose always supporting her, and the "free-lance," generous, artistic Charles. In a conversation with the novelist William Dean Howells, Morse ventured the opinion that Howell's novel *April Hopes* (1887) was based upon the McKim courtship and marriage. Howells, who was Mead's brother-in-law, admitted to Morse that he knew McKim well and had met Annie, but he did not directly confirm Morse's conjecture. The story of the courtship, engagement, and marriage of the unsuited couple in the Howells tale—the man serious, dependable, and charming, and the woman, moody, capricious, and self-righteous—is similar to the real-life situation, although the protagonists do not divorce.[22]

About the time that McKim's marriage was starting to fall apart, Stan's love for ornamentation and the decorative arts and his engaging sociability brought him into the newly organized Tile Club. In the studio of Walter Paris, overlooking Union Square, a dozen New York artists in the early autumn of 1877 formed a club for decorating tiles; within a short time, other artists, including Stan, were invited to join. Each week on Wednesday evening, the artists met at one of their studios for companionship and mutual criticism as they painted tiles. All the tiles decorated on an evening and subsequently fired would go to the host. For a time, the Tilers gathered at the studio of the dwarfish photograpter Napoleon Sarony, where the entrance was guarded by an Egyptian mummy standing upright, the walls were covered by arms and armor, and a stuffed crocodile dangled from the ceiling. The elegant Mrs. Sarony was always stylishly dressed in gowns by Worth of Paris as she greeted her husband's guests. One evening Madame Helena Petrovna Blavatsky, the high priestess of Theosophy, joined the tile painters. There was always a lot of banter at the gatherings; the air was dense with pipe smoke, and cheese, crackers, and beer were passed around. Each tile painter was given a whimsical nickname as his club name. Stan was first christened "the Beaver" and later "the Builder." Eventually the Tilers acquired their own clubhouse behind a residence on West Tenth Street.[23]

For Stan in his early twenties, the association with other artists in the Tile Club brought immersion into the Bohemian community of New York. Many of his primary ties of friendship and conviviality were soon forged with painters, sculptors, and decorators, as well as with architects, and some of these artists were decidedly unconventional in attitudes, behavior, and dress. Although the Tilers were by no means antagonistic to most social conventions, still as artists they were concerned above all for their art, and some were uninterested in the usual ways of making a living.

The neighborhood in which Stan lived with his parents had long been the focus of artistic life in New York City. Since its opening in 1835, the University Building facing on Washington Square had provided rented rooms to artists and writers, and the old Gothic Revival pile was noted for its convivial, artistic atmosphere. Later the Studio Building, designed by Richard Morris Hunt and completed on West Tenth Street in 1858, became a center of artistic life, though by no means was it wildly Bohemian. In the years following, many painters' studios and galleries were set up in the commercial buildings along Broadway below Fourteenth Street, and several restaurants and saloons in the area provided a Bohemian atmosphere for artists. The New York Bohemian community of fellow artists, which Stanford White moved in and out of, always remained important for him.

Since his father's visit to England and Saint-Gaudens's departure for France, Stan had been especially eager to go abroad; by the beginning of 1878, after eight years of training and work with Richardson, he decided to make the journey. He had mastered the fundamentals of his craft, he had saved and borrowed money enough for a stay abroad of several months, and he was now ready to make his life more fully his own, distancing himself for a time from his family to explore a larger world. On February 21, Stan informed Mr. R. that he planned to leave his position for an extended visit to Europe. His employer was understanding and sent back a note, "not without sincere regret," to congratulate him on his proposed trip. "I certainly think," the older architect wrote, "and have for some time past thought it wise and for your best interest to travel and see what the Old World has done for us," though he emphasized that he could "never hope to fill your place to me or in the office." White had long provided responsible, talented, and often highly original support to Richardson in his architectural practice, and no doubt Richardson would feel the loss. But Stan, too, would miss the guidance of the man he most respected and admired.[24]

Saint-Gaudens, who was in Rome for the winter, struggling there with the design for the clothing for the Farragut statue figure, wrote Stan in March that he really needed his friend's help on the pedestal and encouraged him to come to Europe. Gus rejoiced in the sun and warmth of Rome in the winter and hated the thought of returning to "dark, sloppy Paris after this glorious place," but he realized he would have to get back to his several commissions in his Paris workshop. Looking for a firm commitment from Gus to share in the Farragut commission, Stan wrote back that he hoped Gus would let him help out on the pedestal—"then I shall go down to Fame even if it was bad—reviled for making a poor base for a good statue."[25]

That spring, Stan assisted Richardson on the decorations of the Senate chamber in Albany. Following his "last final visit to the abode of the great mogul at Brookline," Stan reported to Gus that Mr. R. and he had "cooked up something pretty decent" for the Senate, and they wanted to let Gus "loose on the walls." If the work for Saint-Gaudens materialized there, then the sculptor, White wrote, would "have a chance to immortalize yourself like Giotto or Michel Angelo." But he also warned Gus not to get his hopes too high and not "to count your chickens before they are hatched," since the commission was not yet firm. When Stan informed Gus that he definitely would soon be on his way to Paris, he suggested that he might ask Gus to find him a cheap room and that he would need Gus's help "to avoid being fleeced" when he arrived. He would also, he wrote, possibly somewhat insecure about overly imposing himself on his older married friend, "test your friendship by boring you a good deal in many ways."[26]

Meanwhile, negotiations continued in New York between White and Governor Morgan concerning the Morgan family tomb project, on which Saint-Gaudens was working. White felt their client was being crafty and had "gouged" him out of half his commission, since Morgan was absolutely adamant that White could have only a five percent commission on the tomb pedestal. Stanny reported to Gus that he had "swallowed . . . pride and principles and accepted his damned five percent," remembering that he himself was poor and young and had already "run in debt to get abroad." He would have to take what he could get. Stan's best news for Gus was that Helena de Kay Gilder, the painter in whose studio-house the Society of American Artists had been established, had expressed a wish to meet him, and he had called on her. She had given Stan a photograph of her baby to take to Gus in Paris, though Stan, who like his father was much attracted by feminine beauty, wished that she had given him one of herself. "Oh! but isn't she lovely, isn't she perfectly charming, & sweet?"[27]

As he completed his final work for Richardson and concluded the negotiations with Morgan, Stan made plans to sail from New York on June 18, 1878. As one arrangement, he took out a thirty-five-year life insurance policy for $2,000 on himself; included in the terms of the policy was an agreement by the Mutual Life Insurance Company that White might travel to Europe while holding the policy. On June 21 he wrote Gus to thank him for the offer of a "bunk" in Paris but had to inform him that he had been obliged to put off his departure in order to complete the Morgan tomb drawings to send out for contract estimates. He promised, however, that he would leave on July 3 on the French steamer *Perière*. Moreover, he had a splendid surprise: McKim, who just recently had been legally separated from his wife, would be accompanying him. "I am tickled to death," Stan wrote. They were scheduled to land at Le Havre and would take an express train on to Paris, arriving on July 15 or 16. "I will pay my respects to you immediately."[28]

4

The Discovery of Europe

❦

S tan and Charley were delighted with the *Perière*, "a fine vessel and very fast, bouncing along at the rate of 15 knots an hour. . . . No one could wish a better ship." Final preparations for their journey had been hectic, but they had a good send-off, sailing from New York on Wednesday, July 3, 1878. For Stan, now twenty-four years old, there were no regrets about leaving his family and his work, only excited anticipation of what the weeks ahead would hold.

Starting out on his voyage across the Atlantic, Stan was about to share in a common experience of nineteenth-century Americans: the discovery of Europe. Just as his father for years before his trip to England had wanted to visit places he had known only through books and photographs, Stan and countless other Americans had long awaited their own introductions to the Continent and the British Isles. Aboard ship moving eastward, they eagerly anticipated interesting explorations and exciting discoveries that would bring pleasure and amusement and enrich their lives. For some Americans the trip to Europe was chiefly a pilgrimage to shrines of culture. For others it was something of a fashionable necessity, undertaken to enhance social position. For still others, like Stan, it was primarily a means of enlarging experience and furthering education.

In a long letter to his mother begun soon after departure, Stan wrote that McKim and he were "in splendid stomach and spirits," enjoying the abundant food and drink available aboard ship. The second day out, he reported, they were awakened "by the most frightful noise and commotion," and Stan, convinced that the ship was foundering, jumped out of bed and ran wildly to the deck clad in just his shirt, only to discover that the noise was a salute honoring America's Independence Day. The female cabin attendant was horrified at his state of undress, and Stan retreated hastily to his quarters.[1]

The stern-faced, reticent captain of the *Perière* impressed Stan as "a thorough gentleman," but Stan felt "the crew might be better. . . . As for the other passengers—good God!" Other than McKim and himself and except for the "round, fat, jolly and sleek" Archbishop of Sydney and his "very tall and slim" assistant, Monsieur l'Abbé, "the rest don't matter." Most of them were "an assortment of Cook's tourists," who, when they weren't being seasick, were single-mindedly trying to learn French from "a great donkey" of a professor. Later on in the voyage, however, Stan did become friendly with fellow passengers from New York and Washington, who, he admitted, were "very nice people." And there were "three pretty Spanish girls aboard; but, alas, they [spoke] only their own tongue."

McKim, who had made the crossing twice before, was pleased that he wasn't seasick; he also had the advantage over Stan of knowing French and being able to deal with the waiters. By the fourth day, the ship began to pitch, and the surrounding air turned cold as the ship began to traverse the Grand Banks; the ship's foghorn blasted forth like a call to awaken "the souls of the damned . . . to eternal torture." That night a storm hit. The waves soon reached high above the ship, and even Stan, who so far had proved a hardy sailor, began to wonder whether they would stay afloat. McKim dragged about, his discomfort "past a joke," although he was relieved now and then by "unstinted applications of chloral mixture" prescribed by the ship's doctor. The air in the staterooms with the portholes shut was intolerable, and Stan came down with a nasty cold.

Finally, after days of discomfort and being tossed about, the travelers observed a welcome sight, the distant shore of England, and on Saturday morning, July 13, they landed at Le Havre. The two young voyagers quickly recovered and were ravenously hungry. As soon as they had gone through customs and were on shore they treated themselves to a huge breakfast of fresh fish and fruit and vegetables: "Nothing ever tasted so good before." Then off by train they went to Paris, a trip "delightful beyond description," even though they felt too tired really to enjoy it.

Arriving in Paris, Stanny and Charley took rooms at the Hôtel Corneille, an inexpensive hostelry in the Latin Quarter, and after settling in enjoyed a splendid dinner at Foyot's, compared to which, Stan wrote home, "all the grub that I had ever eaten before seemed but poor stuff." Following that memorable meal they indulged in a prolonged soak at a public bathhouse, where they "left behind about a quarter of an inch" of themselves in the tubs.

The next day the two Americans set off on a round of sightseeing and entertainments. For young White, accustomed to the grime and dirt, the mostly narrow and crowded streets, and the commercial bustle of New York, Paris was a revelation. In the central area of the vast city, the broad, tree-lined boulevards, built on the site of old fortifications, the network of avenues, the large squares and the great circles, and the many parks and gardens gave a feeling of openness very different from New York. The boulevards were filled with traffic, and crowds of people sauntered along the sidewalks, yet there was little congestion. The countless café terraces spilling onto the wide sidewalks, the luxurious shops, often mirrored and glass-fronted, the many theaters and restaurants, and the elegant residences suggested vast wealth and a far more leisurely pace of life than New Yorkers generally experienced. At night the central city streets glowed from the many gas lamps and the bright illumination of shop and theater fronts. The City of Light under the Third Republic was in a festive mood in 1878, for most of the scars of the damage that had occurred in the Franco-Prussian War of 1870–71 and in the subsequent attack on civic monuments by the revolutionary communards had been repaired or the structures rebuilt. Three years earlier the Paris Opera had been inaugurated, and just a year before the Avenue de l'Opéra had been opened to become the most fashionable street of the city. Celebrating the recovery, an international Exposition was installed in the huge Trocadero Palace, styled with Spanish, Moorish, and classical elements, facing the Champ de Mars. Visitors thronged to the city for the Exposition.

Their first day in Paris, Stanny and Charles had "one continuous bum"—beginning with Sunday morning services at St. Germain-des-Pres and ending that evening at the Theatre Français, where they watched a three-drama program, including the tragedy *Phèdre,* featuring Sarah Bernhardt, who "played magnificently." The Paris Salon featuring selected new art works was, Stan felt, "not at all interesting," but the *Opéra Comique* provided "the most perfect performance" he had ever seen. During the week that followed, afternoons at the Paris Exposition, visits to the Louvre, concerts, and rendezvous with other Americans introduced them to Paris. Although the exhibits at the Exposition were "a little larger and more grandiose, but not much better" than those at the Philadelphia Exposition two years earlier, the art collection was "the greatest exhibit of modern paintings ever held." They attended an artists' *Bal de Nuit,* but Stan found it disappointing and a "pretty poor performance" and vowed not to go again. They soon changed their rooms to No. 1 Rue Fleurus, a "very pleasant 'tinnement' " in the Latin Quarter. All in all, he wrote home, they were "satisfied with everything and everybody, and [were] generally having as good a time as it is possible" and, he reassured his parents, they were "both horribly virtuous, so far."

Saint-Gaudens and his wife, Augusta (Gussie), had leased a substantial apartment at No. 3 Rue Herschel, not far from the sculptor's large studio in the Rue Notre Dame des Champs, where he was working on the Farragut statue. From the long windows of the main room of the apartment they could look out on the Church of St. Sulpice. Gussie Saint-Gaudens wrote her mother a few days after Stanny's arrival in Paris that after "Mr. White" had taken a short trip to Brittany he would move into the studio. Gus was having the place cleaned up and whitewashed. Maitland Armstrong, a New York artist who was serving as director of American fine arts for the Paris Exposition, was staying with them in the apartment, along with Gus's brother Louis, also a sculptor. At times, for Gussie, there were just too many people around, and she complained to her mother that she really wanted her husband more to herself: "There are so many young men here all the time in the evening that it seems as if I see very little of him." The Saint-Gaudenses' marriage would suffer continuing strains.[2]

Ever since he was a student in Paris, Gus had wanted to take a hiking tour in the south of France. When Stanny and Charley came to him one day and proposed that they go off to southern France at once, Gus at first demurred, since he momentarily expected some Americans at the studio to inspect the preliminary work on the Farragut statue. The visitors, it turned out, did not particularly like what they saw, but Gus did not take their views very seriously. A short time later, however, when some fellow sculptors came by to see the work and made fun of the statue's legs, their criticism was too much for him. Impetuously "lifting off the head, [he] toppled the legs and torso to the floor where they smashed into a thousand pieces. 'Come on,' he said to White and McKim: 'I'll go to Hades with you fellows now.' "[3]

On Friday, August 2, the three redheads started out from Paris for an excursion through a good part of central and southern France. To economize and see more of the people, they traveled third class. Gussie, writing to her mother, did not know just how she could "get on without *my* other half" but was certain her husband would "have a splendid time" with his friends. "It's really a business trip," she wrote, "as

McKim wants him to do some bas-reliefs on something he is going to be the architect of, and they must see different styles of architecture together.''[4]

The three friends enjoyed ''absolutely perfect'' weather for their entire ''business trip.'' Most of the inns they stayed at were not very clean, but they were ''tolerable,'' and the food, Stanny reported to his family, was ''most excellent,'' especially the wine and the cheese. Fontainebleau, near Paris, held them only briefly—''the castle has a homelike air''— then on to Moret, ''a lovely little walled town with old gate towers,'' and Sens, ''dirty and decayed without being lovely, but with a very fine cathedral.'' They spent their first Sunday in Dijon, where they ''went to church three or four times.'' At Beaune, next on their itinerary, they ''came across two very attractive and inseparable things—good wine and pretty women,'' the latter all dressed in the latest Parisian fashions. Stanny was fascinated at Beaune by the Hôtel Dieu hospital, where they ''were received with the utmost courtesy, and welcomed into the grand old kitchen by a fair sister, with her sleeves rolled up to her shoulders, and a huge soup ladle in her hand.'' The hospital was ''clean and sweet,'' and its courtyard, filled with young orange trees, was ''quiet as a cloister.'' Leaving Beaune by train on the route to Lyons, they purchased a bottle of old wine, consumed it in the carriage, and got ''quite tight.''[5]

Lyons, large and bustling, was ''a sort of third-rate Paris'' and decidedly ''uninteresting.'' The three friends only remained overnight. Routed out of their beds the next morning at five o'clock, they boarded a 275-foot-long river boat for a twelve-hour trip down the Rhône. The current was tremendously swift, but the discomforts of the craft's sidewise lurching and its running aground once and the pervasive smell of garlic were eased for them by bottles of sparkling wine: France, they vowed as they drank each other's health, ''ish mosh magnifishent countrish'' they ever saw. Avignon that evening provided a welcome and peaceful respite from the hectic trip down the Rhône. Dominated by the great papal palace, then being used as a barracks, Avignon was ''by far the most impressive town we were in.'' At Arles, their next stop, the women dressed strikingly in black and white were more worthy of note for White than the Roman ruins there. Nearby, at Gilles, they admired the twelfth-century church with its triple porch, which years later was to inspire White's St. Bartholomew's Church porch in New York. A cleric took them through the church, presenting them with medals of St. Gilles, while at the same time denouncing Protestants in general and Huguenots in particular for the damage they had done to the building.

Reaching Nîmes, ''thriving'' and ''very beautiful,'' the travelers refreshed themselves in a swimming-bath filled with water brought by a Roman aqueduct from the Rhône, 30 miles distant. At the amphitheater in Nîmes, "the most perfect in the world," the Americans sat in the top row of seats and for a few moments became ancient Romans. Then, while Gus and Charley remained on top, Stanny "rushed madly into the arena, struck an attitude, and commenced declaiming" and was perfectly audible to his friends above; before the guardian appeared and chased him out, he "stabbed five or six gladiators." From Nîmes they caught a tantalizing glimpse of the Mediterranean in the distance and started northward by train along a wild and mountainous route to Langogne. For the next segment of the journey, they rode on the roof of a stagecoach through mountains that reminded Stan of the Catskills, to Le Puy, "perhaps the most strikingly peculiar town in France," dominated by two steep peaks, one of them crowned by "a great big hideous tin Virgin." Stanny hated the place and could only recall it with a shudder: "Of all low, dirty, nasty, ill-smelling, filthy places that I have come across, Le Puy exceeds them all."

Tours, reached by way of Clermont, Moulins, and Bourges, brought them into the Loire Valley château country, where "the best French is spoken." There, "the loveliest of landladies" greeted them at their hotel. But because of the confusingly arranged hallways Stan had trouble, three or four times, finding his room at this inn, and each time he went downstairs to get directions he ran into Gus and Charley "on the same errand."

Back in Paris, on August 13, the travelers refreshed themselves in a Turkish bath, donned clean clothes, and again enjoyed a superb dinner at Foyot's restaurant. Stan felt almost as if he were at home. "In spite of its wickedness," he moralized, "I am getting to have the appreciation which all good Americans have for Paris, and shall leave it for the last time with sorrow in my heart." Although he was coming to love Paris, he had some reservations about the French people, especially those he had encountered in the South—"the politer they became the more they lied"—certainly quite a contrast to the Bretons in the North, who "though rough are absolutely honest." The old ways were changing rapidly in the new republic, yet many Frenchmen were true to the past, he thought, and to Stan that past was better. Gussie, in her regular Friday letter, reassured her mother in her matter-of-fact way that "Aug returned Tuesday night, having had a most successful trip. He feels that he has learned a great deal from traveling with his architect friends."[6]

To commemorate the excursion, Saint-Gaudens designed and executed two small bronzes. The first was a rectangular plaque dated August

1878 honoring "My Friend. Charles F. Mackim [sic]. Architect," with a delicate low-relief profile of McKim in a formal pose, facing to the right. The plaque is also inscribed as follows: "In Souvenir of the ten jolly days I passed with you and the illustrious Stanford White in the south of France." The second bronze was a circular medallion some 6 inches in diameter in low relief, containing caricatures of White, Saint-Gaudens, and McKim, along with decorations and pseudo-Latin phrases. Around the rim of the medal on a narrow band is a phrase that might be translated as: "This medal is in honor of an eleven days' journey in southern France in the month of the Crab, 1878." This is followed by place names and letters, summarizing the itinerary of the excursion. At the lower left of the face of the medallion is a profile sketch of the sculptor himself, the nose and beard sloping sharply to points, with a pinprick for an eye, a sketch that the sculptor often later used as his signature. At the lower right, facing Saint-Gaudens, is the head of McKim, also in profile, characterized by a massive domed cranium with the facial features all crowded together. Above, at the top center, floats the head of White, defined only by his bushy hair, mustache, bearded chin, and large round eyes, looking something like a porcupine. Close to Saint-Gaudens's chin a sculptor's mallet is depicted, while next to McKim are an architect's dividers. Below White a large T-square separates the two profiles. Small reliefs of the St. Gilles façade and a wellhead and an incised sketch of the Pont St. Esprit on the Rhône are placed between the heads.[7]

The phrases on the circular medallion are cryptic. The words "DAMVS SOLVM" appear beside White's head, and "TICKLEVM FVRIO" above Saint-Gaudens's profile and "VA SECHAS" above McKim's portrait. A great many years later, Lawrence White, Stanford's son, explained that the words "Damus Solum" referred to an incident on the excursion when White got into an argument with a railroad conductor because he refused to leave a compartment reserved for women. "Tickleum furio," he said, alluded to a vigorous tickling episode Saint-Gaudens indulged in, while "Va Sechas" was said to refer to an incident in a train when McKim reproved a misbehaving child and was himself told by the child's mother: "Ça va secher" ("Go dry up"). At the base of the T-square is clearly incised "KMA," which, both in abbreviation and spelled out as "Kiss My Ass," would be used frequently by Gus and Stan in their letters to each other.[8]

On his return to Paris, Stan was invited to stay in the Saint-Gaudens's apartment: It became his home base, to which he returned from several sightseeing and sketching trips away from the city. McKim remained in Paris for a short time but in September returned to New York. Stan hired a French teacher, who, while Stan was in Paris, came "relentlessly" to the apartment every morning.

In the following months, White's architectural and artistic education was furthered considerably as he discovered much for himself and experienced directly places, buildings, and paintings he had previously only read about or seen photographs of. Unlike his father, whose interests on his visit to England, it turned out, had been mainly in the upper-class social life he encountered, Stanny's concerns were primarily aesthetic. He kept his pencils, paints, and brushes close at hand, and eventually filled six large scrapbooks with drawings and watercolors. He was especially intrigued by picturesque towers and the silhouettes of old buildings. Textures of surfaces, the play of light and shadow over irregular planes, and unusual decorative details all attracted him, as he strove to capture architectural effects that he might recall and possibly make use of later on.[9]

In October, Stan explored Normandy, stopping at the cathedral city of Rouen on his return to Paris. A letter to his father expressed some loneliness when traveling by himself, weariness after moving about so much, and, indeed, already a decided homesickness: "As soon as my money gives out, I shall be home—and be very, very glad to get there." Yet, he reported, he was enjoying himself, he still had funds enough to travel, and the living conditions he encountered were "always passable," though the odor of the well-marked water closets in the hotels was something of a trial.[10]

Another excursion in early November took Stan, traveling alone once more, to Creil, where he was kept awake until the wee hours of the morning by a noisy ball in the hotel, and then on to Amiens to see the magnificent Gothic cathedral. Douai, in the northeastern corner of France, was "a wretched little French town," but there he saw a portrait by Paul Veronese that nearly made him burst into tears: "To think that so lovely a thing could be done, and I could not do it!" Close by, he stopped at Lille, where in the museum a wax head, attributed to Raphael, had "the loveliest face ever conceived by man." Indeed, he wrote to his mother, "architecture seems but poor stuff compared with things like this." A few days later he was in the formerly "mighty city of Bruges—mighty once, somewhat melancholy now," only a shadow of what it once had been and filled with paupers. At Bruges "the architecture and the old town are enough to set you wild; but when you add to these the pictures, all there is to do is to gasp for breath and die quietly." He loved Bruges and regretted that he would have to leave the place "half-digested" to move on. Ghent was "not one tenth as interesting as Bruges," though *The Adoration of the Immaculate Lamb* by Jan and Hubert Van Eyck was "well worth, alone, a visit to Belgium, even to Europe." In Brussels, "a bully place," on November 9, Stanny splurged on an expensive ticket for a performance of *The Barber of Seville,* with the celebrated Adelina Patti, who sang "with feeling (sometimes) but not with taste." At Antwerp, he "fairly gorged" himself on the paintings of Rubens, with "heaps of fat legs and brawny arms, blear-eyed and frowsy women whose modesty is the most fragile kind."[11]

After several days of moving about, it was a pleasure to return to Paris and his room with the Saint-Gaudenses, even though he had come to realize that he just did not like Gussie. He wrote his mother:

> I hug St. Gaudens like a bear every time I see him, and would his wife, if she was pretty—but she ain't—so I don't. She is very kind, however; asks me to dinner, mends my clothes, and does all manner of things. She is an animated clothes-rack, slightly deaf—a double-barrelled Yankee, and mean to that extent that no comparison will suffice. Why Fate should have ordained that such a man should be harnessed to such a woman, Heaven only knows. Nevertheless, she has been very kind to me, and I ought to be ashamed of myself for saying anything against her.

Obviously Stan felt, as well, that Gussie, to some extent, stood between him and Gus. By contrast, Eugenie Homer, Gussie's sister, staying with them for a time in the apartment, delighted Stan, and he enjoyed escorting her around the city.[12]

In early December, White visited Rheims, "the most historical city in France." Feeling lonely and wanting to share the architectural glories and the great wines of Rheims, he telegraphed Saint-Gaudens to come and join him. Gus obliged and brought along his young sister-in-law. Gussie had decided it would be proper for Genie to accompany her husband only if the young lady wore a bonnet and a plain gold ring on her left hand. At the hotel, while Gus and Stanny drank champagne, Genie roasted chestnuts and apples in the fire. "Such a jolly time as we had in our (St. G's and my) room!" Stan considered her lovely, though he also characterized her as "the most self-possessed young lady I ever came across." She was a feminist, a "Boston girl," and Stan and she got into "a tremendous row" over women's rights; nonetheless, she obliged him by sewing buttons on his shirts and darning his socks. The following morning they visited the great Rheims cathedral, sketching the carved figures on the west front and overspending on photographs of architectural details. In the afternoon they took a train to Laon, a picturesque hill town, where an elderly attendant guided them through the galleries of the Gothic church. Gus and Genie, their money running out, went back to Paris from Laon, while Stan returned to Rheims.[13]

A few days later, a sketching trip to Beauvais was "a little too heroic" on account of the cold. Stanford almost froze stiff inside the Beauvais cathedral, and putting himself between sheets at night was like lying down "between two marble slabs." To make up for such discomforts while traveling, he liked to pamper himself, attending to his personal comfort whenever he could in food, drink, and comfortable accommodations. "Traveling alone makes you very selfish," he wrote home. "I am as careful of my personal comfort (so long as it doesn't cost anything) as the D_____ himself would be." He regretted, however, that he did not have more of an opportunity to improve his French, frequently embarrassed that he was too timid to join in the general conversation at mealtimes. Otherwise, he was managing well enough with the language, and had "got to the state of laughing at people for not understanding" what he was trying to say.[14]

On Christmas Eve, back in Paris, Stan joined Gus in shopping for presents and greenery to decorate the apartment, and after supper they and some friends joined the throngs strolling on the boulevards before a midnight visit to St. Sulpice for Christmas music. Stan bought some mistletoe, which he hung in the Saint-Gaudenses' parlor, and on Christmas Day, as games were being played, he and Louis Saint-Gaudens tried unsuccessfully to maneuver some of the ladies under the mistletoe. William Gedney Bunce, an American painter, who worked in a corner of Gus's studio, was often at the apartment that winter, and Samuel Clemens, who arrived in Paris on February 28, occasionally joined them for an evening. Clemens, who had published *Tom Sawyer* two years before, always smoked one big cigar after another. His pontifications on the nature of art usually signaled the close of what were always highly sociable evenings.[15]

During the early months of 1879, Stan helped Gus at the studio with the Farragut statue and the Morgan tomb commissions. Both artists were committed to creating for the Farragut something new and different from the lifeless, uninteresting public monuments of the time, realizing all the while, of course, the importance of the work for New York City and for their own careers. The Farragut would be a major statue, prominently placed (though in a location yet to be determined), and its designers would obviously gain public notice. By mid-February, Gus reported back to John Dix of the Farragut Commission that he was "doing every-thing in [his] power to try and do something good and to break away from the regular conventional statues." White's studies for the pedestal, Gus wrote, would "be very good indeed and very original." White, he affirmed, "has a good deal of talent and discretion, and I am delighted that he is helping me in this work." Saint-Gaudens hoped to have the statue completed in two or three months and could then send on photo-graphs to the commission. By then the two artists were trying out the idea of a high circular stone seat for the statue base. At the end of February Gussie wrote to her mother that Gus and Stan had "put up the whole thing in paper in the studio so as to get an idea of the proportions, and they have now arrived at a satisfactory result. But what a work it all is!"[16]

Meanwhile, Stanford savored such delights of Paris as the Louvre, the Cluny Museum, the Opéra, the Comédie Française, and the Cirque d'Hiver, often escorting Gus's sister-in-law on an evening. One Saturday night, Gus, Stan, and Bunce, the painter, left Gussie and Genie at the apartment at midnight to attend a masked ball at the opera house and did not return home until half past six the following morning. Gus reported by letter to his mother-in-law that on their night on the town they had had "a splendid time." Stan kept talking about going to Italy, but Gussie wrote again and again to her mother that he was still with them and helping with the Farragut. Stan was obviously enjoying Paris immensely and hated to leave: "Not in this world is it possible to find another place where your wants, intellectual and physical, are so catered to; nor another place, such being the case, where you accomplish so little." Above all, he emphasized to his parents, Paris had "pooty gals," a subject that no doubt interested his father.[17]

For some time Saint-Gaudens had trouble modeling the legs of the Farragut figure, but that problem was at least partially solved when Richard Watson Gilder and his wife arrived in Paris, and Gilder was persuaded to pose for the legs. Suddenly, in March, while working on the Farragut, Gus fell very ill from a severe intestinal inflammation. He was racked by pain and ran a high fever. "It was all Mr. White, Louis, and I could do," Gussie wrote her mother, "to take care of him night and day." Once again, as with Henry Casey, Stan served as a nurse to a good friend. Genie, meanwhile, had left Paris to visit Italy. By early April Gus was on the mend, and he and his wife, accompanied by White, went to St.-Germain-en-Laye for the sculptor's recuperation. In early May, Gus and Stan visited Chartres, leaving Gussie behind in Paris; although "the cathedral was superb," they "had a pretty dismal time'' because of inclement weather. Finally, on May 8, Gussie arranged for ''an extra fine dinner,'' since White would be leaving for Italy the next day. Gus planned to join him there.[18]

The two friends traveled together in northern Italy, visiting Verona, Venice, and Carrara. Saint-Gaudens prepared a small sketchbook with notes and drawings of Italian buildings, paintings, and statuary in the summer of 1879, but it is not certain that White was with him at the time all the entries were made. From later correspondence it is evident that the two men had a disagreement of sorts while in Italy, though they did not let the incident interfere in the long run with their friendship. By June 11, White was in Rome and very busy trying to take in what he could of the Eternal City in the limited time he had available. ''My time is so short here I grudge every moment,'' he wrote his mother, but, ever the dutiful son, he reassured her that he was ''taking quinine, eating regularly, and carrying an overcoat to put on whenever [he went] into the churches and galleries.'' He journeyed south to Naples, hoping to view some volcanic activity at Mount Vesuvius, and on his way north stopped once again at Rome. By early July he was in Florence, already anticipating that he would be back home before long.[19]

White wrote his mother from Paris on August 15 that he would remain there but a few more days before going to London. Once more he and Gus worked on the Farragut Monument. At this time Gus wrote the Farragut Committee in New York that White on his return would have full power to arrange for the pedestal and would inform the committee of the progress on the statue. Stanny planned to sail from Liverpool on August 23. After thirteen months in Europe, he was getting tired of moving about, ''the prey of hotel-keepers, porters, beggars, pretty girls, and the host of spiders that lay in wait for the unwary traveller.'' In other words, obviously eager to see his family, he would be ''devilish glad to get back home again . . . a 'pooty' nice place after all.''[20]

London fascinated White. He discovered ''oceans of things there— far more than in Paris or indeed any place'' he had previously visited. Standing in front of the Greek and Assyrian bas-reliefs at the British Museum, he felt his ''hair alternately stand up and flatten down,'' so exciting were they. If only he might obtain casts of some of them, he would be ''a happy man for life.'' The Renaissance panels at the South Kensington Museum were a great treat as well. ''Never was such a place as London!'' A lifetime would be ''too short a time in which to explore that ancient—and by us neglected—city.''[21]

The voyage westward across the Atlantic, however, was a tremendous letdown from the excitement and the rush of impressions of the previous weeks. On board the *Olympus,* there was "no amusement, nobody to talk to." He felt so "dead of *ennui*" that he could not even read, write, or draw. One day when he did attempt to sketch, eleven old maids aboard the ship crowded about and made such inane comments, while all the time "sighing in admiration and wonder," that he had to stop his work. After leaving Queenstown (Cobh), Ireland, the ship encountered a roaring storm, and for five days they were battered about, the steerage hatchway was crushed, and the stairway to the hurricane deck was swept away. Stan joked each day with the ship's officers about the storm, trying to buoy up his own courage by minimizing its severity, only to have the third officer finally declare in exasperation to him, "Good heavens, sir! What *would* you like? I think you would like to sink the ship." Next to the storm, the greatest diversion on the voyage for Stan came in his encounters with "a she doctor" who was a sister of the notorious Victoria Woodhull and Tennessee Claflin, the feminist reformers. Strong-willed, aggressively opinionated, and a outspoken feminist herself, she was exactly the type of woman Stan most disliked. The inevitable resulted, and he "had a frightful row with the Woodhull woman." His dislike was compounded when he thought that she had purposely hidden a book he was reading and in which he had placed letters because of her exasperation with him. By Friday evening, September 5, the ship lay in quarantine in New York harbor, and the next day the "frightful trip" was at an end.[22]

Three days later, Stan announced in a letter to Gus that he had "gone into partnership with McKim and Mead." They were establishing a new architectural firm.[23]

5

A New Beginning

During his fourteen months abroad White explored châteaux, palaces, and churches; visited painting galleries and art collections; investigated antiques stores and shops specializing in the decorative arts; and immersed himself in the Bohemian life of Paris. His travel experiences were tremendously enriching, enlarging his vision of art and deepening his aesthetic sensibility. In his explorations he especially delighted in the picturesque—a jagged tower ruin, the silhouette of an old church spire, a winding street lined by ancient houses, built up and added to over time—and was particularly drawn to romantic remnants of the Middle Ages. Richardson had introduced him to the Romanesque, forcefully dignified, relatively simple, and yet highly picturesque, and in Europe he came upon the pictorial beauties and grandeur of the Gothic. At this time the balanced, symmetrically ordered structures of the classical Renaissance tradition had less appeal for him.

But whatever he saw, Stan took pleasure in ornamentation—in finely wrought decorative touches, in the fashioning of rich and varied materials, and in the contrasts and complements of different colors. His artistic experiences in Europe influenced the design work he soon undertook in his new firm, albeit limited, as it necessarily was, by clients' instructions and costs. White's vision of the possibilities of opulent ornamentation would permeate his work throughout his career.

Stan's discovery of Europe came at a particularly fortunate time, when he had already mastered the fundamentals of his craft. Like architectural students who lived in Paris and studied at the Ecole des Beaux-Arts, he gained a great deal just from being in Paris and experiencing the beauties and savoring the artistic traditions of the city. The months in Paris, moreover, expanded his stimulating friendship with Saint-Gaudens, providing him with the opportunity to share and question creative ideas with another gifted artist. The visit to Europe, as well, brought a hiatus from the day-to-day work that had so absorbed him for the previous eight years, allowing him to reflect on who he was and what he might be able to do. White's "grand tour" in a way provided a retreat from making a living so that he might better set about to make a life.

Above all, the European journey both deepened his taste for the beautiful and stimulated his appetite for experiencing beauty even more fully. With very limited funds available to him, he could do little more on this first visit than look at—perhaps touch as well—the objects, large and small, that delighted him. Later on, as his position became established, his professional clientele built up, and he acquired financial resources, he could gratify his aesthetic needs more directly by buying things for himself. His father, who collected musical instruments and rare books, and Richardson, a collector of fine furniture, paintings, and art objects, provided models for him to emulate. In a few years, Stan's desire to acquire beautiful objects would become a passion, almost a compulsion, which ultimately would have disastrous results.

William Mead had visited Paris briefly in the spring, and it is likely the two friends had seen each other then. Possibly at that time Mead first broached to Stan the proposition of joining with him and McKim. A few months later, in July 1879, when Annie Bigelow McKim filed for divorce after two years of separation from Charley, the position of her brother in the firm of McKim, Mead & Bigelow became uncomfortable, and Bigelow withdrew. With his departure, Mead wrote Stan and formally invited him to join the firm as a partner in place of Bigelow, setting forth terms for his participation. McKim, who knew White better than Mead did, was well aware that Stan was deficient in systematic architectural training, but to his credit, as Charley said to Mead, he could "draw like a house a fire!" Meanwhile, Sidney V. Stratton and Joseph Morrill Wells, both of whom had worked with Richard Morris Hunt, had come to work for the firm; Stratton's name by early fall shared the firm's letterhead, appearing even above White's on some of the stationery. At first Stan was apprehensive about his ability to make a living on the terms offered him, but he realized, as he wrote Saint-Gaudens after returning to New York: "It really after all was quite as liberal as I could expect for the first year." If he could pick up "a little decoration work outside the office," he felt he would be able to manage. Mead indicated that White accepted the proposition "with great enthusiasm."[1]

Although no record survives of the proposition first offered White, a memoir does exist of the articles of co-partnership, dated June 21, 1880, establishing terms for the year beginning July 1. By the agreement, the net receipts of the firm, after expenses, were to be divided 42 percent to McKim, 33 percent to Mead, and 25 percent to White. The terms offered to Stan the first months in 1879 most likely were less favorable and were justified by his youth and lack of formal training. White himself later recalled that the partnership of McKim, Mead & White was formed in 1881, which was probably the time, two years later, when an equal-thirds partnership was agreed upon.[2]

On Monday, September 8, 1879, two days after arriving back in New York, Stan went to work at 57 Broadway. "For the first week," he wrote Gus in Paris, "I had my hands & my head as full as I can wish of things to do and think over." Not only did he at once become deeply involved in the work of the office, but there were the contracts to be negotiated concerning the Farragut Monument. He spoke to Richardson and Frederick Law Olmsted about the Farragut and showed them the new drawings of the design, which both liked better than the preliminary sketches. Richardson, Stan reported to Gus, still wanted the sculptor to work on the Albany Capitol, even though the older architect had not yet written him about it.[3]

Although Stan found himself nearly overwhelmed by his work at the McKim, Mead & White office in those first months, he managed to carry on an extensive correspondence with Gus in Paris, keeping the sculptor informed of the Farragut Committee's responses, while working out details of the design and arrangements for the placement of the monument. At one point Saint-Gaudens wrote that he felt "completely and thoroughly befuddled and disgusted with Farragut," but his very uncertainty made him think that "therefore it must be very good." Both artists were well aware that what they were doing—inspired by Italian Renaissance statuary and benches—was decidedly different from current standards of American public sculpture, then characterized by idealized figures stuck atop boxlike pedestals with simple moldings. Both believed that if they could carry off their ideas the work would make a tremendous stir because of the unusual configuration of the monument. As the design neared completion, Stan grew more and more excited about it: "I am just as much interested in the success of the pedestal as you are," he wrote Gus, "Nor, alas! shall I see many such chances in my life to do work in so entirely an artistic spirit unhampered by the—well, small

Hells that encircle us on every side, women who want closets, for instance." He could, in a sense, "let himself go" on this pedestal design and make it a personal artistic statement in a way that was not always so possible with the many conventional details of house construction and the demands of clients.[4]

Yet the Farragut Monument was becoming costly—more so than had originally been allowed for—which was a sticking point for the committee. White attempted to explain to John J. Cisco of the committee just what they were trying to do in getting away from "the ordinary unsupported monolithic pedestal" and in utilizing instead a hemisphere with low relief figures below the statue. "There is," White wrote, "no question but that this would be infinitely more original and artistic and a far greater ornament to the city than the regulation pedestal." For Stan, civic sculpture must be noticed, and he was certain that the fully integrated statue and pedestal that he and Gus were making would be looked at and commented on. To expedite the project, Gus proposed to model the relief figures without compensation, and Stan agreed to contribute his work without a commission. Although they were eventually paid commissions, both men spent some of their own money to have the monument work completed. In mid-October, Stan wrote Gus that if he wanted to go back to a "chaste and inexpensive pedestal" he would agree, for Gus was "the boss" on the project. Obviously, though, White preferred to move ahead with their striking new design.[5]

The architect was eager to obtain additional criticism concerning the Farragut design besides that from Richardson and Olmsted. He especially wanted the opinion of his close friend George Fletcher Babb, the architect "on whose judgment I most rely," who "had more feeling for delicate and beautiful detail than anyone yet born on this side of the water," as well as from his longtime adviser, the painter John La Farge. When La Farge saw the drawings he suggested removing the rise from the wall behind the seat below the statue, but Babb, on the contrary, felt that the rise should stay or else the pedestal would look too heavy. As a consequence, White told Gus, "as I care too much for Babb's opinion, & my conscience would never have forgiven me if I got the pedestal too heavy I began floundering around trying to improve matters until McKim came along & said, 'You're a damn fool, you've got a good thing. Why don't you stick to it?' So I've stuck to it." But he did make the back somewhat flatter than the original conception and the pedestal broader and slightly lower. With these changes, "Babb [now] approves, everybody approves, & I am consequently happy." Regarding the proposed incised ocean waves on the pedestal, Stan urged Gus to "do just as you darn please & it will be sure to be bully," closing the letter with "Ever Lovingly." Gus, for his part, left it to Stan to make the final decision on the height of the wall and urged him to move ahead to conclude a contract for the pedestal. The freedom for artistic invention and the possibilities for originality of design and ornamentation made the Farragut immensely important for White. Here, albeit on a small scale but in a work that would be conspicuously placed, he might realize his artistic vision and in so doing, he hoped, gain some public recognition.[6]

White favored a site near the northwest corner of Madison Square Park, while Gus at first wanted the Farragut erected in Union Square, fearful of reflections on the monument from the large Fifth Avenue Hotel across from Madison Square. But by early November 1879, the two artists had decided on the Madison Square site. Articles of agreement for the pedestal work were finally signed on December 13, 1879. Toward the close of the year, Saint-Gaudens had a plaster cast made, and by the following February a plaster mold was taken. A short time later, Gus reported that everything was going well: "I think your fish, sea, seat, the whole thing, will look better than you ever dreamed it would. I'm sure of that."[7]

In a letter the following spring, Stan, greeting his friend with a "Doubly Beloved," apologized that he had not yet sent Mrs. Saint-Gaudens his share of the household expenses incurred during his stay with them in Paris but promised to send the money "pretty damn soon." Tardiness in settling his debts would later become a common feature in White's life. When Gus had written that he was "feeling sorry for things [he had done] in Italy and what not," Stan urged him to stop apologizing: "If ever a man acted well [in Italy], you did, and I ought to have been kicked for many reasons." The air was cleared of the tensions that had occurred on the Italian excursion. Their relationship continued close and harmonious, each greatly admiring and respecting the other's abilities. Saint-Gaudens, another friend believed, "had probably a higher regard for the judgment of Stanford White, who made so many of his pedestals, than for that of any other man."[8]

Shortly afterward, the statue was cast in bronze in Paris and sent on to the United States, and Gus and Augusta returned to New York. Earlier, Gus had entered a plaster copy of the statue in the Paris Salon of 1880 and was awarded an honorable mention. By midsummer the sculptor was established in a studio in the Sherwood Building on Fifty-seventh Street at Sixth Avenue. There he worked on the bas-reliefs for the figures, the emblems, and the lengthy pedestal inscription, which recounted biographical details, prepared by Stan's father. Saint-Gaudens subsequently took a much larger studio at 148 West Thirty-sixth Street and rented a seventh-floor apartment at 22 Washington Place, just to the east of Washington Square, not far from where Stan was living with his parents. During the spring of 1881 the two friends worked together closely, each supporting and stimulating the other, while they oversaw the completion and erection of the monument.[9]

The Farragut Monument was unveiled on May 25, 1881, a bright, sunny day, at a ceremony that included many official participants and a crowd of interested spectators estimated at ten thousand. Saint-Gaudens and White sat on the platform with other dignitaries, including a very proud Richard Grant White. Saint-Gaudens, one observer wrote, looked especially "long faced and solemn" in this "great hour of triumph," which was "the turning point of his career." Flags and bunting were displayed on houses around the square. A Marine guard from the Brooklyn Navy Yard, along with sailors and Marines from American ships, stood nearby at attention. After a prayer, the Secretary of the Navy presented the statue to the city on behalf of the Farragut Monument Association. As a seventeen-gun salute was fired, the draperies covering the monument were drawn aside by sailors who had served with Farragut. Joseph H. Choate, a prominent lawyer-diplomat, then gave the principal address of the day.[10]

As the draperies were pulled away, something entirely new in American sculpture was revealed to the spectators in Madison Square. Here was a remarkable departure from the customary idealized sculptural work of the time. Surmounting the pedestal, the bronze image of Farragut stood firmly resolute, with feet wide apart as if on a rolling deck. A realistic portrait figure in an admiral's uniform, the coat blown aside by the wind, the statue was given a meaning transcending the individual both by the symbolic character of the figure and by the imagery of the pedestal. Constructed of North River bluestone, the pedestal formed a semicircular seat, on either side of a broad pier, which served as the base for the statue. On the central pier, a carved sword cut down through flowing waves, which moved across the high back of the seat on both sides over two low-relief, seated figures representing Loyalty and Courage, virtues associated with Farragut. Next to the figures were the long biographical inscriptions, the lettering modeled so as to enhance the decorative effect. Curving backs of dolphins formed the ends of the seat. Inset in the paving of pebbles in front was a bronze crab with White's name inscribed on its back.[11]

The critical reception of the Farragut Monument was largely enthusiastic. One spectator, who watched the proceedings from the balcony of Delmonico's restaurant just to the north, judged the statue quite simply as "the greatest work of art that had been produced by an American." To Mariana Griswold Van Rensselaer, one of the foremost art critics of the day and a friend of the two artists, the Farragut was "the best monument of its kind the city has to show." The statue, she wrote, possessed a decided "American" flavor, with "the subtle qualities of race and national character . . . strongly prominent." Mrs. Van Rensselaer found the pedestal satisfying, although in her estimation it somehow lacked "perfect adaptation to place and purpose, which is the highest excellence of an architectural creation." For the journalist Richard Watson Gilder, whose legs the admiral shared, the "large and novel" pedestal, however, was perhaps "more interesting" than the statue figure itself. The two artists, Gilder wrote, were men not only of "thorough education and training, but also of genius." An anonymous critic, on the other hand, severely criticized the pedestal for not developing a truly architectural quality. It had a certain "artlessness" about it, which this critic did not find commendable; it was regrettable, in fact, that the sculptor "should not have had the assistance of an architect" in this work. Later evaluations of the Farragut Monument almost always stressed the novel treatment of the base and the skillful integration of statue and pedestal into a unified composition.[12]

Stan and Gus, meanwhile, were continuing their work on the tomb for Governor Morgan and on a monument to Robert Richard Randall, the founder of Sailors' Snug Harbor, a home for aged seamen on Staten Island. Arrangements for both projects proceeded slowly. White had designed the Morgan tomb with three robed angels at the foot of a Greek cross, but the projected cost of the statuary and the tomb proper was so great that Morgan delayed moving ahead for a long while until he felt he could afford the expense. Moreover, for a time there was a question whether the angels would even be acceptable to Morgan and his wife. When someone in the McKim, Mead & White office saw a photograph of Saint-Gaudens's figures, one praying and two playing on the harp and lute, and inquired if they were to represent a musical party and then was shocked to learn they were intended for a tomb, Stanford was very much taken aback. He suggested that Gus write Morgan about his composition and prepare him for the idea of death as a resurrection: "Some people are such God damned asses they always think of death as a gloomy performance instead of a resurrection." Stan himself was enthusiastic about Gus's angels and pronounced them "perfectly lovely." McKim also was enthusiastic, and "even Babb," Stan reported, said " 'H-m-m,' which is lots for him." Already in this early work, there is strong evidence of White's artistic sensibility, his impatience with conventional taste and striving for something daringly different that would stir the viewer. Unfortunately, in August 1884, just as workmen began to erect the tomb in Cedar Hill Cemetery in Hartford, the shed where the pieces were stored caught fire and the work was damaged beyond repair. The Morgan tomb project was never revived. Gus was devastated by the "utter and absolute ruin" of the striking work, and no doubt the blow was severe to Stan as well.[13]

Stan at first imaginatively conceived the Robert Richard Randall Memorial, honoring the benefactor of the home for elderly, retired seamen, as having a 40-foot seat integrated with an ornamented, statue-topped pedestal. But the president of the New York Board of Commerce, who was in charge of the commission and was, according to White, "a perfect blockhead about art and the most pig-headed man I know of," did not want the seat, preferring instead something "as severe and simple as possible." White was annoyed that he could not extend himself in the Randall setting as he had for the Farragut and Morgan pieces, and disliked the plain block pedestal design that the commission decided on. In Paris, Gus had such a difficult time with the statue that he remodeled it on his return to New York. The Randall Monument was erected in 1884 at Sailors' Snug Harbor, Staten Island, but the sculptor and the architect were always dissatisfied with the work.[14]

White was fortunate that the first major architectural project he assisted with in the firm was an important casino, a summer resort recreational center that allowed considerable scope for his inventiveness and for his love of ornamentation. The Newport (Rhode Island) Casino, moreover, inaugurated a long and significant relationship between him and James Gordon Bennett the younger, editor and publisher of the *New York Herald* and other newspapers.

The concept of the casino had arisen out of an incident at the exclusive Newport Reading Room in the late 1870s. Bennett, a member of the Reading Room, had sponsored as a subscriber Captain Henry Augustus Candy, a retired British officer visiting Newport with a polo team. One day, as Candy rode past the Reading Room, someone on the piazza challenged him to ride up the steps into the main hall of the clubhouse; the Britisher forthwith urged his mount up the steps and rode right inside. The Reading Room directors were so incensed that they withdrew Candy's guest privileges. Bennett regarded that action as a personal affront: He resigned his membership and vowed to build a rival clubhouse, the result being his commission in 1879 to McKim, Mead & White for

Bellevue Avenue facilities housing clubrooms, a restaurant, a theater, and tennis courts.[15]

In late October 1879, McKim visited Newport to discuss preliminary plans for the casino and to look over the Bellevue Avenue site adjacent to Richard Morris Hunt's Travers Block, a group of small stores with apartments above, designed in a quaint and cozy medieval-like mode. Some of the general features for the casino had already been decided upon—there would be stores on the Bellevue Avenue frontage, with a slightly projecting second story above, and an arched passageway leading to the casino courtyard. By early December, McKim's plans proved acceptable, and a subscription for memberships was soon under way. "Newport," a local newspaper suggested about the proposal, "can be congratulated in having an aggregation of buildings for the fashionable sports of our summer residents, which cannot be paralleled in the country."[16]

McKim was primarily responsible for the casino design, while White's contributions were particularly evident in the decorative work in the interior and the courtyard. Probably McKim, having devised the general elevations and plans, handed the commission over to Stan to complete. In the realization of the project, three large gables vary the roof line on the street front; the gables, along with shuttered second-story windows, a balcony, and weathered shingles above the first-story brickwork, all give the avenue front something of the character of a large shingle-style residence. The cozy, domestic character of the building harmonizes well with the adjacent intimately scaled Travers Block. The entrance passageway provides access to a picturesque interior courtyard surrounded by piazzas, partially faced by intricately interwoven latticework screens, contributing a variety of textures, solids and voids, and shapes to the walls. A fat shingled clock tower rises near the courtyard entrance. Behind the courtyard—the horseshoe piazza—the architects placed lawn courts, a court tennis building, and a ballroom or theater, which Stan decorated inside in gold, blue, and ivory, "the carving and turning of the woodwork . . . executed with great delicacy and beauty." In the main casino building, a reading room, card room, dining room, and a billiard parlor were installed for the use of club subscribers. Other facilities were open to the public at large. To the critic Mariana Van Rensselaer, the casino was "dignified enough without being formal or pretentious, rural, but not rustic, graceful, intimate, cheerful, with just a touch of fantasy, not out of place in a structure whose ends are distinctly frivolous—a Casino which is a mere summer-house for 'society's' amusement." The Newport Casino opened on July 26, 1880, and at once became the center of fashionable social life in the community, with morning tennis, an orchestra or band regularly playing, and in the evening dancing in the ballroom, sometimes with the galleries above opened for the townspeople, who paid a dollar for the privilege of looking down on the revelers.[17]

Recreational facilities like the Newport Casino would become increasingly important to White, who delighted in the opportunities for inventiveness that club design could bring, and after their completion he often reveled in the entertainments that were offered in his buildings. He would be involved in many commissions for social clubs and became an active member of numerous clubs and associations. In these and other commissions, White's professional and personal lives were brought together. In time this convergence would make it difficult to distinguish the private man from the extravagant creations and the life-style on which they were predicated.

Nearby at Narragansett Pier, Rhode Island, the firm, with McKim in charge, began another important casino in 1883, to be completed three years later. Like Newport across the bay to the east, Narragansett Pier attracted summer visitors from New York, Philadelphia, and Baltimore, but the resort was considered less fashionable and did not favor the ostentatious display of wealth that became so characteristic of Newport. The most striking feature of the Narragansett Pier Casino was the rough-stone masonry arch, spanning Ocean Avenue along the shore, flanked by two large rounded Norman towers. Above the arch, a gallery housed a café and formed a promenade, which was a popular spot for viewing the ocean or for walks to take the air during the evening dances in the ballroom. The main part of the casino stretched back from the arch in a zigzag and contained a ballroom–theater, a restaurant, a private dining room, bowling alleys, shops, and reading and writing parlors, lined by galleries. The roof lines of the casino, dotted with dormers and cupolas, were varied and irregular, suggesting, *Harper's Weekly* observed, "the effect of ravaging winds." To the younger set and newcomers, the Narragansett Pier Casino was regarded "as the crowning glory of a delightful spot." McKim, among the partners, especially liked Narragansett Pier and in later years often vacationed there. White, more sociable and fashion conscious than his partner, favored Newport and enjoyed visiting its casino.[18]

Much smaller than those two casinos, but also serving as a civic recreational center, was the Short Hills Casino at Milburn, New Jersey, commissioned in November 1879 by Stewart Hartshorn for a planned community he was developing. White created the small theater building, while McKim designed a model house for Hartshorn. Known generally as the Short Hills Music Hall, the modest structure was variously used for town meetings, school and church purposes, and theatricals. It was, according to the *New-York Tribune*, "one of the most notable buildings of its kind in the New York suburbs," the locus of many "social gayeties and exceedingly handsome entertainments." Like the other casinos, it became the primary social center for the local gentry and, therefore, served as a cementing force for the community.[19]

Aside from the Newport Casino, the resort town of Newport provided White and other architects with great opportunities to design interesting and innovative buildings. Already by the early 1880s the most fashionable summer resort for well-to-do Americans, Newport toward the close of the century grew into a showplace of luxury and extravagant ostentation. Stanford White moved easily in its opulent ambience; wealthy Newport clients became his friends, and some friends became free-spending clients.

In January 1880, McKim, Mead & White was commissioned by David King, Jr., to remodel his residence on Bellevue Avenue in Newport, close to the casino. The King house, Kingscote, a highly picturesque dwelling, had been designed by the eminent architect Richard Upjohn and built in 1840–41 in the then popular Gothic Revival style, recalling elements of late medieval design. David King, Jr., who had retired very prosperous after fourteen years in the China trade, had acquired the house in 1875, as guardian of the estate of his uncle, who had been judged insane. King and his wife remodeled the place in 1876–77, and in 1880 they decided to enlarge it considerably to enable them to entertain more lavishly, in accord with the changing character of Newport. At that time the kitchen wing was moved some 40 feet out from the house and an addition was built in between. A large dining room, which could also serve as a ballroom, was placed on the ground floor of the new addition, with bedrooms, a hallway, and a bathroom on the second and third floors above.[20]

The 1880–81 addition to Kingscote, though so large as to be out of scale with the original cottage, was integrated well into the house. White designed a new dining room, the most lavish room in the house. Here the walls were paneled in mahogany to the height of a molded plate rail, and the upper walls and ceiling were covered with cork. A massive sideboard was built into the north wall of the room. The east end was formed by a remarkable screen, separating the dining room proper from a foyer; the lower part of the screen was paneled, and the upper part constructed in delicate spool and spindlework with a dahlia motif. A large marble-faced fireplace on the west wall was framed in brass, the chimney covered with green Tiffany glass tiles, and on both sides of the fireplace opaque windows of opalescent blue, green, and gray Tiffany glass bricks were placed. Dahlia designs were sketched both in arched panels above the fireplace and in stained glass panels in a bay window facing south. The effect of this colorful room is that of great opulence, signaled by a variety of materials and textures carefully related to one another, with an interpenetration of spaces—all characteristic of White's work at the time.[21]

Fueled by his exposure to art in Europe, Stan increasingly developed a sensuous quality in his decorative work, as in the Kingscote dining room and in the Watts Sherman house library, rebuilt about the same time, employing fine materials, interesting textures, rich colors, and striking designs. White's love for decoration and interior design, customarily part of the architect's work, was deeply felt, and his gift was no doubt due, in part at least, to his skill in drawing and his attention to detail. The young professional of twenty-seven could make up for some of the limitations of his childhood by reveling in the opulent materials he could now provide his clients. Already in these first years with the firm, White was beginning to serve as an instructor in decoration for his times, a role that would be increasingly important in the years to come.

More central in the firm's projects in the early 1880s were private houses in a picturesque shingle style, the type of work with which White had already had experience in Richardson's office, including several residences in Newport. An important influence on the firm's early domestic designs were colonial American buildings of the seventeenth and early eighteenth centuries of the sort that White, McKim, and Mead had visited on their excursion into New England in 1877. The growing attention of the architects to shingled surfaces echoed this building mode of two centuries earlier. Already in the mid-1870s McKim had begun to use colonial details in house interiors, evoking elements of the American past and striving for a more traditional "American" quality in reaction against the excessive elaboration and fussiness of much midcentury Victorian design. Stan and his partners soon combined colonial touches with Queen Anne stylistic elements from England, ideas that Stan may first have encountered directly in the British Pavilion at the 1876 Philadelphia Centennial Exposition. This stylistic mixture resulted in what has come to be known as the American shingle style.

Characteristic of the 1880s shingle-style houses were an openness and flexibility of interior arrangements, with large doors, giving a flowing quality to the space of halls and rooms, and substantial piazzas and porches for outdoor living. Interior room arrangements often dictated wall shapes and window size and placement, making for exterior asymmetry; towers and turrets, bay windows, gables and arches, ornamented panels, and colored-glass windows, all used in the English Queen Anne, were combined for picturesque effects. Surmounting a stone or brick foundation, the exterior sheathing of unpainted shingles was often arranged in fanciful, decorative patterns. In a time of architectural eclecticism, with a few houses still built in Gothic Revival, Italianate, and Second Empire styles and many in the English Queen Anne or Victorian Gothic, the American shingle-style dwellings stood out in their relative simplicity and strength.[22]

White's talent as a decorator was also evident a short distance to the south of the King house, along Bellevue Avenue, where, in September 1881, the firm began a splendid summer shingle-style residence for Isaac Bell, Jr. Bell was a cotton broker, future United States Minister to the Netherlands, and the brother-in-law of James Gordon Bennett, Jr., builder of the Newport Casino. A deep piazza enveloping the two street fronts of the Bell house created great shadowed first-story voids, which contrasted sharply with the lightness of the second- and third-story shingled surfaces rising into high-peaked gables and sheathing a squat tower with a bell-shaped roof. White was responsible for the attenuated simulated-bamboo posts for piazza supports at both the first-story level and on a two-tiered projection. Inside, the main-floor rooms clustered around the oak-paneled hall, from which a wide staircase rose to the second floor. Stan's intricately carved rosettes and spindles on the inglewood paneling in the hall complemented the Orientalizing motifs found in the bamboo posts of the exterior.[23]

Among the several other shingle-style houses that the firm erected in Newport about the same time, White was primarily responsible for a modest, picturesque cottage for Samuel Tilton on Sunnyside Place, built in 1881–82. Above a rough-faced granite foundation, continuing into the first story on the street front, the architect created a finely wrought shingle covering of varying patterns, inset with wooden panels and, on the north and west, strikingly original stucco mosaics with sunburst and shield designs made from colored glass, pebbles, and shells, a decorative device that White employed several times. As in others of the early 1880s houses, intricately carved paneling, spindlework, and built-in benches and seats characterized the principal rooms, revealing White's penchant for small and unexpected touches, the dramatic surprises of romantic design.

As the reputation of the partners became established and new commissions flooded in, White was engaged as principal architect on several new houses. Considerably larger than the King, Bell, or Tilton houses was the Robert Goelet mansion, Southside, overlooking the Atlantic Ocean on Narragansett Avenue, begun in 1882 and completed in 1884. The entrance façade of the structure was framed by twin bulging towers recessed into the main roof at the top. On the ocean front, Stan created a broad piazza, terminating at both ends in gabled pavilions, the voids at this level echoed by small loggias at the upper story. Stucco panels, glittering with pieces of broken glass, were set into the variously cut shingles forming the striking skin covering of the house. Within, a two-story great hall surrounded by galleries constituted the nucleus of the dwelling.

As with so many of White's projects, the client and the architect became friendly. Goelet, a New York real estate investor, shortly became one of Stanny's close friends. In Goelet's summer cottage as in many of his houses, White with his partners provided a suitable setting for the luxurious and sometimes ostentatious life-style that men of wealth of the Gilded Age often wished to pursue. Within a few years, White himself would be caught up in this sumptuous life-style, sharing the recreations and entertainments of his friends, while emulating their richness of living—and paying a price.

Already a friend at this time in the early 1880s was Samuel Colman, a well-to-do painter, for whom Stan also designed a Newport summer cottage, a structure considerably more modest than Goelet's Southside. The son of a prosperous New York publisher, Colman had studied with the painter Asher B. Durand. His talent, especially in watercolors, was such that at the age of twenty-seven he was elected an associate of the National Academy of Design, and in 1866 he was chosen the first president of the American Water-Color Society. He was also active in the Society of American Artists. For years Colman's New York studio, on Fourth Avenue at Twenty-fifth Street, cluttered with French tapestries, Japanese armor, and Chinese pottery, was a gathering place for artists. White designed the gambrel-roofed Colman cottage in Newport with a richly shingled second story overhanging a deeply recessed veranda; a rubble-coarsed terrace wall extending outward from the veranda provided a substantial base that firmly tied the house to the earth.

In Mamaroneck, New York, the large Charles J. Osborn house, close to the water's edge on Long Island Sound, was one of White's most substantial early designs. Begun in August of 1883 and built in 1884 and 1885, the Osborn project put into a domestic arrangement some of the same elements incorporated into the Narragansett Pier Casino, continuing the theme of rough-textured walls and Norman-style towers that

Richardson had been using. Twin conical-roofed towers connected by a two-tiered loggia above a low-arched entryway formed one end and a separate apartment of the mansion, which extended back in a zigzag plan. Two other towers rose toward the center of the house and, with the two on the ends, enhanced its romantic silhouette. As with the casino, a driveway bisected the structure, the upper stories forming a bridge above. For the towers, the lower story, and the terrace walls, White used rugged quarry-faced graystone, effectively binding the house to the rocky shore. Inside, a large two-story main hall formed the core of the dwelling: The parlor, the reception room, and the dining room all opened into the hall. The firm also designed for Osborn a stable and a gate lodge at Mamaroneck, as well as a mausoleum in Woodlawn Cemetery, the Bronx, New York.[24]

Culminating this romantic, country house mode for White was the shingle-style summer dwelling he created for Joseph H. Choate, on Prospect Hill near Stockbridge, Massachusetts, one of his most elegant early houses. The 26-room Norman mansion, set in a 49-acre estate and surrounded by extensive gardens, was begun in 1885 and completed the following year. Not only did White design the house and superintend its construction, but as with so many of his houses he also advised on its interior decoration and furnishings. Mrs. Choate and her daughters, avid collectors of antiques, filled the house with priceless pieces. Collaborating with White, Frederick MacMonnies sculpted a faun-and-heron fountain for the grounds.

Joseph Choate, a famous, highly successful New York lawyer, who gave the principal speech at the inauguration of the Farragut Monument, became a longtime friend of White. He and his wife called the Stockbridge place "Naumkeag," the Indian name of Salem, Massachusetts, Choate's birthplace, meaning "Haven of Comfort" or "Place of Rest." After completion of the estate, Stan visited Naumkeag several times as a house guest, enjoying the surroundings he had created and the company of Choate, a noted conversationalist, and his closely knit family. By the mid-1880s, White's circle of client-friends was rapidly expanding.[25]

The Choate house was erected with a commanding location on the brink of Prospect Hill. The entrance front, with few openings and terminated by two small conical towers, was built of rough stone at the first-story level and patterned brick above, the entryway almost obscured by a heavy porte-cochère. White opened up the garden side with considerably more fenestration, a large piazza, and shingled walls, to embrace the terrace below and the splendid view to the west. Belying the asymmetrical romantic exterior, the interior of the dwelling was given an almost Georgian formality: The library and parlor, placed on one side of the center hall, balanced the dining room and stair hall on the other. An adjoining wing on the first floor contained the service pantry, a school room, and Choate's private study.

The most unusual domestic project White undertook in the 1880s was the castlelike mansion he designed for Mrs. Mark Hopkins in Great Barrington, Massachusetts, not far from Naumkeag. The widow of the California railroad builder with a vast fortune at her disposal, Mary Sherwood Hopkins undertook to build an ostentatious dwelling for herself in her home town. Inspired by châteaux of the Loire Valley, White created a picturesque and imposing mass dominated by conical towers, soaring chimneys, and steeply pitched rooflines—a European château for a newly rich American plutocrat. Eight months after the Hopkins house was begun and its shell already in place, however, the firm of McKim, Mead & White was abruptly replaced by another designer, Edward Searles, who completed the mansion, married the widow Hopkins, twenty-one years his senior, and shortly thereafter inherited most of her fortune.[26]

In New York, White was also closely involved in the firm's early commissions for city houses. With his partners he brought distinctive touches of artistry and elegance to the urban streets, then mostly lined with monotonous brownstone fronts. By 1880 the city had about 1,165,000 residents, nearly double the population at the time of Stan's birth, and the move northward on Manhattan Island was continuing relentlessly. Demands for luxury housing were rapidly increasing.

The J. Coleman Drayton house on Fifth Avenue near Thirty-fifth Street, built in 1882–83, and the Phillips and Lloyd Phoenix house, close by at 21 East Thirty-third Street and built in 1882–84, were elegant townhouses. Above a rough-faced stone base with a deeply recessed arched entryway, the Drayton house rose in two bays through four and one-half stories, topped by a distinctive hipped roof. The irregular stone frames of the windows as well as the base emphasized the rugged strength of this house. Varied treatment of the windows in the two bays and decorative paneling reinforced the distinctive character of the façade. The four-story brick-faced Phoenix house, by contrast, had a much sparer façade, to which a sumptuous richness was imparted by large panels incised with geometrical designs. Both houses stood out as markedly individual expressions of their designers among the almost uniform, monotonous brownstones of the midtown neighborhood.

The Charles T. Barney double house at 10 East Fifty-fifth Street, erected in 1880–82 for a banker who would become closely involved with Stanford in the years to come, had a much fussier street front, with myriad stylistic elements, including even some Georgian touches. Just a short time after its completion, the Barney house became well known for its interior design; it was called "the best interior in New York from an artistic point of view." George Fletcher Babb, Stan's longtime architect friend, decorated the library of the Barney house.[27]

In Baltimore, White was primarily responsible for a large free-standing townhouse for Ross Winans, completed in 1883. The heir to a fortune gained in railroad construction in Russia, Winans had become acquainted with White in Newport, had been impressed by his early work there, and employed him for the Baltimore house and to decorate the interior of his yacht, which he often sailed from Newport. In the townhouse, White used a light stone for the ground story, quoins, and belt courses and window enframement, and brownstone on the upper walls. A round staircase tower, decorated by a band of leaded windows and sculptured panels, dominated the street façade. Cut into the steeply sloped, slate-covered roof were handsomely ornamented dormer windows, whose shape and enframement were repeated in a regular rhythm elsewhere in the fenestration on the house.

Finally, among these early domestic commissions, the Tiffany house in New York City on the northwest corner of Madison Avenue and Seventy-second Street was White's most remarkable achievement. Design work began on the house in April 1882, but it was not completed until 1885. Built for Charles L. Tiffany, the Union Square jeweler, the house was arranged to contain three separate residences—for him on the first and second floors, for his daughter and her family on the third floor, and for his son, the artist Louis Comfort Tiffany, on the fourth floor and in the vast attic studio above. White had already come to know Louis Tiffany in 1880, when he had worked with him as consulting architect on the Seventh Regiment Armory, which Tiffany, the painter Francis Millet, and others had decorated. Stan again collaborated on the Tiffany family dwelling with his friend, who was actively involved in the project, conceiving the general idea for the great house and decorating the interior.

Set upon a one-and-one-half-story basement faced with dark North River bluestone, the upper part of the house was covered by thin, flat bricks, yellowish and speckled with black. White created these unusual bricks especially for this house, working with craftsmen at the Atlantic Terra Cotta Company in Perth Amboy, New Jersey; they were subsequently known as "Tiffany bricks." The two most distinctive features of the exterior were a turret attached at the street intersection corner of the house, corbeled out from the rugged base and rising through three stories, and the remarkable black tile roof steeply plunging downward over the very high attic. The ceiling of the studio rose to a height of 50 feet above the floor. Access to the house was gained through a low-arched driveway leading to an interior courtyard large enough for a carriage to turn around in; from the driveway and courtyard separate staircases led to the three residences. A smaller house to the north on Madison Avenue was later integrated into the main structure. The picturesque elements of the Tiffany house, especially the textural and color contrasts, the relationship of solids and voids, and the window arrangements clearly related the Tiffany house to Stanny's other early domestic commissions, especially those at Newport.[28]

The Tiffany house attracted a great deal of attention. The British literary critic Edmund Gosse, on a visit to the United States, declared that it was "the most beautiful modern domestic building [he had] almost ever seen . . . the realization of an architect's dream." Gosse likened the Tiffany house to a great seventeenth-century Swiss chalêt, having "a sort of vastness, as if it had grown like a mountain." Mrs. Van Rensselaer also praised the "very beautiful" dwelling as "the most interesting and most promising house we have yet constructed."[29]

White's entry into partnership with McKim and Mead in 1879, as these descriptions of early projects show, brought him immediately into the vanguard of significant architectural activity in the United States. With Bennett's Newport Casino, the additions to Kingscote, the Choate house, the Tiffany house, and the other early projects, he was involved in designs that were soon widely noticed. Already in these first years the firm was becoming recognized as one of the most important in the country, and White's contributions in realizing the needs of wealthy clients and, particularly, in decoration and ornamentation were central in the partnership's body of work.

The press of projects in the office, the problems and tensions of dealing with many clients, the frequent journeys from one ongoing job to another, combined with a very full social life in the city, gave Stan's days an exhausting pace. Although he often complained about the burdens and the pressures, he obviously loved and took great satisfaction in what he was doing. It was evident that he had an insatiable appetite for work and for play.

The operation of the office was made difficult, however, by the frequent absences of one or both of his partners, especially McKim, whose health suffered with the stress from the collapse of his marriage and the bitter court fights that ensued. Stan sympathized with Charley but believed that the blame for most of his partner's troubles could be laid at the door of a strong-minded woman, the type of woman Stan, just like his father, did not care for. To Gus in Paris, shortly before his return to America, the young architect complained: "I cannot tell you how driven I am with business on account of McKim's absence from the office. For the last month I have been nearly frantic, being often at my office till midnight. Poor McKim is much better, but still unable to work. He will have to go abroad again. He will be devilish sorry to miss you." Then, with intense aversion that may have embodied an element of fear as well: "DAMN strong-minded women, say I." Defiantly, he vowed: "I tell you. 'You no catchee me marry!' " That determination would soon be tested.[30]

⑥

57 Broadway

❧

The source of these many designs was the McKim, Mead & White office, located on the west side of lower Broadway just to the south of Trinity Church overlooking Exchange Place. Number 57, a narrow five-story, cast-iron commercial building with Gothic Revival detail, dated from 1850. At first the firm occupied small quarters there, but at some point in the early 1880s, as commissions were growing, McKim, Mead & White took over the entire top floor. Clients making their way to the office and fearful of trusting themselves to the creaking elevator, which had been built into the open stairwell, had to climb up several flights of wooden steps.

On the top story, a small reception room opened into the main drafting room, which occupied most of the floor. A dozen or so large tables were set up for the regular draftsmen, who by the close of the 1880s numbered about seventy-five. Recesses with small tables for senior employees were built along the window side of the main room. Plaster casts of architectural details, Venetian wrought-iron pieces, drawings, and photographs decorated the walls. Cubbyhole offices provided retreats for the partners, but those private offices were so small that the firm members spent most of their time in the drafting rooms. For his private office White acquired an antique cherry desk and a mahogany windsor chair, along with a small cane couch for visitors and a drafting board on horses. Two small drafting rooms, known as the "Holy of Holies," connected with the principal drafting area by a leather-covered swinging door, were reserved for the partners and their chief assistants. Stan's tendency to fling open this door as he rushed out into the main room made standing near it hazardous when he was around. For a dozen years, from 1879 to 1891, the 57 Broadway office was the center of White's life, the place where his creative energies were most focused.[1]

Soon after noon, each working day, the partners and others from the firm customarily dined at a small restaurant, which they called "Spain," a short distance to the south on Broadway. Afterward the men usually took a walk along the seawall around the Battery before returning to work. In the informal talk at meals and on the walks, many young draftsmen who had come to study architecture with McKim, Mead & White absorbed a great deal about the practical aspects of their craft. At times, under the press of work, the draftsmen were asked to put in overtime in the evening; they received a dollar for dinner in a neighborhood restaurant and were expected to return to work until late in the evening without additional pay. An office baseball team brought some of the men together for recreation; occasionally the athletes had a "practice session" in the drafting room, tossing about wads of waste paper. For one "graduate" of the 57 Broadway office, the most enjoyable times there, though, came at the close of short winter days, after many of the men had already left for home, when the lamps were lighted and the hectic pace of the day abated. Then the three partners were "in their best vein," bringing out old volumes to look over architectural details from the past and studying each other's work, gently offering suggestions and voicing sincere appreciation of what the others had done.[2]

In these rooms the office of McKim, Mead & White served as a training ground for a great many American architects. In the view of one man who worked there, this office was "the nursery of a galaxy of talent that, spreading over the country, leavened the architectural thought of a whole generation." Among the most noted of those who "apprenticed" with McKim, Mead & White were Cass Gilbert, John M. Carrère and Thomas Hastings, Henry Bacon, and Edward P. York and Philip Sawyer. During the thirty years from 1879 to 1909, approximately five hundred men worked for the firm, and many of them went on to practice architecture independently and to found their own firms. With its numerous commissions, large staff, and several "graduates" who themselves became prominent, McKim, Mead & White was professionally and stylistically the most influential of all late-nineteenth-century and early-twentieth-century American architectural concerns.[3]

At the center of the office was William Rutherford Mead. Seven years Stan's senior, Mead was the partner who kept things on course, the rudder or balance wheel of the firm, or, as some suggested, "the steersman of the ship,'' referring to the company logo, a ship under sail, with the motto ''Vogue la Galère'' (''Let the ship sail on''). Invariably calm and courteous, the ''extravagantly good-looking'' Mead took care of the practical aspects of both the business details and the designing work in an efficient and painstaking manner that probably would have been impossible for his more artistically creative partners.

Mead hired draftsmen, managed the Saturday night payroll, and let men go when work fell off. He kept the flow of projects moving along, supervised financial arrangements, and took charge of those technical elements of construction—heating, plumbing, and other aspects of building engineering—with which his partners ordinarily did not concern themselves. In the view of the architect Glenn Brown, Mead ''supplied the elements which his partners lacked'' and was ''a necessary factor in [the firm's] success.'' Mead, it was acknowledged, possessed a refined sense of architectural planning, but he did little designing himself, often saying that he had to spend most of his time trying ''to keep his partners from 'making damn fools of themselves.' '' Nonetheless, he did give generously of his time in providing criticism of the others' work, and his practicality was evident in many projects. In manner Mead was soft-spoken and sparing of words; indeed, he was nicknamed ''Dummy,'' an affectionate sobriquet that both his partners often used in notes directed to him. Mead smoked cigars constantly and, one architect who worked at 57 Broadway attested, walked around like ''a friendly bear.'' Yet there was always something aloof about him, a New England reserve perhaps, that kept others at a distance. ''He would joke with you,'' one draftsman recalled, ''but if you tried it with him, somehow your audience melted away.''[4]

Charles McKim, to whom Stan had been close from the time he entered Richardson's office, also tended to be reserved with others, particularly with people he did not know well. In contrast to Mead, McKim had little competence in the business side of architecture, nor was he particularly interested in the practical engineering aspects of building. His concerns were mainly aesthetic, and he brought to his craft a deeply held veneration for architectural traditions that stretched back to antiquity. Of the three partners, McKim was the most scholarly, the one most absorbed by the past, especially the classicism of the Renaissance and, beyond, that of ancient Rome. To his friends, McKim's warmth and charm, his modesty, diffidence, and tenderness, and his lofty idealism were most striking. The lawyer Joseph Choate once wrote: ''I do not believe it was possible to know Charles McKim without loving him, or to have come in personal contact with him without admiring the wonderful features of his character." Some of those associated with him nonetheless considered McKim overly meticulous and even prim in his habits and overly rigid in his viewpoints. Yet he was persuasive. Oftentimes, men would find themselves disagreeing with something McKim favored, only to find that they were soon persuaded, as he won them over by "roundabout paths." In the view of Glenn Brown, who later worked with McKim in Washington, D.C., "He never gave up until he gained his end." By and large, he inspired enthusiasm, devotion, and loyalty in those associated with him.[5]

Always committed to high-quality design, McKim was difficult to work with at times. In the drafting room, McKim thought out loud as he worked through a design, discussing his ideas as he sketched with the draftsmen. "He felt and talked his way toward the solution of a problem." Generally he liked to find a precedent for what he did, so he would send off assistants to research data for him from architectural books in the firm's library. He did not ordinarily make use of T-squares and triangles, favoring freehand drawing, nor did he erase much, apparently just dismissing lines from his mind's eye as he worked over a drawing. He was able to work easily with either hand.[6]

Generally McKim would rapidly make a rough sketch of an architectural idea and then hand it over to a draftsman, sometimes tossing his own sketch into a waste basket after the draftsman had examined it. When the draftsman had developed the idea in a semifinished sketch, McKim customarily responded in a highly positive way, praising the man for what he had accomplished, indeed sometimes calling over other men to see what had been done; but at the same time he would ask the draftsman to erase a line here and redraw something there. The draftsman would redraw over and over, McKim continually expressing great encouragement: "Now you've got it. That's very good. But how about changing this?" Sometimes the alterations went on for hours. When McKim suggested that a drawing be saved and put away, the draftsman knew it did not satisfy him at all and would have to be started anew. Often, the original sketch presented to McKim would be completely different by the time the draftsman got through with it. Those who worked with him had their patience tried by such changes, yet gradually the work was modified until McKim was fully satisfied. And the final result was most certainly not the draftsman's conception nor a copy of any earlier architectural precedent but McKim's own work, expressing his ideas. "Through some hypnotic influence," one architect recalled, "McKim made you think your own design was suggested by him, while all he was really doing was adding, or rather passing his unique skill into your mold."[7]

In contrast to the quiet and laconic Mead and the low-key, deferential McKim, everyone in the office knew when Stanford White was present at 57 Broadway. White was invariably exuberant, bubbling with enthusiasm, always in motion, perpetually talking, usually loudly, setting forth his views in a full, "reverberant" voice, sometimes whistling or even bursting into song. Those expressive traits, along with his height of over 6 feet, 2 inches and his bristling red hair and large drooping mustache, made him not just noticeable but a center of attention and activity. He worked tirelessly, and everyone remarked on his energy and vitality. He could not keep still. When conferring with a client in his private office, his hands were constantly in motion as he gesticulated to emphasize a point or grasped and turned about a small object from his desk. But he had the capacity to make a listener feel special, as if all his energies were focused on the person he was talking with. Like his father, Stanny's manner and intensity attracted attention and interest in public places. In time, as he became known for his buildings, his civic activities, and his widely reported social life, he became a public celebrity, and people on the street would comment to one another: "There goes Stanford White!"[8]

Even at this early stage in his career, White was a commanding figure within the firm. Mead and McKim, though both several years older than he and more experienced as independent designers, accepted their young partner—he was not yet twenty-six when the new firm was founded—as a member of their triumvirate. Clearly he was one of the bosses in the organization. But just as he was "the baby" in his own family—always the favored son, petted and admired—he was now the baby among the partners in the firm, still petted and admired, it would appear. From the beginning, he seemed to expect and require in the office the same sort of attention and admiration accorded to him as a youngster in his family. Certainly many of his personality traits that were so striking in the drafting room were ones that demanded attention. And attention he certainly got, as well as admiration for his undeniable artistic talent.

At the drafting table he worked rapidly, not concerned, as McKim was, with architectural precedents or, as was Mead, with detailed and logical planning. White worked out his ideas directly with a pencil rather than by ongoing discussion, often quickly drawing several very rough sketches, one or two of which he would turn over to a draftsman to be developed. He was spontaneous and instinctive with his forms, much more the artist than the engineer.[9]

In the early years of the firm, White frequently prepared sketches to show a client or a committee. His finished drawings, usually in pastels on colored paper, were carefully executed and displayed "a curious charm and a very personal character." Sometimes the background of a proposed building was "an enchanted dreamland" landscape, giving indication of Stanny's early painterly bent. Yet his concern was always for the final finished structure, not for the design itself. Monroe Hewlett, who was with the firm, wrote: "To work with and under him was to appreciate as never before the fact that the building, not the drawing, is and should be the architect's chief concern." William A. Boring, who joined the McKim, Mead & White office late in the 1880s, likened White to the dashing Benvenuto Cellini: "His flashes of genius dazzled us." His enthusiasm for beauty was communicated in a forceful way to those working with him.[10]

He always seemed to be bursting with ideas about designs, materials, and decoration, and outside the office, as well as in his own drafting rooms, made a striking impression on others in the arts. The story was told that White one day visited a decorator's office to look over a detail drawing made by a young draftsman named Thomas Johnson. When White arrived, Johnson was out to lunch. White's "large energetic figure, dominating, intense personality, seemed to fill the whole office. 'Beautiful!' he exclaimed, 'fine as the Parthenon!' Then, after a second, taking up a piece of tracing paper: 'Dammit, if it isn't, we'll make it so.' " White thereupon rapidly sketched some mouldings and ornament, then compared his sketch and Johnson's detail, and ended by crushing his sketch and dropping it on the floor, exclaiming, while "looking at the original detail!—'Fine! Just as it is,' and abruptly rushed off. When Johnson came in, he picked up the ball of crushed tracing paper, did his own comparing, said 'Better,' and altered the detail to agree with Mr. White's sketch. 'It is a way he has,' said Tom." White's "way" of leaving behind a crumpled drawing with his suggestions was more subtle than was often the case.[11]

In his own office, White was never sparing of criticism; he was generally candid and sometimes brusque, when absorbed in his work. With draftsmen, he was "inclined to wield a very severe stick" if someone failed to do the job he was asked to do or did not measure up to his best. White's uninhibited language, one architect suggested, "would make a longshoreman envious"—and perhaps make a draftsman shrink. From the start, as one of the partners, he could be a trial for those working under him, impatient, demanding, and caught up in his own needs, as he so often was, with a penchant for dramatic self-expression. Some of the draftsmen were annoyed by his mannerisms and his demands. Some were afraid of him. Yet his artistic gift was such that much was forgiven him by his partners and by his assistants.[12]

Particularly in the early years of the firm the three partners worked closely together as a team, complementing each other with their talents: White, the visionary and master of sensuous ornamentation; McKim, a superb designer, imbued with traditions of the past; and Mead, a gifted planner and competent administrator and businessman. Royal Cortissoz, who worked in the office as a young man and with whom Stanny shared an intense love of the music of Beethoven, found that the interchange of ideas among the partners, the draftsmen, and the engineers made the office more like a studio or an atelier than a commercial company selling its professional services. This "team work" was "a thing to delight in by itself." Both McKim and White on occasion emphasized in public ways that the architectural designs of the firm must be credited to the partners jointly. In 1886, White published a rejoinder to the attribution of a Newport house to him alone: "No member of our firm is ever individually responsible for any design which goes out from it." In a private letter, some years later, White asked the publisher Moses King not to attribute any building to a particular partner, since it was "only in one or two instances that we have not *all* had to do with the work which goes from our office." Nonetheless, increasingly with the passage of years, the firm's major commissions were primarily the work of a single partner, assisted by a team of draftsmen assigned to that partner. White, too, carried on considerable private work in small projects unconnected with the firm.[13]

Next to the partners, the most significant person in the office in the 1880s was Joseph Morrill Wells, a talented draftsman and an important figure in the firm's design work. Although the extent of Wells's impact on the designs of the firm cannot be precisely established, it is evident that he had considerable influence and was highly regarded by the partners as well as by many others working in the arts in New York City. Wells was already employed by McKim and Mead when Stan entered the firm, and he and White quickly became close friends.[14]

Wells, in the view of Royal Cortissoz, was "authentically a man of genius . . . both creator and critic, by White's side, the helpful colleague as well as the beloved friend." Quiet, extremely shy, sensitive, and dedicated to his art, he was frequently moody and caustic in his speech. His humor was biting and cynical and tended toward ridicule of superficialities and pretensions. Wells seemed perpetually dissatisfied with his city, with his work, and with himself. At times he complained of being so desperately bored that he wanted to shake things up: "I feel as though I would like to turn on a destructive earthquake, instead of the steam, and destroy the whole town, architects and all," he once wrote. "I am a born fanatic, and if I had no daily occupation, would be a most dangerous

Communist. I may be yet.'' The artist Thomas Dewing in 1884 painted Wells's portrait, showing a remarkably sensitive face; the melancholic eyes, however, appear rather cold, as if revealing something of the architect's skepticism and his need to keep others at a distance. Wells was a direct descendant of Sam Adams, the Revolutionary patriot, but family ancestry counted for little with him. He maintained that a man must make his own way and stand on his own accomplishments. He was desperately poor and had received little formal architectural instruction, but had educated himself well in literature and music as well as in art and architectural history. One account indicates that he studied architecture for a time with Clarence Luce in Roxbury, Massachusetts, and later worked in the offices of Peabody & Stearns in Boston. In New York, he briefly assisted Richard Morris Hunt before joining McKim and Mead. Wells's designing talents were such that his advice was often sought by others.[15]

Wells lived in the Benedict, the apartment building that McKim, Mead & Bigelow had erected on the east side of Washington Square specifically for bachelors. Stan often came there to socialize with Wells and with Mead, who also lived there in the early 1880s. Frequently Stanny and a few other young architect friends gathered in Wells's rooms to spend an evening poring over illustrations in old volumes on Rome during the Renaissance. The architect Bramante was said to be Wells's "god."[16]

Though a subordinate in the firm, Wells attempted to maintain his independence, especially in his working relationship with White, his close friend outside the office. Years later, White's son related an incident that characterized their relationship and showed something of Wells's tendency toward the squelch:

> Wells was working at a draughting table, and my father came running into the room with a large photograph of the façade of the Cathedral of Poitiers, which was a very rich, juicy Romanesque church. He planked it down on Wells's draughting board, and said with great formality: "Mr. Wells,"—they were great friends, but people were not called by their first name in the office at that time—"Mr. Wells, damn it, that building there is as good in its way as the Parthenon." Wells took the pipe out of his mouth and looked up at my father and said, "Stanford,"—which was a terrible breach of etiquette— "Stanford, fried eggs, in their way, are as good as the Parthenon"— and then went on drawing.[17]

The year after the formation of the new firm, Wells took an extended leave to fulfill a long-postponed ambition: a trip to Europe for architectural study. Arriving in England early in July 1880, he traveled about for a time with a young Harvard graduate who, Wells wrote White, complained when they parted that the architect, with his critical and sometimes cynical manner, had "broke all his dreams." Except for some domestic work and the Norman structures, there was "no great architecture" in England, he proclaimed. Paris, subsequently, though "disappointing at first sight," was "a very clever city," and he explored it thoroughly. Going out from Paris, he visited the Loire Valley, which was a joy, because "there you find the best examples of my favorite style." Renaissance architecture, he concluded, was "most convenient to my taste," though he considered Renaissance detail "altogether beyond my powers" to capture in his sketchbook. From Paris, early in 1881, Wells followed Stan's trail of two years before to Italy, where he anticipated "a wind ever soft from the blue heavens" but found instead dismal cold. But as the days warmed, so did his spirits, and from Florence he reported he was having "a grand though not a jolly time, being all alone." One great advantage coming from his European travels, Wells found, was that he felt himself growing in independence in his aesthetic judgments, caring less and less about the opinions of others. Stan likewise had become more independent in his artistic convictions during his European sojourn. Above all, Italy intensified Wells's inclinations toward Renaissance architecture. His passion for Italian Renaissance work would soon have an important impact on McKim, Mead & White.[18]

Wells was passionate about music as well as architecture, and Stan shared his love of music (which was so important in his own family life). After his return from Europe, Wells, with the painter Francis Lathrop and Saint-Gaudens, took such a fancy to a musical group they heard at a beer garden on Broadway in the fall of 1882 that Gus invited the musicians to his studio to give a performance for artist and writer friends. Wells suggested that their musical quality might be improved, however, and in 1883 he arranged for a group of musicians who performed together as the Standard Quartette to play on Sunday afternoons in Saint-Gaudens's studio. Later the Philharmonic Quartette was hired to perform. The concerts featured the music of Beethoven, Mozart, and Shubert and became a regular event from October to May through much of the 1880s. The forty-five or so regulars, including both Stan and for a time his father, McKim, Dewing, and Gilder, were allowed to bring guests to the "smoking concerts"; on rare occasions women were invited to attend. With the Sunday concerts as with other activities outside the office, Stanny socialized with men he worked with as well as, increasingly, with some of his clients. Saint-Gaudens eventually found that preparing his studio for the concerts was so much trouble that he ceased hosting them, but they were continued in Francis Lathrop's painting studio.[19]

Another noteworthy associate in the early years of McKim, Mead & White was Cass Gilbert, who entered the office in September 1880 and served for a time as White's chief assistant. Gilbert at first idolized White, who was six years his senior, "immensely impressed with him as a man of extraordinary ability and of the most attractive and engaging personality." In Gilbert's view, White was truly a genius, "always constructive and helpful" to those around him. Soon after he began work, Gilbert was put on the Randall statue project and was asked to do a perspective drawing. He had a terrible time with the figure, though, and just could not get it right. White, he later reported, took one look at his drawing and "fled in disgust." Saint-Gaudens was in the office that day and offered to draw the figure if Gilbert would do the pedestal; but the sculptor had just as much trouble and finally gave up, telling White in disgust: "Oh hell, Stan! Nobody can draw it. Give me a bit of clay and I'll model it!" Gilbert always loved Gus "for the failure he had made" and his kindly treatment of "a young unknown and inadequate draftsman." Gilbert was frequently sent to supervise out-of-town construction work. In the winter of 1882 he went to Newport to work on various projects as well as to recuperate from an illness. Later that year he went to Baltimore to take charge of the Winans house and yacht projects.[20]

As time went on, Gilbert's view of White began to change. He had, he wrote a friend, "a hearty admiration for [White's] good qualities (and they predominate) but I am getting a little sick of his arrogance, and his claiming all the credit for everything done in his office"—something White never did in public. The pay of $25 a week, Gilbert complained, was low enough and the hours overly long, and the men in the office themselves deserved some of the praise given the work they had done. Gilbert realized that with the frequent absence of his partners, White was constantly overworked, and his fatigue made his temperamental outbursts all the stronger. The spirit of the office, Gilbert felt, had gradually changed since the time he had come in, and things had "somehow gone to seed." Where earlier the office had been "a sort of mutual admiration society," it now seemed that "every man is trying to outdo everyone else" and that jealousy was "the grand passion." Moreover, Gilbert had "heard things and observed things" in White's private character that "make me respect him none the more," a cryptic comment unfortunately not elucidated in the letter. Working closely with White, Gilbert in a fairly short time found Stan a much less heroic figure than he first had believed.[21]

When, toward the end of 1882, Gilbert decided to set up his own practice in St. Paul, Minnesota, where he had grown up, White wrote that he was sorry to see him leave and regretted losing "the valuable help and faithful service" Gilbert had always rendered. White wished him "godspeed" and, with the solicitude of a big brother, suggested that the course his young assistant had chosen would be more to his "ultimate advantage" than remaining as an employee of the firm. Gilbert went on to achieve a brilliant architectural career.[22]

The working partnership of Mead, White, and McKim was, by and large, harmonious: The three men respected each other and got along well together, much more as a collaborative team, however, in the early years than later on. They enjoyed each other's company and often socialized together outside the office, especially McKim and White. It was understood that each of the partners might come and go as he wished, and all of them regularly took long holidays and traveled a good deal, including extended trips to Europe.

At times the organization of the office was chaotic—even Mead realized that. And the office atmosphere was by no means invariably pleasant for the employees working there: White could be overbearing, irritating, and intimidating, McKim, overly perfectionist and subject to nervous prostration, and Mead, cold and aloof. All in all, though, it was the general view that the office provided a highly stimulating environment. Royal Cortissoz, later a prominent journalist and art critic, years after his employment at the firm recalled "the ardor with which men of talent in the formative period enlisted under the banner of White and his partners. . . . Those were exciting days!" The camaraderie, the many talented painters and sculptors who dropped by, and, above all, the sense of crafting work of high artistic merit all created a tremendously "invigorating atmosphere." For the men working with McKim, Mead & White, caught up in the excitement of the many projects, Cortissoz suggested, "architecture was the only art on earth, and its sanctuary was at 57 Broadway."[23]

7

Bessie

⚬

During the early 1880s, as Stan was beginning to make a mark in his profession, he continued to live with his parents. As commissions poured into the 57 Broadway office and with his long work hours and frequent travel from one job to another, along with a social life that kept him on the go in the evenings, the young architect spent little time at home. His father, who had retired from his Custom House position before his trip to England and whose health was poor, complained that he saw little of Stan, so seldom was he around: "I don't see him at breakfast at all, & at dinner only about twice a week. . . . And then after dinner he don't stoppatome more than 10–15 minutes but is off to the Benedick," the bachelor apartment building where Joseph Wells and William Mead lived and where Stan's social life was centered. As Stan's circle of artist friends and well-to-do client friends expanded and as he prospered in his work, the son moved away from the more circumscribed, genteel world of the father. Richard Grant White at times expressed feelings of loneliness, of being left out of things, possibly even resenting that his son was becoming a part of a world of wealth and material show that he himself had long criticized with an outraged envy.[1]

Richard White worried a good deal about Stan, for he felt that young man was working too hard: "I spoke to him about it, & his reply was, 'Well, father'—he always calls me father when he thinks I'm a bore, papa at other times—'the work must be done.' " The elder White believed that the principle was wrong: "Work that can't be done without injury to the doer should be left undone." And, characteristically, he drew a

91

moral lesson: "It is one of the curses of our day, this notion that work is master of the man, not man master of the work. Greed is at the bottom of it." Richard was becoming aware that his younger son was caught up in the drive to success so characteristic of the times.[2]

Richard's letters to his wife, when on occasion she was away from the city, regularly reassured her that he and Stan were being well taken care of by the maid, Kate, and kept her informed of household news. Stan, it seemed, did not like cats and got along badly with their household pet, Nimrod, often stepping on, sitting on, or accidentally kicking the cat. "He doesn't seem to fit into the ways of the poor dumb creatures," Richard wrote. But Stan was at home so little that it was a matter to be noted when he took care of a job around the house, such as mending a rat trap. In his letters, the father's affection for "dear Stan" was always evident: "How good & how charming he is—such a sweet & noble nature," he commented in one letter. The father, it is evident, had much greater need of his son's company than his son had of his.[3]

Out of a father's pride in his younger son and a wish to assist him, even though Stan was already established with his new firm, in April 1881 Richard asked a friend to propose to the Council of the University of the City of New York (later, New York University) that an honorary degree be awarded to Stan later that year. Richard had attended the university and had received a bachelor's degree in 1839, but Stan himself had not been directly associated with the institution, nor had he received any formal advanced education. Richard Grant White's position as a cultural leader and his standing among the members of the council were such that his request was granted. On June 23, 1881, at the Academy of Music, Stanford White received an honorary master of arts degree, the sixty-ninth such degree conferred by the university. Here, certainly, was a remarkable honor accorded to this twenty-seven-year-old, whose professional career was still just getting under way. The award gave young White the distinction of a graduate degree at a time when such an honor was uncommon; possibly, as well, it relieved Richard of some of the guilt he might have harbored for not having provided his son with a university education earlier. Stan later would be deeply involved with his new alma mater and would render important services to the university.[4]

Meanwhile, in the summer of 1880 Stan's social life had taken a new turn. Through McKim he had been introduced to the Smith family of Smithtown, Long Island, including Bessie Springs Smith, who reached the age of eighteen that year. Prescott Hall Butler, whom McKim had come to know when both were at Harvard College, had married Cornelia

Smith, Bessie's eldest sister, and Butler often invited McKim for visits to Smithtown. Butler had commissioned McKim to design a house for him and Cornelia on Smith family property on Moriches Road. As the Butler house was being constructed in 1879 and 1880, Bessie, who was decidedly smitten by her much older brother-in-law, delighted in Charley's visits. McKim, she later wrote, seemed "almost like our older brother." She and another sister, Ella, used to "rush to the kitchen . . . whenever he was expected" to make his favorite ginger cookies. McKim came often, caught up in the vigorous social life of the Smith clan and obviously attracted to Bessie. She and Charley shared an excursion to Montauk Point the summer of 1880; afterward Charley sent her a gift of an umbrella as a "trifling reminder" of their pleasant trip.[5]

Bessie was the youngest of several children of Judge John Lawrence Smith and Sarah Nicoll Clinch Smith. Judge Smith was a direct descendant of the legendary "Bull Rider Smith," who in the seventeenth century had bargained with an Indian chief, Wyandank (Wyandanch), for all the land he could encircle in one day's riding on the back of a bull; he managed to stay on the bull's back from sunrise to sunset and acquired a large parcel of Long Island land. The Smith family had for years been distinguished in public service in New York, while family members had always cherished their ties with the ancestral estate. Bessie's relatives were deeply attached to the area around Smithtown on the north shore of Long Island, and eventually Bessie and three of her sisters settled there.

Bessie was brought up to participate in all the activities of a large rural household. She learned to milk the cows, harness the horses, and help shear the sheep. She later recalled that for her as a child "pig killing" was "the most exciting time of the year," when pigs were slaughtered in the yard and hams and sausages were prepared. Although Bessie maintained that her family was "very poor," they owned a large amount of land, and there were always black servants about to care for the children and to carry on the household chores. For a time she attended a finishing school in New York City.[6]

Bessie adored her forceful father, who, she felt, was "a very remarkable man in every way!" Soon after his marriage to her mother, he had given up a prosperous law practice in New York City to return to Smithtown, when his eyes had given him trouble. He had been told that he had damaged his eyesight by too much smoking, and he thereafter absolutely forbade tobacco to be used in the house. Bessie inherited his dislike for tobacco. He served as a judge of Suffolk County, holding court first in Richmond and later in Smithtown. He had an office directly adjacent to his house, and here clerks studied law with the judge. Two of those young men later married his daughters. Bessie's "favorite of all the law students" was Prescott Hall Butler, who taught her how to read and write and gave her her first sled, ice skates, and tennis racquet, and over the years sent her elaborate valentines and poems.[7]

The judge dominated the lives of his children. He taught them how to swim by throwing them into the water beyond their depth; Bessie took to water quickly, and all her life loved to swim, which she did expertly. Smith served as his children's dentist, pulling out teeth when necessary. They were proud of their strong teeth. He made the children memorize entire chapters from the Bible, and they could recite long passages for years after. He tolerated no nonsense from the children. The household was strictly patriarchal, dominated by the authoritarian judge. The more forceful the judge was, the more Bessie seemed to worship him. Bessie always accepted the notion that males had prerogatives, an attitude very evident in later relationships.[8]

She was striking looking. Rather tall, she possessed an athletic figure that gave her a "Junoesque" appearance, accentuated by pronounced features, a long straight nose, and a wide mouth. Her large dark eyes were very expressive. Her temperament was placid, matter-of-fact, and down-to-earth. Outdoor activities like clam-digging and fishing were her greatest delights. Even as a child, Bessie displayed the ability to sing and whistle simultaneously, an accomplishment that became her favorite parlor stunt in later years.[9]

While overseeing the completion of the Butler house, McKim spoke to Bessie in glowing terms about his younger partner, and eventually Stanford was invited to call. On his first visit, Stan and Bessie enjoyed singing together, and she demonstrated her singing-whistling talent to him. Returning to New York after that first encounter, Stan searched for a song they had both heard and enjoyed and finally found it in a ballad book belonging to his father. Stan had the song copied and sent it along with a basket of fruit to Bessie, asking that "as a reward" she sing it to him "the first time opportunity offers." Bessie was obviously delighted with this attention and promised to learn the song, though she was sure "the reward you ask will not be at all worthy of the trouble you took in getting it for me." Thus began what Prescott Hall Butler described as "a protracted siege."[10]

The siege was indeed long. Stanford paid frequent visits to the Smith family on Long Island to court Bessie, but Bessie, proper and circumspect, kept him at a distance, less interested in a romantic relationship than he. Finally, in February 1882, White decided to remove himself from what was for him an increasingly frustrating situation by going to see his brother Dick, who was then prospecting for gold in New Mexico. His visit no doubt was encouraged by his parents, who wanted to know how their elder son was doing. To Bessie, Stan wrote that he had to give his partners "strong reasons for leaving them," but no one else, not even his mother, knew anything, "save that I go on a vacation—except perhaps Ella [Bessie's sister]—as I have been weak enough to drop one or two despairing words to her, in lack of all other sympathy—for which I beg you will forgive me. . . . After your last letter I furiously resolved that I would not again take advantage of what you told me was but weakness on your part."[11]

Going away might give both him and Bessie a chance to think over their relationship. Also, a trip to the Southwestern frontier to join, even briefly, in prospecting for gold promised to be a novel experience, especially for his circle of friends and acquaintances. He could forsake the largely sedentary artistic life of the past several years for a very active, masculine adventure. Many young American men toward the end of the nineteenth century felt a need to affirm their masculinity in an unmistakable way. "Roughing it" in the West, as Theodore Roosevelt and others discovered, was one way of proving oneself as a man.[12]

Stan was away from New York for more than four months on his "vacation." Arriving in Socorro, New Mexico, along the Rio Grande, in early March, he wrote his mother that Dick was "the same bully fellow he ever was," though his brother's face was "the color of a Chinese lobster" and his vocabulary had expanded to include "some very choice selections out of the New Mexican grammar." In contrast to gregarious, sociable Stan, Dick, now thirty years old, was very much a "loner," most comfortable working by himself, seeing little of others, living in a shanty on the outskirts of the town. His simple dwelling was at least free from the bugs that plagued the crude hotels, but Stan complained about the food: Everything was canned, brought in from elsewhere. The brothers ventured into the mountains, sleeping out in the open, with an Indian scout as guide. All three were armed to the teeth with shotguns, revolvers, and bowie knives. Still, Stan reassured his mother, there was little danger, and all that he lacked was comfortable "summer underclothing." After Dick put his younger brother to work with pick and drill, Stan boasted he had put in ten hours a day for seven straight days as a prospector. Moving about from one site to another, they were fourteen hours in the saddle some days. As Stan wrote his father, he had "about won my spurs from the charge of tenderfootism."[13]

In early April, after the brothers had ventured into the Black Range Mountains for further prospecting, Stan left Dick for a sightseeing trip into northern Mexico. He joined with some traveling companions for a four-day journey by stage to Chihuahua, Mexico; after a short respite, they rode westward some 300 miles across the Sierra Madre to a little place called Batopilas for a week's stay. The trip through the rugged mountains was tiring and dangerous. Twice Stan and his companions had to make sheer descents of several thousand feet on their mules. Yet "the trip was a most beautiful one," and the Indians they encountered turned out to be "the most peaceful set of people in the world." To Stan, the Mexicans, however, were "the meanest people, certainly, I have ever met, and the country [was] full of scamps and rascals." At Batopilas, the travelers came upon a luxurious refuge in an elegant hacienda, where "unprepared for petticoats and champagne" Stan felt uncomfortable in his dirty old clothes. The visitors went deer hunting, and Stan bagged two animals, just missing two others. The placid life at the hacienda provided a sharp contrast to the hectic pace of New York, and after a brief time White felt that he had "inhaled the inherent laziness of the country." After the Americans retraced their route back to New Mexico, Stan remained for a few more days with Dick at Socorro. By mid-June he was in Colorado, making an ascent of Pike's Peak and anticipating his imminent return to New York. A few years later, in 1886, White was to contribute architectural plans for the Ramona School in Santa Fe, New Mexico, the design influenced by the Spanish colonial structures and Indian dwellings he had seen on this trip to the Southwest.[14]

On his return, though immersed in his work, Stanford continued to see Bessie. Even so, the following year, in August and September 1883, Stan made a second long Western trip, this time partially on business and with Gus Saint-Gaudens as his traveling companion. White's decision to take two such extended journeys in those months of courting calls into question the ardor of his and Bessie's romance.

The 1883 trip first brought the two artist friends by rail to New Mexico. They met Dick White at Engle, where they arrived in the middle of the night. Since they had to wait a few hours for a stagecoach to Fort McCrae, they spent the rest of the night in a "sort of mud hut." Accustomed to the discomforts of the region, Stan got along all right here, but Gus, who was obliged to share his room with two roughnecks who "slept armed to the teeth," was, to say the least, alarmed by the conditions, "momentarily expecting to be murdered." Their fitful sleep was terminated when a fire broke out in the general store next door, setting off gunpowder and cartridges. The last leg of the trip to Dick's camp in the Black Range was by horse and muleback, and Gus, completely exhausted, made it no secret that he wished he had not come. At Dick's log cabin, they inspected his mine, hunted for deer, and slept out under the stars. To add to his discomforts, Gus was badly bruised when his gun recoiled on the deer hunt. On the return trip to Engle, the stagecoach driver was so overcome by drink that just as he was falling asleep he handed the reins of the four horses to Gus, who had never before in his life driven a team. But Gus was "master of the situation" and got the stagecoach safely to Engle "half an hour ahead of time."[15]

From New Mexico, Stan and Gus went by train to Los Angeles and then northward to San Francisco, breaking this part of the journey for a horseback ride to visit "a splendid old Spanish mission." The luxurious Palace Hotel in the Bay City was a pleasant respite from the discomforts of the previous days, and the Chinese theater there offered exotic entertainment. A week later, the two friends were in Portland, Oregon, where White had arranged to meet with Henry Villard, for whose railroad, the Northern Pacific, the firm was designing stations. The transcontinental line had just been opened, and Villard had come west with a "collection of English and Yarmen [German] Dukes, Countesses, and high Cockelorum generally," who did not impress White at all favorably. Stan accompanied Villard to Tacoma, "a God-forsaken place at the end of Puget Sound," consisting "chiefly of board shanties and tree stumps," where a railroad station was being erected. The ugliness of Tacoma, however, was mitigated for Stan by the grandeur of Mt. Rainier soaring into the sky. He and Gus returned from Portland to the East on the Northern Pacific by way of St. Paul, forgoing a visit to Yellowstone, which they originally had planned to see. To Bessie, Stan wrote that he was "sick of the West and sick for a sight of you. Boohoo! I wantter go home—and home I am coming as soon as I can." The next time he visited the West, he promised her, his "little puss" would be with him and he would certainly have a much gayer time.[16]

Before the second trip west, Stan and Bessie had secretly agreed to an engagement, and while crossing the plains of Kansas by train, Stan had confided to Gus that he would soon marry. When Stan informed Gus that the coming marriage meant that his "troubles are all over," Gus responded, "Au contraire; they have just begun!" In a letter to Bessie, Stan passed along Gus's remark, indicating that his friend was something of a brute for saying such a thing; but then Bessie was so very "different from [Gus's] cross-grained, clothes-rack of a frau," whom he had always disliked. Back in New York, at the beginning of October, Stan urged Bessie to come to the city for a real "spree" and to bring along her mother and two of her sisters.[17]

After Bessie's father had formally consented on October 11, 1883, friends and family were informed of their engagement. Richard Grant White was highly pleased by the prospect of his younger son's marriage, though he felt as Stan acquired a new family his own life would be "even lonelier than it is now." Prescott Hall Butler congratulated his "little sister" upon the promise of "great future happiness." Stanford, he informed her, was not only his "best friend" but also "as noble, generous and high-minded and as incapable of meanness as any man on earth," well qualified to be "a kind, gentle, and faithful husband" and to make her "a contented, happy, and most fortunate wife." Stan's mother at once wrote her future daughter-in-law, thanking her "for making my boy so happy." Stan's father, she reported, was certainly "more than half in love with [Bessie] himself" and rather "resents it that Stan should presume to cut him out." Both she and her husband, she wrote, were "glad & proud of Stan's choice & very happy in his happiness."[18]

Approaching the age of thirty, Stan was ready to marry and establish his own household, and certainly by that age it was expected that he should settle down with a wife. His older brother had not married, but there is no evidence that Dick had any wish to do so, nor was he financially able to marry. Stan, by contrast, had a substantial income: For the year ending in June 1883, his earnings from the firm's profits were over $12,000, and the following year his company income was up to $18,571; those earnings came at a time when workingmen usually earned less than $500 a year. Stan had the resources to support a wife handsomely indeed. Marriage would mean that he would no longer be the subordinate in the household that he was with his parents. Marriage would mean, as well, that his life-style of bachelor freedom would have to change. That Stan was truly eager to marry is uncertain, however, considering how drawn-out the courtship had been and how the betrothed seemed to lack passion.[19]

It was a time of weddings. Six months before his engagement, White's friend the painter J. Alden Weir, for one, had been married at the Church of the Ascension, and White had served as an usher. Both Stan and his father, along with such friends as Saint-Gaudens, McKim, Gilder, and the painters William Merritt Chase, Wyatt Eaton, and Carroll Beckwith, had celebrated Weir's good fortune at a bachelor dinner at Martinelli's restaurant on Fifth Avenue at Sixteenth Street.[20]

On February 2, 1884, Weir, Saint-Gaudens, Gilder, Butler, and four others together organized a bachelor dinner for Stan, also at Martinelli's. Saint-Gaudens designed the menu card, with a caricature of Stan as a porcupine and the motto: "Who Builds Well, Escapes Hell: Stanford White Builds Aright: Honor his Art, his Head, his Heart." More than fifty of his friends, most of them from the New York art community, including even the reclusive painter Albert Pinkham Ryder, attended the dinner. Joseph Wells, Richard Hunt, William Chase, Frederick Law Olmsted, and Thomas Dewing also were among the guests, as were McKim and Mead, who would himself be married later in 1884. Richard Watson Gilder read some verses he had composed for the occasion, reciting the story of young White—

> I'm a young man
> From Man-hat-tan!
> I'm the tail of the kite
> of McKim, Mead, and White,
> My hair stands up straight,
> I am five minutes late,
> And as usual with me,
> In a terrible hurree!

—at the Gates of Heaven, facing St. Peter, who, it appeared, had decided tastes in architecture. When White affirmed his "personal prejudice" for the Italian Renaissance style and the early Christian, St. Peter welcomed him in. After the verses, White responded briefly to the toasts and congratulations of his friends, and the evening ended with impromptu Spanish dancing on the table tops by two guests, Francis Hopkinson Smith and Loyall Farragut, who refused to stop until they had entangled themselves as well as everyone else with long wreaths of smilax, a green vine used to decorate the room.[21]

The wedding took place on Thursday afternoon, February 7, 1884, at the Church of the Heavenly Rest, according to the rites of the Protestant Episcopal Church. Bishop Abram Newkirk Littlejohn officiated, assisted by the Reverend J. Q. Archdeacon and the Reverend James B. Wetherill, the husband of Bessie's sister Kate. Richard Grant White sent the couple a wedding gift of a soup tureen with the wish, "May you always be happy when this cover is lifted before you." To his bride, Stan presented a necklace he himself had designed and made, decorated by two golden crabs grasping a luminous pearl, and a diamond and ruby bracelet. Gus gave the couple a marble relief plaque picturing Bessie in front of a mirror, arranging her wedding veil. White had seen the work when it was first under way and had criticized it then as "rotten." Saint-Gaudens, upset by the remark, reportedly smashed it to pieces and subsequently began it all over, though he had difficulty modeling Bessie, whom he found cold and "hard," qualities he did not succeed in disguising in the carving. Just as Stan responded negatively to Gus's wife, Gus never really liked Bessie either. On some level, they perhaps perceived their wives as an intrusion on their close friendship.[22]

At the reception following the marriage service, Richard Grant White characteristically became so engrossed in flirting "with a damsel tall & stately, of an aspect fair & gracious" (so Nina reported) that he failed to notice that the bride and groom were leaving, despite the shouting and the showers of rice. The newlyweds took a short trip to Florida, enjoying a brief respite from the New York winter in the sunshine of St. Augustine. A few days after the wedding, apologetic that he had failed to say goodbye, Richard wrote his new daughter-in-law complimenting her on having charmed everyone at the reception "by the show of heartiness and repose of manner" with which she had received congratulations. Soliticious of his younger son as always, he asked her to take care of Stan and help him get some rest, and he expressed impatience for their return. On the evening of his marriage, following the reception, Stan had penned a note to his mother, telling her how much she meant to him, urging her always to tell her troubles to him, and affirming that he would always do what he could to assist her financially, if need be. "You have indeed gained a very lovely daughter—and must always think of me as your loving son."[23]

By early March, the newlyweds were back in New York, and White, preparing for their March 19 departure for Europe, inquired of George Champlin Mason, the secretary of the American Institute of Architects, if he could be sent a certificate of his membership in the Institute "or some paper to that effect with all the seals and red tape possible attached" to help him get into museums while traveling abroad.[24]

Their European wedding trip lasted almost six months, certainly a long period away from the office, especially considering that Stan had been on the job for less than five years. His partners themselves, however, also spent considerable time away from the office. They were understanding and undertook to cover his work. Besides, in both the circle of wealthy clients and friends with whom Stan was more and more involved and his group of artist friends, an extended European wedding trip was commonplace.

Paris, which Stanford knew well, was a "whirlpool"; they had "a very gay time," going to the theater every night. Bessie's uncle Charles Clinch Smith entertained them several times at dinner. In Paris, as elsewhere, Stan searched for furniture, pictures, and other objects to purchase for himself and for others, rushing here and there on the lookout particularly for tapestries for the Osborn house. At the Conservatoire they saw some musical instruments that would, he wrote his mother, "set

Papa's hair on end." Before her wedding trips, Bessie had never been anywhere except Long Island and New York City, so everything was new to her. Stan delighted in showing her sights he was already acquainted with, and he obviously was proud to show her off.[25]

Munich, Stan reported home, "seemed rather tame after Paris," although the streets were lively with soldiers and bands and the city was very colorful. They went on to Vienna, but Constantinople was their primary destination to the east, and it outshone all their expectations. The city was, quite simply, "the most wonderful place in the world." A trip by caïque on the Bosphorus and the Sea of Marmara was an experience Stan believed they would always remember. At Constantinople he impulsively bought a "mosque full of tiles" (which were later lost on a ship that sank near Bermuda) and declared he was "a ruined man." Visiting the Great Bazaar, he at first saw little that he wanted,

> . . . but on pointing out to my guide a mangy old rug on which two greasy Turks were carding wool, and telling him (my guide) that that was the sort of thing I wanted, he asked them the price. They grimaced and said 200 piastres—fifty francs. I, rather as a joke, offered them twenty, and they took me up quick as a wink; and before you could count twenty, I was surrounded by a great crowd of gesticulating Turks, each offering me the carpet on which he had said his prayers—probably for the last thirty years. I bought seven, much to my guide's horror—and I am sure it will be a long time before that corner of the Bazaar settles down to its usual amount of noise.

Bessie was enjoying herself "heartily." Stan had shaved off the beard he had been cultivating, but Bessie did not like the change and, he jokingly reported, thought he looked like an "idiot."[26]

Athens, "an extremely uninteresting city—bright, new and horribly dusty," was a disappointing contrast to the rich and mysterious Oriental atmosphere of Constantinople. Here White discovered some "precious [illuminated] manuscripts" and got them "at great cost of purse and risk of limb," only to lose them later on. There were important classical sites to visit in and around the city. They called on Heinrich Schliemann, the discoverer and excavator of Troy, "a funny little German with a big head," whose house was "frescoed over with scenes from the life of Schliemann."[27]

Next they turned westward to Italy. A steamer took them to Sicily, and in Syracuse White found himself "perfectly ravished" by a Greek

Venus, of which he made several drawings. Then on to Naples and, of course, the usual tourist excursions to Mt. Vesuvius and to Capri.

Rome, in June, was another principal stop, and there Stan could absorb the Renaissance style he was coming to adore, examining more buildings than he had been able to see on his brief visit to the Eternal City in 1879. The charging about to antiques shops accelerated in Rome, and they continued to add to their accumulation of "pottery and broken china," collecting and spending lavishly. They also saw several artist friends there. Stan, Bessie wrote her brother-in-law Prescott Butler, "rushes around the room, then slams the door & shouts back to me— 'tell Prescott I wish I could stay home & write to him too, but I must go see [Elihu] Vedder,' & now I hear his rapid foot-steps & his whistle as he goes down the street. 'Don Giovanni' as usual—my cow-bell I call it, for I always can trace his whereabouts when I hear that." But Bessie was getting a little tired of the frantic pace and so many sights. She felt homesick and expressed a longing to be back with her family sailing and swimming in Long Island Sound.[28]

Venice, which they reached in early July, was a delight—except for the fleas. Bessie was so badly bitten by the creatures that she looked as if she had "the smallpox or some other horrible disease." She and Stan met Waldo Story, a sculptor, and his wife and baby, along with Gedney Bunce, the American painter, who followed them about "always happy, smiling, & making ridiculous jokes with his dry wit." Each evening they were serenaded by gondoliers right under their windows, "with Trovatore & Santa Lucia, always the same things & same discords over & over."

By this time, Bessie had become well aware of one of her husband's most characteristic traits—extravagance:

> You know [she wrote her sister] that Stanford's main idea is never to do anything half-way or to economize in small things—consequently as we, by chance, hit upon the swellest of the hotels, we live accordingly & have the best of the gondolas ever at our disposal—hired by the day—with two men dressed in white & blue suits, & I am forced to appear in my best black silk every night at 'table d'hote'—& in fact, we & Mr. and Mrs. Story are *the* swells. . . . Often in the afternoon we are rowed two miles over to the Lido, a small sort of Fire Island where all Venice goes swimming daily. The rest of the crowd go in the steamboats which run every 15 minutes, but Stan scorns them & will not go near one.[29]

As Bessie was discovering, Stan, with a comfortable income from his architectural practice, was all too ready to spend and spend lavishly, something he had not been able to do in his earlier years. On their wedding trip, the newlyweds enjoyed the pleasures of first-class travel, unlike Stan on his visit to Europe six years earlier. And on this journey he seemed almost unrestrained in buying whatever struck his eye. The flamboyant purchase and the grand gesture were becoming more and more his way. Bessie would have to learn to live with this life-style.

A visit to Switzerland followed. Near St. Moritz, Stan, ready to try anything, climbed onto a glacier but fell and skinned himself badly while coming down. The couple encountered some of Bessie's cousins in the Tyrol, and Bessie was comforted by having at least some of her family about. Hesitant to return to Paris because of reports of a cholera outbreak, they went anyway for a few days, and then stopped for a late August visit in London. From there, Stan announced to his parents by letter the news of Bessie's pregnancy; her baby was expected before the end of the year. On August 30 they sailed for home.[30]

Saint-Gaudens and McKim were at the pier to greet the couple when their ship docked in New York on September 8, and they were joined there by Prescott Butler and Stan's mother and brother. As soon as Bessie disembarked, she went off to Long Island with her mother-in-law, followed soon after by Butler, while Gus, Charley, and Dick waited for Stan to get his luggage and many collectibles taken care of, a tedious conclusion to what had been a pleasant voyage. Finally, some five hours later, they all went off to Solari's for dinner, lingering long over the wine and Stanny's stories.[31]

While Stanford and his bride were still abroad, Joseph Wells, the talented architect working for McKim, Mead & White, wrote an extended letter to his former colleague Cass Gilbert, who was then practicing architecture in St. Paul. Among other matters, Wells made some telling comments about White, whose absence, on his extended honeymoon trip, had been, Wells thought, "productive of delicious quietude and repose for me in particular and the office in general." Wells conceded, though, "that things go better while he is here," since White could "manage draughtsmen" and "get more fair work out of them" than he himself could. Wells wondered, nonetheless, how well Stan would "settle down into the duties of domestic life after his return, as he infallibly must. The novelty is probably already over," he suggested, "and perhaps things can be tided over tolerably until the usual event happens. Then all new sensations will have been exhausted. Nothing more left to be done. How these pernicious Americans do rush through things."[32]

With the passage of years, Wells believed, White and he had moved considerably apart and were "finally in different boats in the architectural stream." White, he thought, did not appear any longer to care for "simplicity, proportion, and unity of effect" in his work, the very qualities that Wells himself judged "the highest in our art." Indeed, Wells had almost come to regard Stan "as a brilliant decorator, not an architect." "From recent developments [White] cares more to make a social figure, than art or friendship. This may seem severe," he went on, "but it is the general verdict. He is fast losing those qualities and traits of character, which made him one of the best of friends," an opinion confirming Gilbert's view two years earlier. In sum, "a person capable of great things allows himself to be led away by small things, until it becomes a worship." Wells did "not look for any further art development in him."[33]

By choosing to marry, Stanny distanced himself from the life-style of the all-male free and independent artistic spirits centered at the Benedict apartments. He necessarily would distance himself from Wells, and Wells seemed to take White's actions almost as a personal affront. Possibly jealousy of someone else coming close to Stan as well as of Stan's professional and social success was partly behind Wells's critical remarks, though much of what he wrote rings true. Wells was right that at times White focused on the sensuous in ornamentation and decoration to the exclusion of larger architectural effects. Stan then and in the years to come, moreover, was sometimes "led away by small things" and did not always give himself the opportunity to show that he was "capable of great things." And his days were chronically a "rush through things," reacting instinctively to the immediate, usually not slowing down to linger and contemplate at leisure what might be done. There can be absolutely no doubt that he was almost obsessed "to make a social figure." Yet White's "qualities and traits of character" continued to attract many friends to him, and he had it in him ultimately to achieve far more in his art than Wells forecast. How well White would "settle down into the duties of domestic life" once the "novelty" and the "new sensations will have been exhausted" would remain an open question for a while.

8

"Simpler and More Classic Forms"

❦

At the same time in the early 1880s that Stan was courting Bessie, his firm's work took a new direction. The Villard houses project, with which Stan was closely involved, marked a significant turning for McKim, Mead & White to the Italian Renaissance style, a development that had a long-range impact on American design generally. Adaptations of Renaissance work were particularly fitting for the United States toward the end of the nineteenth century, or so many architects, critics, and clients came to believe, for it was widely suggested that American high culture generally was experiencing a renaissance similar to that of Italy centuries earlier. Like the powerful Renaissance princes of Florence and Rome, many newly rich Americans were demanding elegant and sumptuous surroundings that proclaimed their wealth and power. Appropriate models, it was suggested, might be found in Renaissance work. Moreover, in times of considerable turmoil and disorder, an architecture of order, balance, and restraint, deeply rooted in the past, was increasingly appealing to many. More than any other architects, McKim, Mead & White would create the setting for America's turn-of-the-century Age of Elegance, inspired, to a considerable degree, by Italian Renaissance architectural ideas.[1]

In the spring and summer of 1881, Henry Villard, a German-born former newspaperman turned financier and railroad entrepreneur, acquired a plot of New York City land, 200 by 200 feet, fronting on Madison Avenue and extending from Fiftieth to Fifty-first Street, directly to the east of St. Patrick's Cathedral. Villard decided to have six attached houses erected on the lot, including a large residence for himself and his family, all grouped together into one large structure around a central courtyard open to the avenue. Villard was already acquainted with McKim, since Charley's sister Lucy, who died in 1877, had been married to Mrs. Villard's brother, Wendell Phillips Garrison, the son of William Lloyd Garrison, the famed abolitionist. McKim had recently designed a stable and alterations for Villard's country house at Dobbs Ferry, New York.

In the spring of 1882 McKim left New York to visit Portland, Oregon, for work on a hotel, a station, and a hospital for Villard's Northern Pacific Railroad, and the Villard project on Madison Avenue was turned over to White, who began preliminary study of the plan and design. In a short time, however, Stan too left New York for his first trip to the Southwest to visit his brother. The Villard houses project was turned over to Joseph Wells, who agreed to undertake the commission with the understanding that he would have a free hand in the exterior design, though incorporating the general plan on which McKim and White had already decided. Henry Villard and Wells disagreed on some details, but the architect worked harmoniously with the client, and the ultimate design was largely what Wells had conceived. The Palazzo Cancelleria in Rome, then attributed to Bramante, was one of Wells's passions, and he decided to fashion the exterior of the Villard houses after that Renaissance structure, using both general ideas and decorative details. Wells's predilection for Italian Renaissance architecture had been greatly strengthened by his 1880 trip to Europe.[2]

Construction of the elegant, grouped houses began in May 1882, and by mid-December 1883 Villard was able to move into his own residence at 451 Madison Avenue, in the south wing of the complex. Yet the entrepreneur had spent so lavishly on this project—at just about the same time he was compelled to use his own funds to shore up the Northern Pacific Railroad—that most of his fortune was drained away. Hostile press accounts accused him of luxuriating in "a princely edifice" while countless stockholders were losing the fortunes they had entrusted to his company. Villard was soon forced out of the railroad presidency, and he saw his house and other property transferred to trustees. In the spring of 1884, after only three months of occupancy, Villard and his family were obliged to vacate the Madison Avenue mansion and return to Dobbs Ferry. In an era of rapidly fluctuating fortunes, Villard was by no means alone in the sudden loss of much of his wealth. A few years later Villard's financial situation improved, and he returned to control of the Northern Pacific Railroad, but in the depression of the 1890s the railroad failed and he again lost most of what he had. He never returned to his Madison Avenue mansion.[3]

In the six attached houses, Wells and his firm made a vigorous statement for formal symmetry and order and for direct historical reference. In so doing they abandoned the picturesque, more informal, freely inventive mode that had largely characterized the firm's previous work, as in the Newport Casino, Robert Goelet's Southside in Newport, and the Tiffany house in New York, and that, in one style or another, had dominated American architecture since the heyday of the Greek Revival in the earlier part of the nineteenth century. With his interest in antiquity and the Renaissance, McKim, of course, found this adaptation of Renaissance elements highly congenial. White, too, from this time onward largely devoted himself to more formal, balanced creations, with structural and decorative details usually inspired by Italian Renaissance precedents.

A highly dignified composition, with an overall unity of design, the Villard houses group was provided with an impressive monumental character. The exterior walls, rusticated with massive blocks of stone separated by deep joints at the lower floors, were covered higher up by smoothly dressed masonry, all in Belleville brownstone. Stone courses at the level of the window sills defined the floor levels. The third-floor windows were boldly enframed, recalling those of the Cancelleria Palace, while a projecting cornice in an Italian mode topped the structure. Small second-story balconies overlooked the courtyard at the central points of the wings. In the center section at the rear of the courtyard, five arches formed a loggia at ground level, with paired windows on the floors above. For the front of the courtyard, a wrought-iron fence was erected to the sides of a central gateway, which was framed by two squared uprights supporting globes and a graceful arch carrying a lantern. To the critic Mariana Van Rensselaer, the original Villard houses composition was "very quiet, a little cold, perhaps a little tame but . . . extremely refined."[4]

White's hand was in striking evidence in the interiors of Villard's dwelling, the largest and most elaborate of the six houses. The thirty-year-old White directed the interior work, bringing in his close friends Gus and Louis Saint-Gaudens, Francis Lathrop, and David Maitland Armstrong, as well as several other decorators and craftsmen, to assist him. Here was a collaborative endeavor of the sort that Stan particularly enjoyed, one in which he could gratify his passion for sculpture, decorative materials, and expensive objects. White had almost unlimited funds to work with and could indulge himself exuberantly in the decorative work.

From the entrance vestibule, a visitor entered the main vaulted-ceiling hall, from which the principal rooms of the floor opened. Gus Saint-Gaudens designed a great marble fireplace and an ornamental sculpture of a woman with two children for the hall. At the east end of the main hall was a large two-story, barrel-vaulted music room, in which the lower wall section, some 8 feet high, was carved in low relief, with designs of musical instruments and garlands. A musicians' gallery at one end was surmounted by a band of five plaster panels of "singing boys," modeled after the "Cantori" of Lucca della Robbia, while a second band of panels decorated the opposite wall. To one early visitor, "Aladdin's lamp never revealed a hall more magnificent": The music room was "the chef d'oeuvre of the decorators' art." Adjacent to the music room was the dining room, part of which could be closed off as a breakfast room; it had walls covered by intricately carved dark English oak, inlaid with mahogany, with three sybil figures above the great fireplace. On the Madison Avenue side of the mansion, a reception room flanked by two drawing rooms could be combined into one large area for entertaining; this impressive space was ornamented by plaster ceiling decorations, elaborate mahogany marquetry, red-stained cherry wood paneling, and inlays of mother-of-pearl. The grand staircase in yellow marble, rising from the hall to the upper floors, with steps 12 feet broad, was faced on the opposite wall by a large clock with signs of the zodiac, designed by Stan and Gus. Wells, who had suggested to Gilbert that White was a better decorator than an architect, felt that he could give "almost unqualified praise" to White's dining room and the hall staircase—"decidedly the most beautiful interior work in this country in spite of all defects." The staircase, Wells judged, was "quite noble—and entirely worthy of the house." Villard, it was estimated, spent more than a million dollars on the construction and decoration of his short-time residence.[5]

In 1886, Villard's house was sold to Mrs. Whitelaw Reid, the daughter of Darius Ogden Mills, who had made a vast fortune in Western mining ventures. White's earlier performance at the house was so impressive that, not surprisingly, he was Elisabeth Mills Reid's choice for additional interior work. Mrs. Reid, whose father had purchased the *New-York Tribune* and had appointed her husband its editor, was used to having her way and getting what she wanted. A strong-minded woman, she was not an easy client to work with, but Stan got along with her and succeeded in finishing the interior to her satisfaction. He designed a new ornately paneled ceiling for the music room, where John La Farge, who years earlier had counseled him on choosing an architectural career, painted lunettes. He also rebuilt the front drawing rooms and reception room into one large room, with marble columns and pilasters topped by gilded Corinthian capitals, and had the old interiors removed to the Reids' country house, Ophir Hall, in Westchester County.[6]

Mrs. Reid also entrusted White with selecting many of the furnishings for her homes. Indulging his taste for the opulent, he selected furniture, tapestries, rugs, as well as woodwork and tiles both for 451 Madison Avenue and for the Reids' country place. In 1888 Reid was named United States Minister to France while major reconstruction was still going on at both places. Considerable trans-Atlantic correspondence concerning the arrangements thereafter took place. Various acts of generosity and gestures of friendliness on White's part helped keep him in the good graces of the Reids. "I hope," he wrote Reid in January 1888, "you will notice that there has been no commission charged on our part on the rug. I am too proud of getting it in the [music] room, to treat it in any other way than a matter of pleasure to me, as I hope it is to you and Mrs. Reid." With his passion for beauty, Stan loved to be able to share beautiful things with others. Of course his firm, or he personally, made commissions on most of the objects. For all White's graciousness, Reid nevertheless was often annoyed with the slow pace of the work: "I will not consent to having this little piece of work dragging along, as so many others have. [The men] should get out before I want to use the house." For a time, Stan himself labored long hours into the night to accommodate him.[7]

The Reids enjoyed showing off their house. Even before the interior decoration on the Madison Avenue mansion was fully completed, Reid, then back in New York, invited White and others from the art community and various of his own friends one evening to a housewarming. White later reported that all the guests were so *"delighted* with the house" and "the good cheer" they had enjoyed with Reid that on the way home after the party they all stopped off to drink Reid's health—"except John Hay, who wandered off." By commissioning White to decorate and furnish their prominently placed mansion, the Reids gave the architect a splendid opportunity to show New Yorkers what he was capable of doing. What he did was widely noticed.[8]

In recommending artists for work on Reid's house, Stan, as was customary, helped out some of his friends. To his longtime painter friend Edwin Austin Abbey in England, Stan wrote in September 1895 suggesting he had had "a sneaking idea of trying to work Whitelaw Reid for a panel over his dining room fireplace." He was not certain that Reid would "take the fly," but he wanted to know if Abbey would want to do it, suggesting that he supposed he "could screw [Reid] up from three to five thousand dollars" for the work. Abbey eagerly accepted the commission that was eventually offered him for a fee of $5,000 and sent sketches to the newspaperman. White had thought that a feast might be an appropriate subject for the dining room panel, but Abbey was inclined toward a dance, and Reid liked the sketches he sent on that theme. By March 1897, the Abbey picture, titled *The Pavanne,* was finished and sent to New York, where it was exhibited at the National Academy of Design. When the panel was installed, White was delighted: "Every time I see it I fall more and more in love with it." He even suggested that it be copied in a tapestry, but that was not done. Reid immensely admired Abbey's picture and thought it particularly charming under natural light.[9]

White was immensely proud of the Villard house group, even though he was not primarily responsible for the exterior design. Some years later, after his principal involvement there, he ranked the complex among the best things that the firm had designed. The Villard house group, in White's view, was "the beginning of any good work that we may have done . . . designed on simple and dignified classic lines, which we have ever since endeavored to follow." Henceforth, he suggested, the firm would "keep to simpler and more classic forms" than had previously been the case. The death in April 1886 of H. H. Richardson, who had so influenced the firm's more picturesque earlier work, perhaps made easier their turning for inspiration to the art of the Renaissance tradition.[10]

Simultaneous with the Villard houses commission in the early 1880s, White worked on another important New York project that also referred back to Italian Renaissance sources. The American Safe Deposit Company and Columbia Bank Building on the southeast corner of Fifth Avenue and Forty-second Street, at what would later become one of the city's busiest intersections, was a six-story structure with banking rooms on the lower levels and offices and bachelor apartments on the upper floors. On the long street side, just under the boldly projecting cornice, wide bays, extending outward from the wall plane, rose into attic-level loggias in an Italian Renaissance mode. The rusticated stonework of the high base, the brick of the upper walls, and the rich terracotta panels alternating vertically between the principal windows provided interesting textural contrasts, the variety and the ornamentation giving the building "an air of gaiety" that would later characterize White's Madison Square Garden.[11]

Artistic collaboration and Renaissance aesthetic ideas were also central to a project in the Church of the Ascension in New York, begun in September 1885. For the Reverend E. Winchester Donald, Stan teamed up with John La Farge, Maitland Armstrong, and Louis Saint-Gaudens to redecorate the chancel of the small Episcopal church in a Renaissance mode. Designed by Richard Upjohn, the building was a splendid example of an early 1840s Gothic Revival church and one of the principal ornaments of lower Fifth Avenue. White, who once said he considered this his "own church," though he realized he was looked upon "as a doubtful member," was responsible for the general conception in the chancel and for the architectural setting for La Farge's wall mural of *The Ascension*. The painter had recently visited Japan with the historian Henry Adams, and the setting for the figures seems to have been inspired by what he had absorbed on his travels. For White's Siena marble screen on the lower part of the chancel wall, Louis Saint-Gaudens provided two angels sculptured in high relief, while Armstrong created mosaics of kneeling angels. Although La Farge began his mural in 1887, the work dragged on and on for many months, much to the consternation of the Reverend Donald, who at one point exclaimed that, despite his being a clergyman, he had to agree with White that the delay was "perfectly hellish." The figures in the mural were derived from the work of Masaccio and Raphael, yet La Farge succeeded in creating a striking personal interpretation of the subject that contemporaries not infrequently proclaimed "a masterpiece."[12]

Another important collaborative project Stan directed, going on from 1887 to 1890, was the Renaissance-style chancel renovation of the Church of St. Paul the Apostle on Columbus Avenue at Sixtieth Street in New York City. The stark basilica-type Roman Catholic church had been designed by Jeremiah O'Rourke and built from 1876 to 1885. White designed a large high altar covered by a great canopied structure or *baldacchino,* with columns of colored porphyry, and inlaid with onyx, alabaster, and gold and marble mosaic, looking as if it belonged in St. Peter's in Rome, as well as more modest side altars dedicated to St. Joseph and the Blessed Virgin. Large stained-glass windows by John La Farge were installed behind the main altar. Frederick William MacMonnies created sculptures of kneeling angels; Philip Martiny an altar lamp; and Robert Reid murals. One critic of the work suggested that "these artists who have contributed to the decorative features of the Paulist Church through their genius mark an epoch in American art." Indeed, "no such scheme of church decoration [had] been inaugurated since the days of Raphael and the Italian Renaissance." Here, the critic forecast, was "a potent influence for the future," referring to the idea that America was becoming the modern-day equivalent to glorious High Renaissance Italy.[13]

A Baltimore church commission designed by White about this time was, by contrast, more in keeping with the firm's earlier work. The First Methodist Episcopal Church, a rugged granite masonry building, was derived from Romanesque and early Christian sources in a style

111

that some clients continued to believe most appropriate for religious structures. The exterior was dominated by an inordinately tall, square corner tower, topped by a rather awkward conical roof, while the interior space focused on a large oval auditorium surrounded by classrooms, offices, and a chapel. Dedicated on November 6, 1887, the Baltimore Methodist Church was planned to be integrated with other nearby buildings for a women's college. Stan subsequently designed several buildings for Goucher College, of which a small gymnasium and a Latin School building were erected.

At that time, as characteristically throughout White's career, friends in New York became regular clients. Stan's social associations with Robert Goelet, for whom in 1882 he had created the Newport summer cottage Southside, led to extensive further work for him and his brother, Ogden Goelet, in New York in the mid-1880s. Robert and Ogden Goelet were heirs to a large fortune in Manhattan real estate. Like many other plutocrats in the Gilded Age, they not only husbanded their properties with care and developed them profitably but also put on a conspicuous display in their homes, their possessions, and their style of living. The two brothers' wives were social rivals and vied in trying to outdo each other in entertainments and display. The brothers were early benefactors of the Metropolitan Opera, and both maintained boxes in the newly built opera house.

In 1885, the Goelets commissioned McKim, Mead & White to design a large commercial building on property they owned on the southeast corner of Broadway at Twentieth Street. Following White's design, a high base of two-story arches supported a shaft of three stories, topped by a full-story attic and an ornamented frieze and cornice. By this time the tripartite division into a well-defined base, shaft, and attic was becoming the characteristic design for tall commercial structures. The intersection corner of the Goelet Building was gently curved, and the three corner arches at the base level defined the principal entryway there. Additional stories were added early in the twentieth century. Prominently placed on the principal shopping street of the city, the Goelet Building was widely noticed.

Stan soon became, in effect, the Goelet family architect. For them he also created in the mid-1880s a private office building at 9 West Seventeenth Street, a picturesque structure not in keeping stylistically with most of the firm's work by that time. The small two-and-one-half-story structure was designed in a quaint seventeenth-century domestic Dutch mode, with a polychrome front, a high-rising dormer, and stepped gables. To one observer the small building was "so extreme as to be comical," but still, "altogether the front is a very jolly performance." The talented architect again demonstrated here how flexible and accommodating he could be, moving from one style to another. Robert Goelet was a dedicated yachtsman, and in 1896 Stan created a huge racing trophy—the Goelet Schooner Cup—for him. White was also charged with the Goelet family mausoleum in Woodlawn Cemetery in the Bronx.[14]

Nearby, on the northwest corner of Fifth Avenue and Sixteenth Street, White designed for the Goelet interests a substantial structure rented largely to the Judge Publishing Company and known as the Judge Building. An eleven-story multi-use building in yellow brick and gray stone, the Judge Building extended nearly 100 feet on the avenue and some 150 feet on the street side. Like the Goelet Building, the Judge displayed a rounded corner at the street intersection and featured highly contrasting walls and trim. When Edwin Austin Abbey returned from England to New York in 1890, he moved into the newly completed Judge Building, taking a fifth-floor studio to which White brought antique furniture and easels for the painter's use and old tapestries and other art objects to decorate the room, an act of generosity the architect often undertook for artist friends. The Judge Building was plagued by problems, however, including such intense vibrations from street traffic that some subtenants moved out.[15]

Larger and more central to the life of the city was the Hotel Imperial on the southeast corner of Broadway and Thirty-second Street, which had something of a Renaissance Florentine palazzo look. The Goelets commissioned White to design the luxurious nine-story, 300-room hotel in 1888; it was opened on September 1, 1890, and a large addition was completed in 1894. Above the white marble base, the exterior walls were covered by a light buff brick set in horizontal bands. Three prominent terra cotta sill courses divided the building walls into two-story segments and formed a base for the highly ornamented attic frieze. Two-story arched window bays at the base gave the suggestion of a loggia open to the street and emphasized the receptive social character of the building. Inside, the public rooms were, as a night clerk at the hotel exclaimed, "out o' sight," for White had let himself go in a binge of opulent décor. The lavishly decorated main floor featured mosaic pavements and stuccoed ceilings. Rich marble stairs led to the elaborate dining rooms on the floor above. The principal restaurant had ivory and gold walls, and the café was wainscoted with black walnut paneling, which helped to set off a bar inlaid with onyx. White commissioned his friends Robert Reid and Thomas Dewing to prepare murals for the café; Abbey also painted a large mural there of Bowling Green in the early days of the Dutch. McKim, highly enthusiastic about the Hotel Imperial, called it "simply bully," and many observers at the time agreed with him.[16]

Meanwhile, the most important commission of the 1880s for McKim, Mead & White was under way. To many contemporaries and to later architectural historians, the Boston Public Library stood foremost among the hundreds of projects the firm completed. The Renaissance-style library was Charles McKim's creation, and for several years McKim gave his primary energies to the project, both designing the library and directing the long, complex, and ultimately successful negotiations with trustees, city officials, contractors, and artistic contributors.

Following the breakup of his marriage some years earlier, McKim had suffered from chronically poor health and was often absent from the office so that Stan and Mead had to cover for him. Excessive perfectionism in his working habits may have exacerbated his physical troubles. For a time in the early 1880s, he was placed on a milk diet because of stomach disorders. Then, in September 1883, McKim became acquainted with Julia Amory Appleton of Boston, who shortly commissioned the architect to design a country house for her and her sister, Marian Alice, in Lenox, Massachusetts. As the Lenox house took shape, McKim saw a good deal of the "fair, handsome, majestically tall" Julia Appleton. Their friendship blossomed into a romance, and on June 25, 1885, they were married in the newly completed Lenox residence at a double ceremony in which her sister was also wed. The McKims left almost immediately for a honeymoon trip to England, Holland, Belgium, and Switzerland.[17]

After their return, McKim seriously contemplated relocating permanently in Boston. His wife owned an elegant double house on Beacon Street, and her family and best friends were mostly there. In a "strictly confidential" letter to Charles Rutan of Richardson's office in late December 1885, McKim discreetly asked the Boston architect about finding an associate to work with him and take charge of a possible Boston office—"a practical man whose abilities would be of a business kind, say 30 to 40 years old, and whose experience and training might resemble your own." The firm's business was growing in New England and increasingly required his presence in Boston. There seemed to be, McKim suggested, "a possibility of our removing permanently to Boston some day. . . . I would then become either the representative of our concern in Boston or practice architecture in my own name."[18]

Tragedy struck McKim a year or so later: On January 3, 1887, at their New York house at 9 West Thirty-fifth Street, Julia McKim died while giving birth to a stillborn child. A funeral was held in Boston at

Trinity Church, and Julia was buried at Mount Auburn Cemetery in Cambridge. McKim later contributed a stained-glass window designed by John La Farge to Trinity Church as a memorial to his second wife. Terribly distraught following Julia's death, McKim resolved to leave New York and move permanently to Boston: "Since my wife's death I do not feel that I could under any circumstances remain in New York," he wrote Rutan. He was still uncertain, though, as to whether he would open a Boston office for the firm or, alternatively, "begin alone." At the time, he did not want Mead and White to know what he was contemplating, obviously not quite ready to make a final decision. His second course would have had momentous consequences for his partners and would, in effect, have destroyed the firm.[19]

In a sense, the decision was made for him. A new Boston Public Library had been planned for some time, and already work had started at a prominent site on Copley Square, across from Richardson's Trinity Church. The first architectural plans proved useless, however, and construction was stopped. At that point Samuel A. B. Abbott, one of the library trustees and a cousin of Julia Appleton McKim, suggested that McKim and his firm were the ones to plan for the library and undertake a new design. A contract was signed in March 1887. Drawings McKim prepared were approved, and foundation work was begun the next year. The cornerstone of the library was laid on November 28, 1888, and the library was opened on March 11, 1895. On Beacon Street, the Appleton house, which Charley had inherited from Julia, was partially converted into the Boston office of McKim, Mead & White. Here McKim took charge of the library project, supervising draftsmen and overseeing erection of the complex Renaissance-classic building. Characteristically, McKim at times so agonized over the work that Mead lost patience with him. As the library moved toward completion, countless problems arose, but no doubt his absorption in the difficult work helped McKim through the anguish of his personal loss. One minor crisis occurred when someone in the Boston office provided a list of historic names chiseled on the main front of the library, so arranged as to form by their first letters an acrostic of McKim, Mead & White. The outcry in the press when this whimsy was discovered was tremendous. Stan was highly indignant over the trick, and McKim immediately had the offending names removed.[20]

Several McKim, Mead & White projects during the middle and late 1880s thus embodied a significant turning away from the earlier more romantic and picturesque modes to embrace elements of Renaissance classicism. Some of the firm's subsequent work went back farther for inspiration, directly to classical antiquity. It may well have been that the reason and order, balance and restraint, and decorum and monumentality of Renaissance styling were increasingly appealing to the architects as they themselves were often caught up in personal problems, tensions, and tragedies and some loss of control in their own lives and, simultaneously, as the disorders and often seeming chaos of urban industrial America became more pronounced toward the close of the century. The sense of working within a long and established tradition could give the architects a certain comfort and security they might cling to in their creative, energy-draining professional work.

During the 1880s Stan and his partners completed a body of important work and built up a reputation for architecture of a consistently high quality. By the end of the decade, McKim, Mead & White had become one of the best known of American architectural firms. The professional reputations of the partners were firmly established. At the same time, Stan, especially among the three men, was increasingly taking a leading role in the artistic, social, and civic life of New York City.

9

Family Ties

R eturning to New York from their wedding journey in September 1884, Stan and his bride first moved into rooms at 2 East Fifteenth Street but soon rented a small brownstone house at 56 West Twentieth Street, close to Sixth Avenue. They would live in that house for more than seven years. Stan had a trip of about 3 miles between home and the McKim, Mead & White offices on lower Broadway; riding each morning on the crowded elevated railway or in the horse cars actually gave him time for relaxation before he was caught up in the hectic pace of the drafting rooms and the countless decisions he had to make for ongoing projects. On his return to New York, well established professionally, White could take considerable satisfaction in the buildings he had already completed and in the several projects he would soon be working on with his partners.

Now a married man entering his thirties, Stan would have to "settle down into the duties of domestic life." Others around him, besides his colleague Joseph Wells, probably wondered how well he would adjust to his new condition. Changing from his earlier bachelor freedom into marriage, with new family and household responsibilities, obviously would necessitate substantial alterations in life-style for him. No longer had he just himself to consider in his free time, but the interests and wishes of his "frau," as he sometimes referred to Bessie, would have to concern him. Bessie, who was almost nine years younger than her husband, had grown up in a family dominated by a strong father and was accustomed to a subordinate role in the household. When she and Stan settled in New York, she took on the new role of mistress of her own household, so she too had adjustments to make. The responsibilities of family life took on additional dimensions for both of them on December

117

22, when Bessie gave birth to a son. The proud parents named the baby Richard Grant White after Stan's father.

Stanford was delighted by the birth of his son, though perhaps not fully aware of what the responsibilities of parenthood might involve for him. Stan's father immediately wrote Bessie congratulating her on the birth of his namesake grandson: "You have done splendidly. . . . God bless you and your boy, & forgive you for making a grandmother of your little Momma. It matters not now what is made of your loving Big Papa." Richard Grant White was immensely pleased that his name would be carried on by a new generation.[1]

Stan's joy in his baby came on top of his satisfaction at seeing his father finally gain some recognition for his literary endeavors. The elder White's edition of Shakespeare's plays had become a standard American work; *Words and Their Uses* was going through edition after edition; *Every-day English* was selling well; *England Without and Within* had received critical praise; and *The Fate of Mansfield Humphreys* was eliciting enthusiastic letters from readers, especially from England, bringing "from strangers expressions of higher satisfaction than any book [he] ever wrote." Richard White had joined with other prominent writers to organize the Authors' Club, and as host to the club at his home was reported to have been "quite assiduous in attending to the interest of the members." He had been honored in an 1883 Society of American Artists' exhibit, which featured his likeness in *Portrait of a Gentleman* by the painter J. Alden Weir. Gratifying to both Stan and his father, as well, was an 1884 poll conducted by a new journal *The Critic and Good Literature,* which invited readers to choose the forty Americans most qualified to be members of an American Academy. Richard Grant White placed tenth on the readers' list, well ahead of Henry James, Mark Twain, and Walt Whitman.[2]

The elder White's professional and family satisfactions, though, were, as always, tempered by his chronic unhappiness with his city, his country, and the American people. Journalistic excoriations of American society and culture seem to have become an integral part of his outlook and nature. The social life of New York, he complained in the *Times,* was "a society of display only." Costly entertainments had become commonplace, but such affairs lacked true hospitality and sociability and were only aimed at effect. Manners continued to deteriorate. New Yorkers no longer deferred to character, good breeding, or ability, but only to money and power. And the low level of American culture was lamentable. White explained in the *Century* magazine that he had declined to write a history of music in America, as he had been asked to do, because there was in fact no American music to write about. He went on to observe that the New England psalm-book makers and singing school masters seemed "about as much in place in the history of musical art as a critical discourse of the whooping of Indians would be." America, for Richard Grant White, ran a poor second to the Old World.[3]

In the latter part of 1884, Stan was dismayed by his father's severe decline in health. In November the elder White suffered a heart seizure and fainting spell. To a friend in England, Richard later wrote that he felt "as if some giant hand had my heart in its grip." He groaned and staggered and began to fall when Stan, who was nearby, caught him. "I was not so far gone then that I lost sweet consciousness of feeling his strong arms around me before I vanished." He recovered sufficiently to play music by Haydn with his string quartet the next February, but he gradually grew weaker and eventually was unable to take nourishment. Congestion of the lungs at last brought his life to a close. Richard Grant White died at his home on April 8, 1885. His funeral took place two days later at St. Marks Episcopal Church, and he was buried in Rosedale Cemetery, East Orange, New Jersey. Stanford designed a simple tombstone for his father's grave.[4]

Richard Grant White had always shown warm affection for his younger son, favoring him over his elder brother and giving him advice and support. He had helped Stanford choose a career and find a place to begin his training. He had assisted him, now and then, with his work, as with the Farragut Monument inscription, and he had helped him improve his position in the city by arranging for Stan's graduate degree in 1881 at the University of the City of New York. The father had always provided the son in his creative activities with a model of hard work, commitment, and rigorous standards, evident in his prodigious literary output (one biographer lists some 750 books and articles he authored). Similarly, Richard Grant White's love of beauty, his discriminating taste, and his appreciation of the art and high culture of the European past had nurtured his son in his youth and shaped Stan's own passion for art.[5]

But the father had left much else as well: Stanford's inheritance included less pleasant aspects of the elder White about which Stan would develop a certain ambivalence. Although Richard Grant White achieved some public recognition, his persona was not particularly sympathetic. Over the years widespread fame, a consistently positive public image, and substantial financial rewards, all of which he greatly wanted, had eluded him. Throughout his adult life he had accounted himself pretty much a failure. The genteel poverty of his adult years was particularly galling to him since as a child he had been raised in great comfort and had

119

been led to expect a life of gentlemanly ease. Chronically dissatisfied with his lot, hypercritical of his culture, out of place most everywhere—such characteristics did not make him an especially pleasant or easygoing companion. Stan would distance himself from those aspects of his father; indeed, he would embrace their opposites—joviality, indulgence, sociability. Yet the father's intense desire for recognition and for wealth and the fine things it could bring became dominating passions for the son. Like his father, Stanny craved wealth and fame. In time he would gain considerable riches and become one of the best known of New Yorkers, but his hold on both his wealth and his good name, like his father's, would be precarious.

There was yet another dimension of the father's legacy to his son: his attitude toward and relationships with women and marriage. Richard Grant White's distaste for strong-minded females and his attraction to young women who looked to him for protection became a strong motif in Stan's life as well. His father's extramarital liaison—which Stan no doubt knew of—presented a model of marital fidelity that would strongly shape his own life.

In the very difficult time following his father's death, Stan became a strong support for his mother. He took charge of the many details in settling his father's estate and became something of the strong, protecting male figure that Alexina, like Bessie, apparently needed. He was appointed administrator of his father's estate and supervised a sale late in the year of valuables his father had collected. A catalogue was printed of the sale items, including 1,900 books and pamphlets, 127 engravings, 30 oil paintings, and several musical instruments. The sale brought only slightly more than $3,000, which failed to match the legal costs, funeral expenses, and other debts of $5,220 of the estate. Other than a small income from book royalties, Alexina White was without resources and dependent on her younger son. Stanford invited his mother to come to live with him and Bessie.[6]

From 1885 onward, Alexina White shared the homes of her son and daughter-in-law, and after Stan's death she would reside with Bessie. Alexina's older brother, Charles Graham Mease, who impressed Bessie as "a beautiful old man with a head like Carlyle," also came for long periods to live with Stanford and Bessie. His health was excellent, and he took pride in his daily 2-mile walk and his vigorous exercises, which each morning shook the whole house. Mease died in 1913 at the age of ninety-two. Bringing Stan's mother and, later, his uncle into her small house and having two people of an older generation always about must have been difficult for Bessie—certainly more than she had bargained for when she was married the year before. But Bessie cheerfully accepted the situation: a multigenerational household was normal for the times.

Stan always remained fairly close to his "Mama," who sometimes vied with Bessie for his attention and affection. Alexina occasionally sent her son notes complaining that Bessie was ignoring her wishes or slighting her. Alexina White herself was known to be condescending at times toward Bessie. She was more widely read than her daughter-in-law, more interested in intellectual pursuits, and indifferent toward Bessie's love of fishing, horseback riding, and the outdoors. During their close relationship over thirty-five years, prolonged tensions periodically arose between the two women, and they sometimes did not speak to each other for days on end.[7]

Just as Stan was beginning to get over the shock of his father's death, another family tragedy occurred. Four months after the death of Richard White, on August 9, 1885, during "an epidemic of so-called cholera," Stan's and Bessie's son, seven and one-half months old, suddenly died at Smithtown, Long Island. The baby was buried in the Smith family plot behind the small church at St. James. Within a short time, Stan had lost both his principal tie to the past and his familial hopes for the future.

The death of the baby was obviously a terrible shock to the parents. For the father, caught up in the routines of the busy office, the loss probably was easier to bear than it was for the mother. But Bessie found some solace being near her own family, close to her sisters, in the place she loved best, the north shore of Long Island. Late in the summer of 1885, the Whites rented a small wooden farmhouse on what was known as Carmen's Hill at St. James, near Smithtown, overlooking Crane Neck and Long Island Sound. As a child Bessie had loved this spot above the harbor, said to be the highest point for miles around. The view, Bessie, later recalled, "became a passion with me," and when she was married her father told Stanford that he was certain Bessie "never would be happy or content to live anywhere else but on top of 'Carmen's Hill.' " Bessie's sisters Cornelia (Mrs. Prescott Hall Butler) and Ella (Mrs. Devereux Emmet) lived on adjoining properties, and Kate Wetherill, another sister, was close by. In the years following, Stanford and Bessie would spend a part of each summer at the St. James farmhouse.[8]

A trip to the South early in 1886 also diverted the Whites from the pain of the loss of their child. They lingered briefly in South Carolina: "We were both wild over Charleston," Stan wrote his mother. "It is a most lovely old city with about the swellest old houses I have ever seen on this side of the water." Visits in Savannah and Jacksonville gave them further respite from the Northern winter and the sad associations with home.[9]

Some months later an event occurred that had an important impact on their lives. On October 25, 1886, Bessie's great aunt Cornelia Clinch Stewart, the widow of A. T. Stewart, the dry goods store magnate, and probably the richest woman in the United States, died in her marble mansion on Thirty-fourth Street and Fifth Avenue. Three days later, Stan and Bessie were present for a prayer service at the Stewart house and for the funeral that followed at the Protestant Episcopal cathedral in Garden City, New York. After the death in 1876 of her husband, who had left a good part of his estate of between $30 and $40 million to his widow, Mrs. Stewart had had the large cathedral erected on Long Island. A few days after Mrs. Stewart's funeral, the reading of her will revealed that, among other bequests, she had made an outright bequest of $100,000 to Bessie White and had given a sum of $250,000 outright and one-quarter of the residual of her estate to Bessie's mother, Sarah Nicoll Smith. The *New York Times* estimated that Sarah Smith's inheritance from her aunt would be nearly $5 million.[10]

The pain of the baby's loss was eased the following year by the birth of a second son on September 26, 1887, at the Whites' home on West Twentieth Street. Lawrence Grant White would be Stan's and Bessie's only living child. Congratulations were showered on the parents, including a pathetic note from Stan's brother Dick at the mines in Hermosa, New Mexico:

My Dear Brother,

I give you joy of your newly born boy and drink to his health in a bottle of white New Mexico wine; perhaps I may get tight as I sit by my open fire, for I have no company to drink with me and become hilarious, so I work at the fire, poke it, and make merry with it for company. So here's health and happiness to Bess and the Boy and you.[11]

Soon after the birth of their second son, Stanny was reported to have asked his wife to take primary responsibility for raising Larry until he was eighteen years old, at which time, he promised, he would take over the youth's training. He believed that caring for children was women's work, and he wanted no intrusions into his professional life. White showed a reluctance to involve himself in the day-to-day responsibilities of fatherhood, just as his own father years earlier had distanced himself from his first-born son. In correspondence, Stan referred to his son as *"her* little boy."[12]

Bessie's life centered on Larry, whom she coddled, protected, and adored. Bessie took delight in the clothing she selected for Larry, and, in the style of the times, Larry wore dresses even after he was five years old. As a young lad, he always appeared with white cotton gloves on outings in the park, and other children considered him something of a sissy. The painter Edward Simmons, whose own sons were close to Larry in age, once remonstrated with Stanford because Larry's nursemaid was so overprotective as not to let the boy get his feet wet or walk on the grass in the park. White exploded and immediately fired the nursemaid; possibly he was sensitive to an implication in the criticism regarding how little he had to do with raising his son. While Larry was only six years old and attending the Allen School on Fifth Avenue, his father applied for his admission to St. Mark's, an elite boarding school in Southborough, Massachusetts, to which many upper-class New Yorkers sent their sons. Larry in time attended St. Mark's, where he did well in academic subjects but disliked athletics intensely.[13]

In 1887, the year of Larry's birth, Stan was invited to become a member of the Restigouche Salmon Club. His sponsor was his friend and Newport and New York client, Robert Goelet. "Preeminent" among gentlemen's sporting clubs, the Restigouche Salmon Club leased a large tract along the Matapedia and Restigouche rivers on the Gaspé Peninsula in Quebec Province and provided lodge accommodations for members and their guests. Prominent American socialites and wealthy businessmen, including several of Stan's friends, were members, and often two or more of them arranged to take a vacation there together for fishing, canoeing, and relaxation. Members could keep their own fishing gear and canoes at the club and hire the services of local guides for extended expeditions along the rivers and streams of the region. White had first visited the club in the summer of 1885, shortly before the death of his first child, and thereafter he returned once or twice every year, staying for three or four weeks each time. Like his 1886 election to the Century Association, a prestigious New York club of men devoted to the arts, White's election to the Restigouche Club a year later was a significant step in his rising social position, so important for him during those years; the contacts to be made in both groups could be useful to him in a professional way. On joining, Stan paid an initiation fee of $200 and purchased a $5,000 share in the club; thereafter he paid his portion of assessments levied on members for the upkeep of the facilities. A few very wealthy men had private lodges at the club. In 1897 White designed

Kedgewick Lodge for William K. Vanderbilt, with whom he sometimes fished. In 1895 he designed a big lodge for Camp Harmony on the Restigouche. For some years, Stanny served as a director of the salmon club.[14]

Stan's family accompanied him to the Restigouche Club a few times. In the summer of 1890 Bessie and Larry, who was then not quite three, along with Larry's nurse, went with Stan to the camp. Again, in the early summer of 1897, Bessie joined her husband there on vacation with Larry and a nursemaid-helper; the expedition that year was on a grand scale, with several other members besides the Whites and eight or ten guides hired for the party. Stan had consistently poor luck on the waters that summer, however, and caught only eighteen fish, as against 111 the year before. Bessie, on the other hand, had the good luck to land on her first try a 43-pound salmon, which was said to be "the largest actually authenticated fish ever killed by the Restigouche Salmon Club" up to that time. The biggest fish Stan ever caught weighed 39½ pounds. Years later, Larry White remembered "quite vividly and with the greatest pleasure" that second vacation fishing holiday, floating lazily down the river on a houseboat and fishing in various pools as they went along. Many times, after his fishing trips, Stan sent presents of salmon to friends and clients. Sometimes the fish were delayed in transit and arrived too late to be eaten, much to his annoyance. The time Stan spent each year at the salmon club was, according to Mead, "something he always looked forward to and out of which he took the greatest pleasure in his life."[15]

An extended European holiday in 1889, their first visit since the wedding trip of 1884, brought the Whites to the Continent and England for three months. In May White had fallen ill and was "very sick in bed," confined to his home for ten days. He felt that he badly needed a long holiday. Accompanied by Bessie and Larry as well as his mother, Stan left New York on July 6 on the steamship *Gascogne,* bound for France. Stan had urged Saint-Gaudens to go with them on the same steamer. Gus had declined, but the sculptor did follow shortly. That summer Paris was filled with visitors enjoying the International Exposition, dominated by Gustave Eiffel's spectacular iron-latticework tower, the tallest structure in all Europe. With his family along, the carefree times White had enjoyed ten years earlier were not so possible on this trip.[16]

In Paris White ransacked antique shops for objects for himself and for pieces he might place in others' houses. William C. Whitney, for whom Stan was altering a large house on Fifty-seventh Street at Fifth Avenue, had commissioned the architect to purchase art objects. In Paris also, Stan encountered the American painter J. Alden Weir and got Weir to persuade the French artist Puvis de Chavannes to agree to work on decorations for McKim's Boston Public Library. In mid-August the Whites traveled on to Switzerland, and from there Stan made a brief excursion to Florence, to consult with his local art and antiques agent, and to Rome to visit the painter Elihu Vedder and his wife and arrange for a collection of plaster casts for the Metropolitan Museum of Art. Larry, not yet two at the time, became ill for some weeks in late summer. His condition was a cause of anxiety for his parents, who still felt deeply the loss of their first son. From New York, McKim reassured his partner by letter that all was busy and going well in the office with "no mishaps and no trouble of any sort." The University Club, which he had designed, was moving along, he reported. As always, he sent his love to Bessie. The Whites returned to Paris in early September and then stopped in London for two weeks, going overnight to the country to visit with the painters John Singer Sargent and Edwin Austin Abbey. Sailing on the first of October, Stan was back in the office by October 10.[17]

Family ties were loosened at the close of the decade as death took its further toll. Bessie's father, Judge John Lawrence Smith, died in 1889. In April 1890 Bessie's mother, Sarah Nicoll Smith, succumbed to pneumonia at the age of sixty-six, within a week of the death of one of Bessie's nieces. With those almost simultaneous deaths, they "had a terrible time," Stan wrote his brother Dick in New Mexico.[18]

The death of her parents brought a substantial additional inheritance to Bessie, most of it from the Stewart estate that had come to her mother in 1886. All in all, it is probable that Bessie eventually inherited directly from the Stewart estate and from the estates of her parents more than half a million dollars in money and property. Stanford was named trustee for Bessie in the matter of the Stewart estate and took charge of her interest in the inherited properties, in which she held a five–ninety-fifths share. Bessie's substantial inheritance had a significant impact on the Whites' style of living and on the relationship between them. It was always understood that the former Stewart properties and the inherited money were hers. The inheritance gave Bessie an awareness that she was by no means dependent on her husband for her needs. Indeed, he was dependent on her for some of the things he wanted. Within a few years of their wedding, she had ceased to be a young female who needed support and protection, the kind of woman that Stan, like his father, was most drawn to.

The management and division of the Stewart estate involved complex legal negotiations for many years. A suit by Irish heirs complicated matters. Some of the properties needed extraordinary expenditures for improvements, and it was often difficult when the properties were held jointly among several owners to get agreement on what to do. Among some 130 properties, Bessie shared in ownership of the Park Avenue Hotel, the Metropolitan Hotel, Niblo's Theater, and the former Stewart mansion in New York City, along with the Grand Union Hotel in Saratoga Springs; properties in Garden City, Long Island; and a large farm and quarry in Westchester County. For years, Stan immersed himself in questions concerning the properties in correspondence with his lawyers and with William A. White & Sons, the real estate firm, which acted as agents for the Stewart properties. An 1893 appraisal of the Stewart estate properties just in New York City arrived at a total value of $6,320,520. Bessie gained full ownership of buildings near Washington Square at 110 Bleecker Street and at 179 Greene Street, among others. She had them torn down and rebuilt, taking out a $50,000 mortgage on the two buildings in 1897. Stanford supervised the investment of his wife's money as her agent and with her consent. In the early 1890s, for example, he put funds into Madison Square Garden shares, bonds of the Century Association, loans to the Restigouche Salmon Club, and the property at St. James, all of which were of direct concern to him. Although it was Bessie's money, White could give others the impression that he had funds available to put where he wished. No evidence has been found to indicate that Bessie objected to the way he used her money.[19]

Bessie's fortune allowed Stan to become a country gentleman. In 1892 the Whites purchased a parcel of some 50 acres centered upon and including the St. James farmhouse they had rented since 1885. Subsequently they acquired additional acreage. The original farmhouse, after some years, became the core of a much rebuilt and considerably expanded country house, eventually surrounded by gardens, including a formal boxwood garden, which gave the place its name, Box Hill.[20]

In the earliest years of the Whites' residence, not much had been done to the rental property, although Stanford's hand was in evidence from the beginning. A handwritten extract from the *Long Islander* in the White Collection at the New-York Historical Society—possibly coming from White himself—describes complaints by the "Rev. Timothy O'Slap," who in company with the wife of a parishioner one day came upon "a low and curious seat," near the house that "S— W—," "the husband of one of the daughters of Judge S—," had taken for the summer, "surrounded by classic statues absolutely devoid of all clothing and standing out in shameless and conspicuous nudity among the green trees."

At the sight of those objects, the clergyman and his companion "fled in confusion." The following day, the Reverend O'Slap summoned a meeting of villagers who sent a remonstrating letter to S— W—. He in turn, it was reported, informed a committee calling on him "to mind their own business." When the Reverend O'Slap and some villagers attempted to destroy "the offensive statues," they were driven away by a large dog. The excerpt concludes with the sanctimonious hope "that this attempt to introduce the immorality of Italy and of France into our midst will be resisted to the end. The honor of Long Island must be upheld and the purity of her daughters assured, at all hazards"— the sardonic moralizing here sounding much like White himself.[21]

The main programs of alterations at Box Hill took place soon after its purchase in 1893 and 1894 and again in 1899, when the house was considerably enlarged. But improvements went on almost continuously, and Stan was involved in one project or another at the Box Hill estate for the rest of his life. When not concerned with the main house, he was instructing workmen on terracing the grounds, rebuilding the roads, or constructing barns, an ice house, a pump house, greenhouses, or a pergola. Lionel Moses from the New York office was entrusted with executing much of the work of remodeling the house and designing and erecting the outbuildings. The passion for improvement and the energy Stanford expended on the country estate was characteristic of his work on many of his projects.

As the alterations went on, the old farmhouse disappeared, swallowed up in a much larger two-and-one-half-story structure. As finally enlarged, at the close of the century, the rebuilt house centered on an entry hall extending from front to rear, with an **L**-shaped extension for the staircase in the front. A large parlor, with windows on three sides, was built to the left of the entry hall, while the dining room, one wall in tiles, opened on the other side to the rear of the stairhall. The pantry, kitchen, and servants' hall occupied the wing beyond the dining room, at the right end of the house. On the second floor of the house, as it was enlarged in 1899, there were bedrooms for Stan and for Bessie, Alexina White's room, and three guest rooms, and the attic floor contained the nursery and four servants' rooms. The house was sited with an eye to the view out over the blue waters of the bay and sound. The openness of the parlor, the large enveloping porches, and the homey, informal, comfortable character of the house all proclaimed that this was a place for summer living. Bessie, Larry, and Alexina White regularly spent the summer and early fall months at St. James, and during their residence Stan customarily came out for weekends and sometimes for a longer stay. Occasionally he failed to arrive when expected because of the press of work or perhaps a social engagement in the city; his absence was always a disappointment for his wife and son.[22]

For White, Box Hill was a place for relaxation, a place to release some of his energy and to entertain friends. The highpoint of the summer season was the Fourth of July, with picnics, boating, fishing, and, always, fireworks. Stan took great delight in activities of the Fourth. Weeks beforehand he would begin detailed planning with fireworks sellers to get the effects he wanted from fountains of colored fire and rockets of green, yellow, and red. Like his brother-in-law Devereux Emmet, on the adjoining place, Stan eventually had a nine-hole golf course laid out on the property. McKim came frequently to Box Hill for summer weekends, after the death of his second wife, and joined Stanny there for a round or two of golf. One Fourth of July, when Stanny arrived at Box Hill, he discovered that all his family and guests, including McKim, were out yachting, so he went around the golf course by himself, with his gardener as caddy, making some splendid drives. After McKim returned from the boating expedition, Stanny insisted that they play the course together, and he "not only got licked, but did not make a single decent drive. Golf is a great game," he concluded.[23]

The enlargement and development of the St. James estate provided an elegant country retreat for White and his family. Before he was forty, then, Stanford White, city-born and city-bred, had to some degree joined the rural gentry of Long Island, with his country seat, his gardens and greenhouses, and his pastures and barns. As lord of the manor, he might deal more confidently with his many wealthy clients at their social level. Although the property was purchased with Bessie's money and he always acknowledged that it was her place, no doubt the estate gave Stan a sense of rootedness and residential stability that he had never before experienced in his life. With this home, he had acquired something that his father had not been able to have since his childhood in Brooklyn. And by providing a comfortable domicile for his mother at Box Hill, he had become materially successful in a way her husband had not been.

About the time of the purchase of the St. James property, the Whites also acquired a new home in the city. In January 1892 the trustees of the William C. Rhinelander estate, owners of the brownstone at 56 West Twentieth Street, which the Whites rented, notified the tenants that they planned to erect a new building on the southeast corner of Sixth Avenue and Twentieth Street and would take possession of the house on May 1 to have it razed. White soon deluged real estate agents with inquiries about houses for sale somewhere between Thirty-fourth and Fortieth streets and between Fifth and Park avenues. He hoped to acquire two adjoining houses, one of them for his brother-in-law Prescott Hall Butler and family. White indicated a willingness to consider houses that might require considerable alterations. Prices were high, and nothing he looked at seemed suitable, so by the end of March he began considering property to rent. In late April he concluded a rental agreement at $3,500 a year with Henry A. C. Taylor for the house at 119 East Twenty-first Street, on the north side of Gramercy Park. Taylor himself occupied the large house adjacent to the east, at the corner of Lexington Avenue. White was already acquainted with the wealthy Taylor: Some years earlier, in 1886, McKim had designed a large and striking colonial revival summer house for him in Newport, and in 1891 Stan's partner had begun work on a large townhouse for Taylor on East Seventy-first Street.[24]

On May 24, 1892, the Whites moved into their Twenty-first Street house. The Gramercy Park residence was more spacious than the family's former house and in a much more fashionable neighborhood. Here was an urban residence considerably more appropriate for an architect who was becoming very well known than the small brownstone near Sixth Avenue. Stan asked friends to return to him furniture and tapestries he had previously loaned out, to place in the new house. Sometime later he tried to purchase the house, valued at about $60,000, but Taylor did not wish to sell; nonetheless, Stan did make repairs and minor alterations. In 1894 he had the property wired for electricity, but two years passed before the lighting system was in full operation. For six years this was the Whites' townhouse.[25]

As Stanford's social status rose during those years, his brother Dick remained a burden and a continuing source of concern. About the time of his marriage, in 1884, Stan had joined with others in New York to purchase New Mexico mine properties, which Dick was employed to develop or, in some instances, to attempt to resell. Speculations in gold, silver, and lead mining claims were an important source of income for many American investors. But the other New York backers had persistent doubts about Dick White's astuteness in assessing the value of such properties and about his financial ability. The accounts of expenditures Dick sent back to New York were often confused or unintelligible. Stan attempted to mediate between the other investors and his brother, though he was well aware of Dick's failings. Matters were made no easier by Dick's lurid and inflammatory comments about his backers and his frequent demands on Stan, whose patience was often sorely tried. To improve his situation, Dick tried to get a marshal's appointment in the New

Mexico Territory. Stan asked various friends and acquaintances to support the appointment, but Dick failed to get the position.[26]

By the fall of 1888, Stan wanted nothing more than to be rid of the headache of the Western mines. The following February he made a quit deed whereby he turned over to Dick, "making over to you all right, title and interest in all or any property possessed by me or of which I am the alleged possessor in New Mexico for the vast sum of one dollar." Stan had had enough: "For God's sake give us a rest!" Dick had been "an utter and double-barrelled idiot" for his attacks on the investors. "Let us cork up," and let matters rest.[27]

Dick White eventually divested himself of his holdings in the New Mexico mines, though he continued to style himself a consultant on mining, mill sites, and other properties, advising as to their purchase, working, and development. Things still did not go well for him, however, and by the early 1890s Stan was regularly sending his older brother $50 a month for support, which he would continue to do for years. He also made inquiries to find some way for Dick to earn his own living: "I would willingly become responsible for him in any position that would require trust, and also would willingly pay his salary for the first year and anything he would need to get a little experience before he could be of much service." In effect, Stan had become a father to his floundering, lonely older brother. To a New York friend, Stan suggested that Dick would be better off in the West than in New York, since "it makes him too unhappy to occupy a subordinate position amongst his friends." Obviously, as well, Dick would be less of an embarrassment to Stan away from the city. When Dick on occasion came to New York to see his mother and brother, Stanny arranged for him to go to Brooks Brothers and other stores to be outfitted properly for the city, and for cash to be made available for him at the firm's office. On such visits, Stan included his brother in some of his social activities, though Dick's silent, withdrawn manner did not make him a particularly attractive dinner or theater companion.[28]

When Bessie was in the city, she sometimes joined her husband for dinners with his friends, either at their own home or in restaurants. Newspaper accounts of the late 1880s and early 1890s now and then noted the presence of Mr. and Mrs. Stanford White at social events. At a National Academy of Design ball in February 1889, Stan appeared in a full coat of mail, while Bessie was garbed as a princess of Byzantium. On the March 1892 evening that the "capricious" Carmencita danced at R. C. Miner's studio in honor of Henry Adams's friend Mrs. Don Cameron of Washington, D.C., the Whites were present in the "artistic and sympathetic audience.'' While still in her late twenties, Bessie occasionally was prevailed upon to serve as a patroness of charity fundraisers, such as that of the Summer Rest Society, which provided holiday accommodations for working women outside the city. But she was far less interested in social gatherings or in having her presence noted here or there than her husband was. She sometimes begged off going out and, of course, she was away from the city for several months each year. Newspaper accounts of society doings often reported on Mr. Stanford White with no mention of his wife. At the fashionable Patriarchs' Ball, held in Delmonico's Ballroom on January 5, 1891, at which "society had its leading representatives present," Stanny was there. Bessie was not.[29]

The very heavy work load for White in the office, his family obligations and concerns, and his strenuous program of social activities took their toll in frequent bouts of illness. A succession of winter colds early in 1890 prompted his doctor to order him south; for a short respite in March, Bessie and Stan journeyed to Asheville, North Carolina. Far more serious was an attack of the grippe in late December 1891, followed by a severe urinary tract and bladder infection in January 1892. For five weeks White was confined to his house. A week's stay in Florida did not help much, and in February he reported that the "water works are still not much better" and that he was "still not 'out of the woods.' '' He underwent minor surgery twice in February. In April, just at the time he and Bessie were preparing to move to Gramercy Park, he complained that he was still quite sick. A month later, however, after the move, he was feeling better and, at the age of thirty-eight, could report that he had "had such a long experience" with himself that he knew he was "tougher than a pine knot." For his fishing excursion to Canada in June he had 75 quarts of Poland Spring sparkling water sent ahead for him. But despite the holiday respite and the regime of mineral water, his health remained precarious. Later in 1892 he would suffer a serious relapse.[30]

In less than a decade, since the time of his marriage, Stanford White had become a widely noticed figure on the New York social scene and had clearly gained a place for himself in the upper social set. He had been accepted in elite clubs and was close to many socially prominent New Yorkers. As Joseph Wells had surmised, Stan did indeed care "to make a social figure," and he had succeeded brilliantly.

But at the same time, White continued to maintain close ties with old friends in the artist community from his bachelor days. Just four years after his marriage, he secretly returned to join again in the free and open artist life that had been important to him in earlier years. From May 1888 at the latest to November 1889, and probably beyond that, White, Gus Saint-Gaudens, Thomas Dewing, Louis Saint-Gaudens, Frank Lathrop, and Joseph Wells were joined together in the "Sewer Club," a name suggestive of scandalous pursuits. The six artist members of the Sewer Club jointly rented a room in the Benedict on Washington Square, where Wells lived. The surviving account of dues and expenses indicates that Stan and Gus, in effect, financed the club. Stan was paying part of Dewing's share and the shares of the other three, who were already behind on their dues as of November 1, 1888. In January 1891, the records indicate, White arranged for another hideaway in room 8 of the Holbein Building at 146 West Fifty-fifth Street. Furnishings from the Benedict room were moved there. For a time Dewing shared with Stan the rental of this uptown room, which with other Holbein studio-hideaways that followed became known in White's inner circle as the "Morgue," another highly suggestive name, implying a deadness to the world outside. The Sewer Club and the Morgue provided private retreats, which, it cannot be doubted, were used for sexual liaisons. A man of enormous appetites, hungry for excitement, delighting in the unconventional and in shocking others, Stan was already unwilling to accept the limitations of a monogamous union. Joseph Wells at the time of Stanford's marriage had wondered how well White would "settle down into the duties of domestic life" once "all new sensations" had been exhausted. He now had his answer.[31]

Stan and his close artist friends saw themselves in those secret hideaways participating in the Bohemian artist tradition of full personal freedom, not bound by accepted morality, challenging the routines of the staid and the conventional. In life as in art, Stanford White believed in freedom, "in every person doing as they darn please." Doing as they "darn please" in defiance of social conventions might mean, of course, that someone would be hurt.[32]

10

The Consummate Clubman

All-male social gatherings were important, perhaps even essential, for Stanford White. Although over the years Stan arranged and attended countless parties for friends of both sexes, often went to balls, and organized excursions for male and female acquaintances, he had a strong need to be with "the boys" at dinners and nights on the town. An all-male group met certain needs for him that a mixed social gathering did not: conviviality of longtime friends, shared attitudes and feelings, an openness to indulgence and adventure, and the freedom to use less than genteel language. Besides the hideaways, New York gentlemen's clubs came to provide him with the all-male environment he seemed to crave.

For many upper-class and upper-middle-class men, the gentlemen's clubs became homes away from home, where many showed up every day and spent a good part of their lives. Some clubs were highly elitist and limited to socially prominent men from old New York families, while others brought together men interested in the arts, in politics, or in athletic pursuits. Most men in White's circle belonged to several. Stan carried club participation, as he would do with other areas of his life, to extremes. He belonged to more than fifty men's clubs, societies, and organizations.

White was the consummate clubman. Sociable, outgoing, well-bred yet never stuffy, with good connections and the appearance, the manners, and the wherewithal of a gentleman, he was invited into most of the elite clubs of New York and became a nonresident member of several outside the city. He assisted in founding several clubs, and newly formed organizations sought him out as a member. He was active on committees in several of his groups. He wrote countless recommendations for friends and acquaintances seeking membership and energetically cultivated friendship and fellowship within his clubs. Stan strongly believed "to make a club successful that the social side must be considered first, and in the majority of cases to the detriment of any serious purpose." Clubs became an essential part of Stan's life as places to go for lunch or dinner or to spend an evening, as retreats from the pressures of business and from family cares, and as centers of close fellowship. With Bessie and Larry at Box Hill for so many months each year, the clubs were at times almost his primary homes. In his favorite clubs he could be sure of meeting not only longtime friends but also congenial men he did not yet know, who might become new friends. Fellow club members often became his clients.[1]

White designed some of the principal clubhouses of New York, most notably those for the Century Association and the Metropolitan Club, besides that for The Players. (McKim, who was also a confirmed clubman, designed the University and Harvard clubhouses in New York and the Algonquin in Boston.) Stan's commitment to club life gave him a sensitivity to members' needs—a pleasing arrangement of rooms, provisions for suitable facilities and amenities, appropriate furnishings and décor, and special entertainments and celebrations. His professional efforts, combined with his social participation, made White one of the most effective shapers of the characteristic way of life for the "clubbable" men of the city around the turn of the century.

The Tile Club introduced him to the conviviality, good fellowship, and friendship a club could provide. The Tile Club had a rather unconventional atmosphere, which Stan enjoyed, though the members were, by and large, serious, hard-working professionals. A few of them were at the same time members of elite gentlemen's clubs. As the "Beaver" or the "Builder," Stanny joined enthusiastically in the weekly gatherings at which the members painted on tiles amid a buzz of storytelling, professional shop talk, and gossip, occasionally stilled for performances by a singer or a violinist. Among Stan's Tiler friends were Saint-Gaudens, Winslow Homer, Elihu Vedder, William Merritt Chase, Francis Millet, J. Alden Weir, John Twachtman, Francis Hopkinson Smith, and Edwin Austin Abbey.

When Abbey returned from England in 1881 and took a studio with Alfred Parsons at 58½ West Tenth Street, he put his quarters at the disposal of the Tile Club members in the evenings. Later the space was taken over for the Tilers' sole use. The clubroom occupied the parlor floor of a tiny house behind a larger red brick house facing on Tenth Street. It was reached by a dark, low, and narrow passageway leading to a small rear courtyard, on which the clubhouse fronted. Stan was entrusted with decorating the clubroom. He designed white tiled fireplaces for each end of the room and paneled the walls in rich redwood. Around the room he hung decorative brass and pewter pieces and small paintings and etchings, which he and other members had created. Tilers and their guests were delighted with the cozy, homey atmosphere.

The fare at earlier gatherings in members' studios had been confined to cheese, crackers, and beer. At the new clubhouse it was enlarged to full dinners of steak, duck, and skewered meats, prepared by a black cook in the basement kitchen or by the Tilers themselves, cooking on grills arranged over the open fire. After members had gathered on an evening, it became the custom that "the whole band, linking arms, danced three times around the ellipse of the large table, silently and with a kind of formality. This accolade effected, they all fell to upon the nourishment set before them." As they dined, Tilers regaled fellow members with stories of the whereabouts and doings of others who were out of the city. Late in the evening, a supper of Welsh rarebit or oysters was served. By midnight they adjourned. The 1886 *Book of the Tile Club,* boasting a sumptuous cover designed by White, convincingly conveyed the atmosphere of camaraderie of the club gatherings. Soon after its publication, ironically, the Tile Club disbanded. The cause, according to gossip, was the abrasive personality of Francis Hopkinson Smith, the "Owl," who had been its leading figure.[2]

The demise of the Tile Club made a project for a new club on the south side of Gramercy Park all the more attractive to White. The famous actor Edwin Booth (a brother of John Wilkes Booth) had for some time planned to establish a library on the American theater; by 1887 that idea had evolved into a proposal for a club for men involved with the theater and the arts. Here, Booth foresaw, actors, dramatists, managers, producers, and even critics might mingle with painters, writers, musicians, and architects. The clubhouse, with bedrooms and meal service, might become, as well, a real home for what was often a homeless and ever traveling profession. When Booth acquired 16 Gramercy Park, a townhouse with Gothic Revival detail dating from before 1846, he invited Stanny to look it over. After White inspected the house and made suggestions for its remodeling, Booth asked him to undertake transforming the building into suitable accommodations for the club. Booth financed the $25,000 remodeling project himself. The Players Club was organized, with Stan a member from the start.[3]

White worked on the house over several months in 1888. He attempted to create a comfortable, homelike atmosphere for what he felt would be a congenial group of artists. Several structural changes were made, the most conspicuous being the removal of the high stoop, which was replaced by a new basement entrance, and the erection of a two-story colonnade and porch in the Italian Renaissance style, decorated with two huge projecting wrought-iron lanterns and handsome wrought-iron balconies. White involved himself not only with rebuilding and strengthening the house—shoring up the walls, inserting iron beams and posts, shifting room partitions, and putting in new fireplaces—but also with decoration of the rooms and furnishing and equipping the whole clubhouse, even down to the pots and pans, mugs, and platters. Stan arranged for his friend Francis Lathrop to provide glasswork and a skylight, and he persuaded the painter John Singer Sargent to prepare a portrait of Booth for the building.

Late in the evening on the final day of 1888, White joined with more than a hundred other men who had assembled to inaugurate their remarkable new clubhouse on the south side of Gramercy Park. Highly enthusiastic about the building, members were especially impressed by the "mellow," friendly, lived-in look of the rooms. Toward midnight Edwin Booth, the first president of the group, in a brief speech "marked by deep feeling, great dignity, and winning sweetness of manner," presented the title deed of the clubhouse with its contents to the members. Augustin Daly, a theatrical producer and vice president, responded to Booth and accepted the gift. Following a few other remarks, a loving cup filled with wine was passed about the rooms as each member took a sip, and the supper room was opened. The Players, inaugurated just as the year 1889 began, was always White's favorite club.[4]

The modest exterior of The Players clubhouse belied the artful and commodious interior. From the basement entrance level, with a billiard room and a wine room, a broad oaken staircase was built to the main hall, dominated by a massive fireplace with two great firedog andirons. The mantel was ornamented by an intricate frieze of masks, Tragedy and Comedy, with an arabesque in white and gold. Booth memorabilia and theatrical portraits were placed about the hall and other rooms. On this main floor, reading and writing rooms overlooked the park, while to the rear of the house, facing a small garden, White placed the grill room, "suggestive of an ancient English tavern," decorated with shelves lined with pewter and glass, old blue Delft platters, and Toby jugs, and chimney pieces ornamented by a boar's head and by antlers. The floor above included the library, with a splendid collection of books and other materials on drama and the theater, as well as playbills, manuscripts, and other items associated with Booth. Upstairs were the founder's private rooms and other bedrooms. White undertook further alterations on the clubhouse in 1889, 1904, and 1906, including a considerably expanded dining room. The house was enlarged so as to occupy the former backyard area.[5]

From its inception, The Players was an extension of home for Stan. After his move in 1892 to the north side of Gramercy Park it was especially convenient for him. Appropriately, he served on the House Committee, and Bessie was occasionally there, coming to the annual receptions and Ladies' Days. Stan proposed several friends for the club, among them Francis Lathrop and Caryl Coleman, the artists; Charles T. Barney, a banker; Prescott Hall Butler, his lawyer brother-in-law; Robert U. Johnson, an editor of *Century* magazine; and Reginald de Koven, the composer. As a sponsor for Nicola Tesla White wrote that the inventor was "one of the great geniuses and most remarkable men who have ever had anything to do with electricity. . . . It is as much of an honor to propose him for membership as his membership would be an addition to the club." When one acquaintance whom he did not wish to see in the club asked for his support as a seconder, Stan begged off with the excuse that he had already served so many in that capacity that his name no longer carried much weight. White relished the sociability there. The Players was not a place where members buried themselves in newspapers or refused to socialize with anyone except old friends. As one member wrote, "The Players, to those whose appetites had not been spoiled and who wanted to be amused and entertained above all, was the best club in New York."[6]

Stan went regularly on New Year's Eve, Founder's Night, when the members came together to honor Booth. On December 31, 1892, the *New York Times* reported: "It was a remarkable collection of men that stood in groups in the various rooms, about the great hall, and on the winding stairs." Grover Cleveland, President-elect of the United States, addressed the group and greeted Booth at the opening of the new year. The actors Joseph Jefferson and John Drew were there, as were the artists Eastman Johnson, Louis Tiffany, Charles Dana Gibson, and Frederic Remington; the writers Richard Watson Gilder, Thomas Bailey Aldrich, and Edmund Clarence Stedman; J. P. Morgan, the banker; and Stan and Gus. "Here were the leaders in the drama and its kindred arts, literature, painting, and sculpture, gathered to show their love and respect for the man in whose mind was born the project that has linked them all together and whose hand it was that gave the place where they are so joined."[7]

Among his several clubs, Stan came to frequent The Players most, sometimes going there for dinner and customarily stopping by late in the evening. On Saturday nights, he wrote a friend in 1891, "I am as a rule there from an hour before midnight to early morning." Saint-Gaudens, Thomas Dewing, and a few others joined White so often late Saturday evening at The Players, where they refreshed themselves with rarebit, oysters, and champagne, that they called themselves the "Saturday Night Club." Especially during the months that Bessie was living on Long Island, Stan regularly arranged to meet friends in the early evening for drinks at The Players before going on to the Union Club, Delmonico's, or Martin's restaurant for dinner, followed by what Stan called "bumming round town." The latter part of the evening might include visits "with the boys" to a music hall or a variety show performance, stopping by a boxing match, sometimes attending a musical concert, moving on to the Opera House, and then returning to The Players, always with considerable drinking. By the 1890s the late evening might involve a prearranged meeting with a young actress or dancer and a midnight supper at the Morgue or another hideaway. The tremendous energy that White gave to his creative life burst forth as well in his social activities: His appetites for play and for work were enormous.[8]

White included a sitting room and bedroom for Booth on the top floor, overlooking the park. When the actor died in June 1893, Stan joined a group of more than a hundred Players to walk from the clubhouse to the Little Church Around the Corner, the actors' church, on Twenty-ninth Street for the funeral service. The architect subsequently designed a stone monument in the form of an Athenian monolith for Booth's grave in Mt. Auburn Cemetery, Cambridge, Massachusetts. Booth's rooms at The Players were kept exactly as he had left them.[9]

When a commission came in 1885 to McKim, Mead & White for a New York clubhouse for the Freundschaft Society, an association for well-to-do families of German origin, Stan was attracted to the idea and undertook the project. A stately, three-story Italian Renaissance structure facing on Seventy-second Street at Park Avenue, the building was set upon a basement and first-story foundation of alternate bands of Scottish sandstone and reddish speckled brick and boasted very high windows on the upper stories, giving an indication of the handsomely styled, spacious rooms within. The first floor included a reception room, a reading room, committee rooms, and a ladies' reception room and restaurant. Dining rooms largely occupied the second floor, while on the third floor was "the special glory of the building": a large ballroom decorated in a Louis XV style, the sumptuous décor characteristic of

Stan's work. A wine cellar and German drinking room were placed in the basement. When the Freundschaft clubhouse was inaugurated on January 3, 1889, just after The Players was opened, the *Commercial Advertiser* praised the use of the Italian Renaissance mode here, congratulating the city "on possessing an ornament to its street architecture of a style which is too rare among us and yet admirably adapted to the conditions of this city." The firm's use of the Renaissance style, here as elsewhere, brought dignity, monumentality, and ordered formality to the often chaotic city streets, along with associations of noble patronage that flattered the modern-day clients. The Freundschaft Clubhouse, it was pointed out, had within an air of "comfort, roominess, and elegance" with "the stamp of German nationality" throughout. White had a glorious time at the opening of the German club, socializing, drinking heavily (as was increasingly his way), and staying up until five o'clock in the morning, overindulging even more than usual, so that he "was consequently a wreck" the day after.[10]

Considerably larger than The Players and more elegant and carefully composed than the Freundschaft Society was the new clubhouse for the Century Association at 7 West Forty-third Street, opened in January 1891. Stan, whose father had been blackballed by the Century Association, had been elected to the prestigious club in 1886, four years after McKim had joined. Like his membership in The Players, he found much that was congenial to him in this association devoted to "authors, artists, and amateurs of letters and the fine arts." The Century Association had been founded in 1847 by a group within the Sketch Club, which had originated in 1829. The name was derived from the number of one hundred men engaged or interested in the fine arts who were originally invited to join in forming the new group. By 1890 the limit of membership had been raised to eight hundred. Since 1857, the Century had occupied intimate, cozy quarters at 109 East Fifteenth Street, the fifth home from the time of its founding, a clubhouse "hallowed by so many associations" of famous foreign visitors, such as Thackeray, Dickens, and Matthew Arnold, as well as of prominent American artists and writers. Many members were reluctant to leave the pleasant old home, but the limited space, expanding membership, and increasingly out-of-the-way location led to the decision to erect a new clubhouse. The Century building committee on May 10, 1889, invited McKim, Mead & White to submit plans and specifications for a clubhouse on Forty-third Street, not to exceed $150,000 in cost.[11]

White immediately got to work determining on the building dimensions, planning the interior, and sketching out ideas for the street façade of the new Century clubhouse. The lot had a frontage of 100 feet, and the main body of the building, he decided, should go back some 55 feet, with an extension to the rear housing a large gallery for pictures and below it a billiard room. But White's work on the design soon had to cease when he left with his family for Europe on July 6, 1889. During his absence the Century design was turned over to Joseph Wells. Preliminary work on the site moved rapidly ahead, and by late September the foundations were "well along." McKim was "proud" of White's design and felt, as he wrote Stan in Europe, "that Wells' interpretation of it is a most happy effect, without in any way having disturbed the scheme." Work on the building, McKim reported, "has boomed. . . . Everyone is delighted, and the building promises to be our high water mark."[12]

A high water mark it certainly was, but construction of the Century clubhouse ran into many difficulties. After his return from Europe, White, as usual, immersed himself in the countless details of construction and furnishings. Norcross Brothers, the general contractors, however, complained early on that they were in the dark about many details of the building, mainly, it seems, because of Wells's carelessness. Wells, they charged, could not decide on cutting washes in stones at the front entrance, and the stones were delivered without having been cut. Someone "who knows how to exercise a little common sense in the matter," it was suggested, had to be in charge at the site. Norcross had to have precise, completed plans in order to proceed; otherwise, "we do not propose to waste any more time fooling with this Century Club." Later on Francis Lathrop, who was doing glasswork above the picture gallery, complained that workmen were trampling over the edges of the uncompleted skylights. Costs shot up more than one-third beyond the original projection, something not unusual in White's projects, but nonetheless a touchy matter that particularly concerned J. Hampden Robb, the Century Association treasurer and at the same time White's client for a large private house on Park Avenue. Many members complained about "the slow progress of the work."[13]

Yet what was rising on the drab mid-Manhattan block was remarkable. Stately and dignified, the four-story Italian Renaissance palazzo-style façade of stone, terra cotta, and thin Roman brick provides a note of lavish elegance to the streetscape. A high two-story, rusticated-masonry base, with deep embrasures for the monumental doorway and windows, supports an upper section centering on a loggia porch, with a high-arched central opening flanked by lower rectangular openings in a Palladian style. The four large rectangular windows of the principal story, set between elaborated pilasters, are decoratively joined to handsomely wreathed bull's-eye windows above. An elaborated cornice and balustrade crown the building. Less austere and more free and open than the Villard houses, the Century façade has a lively character, with its highly individual selection of rich classical architectural details, the many elements harmoniously integrated. Russell Sturgis, who rather critically reviewed the work of McKim, Mead & White in 1895, was highly complimentary about the Century front, commenting on its "graceful proportions" and judging finally that "the massing of the whole, solids and openings, lights and darks, horizontals and verticals, seems as good as it could be."[14]

The new Century Association clubhouse was ready for occupancy in January 1891. Far more spacious and much less intimate than the former quarters, it was "cold in its first effects," one member thought. The ground level included an entrance hall, offices, a cloakroom, a reception room, and a committee room. At the mezzanine level to the rear was the large art gallery, a central feature of the clubhouse. Reading, writing, and smoking rooms were on the second-floor level, while the third floor included the library, the grill room, a private dining room, and a committee room. The kitchen and servants' rooms were placed on the uppermost level. It was originally planned that the roof might be used as a summer outdoor garden.[15]

Since the mid-nineteenth century, the Century Association had been a center of cultural life in New York City, and election to it was, many felt, a badge of recognition of cultural achievement. According to Henry Holt, the publisher, after the Civil War "there was in the city hardly a man of eminence in literature, art, or science, who did not belong to the Century." The fun there, he related, was "simply colossal," and it remained for him in his old age "the most enjoyable club still." Mark Twain, who did not become a member, found the Century swell-headed and stuffy, "the most unspeakably respectable club in the United States, perhaps." The Twelfth Night revels had become a cherished tradition of the club, and for some years Stanford joined in the festivities; he prepared the decorations for January 6, 1895, assisted by John La Farge and Thomas Hastings. White sponsored and supported a great many friends for Century membership, including Cornelius Vanderbilt II, though he expressed some doubt that Vanderbilt, just because he was a Vanderbilt, would be elected "to a Club composed of such hermit crabs as the Century." After 1900 Stan's interest in the Century Association fell off, and he seldom went there. Following an encounter one day with "fifteen members sound asleep out of seventeen who were in the club, I have given it a wide berth," he reported.[16]

Far grander than The Players or the Century clubhouses was the home for the Metropolitan Club, located on the northeast corner of Fifth Avenue at Sixtieth Street. Known popularly as "the Millionaires' Club," it prided itself on a membership that included the richest and most powerful men of the day. The restrained elegance of the Italian Renaissance structure, at a prominent location overlooking the plaza just off the southeast corner of Central Park, no doubt helped to impress the Metropolitan Club, along with McKim's sumptuous University Club (1899), six blocks south on Fifth Avenue, upon the minds of the nonmember public as the prototypical examples of elite New York clubs. The costly materials used in the Metropolitan and the luxuriousness of its rooms led the *New York Evening Sun* to characterize it as "the most palatial club house in New York."[17]

The Metropolitan Club had its origins in a growing dissatisfaction among certain members of the old, socially conservative Union Club respecting the policies of the board of directors, who frequently blackballed proposed members. When J. P. Morgan, the powerful banker, proposed a business associate for the Union Club and learned that his friend had been turned down, he reputedly became very angry, especially when the information was leaked to the press. William K. Vanderbilt had a similar experience in having his brother-in-law turned down. Those two and several others resolved to establish a new club, larger and more comfortable than the Union, where they could enjoy one another's company and bring in their friends. Much of the planning for the new club was undertaken by William Watts Sherman, the owner of the Newport cottage on which White had worked years earlier when he was in Richardson's office. On February 20, 1891, Sherman gave a dinner at the Knickerbocker Club for the purpose of organizing the new association, which a short time later was named the Metropolitan Club. Morgan was chosen as president, and Sherman as secretary. Morgan summoned White and reportedly said, "Build a club fit for gentlemen. Damn the expense!" In a short time about seven hundred members were enrolled, and they pledged nearly $2 million to build and furnish a clubhouse. White and McKim were invited to become dues-paying charter members. On May 9, 1891, after the site was acquired, Stan was commissioned by the board to design the clubhouse.[18]

Stanford's friend and client Robert Goelet headed the building committee and worked closely with him and with the contractor, David H. King, Jr., who constructed many McKim, Mead & White buildings. Henry A. C. Taylor, the Whites' landlord for the Twenty-first Street house from May 1892, as chairman of the executive committee, was also continuously involved with the clubhouse construction. Several members made suggestions for the structure, including William K. Vanderbilt, who offered his ideas on a suitable design. At that time, when so many other projects were going on in the office, White became deeply immersed not only in the original design but also with the countless details of the interior decoration and furnishing of the building. William Kendall, then White's principal assistant, helped with planning the exterior and executed many of the detail drawings.[19]

As with most of the firm's work, once the Metropolitan Club project got under way pressures were intense to move ahead as rapidly as possible. Complications arose, however, because of the rush and delays on decisions of details in the interior; indeed, the foundations were laid and the exterior partly completed before the interior arrangements had been finally decided upon and the drawings made. And that, one associate in the office felt, was not good architectural practice. Elbridge T. Gerry, whose mansion directly north of the Metropolitan Club was being built at the same time, was frequently upset over the larger construction project next to his house. Through his architect, Richard Morris Hunt, Gerry expressed his annoyance with a gatepost set up on the boundary of his property and with the unloading of construction materials for the Metropolitan in front of his house. Hunt and White always got along well and attempted to coordinate their endeavors on the Sixtieth–Sixty-first-Street sites.[20]

By January 1894, as the interior work was being completed, Stan felt himself "nearly driven to death on the Metropolitan Club," trying to get everything finished for the opening. In February he reported that he had "practically lived the whole of the last two weeks" there so that it could be turned over. Henry Taylor proposed that a press day be held just before the opening reception but "avoiding *absolutely* all mention of cost," an especially sensitive issue as the general depression following the panic of 1893 deepened and conditions were increasingly desperate for many in the city—something that Stan, immersed in luxury, seemed generally to ignore. A final push the evening before the building was scheduled to be turned over to the club involved bringing in nonunion workers after hours to install the fireplace mantels, which the union men had refused to handle because the stonework had not been polished in New York State. A regular army of workers carted the mantels from the Hudson River docks and carefully brought them inside the clubhouse to be set in place, while women with mops and other cleaning equipment stood by to clean up anything dropped on the polished floors or spattered on the walls. All the work was successfully finished, the building was delivered the following morning to the building committee, and Stan reportedly collected on a bet that everything would be completed on time.[21]

On February 27, 1894, when the Metropolitan Club was opened,

White stood at the entrance with J. P. Morgan to receive members and their guests. White smiled radiantly: "That he was proud of the clubhouse which was designed by him was evident." The members as well, no doubt, were proud of their quarters. Styled as a four-story palazzo of the Italian Renaissance, the club was faced with Tuckahoe and Vermont marble and was particularly distinguished by a striking marble and copper cornice projecting some 6 feet outward. The building extended some 90 feet on Fifth Avenue and some 142 feet on Sixtieth Street. At the east end a courtyard, entered through a colonnaded gateway, provided carriage access to the principal entrance. Behind the courtyard stood an extension of the main building, two stories high, the upper part containing the library and the ground level dining facilities for ladies and visitors.[22]

From outside and inside vaulted vestibules, members and their guests ascended a few steps to the sumptuous great central hall, "the main feature of the club," measuring some 52 by 55 feet and with a 45-foot ceiling, the walls lined with marble, and columned at the second-story gallery level. A huge double staircase rose on the north side of the hall; above it were five stained glass windows designed by David Maitland Armstrong. The ceiling was deeply coffered and painted in gold. West of the great hall was the main lounge, overlooking Fifth Avenue, decorated in a Louis XIII style, richly paneled in oak and staff. On the second floor the billiard and card rooms, reading rooms, and the Venetian-style library were placed around the upper part of the great hall. Stan's friend, the painter Edward Simmons, decorated the library ceiling. The main dining room overlooked Fifth Avenue on the third floor, where private dining rooms and a smoking room were also installed. The fourth floor contained apartments for members, with the kitchen and servants' rooms on the level above. Like the Century, the Metropolitan Club was originally planned to have a roof garden, but that plan was not implemented. Storerooms, wine cellars, committee rooms, a bowling alley, and service rooms made up the basement. An annex was constructed from a converted townhouse to the east of the courtyard in 1912. As with his other clubs, Stan brought several friends and acquaintances into the Metropolitan, doing favors for others while ensuring that at least a segment of the membership would be especially compatible to him.[23]

Two other projects involved White in clubs personally important to him. Like The Players, The Lambs was primarily an association of men involved with or interested in the theater. The theatrical world took on increasing importance for Stan after the inauguration of the Madison Square Garden arena in 1890, and he was a member of The Lambs. In 1896 he was asked to make alterations in an existing building

at 70 West Thirty-sixth Street for a new Lambs clubhouse. H. Van
Buren Magonigle, who had recently returned to the McKim, Mead &
White office after study in Rome and Paris and a long stay in Athens,
assisted with the drawings. Magonigle later recalled that he had dallied
so long over the work, trying to make it perfect, that Stanford finally
screamed at him in exasperation: "For godssake, Magonigle, push this
along! This isn't the Parthenon, it's only made of tin!" referring to a
bay window frame. Stan contributed his own services for the design,
for which he requested only repayment of out-of-pocket expenses for
the alterations work. In gratitude for all he had done, the directors of
The Lambs elected Stan and his partners life members of the club.
One summer White sent back from Canada a portion of his salmon
catch for a club feast. He served as a member of the Art and the Building
committees, and when another home was needed for The Lambs he
was selected to create it.[24]

The new Lambs clubhouse, in the heart of what had become New
York's theater district, at 128–130 West Forty-fourth Street, was completed in time for the Christmas Gambol of 1904. A narrow, six-story
building in a Georgian Revival mode, the clubhouse included a reception
room, a grill room, a bar and billiard room, and club offices on the
ground level; a lounging room, reading room, and dining room on the
second floor; a library and a private theater–assembly room on the third
floor; and bedrooms for members on the three upper floors. The somberly
restrained façade, marble-covered at the basement level and at the second
level, featured pressed bricks with glazed headers and terra cotta trim
on the upper part. High glass windows set behind a screen of columns
were placed to lighten the lower part of the building and yet signify
the importance of the main-floor rooms. Ram's-head decorations provided
a playful note on the third- and fourth-story exterior. The overall elegance
of the building was emphasized by the ornamental festoons at the central
fourth-story window and the balustrade above the fifth level, screening
the attic story from the street.[25]

The Brook, another of White's principal clubs, had its origins with a
group of Century Association members, who late one evening in the
winter of 1902, while exchanging stories in the Century's reading room,
were interrupted at midnight when the lights were dimmed, the servants'
way of making it known that the clubhouse was closing. Stan chanced
to be there that evening, and he and others agreed that the solution to
the problem of early closing might be a new club with continuous service,
night and day. Other men were approached, and an organizational meeting
was held. Subsequently, at a meeting in the parlors of the Hotel Martin,

officers were chosen and a name selected. Since the purpose was continuous service, someone suggested The Brook as a name ("Men may come and men may go / But I go on forever.") Quarters were leased at 6 East Thirty-fifth Street, and Stan was invited to provide suitable alterations there. The clubhouse was ready for the members by the end of August 1904.[26]

Within a short time, however, B. Altman, the retailer, sought to buy up the house for his enlarged department store, and the club agreed to turn over the lease to him for $35,000. Property was purchased at 7 East Fortieth Street and adjoining at 10 and 12 East Forty-first Street. Once again, White was charged with alterations for a new clubhouse, which was opened to members on May 1, 1905. The four-story brownstone, set on a high basement, was rebuilt with a sober, classical façade, on which the principal floor was emphasized by large areas of glass divided by free-standing Ionic columns supporting an entablature and balustrade. Rare books, fine furniture, and oil paintings of early American scenes were purchased for the new clubhouse.

Stanford was named a governor of The Brook and there could enjoy the company of men compatible to him well into the wee hours whenever he wished. Stan eventually persuaded Saint-Gaudens, less of a clubman than he, to join The Brook, using the argument that the sculptor was needed not for his money but "as a nest egg and an attraction for a dozen men whom we want in." Stan's description of The Brook for Gus's benefit encapsulated his views of the principal clubs then in existence: "not all society men, like the Knickerbocker, or men of the world, like the Union and Metropolitan, or a degenerate lunch club, like The Players, or one where mainly bum actors congregate, like The Lambs, or a Sleepy Hollow, like the Century," but rather "a very quiet small club . . . where you will always be sure, from lunch time to two or three in the morning to find three or four men you will always be glad to see, and no one that you will not be glad to see." Gus contributed models of two of his works in lieu of an initiation fee.[27]

Two other clubhouses, the Harmonie and the Colony, complete the roster of White's la'er club designs. Directly opposite the Metropolitan Club on East Sixtieth Street, the Harmonie Club, squeezed between large buildings on both sides, is rather outclassed by its more showy neighbor across the street, yet the clubhouse holds its own on the crowded side street. It was designed and built from 1904 to 1907. With a very spare lower half centering on a two-story porch and a much more ornate upper part encompassing a wealth of classical detail, the façade lacks integrity: The two parts do not relate well to each other, while the four pairs of elaborated pilasters on the upper part seem overdone and without purpose. Nevertheless, like interiors in the other clubhouses by White and McKim, the Harmonie rooms were well adapted to the needs of the members, with a warm and comfortable character.[28]

The Colony was the first clubhouse built for a women's organization in New York City. In the summer of 1902 several prominent New York women, led by Mrs. J. Borden Harriman, decided that like the men of the city, women also had need of a place to go for company and recreation. The club they were planning would aim "to unite in one organization leading women in the business, the social, the artistic, the literary, the theatrical worlds and to give them a club home where they can enjoy social pleasures and athletic privileges." An organizational committee was formed by the end of 1903, led by Mrs. Harriman. Actively assisting were some of her friends, including especially Anne Morgan, whose father, J. P. Morgan, served on the men's advisory committee; Mrs. Thomas Hastings, wife of the architect; and Helen Barney, whose father, the banker Charles T. Barney, chaired the building committee.[29]

A lot was acquired on the west side of Madison Avenue north of Thirtieth Street, and there, closely supervised by Charles Barney, the six-story Federal Revival clubhouse was erected and made ready for occupancy by the middle of March 1907. When White began working on the design in 1905, he had the building committee "look and study with him the old examples of colonial architecture from which he was drawing his inspiration." He chose as a source the façade from the Nathaniel Russell house in Charleston, South Carolina, and selected for the walls a pinkish gray brick that was laid with only the headers exposed. White limestone was used for the window trim, the cornice, and the stones at the corners. A long porch extended the width of the ground level. The wrought-iron railing of the balcony above the porch, echoed by a small upper balcony and by the lacy trellis of the roof garden above the steeply pitched attic roof, helped bind the elements of the building together. The large second- and third-story space was expressed on the exterior by five arched window openings with French doors giving onto the balcony.[30]

Inside, on the first floor, a reception hall and library, a large tea room with trellised decorations, and a card room served the members. Above, a large two-story assembly room, used for concerts, lectures, meetings, and dances, faced the street, while a two-story gymnasium, with a running track and squash and basketball courts, was located on the back of the building. The basement contained a swimming pool and baths, while the kitchen and dining rooms were located on the upper floors at the top of the clubhouse. Elsie de Wolfe, who had been on the stage and privately had tried her hand at decorating, on White's recommendation, had responsibility for the interior décor, the most striking of her work being the trellised tea room and the swimming pool, lighted from above with a ceiling covered by a trellis and imparting a grape-arbor effect. Male guests had to come into the clubhouse by a separate entrance and were taken by a "strangers' elevator" to the "strangers' dining room," where they could be entertained by members at lunch and dinner. The combination of sobriety and delicacy at the Colony clubhouse—rather different from most of White's more ornate and grander men's clubhouses—was often commented upon.[31]

Always gregarious and very much the joiner (in this regard, very unlike his father and his brother), Stanford eventually would come to the realization that the social and the financial demands on him from his many clubs and associations were too burdensome to be kept up. In club life, as in other ways, Stanford had been too extravagant, had extended himself too far. By the close of the century, he began to feel that he had "tried to do too much" and endeavored "to drop out of things as much as possible" by refusing offices and committee assignments in several clubs and by resigning from others in which he had not taken an active role. A primary creator of New York club life, in only a few years he became something of a victim of its many demands.[32]

Even more important for White's public image than the gentlemen's clubs he designed, however, was the great pleasure palace just off Madison Square he created for New Yorkers in general. Madison Square Garden would be a central institution of his life, and he would be tied to it in many ways. There, ultimately, the several lives of Stanford White would be brought together.

At the time of Stanford White's birth on November 9, 1853, his father, Richard Grant White (1822–85), was already a well-known journalist-critic in New York City. His mother, Alexina Mease White (1830–1921), wrote poetry, including verses about young Stanny.

Stanny entered the New York architectural office of Henry Hobson Richardson—one of the most talented architects of the time—in 1870, when he was only sixteen. In 1874, Richardson moved his studio-office from New York to Brookline, Massachusetts. White frequently worked there *(below, last row, second from right)*, guided by Richardson and accepted into the senior architect's extended family.

After a long European trip in 1878-79, Stanny returned to New York to form, at the age of twenty-five, a partnership with Charles F. McKim and William Rutherford Mead as the architectural firm of McKim, Mead & White. From its office and drafting rooms on the top floor of 57 Broadway, near the Battery, a huge number of projects poured forth.

Recreational casinos were important in the early work of McKim, Mead & White. Stanford collaborated with McKim on the Newport (R.I.) Casino *(above)*, including intricate trellis screens in the front courtyard. White was also involved with the striking design for the Narragansett Pier Casino *(below)*, its rugged towers and arches and intricate roofline echoing the rocky ocean shore near the Rhode Island resort community.

Many of Stanford's early designs were for private homes. Naumkeag *(above)*, the country house of Joseph Choate, a prominent lawyer and diplomat, near Stockbridge, Massachusetts, was one of White's most successful early houses. The Tiffany house *(below)*, created for White's friend Louis Comfort Tiffany and his family, stood on Madison Avenue at Seventy-second Street in New York and was one of the most admired urban residences of the late nineteenth century.

Stanny first became acquainted with the sculptor Augustus Saint-Gaudens in New York in 1875. On his 1878–79 visit to Europe, White made the Saint-Gaudenses' apartment in Paris his headquarters. The two artists collaborated on many projects, starting with the important monument to Admiral David G. Farragut, erected in 1881 in New York's Madison Square Park.

White was also noted as one of the most talented and sought-after decorators of his day. The Watts Sherman house library *(above)* in Newport shows White's skill in designing ornamented wood surfaces. The Kingscote dining room *(below)*, also in Newport, illustrates his talent in bringing together rich textures, varied colors, and an unusual juxtaposition of decorative elements.

In February 1884, after an extended courtship, White married Bessie Springs Smith of Smithtown, Long Island. For a time before his marriage, White sported a luxuriant beard as well as a mustache. Bessie was photographed arranging her wedding dress just before the ceremony.

Stanford White was called upon to provide decorations for various public celebrations in New York City. The April 1889 centennial of George Washington's first inauguration as president was the occasion for White's arch *(above)*, spanning lower Fifth Avenue. An enthusiastic public response led to the erection of a permanent Washington Memorial Arch *(below)* in Washington Square, designed by White and dedicated in 1895. Through the arch opening White's Judson Church and Tower are visible.

Madison Square Garden, a large entertainment center, was one of White's most important contributions to New York's social life. In the large arena, concerts, balls, exhibitions, horse shows, and such elaborate amusements as a re-creation of Venice and its waterways took place. Showman and impresario, White often had a hand in producing the entertainments offered at the Garden.

The most striking architectural feature of Madison Square Garden was the Tower—in which White kept a private apartment—topped by a statue of Diana created by Augustus Saint-Gaudens. When the first version of Diana proved too large, it was replaced by a smaller and more graceful figure. In the elaborate exterior ornamentation of the Garden, White attempted to express something of the joyous and playful character he hoped the building would convey.

White was both a member and designer of several gentlemen's clubhouses. Facing Gramercy Park, The Players, primarily for actors and others interested in the theater, was White's favorite club *(above)*. White was also largely responsible for the design of the Century Association clubhouse *(below),* on West Forty-third Street, an elite club for artists and amateurs in the arts.

White's reputation for creating elegant clubhouses led to an invitation to design the opulent Metropolitan Club *(above)*, on Fifth Avenue at Sixtieth Street, which he created in an Italianate design. Often called "the Millionaires' Club," it boasted some of the most luxurious rooms in New York. White also designed the Colony Club *(below)*, on Madison Avenue, the first New York club for women.

In the 1890s, White created several important commercial structures in New York City. The Herald Building *(above)*, located just north of the busy intersection of Broadway and Sixth Avenue at Thirty-fourth Street, housed the editorial offices and printing plant of the *New York Herald,* published by James Gordon Bennett. The Bowery Savings Bank *(below),* on the Bowery at Grand Street, was one of White's most stately buildings in neoclassical style, and its main banking room remains one of the most impressive interior spaces in New York.

White's delight in creating recreational structures was manifest in his design for Sherry's Hotel on Fifth Avenue and Forty-fourth Street, which housed one of the most fashionable restaurants in the city. Its ballroom was the scene of many elaborate Gilded Age parties, at which White himself often was present.

White created a trellised arch at Twenty-second Street and Fifth Avenue and designed the street decorations northward along the avenue, for the four-hundredth anniversary of Columbus's discovery of America. He delighted in the great entertainments of the day; surrounded by friends, often on the dance floor, he was a ubiquitous presence in upper-class New York social life.

11

"A Permanent Ornament to the City"

The several gentlemen's clubhouses that McKim, Mead & White built, along with their casinos, hotels, and restaurants, were in part a response to the needs and demands of the vast new wealth arising from late-nineteenth-century American industrial, commercial, and financial development. As New York City mushroomed in population and wealth toward the end of the century, new recreational and entertainment facilities for the public at large were also needed. The idea of erecting a large entertainment center or pleasure garden serving varied needs for New Yorkers greatly appealed to White, who loved "good times" and whose taste for the fanciful and extravagant might be indulged in its creation.

By mid-June of 1887, Stan was already "working day and night for a building for the Madison Square Garden site," a design he had started on a year or so earlier. The commission for the large, complex structure was awarded to McKim, Mead & White in 1887, but construction did not begin until late in the summer of 1889. What eventually was erected was the firm's most important public structure in New York in those end-of-century years, the building that, in one critic's words, "most conspicuously increases the beauty" of the city and, of all his works, the one that most fully reflected its designer, Stanford White.[1]

The site chosen for the Garden was adjacent to the northeast corner of Madison Square, which by the latter years of the century, as the population center moved northward, had become the social and entertainment center of New York. Many years earlier, in 1836, Madison Square had been designated as a park by the City Council. In the 1840s a group of men who called themselves the Knickerbocker Base Ball Club regularly got together there for ball games, and in 1845 the club devised formal rules for baseball. In 1853 the fashionable Madison Square Presbyterian Church was built on the east side of the park. The seven-story Fifth Avenue Hotel, opened to the public in 1859, faced the square from the west and was the first of several fashionable hostelries in the area. Subsequently the St. James, the Hoffman House, the Brunswick, and the Albemarle hotels were built close to the square. Several well-to-do families occupied luxurious houses on the north and east sides of the square. Leonard Jerome's mansion at the northeast corner was converted into a clubhouse by the Union League after the Civil War and later housed the Turf, the Madison, and the University clubs. To the south on Twenty-third Street were the exhibit halls of the American Art Association. The Saint-Gaudens–White Farragut statue, erected close to the northwest corner of the square, was thus at the center of a fashionable and lively neighborhood.[2]

Northeast of the square, on the block bounded by Madison and Fourth avenues from Twenty-sixth Street to Twenty-seventh Street, the New York, New Haven & Harlem Railroad had erected a freight depot in 1837 and an adjoining passenger station to the north in 1857. Horse teams pulled trains from that station northward to railyards at Thirty-second Street and later north of Forty-second Street, where steam locomotives were attached for the runs to Albany and to Boston. After Grand Central Station, with terminal rail facilities, was erected north of Forty-second Street in 1871, P. T. Barnum, the showman, leased the abandoned buildings near Madison Square from the railroad and rebuilt the old station and train shed into a large arena, partly open to the sky. It was inaugurated as the Great Roman Hippodrome in 1874. The following year, Patrick Gilmore, a bandmaster, acquired the lease and renamed the arena Gilmore's Garden. It was used for band concerts and also subleased for dog shows, horticultural exhibits, religious revival and temperance meetings, yearly visits of the circus, and boxing matches. After Gilmore's lease expired in 1878, the New York Central Railroad took over the arena and called it Madison Square Garden. A variety of events continued to be held there, the most important being the annual National Horse Show. But the old building was grimy, drafty, and impossibly cold in the winter, and it was rumored to be a firetrap as well.

When the Vanderbilt interests controlling the New York Central announced their decision to tear down the Garden, a syndicate set up by officers of the National Horse Show Association purchased the property for $400,000. A newly organized Madison Square Garden Corporation floated a stock issue to finance the construction of a large, comfortable arena and other facilities to be used for horse shows and other events. William F. Wharton, who served as manager, acquired the largest number of shares. J. P. Morgan bought a large block of shares and was chosen to be president of the corporation. White was acquainted with other board members, whom he made aware of his interest in the project; he was elected to the board of directors and later served as vice president. Stan's portion of his firm's profit distribution was $47,000 for the year ending June 30, 1890, an all-time high to that point, so he had money to spare. He eventually built up his Garden investment to 1,100 shares, some of them purchased with his wife's money. The firm of McKim, Mead & White acquired 350 shares.[3]

More than anyone else White was responsible for the new Madison Square Garden. Like many others, he felt there was a need for large-scale recreational and entertainment facilities for the city. His involvement in the Madison Square Garden Corporation and his enthusiasm for the project made it almost a foregone conclusion that he would be selected to design the new center. His gift for ornamentation, his sense of the theatrical, and his love of amusement made White a good choice; within the firm, he took over direction of the project from the beginning. The Garden project occupied him professionally for a good part of the two years before construction actually started and continued to take much of his time for years afterward.

White's planning on the Garden was interrupted by his three-month holiday in Europe with Bessie, Larry, and his mother in the late summer of 1889. To his dismay, shortly after he left New York, construction suddenly began to move ahead, which he had not anticipated. He felt that "after hollering after the hounds" for so long it was rather hard not to be there when the project was finally getting off the ground, and he wrote Mead, who took charge in his absence, that his "heart was pretty well in the job" and he was ready to come back if necessary. He urged Mead to put "Wellzey" (Joseph M. Wells) to work on "a treatment of the lower part of the Tower" and sent along a sketch of what he wanted done. David King, the contractor, had agreed to build the Garden in accordance with the firm's early drawings for a little over a million dollars and promised to have the amphitheater ready by the following March. Mead from New York assured Stan that he would direct the work "the best I know how" but admitted that he lacked detailed information about what had already gone on. In one letter from Europe, White urged Mead to include a sunken tank in the middle of the arena "which water could be used for aquatic shows especially ones in which girls wear skin tights." He also wanted an open promenade around the upper level of the amphitheater for strolling and visiting during intermissions. He suggested lining the inside of the arena with yellow brick.[4]

Just as he and his family were about to move out of Paris for Switzerland, Stan sent "Dummy" Mead, for his guidance, a detailed half cross-section of the Garden building with comments and suggestions. Costs, he suggested, might be lowered by cutting down on the exterior terra cotta ornamentation, though he was reluctant to make the changes. It was essential, he believed, to have the Madison Avenue entrance side of the building "fairly rich in detail and to keep the character of the building running all around." He urged Mead to put in a wider skylight in order to get all the light he could for the arena. Once more, he asked Mead to "be sure & have Wells make the Tower." He speculated grandly that he might have terra cotta copies made of the bronze horses from St. Marks in Venice for the Garden, which he did not carry through. In a return letter, Mead reassured Stan about practical details and indicated that the firm had "a bully force of men for you when you return." Teunis Van der Bent from the office was supervising the project ("he is a treasure"), and other draftsmen were already involved with working drawings, elevations, and terra cotta designs. Mead wrote that he would be only too happy to have White, on his return, deal with David King, the contractor, who was "a rusher."[5]

In the fall, after White's return from Europe, work on the Garden moved ahead rapidly. Wells's design work for the Garden and his work at the same time on the Century Club, as well as the earlier strikingly successful Villard houses, greatly impressed all three partners. McKim remarked that Wells stood "alone in the profession for thoroughness and a scholarly ability" and that the office was increasingly obligated to him for his contributions. In December 1889, therefore, McKim suggested to White that Wells be presented with a share of the firm and made a partner. Wells was, McKim wrote, "wretchedly poor and badly provided for, without a home or any of the good things of this world." To make him a partner "would be only a fair requital of his invaluable services to the office, past and to come, and of the esteem in which we all hold him." But when a share was offered to the draftsman, he declined on the ground that he could not afford to sign his name "to so much damned bad work." No doubt the refusal showed a whimsical perversity in Wells's character, along with his wry humor, but probably even more it betokened a reluctance to tie himself closely to the others and to be forced into positions of general responsibility. As a partner Wells would have lost some of his personal freedom.[6]

Within a very short time, late in January 1890, Wells fell ill with influenza complicated by pleurisy and was confined to his room at the Benedict. His condition rapidly deteriorated. On February 2 he died of pneumonia at the age of thirty-seven. Wells's untimely death was a blow to those who had worked with him. McKim later said that he had learned more from Wells than from any other source. From St. Paul, Minnesota, Cass Gilbert wrote of his sorrow and expressed his sympathy to Stan, who had been "nearer to him in friendship" than anyone else. A proposal was made to establish an architectural collection commemorating Wells at the new Boston Public Library, but nothing came of the suggestion. Two years after Wells's death, Saint-Gaudens began an annual studio concert in the architect's memory, inviting the group that had formerly attended the Sunday studio musicales to listen to the Beethoven quartets that Wells had loved so much. White designed a stone for his friend's grave in the Oak Grove Cemetery in Medford, Massachusetts, but his original design was rejected by the cemetery trustees as "an unsightly affair" and had to be modified. White later extolled Wells as "an architect whose ability was of the highest order . . . and his hand was seen all through our work while he lived"; White suggested, though, that Wells "had the temperament which make artists unfit to cope with the world, and which, therefore, kept them always as assistants rather than principals."[7]

By the spring of 1890 Stan was almost fully absorbed with his work on the Garden: "I am not worth much myself at night," he wrote to Gus, "on account of the Garden, which is enough work for one man without having anything else to do." It took a herculean effort to get the amphitheater ready for the scheduled mid-June opening; moreover, the management asked Stan, who knew the arena and its possibilities better than anyone else, to help plan and arrange for the inaugural performance. Some New York theatrical producers, fearing competition from the new facility, put obstacles in the way of getting everything set for the opening. For a time the city theatrical license was held up. Costumes brought from Europe for the dancers were seized by customs agents with the charge of attempted smuggling, and substantial duties and fines had to be paid to have them released.[8]

Despite the many difficulties, the Garden arena opened on the evening of June 16, 1890, inaugurating what came to be for some time the most important entertainment and recreational center of the city. Some 12,000 persons attended the gala event, including, besides the proud thirty-six-year-old architect, Roosevelts, Vanderbilts, Cuttings, and Van Rensselaers, as well as the Vice President of the United States, Levi P. Morton. The glitter of jewelry was much in evidence. One reporter commented that "swelldom predominated—the lower element being conspicuous by its absence." General William T. Sherman of Civil War fame, his tall figure slightly bent, as "amiable and unaffected as a happy boy," was especially delighted with the Garden. "I can conceive of nothing more perfect," he said. Another opening-night patron, however, feeling that the grand style had gone too far, suggested that "there's too much barn about it."[9]

From the principal entrance on Madison Avenue, the first-nighters moved through a long entrance lobby lined with polished yellow Siena marble, emerging into the huge and colorful amphitheater, said to be the largest such arena in the United States. Gold and white terra cotta tiles, rather than yellow as originally suggested, decorated most interior walls, with some surfaces painted pale red. Two tiers of seats rose along the sides, and three tiers of boxes, trimmed in maroon plush, filled the ends of the vast room. Some 10,000 spectators could be seated comfortably in the amphitheater, and there was standing room or, for some events, floor seating for up to 4,000 more. An upper-level promenade, well utilized for strolling, gazing, and visiting, extended around the circuit of the arena. The high roof was spectacularly supported by twenty-eight large columns, with exposed steel trusses, lined with incandescent lights, reaching about 180 feet from side to side. At the center of the roof, an enormous skylight could, as if by magic, be rolled aside by machinery. That was done during the opening performance, but it occurred so quietly that most spectators were not even aware of the change until they noticed the cool night air. As in ancient arenas, provision was made for flooding the floor for water spectacles. As at the Roman Colosseum, animal stables to be used for the horse shows and circus performances were placed in the basement below. Here was a bit of ancient Rome, transformed, modernized, and brought to Gilded Age New York!

The inaugural performance at the Garden received a mixed reception from audience and critics alike. Congestion in the entryway passage irritated many of those who were trying to enter the Garden at about the same time. Eduard Strauss, Johann's brother, conducted a forty-three-piece Viennese orchestra, which some patrons thought made too small a sound for the huge space. Two ballet sequences were presented by European performers, one entitled *Choosing of the National Flower* and the other *Peace and War*. Although the dances were rather conventional, they aroused the indignation of one newspaper critic, who found in them "much that was inartistic and almost indecent." The showy ushers' uniforms, which White himself, involved even in small details, had designed—orange cutaway, swallowtail coats, orange trousers, cardinal-red waistcoats ornamented by huge silver buttons—struck some critics as gaudy and even ridiculous.[10]

For all the criticisms, the building itself was almost universally praised, and everyone seemed pleased about the way the Garden fulfilled a distinct need. The *New York Daily Graphic*'s assessment was typical: Here is "an amusement palace in which all classes of the public can meet in harmony upon a common ground. In its architectural beauty, its vastness and substantiality, the new Madison Square Garden surpasses every other amusement structure in America. [It is] a structure unrivalled in its way, a permanent ornament to the city, one designed to serve an important purpose in the amusement and instruction of the public." Another newspaper termed the Garden quite simply "a great municipal possession"; it will be "a municipal institution, prized at home and famous all over the world . . . a constant and permanent force to elevate, refine and refresh all who gaze upon it." No other building in the United States designed for a similar purpose could compare with "this masterpiece of Mr. Stanford White."[11]

Mrs. Van Rensselaer, the architectural critic, pronounced the new Garden amphitheater "entirely successful," with decidedly "agreeable proportions," although with its exposed steel columns and trusses, unless decorated for a special occasion, it looked rather "thin and bare" to her, especially in daylight. At night, however, the garlands of electric lights added a necessary softness, while accentuating the architectural elements of the space. The arena was best seen, she wrote, with crowds of people.[12]

White above all wanted his palace of pleasure to look festive. For the exterior he chose a Spanish Renaissance mode, lavishly ornamenting many of the surfaces in a lively, sumptuous design. The entrance façade on Madison Avenue was especially ornate. Covering an entire city block, the structure rose to a height of 60 feet, the exterior walls of buff-colored brick and decorated with white terra cotta. Tall arched windows surmounted by bull's-eye openings identified the large interior spaces. A colonnade stood at the roof edge, and from it rose eight picturesque columned and domed belvederes and, later on, the soaring, elegant Tower, the crowning feature of the Garden.

A year after the arena was opened, an arcade, providing shelter for arriving and departing audiences, was completed along the Madison Avenue front and extending eastward along the side streets for 100 feet. Permission from the city for erecting the arcade had been delayed for some time, possibly because of fears that it might become the haunt of prostitutes and pickpockets; ultimately special enabling state legislation was required before the arcade could be erected. Certain members of the real estate fraternity were said to be worried that the arcade idea might catch on in the city and by cutting off light hurt potential rental rates for stores at street level.[13]

The arena occupied about two-thirds of the building, with other public facilities provided for in the remainder. For the Madison Avenue end, a restaurant was to go in the southwest corner and a theater in the northwest corner on the ground floor. The restaurant was offered to both Delmonico's and Sherry's, but neither would establish a branch there, even though no rent would be charged, because of the need to vary the menu from night to night as the different events drew different classes of people to the Garden. The restaurant space was therefore used intermittently for an exhibition hall. The Madison Square Garden Theater was opened at the end of September 1890 with a production of *Doctor Bill,* a popular farce. Although the theater seated 1,200 on the main floor and in the gallery, it had an intimate atmosphere. Luxurious in design, the interior was colored in white, gold, and light brown, the seats and carpet a deep red. The large stage was richly framed, with an allegorical "Angel of Fame" set in the proscenium arch. A small colonnade was placed on the right side of the room and another above it in the gallery. To Mrs. Van Rensselaer, the Garden theater was "prettier and more truly architectural in its charm than any other in New York [marked by] its unusual air of joyousness combined with refinement."[14]

On the second story, at the Madison Avenue end, a concert or music hall was designed for the area above the restaurant space. The concert hall was completed in the late summer of 1890 and inaugurated in September with a New England Society dinner, presided over by J. P. Morgan. Small galleries with adjacent supper rooms overlooked the hall on two sides. Decorated by White in Louis XVI style in gold and white, the concert hall was widely praised for its harmony of proportions and its sumptuous molded decorations, including figures modeled by the sculptor Philip Martiny. The concert hall was designed to accommodate up to 1,500 or 1,600 people and was to serve, as well, as a ballroom for the fashionable Assembly Balls, which White often attended.

But the Tower most fully defined the image of the pleasure palace for New Yorkers. For a time it was doubtful that the Tower would even be erected. After the contract for the Garden had been let, the directors found expenses mounting so high that they decided not to proceed with the Tower. When White learned of the decision, he was furious and complained personally to each director in turn, adamant that the Tower was essential for the building and necessary for its success. White made such a row that David King, the contractor, finally decided it was imperative to "shut him up somehow." He agreed to put up half of the money for the Tower himself if the directors would raise the rest. Soon, with some $450,000 arranged for, the Tower work proceeded.[15]

White's inspiration for the Garden Tower was the 275-foot Giralda of the cathedral in Seville, Spain, a Moorish tower dating from the mid-twelfth century surmounted by a belfry in a late Renaissance style added in the mid-sixteenth century and topped by a revolving figure of Faith. Unlike the mixture of styles in the Spanish structure, though, the Garden Tower had a unity of design and was well integrated into the main building below, the topmost features echoing the belvedere structures on the roof below. Whereas its prototype crowned a house of worship devoted to spiritual matters, White's Tower, as befitted the times, capped a house of entertainment, a monument to secular concerns.

The Garden Tower rose some 341 feet to the base of its pinnacle statue, moving from a heavier and solider lower section into lighter, more open, and more decorated upper parts. At the foot, the Tower measured 38 feet on each exterior side, but the very thick walls at the base left an inner space of only about 30 feet on a side. An elevator shaft encircled by a narrow staircase rose from the street level to the Roof Garden loggia. Above, seven stories of small apartments (floors two through eight) were arranged in the lower part of the Tower proper, which was topped by an upper loggia level, where a café was planned. From here, a winding staircase rose to a platform guarded by a parapet. Another winding staircase led to a chamber lighted from above, and from here a ladder rose to a small balcony. From the very high balcony, visitors had a splendid view over the city. Usually a guard was posted to watch over the visitors and point out features of the cityscape.

To cap the Tower, following the precedent of the Spanish cathedral, White asked Saint-Gaudens to help him give New Yorkers a real treat by erecting there, largely at their personal expense, a revolving statue. White agreed to pay for making the statue if Gus would sculpt the model for it. Here, soaring above the city, would be a sculptural piece that would impress New Yorkers far more even than the Farragut Monument, which had been unveiled in the Square below ten years earlier. Saint-Gaudens "eagerly grasped the opportunity," since he liked creating ideal figures and realized the public impact such a conspicuous work would make, while Stan was certainly aware that the figure planned would flout conventions, arouse controversy, and cause both men to be talked about. The Diana "was purely a labor of love" for Stan and Gus; they really enjoyed working on it. The goddess of hunting and of the moon that Gus created was an 18-foot-high figure of beaten sheet copper fastened to a wrought-iron pipe frame, the whole weighing about 1,800 pounds. Poised on her left foot set on a large rotating ball socket, with her right leg extended back, the full-breasted goddess rotated like a weathervane and would turn, facing into the wind, with only a quarter-pound of wind pressure. Her left hand held a bow, while her right grasped the shaft of an arrow. Strands of drapery billowed behind the shoulders of the otherwise nude figure. The statue was set upon a crescent moon of plate glass, some 12 feet from tip to tip, which was lighted from within by 66 incandescent lamps.[16]

Early in October 1891, a temporary derrick raised the gilded copper figure with its crescent, swathed in flannel covering, to the summit of the Tower. Stan was delighted to have this crowning touch for the yet unfinished Tower in place and was sure, when all was done, it would look "bully." But, he wrote Gus, he had some doubts: "My heart contracts at times, however, at the thought that it is going to be too big." In appreciation for the care the crew took in the difficult job of putting the statue in place, Stan presented the foreman of the crew with an inscribed gold charm and chain for his watch.[17]

When "her swaddling clothes" were removed, the very naked Diana at once became "one of the famous of New Yorkers, and certainly one of the most popular." All around Madison Square, people paused to gaze up at the "fine and shining creature." Indeed, in front of the Fifth Avenue Hotel pedestrians were cautioned to walk "circumspectively" lest one "collide with someone else while both are gazing at the golden girl." The *New York Mercury* reported that a great many newcomers had suddenly appeared in the square, which formerly was "famous as the daily gathering-place for children":

> In their place the square is now the daily haunt of bald-headed clubmen armed with field glasses and of every variety of local dude, from the Delmonico elegant to the Casino Johnny. Where babyhood once disported itself, brandy and watery elderly gentlemen and young men with pop eyes and slender legs linger in listless idleness. Other young men with pop eyes and slender legs and older men with no business to speak of, who are evidently visitors to the city, appear and after lingering for a time pass away. So complete a transformation in the frequenters of this famous public place could not, perhaps, have been imagined possible by the wildest flights of fancy, and a Mercury

reporter remarked as much to a park policeman. That functionary, who was gloomily wrestling with the temptation to club a Hoboken dude and find out whether he was stuffed, replied:

"It's all along of her."

"People as has kids," said the park policeman, "says as how she is immoralizing and they won't let the young ones come here no more. Not as I blame 'em much, either, for," concluded the moral sparrow chaser, "I consider her a reg'lar brazen image myself, and I don't think no such statue should be allowed in a public place."[18]

The Tower was opened to the public on November 2, 1891. David King's son, Van Rensselaer King, had the honor of being the first person to ascend the Tower at the opening, taking the elevator to the upper loggia and then climbing the stairs to the uppermost public viewing platform. That evening White arranged for a spectacle of electric light at the Garden, the first large-scale American demonstration of the possibilities of light as decoration. Some 6,600 incandescent bulbs were placed on the outer walls of the Garden base, and 1,400 more were arranged to outline the Tower. One hundred arc lights were positioned to highlight architectural features, and two powerful searchlights were directed toward the statue on the pinnacle so that the gold figure glittered against the night sky.[19]

The focus of light on the golden figure was spectacular, something never done before, and, with the many lights below, called attention to White's palace of pleasure in a highly dramatic way. The Garden was noticed and talked about, and White, as its creator, was a center of attention in the city. The widespread fame that had eluded his father was now his. Had it been possible, it is perhaps not too outrageous to suggest that White himself might have enjoyed being for a time on the high perch, in Diana's place, with the searchlights focused on him.

The response to the Tower was immensely enthusiastic. Edward Hancock Bowen, the editor of a real estate journal, said "the exquisite proportions and graceful lines of the tower" were "the finest thing of its kind in the country." He wrote White, "I always gaze upon it with great admiration whenever in the neighborhood, especially from the Square." One newspaper editorial lauded "the capitalists" who had made possible this "architectural triumph": "The creation of Diana's Tower—as everyone calls it now—was an act of beneficence for which the directors of the Madison Square Garden Company deserve the warmest thanks of the public." The soaring structure was, moreover, a testimony "to the progressive spirit of a city which is always quick to give its support to an enterprise that reflects upon its dignity as a municipality." In the view of the *New York Sun,* the Tower quite simply was "the greatest artistic achievement of the nineteenth century . . . unrivalled by any creation of art in now many centuries." Its creator had won "an imperishable name" by his design: "If this community can put any token of honor and esteem on Stanford White, now is the time to do it."[20]

From Greenwich, Connecticut, a correspondent wrote White that "in roaming around the horizon yesterday with my telescope" he had sighted "your beautiful Tower" from his country house. "To make sure of the Tower, I fixed the glass & after dark found it focused on a beautiful shaft of light unlike anything else on the land, sea, or firmament." Before this sighting, it had not been thought possible to see New York City from Greenwich, though no doubt "this beautiful Tower," he speculated, could be seen at even greater distances.[21]

Delighted with the reception of the Tower and Diana but now convinced that he and Gus had erred in making the figure too large, Stan decided that "a new figure must be made proportionate to the Tower." He had not anticipated that Diana "would become such a noticeable and prominent feature" of the neighborhood landscape. One Saturday afternoon, when the staff had left the office for the day, White and his assistant Frank Hoppin made a silhouette of the Tower and several silhouettes of different sizes of the Diana in an attempt to decide on the most suitable height for a new version. McKim, working there that afternoon and only too aware of the disproportionate size of the figure, came out of his private office as Stan was striding back and forth to chide his partner gently. "Stan," he said, "that was a very beautiful pedestal you made for Saint-Gaudens' statue, but I thought that he was going to make a finial for your Tower." McKim hastily retreated to his office "shaking with laughter at the explosive sounds that followed." After eleven months on her perch, Diana was taken down.[22]

The figure was sent to the foundry in Salem, Ohio, where it had been originally cast, to prepare it for a new temporary home in Chicago. The influential Mrs. Potter Palmer had requested the statue for the Women's Building at the World's Columbian Exposition, which would open in May 1893, but there was no suitable pinnacle for it on that structure. Meanwhile, a vigorous outpouring of protest arose in Chicago at exhibiting the nude figure at the fair. Some suggested that if it were put up there, Diana would have to be provided with a long dress and other appropriate clothing. Spokespersons for the Women's Christian Temperance Union were especially upset about allowing Diana to come to the fair: "It would be a sad commentary on our present civilization to exhibit anything like that!'' White himself, outraged at the attacks on Diana, spoke out in her defense: ''It's all bunk for these people to say that Diana is indecent.'' Eventually the figure was erected atop the large Agriculture Building, which McKim had designed, and remained there throughout the 1893 exposition.[23]

The second Diana, placed atop the Tower in November 1893, was lovelier than the first, most people felt, and at 13 feet in height more appropriate in size. Again a nude figure, somewhat slimmer as well as simpler and more graceful than the first, the second Diana was balanced on a small sphere on the toes of her left foot, her right leg extending back; her left arm extended forward with the bow, and her right hand pulled the bow string. Drapery was swathed about her left shoulder and waist. The crescent of the first Diana was left out this time. White and Saint-Gaudens themselves bore the $5,000–$6,000 cost of having the replacement statue made and put up. Around 1905, a severe thunderstorm broke off the drapery from the figure; subsequently the statue was fastened down and no longer served as a weathervane.[24]

The second Diana became the inspiration for O. Henry's ''The Lady Higher Up,'' published on July 24, 1904, in the *New York Sunday World Magazine*. In the short story, Diana chats with the lady in the harbor, the Statue of Liberty, who is envious of all the exciting events that take place in Diana's home, Madison Square Garden: ''Ye have the best job for a statue in the whole town, Miss Diana.'' More sophisticated than Miss Liberty, Diana ridicules the harbor statue's ''Mother Hubbard'' and brags about her own fashionableness: ''I think those sculptor guys ought to be held for damages for putting iron or marble clothes on a lady. That's where Mr. St. Gaudens was wise. I'm always a little ahead of the styles; but they're coming my way pretty fast.''[25]

The Roof Garden, which years later would provide the backdrop for the final scene of White's life, was the last part of Madison Square Garden to open. Occupying an area of about 200 by 80 feet at the Madison Avenue end of the building, the Roof Garden accommodated some three hundred tables and provided customers with drinks, supper, and light entertainment. A stage was placed to the east, and arcades surrounded the area open to the sky. Varicolored electric lights and Chinese lanterns were strung about, fountains played here and there, and a profusion of flowers and shrubs decorated the rooftop. On opening night, May 30, 1892, a festive crowd gathered on the roof to enjoy Spanish shadow dancers and a group of mandolin players. White was there in the crowd, enjoying the congratulations he received. But late in the evening, when the entertainments in the amphitheater, concert hall, and theater ended and many people from those places came upstairs, the Roof Garden became overcrowded; the planners had not anticipated the large crowds that might simultaneously converge on the facility. In the crush, hats were smashed, women's dresses torn, and many feared that panic might break out. Subsequently, new exits were added to make the Roof Garden less congested and less dangerous.

With the arena, the theater, the concert hall, and the Roof Garden, Madison Square Garden became for a time the most important place of entertainment in New York. The program of events in the Garden was diverse. Yet the building was not a long-term financial success; indeed, in many years mortgage payments and other fixed costs exceeded income. The lavishly conceived and elaborately ornamented facilities had been expensive. In his professional work as in his private life, flamboyance, extravagance, and the striking gesture were White's hallmarks, and the Garden embodied them all. Possibly a more modest, simpler, less showy building would have been financially more viable. An additional problem for the Garden was that the city's entertainment was continuing to move northward, and in the later 1890s most of the theaters, fashionable restaurants, and cabarets were rising around Forty-second Street and Seventh Avenue, leaving the Garden somewhat out of the way. Nonetheless, the elaborate, joyous character of the Garden and the many expensively conceived productions still attracted many patrons.

At times the financial troubles of the Madison Square Garden Company created uncertainty about the future of the building. Controversy erupted at the annual meeting of stockholders in May 1893, when a group of minority stockholders, headed by James A. Bailey, "the Napoleon of Circusdom," charged the management, supported by the majority stockholders, with gross extravagance and mismanagement, charges that were not specifically substantiated. Since the Garden had opened it had not yet paid any dividends to stockholders and had managed to make a profit of less than $3,000 for the twelve months ending in April 1893. The meeting ended with the appointment of a committee to arrange for the sale of the building. The following month, however, the decision to sell was reversed, largely because the Horse Show Association had arranged for a five-year arena rental. Proposals to dispose of the facility, nonetheless, were to come up again later on. For a time, though, the Garden could develop further along the course that had been established. "In two short years the Garden has become the most useful public building known in the city," the *Providence Journal* editorialized; "its sale would be a serious loss."[26]

As a director, White was intimately involved with many operations of the Garden and was often called upon to help plan and even design productions for the arena. Newspaper accounts often noted his presence at events held in the arena and in the concert hall and theater. White's name, indeed, was more often and more closely associated with the Garden than that of any other person. The Garden, one manager wrote him, is "a great monument to your wonderful talent & taste; & your unflagging devotion to it has so contributed to its success—in fact to its very existence—that no words of praise from me could be adequate to express my feelings."[27]

As adviser on and actual producer of extravaganzas at the Garden arena, Stanford White in the early 1890s was venturing into yet another world, that of the theater. Flamboyant and often theatrical in manner, aware that many of his urban buildings in effect served as street scenery before which the daily drama of city life was played, Stanford White was attracted to and found himself very much at home in the world of the theater. The Garden served him as a great stage, and he enjoyed providing spectacles for it. His introduction to the theater at the Garden was the beginning of a lifelong passion. In time he became friendly with many producers, entertainers, musicians, actors and actresses, and others associated with the theater. He soon became the producer of extravaganzas for the city at large.

One of the early events held in the Garden amphitheater was the Actors' Fund Fair, which Stan supervised and largely designed, contributing his services, along with a $100 donation, to help the fund. Visitors entered the arena under a triumphal arch flanked by a classic exedra and a semicircular arched colonnade. An entire village, with streets and shops, was erected on the floor of the arena. Here, visitors found a representation of Shakespeare's house at Stratford-on-Avon, models of the Globe Theater and other playhouses, a Japanese tea house, a pagoda, a small mosque, and several booths set up by the commercial theaters of New York. One of the best exhibits was a representation of Dickens's Old Curiosity Shop, operated by the Women's Press Club and designed by the painter William Merritt Chase. At the opening on May 2, 1892, the actor Edwin Booth was introduced, and Joseph Jefferson, another famous thespian, made a witty speech. Belles of society presided over the many booths. The press called the fair a great success, repeatedly describing it as "a scene from fairyland." Stanford was lauded for "his zealous and most skillful work in planning and superintending the construction of the pretty village." He was elected an honorary member of the Actors' Fund Association.[28]

In November 1892, Bessie White was invited to serve as a patroness of the Chrysanthemum Show. Along with well-known figures in the New York worlds of business and society, the Whites took a box for the show and were spotted by the press moving along "with the current of humanity in the promenade," while "John Jacob Astor and Mrs. Astor sniffed the fragrant atmosphere from a box" and "Mr. and Mrs. J. Pierpont Morgan strolled around in the crowd." Even Abe Hummel, a dwarflike lawyer of questionable reputation on whom Stan would call for assistance in later years, was there. A large "floral representation of the Washington Arch with figures of green smilax and lily buds" was "the chief glory of the show." Young ladies in brilliant satin Japanese kimonos looking "quite bizarre" served as attendants. Other flower shows, as well as poultry shows, dog shows, cat shows, boxing, circuses, and Christmas toy shows were held in the arena. In 1895 White, who was characterized as "something of a farmer himself," arranged a farm show there, with pigsties, cowpens, and hen roosts. A Saturday matinee in February 1894 brought "New York's First Children's Monster Musical Congress" to the Garden. One summer the arena became a miniature Venice, with patrons floating about in gondolas.[29]

The annual Horse Show at the Garden was a highpoint of the New York social season. For the mid-November show in 1892, the Whites took a $550 box. Bessie usually attended the horse shows with Stan, and friends from the worlds of art and society joined them. Box holders were listed in the program so that everyone could see who was who. Spectators moving about the promenade looked carefully to see what members of the fashionable set were wearing: It was considered *de rigueur* for the ladies to have different outfits at each performance during the weeklong show. The entire neighborhood of the Garden took notice of the Horse Show. Shop windows displayed the blue and yellow colors of the Horse Show Association, while restaurants and hotels were decorated with violets and chrysanthemums, the official flowers of the show. One commentator wrote, "No other city ever presents a complex spectacle just like this; and it would be impossible here without a building just like our Garden."[30]

The opening of Madison Square Garden inspired a proposal for a small permanent circus building for the city, like that in Paris. Early in 1892 White, the builder David King, Robert Goelet, Perry Belmont, and a few others discussed the idea and sent around a circular to friends who they thought might be willing to subscribe to the project. Several sites were considered, and White was reported to have made rough sketches of plans suited to the different sites. It was estimated that the circus building would cost about $600,000. When Hermann Oelrichs, a friend and later a client of White, received the circular, he wrote to wish Stan well on the project (though not offering to invest in it) and added that he believed White and King were "better fitted to start and run a circus" than anyone else in New York, with the possible exception of the owner of Niblo's Gardens. Whatever they did with the circus, Oelrichs felt, would be "first class" and elevated "to the highest moral plane." But White was occupied with so many undertakings, and the interest of possible investors was so lukewarm, that the project was dropped. The scheme was revived in 1896 by one Alexander Comstock of New York, who reportedly got plans from McKim, Mead & White for a great amusement palace, featuring space for a winter circus, a palm garden, and a roof garden. "Many of the best people in town are to be stockholders," it was reported. But this scheme, too, came to nothing.[31]

As the Tower was being completed, Stan considered taking one of the small apartments there for his own use, thus identifying himself even more fully with the Garden by making it a home. When the Whites' house on West Twentieth Street was to be razed and they learned that they had to vacate by May 1, 1892, Stan applied to the Garden manager for a Tower studio, planning to stay there during the summer while Bessie and Larry were at St. James and before the new rented house on East Twenty-first Street was ready. He selected the sixth-floor apartment and soon had it fitted up, painting the walls in shades of umber, sienna, vermilion, and chrome yellow. Daniel Chester French, the sculptor, already had a Tower studio, which White had briefly used as an office while the Roof Garden was nearing completion. The inventor Peter Cooper Hewitt, a grandson of the ironmaster Peter Cooper and son of a former mayor of the city, took another Tower room, setting up an experimental laboratory where he worked on the Mercury vapor lamp, the wireless, and X-rays. Henry Randall, an architect, occupied the fourth-floor studio. Although White at first thought it might be difficult to live there because of problems of getting part-time cleaning and other services, he brought in furniture and had a three-quarters-size bed installed. Very soon, much to his annoyance, stories appeared in the press about the prominent architect taking the Tower studio. He promptly had his name removed from the directory board at the street entrance. Seven years later, in 1899, White moved his pied-à-terre from the sixth floor to the uppermost eighth floor, which Mrs. Robert Goelet, a painter, had occupied for some years, and in a kind of musical chairs move, Cooper Hewitt took over White's former studio.[32]

The eighth-floor studio, like the one he had occupied two floors below, was wrapped around the steep winding staircase and elevator shaft. A vestibule led from the elevator to the entry on the left. To the right, another door opened onto a kitchenette, with an electric oven. A small pantry and a bathroom adjoined the main room. In the intimate Tower studio, White gathered together some of his smaller choice art treasures—tapestries, paintings, Oriental rugs, carved divans and chairs, and leopard and tiger skins. A crystal globe hung from the ceiling, diffusing a mellow light through the room. Other lamps were scattered about to provide artful lighting effects. A cardinal's hat partially concealed one light. An upright Steinway piano, out of tune much of the time, stood along one wall, a copy of MacMonnies's *Bacchante* on top. Nearby was an oblong aquarium stocked with Japanese fish, which frequently were so neglected by White's servants, who came in to clean the place, that they died. Heavy draperies could be pulled across the windows but usually were fastened back, for the view was spectacular, and in the summer guests could look down from the west and north windows over the Roof Garden below, taking in the performances from the unusual perspective.[33]

The Tower studio became White's best-known retreat and his principal alternate New York home for years, and he took great delight in it. The Tower room, he wrote a friend soon after moving into the sixth-floor studio, had "turned out a *great* success. Indeed, I don't know of anything so 'chic' or like it in the world. It is quite like Fairyland."[34]

For White, not only the Tower studio but the Garden itself became a Fairyland, a magic place where dreams and fantasies might be realized. In his Tower room, high above yet hidden away from the city, he could create a very private life that catered to his secret fantasies, as he was already doing in rented studios elsewhere. In the public parts of the Garden, he could invent fantasies that enlarged the lives of those who came there, taking them away from their everyday cares and immersing them in a world of the imagination. In the building as a whole, he produced an evocative object of beauty for the streetscape of the city. The architect as showman had created a world of pleasure and delight for New Yorkers and for himself.

12

"Municipal Commissioner of Public Beauty"

୧୨

The final years of the nineteenth century, as New York City, mirroring the country at large, mushroomed in population with a huge immigrant influx and an ever more heterogeneous populace, were times of great turmoil. Municipal services were often unable to meet soaring demands, housing for the poor became ever more crowded and wretched, and the vast disparities of wealth grew increasingly evident. Life in the metropolis seemed increasingly fragmented as many old bonds of community life disappeared. There were countercurrents to fragmentation, however: Large-circulation cheap newspapers featuring local news and gossip, public school education, the entertainments of vaudeville and baseball—both widely attended—and the dazzling spread of goods in the large department stores no doubt gave many city people a sense of sharing in communal experiences. By the early 1890s Madison Square Garden, Stanford White's glittering public entertainment palace, within whose walls all classes of New Yorkers could gather on common ground, also served as a unifying element in city life. Important as well in bringing city residents together in shared experiences were celebrations that commemorated past events and reinforced historical memories and traditions. Stanford White, a formidable impresario, became a central figure in New York's expanding civic life and celebrations.[1]

White's talents were in great demand. Increasingly prominent in the New York art community, he was recognized as a highly imaginative, exceptionally able, and seemingly tireless worker who could get things done. His sense of style, his educated taste, his many contacts, and his ability to put his hands on what was needed made him much sought after. Generous with his time, his talent, and his money, he seemed driven to create what would be seen and talked about. He had a need to perform and to be praised. In many ways he reflected, indeed personified, the character of the end-of-century city—energetic, fast-moving, outgoing, driven to accomplish, using wealth for display, often doing too much too fast, and at times with reckless abandon.

As much as anything else, White's 1889 Washington Arch and the permanent Washington Memorial Arch that followed established his credentials for civic decoration and embellishment.

The story of the arch begins in the mid-1880s, when planning started for a commemoration of the hundredth anniversary of George Washington's first inaugural as president on April 30, 1789, at Federal Hall on Wall Street. Early in 1884, the New-York Historical Society proposed ceremonies marking the centennial, and the Chamber of Commerce soon followed in urging a suitable celebration. Late in 1887 a number of New Yorkers organized themselves in several committees to plan for the Inaugural Centennial. For the festivities, William Rhinelander Stewart, a wealthy lawyer and real estate investor and a resident on the northwest side of Washington Square, conceived of a temporary triumphal arch to be erected over lower Fifth Avenue. Other temporary arches were planned for Wall Street and Fifth Avenue at Twenty-third and Twenty-sixth streets. Stewart soon raised more than $2,500 from residents around the square to pay for the Fifth Avenue arch, and the Centennial Art and Exhibition Committee commissioned Stanford White to design it.

The 1889 Centennial turned out to be a grand affair indeed: New York put on a big party to celebrate this important civic and national anniversary, and White, with his penchant for the spectacular and love of festivities, was right in the spirit of the celebration. President Benjamin Harrison was rowed by thirteen sailors in a decorated barge from Elizabethtown, New Jersey, to the foot of Wall Street to lead the commemoration— three days of naval and military parades, civic receptions, church services, an industrial and civic parade, an open-air concert, an exhibition of Washington memorabilia, a Centennial ball, and, of course, lots of fireworks. Stan was asked to design the cover for the Centennial souvenir program and the title page for the Centennial celebration history. Saint-Gaudens would design the Washington medals.

White's temporary 1889 arch spanned Fifth Avenue about 100 feet north of Washington Square, between the two corner houses. A wooden structure painted ivory white, with a frieze of garlands and papier-maché wreaths of laurel, it was topped by a balustrade and a pedestal on which stood a curious old wooden statue of George Washington, about 8 feet high, dressed in a Continental uniform and painted in bright colors. White had discovered the figure in an antique dealer's shop and arranged to have it placed on the arch. Tradition had it that the statue originally had been set up on the Battery in 1792, where it stood for several years. Below the statue, as well as on the arch piers, flags were clustered; the keystones supported large stuffed bald eagles; and streamers of bunting were draped across the upper part of the opening. The piers of the arch were made slender to keep encroachments on the two sidewalks at a minimum. At night several hundred small electric lights powered by a nearby generator outlined the arch, probably the earliest use of electric lights for outdoor decorative purposes.[2]

The temporary arch was a stunning success. The brightly colored statue, the flags and bunting, and the incredible electric lights all drew attention to the imaginatively conceived arch, the work of a master showman. A writer in the *Boston Evening Gazette* reported that the arch had become "one of the chief points of interest in the city, and ragged urchins as well as the rich and great stand gazing upon it in admiration." Another commentator declared that "every one immediately concerned must have been a little surprised at the immediate popular success of this unpretentious wooden arch; it was, in a sense, the success of the celebration, and the suggestion was soon made," he went on, "and, as soon as made, enthusiastically received by every one, to perpetuate the arch in marble, as a permanent record of the event."[3]

A special Committee on the Erection of the Memorial Arch at Washington Square was organized. Henry G. Marquand, the president of the Metropolitan Museum of Art, chaired the committee. Stan's longtime friend and client Richard Watson Gilder, poet and editor of the *Century* magazine, served as secretary and coordinator of the project, while William Rhinelander Stewart, as treasurer, was charged with raising funds. Among the other committee members were such prominent figures as Richard Morris Hunt, who lived close by at 2 Washington Square North; the painter Daniel Huntington; Levi P. Morton, Vice President of the United States; and Grover Cleveland, who had recently left the presidency after his first term of office.

White at first proposed retaining the temporary arch design and erecting the permanent arch at the same location, but he soon agreed to the park site in Washington Square that others favored and recognized that changes would have to be made, especially enlargement of the piers. He wanted, if possible, to see how an arch would look in the new location at the north edge of the square and briefly considered having the temporary arch moved to the proposed site. But moving the wooden structure would have been hazardous and might also have necessitated cutting down some large trees, so the idea was abandoned. White submitted three designs to the arch committee, which made no choice. Instead, the members placed their full confidence in the architect's taste and discretion: White "should himself decide on the final design for the Arch." In accord with the design he selected, White supervised preparation of a marble model of the new arch.[4]

Groundbreaking for the arch took place on April 30, 1890. Henry Marquand, the chairman of the committee, stepped down into a small hole made by raising some paving blocks in the park and spaded out a little dirt. He then declared that he was "bursting to say something on this great occasion, but it is forbidden by the committee." The *New York Times* reported that despite the committee's stricture, he did go on to say: " 'As great oaks from little acorns grow, so I expect from this little beginning great things for the city of New York. In digging out this foundation I wish to stipulate that all gold and silver discovered shall go to the committee for the erection of the arch.' Cheers were proposed by Richard Watson Gilder, and heartily given." Workmen digging for the foundation did not discover any gold or silver, but they did find many bones, decayed coffins, and headstones from an old burial place dating from 1803, about 10 feet below the ground surface. The bones were reinterred.[5]

A month later, on Decoration Day, May 30, 1890, the cornerstone was laid. White had arranged for a small copper box for medals, coins, and newspaper articles to be placed within the hollow cornerstone. The ceremony was again impressive: Some five or six thousand spectators watched the First Brigade of the New York State National Guard escort the dignitaries to the site. After a prayer and a choral hymn, Chairman Marquand delivered a formal address—this time allowed by the committee—in which he declared that the monument "should be historical and instructive and prove a popular expression for [feelings] of civic pride. It signifies also the beginning of a new and pure taste in the art of architecture. This is the arch of peace and good-will to men," he went on. "It will bring the rich and poor together in one common bond of patriotic feeling, and prove a poem in stone for our fellow citizens of all time." At the close of the ceremony, the grandmaster of the Masons in New York sealed the cornerstone with traditional Masonic ritual.[6]

Financial support for the arch came from a variety of sources. White contributed his professional services, as did David H. King, the builder, who took no profit on his work. The wealthy Rhinelander sisters, who lived in the corner house east of Fifth Avenue, gave $1,000 each; Cornelius

Vanderbilt, George Washington Vanderbilt, and their mother, Mrs. William H. Vanderbilt, each donated $1,000; John D. Rockefeller contributed $500; while Andrew Carnegie sent $250 and Mayor Hugh Grant, $100, among others. But not only the well-to-do provided support: the Society of American Artists raised $150 among its members; the Seventh Regiment of the National Guard donated $443; and draftsmen in the office of McKim, Mead & White contributed $130. A great number of small contributions came in, making this a truly general public endeavor. At the Madison Square Theater, the actor Joseph Jefferson starred in a benefit performance for the arch fund, while the New York University Glee Club offered its "services for any entertainment for raising money for . . . the speedy erection of this fitting monument." The largest single contribution, however, came from out-of-towners. At the Metropolitan Opera House on March 27, 1892, Gilder's friend the Polish pianist Ignace Jan Paderewski, who had made his first American concert appearance a few months earlier, assisted by the Boston Symphony Orchestra through the generosity of Colonel Higginson, gave a concert that brought more than $4,000 to the fund. Paderewski's gift, the arch committee noted, was "not only a most generous act on his part, but also another token of the sympathy existing between the people of Poland and of America in their common love of human liberty and free institutions."[7]

The final blocks of the arch were set in place on April 5, 1892. The next day Gilder wrote to Paderewski in Europe: "Yesterday Mr. Stewart, the treasurer, Mr. Stanford White, the architect, and myself, climbed up three ladders and laid the last three stones of the structure, while Mrs. Steward, Mrs. White, and Mrs. Gilder waved their handkerchiefs from below! Our own initials were carved on hidden parts of these stones, and a large P for Paderewski took its place among the rest. So your initial is built into the very structure of the monument, and as long as the history of the arch is remembered, your generous deed will be kept in mind."[8]

It was some time before the arch was finished. More of the carving and the lettering remained to be done. The sculptor Frederick William MacMonnies, who lived in Paris, was responsible for much of the sculptural decoration, including the angel-like figures in the spandrels. William Rhinelander Stewart suggested that his wife and Mrs. White be used as models for the faces of the two figures on the north face of the arch and repeatedly asked that his wife be used for the one to the west, nearer the Stewarts' residence. MacMonnies copied photographs of the two women. Stan was insistent that MacMonnies get a good likeness of Mrs. Stewart, though for the representation of his own wife, he wrote

171

the sculptor: "You are free to do what you choose." The figure that Mrs. Stewart modeled, it turned out, represented "Peace," above the statue of Washington as President, while Bessie was the model for "War," above the statue of Washington as Commander-in-Chief.[9]

The dedication of the Washington Memorial Arch was scheduled for April 30, 1895, but had to be postponed to May 4 because of heavy rain. The city made an impressive public cultural event of the dedication, the ceremonies evincing the civic pride so many New Yorkers felt and that White had captured so brilliantly in his work. National Guardsmen and a naval brigade paraded down Fifth Avenue to Washington Square, where now-Governor Levi Morton, a member of the arch committee, and other dignitaries had gathered.

In his address Henry Marquand this time emphasized the popular support for the monument signified by the "widely distributed sources" of contributions and suggested that the arch itself had become a lesson, "teaching the great principles of art to consist in simplicity, beauty of form, adaptation to use, and appropriateness of situation." Above all, he stressed, the ceremony affirmed the arch as a perpetuation of Washington's fame and as a symbol of the birth of "our free and enlightened government." Toward the close of the dedication, William Rhinelander Stewart turned over to Mayor William L. Strong, who had also been a member of the arch committee, the key to the little right pier door of what Stewart called this "beautiful civic monument which Stanford White's genius conceived."[10]

In design the more than 70-foot-high Washington Memorial Arch echoes something of the character of the Arc de Triomphe erected in Paris early in the nineteenth century, though it is smaller in scale, considerably more delicate, and less ornamented. White himself suggested that his marble arch was "Roman" in style, and he was especially proud that it had a larger span than any single-opening arch of antiquity. His work, he stressed, was without columns and was lighter and had a less prominent attic than ancient arches. He seemed confident that as his work was compared with the best-known arch of his own century and the principal arches of antiquity, it would not be found wanting in artistry and grandeur.[11]

The writer Henry James, on his visit early in the twentieth century to the scenes of his childhood, however, disparaged what he termed "the lamentable little arch" bestriding "the beginnings of Washington Square," looking so "poor and lonely" in its "unsupported and unaffiliated state"; a truly "melancholy monument," he called the arch, then still without its statues of Washington on the north side. But most early responses to the arch were highly positive. One man, who styled himself "only a merchant down town," wrote White that he was given "pleasure in the morning as I pass through Washington Square [just] to look upon your successful work." Through the years, the arch became one of the principal identifying icons of New York City as an imposing part of the urban landscape.[12]

Across Washington Square from the arch, at the southwest corner of Thompson Street, Judson Memorial Church, built at the same time, was another major contribution by White to the New York cityscape. Judson Church, the conjoined tower, and Judson Hall have been prominent landmarks since their construction, and the buildings have contributed importantly to the life of Greenwich Village.

The church project was initiated by the Reverend Edward Judson as a memorial to his father, Adoniram Judson, a Baptist missionary. The father, a native of Massachusetts, had precociously chosen his career by the age of four, when he began preaching to neighborhood children. In his early twenties he went to Burma, where for some forty years he worked as a missionary and became known as "Jesus Christ's man" on account of his aggressive spreading of the gospel. He published a grammar of the Burmese language and translated the Bible into that tongue. Three Mrs. Judsons sequentially supported his endeavors and were eventually honored in three memorial windows in the church. Erected on the south side of Washington Square at the edge of a district of tenement houses, the church, it was hoped, would serve both the poor and the well-to-do, and many persons "interested in keeping vice away from the historic plaza opposite which it stands . . . contributed to its erection." The cornerstone was laid on June 30, 1890, and the church was opened for services on February 7, 1891.[13]

White chose a mixture of Italian Renaissance and Romanesque elements for the design of the basilica-like Judson Church. He faced it with yellowish-brown brick and pale yellow terra cotta trim and topped it with a sharply defined gable roof. A ten-story square tower was erected next to the church and was attached on the other side to a substantial structure originally planned as an apartment building for Baptist bachelor educators and clergymen. The rents were expected to provide income to help support the church.

Judson Hall, including the tower, begun in 1890 and completed in 1895, was built by James Knott, the founder of a hotel chain, for the church. When completed, it became the Hotel Judson, and over the years would be the home of many notable artists and writers. A large two-story studio looking out over the square was used at one time by the painter John Sloan, while Frank Norris, the novelist, is said to have worked on *The Pit* in one of the tower rooms.[14]

As designed by White, the church, the tower, and the hall created an impressive scenic backdrop for part of the south side of the public square, the three architectural elements bound together into a single yet varied composition by strong horizontal rusticated bands. The richest terra cotta ornamentation was placed on the hooded entryway between the church proper and the tower. The windows of the upper tower stories suggestively echoed the tall arched windows and panels of the church itself, while a high, open loggia at the uppermost level of the tower, topped by a richly decorated cornice, provided a graceful skyline feature.

White's work on the Washington Centennial first associated him with civic beautification for New Yorkers, and before he turned forty he was subsequently called upon several times to provide expert advice about civic projects. When the editors of the *New York World* in 1891 proposed converting "the now unsightly and unprofitable reservoir" on Fifth Avenue at Forty-second Street into an elevated pleasure garden, White was asked for his views. His response was enthusiastic; he pronounced the proposal "a most magnificent and praiseworthy undertaking" that would be a great improvement on a decided eyesore. "No greater benefit could befall the public than give them this magnificent air garden." The "air garden" came to nothing, but when the reservoir was removed some years later, his firm entered competition for the New York Public Library on the site. Stanford had at least two carloads of rough-faced stone from the disassembled reservoir shipped to Box Hill for use as garden walls; some tangible associations of old New York were thus built into the Whites' Long Island estate.[15]

In 1892 the editor of *The Forum* invited White to prepare an article on the general subject of "How New York May Be Made as Impressive and Beautiful a City as the Metropolis of the United States Ought to Be." The idea was to review work done recently and to suggest "practical improvements" that might be made. White, who disliked writing, refused to prepare the article. He was, as he once privately suggested, "very shy of being entrapped in print." It seemed to him "that the man who *does* things is not the one to *write* about them, while the man who can *say* things, as a rule, knows nothing about them, and it is for this reason that writing on art is a delusion and a snare." Unlike his father, who had written a good deal but created little that was lasting, White believed that he could express himself far better with his drawing pencils than in words and that his drawings could be early steps in creating something permanent. Perhaps in his way he was saying that the architect son ultimately would surpass the journalist-critic father.[16]

As an experienced civic decorator, Stanford was an obvious person to provide artistic guidance and leadership for the next important New York civic celebration. The four hundredth anniversary of Columbus's discovery of America was the occasion for a national commemoration, most notably the World's Columbian Exposition in Chicago. Although New York lost out to Chicago as the site for the world's fair, New Yorkers were determined to observe the quadricentennial in an appropriate and festive way. The October 1892 Columbian celebration, organized by a Committee of One Hundred, was extensive and no doubt provided an important strengthening of community ties in the shared activities.

White became a primary participant in the proceedings and again received much publicity and praise for his civic design endeavors. Perry Belmont, as chairman of the Sub-Committee on Art, appointed an Honorary Advisory Committee, which included White, Hunt, Saint-Gaudens, La Farge, William Merritt Chase, the designer Louis C. Tiffany, and the sculptor John Quincy Adams Ward. White was appointed to take charge of the decorations along Fifth Avenue, the line of march for the Columbian parades. White, Hunt, and La Farge were charged with selecting designs for temporary arches, and White and Tiffany were made primarily responsible for a pamphlet advising property owners on appropriate decorations for stores, clubs, and houses.

Preparations for the Columbian festivities proceeded at a hectic pace in the summer of 1892, while White was temporarily staying in the Tower apartment. In August he planned for a brief trip to Europe the following month, inviting the architect Thomas Hastings to accompany him, but his heavy workload forced him to cancel the excursion. McKim was then in Chicago much of the time supervising the firm's work for the exposition, and Mead was frequently away from the city. Bessie was summering at Box Hill, where Stan usually spent short weekends. White felt absolutely "driven" by the press of his work. Referring to the entertainments at Madison Square Garden, he lamented, "If it were not for the Roof Garden & the Ballet Girls to cheer me up, I should have been dead long ago." He did travel to New Orleans in early September to see James J. Corbett defeat John L. Sullivan, losing $100 on the boxing match, and he and Bessie, with McKim and the Butlers, spent the second week of September near Lake Placid in the Adirondacks, where the Whites, the Emmets, the Butlers, the Wetherills, and Henry Howland had purchased land together.[17]

For the Columbian celebration, the New York art committee supervised the erection of a statue of Columbus at the crossing of Fifty-ninth Street, Broadway, and Eighth Avenue. The committee also authorized two temporary arches over Fifth Avenue. For Fifty-ninth Street, at the southeastern corner of Central Park, it selected a design by a young Columbia College architectural student, a high wooden arch with plaster and papier-maché figures, to span the avenue. For Twenty-second Street, White created an elaborate trellis arch, supported by twelve columns, 20-feet high, decorated with flags, banners, and bunting and filled at night with lighted lanterns, providing a festive note to the area just south of Madison Square. From there northward to Thirty-fourth Street along Fifth Avenue, White had one hundred 60-foot poles erected, topped by spheres and eagles, carrying flags, shields, and streamers, and supporting Venetian lanterns on wires strung across the street. "The delicately tinted lights stretched away until they were dim in the distance and twinkled like as many stars," it was reported—though "before the pageant had arrived, they had most of them gone out."[18]

At Madison Square Garden, in a characteristic grand gesture, White arranged at his own expense for the illumination of the Tower with red, white, blue, and green lights, and for a fireworks display from the Roof Garden. He also supervised the nighttime illumination of City Hall, arranged for Japanese lanterns to be hung from tree branches in Madison Square, and had the Washington Memorial Arch lighted. The view from the summit of the arch was so tempting that during the celebration revelers broke the door open and climbed to the top. A loan exhibition of art works was hastily organized at the National Academy of Design in conjunction with the Columbian events; when response to requests for paintings to exhibit was poor, the committee drew on White's private collection and that of his friend Thomas B. Clarke, among others. A few of Stan's own sketches, still a hobby for him, were included in the display, along with architectural drawings from the McKim, Mead & White office.[19]

In many ways, then, White contributed his time, energy, talents, and even his possessions to make the celebration a success. Newspaper reports were highly enthusiastic. A Boston paper judged White, the main producer of the civic extravaganza, as "the master spirit of these unusually artistic decorations," while *Harper's Weekly* suggested that he should be acclaimed as "Municipal Commissioner of Public Beauty."[20]

After laboring on the trellis arch the entire week before the celebration and then, in his compulsion for work, staying up all night for two nights running—one night in the rain—with no sleep for forty-eight hours, Stan gave out just before Columbus Day and was "in howling pain all through the night," possibly the effect of a bleeding stomach ulcer. For five weeks he was confined to his bed, for a time "packed in ice and under morphine." After he was able to get about, he still remained under the weather for several weeks, "hors de combat," unable for a time to "eat or drink a mouthful." He had minor surgery and was required to visit his doctor daily. During seventeen days before Christmas he was put on a strict milk diet, "visibly wilting under the treatment. . . . The little buzz-saw inside of me," he reported, "is still going on in an unpleasant manner." An abcess in his ear compounded the distress from the gastral problem. The tension of carrying on so many projects, the periods of intense unstinting work, and, increasingly, a crowded social schedule with overindulgence in food and drink, compounded later on with financial worries, would precipitate severe illness again and again in the years to come.[21]

Many friends wrote notes wishing him a speedy recovery. Abbott Thayer, the painter, suggested in a letter that "when old White gets sick, it seems as if about half the art in the world were sick. Do hurry up and get well again. You are a sort of artist eagle, and I need to see you always in the sky." McKim was doubtful that his "artist eagle" partner could be persuaded to rest on his perch and take care of himself in order to recover fully. In the midst of this illness, Dr. Thomas S. Robertson, White's physician, presented his bill for $800 for services over more than a year, but apologized at the same time for sending "this or any bill"; he was "in a little hole" and needed the money. When White promptly paid the bill, the doctor responded that it was "such fun & pleasure to be with you & attend you" that he was sorry he had to ask him for any money at all.[22]

A complete change seemed to be in order, and so the deferred trip to Europe was now accomplished. On January 14, 1893, Stanford, Bessie, and Larry were once again on their way abroad. White engaged cabins on the French steamship *Champagne* and employed a stewardess to look after five-year-old Larry during the voyage. In Paris, Stan consulted with doctors about his condition and spent some time with Frederick MacMonnies, then working on the Washington Arch sculptures as well as on statuary for Prospect Park in Brooklyn. Later on, in Florence, White visited the antiquities dealers with whom he regularly dealt and arranged for a miscellany of objects to be sent back to New York.

The high point of the four-month holiday in 1893 was a March trip to Egypt with Ella and Devereux Emmet, Bessie's sister and brother-in-law, the Emmets' child, and a Scottish nurse. While visiting the pyramids near Cairo, Stan encountered the reporter and author Richard Harding Davis, whom he had come to know in New York, and with the Emmets they climbed to the top of the Pyramid of Cheops. On reaching the summit, Stan informed Davis that they were a hundred feet higher than Diana atop Madison Square Garden. Years later, Larry White recalled dashing about the crowded streets of Cairo in a carriage with two runners ahead of the vehicle and the driver using a whip and screaming and cursing all the while to make their way through the throngs of people. The Whites and Emmets hired a dahabeyah to go up the Nile River as far as Aswan, taking with them as a guide a Syrian Christian named Joseph Haik, "absolutely the most splendid fellow imaginable." The boat was small and crowded, and rats got aboard and chewed up all of Bessie's shoes, much to her annoyance. All in all, however, Stan found the trip up the Nile, away from his work and the hectic life he led in New York, "the best rest in the world," something he sorely needed at the time. From Africa Stan, always the collector, brought home spears from the black natives at Aswan, a part of a mummy's body, and "all kinds of queer things."[23]

The Nile journey had one unforeseen consequence, however. Stanford liked their guide so much that he generously presented him with his combined double-barreled shotgun and rifle. Since the caliber was unusual and Haik was unable to find appropriate cartridges, Stan later sent empty shells to him, which the guide could have loaded in Syria. The express company attempted to pass the shells through customs as "pieces of dinner service." When the deception was discovered, the unsuspecting Haik was clapped in jail, and White had to petition the Egyptian envoy in the United States to intercede and get the poor fellow released. Haik was eventually freed, with no harm done, and White recommended him highly to other Americans about to visit Egypt.[24]

In April the Whites were back in Paris and once more met Richard Harding Davis, with whom they visited Versailles. In London, subsequently, Stan went on a buying spree and carefully replenished his wardrobe. Stan and Bessie attended the London wedding of Julia Chamberlain to Robert Winthrop Chanler, a member of a family with which they had many ties. Davis joined them in London and escorted Bessie around the city "in proper style," introducing her to the Lord Chief Justice, whom he had come to know the year before, and arranging for the Home Secretary to take her on a tour of the House of Commons. No doubt Bessie enjoyed the attentions she received and found the tours of London enlightening; she came to have a passion for learning dates in English history and lines of British rulers. The Whites, in their turn, generously treated Davis to meal after meal. They visited Edwin Austin Abbey and his wife, and enjoyed John Singer Sargent's hospitality at his studio. The pleasure of the London visit was marred, however, by White's loss of his purse; Scotland Yard was put on the case, but there is no evidence that his property was recovered. On May 13, 1893, Stanford was back in New York, "looking well and happy," McKim reported.[25]

White's extended absence in Europe and Africa, following upon his long and severe illness in the fall and winter, had made many New Yorkers more than ever aware of what his presence and his friendship meant to them. Shortly after his return, therefore, some of White's male friends honored him with a dinner in one of the supper rooms in the music hall at Madison Square Garden, followed by coffee in the Tower studio. As one of the men he knew well wrote White that spring: "There is one thing . . . that will not change, and you can depend on that, and that's the friendship of your friends! You can always count upon them."[26]

A few days after the dinner, Stan, Bessie, and Larry boarded a train for Chicago for a visit to the World's Columbian Exposition. Stan had intended to stay for only a couple of days, but he ended up remaining for ten. The previous October he had planned to attend the dedicatory ceremonies, but his illness then had prevented him from going. For months, however, he had been involved in preparations for the fair. He served on the Advisory Committee on Fine Arts for both New York State and Pennsylvania, helping to choose local architectural drawings for exhibit. He created the designs for the small White Star Lines pavilion and for the Puck Building at the fair, and the firm also did a booth for the American Cotton Oil Company. McKim was primarily responsible for the designs of the huge Agriculture Building and the impressive New York State Building, though Stan also had a hand in both commissions. White's work on the New York State Building was, in fact, widely praised; the *New York Press* called the interior a "color study by Mr. Stanford White . . . daring in its splendor." The first Diana, removed from the Tower at Madison Square Garden, stood resolute and conspicuous atop the Agriculture Building. From his private collection, White sent paintings by Kenyon Cox and Thomas Dewing for exhibit at the fair.[27]

White and his family had "a bully time" in Chicago. Years later Larry would recall how they had been "handsomely treated by the officials" of the fair. Stan himself thanked his Chicago friends for the good times there, which involved several nights on the town for him: "You fellows came nearer laying me out in Chicago than I was ever laid out before. . . . I didn't go to bed for five days running until dawn and came home a wreck." The Court of Honor, he thought, was tremendously impressive, especially at night, when the thousands of electric lights and the gondolas with their lanterns were "almost the finest thing I have ever seen in my life.'' Stan returned ''with my Frau'' in October for a second visit of several days. At the close of the exposition he arranged to purchase the Javanese Commissioner's house from the fair and had it taken apart and shipped to Box Hill for reassembly on the grounds as a summer house.[28]

A sour note echoing through the exposition summer of 1893 was occasioned by Dick White's further misadventures. Richard Mansfield White had been named Commissioner for the Territory of New Mexico to the exposition and went to Chicago to supervise the territorial exhibit. Suddenly, in the spring, he was removed from his position by the governor of New Mexico, acting on the unanimous request of the New Mexico Board of Managers, which had charged him with ''constantly bringing the Territory into discredit'' and doing ''everything in his power to retard the action of the board and hinder a creditable exhibit from this Territory.'' Dick had apparently ignored the managers and had made all decisions on his own. In the usual pattern, Stan came to his older brother's defense. He wrote President Grover Cleveland to protest ''the injustice'' done while at the same time chastening Dick for the ''lurid character'' of his letters and urging him to get a lawyer to find out precisely what recourse he might have. Letters of appeal were sent to the Attorney General and the President, but Dick White's position was untenable. The public rebuke was a devastating humiliation for him.[29]

As Dick's reputation went down, Stanford's fame was soaring. By the time he turned forty in November 1893, he had created a substantial body of important work, with one acclaimed achievement after another. His work on the Washington Centennial, Madison Square Garden, the Washington Memorial Arch, the Columbian Quadricentennial, and the Chicago fair, along with a great many other commissions, had made him a figure of considerable public renown.

Following the Columbian quadricentennial projects, however, protracted legal controversy over payments due to subcontractors on the decorations became a long-term source of tension for him. Several subcontractors, whom White had hired, had gone over their estimated costs, and the Committee on Art had refused to reimburse them. At his own expense and with a good deal of trouble, White had to hire counsel to negotiate payments. At one point he resolved ''after such a burning'' not to ''put my foot in the fire again.'' ''Nothing,'' he affirmed, ''would induce me to try decorating the city again.'' But he would not keep that resolution.[30]

Decorating the city brought White considerable acclaim, but just as gratifying in some ways were several memorial projects on which he

180

worked, most of them outside New York, collaborating with Gus Saint-Gaudens and "Willie" MacMonnies. On a small scale, in those works he was in a way becoming something of a "commissioner of public beauty" for the nation.

13

With Gus and Willie

⌘

I n the late nineteenth century many Americans, it seemed, had a passion for sculpture. Countless civic monuments commemorating American statesmen and military heroes were erected, and figures of the past were often celebrated in settings of imposing grandeur, even in small towns. Gravestone monuments were embellished with increasingly elaborate sculptural decoration. City dwellers flocked to displays of casts of antique sculpture in the newly established museums, while Americans traveling abroad accumulated photographs of European monuments and statuary. The greatest of American statues, the Statue of Liberty, honoring ideals of freedom and independence and of American openness to immigration, was inaugurated with widespread acclaim in 1886. The vogue for sculpture, identifying heroes, memorializing the past, and creating symbols of communal and national identification, was an important artistic countercurrent to the pervasive materialism of the Gilded Age.

From the unveiling of the Farragut Monument in Madison Square in 1881, White's reputation for artful monument work was firmly established. Some of his subsequent projects embellished New York, although most of his monuments and memorials were erected outside the city. Stan's conviction that artists working in different media should join together in creative endeavors and his commitment to beautifying public places naturally led him to work on several civic projects, which required mastery of materials and pedestal motifs as well as a skilled eye for site placement. On larger projects he collaborated closely with an experienced sculptor, most often with Saint-Gaudens or with Gus's onetime pupil Frederick William MacMonnies. White also designed many lesser pieces, often working alone. Sometimes he did not even charge a fee for the sketches. Many were cemetery monuments or gravestones, prepared at the request of friends and, occasionally, strangers. He clearly relished the challenge of creating monuments and memorial plaques.

In his monument and statuary work, White, like other American architects involved in such collaborations, customarily formulated the primary decisions as to the overall composition and then undertook the detailed planning and designing of the architectural elements, working closely with the sculptor. McKim, too, did important collaborative monument work with Saint-Gaudens, including, most significantly, the impressive Shaw Memorial (1897) near the Boston statehouse and the great Sherman Monument (1903) on the Plaza in New York City, but White was involved in many more such projects. The monument work came to him as personal commissions rather than to the firm.

Stan's collaboration with Gus Saint-Gaudens seemed a natural outgrowth of their long-standing friendship, nourished by their mutual passion for art and architecture and their love of good times. Following his marriage and move to Europe in 1877, Saint-Gaudens spent three years in France and Italy but returned to live in New York in 1880. The next year he took an apartment with his wife and young son Homer at 22 Washington Place, close to Washington Square, not far from where Stan was then living. The sculptor set up his main studio at 148 West Thirty-sixth Street and rented three smaller workplaces. While he lived in New York, Gus was Stan's closest male companion. Over the years, Augusta Saint-Gaudens, seeking cures for ill health and nervous complaints and distancing herself for long periods from a difficult marriage, was often away from the city, taking Homer with her, frequently for months at a time. Because Augusta and Bessie White were both out of town frequently, the two men spent all the more time together.

Especially in the late 1880s and early 1890s, Gus and Stan saw a great deal of each other, at times daily. Notes went back and forth between Gus's studio and Stan's office, sometimes two or three communications a day, checking on their joint work, arranging for dinners, and planning ahead for an excursion or an evening "spree." Their notes at times were direct and straightforward about business matters, but more often they were playful and filled with expressions both of endearment and of ribald sexual imagery and expression, often with homoerotic overtones. Gus customarily used the salutation "Darling" or "Beloved Beauty" to Stan, who himself greeted Gus with "Sweetest" or "Doubly Beloved." The "KMA" incised on the caricature medallion commemorating the 1878 journey in southern France was the usual closing phrase for both men's notes and letters, though Gus, like an overgrown adolescent savoring naughty words, sometimes spelled out "KISS MY ASS," "Bai-sez mon cul," "Baccio il mio culla, ti dice," "Kiss me where I can't," "Once more and for the 5999th time you can kiss me," or, less endear-ingly, "Merde." On occasion Gus would draw a large, phallic "A" with eyes and mouth for a signature; more often he signed with the caricature of a few telling lines that emphasized his sharply defined and sloping facial features. Stan frequently drew his caricature signature on his notes as two round eyes staring out under hair on end, sometimes including a broadly grinning mouth.[1]

Their enjoyment of each other made working together as natural as playing together. The positive public response to their Farragut Monument led almost at once to another large project. A Chicago committee formed to commission a statue of Abraham Lincoln, provided for by a $40,000 bequest, was so impressed by the piece in Madison Square that the members resolved to have Saint-Gaudens do the work for their city. When the project was awarded to him, Gus asked Stan to join him. The fact that the commission came to the sculptor, who then invited the architect to assist him, implying that he had subordinate status, may have been irritating to Stan, but in such monument projects the architect's work was commonly perceived as secondary.

In mid-August of 1883, Gus and Stan visited the proposed site in Chicago's Lincoln Park, and late the next year they signed a contract for the work. Gus subsequently created an 11½-foot statue of Lincoln, the head and hands modeled from life casts taken many years earlier, while Stan planned the pedestal and the accessory features. The statue was unveiled on October 22, 1887. Set on a granite pedestal on a raised platform, the highly dignified figure of the president stands before a chair, lost in thought, his head slightly bowed; a 60-foot-long exedra bench curves around behind the figure, framing the sculpture. The impres-sive integration of the sculptural and architectural elements in this project, as was the case in the Farragut Monument, is indicative of the two artists' harmonious working relationship. To the critic Mariana Van Rens-selaer, the Lincoln composition was "not only our best likeness of Abra-ham Lincoln, but our finest work of monumental art."[2]

Simultaneously with the Lincoln commission in Chicago, Gus and Stan were engaged on a major statuary project in Springfield, Massachu-setts. In 1881 Chester W. Chapin, president of the Boston & Albany Railroad, commissioned a statue of his ancestor Deacon Samuel Chapin (1595–1675), a founder of Springfield. Set on a circular granite base, the heroic bronze figure of Deacon Chapin, his cloak blown back, strides forward as if going to church, a Bible grasped in his left arm and a

185

walking staff in his right hand. *The Puritan* was unveiled a month after the *Standing Lincoln,* on November 24, 1887. Stan, with an eye for the landscape setting, designed a small park for the statue, which he placed at one end, with a fountain and bronze turtles at the opposite end, balancing the statue, and a marble bench between the two configurations. He had white birch trees and a pine hedge planted along the sides to enclose the park.[3]

Far different in spirit from the Farragut, the *Standing Lincoln,* and *The Puritan* were the two Diana figures, erected sequentially atop Madison Square Garden Tower. Once again in this project the two artists' working relationship was harmonious and for White especially pleasant since he, in effect, was the client who commissioned the work for his own building. Both men took delight in the prominently placed figures and the considerable controversy they aroused.

The White–Saint-Gaudens artistic collaboration was brought to its most significant fulfillment in the Adams Memorial, erected in 1891 in Rock Creek Cemetery in Washington, D.C. Generally acknowledged as Saint-Gaudens's masterpiece, the mysterious, brooding, evocative figure of the Memorial is surely one of the greatest achievements in American art. White, responsible for the architectural elements, worked closely with Gus over several years on the evolution of the design. The impact of Saint-Gaudens's figure is immensely enhanced by White's architecture, set in a serene and isolated bower.

Henry Adams, grandson and great-grandson of presidents, biographer, historian, and essayist, commissioned the monument from the two artists just as he was starting out on a trip to the Far East, in June 1886, with the painter John La Farge. It was conceived as a memorial to his wife, Marian Hooper Adams, who had taken her own life the previous year. Scholarly, introspective, and reserved, the patrician Adams at the start had some doubts as to whether Saint-Gaudens could realize the concept he had in mind. Probably his reservations had more to do with the exuberant, fun-loving, often impulsive White, their temperaments being so very different. Yet what the two artists created ultimately seemed to satisfy the fastidious Adams.

It was some time before the project got under way. By the fall of 1887 Saint-Gaudens had made preliminary sketches for the figure; however, Stan did not get a look at them until January 1888. When he did see them, he objected to references in some sketches to Socrates, who had committed suicide. Still, he wrote to Adams that he was "very proud of the design" and that two of Gus's sketches seemed "very stunning." He hoped that Adams would let him know if he were coming to New York so that they could move ahead. That summer Stan completed preliminary drawings for the architectural setting and made arrangements for marble for the platform, steps, and seat. He continued to keep in close touch by letter with Adams and sent him a present of a large salmon from the Restigouche camp in Canada. Gus sought out La Farge for advice on the figure he was planning, and in November 1888 he began work on a 2-foot model of the piece. When Adams came to New York to see the model that December, he decided he should stay out of the project from then on and leave the designing fully up to the sculptor and the architect. A contract was finally signed on December 11, 1888.[4]

Saint-Gaudens continued to move slowly with the work and, uncharacteristically, was reluctant to let Stan see how it was developing, a possible indication of tension arising between the two men regarding their collaborative roles as joint creators and critics of each other's work. In the spring of 1889 Stan wrote Adams that the full-size figure Gus was then preparing was "very impressive, and simple and mysterious," but he had to admit that he had "not had a real look at it" and doubted that Gus would let even Adams see it at that stage. Although the figure was inspired by Eastern religious ideas of Nirvana, some of the plastic conceptions were derived from Michelangelo's Sistine Chapel lunette figures. The Adams Memorial work ceased for a time in the late summer of 1889, when Stan and his family and Gus visited Europe, but by October White reported to Adams that Saint-Gaudens was "working like a beaver on your figure." Norcross Brothers supplied the stone for the Memorial and arranged for the carving and polishing right in the quarry. As the figure neared completion, Gus suggested and Stan agreed that it should be placed on a rock of granite rather than a bronze base, as originally planned, so the setting was changed slightly. Adams was traveling in the South Pacific in March 1891 when the figure was finally set in place.[5]

The Adams Memorial marks the site of the grave of Marian Adams and the later burial place of her husband. There are no inscriptions. Enclosed by a thick wall of holly shrubs and cedar trees, the Memorial rests on a hexagonal platform, some 20 by 28 feet, raised a step or two above the ground level. The brooding figure, shrouded under an enveloping cloak, the face resting on the right arm and hand, is seated on a boulder, with a stone footrest. (The head covering and the position of the right arm recall the plaque of Bessie White that Gus created as a wedding present for the Whites in 1884.) A polished pink granite stele, topping by moldings, forms a backdrop to the figure. Opposite the statue on three sides is a stone bench, where viewers can sit insulated by the surrounding greenery from the world outside and contemplate the figure. Adams liked the name *The Peace of God* for the work and suggested that "the whole meaning and feeling of the figure [was] in its universality and anonymity." Saint-Gaudens, too, believed that this name best expressed what he had wished to convey.[6]

Before Adams finally saw the monument in place, he was critical about the progress of the work, writing from the South Pacific to his confidante Elizabeth Cameron that nothing had distressed him as had Saint-Gaudens's and White's "outrageous disregard of my feelings in this matter." Like many of the sculptor's commissions, the project took years to complete, and the delay, understandably, was annoying to the meticulous Adams. Whimsically, the historian suggested that he would like to club them over their heads "and put them under their own structure." When, however, his close friend and next-door neighbor John Hay reported enthusiastically by letter on the Memorial after it was in place, Adams felt relieved and wrote back that from a photograph it was "at least not hostile" to his idea. He judged that White, who he felt had little understanding of Oriental concepts, had gone astray, though his mistakes on the architectural setting were "not so serious as to overbalance the merits." On his return, after visiting the Memorial, Adams's attitude toward the piece became more positive. He often sat on the bench and watched visitors who came there and listened to their various responses: "The interest of the figure was not in its meaning, but in the responses of the observers," he commented. "Like all great artists, Saint-Gaudens held up the mirror and no more." In his autobiography, Adams cryptically suggested that the meaning of the figure was "the one commonplace about it—the oldest idea known to human thought."[7]

Despite the important Adams Memorial and a great many other commissions, Saint-Gaudens perpetually claimed he was broke, and he often asked his architect friend to lend him $100 or $200 to tide him over for a short time. Stan invariably helped him out. At least one larger loan extended over several years. In 1885, the Saint-Gaudenses began to spend summers in Cornish, New Hampshire, renting there a former inn and large property, which Gus purchased in 1891. Gus's expenses for studio rents, materials, models, and assistants, as well as the costs of maintaining the Cornish estate were substantial, and income anticipated from commissions was often in arrears. "Thank you a thousand times for the money, which I will return on Saturday. That G. D. Gen'l. Viele of the Cooper Committee is the cause of my being bust," Gus wrote Stan on one such occasion when money he was owed was not forthcoming.[8]

When he was at Cornish, Gus asked White to see that letters sent to him at The Players clubhouse would be discreetly forwarded to him, usually directing that such letters be sent in an outer envelope addressed to his favorite niece, whose mail he would then collect or arrange to have sent to him. As with others of White's circle, there were matters he did not wish his wife to know about. Saint-Gaudens was said to be involved over the years in several serious extended love affairs. The most long-lasting was his relationship beginning around 1881 with the Swedish-born Davida Clark, his principal model for many years. In 1889, Davida gave birth to their son, who was named Louis Clark and familiarly called "Novy." For some time Gus supported the second family unbeknownst to his wife. When Augusta finally learned of the other family—perhaps in 1892—and their relationship came to a crisis, he pleaded forgiveness. The Saint-Gaudenses were reconciled and remained married, though with long periods of separation. The sculptor continued to support his second family, whom he settled in Connecticut, and he visited them regularly until the last year of his life. Stan was well aware of Gus's affairs and was, perhaps, especially sympathetic since he so intensely disliked Gus's wife.[9]

In another major collaboration, following the Henry Adams commission, Gus and Stan planned a striking memorial to the martyred President James Garfield for Fairmont Park, Philadelphia. Gus prepared a bronze bust of Garfield, which was placed on a marble base and shaft designed by White; in front of the shaft, an idealized bronze female figure of the Republic holds an oval shield emblazoned with the President's name. Stan was "perfectly delighted" with the Garfield Monument, unveiled on May 30, 1896, and felt that the heroic bust and the idealized figure made the monument "a charming work of art," truly giving "pleasure to the eye" in a way that statuary in modern dress rarely did. In a note to Gus, accompanying his bill for 2 percent of the total cost of the materials and preparation of the monument (his commission for the architectural work) and for travel expenses and photographs, Stan asserted proudly: "I almost think it is the best thing that we have done together."[10]

Soon after the *Standing Lincoln,* the two friends had begun another substantial project for Chicago. Early in 1887, the Illinois state legislature appropriated $50,000 for a monument honoring General John A. Logan (1826–86), a Union army hero in the Civil War and later a senator from Illinois. In September 1888, the commission was awarded to Saint-Gaudens, who, assisted by Alexander P. Procter, who modeled the horse, began work on a colossal equestrian statue representing General Logan as he rallied his troops at a crucial moment in the Battle of Atlanta, holding the regimental flag in his right hand. As was becoming the pattern with Gus, it took an excessively long time for him to be satisfied with his design for the figure. Stan did not feel he could start planning the pedestal until Gus had the figure worked out, and not until June 1895 did he visit Chicago to look over available sites and begin sketches for the pedestal.[11]

A prominent location in Grant Park facing Michigan Avenue was decided upon for what was said to be the largest equestrian statue in the United States. For the Logan figure, White, in a burst of showmanship, created an oval pedestal, 27 by 31 feet, of pale pink and green granite spectacularly set atop a terraced hillock nearly 100 feet in length. Eagles and laurel wreaths decorated the pedestal, along with the names of battles in which General Logan fought. The architectural setting and the equestrian figure were skillfully merged in a striking work of art. Despite the delays on the huge project, Stan and Gus once again skillfully integrated their ideas and worked well together along with Daniel Burnham, the Chicago architect, who supervised construction of the pedestal and placement of the equestrian bronze. The Logan was unveiled on July 22, 1897, in an impressive ceremony which Stan attended.

On their commission, awarded in 1894, for a statue honoring Peter Cooper, the inventor, ironmaster, and founder of the Cooper Union, however, the artistic collaboration of the two artists was not so smooth as it had been in earlier projects. Both men agonized considerably over the work. Gus prepared countless sketches of the Cooper figure and of Stan's proposed architectural settings, soliciting the advice of their friend the architect George Fletcher Babb, before the two men came to a final agreement. The statue was unveiled on May 29, 1897. As erected, the 8½-foot-high seated bronze figure of Cooper is almost overwhelmed by the architectural setting. The statue rests on a Knoxville marble base 6 feet square and 8 feet high; the base is placed on a 4-foot-high platform of steps of Milford pink granite some 22 by 24 feet; and above the figure rises a large half-canopied niche supported by Ionic columns of pink Milford granite, with the bases, capitals, and entablatures of Knoxville marble. Saint-Gaudens afterward expressed dissatisfaction with the Cooper Memorial, believing that the architectural elements jarred with the realistic portrait statue.[12]

Six months after the Cooper was unveiled, in November 1897, Gus, who for some time had wanted to return to Europe, where he had begun his career, left New York for Paris. He remained there for three years. Some time before Gus went abroad, though, another collaborative endeavor brought the two artists back to Trinity Church in Boston, on which they had first worked many years before under Richardson. Following the death of the Reverend Phillips Brooks in 1893, a fund was raised from the congregation of Trinity Church for a monument commemorating the former minister and Episcopal bishop. The commission was awarded to Saint-Gaudens, who invited White to work with him.

White struggled over the Brooks Monument, rejecting in May 1894 as unsuitable anything Gothic or Romanesque in style for the architectural elements, since he did not feel comfortable with either of those modes, despite the fact that Trinity was generally Romanesque in style. Only a classic-like design or an early Christian style, assimilated with Renaissance elements, White maintained, would be appropriate. Two years later, after Gus had sketched figures for the monument, Stan was still uncertain as to how to proceed. Although he had come to favor a linteled or canopied setting, he suggested that Gus should make the final decision among different drawings sent to him. Stan feared that Gus actually preferred a reredos (altar screen) setting with the figures in relief, which he himself did not want, and he suggested to Gus that if they could not come to an agreement on the work in a way that satisfied the sculptor, he was willing to have his name "disconnected from the monument." By the time this project was advancing, their excellent working relationship of earlier years had eroded considerably. White reported that Saint-Gaudens at times expressed annoyance at having a " 'bête noire' of an architect to interfere" with him. Perhaps it was White's need to be at the center of any project he was engaged on that weakened their collaboration; however, the tension did not extend to their social life, and they remained close friends.[13]

Saint-Gaudens delayed moving ahead with the Brooks commission for years, possibly reluctant to bring the artistic disagreement with Stan to a head. A model that he finally completed in 1902 was destroyed in a fire at his studio in 1904, and when he started to work on the Brooks again he insisted, though then quite ill, on doing all the modeling with his own hands. Only with the figures once more finished did Stan go back to his work on the setting. The Brooks Monument was not completed until 1910, years after the deaths of its two creators. In the monument as erected, the fiery clergyman is portrayed with his right hand raised in a gesture of blessing, his left arm grasping a Bible on a lectern. A veiled figure of Christ stands behind and to the left of the minister and touches Brooks's left shoulder. Behind and above is a large cross. The figures are set on a high inscribed base, from which rises a large semicircular colonnade roofed by a half-dome canopy, the setting White had favored many years earlier. Stan had had his way on the architectural setting, and, as with the Cooper, the highly elaborated setting jars with and almost overwhelms the statuary. White had clearly demonstrated that his contribution was equally important to that of the sculptor but, it would seem, to the artistic detriment of the work.[14]

At the turn of the century White became involved with a large-scale plan for a memorial for the city of Detroit. In conjunction with the forthcoming observance of the Detroit bicentennial, several prominent residents in 1899 decided that a commemorative architectural embellishment would be appropriate for the city. Stanford's close friend and sometimes drinking companion, Charles Lang Freer, a Detroit industrialist and art collector, was influential in having White invited to design the memorial, suggesting artistic collaboration with Saint-Gaudens, Frederick MacMonnies, and the painters Thomas Dewing and Dwight Tryon. Freer and the mayor of Detroit came to New York to urge the architect to submit a plan as soon as possible. After White subsequently visited Detroit and looked over possible sites, the committee settled on a location in Island Park on Belle Isle in the Detroit River, a place the members felt symbolized the trade routes to the west. A limit of a million dollars was set for the imposing project.

For a time, Stan worked day and night to get drawings ready, and in late February 1900 he returned to Detroit with his proposal. For the scheme, he grandiosely planned a huge, 220-foot Doric column supporting a tripod to be used as a torchlight and surrounded by sculptural groups and a colonnade centered by a statue of the explorer Cadillac, who had founded the city in 1701. The drawings were displayed in the Detroit Art Museum, where the architect was invited to explain his project to a large audience. White hated speaking in public, and this talk was, as always, a trial for him. He was embarrassed, too, by the tremendously enthusiastic reception accorded to him, especially his introduction by the mayor, who praised him as the equal of Michelangelo and lauded him as the noted architect of New York's Dewey Arch—which he had not designed. Back home in New York, Stan wrote to Gus in Paris, finally informing him about the project and suggesting that it would certainly appeal to him and that it was "a great thing for an American city to put through such a design—so entirely artistic and uncommercial." Stan expressed doubts, however, as to whether the money could be raised by popular subscription. Indeed, five months later the project was abandoned because of lack of public interest and funding. Stan was paid for his work, but he was disappointed that such "a glorious opportunity" for a civic memorial had been lost.[15]

Besides the larger civic pieces, Stan and Gus collaborated on lesser projects, mostly memorials for cemeteries, often done for friends, and sometimes without a fee. Some of the cemetery commissions were substantial mausoleums, similar to countless others being erected for well-to-do Americans. Others were merely decorated gravestones, frequently with classical motifs and usually handsomely lettered. Altogether Gus and Stan collaborated on more than thirty commissions. Louis Saint-Gaudens assisted his brother and White on some of them.

White's other principal collaborator on monuments and memorials, Frederick William MacMonnies, was the son of a wealthy New York grain merchant who had lost his fortune in the Civil War. "Willie" MacMonnies had begun to train for his career by serving informally as an apprentice to Saint-Gaudens. He had first visited Saint-Gaudens's New York studio in 1881 as a sixteen-year-old, while the Farragut Monument was being completed. Soon after, the sculptor hired him to run errands, keep the studio clean, and do secretarial chores. The young man quickly demonstrated such a remarkable artistic talent that he was hired by Gus as an apprentice-assistant. White first came to know him as Gus's pupil. Willie enrolled in classes at the Cooper Union and studied his craft at the National Academy of Design and the Art Students League, while continuing for about three years in Saint-Gaudens's employ. In 1884 McKim assisted MacMonnies financially so that the young sculptor could go to Europe. In Paris he was successful in gaining admission to the Ecole des Beaux-Arts. Returning to New York a few years later, MacMonnies (who with reddish hair and a prominent nose came to resemble Saint-Gaudens physically) worked again briefly for the older sculptor, but he shortly struck out on his own.[16]

Stan and Willie hit it off well, and White helped the immensely talented young sculptor, more than ten years his junior, establish an independent career. In 1887 Stan invited MacMonnies to assist him in his renovations of the chancel of the Church of St. Paul the Apostle on Columbus Avenue and West Sixtieth Street in New York, providing kneeling angels for the altar. Soon after that White got him a commission for a statuary fountain for Edward D. Adams at Seabright, New Jersey, and subsequently Stan was responsible for a fountain commission from Joseph Choate for his country house near Stockbridge, Massachusetts. Stanford probably found working with a younger man, not yet set in his ways and or at the top of his field, more pleasant than his collaboration with Saint-Gaudens. With MacMonnies, he would be the senior partner, with the more influential voice in collaborative endeavors. Moreover, commissions were not so likely to drag on and on, as was the case with the overworked, perfectionist Saint-Gaudens. White and MacMonnies became close friends, and Stan included the young man in his evenings on the town.

In 1889 MacMonnies received a Sons of the American Revolution commission for a statue honoring Nathan Hale for New York's City Hall Park, and White designed an elegant cylindrical granite base for the statue. In White's view, MacMonnies's Hale figure was "a striking, lifelike and ideal representation of the man, and a work of art in every sense," a statue that would "hold its own in fearlessness of conception and artistic character with any portrait-statue of modern times."[17]

The following year White entered a competition for a monument at the United States Military Academy to commemorate the men and officers of the regular army who were killed in battle or died of wounds in the Civil War. The project had originally been instituted in 1863, in the midst of the war, but had been abandoned; subscriptions to a fund for the memorial had nevertheless mounted up, reaching some $63,000. For the 1890 competition, a committee consisting of Richard Morris Hunt, Saint-Gaudens, and Arthur Rotch of Boston, appointed to judge the entries, chose White's proposal. Stan, it turned out, was embarrassed about his hastily designed entry. In a letter to Gus, he apologized for the drawings, which, he felt, "looked like hell," but the press of work on Madison Square Garden at the time had prevented him from giving the competition enough attention. He emphasized, though, that he believed his concept of a column was "the finest thing to do for the site and purpose." He had long been "aching to do a column" and promised to "bust myself on it."[18]

For the monument, planned for a dramatic site at West Point on a cliff overlooking the Hudson River, Stan devised a monolith shaft of polished pink granite, 46 feet high and 5½ feet in diameter, surmounted by a figure of Victory, which he asked MacMonnies to prepare. A broad circular base surrounded by flights of steps supported the column; figures of eagles were placed at the base. White's first instructions about the statue to MacMonnies were vague, possibly because of the press of work he was involved with and the little attention he could give to the project. Many months after information first reached him, the sculptor in Paris was still trying to find out if the Victory figure was to stand on a ball, and if so, whether the ball would be of marble or copper. A granite sphere was decided upon. The huge monolith, said at the time to be the largest single piece of polished stone then erected, was cut and polished at Stony Creek, Connecticut, and set in place by Norcross Brothers.[19]

Battle Monument was completed in March 1894, but when Stan first saw it in place he reportedly "fell flat on the Parade Ground." MacMonnies's hammered copper Victory figure, the right foot extending back with garments blowing in the wind, was much too large, out of proportion to the column, and immodest in pose. Stan was blunt: "It was the most awful looking thing I ever saw." Like the first Diana on Madison Square Garden, the Victory had to be replaced. The architect had failed to provide full and clear instructions as to what he wanted for the monument. White promised that his firm would pay all expenses for a smaller and more modest statue and for its installation. He asked Willie to keep the replacement figure "severe and architectural" and to have both feet placed on the sphere; drapery for the smaller figure was to be more modestly arranged. By late 1896 the new figure, known as Fame, was in place, and the names of the Civil War casualties had been carved. The impressive Battle Monument was dedicated on May 31, 1897. The superintendent of the Military Academy was unreserved in his praise: "Artistically it represents the genius of architects and a sculptor who have no living superiors."[20]

By this time MacMonnies was married and had decided to make his permanent home in Paris, where he found living and working much more pleasant than in the United States. The young sculptor soon became a man-about-town in Paris, and on his visits to Paris Stan always saw a great deal of him. The two of them enjoyed "gorgeous sprees" together. From his Paris studio, Willie collaborated with Stan on the Washington Memorial Arch and on the Bowery Savings Bank, for which he created figures for the pediments. In both projects, White was the client commissioning his younger artist collaborator to do the work. MacMonnies's large Columbian Fountain for the Chicago fair in 1893, a commission he owed to his former teacher, Gus, was conspicuously sited in the basin in the Court of Honor and brought him considerable public attention. In time, however, Saint-Gaudens became openly critical of his former pupil, not disguising his envy of the attention and commissions the young man was getting.[21]

Stan was instrumental in obtaining MacMonnies the commissions for several projects in Prospect Park, Brooklyn. For the entrance to the park at Grand Army Plaza, the sculptor in Paris, working with the architect in New York, created a large bronze Quadriga piece consisting of a central female figure carrying a banner and a sword, four horses, and two winged-victory figures, which was placed atop the monumental Soldiers' and Sailors' Memorial Arch by John H. Duncan, and on the south pedestals two groups representing the Navy and the Army. As originally conceived, MacMonnies's figures seemed far too large to White, who had to suggest diplomatically to his partner that they be scaled down, once again repeating the experience of the first Diana and the

West Point Victory. White designed bases for the pedestal pieces as well as four 50-foot Doric columns, topped by eagles by MacMonnies to frame the arch, along with railings, lamp standards, urns, and two small Tuscan-columned temples. Much of this elaborate composition was erected in 1895. At the southern Park Circle entrance to Prospect Park, MacMonnies's Horse Tamers were completed in 1899 on pedestals designed by White, and the two men also collaborated on several smaller projects for Prospect Park. There also White's Maryland Society Battle Monument, a slender polished granite Corinthian column set on a high base surmounted by a marble globe, commemorating Maryland Revolutionary War soldiers who participated in the Battle of Long Island, was completed in 1895. Close by, McKim's huge Brooklyn Museum was being built at the same time as many of the Prospect Park decorative structures and monuments with which White was involved.[22]

Stan took delight in Willie's skill as a sculptor and encouraged him in his work. "You are," he once wrote, "a radiating genius if there ever was one." For the interior courtyard of the Boston Public Library, the free-spirited, fun-loving MacMonnies created a small dancing bacchante for McKim. The outcry in Boston over the unclothed figure, however, was so intense that McKim decided to remove it. After consulting with Stan, Gus, and others, he presented it to the Metropolitan Museum of Art. "Removed from Puritan surroundings to the metropolis, where she belongs," McKim wrote MacMonnies in Paris, "I think we may regard the question of her virtue as settled for all time." Willie prepared two small copies of the bacchante for Stan, one of them a present for Bessie.[23]

The gift of the statuettes was emblematic of the congenial artistic collaboration that had developed between Stan and Willie. Earlier, Stan's close professional working relationship with Saint-Gaudens in the 1880s and early 1890s was reflected in the remarkable integration of architectural and statuary elements in their projects. In his late twenties and his thirties, Stan was willing to take second place as architectural collaborator to the older, talented sculptor. Although the two men remained friends and social companions, Stan by his forties became more assertive about what he wanted in architectural settings, less willing to subordinate his ideas to those of the sculptor, as was evident in the Cooper and the Brooks projects. The results were less harmonious and less felicitous than the earlier works. But Stan's high esteem for Gus's genius as a sculptor never wavered; when asked his views about American sculptors, Stan still considered Gus "altogether the greatest artist living, and one whose work will last forever." By the mid-1890s, though, Stan seemed to find working with MacMonnies, several years his junior, far more to his liking. Their collaborations, mostly secured as commissions by White, generally went smoothly; moreover, the younger sculptor did not drag things out as Gus was doing. In most of the collaborations with MacMonnies, as in Battle Monument and the Washington Arch, the architectural elements dominated the sculpture, something White had come to favor.[24]

These several monuments and memorials, many in the mid-1890s, were but a small part of White's full body of work in the end-of-century years. His commissions were numerous and varied. A large new office, conveniently located, facilitated the operations of the firm and White's own professional endeavors.

14

160 Fifth Avenue

❧

B y early May of 1894, McKim, Mead & White was installed in spacious new offices. Here White would orchestrate the elements of his art for a dozen years. The old office at 57 Broadway, rather removed from the centers of commercial and construction activity in the city, had for years been inconvenient for many clients. The steady northward march of residential and commercial development on the island of Manhattan had left the firm stranded in an alien neighborhood, one largely devoted to finance and international trade. The lower Broadway building, moreover, was small, and the top-floor space inadequate for the needs of the firm. In May 1891 McKim, Mead & White moved some 3 miles northward and took over the top floor of the former Herter family mansion at 1 West Twentieth Street, on the northwest corner of Fifth Avenue. The firm's tenancy there lasted just three years, for the owners of the building decided to replace it with a substantial commercial structure and gave notice that the premises had to be vacated by May 1, 1894. The architects moved just around the block to the large Mohawk Building at 160 Fifth Avenue, at the southwest corner of the Twenty-first Street intersection. Here the firm leased the entire fifth floor and sublet a small space to Norcross Brothers, the building contractors, who worked closely with the architects. In the office space at 160 Fifth Avenue, White and his partners established a new working home, well fitted for the design of the many substantial and truly grand projects with which they were involved.[1]

The Mohawk Building provided larger and more comfortable quarters than the intimate rooms at 57 Broadway, where the partners had worked so closely together on the firm's projects. Visitors entered a small outer office where deliverymen with packages, contractors bringing blueprints, salesmen with catalogues, and clients seeking advice were asked to wait. Near the entry, George F. Martin, the firm's bookkeeper and paymaster, had a caged-off area where he worked standing up at an old-fashioned desk. An office boy took in letters of introduction, and selected visitors were then ushered into the large, dignified reception room overlooking Fifth Avenue. Antique French and English furniture filled the room, and drawings and photographs of the firm's work decorated the walls. After a time the client or business associate might be escorted to the private office of one of the partners. The formalities of reception reflected the status and prestige of the firm, which had become the largest architectural firm in the country, and, indeed, in the world.[2]

The drafting room occupied most of the floor and had six windowed alcoves along one side for senior draftsmen. Some 75 or 80 junior draftsmen might be accommodated in the open area, though the room was so poorly ventilated that some complained it was "unhealthy" and lessened their working efficiency. Scattered about the drafting room were many large, well-bound volumes of architectural history, which, an English visitor noted, were "in daily use by the men." In one corner of the drafting room, an area was partitioned off for the specifications man, who customarily put up drawings for a particular project on linen roller shades and used opera glasses to study them while organizing and dictating the specifications. Roof space on the building was in later years leased for a shed, where blueprints were made, photographs were developed, and building models were occasionally constructed. A short time after the move, McKim wrote to "Dummy," who was in Europe and had not yet seen the space, that the office was "not quite so light as the old one but is better arranged and everyone seems to like it."[3]

In his private room, the tall, red-haired White, with his drooping mustache, worked standing up and leaning over a chest-high, 8-foot-long counter; he took care of correspondence by scrawling a few words of response on letters and notes to his secretaries to indicate what he wanted done. At the window he had a mirror set at an angle so that he could tell if a cab he ordered had arrived or observe who was on the way up to the office. After the turn of the century, he increasingly made use of the telephone for business, though the instrument was often unreliable and gave him considerable annoyance. Time and again he fired off a vigorous letter of complaint to the general manager of the New York Telephone Company about the service. April 13, 1901: "I cannot but look at the telephone as a matter of exasperation instead of use as far as this morning's work is concerned," having been "cut off *seven times* this morning talking." To lessen the noise for others when he was on the phone and to gain the privacy he wanted for his social calls, he had a cork-lined telephone booth installed in 1904 in his private office. Once when the telephone did not perform to his satisfaction, in a burst of temper he ripped out the wires and kicked out the side of the booth.[4]

Everyone in the office commented on his incessant loudness, which, of course, called attention to him. His voice was naturally strong and carried well and, excitable as he frequently was, it was often raised. So persistently did he whoop and holler in the office that for a time he was nicknamed "the Indian" by the staff. White's international telex code was "Giddydoll."[5]

Because Stanford realized his partners might be bothered by the noise he made, he asked McKim, who had the somewhat secluded corner room, to exchange private offices with him. All Charley wanted in a room, he wrote in a note to Stan, was "a place where I could be quiet." A switch was made, and McKim was satisfied with White's former office.[6]

Like his first room, Stanford's new office soon became a jumbled mess and a minor irritant to his fastidious partners. In an attempt to dig out of the chaos of his room, Stan arranged a series of baskets labeled for business letters, memoranda, estimates, and personal letters that "needed immediate attention" and those that "could await consideration." But such attempts to bring order never really seemed to help much. Letters and memoranda were continually disappearing, only to reappear later on. He cautioned art and antiques dealers to stop sending things for him to the office: "It makes my partners very angry to have it turned into a sort of bric-a-brac or furniture shop." At one point Stan jokingly related that Mead had "threatened, unless I put my room in order, to reorganize the firm." Whatever annoyance Stan's noisy and disordered ways might cause his partners was readily forgiven, however, for they were genuinely fond of him and aware of how important he was to the firm. He was still the "baby" among the partners, pampered and indulged.[7]

White employed personal secretaries to assist him with his correspondence and to work with him in the office. While the firm was about to leave 57 Broadway, he asked Goldwin Goldsmith, then a youth of eighteen and already employed as a general office boy for the firm, to serve as his private stenographer. At first Goldsmith was not sure he could satisfy the junior partner, whom he realized was extremely excitable and demanding, but White assured the young man he could do the work, because, Stan said, he did not seem afraid of him as other office help were. In his hyperactive way, White usually dictated letters while walking about, and it was not always easy to get down everything he said. Nevertheless, the two got along well, and Goldsmith was entrusted with signing White's signature and sending out letters he had typed without Stan's review of the final version. Other stenographers came and went, most lasting only a brief time.[8]

By the turn of the century, White employed two private secretaries, Charles Harnett and George E. Rarig, both red-haired, who were privy to their employer's business and to some of his private affairs. Rarig, who did most of the correspondence, was able to decipher White's scrawls on the backs of envelopes and other scraps of paper and to turn them into coherent and literate directives or letters. Harnett, a taciturn, subservient man and something of a mystery figure about the office, where, behind his back, he was called "Red Dog," mostly ran errands for White, picking up theater and opera tickets, tipping doormen at music halls, delivering bunches of violets to woman friends of his employer, taking care of telegrams, arranging for loans and handouts to impecunious artists, and even supplying the architect with pocket money from the bookkeeper. Harnett, it was said, knew more about White's private life than anyone else but was always loyally discreet. He resigned in 1904 and was replaced by Harry Lynke, who was also privy to some of his employer's affairs.[9]

Even with a large staff, organization in the McKim, Mead & White office at times seemed haphazard and chaotic. Mead reportedly once said, "We never had any system and haven't now." Some people who knew the office were astonished at the amount and the quality of work turned out under such conditions. For many years, as at 57 Broadway, Mead continued to supervise the office. He was highly respected and well liked. "He had the faculty of getting the best out of all who worked for him," one architect wrote, and "they did their best for him because they liked him and because he was fair and square." In this man's view, "the somewhat erratic brilliance of White and the sensitive genius of McKim needed the steady going common sense and sympathetic nature of Mead to knit the organization together and make a success of it." White obviously respected the older Mead, who on occasion very firmly laid down the law to him as to what might or might not be done. When on one occasion Stanny proposed that the firm set up its own studio and employ its own architectural modelers, Mead responded in a peremptory way that he "seriously opposed" the scheme and concluded: "See me about this." The idea was not implemented.[10]

By the 1890s, the partners were working less closely together than earlier; each took on different projects and used the services of particular draftsmen who regularly worked for them. Senior draftsmen were put in charge of the jobs, overseeing the work of younger men; the teamwork engendered a sense of communal endeavor and pride in seeing specific structures through to completion. With the largest number of projects by far, a great many of them commissioned by friends, White had the most assistants, and with McKim's uncertain health, he generally carried the largest share of the firm's load. He had his personal workplace at the end of the main drafting room. When he dashed there—he dashed everywhere—he had the habit of sliding the last few feet so that he polished up that strip of floor, making it like glass. One day, while sliding near his table, he ran a large sliver into his foot and as a consequence was forced to pad about in bedroom slippers for several days.[11]

The partners obviously respected one another's abilities and particular work styles, and by the 1890s they customarily kept their distance from each other's work. Only rarely did one partner look over a project another was working on and then would offer criticism only if asked and "in a rather detached way as if he had come in from another office to take a look." McKim, sometimes indecisive, often depressed by his family tragedies, and frequently in poor health, sometimes needed strong encouragement from the others. Soon after his preliminary Boston Public Library studies were completed and accepted but had received some criticism in the press, McKim grew uncertain about the work and contemplated going off to Paris to consider changes. Mead vigorously opposed his leaving, urged him to get started with the design he had made, and encouraged him to take advantage of his strong position. McKim did remain to go ahead with the library.

If the partners disagreed on a matter, it was usually resolved by leaving the decision to the partner most concerned. McKim was particularly accommodating to the others. When White devised a cost estimate for an apartment house considerably below the sum Charley had figured, McKim wrote the client that he and his partner were "in accord about this as in all things." Since White's scheme was less costly in the estimate, McKim "deemed it wiser in every way to ask him to proceed with it. . . . I advise you strongly to be guided by him, knowing as I do his ability to carry out anything which he undertakes." White, it should be pointed out, not infrequently underestimated project costs, a situation resulting in clients' exasperation and complaints.[12]

In the office Stan was "an engine for energy," seemingly never tired, never indifferent to any matter, always moving about and getting involved in one thing after another, traits he had exhibited so excessively in preparing the city decorations for the 1892 Columbian celebrations that his health had been affected. He was frequently critical of, often irritating to, and usually stimulating for those working on projects with him. Many found it exhausting just to be around him. The early morning in the office was relatively quiet, for White seldom came to work until after nine o'clock, and there was a respite in the early afternoon, when he customarily went across the street to the Union Club for a leisurely luncheon. But he seldom left the office until after seven in the evening, and he often returned later, sometimes slipping away from the theater or the opera in full evening dress to work on a new project and sweep up any late-working draftsman into helping him do just what *he* wanted done. Sometimes draftsmen coming to the office in the morning would discover sheets of tracing paper covered with small sketches scattered over a drawing board, one or more of them circled, indicating an idea that White wanted developed. In his later years in the office, Stanford was so busy initiating ideas for and overseeing his many ongoing commissions that he did not make finished drawings himself, although he closely supervised the men working on his projects. Close attention to detail and a sometimes maddening quest for perfection even in the smallest matters were by and large characteristic of his work.[13]

Newcomers to the office staff were terrified of White, unaware of the kindness beneath his explosively intense exterior. "He was very kind, but very exacting," one architect wrote. "Everybody was scared pink when he was around." Often Stan would charge up to a draftsman at work on one of his buildings, loudly demand, "What in God's name is that?" and pronounce what the man was working on "the goddamdest lookin' thing" he had ever seen. Then he would grab a pencil and tracing paper and make a dozen or more sketches of a detail and order the draftsman to work up two or three of them. Usually the poor fellow would have a hard time making out just what was wanted. Frequently, when inspecting someone's work, White twisted his mustache with his fingers, and hairs would fall down on the paper, or he would chew a pencil and spit out splinters. One draftsman, after White had moved away from his table, always used his T-square with an exaggerated fastidiousness to poke away the coarse red mustache hairs that had fallen on his work.[14]

Unlike McKim, Stan was often insensitive to his subordinates' feelings. He seldom complimented draftsmen on their work. Sometimes he was bitingly sarcastic about what they were doing. He demanded the best from those working under him, and when he did not get their best he reprimanded them severely. When Austin W. Lord was working as head draftsman for McKim, Mead & White, he once was unable to satisfy Stanford's countless preemptory demands after long hours of evening toil. He finally told White wearily: "I can't stand it any longer. I am going to leave for good." Stan "gazed at Lord as if stupefied. There was a tense moment, and then White threw his arms around the worn-out draftsman, giving him a hug as he ejaculated—'Goddamit! Don't you know I can't help it!' " Especially when absorbed in his work, White at times seemed childlike, unable to control his behavior and accommodate himself to those about him, but aware that like a brilliant child he would in the end be forgiven.[15]

White was frequently asked how young men might best prepare themselves for an architectural career. Quite aware that he had never had formal, systematic training, he unfailingly suggested a year or more of professional schooling in this country. He especially recommended the course at Columbia College or, alternatively, those at the Massachusetts Institute of Technology or the University of Pennsylvania, followed by study in Paris at the Ecole des Beaux-Arts, "by far the best school in the world." Above all, young men should work on draftsmanship, "because it is in this way only that ideas can be expressed," and should give as much time as possible "to the study of free hand and mechanical drawing." Curiously, he also suggested, despite his interests and influence in such matters, that the study of styles and historical courses "don't amount to much in the end," though it could stimulate interest in building design and usually appealed to young men. Apprenticeship under professionals, such as he had had, could be useful, but formal systematic training, he believed, was absolutely essential for proper preparation. Perhaps at some deep level, White felt a certain inadequacy in his art because of the unsystematic, though practical, training he had had, which may have led to the demands he made upon himself and his highly critical approach to work in the office.[16]

Countless young men interested in an architectural career beseiged the office, begging for employment. The office at 160 Fifth Avenue was widely acknowledged—White's views on the need for formal schooling notwithstanding—to be "the best native training ground for American architects." Regularly, young men who had little or no serious study or experience in the field were taken on as office boys, tracers, or beginning draftsmen. They were allowed to help out, but usually with no salary. After six months or so, a newcomer who had proved himself capable might be put on the payroll. Salaries in any case were rather low, ten to twenty dollars a week, since the firm could easily attract help. For some the experience of working in the prestigious McKim, Mead &

White office compensated for the low pay and the long hours. But not perpetually: Lionel Moses, one of White's senior assistants, once applied to Mead for a raise to twenty-five dollars a week on the grounds that he had been employed by the firm for nearly eleven years and had been at his present salary for four. Mead referred the decision to White, who, loyal to his principal associates, probably supported the raise, though the evidence is inconclusive.[17]

Friends often asked Stan to take on someone who appeared to be clever at drawing or interested in an architectural career. He hated to say no to personal requests of this kind (and many other kinds as well), so some men came into the office, quickly demonstrated their incompetence, and had to be let go. The turnover of the work force was constant. A German whom White hired claimed that he needed an advance to get his drafting instruments out of a pawnshop before he could begin work, and White handed him ten dollars against his salary. That was the last he saw of the man. White considered himself fortunate to be rid of him. Time and again Stanford did what he could to help men who had once been in the office find other jobs. When a woman applied for a position, something almost unheard of in the young profession, Mead laid down the law: "We don't employ lady draughtsmen!" At least two women were on the office roll as stenographers late in the century.[18]

The office at 160 Fifth Avenue was an immensely stimulating place. An Italian, grateful to White for having been privileged to work there a short time, no doubt expressed what many others felt: "Even four months in an office like yours is a revelation to any one who loves art." Especially among the draftsmen there was great camaraderie and evident pride of craftsmanship. Like architectural students preparing drawings for a deadline, they helped each other out when time was pressing and called upon the specialized talents of fellow workers. The draftsmen were considered the elite group in the office. It was felt that at times they looked down on the specification writers and the constructionists who devised the heating and plumbing systems and determined what masonry and steel were needed for a building. But almost everyone who could tell of a past experience in the office recalled that all in all the atmosphere there was congenial—a "happy family," one architect commented.[19]

Occasionally there were office revelries. When the firm was still on West Twentieth Street and won the competition for the Rhode Island state capitol, the office staff decided a celebration was in order. Costumes were pieced together out of detail paper, and a procession was formed.

Frank Hoppin, covered by pontifical robes, wearing a mitre, and holding a T-square high, headed the parade. Similarly garbed acolytes followed. John Howells, Mead's nephew, marched along swinging an old Venetian lamp as if perfuming the air with incense, and Henry Bacon carried a cardboard silhouette of the capitol façade with the inscription ''We have tempted Providence; we have fared Capitolly.'' Others joined the march around the office, all vigorously singing a hymn of celebration:

Onward, all ye Draughtsmen,
　Marching as to War,
With our office T-square
　Going on before.
We are not divided,
　All our office, We,
In all competitions
　Ours the victory. . . .
Foes may struggle vainly,
　We will vanquish all,
For they are not in it,
　They will have to crawl.
Providence is with us
　Thro' the darkest night;
In our blest profession
　We're simply out of sight.[20]

A baseball game at the Polo Grounds on a Thursday afternoon in early October 1894 pitted the firm ''against all comers.'' McKim, who had starred in baseball at Harvard College, pitched for the team; Mead was catcher, and White played shortstop. They lost the game, six to three, because, Stan suggested, the other side brought in a professional pitcher and catcher and put them at a decided disadvantage. But ''the whole gang was up yelling and rooting and we had a hell of a time generally,'' Stan reported. It may have been this same game that a draftsman in the office described with a somewhat different ending. McKim, he related, was still a star player: He caught a fly ball and knocked a home run. White put on quite a show at shortstop, in his white flannel knickbockers, with a huge catcher's mitt on his left hand and a fancy glove on his right. When a sharp hit came his way, he stuck out his foot and stopped the ball, ''but it nearly took his foot off. The shout he gave could have been heard in Brooklyn. He hobbled to the sidelines, threw his mitt at [Lionel] Moses with considerable profanity, and went home in a cab.''[21]

Such recreational outings were rare, however, for an office force that was expected to be committed to long hours of hard work and that produced a larger body of projects than any other late-nineteenth- or early-twentieth-century American architectural firm. From 1879 to 1910 McKim, Mead & White undertook more than seven hundred commissions. The office victory celebration after the Rhode Island State House competition was also a rarity. The firm generally avoided competitions.

Before participating in a competition, the architects had to be satisfied that protection of the entrants' designs was guaranteed. For the Rhode Island State House, Stan felt the terms of entry were fully acceptable: four competitors were invited to submit designs, each was paid $1,000 for the work, the winner would receive the commission, and those who were unsuccessful had their drawings returned. The appointment of the highly respected Richard Morris Hunt as a paid judge was, in effect, a guarantee of a fair and just competition. Only if a competition were "limited and paid," with a professional expert as judge and a provision that the drawings of unsuccessful entrants would be returned and not used in any way would McKim, Mead & White become involved. The adaptation of unsuccessful competition drawings for use by a client was not uncommon before professional standards were generally accepted.[22]

Even more than the other partners, McKim disliked competitions. On at least one occasion when the firm entered a competition he ignored the terms and refused to follow the program. When the firm competed for the large New York Public Library to be constructed on the site of the old reservoir on Fifth Avenue at Forty-second Street, McKim took charge of the work and rented space on the sixth floor of the Mohawk Building solely for developing the firm's proposal. But he found the requirements too limiting and disregarded what had been laid down. Late in 1897 the McKim, Mead & White entry lost out to Thomas Hastings's proposal, which was eventually erected. Hastings had worked for the firm and remained a close friend of the partners, especially White. No doubt Stan's congratulations to Hastings were sincere, yet, in light of the enormous expenditure of time and money in preparing the entry, he told Saint-Gaudens that he greatly regretted "the folly of having gone into such a contest," and then affirmed, "I never want to go into one again." Often when the firm was invited to enter a limited competition—as with the New York Museum of Natural History and the City College of New York—it declined. Fear of losing was probably involved in the decisions, yet possibly the partners also felt that their firm, as the most important and prestigious in the country, should not be judged as others were.[23]

The partners were always adamant that established, acceptable procedures be followed not only in competitions but in business relationships generally. Like other leading architects, led by Richard Morris Hunt, McKim, Mead & White worked to maintain high quality standards for what was still an emerging profession. They believed also that architects had to stand firm to protect their fair rights. Stan wrote to Daniel Burnham, whose large Chicago firm rivaled his own, regarding a program scheme for the Cook County Court House that deviated from the customary standards "that architects of standing accept": "I believe that the only way architects can expect to be treated with proper professional consideration is to stand up in the most unyielding way for their rights."[24]

For its professional services on projects carried to completion, McKim, Mead & White adhered to the fee scale established by the American Institute of Architects: 5 percent of the cost of all work, except that of a decorative character, on which 10 percent was charged. Of the 5 percent charge, 1 percent was allotted for preliminary studies, 2 percent for specifications and working drawings, and 2 percent for superintendence of the job. The firm also charged 5 percent on contracts for the work of experts to design and install electrical, heating, plumbing, and ventilation systems. Often a clerk of the works was employed to supervise the job, and his salary of $125 a month was additional, as were expenses the architects incurred outside the office for a job, as in travel or telegrams. Commission income for the firm was substantial, averaging $168,540 a year during the 1890s, while from profit distributions White earned an average of $28,062 annually during those years.[25]

Not only did the partners feel a responsibility to uphold standards for the architectural profession in general, but they also accepted a particular duty to provide high-quality training for the men who worked for them. As Lionel Moses wrote, the three partners "were always teaching, helping and encouraging all who were in their office" so that when they went forth to practice architecture themselves "they might uphold the standards of the profession as those standards should be upheld." A few of the most talented and loyal staff members who benefited from such training and who stayed on were eventually rewarded with shares in the firm. William T. Partridge of the staff recalled that Burt L. Fenner, Teunis Van der Bent, and William M. Kendall early in the century received a small share of the firm's profits. By 1904 Fenner was in charge of the office, taking over much of the work that Mead had formerly done. On January 1, 1906, Kendall, Fenner, and William S. Richardson, who had for some time worked closely with White, were made partners in the firm, although the shares allotted to them were small in relation to what the senior partners retained. The new partners' names soon appeared on the company stationery directly beneath those of the senior partners; Van der Bent and Daniel T. Webster were listed in a separate category below the partners. In 1909 Van der Bent also became a partner.[26]

Although the founding partners together shaped the character of the firm and contributed to its output, White had become the best known among the three men to the public at large. Many of his commercial and domestic projects of the 1890s attracted a good deal of public attention, and his name was often in the press in connection with New York social life. Despite the frequent irritations he caused his partners and working associates, he managed to create a remarkable and enormous body of work. His dynamic talent and brilliance were such that many young architects clamored to work with him and countless clients sought him out.

15

"The Finest and Most Harmonious Effect"

From the midtown McKim, Mead & White offices—first in the Herter mansion and then in the Mohawk Building—a torrent of designs poured forth in the 1890s. Work continued on several important commissions begun earlier, including the Tower and the Roof Garden of Madison Square Garden, the Metropolitan Club, and the Washington Memorial Arch, which moved toward completion. Many new projects on the drawing boards were just as striking as those and became some of the best known of the firm's works. Although the largest undertakings of the decade were directed by McKim, White was the partner who directed the greatest number of projects and carried the heaviest load of design work and supervision. In the spring of 1894, for instance, Stan had charge of about sixty separate projects, on which he and his assistants were working at one stage or another or were about to begin.[1]

As an experienced architect and a leading figure in his profession, White by his forties had firm ideas about his craft and about what he wanted to accomplish. In some of the new projects, controversies with his clients were provoked by his very grand and even grandiose ideas. As might be expected, White was more successful in getting his way when dealing with well-to-do private clients, whom he knew personally, than on institutional projects, where the work was commissioned by budget-restricted building committees.

For White, during the last decade of the nineteenth century the formally balanced classical tradition, derived from the public buildings of Greece and Rome, with the more ornamented Italian Renaissance derivatives, became ever more important. The classical tradition, which the planners

211

of the 1893 Chicago fair promoted in the design of the great "White City" on the shores of Lake Michigan, was, White believed, the most appropriate architectural mode for the United States on the eve of the twentieth century. As the United States grew in wealth and national strength and became with the Spanish–American War a world imperial power, adaptations of traditional modes of the grand and imposing Roman imperial design seemed to him particularly fitting for multibuilding institutional purposes. Just as White's personal vision was customarily grand, neoclassical traditions could provide a grandness of design for the country at large. Employing the classical-Renaissance mode for public and commercial structures could, as well, help bring a unity and harmony among buildings, turning away from what was all too often a discordant, clashing eclecticism. McKim, who had suggested the overall architectural design style for the Chicago fair and who worked afterward to implement the spread of neoclassicism through his work and through his founding of what became the American Academy in Rome, fully shared that vision.

Two early 1890s New York City commercial structures strikingly demonstrated White's continuing use of the traditional vocabulary: the Renaissance-derived *New York Herald* headquarters and plant and the neoclassical Bowery Savings Bank were important and widely noticed buildings.

James Gordon Bennett, owner of the *Herald,* which he had inherited along with $7 million at his father's death, had long admired White's artistic talent. At the beginning of Stan's association with Mead and McKim, he had contributed importantly to Bennett's Newport Casino, adding elegant decorative touches to what became the social center of the seaside resort. Bennett was greatly impressed by White's work there and soon employed him to design the interior décor for his 227-foot seagoing yacht, *Namouna,* said at that time to be "the largest private yacht afloat." The great ship was described as "fairylike in form, Oriental in the splendor of her decorations, and cozy and comfortable as an old English home in the plan of her appointments." Some years later White was employed to work on the cabin interiors for Bennett's new yacht, the *Lysistrata.*[2]

Bennett, however, spent little time in the United States. A scandalous incident that occurred in New York a few years before the Newport Casino commission, on New Year's Day in 1877, had made him a social pariah. At a party to celebrate his engagement Bennett, responding to a call of nature, had relieved himself in the fireplace (some accounts say it was behind the parlor door or in the open grand piano). His fiancée's brother proceeded to whip him and a duel followed. Bennett was then excluded from New York society. The newspaper owner for the most part turned his back on America and made his home in Paris. Whether in Europe, at sea on his yacht, or on short visits to the United States, Bennett nonetheless kept in close touch with the *Herald* editors and continued to control the policies and general content of the newspaper.

By the beginning of the 1890s Bennett was contemplating a change of home for his newspaper. The old building on Newspaper Row across from City Hall had become increasingly cramped and unsatisfactory. Bennett unexpectedly decided to remove his newspaper headquarters and plant from the lower Manhattan site to a new location uptown. He settled upon the former Seventy-first Regiment Armory, located between Thirty-fifth and Thirty-sixth streets and between Broadway and Sixth Avenue. Bennett planned to remodel the armory, which could be leased for thirty years, putting in large plate glass windows at street level so that passers-by could observe the printing of his newspaper. White was asked to work out schemes both for altering the armory and for an entirely new structure. As his work went on into the summer of 1891, Stan urged Mead, who was then in Paris, to get in touch with Bennett as soon as possible and settle the matter of the *Herald* plant. "The job," White wrote Dummy, "would fit in very nicely now in the office, everything being dull and apparently nothing ahead."[3]

Bennett eventually decided on a new building for the leased site; he suggested a replica of the Doge's Palace in Venice, which would, he believed, provide just the eye-catching headquarters he wanted. Other city newspapers had already erected striking homes, most notably the tall Florentine tower for the *New-York Tribune,* designed by Richard Morris Hunt. White and his partners were willing, though reluctant, to go ahead with a Doge's Palace design, providing, as they telegraphed Bennett, "it can be so arranged that we are relieved of professional responsibility in doing so." Since 1865 the National Academy of Design building, modeled on the Venetian structure, had stood on east Twenty-third Street, and the partners probably felt a similar structure would look imitative. Bennett shortly came around to White's suggestion of a building based on the late fifteenth-century Palazzo del Consiglio in Verona. The new site was prominent, and the Herald Building would become one of the best known of the McKim, Mead & White structures. Bennett's esteem for White at this time was evident in the *Herald*'s praise of the architect as "the one man in New York who seems to be omnipotent in matters pertaining to structural beauty."[4]

Trapezoidal in shape, with the principal entrance on the shortest side facing south to Thirty-fifth Street, the Herald Building was begun late in 1892 and mostly completed the following year. A recessed half-elliptical porch led up a few steps from the entrance to the circular white and gold counting room, from which a broad staircase rose dramatically to the second-story reception room. The first floor also housed the mail room, the delivery room, the upper part of the press room, and the stereotype room, with large windows opening to the Sixth Avenue sidewalk, exposing its operations to public view. From the Broadway side, passers-by could look down into the press room, set in the basement, and observe the show of six huge presses there turning out as many as 90,000 papers an hour. The second floor housed a telegraph room; a library; offices for editors, business managers, and the proprietor; and the large skylighted city department. Bennett's private room on the second-floor entry front had an adjacent bathroom equipped with a magnificent, costly bathtub. In the attic, under the tiled hipped roof, the composing and art departments were housed. The most up-to-date technology in printing and internal communication was utilized for the newspaper plant. This, the *Herald* reported with considerable pride, was "unquestionably the finest newspaper establishment in the world."[5]

In a city that was beginning to press skyward, with new commercial structures piled story over story, the Herald Building, with its modest height, was something of an anomaly. Comfortable in scale, harmonious in proportions, and richly ornamented, the Herald Building, in its Italian Renaissance dress, stood as an oasis of refinement in a visually chaotic commercial and entertainment neighborhood. The deeply recessed street-level arcades, extending around three sides, were carefully integrated with the arched bays and panels in the upper story, while the elaborated and boldly projecting cornice provided a satisfying upper enframement for the sides of the composition. On the entrance front, a clock face and a wind direction indicator were placed at the upper level. At the roof edge a statue of Minerva loomed above a large bell, and every hour two figures representing typesetters and popularly known as "Stuff" and "Guff" struck the bell with hammers. The most unusual and most often remarked-upon features of the exterior, however, were twenty-six bronze owls, each 4 feet high, standing at intervals along the roof edge on 3-foot pedestals. The eye sockets of the owls contained lighted electric globes, which at night winked on and off to the passers-by below, providing, it would seem, the message that owlish wisdom was being processed within and would shortly be disseminated in newspapers for the public.[6]

By August 1893, the Herald Building was ready for occupancy, and the newspaper offices and plant were moved to the new site. The *Scientific American* called the building "an object of varied and surpassing beauty

. . . a crystallized dream of art." The Cincinnati *Commercial Gazette* judged it "a palace for a molder of public opinion, an artistic relief to eyes wearied with hideous structures reared for business purposes only, an ornament to the city." To Charley McKim, always generous to his partners, the Herald Building, like the Century Association clubhouse a few years earlier, was "the high-water mark of this office in design." Bennett himself apparently had some reservations about the structure; though he came to like it, the newspaperman once complained that the Herald Building looked like "an Italian fish market."[7]

As the Herald Building was nearing completion, another of Stan's major commercial structures was beginning to rise. On March 10, 1892, the Plans and Building Committee of the Bowery Savings Bank asked five architectural firms to submit plans for their consideration. A subcommittee recommended final consideration of the McKim, Mead & White plans and those by George B. Post. After considering evaluations of the submissions by Professor William Ware of Columbia College, the committee decided on the McKim, Mead & White proposal.[8]

The neoclassical Bowery Savings Bank, a notable achievement in forceful and monumental composition, was soon acclaimed as the most sumptuous savings bank in New York City. In determining upon the design for the bank, White had sought grandeur and simplicity rather than richness of elaborated detail, although fine woods and marbles were used liberally throughout the building. The main banking room stood on the site of the former bank building on Grand and Elizabeth streets; that magnificent room was joined on the L-shaped plot by a wing that fronted on the Bowery and included the principal entrance. Great colonnaded porticos were placed on both entrance fronts. Just inside the Bowery entrance, waiting rooms for men and for women were created in what was, in effect, an anteroom to the large banking room to the rear. This immensely impressive principal room, nearly 100 feet square, was surrounded by 20 disengaged Corinthian columns, carrying a great entablature that supported an ornamental coffered ceiling, rising some 60 feet. In planning the bank, light, air, and cleanliness were emphasized, owing to the fact that, as a descriptive pamphlet had it, depositors coming from a decidedly varied population (i.e., Lower East Side immigrants) were expected to use the facilities. A partial second story included directors' and committee rooms. As with so many other McKim, Mead & White buildings, David H. King served as building contractor for the Bowery Savings Bank. Willie MacMonnies created the sculptured pediments over the front and side entrances.[9]

Another substantial commercial structure White designed in the early

1890s demonstrated his versatility and skill in adapting to unusual technological requirements. The nine-story Cable Building at the northwest corner of Houston Street and Broadway, completed in 1894, provided headquarters for the Broadway & Seventh Avenue Railroad Company as well as service as a power station for the cable line, which ran on lower Broadway. In the basement, gigantic 32-foot wheels, weighing some 100 tons each, carried the under-street cables that pulled the streetcars. Some of the upper stories were rented out as offices and manufacturing lofts. Recalling motifs of the smaller Goelet Building and of the Renaissance-style Hotel Imperial of a few years earlier, the Cable Building featured a splayed corner facing the intersection, a high base with arches, a four-story midsection shaft rising into arcades, and a rather topheavy attic. The many large mullioned windows gave a cluttered look to the street façades, in contrast to the simpler fronts of the two earlier buildings. The *New York Recorder* noted that the Cable Building stood "peculiar and alone in its artistic merit" but was nonetheless comparable to the Hotel Imperial, "another capital example of the same ornate style." White's styling and ornamentation of substantial commercial structures was being recognized as a characteristic personal touch.[10]

Despite the many projects under way, the nationwide panic and depression beginning in 1893 had considerable, though short-lived, impact on McKim, Mead & White. By the late summer of 1893, new commissions had practically dried up. As Stan wrote, "We, ourselves, are suffering from stagnation and can hardly see a new piece of work ahead of any kind." Draftsmen had to be discharged, even men who had been on the staff for years. By the close of the year, however, "the dull spell which made it necessary for [the firm] to cut [the] force down one-half" appeared to be "giving way to brighter prospects." Big projects came in for Symphony Hall in Boston and for Columbia College, both of which McKim would undertake, as well as important work for White for the University of the City of New York and at the United States Military Academy. Later in the decade several other large projects were begun, including the huge Brooklyn Museum, designed and directed by McKim.[11]

An opportunity for Stan to develop and realize his ideas for a large-scale, basically unified architectural environment came when he was commissioned to create a new home for the University of the City of New York. Since the mid-1830s the university had been housed in a Gothic Revival building on the east side of Washington Square. At the time it was built, the University Building was in a fashionable residential district. Used for offices for organizations and societies, for artists' and writers' studios, and for a secondary school, as well as for classrooms for the university students, the old building had long been a center of intellectual and artistic life in the city. By the 1890s, except for the oasis of Washington Square, the neighborhood had changed over to largely commercial and manufacturing uses.

Early in the decade officials began discussing removal of the undergraduate division of the university to another site. In 1891 Henry M. MacCracken, then vice chancellor, prepared to raise money for a new campus, and a down payment was made for a site in the Bronx, on a hill overlooking the Harlem River. In January 1892 MacCracken, now chancellor, sought out White for professional suggestions on the move, emphasizing the architect's ties to the university by way of his father's studies there and his own honorary degree in 1881.[12]

As he considered the proposal, White contemplated dismantling and then re-erecting the shell of the old Washington Square building on the Bronx site; constructing a new interior for a chapel, library, and science museum; and using it as a centerpiece for the new campus. He also suggested that a large commercial building be erected on the Washington Square site to bring in substantial rental income, with the upper stories also used for university purposes; in style, the lower stories, he proposed, should be "very plain" and the uppermost given "a certain academic exterior." In September 1892 MacCracken wrote to ask the architect if he would, in effect, donate his professional services to the university, in honor of his father; the educator attempted to flatter Stan by writing that "on every hand" people of the university had "appreciated and approved" his asking White's advice. A general plan for the new campus, re-erection of the old University Building, a new science hall, and a large commercial block for the Square were needed.[13]

Stan moved ahead on the project, generously agreeing to work without a fee, but by December 1893 it was determined that to dismantle the old University Building, transport the materials, and re-erect the shell in the Bronx would cost at least a quarter of a million dollars, which was just not available. University officials decided to erect completely new structures for the Bronx campus. The banker Charles T. Barney, a friend of Stan, was asked to join with MacCracken to oversee construction of the new campus, thus ensuring that there would be a shrewd businessman to help direct the undertaking. The Hall of Languages was the first building completed (November 1894) according to White's plans. A dormitory, museum, and science hall were built later. Most important was the library.

Stan had drawings for the library completed by January 1895, but the Library Committee members were not impressed by them. The cost projection was too high, and the grand and ornate rotunda room did not seem appropriate for library purposes. For a time, without consulting White, they considered opening a limited competition, much to White's outrage. None took place. Chancellor MacCracken also was not satisfied with White's library proposal, at least the interior, with its "barn-like rotunda," "dimly lighted" reading room, and "sham marble columns." He asked the architect for alternative plans that he could conscientiously support. Richard Morris Hunt was called in as an outside adviser to mediate the disagreement; Hunt mostly supported White's ideas. Mac-Cracken's suggestion for a much larger skylight than White had proposed for the reading room, however, was adopted, despite Stan's original opposition. The library was financed by contributions from Helen Miller Gould Shepard, the daughter of Jay Gould, the railroad financier.[14]

Meanwhile, the commercial building project for the Washington Square site was awarded to another architect, Alfred Zucker. The lower floors of the building were arranged for the American Book Company, while the law, education, and graduate school of the university occupied the upper three stories. When the university was renamed New York University in 1896, White was asked and agreed to design a seal for the institution; the device he created, based on MacCracken's suggestion, incorporated a torch, like that of the Statue of Liberty Enlightening the World, which would signify New York City, "our locality which we try to enlighten!"[15]

As the plans for the University Heights buildings evolved, Stan was insistent that the campus be treated "as a *single* plot" in order to gain "the finest and most harmonious effect." He urged Chancellor Mac-Cracken, when and if he and the Building Committee could not agree with White's ideas, to bring in outside experts to mediate, as had been done in the early work on the library. Absolutely convinced that his plans were the most suitable for the Bronx Heights campus, White in this and other projects seemed to be more loyal to his artistic vision than to the possible wishes of his client. MacCracken did raise objections here and there to elements of the campus design, but White eventually went along with the educator's suggestions, and no serious controversy developed.[16]

Stan took great pride in the library and the surrounding Hall of Fame, the crown jewels of the new architectural assemblage. Modeled in part on Jefferson's University of Virginia library in an eclectic Roman style, the dignified and monumental Gould Library was the focal point of the campus and, unlike McKim's even more monumental Columbia University Library erected at about the same time, was linked by an ambulatory to lateral structures and thus reached out, in a sense, to embrace the campus in its more rural setting. Montgomery Schuyler, an architecture critic, wrote that White's grouping of academic buildings on University Heights carried out the "collegiate connotation" far more successfully than was the case at Columbia University and brought a feeling for a specific place and a well-realized recalling of "the free and vernacular use of classic forms" of American colonial and Georgian work.[17]

The Gould Memorial Library was one of Stanford White's most important achievements. Construction began in 1897, and the structure was completed in 1899, though interior work went on until 1902. An imposing portico with six Corinthian columns dominates the façade facing the campus, while the other three fronts have limestone Corinthian pilasters set against the yellow brick walls. The body of the building is in the form of a Greek cross with an extended arm on the entrance front. At the apex of the building a drum carries a low saucer dome. Within, a long, narrow barrel-vaulted stairhall leads upward from the vestibule to a portal opening into the large circular reading room in the rotunda. Sixteen green Connemara marble columns, topped by gold-colored metallic Corinthian capitals, support a full upper-member entablature and a balcony, the back wall of which forms the drum, while the intricately coffered dome soars above. Seminar rooms and book stacks are placed on three tiers surrounding the rotunda. From the entrance vestibule, two subsidiary staircases lead downward to the basement chapel under the reading room. True to his vision of a grand neoclassical centerpiece for the university, White designed the interior decorative fixtures as well as the structure itself, attempting to make "the building a complete and whole work of art and one thoroughly homogeneous in style."[18]

Forming a semicircular colonnade around the sides and rear of the Gould Memorial Library, with lateral extensions, is White's Hall of Fame, a terrace ambulatory containing busts of famous Americans. Constructed of granite and limestone and covered by a tiled roof, the neoclassical Hall of Fame provides a promenade with spectacular views of the Harlem River nearby and of Manhattan in the distance. Together, the Hall of Fame and the Gould Library are monuments to White's mastery of classical vocabulary, skillfully adapted for contemporary uses. When a memorial was contemplated for the architect in 1919, bronze doors placed at the entrance of the library were decided upon as most appropriate.

White's work at the United States Military Academy at West Point, New York, was less complete and ultimately less satisfying than the New York University campus. Early in the 1890s, while he was finishing his work on Battle Monument at the Military Academy, Stan learned that Brevet Major General George W. Cullum, a former superintendent of the Military Academy, had just died and left a bequest of $250,000 for a Memorial Hall at West Point. Stan immediately sounded out a friend at the academy about the project: "You know that I have a fair reputation as a fisherman and although fishing in this way is a little out of my line, still a Memorial Hall, and at West Point too, is better game than the salmon, and I hope that if there is any chance, we may get a nibble at it." It took more than a year, but the fish did bite. At a meeting on September 25, 1893, the Trustees of the Memorial Hall, after a limited competition among prominent architects, selected McKim, Mead & White as architects for the building. White's personal connections helped in this case, as so often, to get him the commission.[19]

General Cullum, an 1833 graduate of the Academy, had served as superintendent toward the close of the Civil War and after, from 1864 to 1866. In his will he had stipulated "that the hall was to serve as a repository for statues, busts, portraits, and other memorials to deceased officers and graduates," as well as for flags, plaques, war trophies, paintings, and other objects "giving elevation to the military profession." Facilities were to be provided for receptions and ceremonial occasions, along with rooms for visiting officers and editorial offices for the published register of academy graduates. By June 1894 a site was chosen on the eastern side of the parade ground at the edge of the cliff overlooking the Hudson River.[20]

White undertook the design of the Cullum Memorial, but when the first set of plans was submitted to contractors for estimates on building costs and went over the money allotted, a modified design had to be worked out. After a few months, Colonel Oswald H. Ernst, superintendent of the academy, expressed irritation to McKim, Mead & White over "the interminable delays which have characterized your management of this business" and found the firm's explanations "not satisfactory, of course." For a time, while White was away from the office, Albert Ross, one of his assistants, was put in charge of the rather drawn out project. McKim considered Ross's work on the building "admirable . . . in its essential particulars." White met with the academy committee several times to discuss the plans. After some minor modifications were made, the design was finally accepted, and construction began in February 1896.[21]

As the Cullum Memorial went forward in the late 1890s, Stan gave it a good amount of his attention. He designed the memorial tablets and medallion heads for the assembly halls and arranged for their placement, and he supervised the decorating of the principal rooms by Allard

& Sons. Professor Charles W. Larned, who headed the Cullum Memorial Committee, pressed White to canvass his "millionaire friends" to get them to donate statues of prominent American military figures for the building, but Stan refused. A minor crisis arose after Stan misspelled the word "meritorious" for an interior inscription; when the error was discovered, letter support holes already drilled had to be filled in with marble dust and glue. Cullum Memorial Hall was completed in December 1898 and dedicated on June 12, 1900.[22]

Prominently located to the east of the Academy parade ground, the Cullum Memorial has a cold, austere quality about it, unlike White's work generally. The classical antecedents of the building are emphasized on the principal front by the four colossal half-engaged Ionic columns, the Greek entablature, the pediment-capped entrance, and the ornamented decorations at the roof edge. The river side of the building is more open than the principal front, with a loggia on the first-story level. Reception rooms, service rooms, and an assembly hall were placed on the first floor, and billeting for visitors on the floor below, overlooking the river. In the interior, the great assembly hall takes up the entire second floor. Along the walls of this room, the architect placed portraits, plaques, medallions, and cannon, interspersed between the giant Corinthian columns, while he had flags and banners suspended high along the sides of the room below the intricately coffered ceiling. Here was a highly impressive space for important academy convocations and social events. The building was well received.

The success of the Cullum Memorial led to yet another academy commission. On June 21, 1900, McKim, Mead & White was invited to prepare plans and working drawings for an Officers' Mess and Quarters adjacent to the Memorial. Stan moved ahead with plans for the Officers' Mess on a site immediately south of Cullum Hall; by late October the plans he had sent to an officers' board were returned with proposed changes. When the architect suggested that the authorized sum was insufficient for a suitable building and requested appropriation of additional funds, the superintendent agreed to request a small additional sum. After the Officers' Mess was completed in 1903 at a cost of $103,000, White petulantly expressed the view that it had been "finished in a very meagre way." He resented the constraints of a strictly limited budget for the project, something he did not often have to face.[23]

Meanwhile, Congress in 1902 had authorized a limited architectural competition for an overall redesign of the Military Academy. In October 1902, McKim, Mead & White was invited to participate and submit a master plan for future development. White supervised the firm's May

1903 entry, stating that it was the architects' wish to present "a treatment worthy of the historic associations and natural beauty of the site." The firm's proposal, comprehensive and unified, emphasized that the architects were rejecting the "obsolete form of Tudor Gothic which now obtains in the majority of the existing buildings." Montgomery Schuyler, the influential architectural critic, had suggested that any overall design for West Point should adopt the "Carpenter's Gothic" or the battlemented style of the older buildings on the post. White, on the contrary, proposed that the classic style alone was appropriate for the Military Academy, and he even advocated providing new exteriors for Richard Morris Hunt's gymnasium and academic building and other structures in order to harmonize with a new, overall neoclassic design. "A really great result could not be obtained without the unification in style of all the buildings facing the Campus." White in his plan projected a total, uncompromising vision that took little note of what already had been built at the academy or of practical financial considerations. As at other times in his career, he would impose his vision, unrealistically confident that his grand scheme was the best, indeed the only possible course. Privately, White suggested that if a gothic style were chosen for the academy, Cullum Hall and the Officers' Mess, his own works in neoclassical dress, should be removed. In his plan, White also proposed new houses for officers, new academic and barracks buildings, and an elegant neoclassic chapel lined up on the opposite side of the parade ground from the Cullum Memorial. A huge riding hall would be built on a site against the bluff overlooking the river, its roof forming a terrace, which in effect would extend the parade ground.[24]

When a jury met in May 1903, it spent several days considering the several drawings and descriptions. The jury finally decided on Plan "J," the entry of Cram, Goodhue & Ferguson, associated with Olmsted Brothers. The Gothic Revival style of the winning entry was aimed at harmonizing all new construction with the existing academy buildings and embodied everything that McKim, Mead & White had rejected. To White, "the cheap carpenter's Gothic patch-work" of the winners was, quite simply, "a public calamity," in effect, "a body blow to all those who are striving to raise architecture out of the heterogeneous mush" into which it had fallen. The Military Academy jury had absolutely repudiated his neoclassical vision. Fortunately, the winning architects were more open minded than White, and they kept his own buildings standing.[25]

Two major New York commercial structures in the mid-1890s did not present the constraints on White's vision that he encountered at New York University and at the Military Academy. White's entry for an enlarged headquarters building for the New York Life Insurance Company was chosen in an 1894 limited competition. Already in the late 1880s, McKim, Mead & White, under Mead's direction, had designed two large Midwestern office buildings in Omaha, Nebraska, and in Kansas City, Missouri, for the insurance company. In New York on lower Broadway in successive stages from 1896 to 1899, a long, narrow four-story office building, dating from 1870, was turned into a greatly enlarged structure in accordance with White's designs. To the rear of the original section, twelve stories were built first, harmonizing with work already begun there, and subsequently eight stories were piled above the old building. The resultant unified office building, rising into a handsome three-story arcade at the uppermost level, included well-appointed executive offices, numerous lesser offices, a large banking room, and the sumptuously decorated private Merchants' Club on the top floor. Maitland Armstrong, Stan's longtime friend, did much of the decorative work on the interior. The project went well, as the New York Life officials apparently agreed to all of White's suggestions.

Another prominent commercial structure built at the same time was Sherry's, constructed in 1896–98 for the restaurateur Louis Sherry as his New York showplace. Although the eleven-story building was erected primarily to house a large restaurant, it also included a café, a palm garden, a confectionary shop, three ballrooms, supper rooms, parlors, and a substantial number of bachelors' apartments. For a time Sherry's had a small outdoor terrace on the Fifth Avenue sidewalk, where diners could gaze diagonally across the avenue at Delmonico's, the midtown branch of the other best-known restaurant in the city.

Always the showman, White greatly enjoyed the challenge of creating a fashionable new center for the city, a showplace that would embody the elegance of décor he felt was most appropriate for the social world he was serving and of which he himself was a part. The architect placed Sherry's main restaurant on the street level at the corner and had it richly paneled in oak with a gold overlay and dark green velours on some wall surfaces. Behind the restaurant on the side street, a sumptuous entrance hall and grand staircase led to the principal ballroom on the third floor. Decorated in a Louis XIV mode, the ballroom was one of the most magnificent interior spaces in the city and became the scene of many fashionable entertainments. Small electric lights highlighted the dome and frieze of this three-story room, which was spectacularly lighted by eight huge crystal chandeliers and numerous wall sconces. White arranged for James Wall Finn to paint wall panels and the central ceiling of the ballroom. Adjacent on the west side was a large conservatory, to which ball-goers might retreat. On the exterior, the street fronts of the building had a decidedly "cut-up" look resulting from the strongly accented horizontal divisions between the floors, the banding of the colossal piers, the well-emphasized quoins (corner edge stones) and rusticated surfaces, and the large projecting cornice. Stan and Bessie on occasion patronized the restaurant and sometimes attended parties in Sherry's ballroom. For years Sherry's was a fashionable hub of New York society, its opulence symbolizing so much of the era.[26]

While the projects at New York University and at the Military Academy were moving along, another important collegiate commission materialized. White's endeavors at the University of Virginia involved the challenges of rebuilding one of the most important of early-nineteenth-century American buildings, creating new structures that fitted in with the original buildings, and devising plans for future development of the institution. Here again, as at the Military Academy and at New York University, he turned to the use of classical modes, adapting them skillfully for modern-day educational purposes.

In the middle and latter years of the nineteenth century, as the fields of learning enlarged and the student population expanded, several new academic buildings were erected at the University of Virginia, most of them built with little attention to stylistic coordination with the original buildings designed by Thomas Jefferson, the founder of the university. Created as an "academic village" in the 1820s, the original group was centered on the Rotunda, modeled on Emperor Hadrian's Pantheon in Rome. Two parallel lawn and range wings, with small classroom and lodging pavilions, were extended southward from the Rotunda on either side of a central quadrangle open at the southern end to a spectacular natural vista. The interior of the Rotunda was divided into three floors, the uppermost a reading room and below, oval classrooms on the main floor and in the basement. Each of the original buildings included architectural elements adapted from classical models, which could be used for instructional purposes. The most conspicuous addition to the university was the massive Annex joined by a colonnade to the north side of the Rotunda in the 1850s. Robert Mills, who had studied with Jefferson and had designed the Washington Monument in the nation's capital, created the five-story Annex to include lecture rooms and an exhibition hall and museum. From the time of its construction, however, the Annex had been disparaged as out of keeping with Jefferson's work. By the 1890s the inadequacy of the Rotunda as a general library was recognized, and in June 1894 the faculty recommended that a new library be built and the Rotunda turned into an alumni hall.[27]

The situation at the university was suddenly changed on the morning of October 27, 1895, when a fire, probably started by faulty electrical wiring, broke out in the Annex. Fanned by high winds, the fire quickly spread to the Rotunda, despite efforts to dynamite the colonnade and stop its movement. The Annex was destroyed, as were the wooden dome and most of the interior of the Rotunda. Later that same day, the faculty took steps to keep the university open and to begin restoration of the damaged structures. It was recognized that the fire provided an opportunity, however, not only to rebuild but also to expand and improve the university facilities in harmony with the original design. Within a few days of the fire, Mead wrote a member of the university medical school expressing the firm's interest in this project. A faculty report recommended that the unsightly Annex be removed; that the Rotunda exterior be faithfully restored, but with interior changes for book accommodation from the portico floor upward, and with a new north portico; that a new academic building with a public hall and a new physics laboratory, and engineering and law buildings be erected; and that plans for future university expansion be submitted. The faculty recommended that the Board of Visitors (Trustees) select a nationally known architect to serve as adviser on the project.[28]

McDonald Brothers and the Spooner Construction Company of Louisville, Kentucky, were first employed to remove the Annex ruins and rebuild the Rotunda, but their work was considered inept. The Board of Visitors decided to name a distinguished architect to undertake the restoration and rebuilding. Stanford White was asked to do the work. William Thornton, chairman of the faculty and a member of the building committee, had visited the architect at his office in New York in the fall of 1895, possibly even before the fire, to talk about new construction at the university. On January 18, 1896, White was officially invited to become the architect of the Rotunda reconstruction and of the new buildings. Delighted with the honor, on receipt of the letter of invitation he accepted at once by telegram.[29]

White visited Charlottesville the first week in February. A tight budget and a time limit, first set at eight months, made the construction project difficult, but even more of a challenge was the need to harmonize the new construction and rebuilding with Jefferson's original work. White plunged into the assignment with his usual energy and enthusiasm, well aware, on this occasion, of the financial constraints of the university. He offered to deduct from his fee the amount that had been contracted to pay McDonald Brothers, a generous act that made matters easier for the university.[30]

After White returned to New York from his initial visit, his friend Edward Simmons, the painter, encountered him one evening at The Players. As Simmons later wrote, the architect seemed "puzzled, confused, and silent." When the painter asked him what was the matter, White "started and came out of his mood," then explained with great deference that he had seen Jefferson's original plans for the university when he was in the South. "They're wonderful and I am scared to death. I only hope I can do it right." Such a wavering of self-confidence was decidedly out of character for White, but in this work he was following in the steps of the great Thomas Jefferson. It was surely one of the most challenging and important commissions of his life.[31]

In the next few weeks of 1896, Stan was "nearly driven crazy by the University of Virginia work." McKim was away from the office, and with the rush to get the university project started, along with his other jobs, he did not have "much mind left." In late February White sent suggested alternate plans for the interior of the Rotunda, one for rebuilding it as it had been before the fire, and another opening the interior from the portico floor to the dome, as had been proposed, which he felt Jefferson would have wanted if the building were to be used solely for library purposes. Alternative suggestions were also made on siting the new buildings, one plan for their placement to the side away from the main quadrangle, which White favored so as not to spoil the vista, and the other for their placement at the lower end of the lawn, closing in what would be an enlarged quadrangle. In March he returned to Charlottesville to present his plans.[32]

The restoration of the Rotunda proceeded rapidly. After the ruins of the Annex had been completely removed, a shallow portico with a single row of six columns was attached to the north side of the Rotunda, with a flight of steps leading down to a terrace and the road below. A new fireproof roof was built as a dome. The interior of the building was opened up from the portico floor to the dome by removing the remnants of the former upper floor, thus considerably enlarging the principal space; twenty large Corinthian columns were erected at the portico level, within the Rotunda, their entablature carrying an open gallery. Five book tiers were placed between the range of columns and the outer wall. The interior of the remodeled Rotunda was thus treated similarly to White's New York University library. Terrace wings with library rooms were extended to the sides of the Rotunda at the rear, connecting by open colonnades with the front terraces and forming small courtyards to the east and west.

At the south end of the quadrangle lawn, on an axis with the Rotunda at the opposite end, White had a new courtyard constructed at a level some 20 feet below the level of the bottom step of the Rotunda. A large academic building, named Cabell Hall, was constructed at the south end of the new courtyard, while the Physics Laboratory and the Mechanics Laboratory buildings were built to its sides. The three new buildings were so situated that only the top-story levels fronted at the edge of the courtyard, an abrupt dropoff permitting two and three additional lower floors at the rear. Thus from the quadrangle the new White buildings gave the appearance of low, one-story structures. In the new buildings, he endeavored "as far as possible," he said, "to do nothing, which would injure or break away from the wonderful character of the old buildings." Cabell Hall was centered by a portico on a slightly projecting central segment of one and a half stories, with symmetrical lateral wings. Open covered walkways at the ends of Cabell Hall connecting with the two laboratory buildings preserved something of the vista to the south. Stan also designed a power house, including a foundry and forge, erected behind Cabell Hall, and submitted a proposal for the placement of buildings in future expansion arranged on a cross axis at the lower end of the campus. In all these structures he aimed for the unity of effect that was so important to him.[33]

As the work at the University of Virginia got under way, Stan once more undertook to help out his brother Dick, who for years had been living primarily in New Mexico and styling himself a mining consultant. The architect arranged a position for Dick at Charlottesville as an assistant to the superintendent of the works, Theodore H. Skinner. Stan saw the job as "good training" for Dick "should anything turn up," and it was work that would not in any way injure his interest in the New Mexico mines. The job, Stan suggested to his almost forty-five-year-old brother, would, he hoped, put him "in a quiet frame of mind by being in a place where [he was] under orders and where there was some sort of routine work." Dick was to help out the superintendent in whatever ways he was asked. But, Stan cautioned him, that was all he was to do: He was "not to talk about things to the Contractors, the University authorities, or, in fact, anybody. If there is any talking to do, leave that for Mr. Skinner. This is very important." Stan was well aware how over the years, Dick again and again had got into trouble because of his sharp tongue and imprudent behavior.[34]

Dick began working on December 1, 1896, and remained at the university for some sixteen months. Besides his salary, Stan continued to send his brother spending money, though he complained that with all his expenses and investment losses he himself was "busted" financially.

Dick did take on responsibilities and apparently performed creditable work on the project. In his free time he played golf, rode a good deal, played polo, and even joined a hunt club. But as always Dick was at odds with himself, restless, impatient, looking elsewhere for the big strike. After only a few months in Virginia, he was contemplating a return to the search for gold, this time in the Yukon, where a gold rush had started. Stan promised to "stake" him if he went to the Yukon; when Dick left Virginia in the spring of 1898, Stan gave him a letter of credit for $2,000. By late summer Dick was in Tacoma, Washington, on his way north, and Stan wrote that their mother had become very worried since she had not heard from him. In the family, Stan was still the responsible son, watching over and taking care of his unsuccessful older brother.[35]

A decade after White had first begun the Virginia project, he was asked to take charge of new work at the university, including a house for the president, a dining hall, and an addition to the hospital. He was invited because of "the high esteem in which [his] own beautiful contributions to [the university] have been and will always be held." He soon started planning work on the president's house and the dining hall.[36]

White's reluctance to put pen to paper for publication was overcome with respect to his work at the University of Virginia. Indeed, White's only extended published statement about his work came at this time in an article headed "The Buildings of the University of Virginia" for a local journal, *Corks and Curls*. White's piece was above all a tribute to Thomas Jefferson, "unquestionably one of the most many sided of geniuses." Jefferson, he suggested, was a man "who possessed a creative and designing facility" and "would unquestionably have made a great architect." The Virginian was able to select from the vocabulary of antiquity what was appropriate for his time and purpose, and he created "if not the finest, richest, or most imposing, at least the most exquisite and perfect group of collegiate buildings in the world." If the new work his own firm had done was successful, he pointed out, this was "mainly due to the fact that the architects have rigidly endeavored to carry out and complete the original scheme as laid down by Jefferson, and that in doing so, the work has been to them a work of love." White's heartfelt words indicate how deeply he felt about the importance of the historic project to which he had been privileged to contribute.[37]

White's neoclassicism, so significant for the Bowery Bank, the Military Academy, New York University, and the University of Virginia commissions, emerged in yet another building, also a part of an integrated group of structures. At Naugatuck, Connecticut, near Waterbury, John

Howard Whittemore, a highly successful manufacturer of iron products, employed McKim, Mead & White to design several buildings for his community. In the late 1880s White had already designed for Whittemore a house that included gallery space for his collection of contemporary paintings. A memorial library, a small bank, a grammar school, and a church were all Whittemore philanthropies. They were positioned about a town green to mark a physical center for the community. The most impressive of the Naugatuck buildings was the neoclassical colonnaded public high school, for which White was responsible, set on a small hill overlooking the town center.[38]

By the mid-1890s White's commitment to the classical tradition was firm and deeply held. In his view, the architecture and the sculpture, as well as the literature, of the late nineteenth century were tied to a long tradition flowing forward from the Renaissance, with its roots deeply embedded long before in classical antiquity. The Middle Ages and "the sporadic waves of Gothic and Romanesque must necessarily always be looked upon as alien outgrowths of the whole movement in Art" toward the present, he asserted. Such styles were "absolutely impossible to us."[39]

The most important currents of artistic modernism, White felt, had come from France through the traditions, within the classical mode, of the Ecole des Beaux-Arts, which Richard Morris Hunt had first brought to the United States. According to White, it was "to a certain extent from [Hunt] and through him that the real modern artistic advances in architecture in New York and America could be traced." Indeed, the American "men of ability or prominence now practicing [architecture] are pupils of the Paris School of Fine Arts." Hunt's death on July 31, 1895, deprived the United States of the man generally recognized as its foremost leader of the architectural profession. His loss was felt deeply by the partners, and Stan collaborated with others in planning the Hunt Memorial, erected on Fifth Avenue at Seventieth Street.

The one exception to the "progressive trend" in architecture, in White's view, had been Stan's own mentor, H. H. Richardson, whose "unmodern" style was a "discordant note in this, to a great extent, generally consistent advance in architecture." Richardson's Romanesque style, Stan once remarked, "fine in his own buildings, became atrocious in the hands of his pupils." Mead was reported to have told one of his draftsmen that "Richardson had left the worst legacy to the architects of America than any man he had known." White and his partners, in their commitment to the classical-Renaissance tradition—beginning for them in the early 1880s—had by now turned their backs fully on Richardson and his influence and, in effect, on much of their own earlier work.[40]

His several institutional commissions in neoclassical dress allowed White to put his mark on large-scale projects. With McKim and other architects, he helped establish what became the dominant style for American public architecture during the first half of the twentieth century. Even more outspoken on the matter than White, McKim championed the dignified and monumental neoclassical style, a mode that brought an easily recognized order to building design and that, in recalling the imperialism of ancient Rome, seemed so compatible with the growing power and imperialistic thrust of the United States at the turn of the century. The Rhode Island State House, the Brooklyn Institute of Arts and Sciences, and Pennsylvania Station in New York, along with White's projects and other commissions, further enhanced the firm's reputation as masters of modern neoclassicism.

The considerable acclaim that came from his institutional projects was gratifying for White, but just as important to him were the pleasures coming from the world of art in which his life was so deeply and fully involved.

16

The Business of Art

The intense drive for material wealth in the last decades of the nineteenth century led many Americans to place a new and important premium on the quest for fine art. The fine arts of the past and the present were, of course, closely identified with the acquisition of vast wealth, and as the country was enriched, the commerce in art objects correspondingly flourished. Fine architecture, sculpture, and painting could provide things of beauty for the decoration of American homes and cities and for the pleasure of American plutocrats. There was a widespread assumption in the United States that this relatively new nation was the appropriate heir to the great traditions and treasures of the European past, which could so easily be absorbed by this large and expanding nation with its wealth and power. The arts could enhance the life-styles of the rich as well as serve as models for emulation in the larger society. Bringing heightened aesthetic awareness and sensitivity, the arts might even be a stimulus to moral uplift and renewal as well as an incentive to civic and national betterment.

White, whose love of the arts and commitment to artistic creativity had been deeply felt since his boyhood, shared with many others the vision of encouraging art activities to elevate the general taste and to improve the quality of American life. According to the novelist Edith Wharton, White was one of a handful of "men of exceptional intelligence" who, with their "new ideas" on art, "stirred the stagnant air of old New York." Like other spokesmen for the arts, White at times seemed to have a missionary zeal. His huge success as an architect, his tremendous energy and drive, and his excellent professional and social contacts made it inevitable that he would take a leading role in the New York art community. Royal Cortissoz, his onetime employee and later a well-

231

known journalist and art critic, observed that White was noteworthy as "a prominent member of the chief artistic organizations of this city" and "at every point . . . a brilliant force in the art life of America." This did not, however, preclude his considerable involvement in the commercial side of the arts. A good part of his income was derived from his dealings in art, the commerce of his continuous search for art objects for clients, dealers, and himself. Art meant to Stanford White business as well as pleasure.[1]

Architecture, of course, was the primary focus of White's artistic activity. Stan's dedication to his own profession was always apparent. Elected as a member in 1882 and as a fellow in 1886 of the American Institute of Architects, the national professional organization, he served as a director of the society from 1889 through 1891 under the third president, Richard Morris Hunt. As a director and a member of the executive committee of the AIA, he met often with Hunt and other directors on institute matters.

At the beginning of the twentieth century, McKim, without being consulted, was nominated and elected AIA president. Though reluctant to accept, he served in that office in 1902–3. White was genuinely pleased with the professional recognition that came to his partner. Working to raise standards of design for governmental buildings, McKim was also instrumental as president in acquiring William Thornton's Octagon House in Washington, D.C., as national headquarters for the institute. On his first visit to Octagon House, Stan's enthusiasm for the new quarters was characteristically "unabated," Glenn Brown, the institute's secretary, recalled. Brown had first met Stan more than a quarter of a century earlier on the Cheney Building project.[2]

During the 1880s Stan cooperated with young architects who in 1881 had organized the New York Architectural League with the intent of improving standards of work and bringing about more professional sociability. In November 1886 White served as a juror and ranked league members' drawings, and in January 1887 he took a leading part in the ceremonies at the annual League dinner by responding to the toasts. Over the years he frequently contributed his services as a juror and spoke out in support of safeguards for the rights of architects in competitions.[3]

As an architect at the top of his profession, White was often called upon for advice on building projects and professional matters. He was one of the people asked to give advice on the rebuilding of the Assembly Chamber in the State Capitol at Albany, to serve on an advisory committee to supervise the landscaping and architectural features of the Harlem

River Drive in New York, to join Daniel Burnham and William Robert Ware in judging a proposed design for a fine arts building in Philadelphia, to serve on a subcommittee on sites for a Civic Charter Day celebration, and to participate in making arrangements for the city celebration honoring Admiral George Dewey, the hero of the Spanish–American War. Despite his heavy workload, White usually agreed to take on committee work or judging, no doubt feeling a certain responsibility to his profession and his community because of his position.[4]

White worked closely, too, with art organizations outside his own field, particularly the Metropolitan Museum of Art. By the 1890s the Metropolitan Museum, which had been founded only in 1870, was becoming influential in providing the public with an introduction to some of the main currents of Western art. Part of its educative function was carried on by means of plaster casts of important sculptural pieces held in private collections or on display in museums in Europe. In January 1891 General Louis de Cesnola, director of the Metropolitan Museum, notified White of his appointment to a committee to enlarge the museum's collection of casts. About the same time he was chosen "a fellow for life" of the museum. He subscribed $1,000 to the cast fund and worked diligently to influence friends and acquaintances to subscribe. When Stan asked the painter Elihu Vedder and Mrs. Vedder, then living in Rome, to serve as agents to obtain casts from "Eyetalions," the Vedders were delighted to work with him.[5]

A minor incident at the museum entrance one day occasioned an irritated letter from Stan to Henry Marquand, the president. White had received a Sunday admission card, so one Sunday he showed up for a museum visit and brought along Bessie and McKim. The guard would not let his guests in and treated him "with scorn and derision." An additional card was quickly sent to him. White's complaint about the way he had been treated was not unusual. He expected polite, respectful treatment always, and at times even special consideration, from those who served him, and never hesitated to fire off letters complaining of impoliteness or poor service. There was within him, as there was within his father, a certain sensitivity about his status and reputation that led him to be excessively touchy when he felt he had not been accorded the consideration he believed he merited.[6]

White served as a governor on the executive committee of the National Sculpture Society, too. The Sculpture Society was organized in 1893 by artists and sculptors to improve the quality of their art and, in particular, to promote the sculptural embellishment of public buildings, squares, and parks. For many years the society played an important role in Ameri-

233

can art life, arranging for traditional sculpture in public buildings, national expositions, and civic celebrations. Annual exhibitions by the society promoted traditional sculptural styles in an attempt to serve as a bulwark against currents of modernism. White, who disliked most tendencies of modernism in the visual and plastic arts, enthusiastically supported the activities of the Sculpture Society.[7]

Also organized in the early 1890s to encourage the fine arts in America, with the particular purpose of abolishing all duties on works of art brought in from abroad, was the National Art Association. Under the presidency of the painter Daniel Huntington, the association included White among its leading members. On one occasion Stanford testified before the Ways and Means Committee of the U.S. House of Representatives in favor of the free admission of art works into the country, a measure that would have immensely benefited him personally.[8]

The most influential organization in the New York art world at the time was the National Academy of Design. As a member of the Art Committee and of the Advisory Committee of Artists, Stan assisted in organizing several special exhibitions at the academy's Venetian Gothic building on Fourth Avenue and Twenty-third Street. For a Ladies' Portrait Exhibit in November 1894 to benefit the New York Orthopaedic Hospital, Stan solicited portraits from friends and persuaded several art dealers to contribute tapestries for decoration. He lent the exhibit his own marble plaque of Bessie by Saint-Gaudens and the portrait of his mother by Abbott Thayer. The following year Stan assisted in organizing another exhibition of portraits and contributed some of his own paintings by Daniel Huntington, J. Alden Weir, Thomas Lawrence, and George Romney. He also arranged the decorations for the exhibit rooms.[9]

White's position in the New York art community enhanced his financial success as a liaison between dealers and customers. As a decorator for well-to-do clients, as a collector of paintings and other art objects, and as a large-scale purchaser of art objects for resale, he was constantly involved with art dealers hoping to find outlets for particular pieces.

On his European trips Stan made so many purchases that he had to rent warehouse space for storage in New York. Pieces temporarily placed in his own house, the Tower studio, or another studio were sometimes sold to clients for rooms he was decorating. Both through his own purchases and in directing friends and clients to particular dealers abroad and at home, Stan was an effective catalyst to the international art and antiques trade while earning substantial commissions. Elihu Vedder reportedly said that White "had bought so largely that he had raised the price of antiques all over the Continent." Stan was once reproached for taking so much from Europe to beautify America. His defense was a not uncommon argument: Dominant countries in the past had always taken art works from their predecessors, and Americans, now with a leading place in the world, had the right to gather for their use the spoils of the past.[10]

Stan had favorite dealers in Europe whom he visited regularly and to whom he sent friends who had sought his advice about making purchases abroad. In 1899, when Mrs. John Jacob Astor asked for information and advice about European dealers, he responded with an unusually lengthy and detailed list, discussing not only those dealers who had the best things for sale but also those whom he especially trusted and distrusted. Most dealers gave White a discount on goods he purchased as well as a commission on sales to clients directed to them.[11]

For years White worked closely with Arthur Mario Acton, his agent in Florence, whom he considered honest, "a very nice young fellow," with a mine of information about Italy and good connections. Acton frequently sent White news of dealers and photographs of objects they had for sale and traveled about seeking things the architect might want. He attended auctions where he would bid on White's behalf. When Stanford visited Florence, Acton placed his automobile at White's disposal. Sometimes he traveled to Paris or London to assist White. Acton once sent a watchdog in care of White for William C. Whitney, for whom he had bought extensively. In 1902 Acton acquired a large fifteenth-century villa close to Florence. He was to spend much of the rest of his life restoring Villa La Pietra and its gardens to their onetime Renaissance splendor. Many years later Acton's son, Sir Harold Acton, would donate the sumptuous villa with its art treasures to New York University, for which Stan himself did so much.[12]

The painter Charles C. Coleman, who lived on Capri in the Bay of Naples, was White's chief agent in southern Italy. Coleman frequently got first refusal on things put up for sale in the Naples area, acting on White's behalf. In Rome, White worked with Waldo Story, son of the American expatriate sculptor and man of letters William Wetmore Story. Waldo Story often bought objects for shipment to New York. Figueroa Hernandez served as White's agent in Madrid, but he was far less active than the agents in Italy.

More central to White's daily life than the foreign galleries and dealers were those in New York. Stan regularly stopped at favorite shops, many located on or close to Fifth Avenue in the Twenties, near his office. He enjoyed looking at beautiful things and wanted to keep abreast of what was available. Occasionally he planned the decoration of rooms around objects he found at the dealers' shops. The White correspondence files are filled with countless notes from dealers informing the architect of new things—rugs, paintings, statuary, bronzes, tapestries, old damask and velvet—which they hoped would interest him. As a well-known designer and decorator for the well-to-do, White could make fortunes for dealers as well as for himself, and his patronage was eagerly sought.

Some of the New York galleries with which White dealt were American branches of European antiquaries. Duveen Brothers, Allard & Sons, Durand-Ruel, and Vitall Benguiat were among the firms closely tied to parent establishments in London or Paris. Many of the New York stores were direct importers of rugs and carpets from the Near East, paintings from England, antique furniture and bric-a-brac from France, and rare textiles, pottery, and bronzes from Italy. Several of the ones White frequented carried bolts of the rich antique red velvet that he bought by the hundreds of yards for use as wall covering. A few dealers, such as Thomas B. Clarke and Samuel P. Avery, Jr., carried American paintings, including works by some of White's friends. Some of the art shops he patronized undertook restorations of furniture and old ceilings for him, prepared picture frames following his designs, executed reproductions of marble or bronze work, or copied old embroideries and laces. A few were primarily auction houses where he sometimes bid or had others bid for him and, less often, placed pieces of his own for sale.

The most important of the auction houses for White was the American Art Association, which had display rooms on the south side of Madison Square just east of Broadway. In 1883 Thomas Kirby, who had come to New York from Philadelphia to sell art, took over the American Art Gallery, renaming it the American Art Association. Under Kirby the firm prospered, reaping substantial income from the sale of A. T. Stewart's large art collection in 1887 and from the sales of other exceptional collections. Some American painters prepared works specifically for Kirby's sales. Stan frequently stopped by the Association showrooms, a short walk from his office and his home, and often put in bids on items placed there for auction.[13]

With the dealer-importer Eugene Glaenzer, who specialized in antique stonework, Stanny bought so extensively that he had no place for his purchases and left them on Glaenzer's premises, where he eventually stored other objects as well. Glaenzer had agreed to offer his customers whichever of White's pieces the architect might choose to sell. Stan did work on an addition for Glaenzer's warehouse at 540 West Twenty-first Street, begun in late 1901, "the cost of same to be on joint account," with the extension at White's "entire disposal to place there whatever decorative things [White might] wish to dispose of." Stan became annoyed when he learned it was being said that he and Glaenzer were actually involved in a partnership. Glaenzer assured White that he had not mentioned the architect's name in connection with his business and promised him never to speak to anyone of their "combination." Although much of his income came from dealers' commissions and from the resale of art objects, White never considered himself a merchant, nor did he want others to identify him as one.[14]

Occasionally Stan asked wealthy friends to finance purchases of art objects for him, in effect lending him funds until the pieces were placed. Charles Barney, his financial adviser, friend, and client, sometimes financed purchases for him. Hamilton Twombly, whose mansion and estate buildings at Madison, New Jersey, the firm designed, and for whom Stan acquired magnificent tapestries from the Barberini Collection in Rome through an art dealer in Washington, D.C., agreed in 1895 to advance Stanny $10,000 to buy "the Bardini marbles." Twombly had the option of purchasing the marbles himself at cost if he liked them; if not, he could consider the advance a regular loan. In that way White could avoid a bank loan but take possession of the goods with the prospect of a 10 percent commission.[15]

Nevertheless, after the turn of the century, White's purchases had become so numerous that he often fell in debt to dealers, who dunned him for payment but were usually willing to take his short-term notes for what was due. Small payments on such notes and the issuance of new notes, when the obligations fell due, increasingly became White's way of doing business. Sometimes dealers would offer him items with the specification that "at such reduced figures [they] must be for cash." With some accounts, he fell years behind in payment. Often the same dealers were offering White items for purchase while dunning him to pay his accounts. Thomas J. Blakeslee, in a note of October 17, 1900, from his shop at 353 Fifth Avenue, urged Stan to drop in to see one of the grandest paintings ever to come to New York, while reminding him that his $2,500 note would be due on the following Saturday. Stan could arrange to renew it in full, Blakeslee suggested, or pay a part of the balance. Though White bought art goods lavishly, even recklessly, he rationalized his purchases as good investments that ultimately would pay off.[16]

Not only did Stan have a passion for collecting paintings, furniture, rugs, carved ceilings and other architectural elements, and a variety of precious objects—ransacking, as it were, the galleries and shops, the churches, and the great houses of Europe—but he also enjoyed greatly decorating rooms, frequently giving primary emphasis to things he had himself acquired. Decorative art in his day, White believed, was "at a pretty low ebb all over the world," though "lower here than anywhere else." Standards of decoration were uncertain: "The whole trouble about modern decorative work is that all fine ornamental or conventional work ended a hundred years ago." The problems of the present had to be carefully thought out, he maintained, keeping solutions from the past in mind. Too often, he suggested, clients were in a rush to get things finished instead of taking time to work out the most suitable and aesthetically satisfying décor. Decorating was a considerable challenge for him as well as a source of profit.[17]

For Stan, working things out meant taking time to find the best things available. By providing the best a good example might be set for others to emulate. White believed that fine interior design could serve to raise the general level of taste. Often he himself had to design what was best for a client, and in his private capacity he engaged woodworkers, cabinetmakers, muralists, gilders, glass artisans, plaster workers, and makers of fine fabrics to restore pieces or prepare reproductions that would harmonize with original pieces.

By and large in his major decorative work for the well-to-do, White favored an Italian Renaissance mode. He often made use of an old carved ceiling brought from Italy as a principal feature to set the proportions and scale of a room. He favored the use of antique damask or red velvet, unembellished oak or walnut paneling, or tooled leather to provide a flat and fairly simple wall covering, which set off the three-dimensional architectural elements of a room, such as a highly ornamented fireplace and mantel, door and window enframements, and cornices. Such rooms were usually rather sparsely furnished, in contrast to the typically cluttered Victorian décor, with the main pieces of furniture placed near the center of the room and the secondary pieces scattered about the central grouping. People coming into such a space were expected to be drawn to the center, from where the architectural elements of the room, with the play of light and shadow, could best be seen and appreciated. White was skillful in bringing together the many elements into a unified, well-proportioned ensemble, creating what in essence were highly pictorial stage sets. He planned rooms in a house with a general stylistic unity, taking particular pains to see that they harmonized well and flowed one into another. He considered the transitional effect of a doorway or other opening very important. White was widely recognized for his genius in creating decorative effects; many considered him the foremost American decorator. Through his decorative work for well-to-do New Yorkers, he became an arbiter of taste for his times.[18]

Especially during the 1890s, the architect worked closely with painter friends, wood carvers, and plaster workers to create picture frames. He became so well known in the New York art community for work of this kind that sometimes even painters and collectors he did not know asked for his suggestions or designs. In his frames, Stan shied away from overornamentation and attempted to enhance paintings by relatively simple settings, often of parallel lines and delicately incised wreaths or leaves. The painter-critic Sadakichi Hartmann called White's frames "the most artistic ones I know." A Chicago *Times* critic suggested that "for delicately poetic creations," White's frames were "the best in existence."[19]

White designed frames for such friends as Saint-Gaudens, MacMonnies, and Thomas Dewing, as well as for other artists to whom he was less close. The artists sometimes suggested what they would like in the way of frames for their paintings, but they always deferred to White's judgment. Childe Hassam once wrote him, "You know what to have made better than anyone else." Occasionally an artist asked his advice about cutting a canvas down in size before it was framed. In the early 1890s White employed the skilled woodworker Alexander G. Cabus to execute his frame designs; later he turned to another craftsman, Oscar Rudolph, for such commissions. Stan's usual procedure was to have full-scale drawings of the ornamentation prepared and then to keep in fairly close touch with the craftsmen on the carving, gilding, and burnishing of the frames. It was understood that White's overall designs and the decorative elements were not to be copied for other frames without his consent.[20]

Besides the design of picture frames, Stan undertook a miscellany of other decorative work, most of the commissions "as a matter of personal friendship." Some of the products reached large audiences. For his long-time friend and associate Richard Watson Gilder, White designed covers for *Scribner's Magazine* and the *Century* as well as for the six-volume *Century Dictionary* and for *Battles and Leaders of the Civil War*. He also designed a dictionary stand and a richly carved mantel with the Century Company seal for the business offices on Union Square. He created covers for *Cosmopolitan Magazine,* for a special 1895 issue of the *Architectural Record* on the work of McKim, Mead & White, and for *The National Democratic Review*. White prepared covers for several books, including a cover that won him a medal for the design. He also crafted a machine cabinet for the National Cash Register Company. He did considerable decorative work for private yachts and at least once planned an automobile body. Good design, he believed, could heighten aesthetic awareness and enrich the lives of those touched by it.[21]

White's assistance to fellow artists was legendary. Although in his professional work he looked to the European past for inspiration, he was deeply committed to the more traditional art of his own times as well. Not only did he employ many artists in his architectural work, but also his multitude of connections with dealers were useful in helping artist friends display and sell their works. His recommendations to clients assisted many artists, as did his own purchases, and his reputation for kindness grew.

White was frequently asked to recommend a painter, a sculptor, or another artist for a particular job. In 1898 he was asked for the names of the foremost American sculptors for possible commissions in Philadelphia. White listed Philip Martiny, Karl Bitter, Daniel Chester French, Augustus Saint-Gaudens, Frederick MacMonnies, and Larkin G. Mead. Saint-Gaudens was, in his view, "the greatest artist living. . . . MacMonnies ranks next to him. French is not in his class at all." But Saint-Gaudens, he pointed out, had more work than he could do and was such a perfectionist that it was never certain that he would even finish something he agreed to do. MacMonnies lived abroad. French no doubt was "the best available man." Among other artists, in White's view, Robert Reid was "certainly in the first four or five American painters and decorators," J. W. Finn was "the first decorator in the country," Alfred Q. Collins "the strongest man's portrait painter," Charles Coleman "one of the sweetest artists who ever lived," and Everett Shinn a man of "unquestionable talent."[22]

One young artist Stan assisted was Gertrude Vanderbilt Whitney. On invitation, he went to look at a piece of sculpture she had done, admittedly "with a little dread," but he "was taken off my feet on entering the studio by the life-like appearance of the study and its vigor and pose." When Mrs. Whitney asked who he thought was the best teacher to give her lessons in modeling, Stan recommended her to Daniel Chester French as "a charming girl" with "a real talent for sculpture" and suggested that he would take it as a favor if she could study with French for a few weeks before going abroad. French did take her on, and she "enjoyed the lessons tremendously." White subsequently gave her an introduction to MacMonnies in Paris.[23]

Countless artists sent White notes begging him to favor them with a commission or help them in some way to find work. Many left drawings or paintings at his office in the hope that he would buy the pictures. Julia Brewster impressed him with her watercolors of buildings; he commissioned her to do others and sent a check. When Sadakichi Hartmann persisted in leaving sketch after sketch at his office, however, White finally sent him a small sum and told him not to leave anything else unless he were asked to do so. For some years White was plagued by a penniless artist of small talent named Alfred Brennan, who sent unsolicited sketches along with notes detailing his desperate situation (furniture repossessed, two small children without food, no money whatsoever). Time and again, White sent Brennan money and took fifteen or twenty of his sketches. Eventually White wrote Brennan that he could not buy any more, since his own affairs were in such a snarl. Nonetheless, pictures and letters continued to come, and Stan helped him out again.[24]

Some artist friends asked for loans. Robert Reid, Edward Simmons, William Merritt Chase, and J. Alden Weir, among others, borrowed money from White, and Saint-Gaudens regularly asked for small loans. Strangers, too, wrote to ask for a handout. Other artists borrowed tapestries, a suit of armor, or an old chair from White for use in a painting. Edwin Austin Abbey, on a short stay in New York, furnished an entire studio with objects White sent him. The architect Charles A. Platt asked to borrow books on architecture, including "a very elaborate book by some Frenchman on Italian architecture," because he wanted ideas for a house he was going to build in Vermont. Architects sometimes asked for the loan of the plans of buildings White had designed. Stan's generosity put a great many in his debt. "You are always so ready to do a service to your friends," a fellow architect wrote him, "that I only wish the opportunity would arrive when we could render you one!"[25]

When Dennis Bunker, a painter who had occasionally joined Stanny for evenings on the town, suddenly died around Christmas in 1890, scarcely two months after his marriage, White undertook to help out Bunker's widow. He purchased two pictures Bunker had painted, collected contributions from various friends, and sent $1,000 to her. In addition, he joined with others to purchase a Bunker painting that was donated to the Metropolitan Museum of Art.[26]

Edward Simmons, a painter and a close friend of White, who at times borrowed money from him, recorded in his autobiography several anecdotes about the architect that reveal a good deal about Stan's aid to artists. One day Stan asked Simmons to accompany him uptown. They stopped at a studio building where many artists resided, and Stan asked Simmons to show him where a certain artist lived, a man they both knew was not then at home. Outside the man's room, White knelt down and pushed a roll of bills under the door, and they left hurriedly. When Simmons asked why he had done this, White replied, "You know he needs it. I have it. Why shouldn't I give it to him? But you must never tell." The next day Simmons heard the artist telling a friend that he had returned home the evening before prepared to pack his things, since he was to be evicted, only to find on the floor a roll of bills that saved the day for him. "He died without knowing who had helped him," Simmons related. Another time Simmons and White were leaving The Players and on the sidewalk met a professional beggar well known for always being just a trifle shy of the train fare he needed to get home. With no hesitation, White pulled some silver from his pocket and, "in an embarrassed way," handed it to the beggar. "I suppose," Simmons told him, "you know that you're not really doing him any good. They say he is rich." "Oh," White answered, "you don't understand. Do you suppose I was trying to do him good? I was only trying to justify my own existence." This incident was one of the few indications White gave that his lavish life-style and self-indulgence caused him inner qualms of guilt.[27]

Janet Scudder, a sculptor and former pupil of Saint-Gaudens, was one of many artists who benefited from White's patronage. Gus urged Stan to visit her studio to look at a marble figure she had made and give her work if possible. Scudder herself sent the architect, whom she had met in MacMonnies's Paris studio, an invitation to her Washington Square studio to see her things. White replied curtly that he was much too busy to go about on studio visits. She wrote back to say that she considered her invitation reasonable. A few weeks later she ran into the architect at a busy intersection; he recognized her and right there in the street offered to buy her *Frog Fountain,* which he had seen, on the spot agreed to her price of $1,000, and asked to have the piece sent to his office. This sale gave a great boost to her career.[28]

Some time later, White sent a note asking her to stop at his office at a specified time. When she did so, she was seated in a comfortable chair in the reception room, only to wait and wait.

Then, one of the doors suddenly burst open and Stanford White rushed into the room, shook my hand vigorously and said:
"Oh, Miss Scudder—I wanted to—"

He got no further, for close on his heels appeared his secretary, who said Chicago was calling him on the telephone. He rushed out and I once more sank back into the comfortable chair.

Another half-hour and he burst into the room again.

"Oh, Miss Scudder—I wanted—"

Again the secretary on his heels with some murmured words that carried him off without further explanation!

By this time my anxiety and curiosity to know what he really did want were getting the best of me. The comfortable chair was no longer comfortable; I had to leave it and walk about a bit to keep calm. The third time Mr. White appeared, he had his hands full of sketches which he thrust into mine before any one could possibly call him away.

"Designs for two fountains," he said breathlessly; "Yes—take them along—make sketches for the figures. I've indicated about what I want. Yes—yes—you'll see. Bring them back as soon as you can. Work out your own ideas for them. By the way, I've placed your Frog Fountain in the conservatory of the Chapin house and I want you to have another made in marble for Jim Breese's Long Island garden. Better have three more of the bronzes cast. That will make four. Quite enough of them. You don't want them to get too common. Now—about this design—"

Again that bothersome secretary had appeared and over his shoulder Mr. White called to me: "Bring in the sketches the moment you have them ready. We can talk them over. Good-bye."

Scudder made several more visits to the office to consult with the architect about her project, but each time the same sort of interruptions occurred. "White's existence," she found, "was the most hectic anyone could possibly have lived; and yet he always knew exactly what he wanted and was able to explain his ideas in a most clear, distinct and inspiring manner." To Scudder, White was, unquestionably, "the greatest architect America has ever produced."[29]

Stan often alerted well-to-do friends about paintings and other art works that might interest them. He wrote the broker Henry Poor, for example, about "a stunning thing by Remington" he had just seen: "I thought of it for your room at Tuxedo. They want $400 for it, but it really is a masterpiece of its kind." On occasion White informed J. P. Morgan, the powerful banker, about important art works or collections he had learned were available in Europe, which he hoped might find a home in the United States. The news that Tiepolo frescoes from Venice had been put on the market prompted Stan "naturally to turn to you before any one else for aid" in the hope of getting them into the Metropolitan Museum, though he wrote to a friend that he thought Morgan was "not going to take it up." Morgan had been associated with White on the Madison Square Garden project and the Metropolitan Club, and now and then Stan saw him socially. Their relationship was not close, however, and the architect held the financier-collector in awe. Morgan was closer to McKim, whose private library for the banker, begun in 1902, was one of his great achievements.[30]

White collected both old and contemporary paintings for himself. He preferred most of all ones that exhibited decorative qualities. He chose some "old masters" from Italy for his walls, though the paintings were usually labeled "from the school of" and were loosely connected with the great masters. Two of his most lavish purchases were for Gainsborough's portrait of Lady Carr ($12,500) and Romney's portrait of Lady Hamilton ($8,000). He once said that he preferred paintings that antedated Salvator Rosa, the seventeenth-century Italian, whose works he did not particularly care for. He was not at all interested in Oriental art. Stan collected many works painted by friends, and on occasion he would commission a work from someone he knew. One picture he especially liked was a portrait of himself by Giovanni Boldini, a fashionable Italian painter, and he tried to interest some of his wealthy friends in sitting for Boldini.[31]

White's own collection also contained many paintings of female nudes. Some he commissioned; others were brought to his attention by dealers and friends. He began the systematic acquisition of nudes soon after the attacks on the statue of Diana atop Madison Square Garden. At that time he alerted the dealer Samuel P. Avery that he might be considered "in the market for nudes by any one I like." When commissioning a nude from the artist H. Siddons Mowbray, White wrote: "All I want to impress upon you is the fact that I want you to make the picture alluring enough to scare all the straight-laced people in New York. If I carry out my intention and get a pretty decent little collection of nudes I mean to give it to the Metropolitan Museum to shock everybody for all time." What he especially wanted were small pictures with Cupid and Psyche, Leda and the Swan, or "wood nymphs or something of that sort." It was important to him for the breasts to be firm and "to have her little bubs stick up." Most of the nudes were stored in his office, and some were kept in his bedroom of the townhouse.[32]

An artist named Annie Beebe, whom he did not know, once offered White a "Salon picture" nude. He wrote back that he was no longer collecting nudes, but she persisted and sent him a small copy of the salon painting along with a note. If she could make it known that "Mr. Stanford White had a picture of mine in his possession," she wrote, "it would have great weight with other people about me as a painter." White sent her a check, and she promised to paint him another nude if he decided not to take the picture she sent. After Thomas Dewing finally came through with a nude that he had long promised "would be so alluring and 'lithe' that you would not be able to keep it in your room,'' the picture turned out to be of a girl sitting on the grass with her arms clasped around her legs and her chin resting on her knees. Stan expressed disappointment with Dewing's picture—''it was darned hard work to tell whether it was meant for a girl or a boy''—and the painter became ''quite huffy.'' Dewing obviously had not made ''the nude young, sweet, and alluring.'' And what, Stan wondered, ''are nudes for if they are not for that!'' When the painter Ned Abbey sent him sketches of girls for his choice, Stanny selected one of a pubescent girl ''apparently in distress, as she could count on me every time for 'hellup.' '' Female youth, beauty, innocence, and vulnerability never failed to charm Stanny, just as they had his father.[33]

17

The Social Whirl

A s White moved into his forties, his lively and varied social life intensified. He seemed to have a compulsive need to be on the go all the time. Much of his social life revolved around male companions: at his clubs, on fishing holidays, or in late evening sprees on the town. He could also be seen, however, at dinners, at the theater or the opera, or on yachting parties with friends of both sexes. Though he constantly complained of being "driven" by his professional work, his social activities must have been just as exhausting: "The tread mill goes on merrily," he wrote his brother-in-law Devereux Emmet early in 1895, "and I hope you are having as good a time as I am. If I didn't have to work for my living, it would be all right, but what with dinners, Opera, balls, parties, and the Devil knows what all, I find the nine o'clock to seven o'clock grind harder and harder."[1]

Bessie sometimes accompanied her husband to dinners, the opera, and balls, and occasionally went along with him on yachting parties and country excursions, but she preferred to stay in the country at St. James, near her sisters. She customarily spent at least five months a year there during the summer and early autumn. When she was at Box Hill, until a telephone was installed in 1901, she regularly sent notes to Stanford at the office to arrange for weekend guests in the country, to plan for occasional evenings together in the city, or to settle up their financial accounts, including their shared household expenses. Stan, in turn, wrote to let her know he would be out of town for a few days looking over his projects, to ask that she invite friends out to Box Hill for a weekend, or to arrange for work he wanted done at the country place.

A regular winter activity in the city for the couple was the opera. The new Metropolitan Opera House on Broadway at Fortieth Street had opened its doors to the public in November 1883, with an inaugural performance of Gounod's *Faust*. In the years following, the Metropolitan provided a rich fare of Italian, German, and French operas. The Golden Horseshoe boxes in the splendidly decorated hall were much sought after, and a season rental of a well-located box served as a recognized symbol of social position. For some operagoers the socializing that took place in the boxes was even more important than the performance on the stage. With his passion for music, his love for theatrical spectacles, and his intense sociability, Stan greatly enjoyed evenings at the Met. He came to know some of the leading performers, including Nellie Melba, Lillian Nordica, and Edouard de Rezke, who introduced him to other prominent singers. By the fall of 1890 the Whites had box tickets for the season. In the 1893–94 season they shared a parquet box on Wednesday evenings with the Prescott Hall Butlers, Bessie's sister and her husband. But the next season they changed to the more fashionable Friday evenings and shared a box with the socialite banker Charles Barney and his wife, a signal to all concerned that the Whites indeed were part of New York high society.[2]

After a fire on August 27, 1892, seriously damaged the auditorium and stage of the Metropolitan Opera House, necessitating major reconstruction, a newly formed organization calling itself the Vaudeville Club negotiated rental space for clubrooms in an assembly hall, foyer, and adjacent rooms on the second tier level. The all-male private club would offer a retreat to which members could come during or after a performance of the opera and where light theatrical entertainments, mostly by music hall artists, could be held. The composer Reginald De Koven served as president of the new club, and White was chosen one of the directors.

The Vaudeville Club stage shows, to which wives and other guests might be invited, ordinarily took place after 11:00 P.M., when opera performances had ended and the theaters had let out; the club was thus one of the first nightclubs established in the city. J. Cleveland Cady, the architect of the Opera House, supervised the first alterations for the clubrooms. He installed in the rented space a little theater with a small stage and dressing rooms, private boxes and galleries, a grill room, and a reading room. The clubrooms were ready early in 1893. Soon afterward, however, the new galleries and the dressing rooms were declared a fire hazard. White was charged with their removal, other structural changes, and the decoration of the clubrooms. In return for his services, the architect obtained gift memberships for several friends. Stan became a leading force in the group, willing to take on the duties of an impresario for the Vaudeville members. He arranged for Carmencita to dance there and one evening brought his friends Elsie de Wolfe and Elizabeth Marbury to play and sing. Bessie occasionally attended performances there with her husband. On February 23, 1895, White himself, to much applause, appeared with a group on the Vaudeville stage as Sandow the Strongman, very muscular in tights stuffed with batting, and hefted dumbbells and weights made of papier-maché. Stan delighted in dressing up and role playing. Membership in the Vaudeville Club peaked at about 450, but that number was not sufficient to cover expenses, and the club was disbanded after a few seasons.[3]

Stan's social whirl intensified further in the year 1895. At a wedding in Philadelphia, the forty-one-year-old White was one of the ushers who, like hot-blooded young swains, ventured out in zero weather in the wee hours of the morning to serenade the bridesmaids—unsuccessfully, it appears, since the young women did not even wake up. Stan boasted that the excursion was a great success anyway, because he had "kissed the bride and two bridesmaids and acted in a most scandalous way generally," which seems to have caused him no regrets. Late in the year, the socialite illustrator Charles Dana Gibson was married to the beautiful Irene Langhorne, his chief model for the well-known Gibson girl, in Richmond, Virginia. Stan, who attended the wedding with Bessie, seems to have been more decorous this time.[4]

Much of Stan's social life reinforced ties with artists important to him. At the end of March he organized a banquet honoring the painter John La Farge on his sixtieth birthday at his newly opened Metropolitan Club, and a short time later he arranged an elegant dinner at The Players honoring the painters John Singer Sargent and Edwin Austin Abbey, who were visiting from England. Late April brought what McKim called "the Boston Tea Party," a two-day excursion of forty-two people, including White, in two private railroad cars from New York to inaugurate McKim's impressive Boston Public Library. At the much publicized inaugural banquet, McKim asked Stan, since "he understands the problem," to be Augusta Saint-Gaudens's dinner partner. White graciously agreed, though he had always disliked the difficult, deaf wife of his best friend.[5]

But it was the dinner that White organized, together with his friends Henry W. Poor, a Wall Street broker, and James L. Breese, a wealthy semiprofessional photographer, that led to the greatest publicity of the spring's social events. Planned as a combination birthday party and tenth wedding anniversary celebration honoring John Elliot Cowdin, the May 20 dinner was held at Breese's photography studio. Shortly before the event, when Stan urged the artist Charles Dana Gibson to come, he wrote him that "hell is going to be let loose" there, "but don't tell anybody about it." Individualized dinner cards, with illustrations said to be risqué, were prepared. Breese photographed the placecards and later distributed sets to the guests. The artist John Twachtman etched a seal or device for the menu. Henry Poor wrote Stan a note the evening before the party in which he expressed the hope that "the girls will not back out or funk on us!" but concluded that "everything seems O.K."[6]

Both McKim and Mead were among the more than thirty men at the dinner that evening, as were Gus Saint-Gaudens, the scientist Nicola Tesla, the architect Whitney Warren, the inventor Cooper Hewitt, and the painters J. Alden Weir, Robert Reid, Willard Metcalf, Edward Simmons, and Carroll Beckwith, all among White's close friends. Sherry's catered the elaborate twelve-course dinner, and four banjo players and four jubilee singers provided musical entertainment. Two shapely girls poured the wine, a brunette for the red and a blonde for the white. Champagne was also served with each course. When it was time for dessert, the singers began to chant "Sing a song of sixpence" and servants carried in a huge pie covered by a flaky brown crust. And when the pie was opened, out popped "a bevy of canaries" along with sixteen-year-old Susie Johnson, dressed in filmy black gauze, a stuffed blackbird perched on her head.

The waiters and musicians were sworn to secrecy, but word of the scandalous "Pie Girl Dinner" quickly reached the newspapers. A few months later Joseph Pulitzer's *World,* in an attack on the New York high society that refused to admit its publisher, blasted the "bacchanalian revels in New York fashionable studios" and men who corrupted young girls for their pleasure. Susie Johnson was reported to have begun to pose in the nude for painters and photographers after the May 20 dinner, and then to have abruptly disappeared. Her mother, it was said, searched for her in vain in the studios of the city. Some sensational newspaper accounts years later associated White himself with the girl's downfall and disappearance. As the public criticism intensified, a Chicago friend wrote White that "some of the boys must be having a hard 'row to hoe' at home just at the moment." Whether or not Bessie reacted to the dinner by reproaching her husband, we do not know. More than a decade later, newspapers were reporting that Susie had subsequently married, but when her husband found out about her past he had thrown her out of the house. In one version, friendless and forgotten, she had then killed herself.[7]

The Pie Girl Dinner was in several particulars characteristic of White's private life by that time. Here was the society of male friends, mostly in the arts, whose company he especially enjoyed; they had come together with a good deal of secrecy for an elaborate, heavy dinner, some serious drinking, and sexually titillating entertainment. The scandalous affair certainly appealed to White—just as the shocking Diana perched on her Tower had delighted him. He would decorate his city, he would be a showman, but at the same time he would please himself, never caring that his behavior might well shock or even horrify others.

Shortly after the Pie Girl Dinner, Stanny left New York for his customary early summer fishing trip to the Restigouche camp in Canada. He was not present, therefore, for the groundbreaking ceremony in mid-June at McKim's Columbia University campus, another of the firm's largest and most significant projects. Soon after his return from Canada on July 13, he, Bessie, and Larry embarked on the SS *La Touraine* for a European holiday. Archie Chanler, who had been at the Pie Girl Dinner, and his sisters Elizabeth and Margaret Chanler occupied nearby cabins on the ship. In Paris the Whites took a suite consisting of a parlor and two connecting bedrooms at the Normandy Hotel, and Stan conferred with Willie MacMonnies about their work for Prospect Park in Brooklyn. As was his custom when visiting Paris, he joined the sculptor for evenings on the town.[8]

The primary purpose of the 1895 trip to Europe, however, was a rest and water cure for White at Contrexeville Spa in the Vosges region of eastern France. Like Henry Richardson's intemperance in food and drink, Stan's overindulgence had become a way of life. He increasingly suffered gastrointestinal problems, while his earlier bladder and urinary tract ailments occasionally flared up. For some time Stan had been drinking bottled Contrexeville water, known for its diuretic effects, and had even ordered it stocked at some of his clubs. While Bessie and Larry traveled to the nearby mountains, Stan spent three weeks in near seclusion, drinking only mineral water and eating very little.[9]

Following "the cure," a hurried trip to Lausanne, Lucerne, Venice, and Florence was devoted to the buying of antiques. Back in Paris, White spent a pleasant evening with the painter James A. McNeill Whistler. On August 26 the family left for London, where Stan restocked his wardrobe and went with John Singer Sargent to see Whistler's *Peacock Room*, which, he later wrote the artist, he hoped to arrange to bring to the United States. The family sailed on the *New York* from Southampton on August 31, and the architect was back in the office on September 9. A month after returning, Stan wrote his brother Dick that he felt "fairly well, but my trip to Contrexeville did not do much good"; his gastrointestinal and urinary tract problems were still troubling him.[10]

McKim's health was poor in 1895, too. For some time he had been suffering from a hernia. He had been fitted for a truss but was advised to have an operation. In late October he underwent surgery and remained at home. When he returned to the office in late November, it was for only an hour or two each day. McKim's recovery from his operation was slow, and on December 7 he sailed for Naples for recuperation in Europe. In Rome he was able to take care of business for the American School of Architecture (later the American Academy in Rome), which he had organized. In January he went on to Egypt for an excursion up the Nile River with American friends, following the route that White and his family had taken three years earlier. Charley was back at the office in April 1896. He tried to improve his health by playing golf, riding a bicycle, and occasionally going off for shooting in South Carolina. From that time on, however, McKim's uncertain health would add to Stan's burden of work.[11]

White himself occasionally used his own ailments to his advantage. When summoned for jury duty, Stan regularly had his doctor sign a letter to the effect that his bladder problems precluded his sitting still for an extended period. "He is liable at any time to have to leave the room to relieve his bladder," Dr. John B. Walker wrote on White's behalf, "and it would be dangerous for him to be confined to any place where he could not do this or would have to restrain himself." He was regularly excused. Once when summoned, White informed the commissioner of jurors, enclosing his doctor's letter, that he had "been unable to serve on the Jury for years and was finally stricken from the list." Once more he was excused but not stricken from the rolls, for the matter repeatedly came up.[12]

White might not have been in good enough health in his early forties to sit as a juror, but he was obviously fit enough for a dance floor. Stan's presence, frequently alone, was often noted in newspaper accounts of dancing parties. For a costume party in February 1896 he donned a full suit of armor, probably even more uncomfortable than the coat of mail he once wore to a National Academy of Design costume ball, with Bessie dressed as a Byzantine princess. At the famous Bradley-Martin Ball, which has come to epitomize Gilded Age high society excess, held in February 1897 in the Waldorf-Astoria Grand Ballroom, decorated to resemble the royal court at Versailles, Stan came in a court costume of black velvet jacket, black shoes, white tights, and white doublet. The Bradley-Martins spent so lavishly on their party and were so harshly treated by the press afterward for their ostentatious extravagance that they soon left the country to live in England. It may have been at this ball that the author Richard Harding Davis observed White's lavish attention to a beautiful young woman named Mrs. Starr. Declaring his behavior "drunk and crazy," Davis expressed shock at White's apparent loss of control.[13]

White greatly enjoyed serving as host at late evening supper parties in the Tower studio, usually for eight to sixteen guests. Bessie was occasionally there as hostess, but not often. Stan always took great pains over the food, flowers, and entertainment. He customarily had the food catered by the restaurateur Louis Sherry. He had a florist bring in potted bay and palm trees, azaleas, orchids, bouquets of roses, smilax greenery for draping about, and boutonnières of violets. Sometimes he even had lemon and orange trees brought to the Tower room from his own greenhouses at Box Hill. Tiny lights were arranged to twinkle in the potted trees. Neapolitan mandolinists and singers in costume usually entertained at such parties, though at times he hired music hall artists to perform. When guests arrived at the Tower studio on the evening of April 1, 1896, they found china and flowers, but no food whatsoever. Louis Sherry then appeared and asked the guests to go to his restaurant on Thirty-sixth Street. When they got there, they discovered only a bare table and a placard bearing the words "April Fool." Stan then suggested they go elsewhere, and eventually the party ended up in the basement of Sherry's, where a table was set. A menu "full of surprises" had been selected. Later, everyone returned to the Tower studio for dancing. White always served Moet & Chandon "brut" at his parties, and Dewar's Scotch was available, along with a plentiful supply of sparkling wines, marsala, port, and cognac. Though Stan did not smoke cigars, he attempted to keep the best medium and light cigars on hand. He himself favored Philip Morris cigarettes.[14]

White's small, chic parties in the Tower apartment became widely known. Although not on the elaborate scale of the entertainments of the Astors and the Vanderbilts, White's affairs still shared the Gilded Age obsession with fine food and drink and meticulous care for decorations and arrangements. Invitations to his supper parties were prized, and in his studio above the Garden the "arty" crowd, mixed with figures from the theater and high society, was probably far more amusing than the more conventional dinner party assemblages of the leading New York social figures.

In the spring of 1896 Bessie fell from her bicycle and sprained a ligament in her leg, necessitating a cast and crutches for several weeks. But her recovery was good, and that summer she and Stan often played golf on the nine-hole course at Box Hill and fished together at the Nissequoque Fishing Club lodge nearby. Stan entered a golf match at Islip that October, hoping for a high handicap, and he purchased new golf clubs for himself and "the best set of woman's golf clubs" available "for a tall girl . . . marked B.S.W."[15]

While golf was a private passion for Stan, for some months in 1896 he became involved in a public passion as well. Stan, like many other Americans that year, was caught up in the presidential campaign, the only time he showed anything but political indifference. Nominally Republican, he was stirred by the issues of the election, which focused on the inequities of wealth distribution in the United States. When William Jennings Bryan, the Democratic candidate, came to speak at Madison Square Garden, Stan arranged for Charles Dana Gibson and his bride and her sister, along with his friend James Breese, to join him at a box there. It was necessary to have a box, he wrote Gibson, with decidedly elitist snobbism, "otherwise, you would be torn to pieces by the awful crowd who will be there."[16]

In this "Cross of Gold" campaign, with the populist Bryan seeking full coinage of silver as well as gold, Stan declared that he too was a bimetallist, but he felt that bimetallism had to be established by an international agreement providing uniform coinage standards in all world powers in order to be effective. He also declared, with unconscious irony, that he was "really down on Trusts and the injustice of the accumulation of wealth," which set him at odds with the sources of his firm's income and of the money for his purchases of art. He insisted, however, that for him the overriding issue in the campaign, more pressing than gold or silver coinage or the disparities of wealth, was the danger of demagoguery. That issue landed White's politics safely back in alignment with his party and his wallet. The Republican McKinley struck him as something of a demagogue, but "he happens to stand to me for right and wisdom against wrong and silliness." The Democrat Bryan, in contrast, was "a first-class double-backed, double-faced, self-threading demagogue of the worst kind. His platform is rotten and his associates without standing." Not surprisingly, Stan, confident of the election outcome, decided to have an election night watch party at the Tower studio with "at least two awfully pretty girls" present. Supper for a dozen was ordered. Guests followed the spectacular play of the Garden searchlight from the Tower as its beam changed direction to show the trend of the election returns. McKinley's victory appeared to erase demagoguery and the specter of radical change to White's satisfaction. The political values he admired—protection of wealth and property, leadership by the well-to-do, and a stable social order—seemed secure.[17]

Shortly before the election, White had yet another chance to put his penchant for spectacles on display. In October 1896 he arranged the wedding reception of Alida Chanler and Christopher Temple Emmet, Bessie's nephew, at the large, richly furnished Chanler country house, Rokeby, near Rhinebeck, New York. A special train brought two hundred guests from New York to the wedding ceremony at Christ Church in Red Hook. For the reception, Stanny had large tapestries and banners draped on the front of the mansion and brought in a strolling mandolin band and a Hungarian orchestra for dancing. The festivities went on for hours. Like all productions in which he had a hand, this was a unique and extravagant affair.[18]

Stan's life soon became closely intertwined with the socially elite Chanler family in other ways. Some years earlier, in 1890, Stan and Saint-Gaudens had persuaded John Armstrong ("Archie") Chanler, their frequent social companion and an heir to part of the Astor fortune, to provide funds that would enable promising young American artists to go to Paris for study. A competition decided by jurors was agreed upon, and Stan and Gus were named as jurors and as co-trustees of the fund. The painter Jean-Léon Gérôme agreed to supervise the students' work in Paris. For about fifteen years White administered the Chanler Paris Prize Fund.

Archie Chanler was the eldest of the ten children of Margaret Astor Ward and John Winthrop Chanler. Their mother, who inherited a large fortune and the Rokeby estate at the death of her grandfather, William B. Astor, in 1875, had herself fallen ill at his funeral and died shortly thereafter. Her husband died two years later. The ten orphaned children— the eldest then only fifteen—a notably "hyperactive group" and "furiously individualistic family," stayed on at Rokeby, reared there by tutors and governesses. Archie Chanler was later schooled at Rugby in England and at Columbia College and was admitted to the New York bar in 1885. After extensive travel in Europe, the West Indies, and South America, he returned to live in New York. There he became acquainted with Stan, joining some of the clubs White frequented and often socializing with him.[19]

In 1887, on a visit to Newport, Archie encountered a lovely Southern girl, Amélie Rives, and was smitten. He wangled an invitation to spend Christmas that year at the Rives estate, Castle Hill, near Charlottesville,

Virginia. The Rives family was distinguished: Amélie's grandfather, William Cabell Rives, had studied law with Jefferson and twice served as Minister to France; her father, a godson of Lafayette, was chief of engineers in the Confederate Army during the Civil War. Amélie was a goddaughter of Robert E. Lee. A talented writer, in April 1888 she published *The Quick or the Dead*, a lurid romance with a character in it modeled on Archie; the novel became a best-seller, with some 300,000 copies printed.

Archie and Amélie were married in June 1888. Her family was opposed to the marriage, however, and Amélie soon came to feel that something was wrong, indeed that Archie was mentally unbalanced. Five months after the wedding, they separated. Archie went off to Europe alone. They were back together in Paris again briefly in 1889 but found themselves constantly at odds. Suffering from migraines, Amélie took morphine for relief and soon became addicted. It was on his return to New York in 1890 that Archie provided for the Paris Prize Fund. Amélie went back to Virginia, where she seemed to be wasting away on drugs. Eventually she was placed in the care of the famous physician Dr. S. Weir Mitchell of Philadelphia, who effected her recovery. In October 1895 she divorced Archie in South Dakota. She was married the following February to Prince Pierre Troubetzkoy, an impecunious sculptor. As Princess Troubetzkoy, she continued to write books and plays, some of which were highly successful.

Meanwhile, in the early 1890s, Archie and his brother Winthrop Chanler had established a cotton mill and water power plant along the Roanoke River in Halifax County, North Carolina. White in his professional capacity was called upon to design the buildings for the Roanoke Rapids Power Company and the United Industrial Company, and he also invested in the Chanler enterprise. When Archie, the principal investor, and Winthrop, the second largest investor and president, fell into a dispute over policy at the mill, however, Winthrop resigned from the business. In January 1897 Archie took over as president. Soon after, though, he desired to be relieved from the work in order to devote himself to investigating various psychological phenomena that interested him. Archie thereupon gave Stanford White the power of attorney over the business and the prize fund. For a time the architect also served as president of the North Carolina mill. Archie, whose behavior was becoming more and more strange, claimed he could change the color of his eyes by meditation, and he shut himself in his house, The Merry Mills, to conduct "experiments."[20]

Alarmed at reports of what Archie was doing, Stan went to North Carolina in February 1897 with a physician and persuaded Chanler to return to New York with him for medical treatment. Shortly after their arrival in New York, at the Kensington Hotel, Chanler proceeded to demonstrate that he could go into a trance and reenact the death of Napoleon. His brothers Winthrop and Lewis concluded that Archie had completely lost his mind, and in March they had him committed to Bloomingdale Insane Asylum. White, holding Archie's power of attorney, was urged by the family to have him declared insane, but Stan refused to do so out of loyalty to his friend. White also held power of attorney for Amélie Troubetzkoy, Archie's former wife, in matters relating to her first husband's property in which she had a stake. Two years later, in June 1899, Winthrop and Lewis Chanler succeeded in having Archie ruled insane by the courts. It was reported that Archie by then thought himself to be a silver box tarnished by magnetism. Prescott Hall Butler and, later, his law partner Thomas Sherman were appointed guardians for Archie Chanler, whose estate was very large.

White's loyalty to Archie was not reciprocated. Archie was furious with White and blamed him, along with his brothers, for his incarceration in the Bloomingdale Asylum. His confinement there was actually minimal; he was allowed to leave for brief periods and even kept his own carriage and horses nearby. On Thanksgiving Eve, 1900, however, he left the asylum and did not return. Stan was immediately warned that Archie had escaped and to be on the alert, since Chanler was particularly hostile toward him. It was later discovered that Chanler went to a private sanatorium in Philadelphia and subsequently to Virginia, where he remained, living quietly. In May 1905 Stan, Gus, and Thomas Sherman, the attorney, arranged to have the Paris Prize account turned over to the American Academy in Rome for the support of American art students. Chanler, meanwhile, had sought to recover legal control of his estate and sued in Virginia to have it turned over to him. Eventually he was ruled sane in Virginia and in North Carolina, but he still remained insane under the laws of New York State. In 1906 Chanler published an exposé of the Bloomingdale Asylum in which he concluded that in this "Bastille of the Four Hundred" the rules and procedures alone were enough to drive a sane man crazy.[21]

For several years the Archie Chanler affair greatly complicated Stan's life, burdening him with countless decisions about the North Carolina mill, the Paris Prize Fund, and Archie himself. The various involvements did not benefit White financially but brought only irritation, worry, and the labor of vast correspondence. Loyal and compassionate toward his friend, Stan was increasingly drawn into the large circle of the Chanler family and their Astor relations.

Despite the troubles with Archie Chanler beginning in 1897, that year appears to have been an especially happy one. Stanny and Bessie were often together, enjoying golf and fishing in the country. Business in the office had improved greatly: The firm's commissions income in 1898 from work completed more than doubled that from the previous year. The partners were especially close, as well, and they took great pride in their work. Theirs was by this time indisputably the most important architectural firm in the United States and brought fortune and fame to them all. Although McKim often complained of chronic "dyspepsia" and "catarrh of the stomach," he was feeling much better than before. And, according to McKim, Stan was "looking splendidly and in robust health."[22]

In August the three partners traveled to Quebec for a fortnight of fishing at the Restigouche camp, the only time they all vacationed together. While at the fishing camp, White inspected work he had previously arranged for on William K. Vanderbilt's rustic lodge, and he and the others had great success in catching salmon. They rode to the headwaters of the Restigouche and enjoyed "a perfectly splendid trip down the river." At one point, near the main camp, White "had the great satisfaction of making my horse splash both McKim and Mead successively all over with dirty water, much to their rage and my joy." It was a restful, idyllic time. They reveled in the crisp air of the northern forest, with its luxuriant greenery and wild flowers, its rushing streams and spray-dampened rocks. The peaceful days were free of worry and filled with pleasure: "We had the most magnificent weather all the time, like warm October days, with brilliant moonlight nights, and both McKim and Mead were simply enraptured with the river and the trip." Obviously, Stan felt the same way.[23]

All too soon, however, the peace and pleasure of the summer holiday and the general contentment of those months would pass. From that time onward, White's private life was more and more filled with turmoil, moving out of control. But the turmoil and loss of control in his private life only seemed to spark more creativity and consummate artistry in his professional work.

18

"In a Hole All the Time"

I n the late 1890s, social activities and many new large professional projects greatly increased the pace of White's life. Occasional trips to Europe, a few short holidays in the South, and twice-a-year visits to the Restigouche Salmon Club provided some relief from his frenzied life-style, but at times it seemed as if he were on a carousel revolving faster and faster, spinning out of control. His tendency to spend lavishly became virtually a compulsion. He was living far beyond his means. He was the little boy in the candy store, hands in the display case, gorging himself on all the goodies he could reach. To meet what seemed to be an insatiable need for wealth, Stan began to speculate in stocks and grain futures, often with borrowed money, often recklessly. More and more, too, he seemed to need to be at the center of things, to earn the admiration of a society devoted to grand appearances, the love of display that his own father had condemned. To his painter friend Ned Simmons, he was the artist-child, who "never became an adult."[1]

After the quiet summer of 1897, from September 18 to November 20 Stan traveled to Europe once more, this time primarily on a buying trip. Frederick W. Vanderbilt authorized him to purchase articles of furniture for the mansion McKim had recently designed for him at Hyde Park, New York. Vanderbilt placed $150,000 at White's disposal, and White was to be guided in his purchases by a list of articles furnished by McKim. Stan easily spent all Vanderbilt's money in London, Paris, Florence, Rome, and Venice; freight, duties, and Stan's personal commissions of 10 percent were paid later on. It is conceivable that the occasions when Vanderbilt and other clients provided him with very large sums to purchase goods for them gave White an inflated idea of his own personal spending power.[2]

On this trip, the architect also purchased many things for his own collection, planning to resell some later to clients and to use others for decorating projects. From his Paris headquarters at the elegant Hotel Vendôme, Stan went around to his favorite dealers. Georges Allard of the decorating firm had "several new things of interest" to show him, and one dealer brought a purported Greuze painting for his inspection, something that Henry Duveen in New York had asked him to find. Later in London, he stopped at the Savoy Hotel and again made the rounds of dealers' shops. On his return to New York, White was accorded "the courtesies of the port"; he was "carefully looked after" when his ship docked, "well taken care of by the Customs Department," and not asked directly whether he had anything to declare.[3]

Perhaps the customs authorities would have been less gracious to him had they known of his regular arrangements with European dealers to have goods sent on to him invoiced at sums considerably lower than what had actually been charged. White's conduct in the matter of customs charges was less than honorable, though the practice was commonplace among dealer-importers. Two invoices with different prices were frequently issued for goods imported. When duties were levied on antiquities late in the 1890s, Stan instructed dealers shipping antiquities to enclose invoices for the customs declaration at "about 30 per cent" of the price actually paid. His rationale for setting the invoice price on antiquities so low was that "antiquities are not like new work, but they have a fictitious value, and an antique you might buy of a dealer in Florence, for 10,000 francs, a dealer in Rome might charge you 5,000 for, and it is, therefore, possible to declare the *lowest* price *possible* on antiquities for the Customs House." Dealers from whom he made purchases always had to be instructed to make out the extra set of invoices. White once wrote that the best way he had found to get things over was by sending them in Europe to Allard in Paris or Duveen in London, "without any invoice at all and letting them make their own invoices and get them through in their own way."[4]

The following spring, in 1898, both Stan and Charley fell seriously ill again. Stan came down with influenza and for several weeks was severely limited in what he could do. McKim's chronic stomach trouble flared up, and he suffered from insomnia. For a good part of the spring, Charley stayed in the South. On his return he put in only limited hours at the office. To add to his discomfort, McKim was obliged to move from his long-rented rooms at 9 West Thirty-fifth Street to new quarters. He finally found housing at 9 East Thirty-fifth Street, which he remodeled to suit his needs. His daughter Margaret, with whom he was now reconciled, could stay with him there on visits to New York. Stan felt that because of the difficult winter and spring, he needed his outing in the Canadian wilderness "more than ever." He spent five weeks fishing on the Restigouche and returned, he boasted, "in roaring health," pleased to report to MacMonnies in Paris that now "everything is serene with me."[5]

The "serenity" of Stan's life in 1898 might be questioned, however, for the pressures of his professional work along with many private projects continued and the hectic pace of his social life was unabating. He had entered into negotiations for a new city residence, and he was becoming more and more deeply ensnared in financial speculations. Several years earlier, at the end of the 1880s, he had already begun to play the stock market on a small scale, and an occasional "killing" no doubt fueled his gaming instinct and encouraged him to believe that great wealth, which he like his father before him so coveted, might be his. By the mid-1890s his speculations had increased. Bessie's inheritance from her great aunt and mother provided some of the money for his stock purchases, though Stanford himself was making substantial commissions as an art agent and on resale of goods. Moreover, he was also receiving good profit allocations from the firm—nearly $28,000 for 1895–96 and more than $59,000 for 1896–97, for example—which left him with further funds available for investments. Occasionally he borrowed money to finance stock purchases or bought stocks on margin. In 1894 he contracted a loan for stock purchases from the Knickerbocker Trust Company, secured by bonds that Bessie held; part of it was later paid off by the sale of the Whites' Madison Square Garden bonds. In 1895 he borrowed money on his Restigouche Club share from Prescott Hall Butler. In the summer of 1895 he had about $45,000 available in cash to invest with his broker, Robert Winthrop & Company.[6]

By 1897 White's purchases of stocks and bonds had soared, much of the time on margin, and he was speculating in grain futures as well. Surviving correspondence indicates that he was profiting from his stock investments in 1897, but matters soon changed: In 1898 and 1899 he suffered substantial losses and went into debt to several brokerage houses. Now and then White devised "a little scheme" to borrow on shares he held in order to make additional purchases on margin. In November 1898 he was convinced that "the market is going up and . . . it is a great time for a plunge," so he put in large orders with three or four brokers for railroad, gas company, oil, and iron and coal shares, specifying sale when the stocks rose five points. Some of the investments did well while others went down, but he managed to come out of those ventures with some profit.[7]

In the winter of 1899, however, Stan took "a flyer in sugar and fell into a boiling cauldron of it." As a result, he wrote, he "had the skin all taken off me." His loss was so great that he became physically ill. He lamented that he would have to "begin all over again and reconstruct my little pile." Not only did he get skinned by sugar, but most of his other stocks also plummeted. By the spring he was, he said, "really at my wits end to meet my obligations." On April 10, 1899, he took out a loan of nearly $75,000 with the New York Loan & Improvement Company, arranged by Charles Barney. To add to his distress, his close friend and client Robert Goelet died suddenly that spring on his yacht moored at Naples. In May Stan went to Newport for the arrival of the yacht bringing back Goelet's remains and served as a pallbearer at the funeral. His many worries, he was convinced, contributed to a severe recurrence in June of his bladder and urinary tract infection.[8]

That summer, the forty-five-year-old White decided to increase his life insurance, but at the physical examination he was "in such a nervous state as to affect my health" and was turned down. The following year he approached another life insurance company and was accepted for a $50,000 policy with a high annual premium of $5,636. In a letter to Gus in Paris about his troubles, Stan, no doubt recalling the pleasures of their excursion with McKim in southern France more than twenty years before, when his burdens and worries were so few, wistfully suggested that they might go off "together in Spain or somewhere again."[9]

Six weeks at the Restigouche camp in June 1899 and a shorter second trip in late July gave him much-needed rest. His health was better after the Canadian visits, though his doctor, concerned about the urinary tract problem, was "indulging in some severe treatment to prevent any chance of chronic trouble." In November, plagued by his creditors, White negotiated a demand note from the Manhattan Trust Company for $25,000. Then in December his financial condition worsened, with further losses in the market. Just before Christmas 1899, he wrote MacMonnies in Paris, "I got my head cut off and I fear it will be a long time before it is back on my shoulders again." When asked to contribute to a City Club charity, he responded that "the most deserving object of charity that I know of is myself." He likened his recent forays in the market to a shooting expedition, "but the trouble was that I was the game and not the hunter." To add to his troubles, about this time his arms became covered with the open sores of carbuncles. Robert Reid, the painter whom he had assisted so often, learned of White's disastrous plunges and offered to return a large Spanish tapestry on loan in his studio if it would help Stan out.[10]

While his stock market dealings were taking up more and more of

Stan's energy, he had become involved in negotiations for a new town-house, which it would seem he could then ill afford, even though he had not yet suffered the big losses of 1898–99. For some years the Whites had been trying to get Henry A. C. Taylor, their landlord, to sell them the brownstone they were renting at 119 East Twenty-first Street. Taylor himself had long occupied the larger adjacent house at 121, inherited from his father, on the corner of Lexington Avenue, but in 1896 or 1897 Taylor moved to a new mansion that McKim had designed on East Seventy-first Street. By 1897 Stan was making inquiries about the possible purchase or long-term lease of the corner property.[11]

Early in 1898 White concluded an agreement with Taylor to rent the house at 121 East Twenty-first Street. Even before they moved next door, Stan and Bessie gave a ''Vaudeville Party'' on March 1, 1898, in the corner house in keeping with their usual lavish style of entertaining. The architect had a small stage built at one end of the ballroom of 121 and a wooden passageway connecting the ballroom with the dining room of 119. The Broadway comedians Weber, Fields, and Bernard were hired to entertain the guests. Between the first and second parts of the stage show, Stan arranged for a cinematograph, which necessitated bring-ing in a special electrical line for the house. He assured Taylor that he had received permission from the Board of Underwriters and that the temporary platform inside would in no way ''be the slightest injury to the house.'' The Twenty-first Street houses were two of the earliest in the city to be wired for electricity, and the cinematograph, including pictures of a bull fight, was no doubt one of the earliest such cinematic presentations in a private house anywhere.[12]

As negotiations for the corner property proceeded, White decided that he would like to rent both of Taylor's houses and sublet 119 to his sister-in-law Kate Wetherill, who was looking for a townhouse. Taylor accepted the proposal, and a rental of $6,200 a year plus taxes of about $2,000 was agreed upon for the two houses. Taylor also agreed to take care of some repairs and plantings. It was arranged that minor alterations to be shared by Taylor and White would be made on the corner house. Mrs. Wetherill, who paid White $3,600 in annual rent, occupied the house at 119 for five years, after which her lease was assigned to Mary P. Iselin.[13]

While Bessie remained at St. James through the fall months, Stan took charge of decorating 121, supervising carpeting, masonry, painting, plastering, tiling, plumbing, and the laying of new floors, as well as choosing carpets, wall paper, and curtains. Just as his own clients did, Stan frequently complained to the contractors about their slow progress.

Allard & Sons, who were doing much of the decoration, botched up work on an old Venetian ceiling, which White was having installed in the dining room, by sanding and lacquering it to make it look like new. Stan brought in the painter Everett Shinn to do ceiling murals in other rooms. In this large new house, White was preparing yet another New York stage setting, this time for himself and his family, and the residence he was planning would rival the houses of the wealthiest New Yorkers.[14]

On December 15, 1898, Bessie, Nina, and Larry, together with a retinue of eight servants, moved into the city from Box Hill, joining White at the house, even though work on the first-floor rooms had not yet been completed. As the work went on, the expenses mounted. By January 1899 Stan owed the principal building contractor some $21,000 for work already done, and other contractors also had to be paid. The residence at 121, he wrote his landlord, "will be a most charmingly comfortable house to live in," though he expected his stay to be "very short," because, considering the expense, he anticipated "debtors' prison before the 1st of May." By May, Stan estimated that the cost of rebuilding and restoring the new house was approximately $50,000, with interior decorating work costing $15,000 more. He asked Taylor to take on the payment of half of the cost of restoration, which he would then repay in installments with interest over ten years. Taylor did not accept the proposition. Stan continued to press him for a loan for the work he had had done; the following year he reported that he had spent $80,000 to restore the two houses. The matter would come up again later.[15]

When the alterations, restorations, and decorating of 121 were largely completed, Stan boasted that "as the house now stands, I really think it is as commodious and fine as any but three or four in the city." He knew the great houses of the city well, and his was certainly one of the finest. Although only 32 feet wide, the house extended northward along the west side of Lexington Avenue for 131½ feet. It was large and substantial and soon became widely known as a showplace. In decorating and furnishing his new residence, Stan was creating both the beautiful and opulent ambience he relished and making a statement to New Yorkers about his prominent position in the city. An inventory of household furnishings, paintings, and works of art in the house that White compiled in 1899 listed the major pieces in each room with their estimated worth and arrived at a total valuation just short of $300,000. Had the radical sociologist Thorstein Veblen been aware of White's newly renovated Gramercy Park house, it might have provided him with a striking illustration of "conspicuous consumption" for his mordant and ironic *Theory of the Leisure Class,* published that very year.[16]

From a small vestibule at the front entrance on Twenty-first Street a visitor came into the downstairs entrance hall, with eight marble columns, an antique altar, four ancient sarcophagi, a large stone mantelpiece, and a *mille-fleurs* tapestry placed around the room. To the rear of the lower hall was the reception room, decorated by another *mille-fleurs* tapestry. Farther yet to the rear on the ground floor were the servants' hall, the kitchen, and the laundry. On the floor above, the four large rooms were laid out en suite, providing a vista the full length of the house. The drawing room in the front, with walls covered by red Genoese velvet and with an Italian carved ceiling, housed some of White's most prized paintings, including portraits said to be by Holbein and Romney and portraits of his parents by Daniel Huntington, Abbott Thayer, and Thomas Dewing. An antique mantel and an elaborately carved Venetian mirror were placed within a large door frame set against a wall. Two polar bear skins and a tiger skin were scattered about on the floor. Behind the drawing room was the main hall, with staircases to the lower and upper floors. Four large tapestries graced the walls, and an Italian Renaissance carved stone mantel and overmantel stood there. Behind the hall, the dining room had a richly carved Venetian ceiling, and in an antique marble fountain live trout swam about. Four large Renaissance tapestries covered the walls. Opening into the dining room to the rear was the ballroom or music room, in which musical instruments once belonging to Richard Grant White were displayed.[17]

On the second floor, the green room, a sitting room facing Gramercy Park, was filled with contemporary paintings White had collected, many of them by artist friends. As in the other rooms, antique vases, candlesticks, and bowls were scattered about. Bessie's and Stan's separate bedrooms, each with private bath, were on this floor; Stan had a few of his paintings of nudes in his bedroom, while Bessie in her room enjoyed framed photographs of family and friends, an indication of how the couple's interests diverged. A tile-lined lobby, lighted by stained-glass windows and containing yet another carved sarcophagus, marble statues of Venus and Leda, and ten Italian Renaissance bas-reliefs, led to the large picture gallery at the rear of the house above the music room. An open timber ceiling and a huge stone fireplace gave a sense of spaciousness to the picture gallery. Stuffed animal heads hung from the upper walls and ceiling beams. Paintings attributed to Quentin Matsys, Thomas Lawrence, Tintoretto, Kneller, and Romney lined the walls of

265

the gallery, along with works by White's friends Brush, Dewing, Ryder, Metcalf, Weir, and Sargent. On the third floor, Larry's room was at the front, with guest rooms to the rear. The low-ceilinged top floor held servants' quarters. A stable at 5 Lexington Avenue stood directly behind the house.

While the principal work on the Whites' new Gramercy Park house was being completed, Stan was busy on yet another program of major alterations and new building at Box Hill, which began in the spring and summer of 1899 and continued in 1900 and 1901. Just while his stock market losses were soaring, he recklessly plunged into additional spending on the country estate. Labor was cheap, of course, and Bessie probably paid most of the costs for the Box Hill expansion. Yet Stan seemed compulsively driven to create at his rural residence, as in the rented townhouse, the luxuriant ambience he so urgently needed. Landscaping and terracing were undertaken as well as considerable work on the ancillary structures of the estate, including a new barn and stables, a tank house, an ice house, a pump house, a pergola, and a coachman's cottage. Stones from the former Stewart mansion on Thirty-fourth Street at Fifth Avenue were built into a new wall on the property. A burglar alarm system was installed in the house, as had been done earlier at Twenty-first Street. New greenhouses were erected in which palm, orange, and bay trees were planted.[18]

Like the Whites' Gramercy Park house, Box Hill, after the turn of the century, became widely known as a Stanford White showplace. Visitors who saw the gardens on the estate often complimented White on what he had created there. F. W. Kelsey, a New York City nurseryman, was especially impressed with White's skillful recreation of an Italian garden and his success with his greenhouse trees and plants. Possibly hoping to ingratiate himself and pick up some business, he wrote White: "Your gardening, like your architecture, is original, artistic, and unique." Stan himself once wrote that he took more pride in his orange trees "than my gardens or anything else."[19]

Others became acquainted with the St. James house and property at second hand from magazine articles or book chapters on Box Hill. The author Barr Ferree in *American Estates and Gardens* provided a well-illustrated discussion of the White country place, which he viewed as one of the outstanding country estates in the United States. Ferree described the splendid views of the harbor and sound from the house, the "gently swelling lawns" below the house, the colorful and artfully designed formal garden, and the small Grecian temple, the exedra seat, and the copy of Diana carefully sited on the property. The rich collection of art objects scattered about "this delightful home"—tapestries, mirrors, twisted columns, Turkish rugs, carved chairs and chests, gilded trophies and ornaments of various sorts, and silver ceiling lamps—charmed the author. The dining room, with its wall of Dutch tiles, its majolica plates, and the profusion of silver, china, and cut-glass objects, was of particular interest to him, as was the large living room, with its bamboo-covered walls and ceiling, splendid carpets, tapestries, mirrors and paintings, carved window frames, and twisted columns. Although the living room was probably a housemaid's nightmare, to Ferree "the very multiplicity of its contents, speaks not alone of comfort, but of interest, and real, living interest, in everything it contains." Perhaps, as well as any place, this room embodied the essence of White's mode of interior decorating— taking a miscellany of antique art objects, some of them worked into the architecture of the room itself, and placing them together to create an atmosphere of visual surprises and artful elegance.[20]

Box Hill, as always, was primarily Bessie's domain. In his more intimate correspondence, Stan wrote of the St. James place as "Bessie's house," though the public at large understood it to be *his* estate. Here, Bessie was happiest, and Stan, though deeply involved in rebuilding and enlarging the house, in designing the grounds, and in planning count-less projects around the estate, was something of a visitor, a guest in his own house. As earlier, except for brief summer holidays, Stan seldom came out to Long Island for more than a short weekend of Saturday afternoon and Sunday. Bessie directed the house servants and oversaw the gardeners, coachmen, and groundsmen, and she arranged dinners and weekend parties there. By the turn of the century she had the able assistance of Joseph Gould, the chief gardener, who lived in a cottage on the property and took day-to-day charge of the estate. It was Gould who supervised the work of the contractors who put down new surfaces on the 2,500 feet of primary roads and the 1,200 feet of service roads on the place in 1903.[21]

Bessie lived quietly at St. James. She would see her family and friends who lived nearby, enjoy golf and fishing, and oversee the household. There in the large and comfortable house, she carefully clipped newspaper articles relating to friends and acquaintances. She compiled countless lists of such matters as the rulers of England, the Presidents of the United States, the signs of the zodiac, holidays and anniversaries, the seven wonders of the ancient world and the seven hills of Rome, and "The Best Books in Chronological Order." Self-conscious about the limitations of her formal education, she had a passion for self-improvement and the accessible facts such lists could provide. In her scrapbooks she kept accounts of the fish she, Stan, and Larry had caught. She pasted in jokes and puzzles and copied out homilies: "Rules for a comfortable old age: Eat less. Drink more water. Sleep a great deal and laugh heartily at least once a day." In her latter years Bessie was always reticent about her age; it may be that the scrapbook clippings and notations provided her a means of holding on to the present recorded moment and to feel that she was staying the rush of time. Almost obsessively neat, she labeled small boxes for storing all sorts of odds and ends. She loved parlor games: One July 1905 evening a "Game of Avengers" with Larry and several of his friends was particularly memorable both for the pleasure of being with the young people and for Bessie's winning scores. Lists, labels, and winning game scores could all bring order into her world, helping to wall out the turmoil and disorder that—increasingly after the turn of the century—raged around her husband.[22]

At Box Hill, Stan's elderly mother, Alexina, devoted much of her time to Larry until he went away to St. Mark's School. Larry felt close to his grandmother and later said that she was "very careful" educating him "in music and English and pronunciation and whatnot." Nina's relations with Bessie were sometimes strained. When a water pipe burst one evening, sending a downpour into the dining room, and Nina suggested that the accident had occurred because the windmill continuously pumped water into the water tower, an argument broke out. Nina complained to her son—asking him not to tell Bessie she was writing him about the incident—that whenever she tried to get an explanation of something "no one [i.e., Bessie] is willing to explain if I am mistaken without getting into a passion." Her manner with her adult son was always affectionate and often self-deprecating, a mode of discourse she had learned well in her years with Stan's father. On one occasion she and the maids hunted high and low through Box Hill for some figurines and other objects Stan wanted sent to the city. She hoped that what she did send were the things he wanted. But then, what could he expect? "I am not a conoseur [sic], a dilettante, nor any other wild animal devoted to Art—but only your loving little Mamma."[23]

At the close of the century, Stan's concerns about his stock market losses and increasing indebtedness, along with his health problems, made the diversion of yet another European trip all the more appealing. Getting away from the office and his usual whirl of social activities, and putting behind him, at least for a short time, his day-to-day problems could give him a respite that might bring a sense of renewal. In the summer of 1900 he was forty-six years old, youthful and energetic in some ways, yet also well into middle age, growing heavy, graying, and plagued by repeated illness. At times he expressed astonishment at the way he had got caught up in the hectic, "driven" life he was leading.

After a fortnight fishing in Canada in early June, White left New York on the *Aquitaine* on June 28, 1900, accompanied by Bessie and Larry, taking two deck cabins. On July 6 they reached Paris and stayed at the Normandy Hotel in a suite of two bedrooms and a salon. Stan went almost at once to see Saint-Gaudens, who had been in France for three years working on his Sherman statue and other commissions. Saint-Gaudens's sculpture by then was internationally recognized: the Sherman statue had occupied a place of honor at the Paris Exposition and had received a gold medal, and the sculptor had been named to the Legion of Honor and elected a corresponding member of the Academy of Beaux Arts. For more than two years, though, Gus had been ill, and he had just been diagnosed as having a rectal tumor. Surgery was imperative. Stan helped Gus sail for the United States. Shortly after his return to America, Gus had an operation to remove the cancerous growth at the Massachusetts General Hospital in Boston. A few months later he underwent surgery a second time. Besides helping Gus get the medical attention he needed, Stan in Paris visited the Exposition held that year, and he and his son enjoyed a breathtaking ride in a balloon over the rooftops of the city. The architect made extensive purchases of furnishings and art works for William C. Whitney, Frederick Vanderbilt, and others, and he spent a good deal of time with his collaborator Willie MacMonnies. Larry White, who was clever at drawing like his father, filled a small sketchbook with impressions of European scenes on this trip.[24]

A month or so after the Whites had sailed from New York, McKim also went abroad. Before he left, he apprised "Dummy" of the status of work in progress: Symphony Hall in Boston was "coming on finely" and a large Harvard University commission appeared to be in the offing. The outlook for the firm, McKim suggested, was "certainly gratifying," and, he went on, "it especially pleases me to feel that White's prediction, since the [Boston] Library competition, that 'we are now on the descendent,' is slightly premature." (White some years earlier had apparently been pessimistic that the firm would continue to attract additional big commissions, but the 1890s had been rich with many large projects.) To Stan in Paris, Charley telegraphed that Gus's operation had been completely successful and that at the office all was "serene."[25]

While Bessie and Larry went off on an excursion to the Pyrenees with Nellie and Prescott Butler, Stan "made a lightning trip to Italy," traveling as far as Sicily in the company of Charles Coleman, his Naples agent and painter friend. The visit to Italy was hectic and exhausting, involving "ten nights on the train and only one night in bed." Coleman, however, recalled the trip with White to Sicily as "like a wonderful dream," the view of Mt. Etna especially, "a sight never to be forgotten." In Italy Stan purchased, among other things, a bas-relief of the Annunciation attributed to Mino da Fiesole and an antique life-size marble group, which he had shipped to New York. Later, in England, he arranged for the setting and marble for the large Robert Louis Stevenson Memorial plaque, on which he had worked earlier with Saint-Gaudens. On September 16 the Whites sailed from England on the *Deutschland* and were back home by September 22. They brought through customs eleven trunks filled with purchases. At this juncture, Stan reported, "I had to give a horrible wink to the Custom house officer when he said, 'I suppose you have made no purchases abroad.' I had 'the courtesies of the port,' however, and got through all right." The large Italian sculptural group, when it later arrived, was charged a 20 percent duty as a work of art, but the bas-relief was listed as "a work of manufactured marble" and charged a 50 percent duty. White protested the tariff assessment but lost his case—fair enough, considering how he had cheated customs on the purchases in the trunks![26]

On his return, White reported that he had "had a bully time" on the three-month trip abroad. Almost immediately, though, the demands of work once again were all too pressing. He made a hurried trip to Boston for the opening of Symphony Hall and afterward wrote Gus, then convalescing at Cornish, New Hampshire, to apologize for not having had time to go to see him on that trip: "Perhaps because I am getting old, and still try to do so much and can't do it, but I seem to get more and more behindhand on my work all the time and to be in constant hot water in consequence . . . with the rushing around I am forced to do anyway. I am in a hole all the time."[27]

His financial situation, moreover, had become an unrelenting worry. Along with his stock market speculations, Stan had invested in the spring of 1899 in a flooded copper mine at El Cobre, near Santiago de Cuba, joining with Prescott Hall Butler and William Astor Chanler, a brother of Archie Chanler, who had served with the American forces in Cuba in 1898 and was subsequently elected to Congress. When the owners of the mine were assessed in May 1900 to provide funds for its rehabilitation, Stan had been obliged to borrow from Chanler, giving his shares as security. Chanler had also paid Stan's portion of another assessment while he was in Europe.[28]

White realized he had to get out, for the mine was an additional burden he did not need. His letter to William Chanler that October was despairing: "Since I have been away, matters have been going from bad to worse, and on my return I find my affairs in a desperate state, with unexpected calls for money." Not only was he unable to pay these pressing claims, "but what makes me madder is that the money is simply thrown into the sea. Every attempt I have made to recover myself has proved disastrous and only an additional source of worry and anxiety and outlay. I am at the end of my tether and must chuck everything overboard."[29]

But his financial situation just got worse. In April 1901 things again went badly for him in the market, and he "managed to hit it wrong both ways." Then in May, as the J. P. Morgan and James J. Hill forces battled with Edward H. Harriman and Jacob H. Schiff for control of the Northern Pacific Railroad, that stock was "cornered" and, with short sellers trying to cover their commitments, shot up to $1,000 a share. Panic selling ensued, as the big traders tried to cover themselves. Other stock prices plummeted. White had gambled heavily in oil, mining, and railroad stocks, as always in quest of a big and quick return. In the 1901 panic, he lamented, he was "wiped off the face of the earth." In two days, May 8–9, he lost about $388,000 and was buried in debts to his brokers and bankers. Henry Poor & Company was one of his principal brokers. Stan had some $40,000 to $50,000 of his own art objects in Henry Poor's mansion across Lexington Avenue from his residence, and he could satisfy that debt by turning over the objects to Poor. To James Breese, who helped him out with a substantial loan, he assigned various objects in his house and on loan in Breese's studio as security. Other debts, though, could not be satisfied so easily. As the months passed, White's financial situation deteriorated even further. Finally it dawned on him, he wrote a friend: "The truth is you can't run architecture and stock-jobbing at the same time."[30]

19

"Bachelors for the Evening"

☙

For years, before he moved to Paris in 1897, Gus Saint-Gaudens was Stan's most intimate friend and social companion. The two artists not only shared a great deal in their work—though tensions developed over time in their collaborations—but they also both enjoyed "whooping it up," often with others, in nights on the town. For Stan, a night out with male friends often involved "a glorious spree," heavy drinking, and sometimes the excitement of attractive young women. A particularly memorable spree was often referred to as "a most monumental time."

By the early 1890s White was more and more frequently arranging small dinners and nights on the town for male friends, often artists whom he had known for years, some of them from the time of the Trinity Church decoration. Stan called those longtime friends "the old gang" or "the crowd." When setting up an evening he would promise "just an old-time affair." Gus and his brother Louis, Frank Lathrop, Thomas Dewing, George Babb, Edward Simmons ("Simjaks"), and Robert Reid were regulars in "the gang." McKim, Mead, and Archie Chanler were occasionally with him for evenings on the town, as were George de Forest Brush, Abbott Thayer, and Willie MacMonnies on their visits to New York. By the latter 1890s, friends from the financial and business world often joined Stan for dinner and an evening of carousing—Robert Goelet, Henry Poor, James Breese, and Charles Barney were frequently with him. Another "gang" of Stan's friends was made up of fishing companions from the Restigouche Salmon Club.[1]

273

Stan and a very few close companions, as "bachelors for the evening," for years carried on a secret life of sexual adventures, which were hidden from their families and from most of their friends and acquaintances. The available evidence is spotty about the encounters and involvements of White and his companions in promiscuity, but some of the story can be reconstructed from materials that have been located.

For some years the painter Thomas Dewing was a member of White's innermost circle. A great hulk of a man, two and one-half years older than Stan and considered strikingly handsome, Dewing had started his career in New York from a studio in the University Building the same year that White teamed up with McKim and Mead. He shortly left the city to return in 1881, the year he was married to Maria Oakey, an artist with whom he occasionally collaborated on paintings. Like Saint-Gaudens, he acquired property in Cornish, New Hampshire, where Stan designed a painting studio for him and his wife. He joined the Society of American Artists and was also a full member of the National Academy of Design.

Dewing was noted for his malicious wit. Some people avoided him because he was "quarrelsome, always ready to pick a fight." White considered him "nervous and touchy," and often difficult to deal with; one had to "make allowances for the man's excessive sensitiveness," he said. Dewing, for his part, had reservations about White, whose perpetually exuberant, often frenetic manner bothered him at times. Stan once planned a visit to him in Cornish, and Dewing wrote Charles Freer, the Detroit industrialist, that there was always such a noisy disturbance when White was around that he advised Freer not visit there at the same time. White liked Dewing's paintings and acquired several for his own collection, including one he characterized as "the little girl we were both afraid of." He designed frames for some of Dewing's works and employed him to do ceiling decorations in the Hotel Imperial. By the late 1880s, Dewing was developing a highly personal style, influenced by Japanese art, painting mostly frail, etherealized women in quiet, lonely rooms or in open fields, abstracted from ordinary reality. Dewing did a revealing sketch of Joseph M. Wells and a portrait of Bessie, which Stan greatly admired and occasionally sent out for exhibition.[2]

When he lived in New York during the winter months, Dewing saw a good deal of Stan, enjoying "our Indian summer of life and—gayety." He rented various studios in the city and for a time painted in a Tower room at Madison Square Garden, which White had arranged for him. He often borrowed objects from White to use in his paintings and regularly borrowed money from him. On visits to New York from Cornish, he sometimes stayed with Stan at his house. Like Saint-Gaudens, Dewing asked Stan to see that letters addressed to him at The Players were sent to New England in an outer envelope, marked "For C. A. Platt": "There are just a few letters that might come that I want to be extra careful of." When Dewing moved to Paris in 1895, he reported back to White that he had seen "a good deal of Whistler and MacMonnies" there and that they had had "several *large* times that MacMonnies pronounced the most extraordinary that he ever dreamed of." Charles Freer, who was then in Paris, "had a courier who was way up in the art of providing shows." The "shows" once included what was apparently a salacious male performance, at which they spent "nearly two hours on a balcony watching 7 types jouir in 7 different manners from an old hairy pale-kneed grandfather down to the young Chicago sport who had stage fright." Dewing cautioned Stanny: "Be a little careful how you write." Dewing also made use of Freer in arranging communications with a woman named Molly, trying to keep knowledge of her from his wife.[3]

Beginning in 1888, Dewing had joined with White, Gus, Louis Saint-Gaudens, Frank Lathrop, and Joseph Wells to form the secret "Sewer Club," which met in a rented room in the Benedict Apartments on Washington Square, a likely venue for sexual liaisons. Stan not only helped Dewing out with his club dues but paid for most of the others too. The impecunious Wells was particularly in need of assistance.

It was probably no surprise to Stan that Wells did not pay his dues for the Sewer Club, for the draftsman's financial position had always been precarious. But Wells appeared not to worry about such matters. Like his fellow members, Wells was not one to be bound by social conventions. The often embittered and cynical bachelor rejected marriage as unsuitable for anyone working in the arts. When Cass Gilbert was about to be married, Wells wrote him at length in an effort to discourage him from taking that step. He suggested that an artist's art always declined after marriage, since an artist depended on absolute freedom, which was possible only in a single state. He had said essentially the same thing to Gilbert about White soon after his marriage to Bessie. The considerable misogyny in Wells's advice is evident, but the others in the group not only respected his artistic talent but were very fond of him. Cass Gilbert considered White "nearer to [Wells] in friendship" than any other person, and in Royal Cortissoz's view, Wells was ever the "beloved friend" of White. That he was equally beloved by Saint-Gaudens is evident in the decidedly homoerotic "love" note the sculptor sent to Wells, even addressing him with a feminine identification: "Mon amour adorée, ma belle fille, je n'aime que toi, toi seul au monde— ton beau sourire me fait mourir d'amour."[4]

Thomas Hastings, who worked for McKim, Mead & White before

forming his own firm in partnership with John Carrère in 1885, was another who received "love notes" from Saint-Gaudens. When he worked on the New York Public Library project, he wrote Gus asking for his help in choosing sculptors for the library: "Write me a letter which I can read to Mr. Rives, Mr. Cadwalader, Mayor McClellan and others, that is, do not put too many love words and other things in it, but write me a love letter apart." He signed with his customary "Ever thy beloved." Tommy Hastings's notes to "Dearest Stamford [sic]" always expressed uncommon affection, his closing phrase elaborated to "Ever and ever thy beloved," "Forever and ever thine," "You are an angel," or simply "With love." When White helped him get into The Lambs Club, Tommy wrote Stan: "You are a trump! Thank you ever so much for rushing me in." Then he used an expression fairly commonplace at the time, meaning to treat a friend to drinks or a meal: "If you will meet me there sometime, I will blow you off until you have nothing to stand on." Before the turn of the century, Hastings occasionally joined Stan for a spree in the city.[5]

Hastings and White had much in common in their backgrounds. Like White's family, Hastings's had come to Massachusetts in the 1630s. Six and one-half years younger than Stanford, Hastings had also grown up in New York City in a highly musical family. His grandfather was a writer of hymns, who composed "Rock of Ages," and his father a highly respected Presbyterian minister and president of the Union Theological Seminary, who arranged to have much music in the home. Sensitive and delicate as a child and, like Stan, talented in drawing at an early age, Tommy entered the office of Herter Brothers as a student and draftsman at the age of seventeen. There he worked on decorations for a room at the Seventh Regiment Armory and became a friend of Joseph Wells. In 1880, at the age of twenty, Hastings went to Paris to study architecture at the Ecole des Beaux-Arts. On his return, through the influence of Wells, he went to work as a draftsman for McKim, Mead & White in October 1883. At 57 Broadway he met John M. Carrère, who also had been at the Ecole in Paris, and in 1885 they formed an architectural partnership, first renting a small room at 57 Broadway. Hastings became the designing partner of the firm, while Carrère took charge of office organization and business arrangements. In 1897 Carrère & Hastings won the important commission for the New York Public Library, which was completed in 1911. From its later offices on Madison Avenue at Forty-first Street, the firm undertook a great many significant commissions, mainly in a French Renaissance style, and became in the early years of the twentieth century the most successful and best-known New York architectural firm after McKim, Mead & White.[6]

In the view of Hastings's biographer, the artist and the man in Hastings seemed "inexplicably detached one from the other." He was intense and single-minded in his art, "obeying the mystic guidance of his genius with an almost ruthless energy and devotion." But as a man, he was always open, generous, and good-natured, like "a lovable child," always "gay, irresponsible, affectionate, charming" in talk. The biographer goes on: "He enjoyed his wine and the pleasures of the table, but he had no leaning toward excess. Women were neither an interest nor temptation." Until he was forty he resided in his parents' house.[7]

Tommy's engagement to the wealthy Helen Benedict early in 1900 therefore came as a surprise to his friends. *Town Topics* also expressed surprise and was rather caustic about the bride-to-be: "Miss Benedict has not been looked upon by her friends as matrimonially inclined. She is devoted to country life and to her horses and dogs." The *Town Topics* account continued in its less than sympathetic vein: "In accordance with the fitness of things, the bride, who is one of the best four-in-hand whips in the country, will drive the bridegroom in her brake when they leave on their honeymoon trip. Will this be symbolical of their married life?"[8]

Stan took charge of decorating the church for the Benedict–Hastings wedding in Greenwich, Connecticut, on April 30, 1900. A choir of twenty-six boys from Trinity Church, New York, provided music. Charley McKim served as best man to Hastings, and White was one of the twelve ushers. The bride's only attendant was twelve-year-old Larry White, who served as a page. In later years, Mrs. Hastings lived most of the time with a companion, Miss Jessie Mann, at the Hastings's country house in Old Westbury, Long Island, while Tommy kept a penthouse apartment atop the New York City building that housed his office.

Another prominent architect who always wrote endearingly to White was Whitney Warren, a very handsome red-haired man who dressed so strikingly, often in a great opera cloak and broad-rimmed felt hat and carrying a gold-headed cane, that he created a sensation wherever he went. Both Warren, whose sister married Robert Goelet, and his wife now and then approached Stan for help. Whitney Warren would ask Stan to send draftsmen to help him out of a bind in finishing some work, and Charlotte Warren would urge him to "pull wires" to get her husband commissions. Stan arranged for a Tower room at Madison Square Garden where Warren could work on his designs, and he was helpful in getting him the important commission for the New York Yacht Club on West Forty-fourth Street. When the Yacht Club was finished and Warren was in Paris, he wrote to ask White to help his firm make the new building presentable for the opening. Stan spoke of Warren as "one of de gang" and found him similar to himself in some respects, "though not so bad . . . but pretty nearly," an indication his friend was involved in the same kind of sexual escapades. Curiously, Whitney usually signed his notes to White with the feminine name "Bibi la Poupette" and sometimes referred to himself in letters in the third person as "Bibi."[9]

By the turn of the century, Charles Freer, a close friend and patron of Dewing who went on "sprees" in Paris with Dewing and MacMonnies, was included in White's inner circle. Freer, born in Kingston, New York, had made a large fortune, in partnership with Frank Hecker, in the manufacturing of railroad cars in Detroit, where, a lifelong bachelor, he took a prominent role in civic and art activities. In his thirties he began to collect prints and paintings, eventually acquiring works by several American artists, most especially Dewing. On a trip to London in 1890 Freer met James McNeill Whistler, whom he came to know well and whose work he also began to collect. A trip in 1894–95 to the Far East acquainted him at first hand with Oriental art. In 1900, at the age of forty-five, Freer retired from business with a substantial fortune to devote himself to travel and art collecting. According to his biographer, he "never seemed close to marriage," and though he "cultivated the image of a gay blade" he was always very much "a fussy bachelor." He relaxed in the company of men, enjoying club life in Detroit and in New York, where he became a member of The Players. With a fellow bachelor he acquired a villa on the island of Capri, where they enjoyed "hopelessly indolent days" and saw a good deal of the painter Charles Coleman, White's agent in southern Italy. The Capri villa was filled with antiquities, and Freer and his companion celebrated there what was said to be a Mithraic cult of sun worship. One scholar of Freer and his circle has pointed out that Freer suffered from syphilis, which gradually led to dementia and brought on his death in 1919.[10]

Freer was largely responsible for White's being invited to provide designs for the proposed Detroit Bicentennial Memorial, which was not erected, and he had White create plans for a country house in Sheffield, Massachusetts, he was contemplating but finally decided not to build. Stan did design and supervise the execution of frames for several paintings that Freer purchased. Freer's great collection of art objects, including a number of Whistler's works, among them *The Peacock Room,* was eventually donated to the Smithsonian Institution for the gallery that bears his name. Early in 1906, as Freer planned to house his important art collection in Washington, D.C., he intended to designate White as architect of the gallery.[11]

Another bachelor friend in the White circle was the inventor Nicola Tesla, for whom Stanny designed a curious mushroom-shaped transmission tower and laboratory at Shoreham, on the north shore of Long Island, completed in 1902. White had known Tesla for some years, since his work on a Niagara Falls generating plant in the early 1890s. White sponsored the scientist for The Players; when elected a member, Tesla became a regular at the clubhouse. White was in awe of Tesla's scientific and technical accomplishments and was tremendously impressed on visits to the Manhattan laboratory where the scientist demonstrated electrical phenomena. Larry and Bessie went along on one such visit, and when Tesla demonstrated taking very high voltage and low amperage in his body and lighting tubes held in his hands, Larry "thought that was absolute magic" and begged his mother to let him try it, but Bessie would not allow it. Tesla's wireless transmission tower on Long Island served for experiments but was abandoned in 1903 and later razed. Stan occasionally invited Tesla for a weekend at Box Hill, reportedly loaned him substantial sums of money, and often included him in stag parties at the Tower studio. Tesla's biographer speculates about "whispers that he was a homosexual" and states that Tesla's "relative indifference to women continued to be a subject of international gossip" for many years.[12]

Stan's closest buddy and most kindred spirit in New York in the years when Gus was no longer living there was James Lawrence Breese, a wealthy stockbroker, whose private fortune supported his hobby and part-time profession of photography. Breese operated the Carbon Studio on the ground floor of his townhouse at 5 West Sixteenth Street, assisted for a time by Rudolf Eickemeyer, Jr., who would become one of the most gifted photographers of the early twentieth century. The Carbon Studio was both a place for taking photographs, many of which White and his friends collected, and a place of rendezvous for nights on the town, teas with young ladies, and parties like the Pie Girl Dinner. *Town Topics* called the men who gathered at the Breese studio "the Carbonites." Rumors about what went on there abounded. It was an open secret that Breese sometimes persuaded young women to pose in the nude for his camera, and he circulated some of the photographs among White's friends "as a pleasant reminder" of "days and nights gone by." Stan sponsored Breese for The Players as "a gentleman of culture and refinement" and "perhaps the best amateur photographer in America." He twice proposed Breese for the Century Association, though he eventually withdrew his name. Bessie liked Breese, and sometimes she and Stan enjoyed a dinner party with him and his wife. More often, however, Stan and Breese were "bachelors for the evening" when they were together.

Some of their notes to each other hint at extramarital pleasures: "Why don't you dine with us at seven-thirty and go to see the sporting show and do some other sporting afterwards?" "I am with you tonight for anything."[13]

The life-styles, personality types, and language of endearment in White's intimate circle, along with attitudes toward women, unconventional marriages, and "gay blade" bachelorhood of some members, raise the question of their sexual orientation. Today, some of the words and expressions commonplace in Stan's crowd suggest sexual intimacy, yet it must be stressed that same-sex endearing modes of address were nothing out of the ordinary in the late Victorian period. For the most part they were probably not associated with physical sexuality. The prevalence, as in the Saint-Gaudens–White correspondence, of sexual words, images, and even explicit anatomical drawings relating to male sexuality, however, should be noted. One surviving letter from Saint-Gaudens to Stan is decorated with thirteen phalluses. On another occasion, Gus wrote Stan, "I'm your man to dine, drink, Fuck, bugger or such, metaphorically speaking." In one letter Stan expanded the usual "K.M.A." to include, as well, "S.M.A.—S.M.B.—S.M.C.," followed by "G.T.H." By contrast, there are few erotic words, images, or drawings relating to female sexuality. No doubt some in the group, including Tesla and most likely Wells and Freer, were homosexual. Others, like Saint-Gaudens, Hastings, and Warren, probably had bisexual inclinations.[14]

That there was a bisexual element in White's nature seems evident. People often commented on Stan's "feminine tenderness" toward his close friends and on the caring and nurture that went into his friendships. White's correspondence, however, is filled with references to "girls"— almost never "women"—and his known liaisons were with females. Like his father, Stan was attracted to young women; his female ideal-type seemed to be a lithe, tiny-breasted, late adolescent girl. White's attraction to adolescent and postadolescent girls was already evident in his courting of Bessie, which began when she was about eighteen. Mature, voluptuous, full-bosomed women of the Lillian Russell type, so popular in the 1890s, did not appeal to him. Nor did he have much interest in the athletic, large-bosomed, large-hipped Gibson Girl popular after the turn of the century. Once White indicated in confidence that "the most beautiful body was that of a twelve year old boy." Although it is possible that some of "the scenes of mirth and physiological interest and investigations" that went on in the various rented hideaways involved young males, no direct evidence on that point has been located. The evidence available would indicate that White himself remained heterosexual in his activities.[15]

The dynamics of White's philandering and his choice of late adolescent girls might be taken to suggest, conventionally, that the architect by his near-compulsive behavior was trying to hide from others as well as from himself strong homosexual tendencies. Considering the sexual inclinations of some of his friends, the contacts he would have been able to make through them, and the several hideaways available to him, it would seem that he could easily have indulged any homosexual urges in secret, if he wanted to. Stan's focus on young women was consistent enough for a conclusion that it indicated his true sexual preference. His collection of female nude paintings, later remarks by people who had observed him on the city streets, and the comments of young women who knew him support that view. He was, moreover, following the example of his father, though going far beyond what his father had managed.

White pursued an unconventional, self-indulgent, secret sexual lifestyle. His stated belief in full freedom for the individual, the argument that everyone should be able to do as he wished, was more a rationalization than a moral defense for what he was doing. Indeed he sometimes jokingly intimated, albeit with a certain pride, that he was "pretty bad." Certainly his philandering could be hurtful to his young partners, his wife, and others. At least once he apparently had to "pay off" a young woman who considered herself aggrieved by his actions. But he was known to be generous to the young women with whom he was involved. By and large, sexual activities were not a moral issue for White.

Besides photographs of young women, volumes of erotica were popular items to be passed from hand to hand among White's cronies. Like his father, Stan became a serious collector of erotica. He usually carried along some "dirty" books on his trips to the fishing camp in Canada, which he shared with friends. His frequent fishing companion Arthur Weekes, who signed a surviving note to Stan with a caricature phallus worked into his name, took great pleasure in *The Woman of Fire*, which Stan had lent him. Henry Poor, who also collected erotica, sent some books to Saint-Gaudens, who read them and turned them over to Stan. Poor cautioned Stan to make sure, when he finished with them, that the books were returned to Poor's Wall Street office rather than to his residence, where an inquisitive member of the family might come upon them in his absence. Booksellers from New York, London, and Philadelphia, as well as private collectors, regularly offered White volumes that might interest him, including such well-known works as *The Memoirs of Casanova*, characterized by Stan as "the worst bethumbed book in

the Century Club library." On one occasion White tried unsuccessfully
to retrieve a book called *Fantastic Tales,* translated from the French,
which he had carelessly left on a train from Southampton.[16]

Regardless of his private interest in erotica, in public life Stan was
noted for his gallantry toward women. A great many women, both in
high society and in the demimonde, found his attentions and flirtations
charming. One decidedly respectable lady once wrote to tell him how
much she liked his "way of calling me bad names." His carefully chosen
gifts delighted women friends. Still, a tone of condescension toward
women, as if they were mere objects of pleasure, permeates some of
the more intimate correspondence by White and his friends. They shared
an attitude that wives were often troublesome, and at times the best
thing to do was to slip away from them. One fellow architect, lamenting
about "the fool wife," wrote Stan that "none but wise men should
marry, for they don't leave their affairs in their wives' hands." In a
letter to a Midwestern friend, Stan himself was blunt, with a certain
masculine bravado, about a forthcoming visit: "My real object [in coming
to Chicago], as you well know, would be prairie *chicken* hunting, as I
understand they can still be found in Chicago." To another Chicagoan
he wrote: "Girls are always disturbing except in one position."[17]

White's relationship over several years with Ruth Dennis, though,
involved many more dimensions than the blustering dictum sent to Chicago. Elements of their relationship were found in others of Stan's affairs,
and the Dennis situation foreshadowed much that would occur a few
years later with Evelyn Nesbit. It was at the Vaudeville Club in the
Metropolitan Opera House one evening early in 1895 that Stan first
encountered sixteen-year-old Ruthie Dennis, who had been booked there
for an acrobatic dance. After her first performance at the club, White
sought her out to compliment her and bent down to kiss her hand, a
gesture she found exciting. The tall, red-haired, smiling man, she later
wrote in her autobiography, "was my first contact with a world I knew
nothing about, a great social world that lay outside my experience, but
not outside my curiosity." A few weeks later White found out where
Ruthie lived and invited her and her mother to accompany him to the
masked "French Ball" at Madison Square Garden. Mrs. Dennis made
a black Spanish dress for her daughter, pinned up Ruth's hair to make
her look older, and watched her closely on the dance floor from her
seat in White's box. Stan danced with Ruth only once or twice but
arranged for her to have partners all evening. With the happy crowd,
swept along by the music and the attention she was getting, Ruth felt
she was "in heaven." From that evening on, White moved through

her life, she later recalled, "with a strange tenderness and aloofness." He called her "his little 'Wild Flower,'" and often sent her notes and bouquets of violets or American Beauty roses by special messenger. He was "unbelievably kind" to Ruth and "commanded my adoration." She recalled him as "a beautiful spirit, a great artist and a fascinating man whom I ringed about with a halo of idealism."[18]

For many years Stan assisted Ruth with her career. He brought her to the Tower studio one April evening in 1895 with the opera stars Nordica, Melba, and de Rezke present, to dance, pose, and do imitations for the guests. He tried to secure her an engagement at the Roof Garden. He also helped arrange for her to audition at Palmer's Theatre, where A. M. Palmer, the owner, was "well pleased" with her trial, promised her a part in a show, and gave her a salary advance. When Ruth informed Stan of the good news, she sent along "some country wild flowers from a country wild flower" and asked him to attend her opening performance "and help make it a success" by bringing along "a small brigade" of his friends. But within a day or two the business manager of the theater let Ruth go without the two weeks' salary called for in her contract. Strapped for money, Mrs. Dennis wrote to ask the architect for a loan to help them out. When White immediately sent them money, Mrs. Dennis wrote back very grateful about "the prompt and delicate way" he had responded to her request. His answer, she went on, showed "that God still lives," and she naïvely commended "the unselfishness" he had shown toward her daughter "without exacting any return from her. Most men are not so. It only increases her respect and affection for you." She hoped he would come visit them soon at their boarding house.[19]

Meanwhile James Breese, also entranced by young Ruth's performance at the Vaudeville Club, had invited her to come to the Carbon Studio to be photographed. On her first visit Breese brought out some decorative hats, fichus, and veils. He suggested that she looked like an "early Gainsborough" as he posed her in a wine-colored hat and a fichu around her shoulders. On her second visit, she later wrote, Breese seemed agitated but finally asked her, "in a charming, caressing voice," if she would pose in the nude. He was anxious, he told her, to capture in a photograph what he was sure was her "beautiful body with long lines." Although Ruth was "in a flutter of indecision" at the proposal, her vanity won out over her reluctance, and she "very chastely stepped out of my clothes." After the pictures were taken, she put on her clothes, left the studio, and did not see the photographer again for several years.[20]

For many months Stan also did not see Ruth, who was then living with her mother in Brooklyn. When he eventually wrote her mother to inquire about her, Mrs. Dennis responded that her daughter did not have any engagements and was very restless. White then sent her "a gorgeous bicycle, a shining black miracle of wheels and steering gear." Ruth was enchanted. She rode her new bicycle all over Brooklyn, from Prospect Park to the ocean, and across the Brooklyn Bridge to Manhattan. She even entered a six-day bicycle race at Madison Square Garden and came in among the top finalists.[21]

In 1900 Ruth met David Belasco, the theatrical impresario, who hired her to play a minor role in an American company then performing in London. Mrs. Dennis called on White to tell him of her worries about Ruthie going abroad. White reassured her that he would be in London that summer on a visit and sent money for return fare for her to have on hand. He also asked a friend to keep an eye on Ruth during the sea voyage to England.

When White got to England that summer he saw Ruth several times. On one occasion,

> Stanford had come to the stage door to get me after the performance. He was on his way to Paris and wanted me to have supper with him. After supper he took me to his suite at the Cecil. We were sitting on a couch when his valet came into the room to bring him some cigarettes. As he started to go he turned and said, "Will you have breakfast for one or two, sir?"
>
> Stanford laughed about this for hours. He said the look on my face was something to conjure with. When the man left he threw his head in a characteristic way and roared.

Belasco, also in London, noticed White's attentions to Ruth and suggested that the architect help back her to become a comedy star.[22]

By then Ruth was aware, she later revealed, that White wanted her as his mistress. Unprepared for such a step, she did not see him again for about six years. She returned to New York to pursue a career as an actress and dancer. In early 1906, billed as Ruth St. Denis, she created a sensation in her version of an Indian temple dance. Society invitations flowed in, and her fame as a dancer was established. White saw her perform at the Waldorf-Astoria later that year and rushed backstage afterward to congratulate her. Bessie knew about her husband's friendship with Ruth. In fact, on June 2, 1906, Stan sent Bessie a note telling her how to get in touch with the dancer.[23]

Ruth realized that she "was only one of the many girls of the stage whom he befriended." There were many more—how many we do not know—most of them quite young, though perhaps not so innocent as

Ruthie was when she first met White. Like Ruth, most of the women Stan befriended were young, attractive, svelte actresses or dancers, usually just starting out on the stage and in need of help and protection. Like Ruth and her mother, his young girl friends often turned to him for assistance. He attempted to aid some of them in their careers, as he had tried to help Ruth, with appeals to theater managers and impresarios on their behalf, gifts of rent or board money when funds ran low between engagements, and even arrangements for dental and medical care. Sometimes, as with Ruth, he sought out and came to know the young woman's mother. He sent flowers to countless girls and made gifts of jewelry to many, for years running up huge bills with florists and jewelers. He often arranged to have the girls photographed and collected the photographs. Some of them came to parties at the Tower apartment or accompanied him to one of the other hideaways he rented. With some of them, like Ruth, he probably made no explicit sexual approaches, content to enjoy their companionship around the city, but with others he was no doubt sexually intimate. After the turn of the century the number of liaisons increased; the surviving correspondence includes more and more mentions of girls' names. Comments by taxi drivers and others after White's death indicate that his involvements with young actresses and dancers were widely known about and commented on.[24]

Bessie was probably aware of her husband's transgressions. As to how she reacted—whether with anger, sorrow, or resignation—the record is silent. Nor is there any evidence that she and Stan came to a serious confrontation over his life-style and his infidelities. Bessie could live as she wished, indeed very comfortably, at Box Hill much of the time, where she need not be bothered by gossip or awkward encounters. Stanford himself disliked quarreling intensely: "Rows are the things of all others," he once wrote, "I hate in this world." Stan and Bessie continued to show affection for each other, even though a formal tone that crept into some of their notes was evidence of occasional strains. At times "My darling Bess, . . . Lovingly, Stan" became "Dear Bess, . . . Stanford," and "Lovingly, Bess" was replaced by "Yours, B. S. White." It would seem that Bessie accepted the fact that her flamboyant, impulsive, self-indulgent husband had needs different from her own. She appreciated his kindness and generosity to others and obviously had some understanding of and feeling for his artistic creativity. Bessie, the daughter of Judge Smith of Smithtown, had learned early in life that males have prerogatives. Saint-Gaudens once told his own wife about his admiration for Bessie White's "quiet dignity" in the face of Stan's infidelities.[25]

After the births of two sons, and with the passage of the years, Bessie's figure filled out generously, which could have made her less physically attractive to her husband than she had been when younger. An aprocryphal story that Stan once wrote "Fat is Fatal" in a note to Bessie has some credibility. Bessie and Stan lived apart for increasingly long periods; by the late 1890s they had separate bedrooms at home and arranged for separate rooms when traveling together. Their separate financial accounts and property reinforced their division. Bessie's inherited wealth probably made her less attractive to her husband, allured as he was by dependency in girls. Even so, of course, he found her money useful to invest and to spend.

Because he was well known in New York, dressed expensively, and wore jewelry, White had to be careful where he went. He probably had the good sense to stay out of the less reputable places of assignation in the city, most of them by the late century grouped along the Bowery south of Houston Street or in the part of the city known as the Tenderloin, centering along Broadway and Sixth and Seventh avenues, from Fourteenth Street to Forty-second Street. The Whites' West Twentieth Street house, rented to 1892, was right on the edge of the Tenderloin, and Stan was surely aware of some of the establishments in the neighborhood. By 1900 the prostitute population of the city was estimated at some 25,000. White did make visits to the Bowery in the early 1890s, according to Dewing, but later gave his attentions mostly to young women uptown connected with the theater.[26]

Particularly after the turn of the century, White went to the theater, usually to musicals, as many as a dozen or more times a month. He ran up large bills with ticket agencies. He came to know well many prominent people in the theater, including the actresses Ethel Barrymore and Ellen Terry and the producer Daniel Frohman. His theatrical friends invited him to parties where he could meet the young actresses and dancers whose company he enjoyed. He was a director of the Vaudeville Club and the Strollers Club and active in The Players and The Lambs; theatrical evenings at those clubs delighted him. Although not a "stage-door Johnny," he would sometimes appear at the stage entrance to a theater. Most often he sent cabs to pick up his companions and take them to meet him at some private place, where business associates, acquaintances, or journalists would be unlikely to observe him. White avoided the lavish so-called lobster palace restaurants around Longacre Square, which many society men frequented openly with actresses and chorus girls.

When he kept company with young women from the theater, White was doing just what many of his well-to-do male contemporaries were doing, and no doubt being more gracious and charming about it than most. The response of one young woman to a White invitation is revelatory:

> *Dear Angel Writer—*
> I cannot resist you, so come for me at any time you please. I have asked two particular friends to dine and they will think me crazy & probably cut my acquaintance, but never I mind! I will go with you—[27]

Like Ruth St. Denis, many of the girls were asked to pose for photographs. After the turn of the century Rudolf Eickemeyer, who had worked with Breese at the Carbon Studio and later opened his own studio on Fifth Avenue, did much of the photography for White, although other professionals took pictures for him too. White regularly ordered a dozen or more 8-by-10 platinum prints of each girl's picture, some of them in the nude; Eickemeyer gave him a 25 percent discount. The copies were passed around or given outright to friends, and framed to be hung in White's retreats.[28]

Stan suggested to some young women that they visit a dentist before being photographed. Dr. Frank M. McCarty, whose office was on Forty-ninth Street and later on West End Avenue, did dental work at Stan's behest. White also arranged for professional services by medical doctors for a few of his young friends. He once asked Dr. P. E. D. Malcolm, to whom he sent several young women, to "fix up" Miss May de Souza, who "sings like a bird and has a bad throat and cold" and was scheduled to open the following week at the Majestic Theatre. The bills were sent on to White.[29]

Although White's dalliances with young women of the theater were widely known, he was able to acquire some insurance against sensational press exploitation of his affairs. Like many others, he paid for the silence, or at least a muted voice, of Colonel William d'Alton Mann. Mann, a former Civil War cavalry officer from Michigan, had settled after the war in Mobile, Alabama, where he had established a cottonseed mill and refinery, promoted railroads, and published newspapers. In 1891 he acquired *Town Topics* from his brother. Colonel Mann moved to New York and proceeded to make that publication the city's leading vehicle of gossip. Its attention was directed at the doings of the rich and the socially prominent, not only in New York City but all over the country.

The colonel was soon a familiar figure around town. His frock coat, plug hat, red bow tie, long, snowy beard, white whiskers, and large red nose made him easy to recognize. He was noted for a gargantuan appetite and a peculiar way of grunting "Woof! Woof!" to signal approval while dining, watching the opera, or appraising horse flesh at the horse show.

Colonel Mann's gossip sheet, fueled by tips from informants, employed a style marked by subtle innuendo, circumlocution, and verbal winks and nods. The colonel and his advisers were careful to avoid any statement in print that might be found libelous, but regular subscribers knew how to read between the lines. Many of his "best stories," however, never appeared in print: Their subjects were invited to stop by the office to check on galleys, and in return for "loans" to the colonel or other favors the stories were not printed.

White was among several prominent Americans invited in 1901 to subscribe to a lavish book entitled *Fads and Fancies of Representative Americans,* with illustrated biographical sketches. Somewhat reluctantly, Stanford agreed to pay the $1,500 charge to be included in the book and to own a copy. He later had a hard time making the payment to Mann and was dunned several times. The colonel admitted that he made a profit of some $90,000 on the book. It was also known that he always kept a pistol handy.

The sketch in *Fads and Fancies* characterized White as "possessing the restless energy, the thirst to accomplish, of the man of deeds" yet "artistic to his finger-tips," very much "the poetic dreamer." He would be, the sketch continued, "a curious study to the psychologist." The architect was also called "an unceasing source of surprise to those who have followed his career," which perhaps was a hint that Colonel Mann's informants had been keeping an eye on White's secret life. In the early years of the century White, as one of "the immunes," was seldom mentioned in *Town Topics,* and references to him were usually complimentary or amusing.[30]

A psychologist making a "curious study" of White would surely have remarked upon his several New York hideaways. The room rented by the Sewer Club in the late 1880s was probably the earliest of them. Far more conspicuous was the Tower studio at Madison Square Garden, which he acquired in May 1892; his occupancy of the Tower room was extensively publicized, so it lacked the privacy he often wanted. Then there were the Holbein Studio Building rooms, on West Fifty-fifth Street, beginning in January 1891. In August 1893 White changed to a second studio, also in the Holbein, room 1 at 139 West Fifty-fifth Street, for which he shared the rent with the contractor David H. King, Jr. By the mid-1890s White and some of his friends were using the

Holbein studio often. Indeed, Louis Sherry, the restaurateur and caterer, was instructed to keep separate accounts for his services at the White family residence on Twenty-first Street, at the Tower apartment, and at the West Fifty-fifth Street studio. Thomas Dewing often visited the room, which was referred to as "The Morgue" or the "Uptown Branch." A servant named John took care of the studio for years, and "scenes of mirth and physiological interest and investigations" (in Dewing's words) made the studio a welcome refuge. Some time before October 1, 1898, Stanford and David King took yet another Holbein room, also "The Morgue," Studio 3 at 154 West Fifty-fifth Street. The Morgue, Stan wrote King, was always a convenient place for "the gang" to "use in a pinch when other places fail." Toward the end of the 1890s Stan and King seldom went to the Holbein studio and contemplated giving it up, but they were still renting and sharing it as late as 1905.[31]

One reason White used The Morgue less was that he had acquired another hideaway, far more commodious and much more convenient to his home, his office, and The Players. With J. D. "Jack" Cheever, a Wall Street broker in the office of Henry Poor & Co., White took the two upper floors of 22 West Twenty-fourth Street, above F. A. O. Schwarz's toy store. Already by December 1897 White was involved in renovations and decorations of the premises that would become widely known as his most "infamous" haunt. In the summer of 1899 White arranged for rigging to be mounted on the roof of the Twenty-fourth Street building to haul an old marble mantel up to the apartment, and for some months after that he was involved with the installation of a gas furnace and new heating ducts for the several rooms. It was a time of financial strain for White. Cheever paid many of the bills for fixing up the apartment, and by late 1901 he was dunning Stan for something on his share of the expenses. In 1902 White had large orders of his favorite champagne delivered to the apartment, as well as to his house and the Tower room, and the hideaway was used regularly. But late in the spring of 1903 he had the marble mantel removed and sent to storage, and White and Cheever vacated the apartment on May 1 to make way for new tenants.[32]

Meanwhile, always looking for privacy and convenience, he had acquired in 1901 yet another studio at 134 East Twenty-second Street, only a short distance from his townhouse. He shared the new hideaway with Henry W. Poor, whose elegant double residence, which Stan had rebuilt and decorated, was almost immediately adjacent to the south, facing on Twenty-first Street. The architect had a large four-poster bed with other furniture brought in to the studio and arranged an artful alcove and a "shadow closet for pictures." In addition, in 1904 White sublet a studio of two small rooms in the Bryant Park Studio building at 80 West Fortieth Street. Again he arranged for decoration of the studio. Finally, cryptic references in the White correspondence give clues to other studios he held briefly in this compulsive search for private spaces for his clandestine rendezvous. In 1900, for example, he rented an apartment on Seventh Avenue, but "the desperate condition" of his finances after his return from Europe that year forced him to give up that place. Later that year Jim Breese temporarily made available to White the place he referred to as "the Decoy." As he turned the apartment over, Breese warned Stan not to "take anyone that will talk about it." In 1903 Stan also shared the rental of a small place with Thomas B. Clarke, an art dealer, a collector, and White's client, and sometimes he borrowed artist friends' studios for a few hours. At the Mohawk Building, which housed his firm's office, Stan rented a hideaway office for his private use on the sixth floor, a retreat away from the bustle and interruptions on the fifth floor. Here he had a large old desk, which Bessie prized, and kept many of the private possessions, such as books and photographs, that he did not wish those in the main office to know about.[33]

The likelihood that the several studio hideaways were used not just for creative work or business but also for sexual rendezvous is strong. The many moves from place to place indicate that the occupants wanted to keep their doings as secret as possible. The rooms, it is evident, were frequently in use. As Stan wrote Gus in Paris early in 1899, while complaining about his financial "mess," "All the boys are well & that thing ending in 'ing' goes on merrily."[34]

The Great Houses

The half-century after Stanford White's birth had seen the United States split apart by the Civil War and then painfully brought back together in the Reconstruction era. In the postwar years the country underwent tremendous economic growth, with a greatly expanded transportation system, vast industrial development, and large-scale urban expansion. In population as well as wealth, the United States grew markedly in the late-century years. By 1900 the continental United States included 76 million people, two-fifths living in urban places, three-fifths in rural areas. Although earnings remained modest for most Americans—the American workingman averaged annual earnings of less than $500— some Americans were accumulating huge fortunes. Disparities of wealth, social injustice, and the exploition of workers increasingly concerned many Americans, and the turn-of-the-century years were times of great turmoil and social protest. White and his circle were largely insulated by their money and possessions from the social unrest.

As wealth piled up in the hands of owner-investors, coming not only from the transportation, industrial, and commercial expansion but also from soaring real estate values, many among the new very rich (most of whom started their careers from comfortable family fortunes) sought public and private recognition for the positions to which they thought their great wealth entitled them. Some Americans who had acquired great fortunes probably expected an exceptionally large new house to relieve some of the uncertainty about their place in the society, provide a highly visible sign of achievement, as well as gratify their pride and ambition. For some a great house, besides its symbolic value, could give a sense of stability and permanence as a place where a family might be rooted for generations to come. Architects enjoyed designing such houses. They offered opportunities for creative indulgence and brought in large fees. Although contemporary writers on architecture generally took delight in such lavish structures, with their richness of architectural ideas, social critics of the time often denounced the expenditures on the grand houses as wasteful of resources, undemocratic, and socially useless. The great mansions of the very rich contrasted all too sharply with the dwellings of most Americans, especially the wretched, crowded housing of the urban poor.[1]

Like other fashionable architects of the late nineteenth and the early twentieth centuries, White and his partners devoted a good part of their artistic energies to the design of large country houses and city mansions. Richard Morris Hunt had led the way in creating great houses for the very rich in the late 1880s and the early 1890s, when he designed several of the largest and most lavish of the American mansions. The three members of the firm admired Hunt, applauded his taste, and probably envied his good fortune in getting such commissions. Stan especially delighted in working on big residential projects, which suited his interests and his temperament. For this new aristocracy of wealth, White created some of the most opulent private houses ever built in the United States, drawing inspiration from the European past. His love of ornamentation, penchant for display, and fondness for fine materials, fabrics, and furnishings made White the ideal architect for such grand houses.[2]

Committed to his vision, confident of his artistic standards and taste, and endowed with a commanding personality, White generally directed his clients into what *he* felt was most appropriate for their needs. Extravagant in his private life, White was also extravagant as a designer for others. His clients generally acceded to his suggestions, which often sent expenses beyond the agreed budget, an outcome not uncommon for architects then and later. The higher the costs, the more money was earned for the firm. The great houses were projects of the firm, whose usual fee was 5 percent of the cost of the project; Stan's income from the firm was based on the profits of the partnership during a fiscal year, not the direct cost of the houses. Nevertheless, both he and the firm profited from the lavish expenditures.[3]

For many of the great house projects, White worked most closely with the woman of the household, whose particular concern was how the dwelling would function to enhance family life and social display. There is no evidence that his female clients as a rule were more easily swayed by his suggestions than male clients, but some apparently were. His relations with clients of both sexes were generally harmonious and more often than not grew into personal friendship. Many of his clients, of course, he already knew socially before they engaged him.

With McKim in 1889–91 Stan planned a remarkable house at Newport for Commodore E. D. Morgan, a dedicated yachtsman and the grandson of the Governor Morgan for whom Stan and Gus had designed the Hartford tomb early in their careers. By the late nineteenth century, Newport had become the most important summer resort for wealthy Americans who aspired to social eminence. The lovely seaside town had long been a favorite summer retreat for Bostonians and well-to-do Southerners, many of whom came to stay for long periods in one of the comfortable hotels. Toward the close of the century, more and more New Yorkers went there in the summer. People of means and fashion began to vie with one another in the sumptuousness of their summer "cottages," many of which were opened for only a few weeks a year and were used mainly for large-scale entertaining and display.

The location chosen for Morgan's "cottage" was a rocky bluff overlooking the harbor to the east of Fort Adams. From the land side the Morgan house, Beacon Rock, looks today like a dramatically sited classical temple. The house dominates the site instead of being tied to it organically like the contemporaneous Indian Springs, a Newport house overlooking the ocean designed by Hunt. On the entrance front of Beacon Rock two colonnaded wings, housing servants' rooms on one side and family and guest bedrooms on the other, push forward from the main body of the house. The formality of the land side contrasts markedly with the less formal arrangement on the harbor side. Here are swelling bays and a semicircular Doric colonnaded veranda. This elegant residence was costly: In contemporary dollars, it cost $238,337, which today would equal forty to fifty times that amount. In August 1893 Morgan opened his mansion to 250 captains and guests of the New York Yacht Club. The house and grounds were illuminated for the occasion with hundreds of electric lights.[4]

Mead and White collaborated in 1892–95 on a large house in Scarborough, New York, named Woodlea, for Mrs. Elliott Shepard, a daughter of William H. Vanderbilt. Erected on a commanding site with a sweeping view of the Hudson River between Tarrytown and Ossining, the Shepard mansion was surrounded by more than 500 acres of grounds. With some sixty-five rooms, many of them huge, the mansion was big enough to provide space for a house party of more than one hundred guests. "Immensity," it was said, "is one of the chief characteristics of the house.'' The symmetrical exterior of buff brick with carved sandstone and marble trim, styled with projecting pedimented pavilions, a second-level balustrade, and an elaborated cornice, was reminiscent of American eighteenth-century Georgian designs. From the semicircular porch on the river front, rolling shaded lawns swept down toward the river. Formal gardens were laid out to the north of the mansion.[5]

Not far from Woodlea was Ophir Hall, at Purchase, New York, in Westchester County, the country home of Whitelaw and Elisabeth Mills Reid. White had worked for the Reids at the southernmost Villard house on Madison Avenue in New York City, beginning in 1886. Just the next year the Reids acquired the country estate known as Ophir Farm. Ben Halladay, the original owner, had erected a gray granite house of more than eighty rooms, along with several outbuildings. After a fire in July 1888 almost completely destroyed the mansion, Reid's father-in-law, Darius Ogden Mills, who had amassed a fortune in Western mining, helped finance the rebuilding of Ophir Hall. The Reids invited White to plan and supervise the reconstruction, which was mostly completed, with the country mansion ready for occupancy, in 1890. White's interior decoration there, his work on a gatekeeper's lodge, and other estate projects in which he had a hand went on, however, through much of the rest of the decade. Frederick Law Olmsted designed the grounds, laying out woods, pasturelands, fields, ponds, and a small formal garden; thirty gardeners were employed to care for the place. Stan was often at Ophir Farm to supervise the work under way, and he and Bessie on occasion visited there as guests of the Reids.

White had the three-story mansion rebuilt in its original Norman castle style, the walls battlemented as if to provide defense against invaders, with a five-story tower. It was a decidedly anachronistic style for 1890s America and for White himself, but it was like many of White's other mansions in having strong associations with traditions of European nobility, which both the architect and his clients relished. The plan of the mansion was centered on a great hall walled with pink Georgian marble. To the left of the hall, White created an octagonal reception room finished in richly inlaid mahogany, and behind it his fellow architect George Fletcher Babb designed a large dining room in mahogany and embossed leather. To the rear on the same side, the architect placed the kitchen and servants' wing. On the other side of the hall he placed the main drawing room, a sitting room, and, to the rear, the library wing, including an office, which Reid himself designed. On the second floor one bedroom was set aside exclusively for the use of Darius Mills on visits to his daughter's residence. A billiard room and bowling alley were built in the basement. Telegraph lines connected the sumptuous Ophir Hall directly with the editorial offices of the *New-York Tribune*.[6]

To supervise the interior work at Ophir Hall, White put H. Van Buren Magonigle and, in turn, Lionel Moses, from the McKim, Mead & White office in charge. Magonigle usually traveled from the White Plains station to the Reid place by horse and buggy; a horse named Walter, which had the curious habit of galloping down every hill, regularly fell to his lot. On one of Stan's inspection trips, he took the reins as Walter started out from the station, and, true to form, the horse started down the first hill at a gallop. Whereupon, Magonigle related,

. . . White gave a wild yell, rose to his feet, and leaning far out over the dashboard urged Walter on with whip and voice. Walter was quite blown when we got there, but he galloped down all the hills coming back just the same. The exhilaration of our mad ride abode with White; we entered the drawing room which had an elaborately coffered ceiling and at every intersection I had put a rosette; they hung down all over like a lot of stalactites and made the ceiling look as though it had broken out with some kind of eruption. White gave one look. "Well if that isn't the goddamndest lookin' ceiling I ever saw—gimme a hammer! gimme a hammer!! gimme a ladder!! gimme a ladder!!!" When these were hastily provided he seized the hammer, climbed the ladder like ascending smoke and proceeded to lay about him, knocking off rosettes; they fell with satisfactory crashes; White gave a whoop of delight, and knocked off some more, each with a yell, until he had cleared a space leaving certain ones sufficient for accent. He came down and handed back the hammer, saying, "There! Take off the rest of 'em!" The ceiling was much improved by the deletions, although in his enthusiasm he did a lot of damage to other parts of it. The workmen thought he was "looney"—a favorite expression of White's own.[7]

White, as always, had his own ideas of fitting décor, and with characteristic impatience, stimulated by the wild ride, he impetuously, dramatically, and rather carelessly demonstrated what should be done. Others had to clean up the mess.

As was his wont in such extravagant jobs, White acted as patron himself and brought some of his artist friends to work at Ophir Hall, arranging for Francis Lathrop to make leaded glass windows and for George W. Maynard and H. Siddons Mowbray to do ceiling paintings. He also arranged for sculpture commissions for Willie MacMonnies. Reid was particularly delighted with Stan's gatekeeper's lodge at the

White Plains Road entrance to the farm and with a picturesque sundial the architect designed, though it was not accurately placed at first. Reid, however, had qualms about a barn that William Mead was working on; he expressed the common complaint of clients that "with the general tendencies of architects, he may be giving me a much finer thing than I want, or rather much finer than I want to pay for." Among the partners, White was the one who most often went beyond the limits on spending that had been set by the clients, carried along by his vision of opulence and grandeur.[8]

While a part of Darius Mills's Western mining fortune was going into the Reids' country place at Ophir Farm and their city home on Madison Avenue, another portion was put into a mansion at Staatsburg, New York, north of Hyde Park, for Elisabeth Reid's brother and his wife, Ogden and Ruth Livingston Mills. In 1888 Ruth Livingston Mills inherited a Greek Revival house, which had been built in 1832 on a knoll overlooking the Hudson Valley by her great-grandfather, Morgan Lewis, the third Governor of New York. The Millses retained McKim, Mead & White to remodel and enlarge the house, with Stan the partner in charge. As rebuilt, the old house completely disappeared into a palatial new structure. Two wings were added on either side of the original building and integrated into the older interiors. Completed in 1897, the sixty-five-room Mills mansion was modeled on the exterior from the north façade of the White House, with a large, elegant portico dominating the entrance front. Symmetrical fenestration, decorative panels and swags, an elaborated cornice, and a roof edge balustrade all emphasized the formal, rather austere character of the main front. Within, the principal rooms echoed the exterior neoclassical formality; they were richly decorated with oak paneling, ornate marble fireplaces, gilded ceilings, and furniture in the styles of Louis XV and Louis XVI. The Mills family customarily made use of the mansion for only a few weeks in the autumn.[9]

Just as elegant and imposing, though more open and inviting, was Rosecliff, a summer residence built for Hermann and Theresa Oelrichs, overlooking the Atlantic Ocean in Newport. White's design for Rosecliff resulted in one of the most beautiful of the Newport "cottages," and it quickly became a showplace of the resort city. White began work on Rosecliff in 1897, though by this time he was feeling a certain reluctance to undertake private houses outside of New York, since he had more than enough work to do in the city; indeed, he indicated later that the firm would turn down commissions for country houses except "for intimate personal friends or old clients we are unable to refuse." Stan had been acquainted with "Tessie" Oelrichs for some time, however, occasionally even sending flowers to her city residence on the northeast corner of Fifth Avenue and Fifty-seventh Street. Like Ogden Mills, Tessie Oelrichs was the heir to a large fortune derived from Western mining ventures. Her father, James Graham Fair, a former senator from Nevada, had garnered great wealth from the silver-rich Comstock Lode near Virginia City, Nevada. In 1890, when she married Oelrichs, Fair gave his daughter Tessie a million dollars. The following year, the Oelrichs, joined by Tessie's sister Virginia Fair, purchased the former estate of George Bancroft, a historian and diplomat. Bancroft, who had cultivated magnificent rosebushes on his Newport property, had named the place Rosecliff.[10]

Although Rosecliff would not be completed until 1902, Mrs. Oelrichs decided after the house was only partially finished that she could no longer wait to show it off, and in August 1900 she opened her ballroom for a dinner party for 112 guests. A year later she gave a garden party, with a full circus for entertainment, in honor of her son's tenth birthday. Thereafter Tessie entertained frequently and lavishly at Rosecliff, the most famous of her parties being the "Bal Blanc" in August 1904. For the Bal Blanc, the hostess planned for everything to be white, like the exterior of her house. Thousands of white flowers were massed in the rooms, and the female guests were asked to wear white gowns. Both Tessie and her sister Virginia, by this time Mrs. William K. Vanderbilt, Jr., wore lavish white gowns, with pearls and diamonds as jewelry. The favors given to the guests were all of white or silver. For another of her parties, Mrs. Oelrichs had a small fleet of model ships constructed and floated on the ocean close to shore to give the illusion of a harbor. As one of White's more spectacular showplaces, Rosecliff seemed particularly suitable for Tessie Oelrich's own extravagant entertainments.[11]

With visual reminiscences of the Grand Trianon Palace at Versailles, Rosecliff, like White's work generally, impresses the visitor today as exceptionally harmonious in its proportions. The mansion is **H**-shaped in plan, with shallow terraces occupying the voids on both sides between the wings. The exterior walls are covered by china-glazed terra cotta, near white and looking like marble from a distance. The high first-story exterior is characterized by the rhythmical play of high, round-arched windows, separated laterally by Ionic pilasters and topped by an elaborated entablature. On the recessed central segment of the entrance front, a slightly projecting colonnade of coupled Ionic columns accentuates the vertical rhythm of the pilasters. The half-height second-story rectangular fenestration repeats the rhythms of the openings and pilasters below. A more delicate entablature above the upper story supports a balustrade, which hides the recessed, low-roofed attic floor from view below. The entry wing on the right side is given a slight emphasis by the foliage of wrought ironwork on the entrance door and flanking windows and the projecting iron canopy and lanterns.

Guests coming to a reception or a party at the mansion proceeded up a shallow flight of steps to a large vestibule at the main floor level. Directly in front they faced a magnificent wall screen with a Palladian arch opening into the stair hall, into which the grand staircase on the right dramatically cascaded from above like a waterfall. The sinuous staircase divided at a landing, dominated above by a large arched window, and continued its rise, doubling back on either side to the upper floor hall. The opening outlined by the ceiling of the stair hall and the undersides of the two upper staircase portions formed the shape of a heart, the architect's gallant gesture to his client.

Behind the stair hall, facing the ocean, White placed the reception room, where Tessie Oelrichs received her guests; it was decorated with a coffered ceiling and a huge late Gothic chimney piece with allegorical panels. From both the stair hall and the reception salon, visitors might move into the living room or ballroom, 40 by 80 feet, in the central bar of the **H,** decorated in Louis XV style and eminently suited to elaborate social gatherings. High French windows led to terraces on both sides and could be opened so as to enlarge the area for entertainment, bringing the indoors out; an awning was customarily stretched out over the sea-facing terrace to protect guests there from inclement weather. Opposite the entrance wing guests came for refreshments to the Louis XVI-style dining room on the entrance front and for relaxation to the billiard room (later used as a library) on the sea front. House guests were accommodated on the second floor, centered on a gallery 18 feet wide and 100 feet long, where nine bedrooms were located. Servants' rooms occupied the recessed attic floor. The house was a small palace made for guests and entertainment.[12]

As the work on Rosecliff neared completion, the architect had arranged for a large tapestry from Duveen's shop in New York to be hung in the salon without Mrs. Oelrich's knowing about it. He had designed a wall panel in the room just the size for that particular tapestry, and planned to hang it there when the room was finished. To a friend, he wrote, "I felt almost sure that, when she saw it, it would please her and she would take it." But Tessie decided against it. The "cost of her house is running so beyond her expectations that she would not consider the question of buying tapestries now at all." Cost overruns and appeals to clients to acquire certain art works for rooms he was decorating were not at all unusual for White, arrogant though they might seem. As arbiter of taste for his times, he would guide his clients in beauty and appropriateness and, if need be, would impose his vision. Occasionally clients resisted, but by and large they went along with what he suggested. They trusted his taste and valued what he could do for their prestige.[13]

Related to Rosecliff's style and looking back as well to Versailles was a pavilion combining recreational facilities and guest rooms that White designed for John Jacob Astor IV at his country estate Ferncliff, near Rhinebeck, New York, in the Hudson River Valley. The pavilion was begun in 1898 and built in 1902–4. High-arched French windows divided by paired pilasters on the wings and paired columns in the vestibule provided a regular rhythm to the entrance front; above, a full entablature supported an elegant roof-edge balustrade. A visitor arriving by carriage might drive right into the recessed enclosed vestibule court on the entrance front. An ornate lounging room, 40 by 60 feet, in the center of the building gave access to the large vaulted, two-story, skylighted tennis court in the back; to the left were a marble swimming pool, squash courts, and men's dressing rooms, and, to the right, women's dressing facilities, five guest bedrooms, and a sitting room. For some reason, the Ferncliff commission led to a dispute with the owners, and White admitted afterward that he was "not on architectural speaking terms" with the Astors "owing to the rumpus over their athletic courts at Rhinebeck."[14]

Considerably larger and grander than Rosecliff and the recreational building at Ferncliff was Harbor Hill, which White designed for Katherine and Clarence Mackay near Roslyn, on the north shore of Long Island. Clarence Mackay was the son of John William Mackay, who had made a huge fortune from the Comstock Lode as a partner of James Fair, Tessie Oelrich's father. The senior Mackay had shrewdly invested his silver earnings in cable and telegraph companies, and on his death his son inherited a fortune said to be $500 million, mostly in silver mines and communications companies. A goodly sum—close to a million dollars (or, again, between forty and fifty times that today)—from the Mackay fortune went into the construction and furnishing of Harbor Hill, the largest house that White designed. From its superb elevated site, reputedly the highest point on Long Island, both the distant Atlantic Ocean and nearby Long Island Sound could be seen.

As on many of his domestic projects, the woman of the family was White's client. Katherine Duer Mackay was guided by the architect, but she decidedly had a mind of her own on architectural as well as other matters (she was an early feminist) and had considerable impact on the project, sometimes overruling White's suggestions. A strong-minded woman, she was a match for the strong-minded architect, but they got along well. Stan persuaded her, as he did other clients, to go on to ever larger expenditures for her great house, much to the irritation of Clarence Mackay, who paid the bills and often remonstrated with his wife and the architect about the expense of the project. At least once White attempted to reassure Mackay that he was getting a fine house, "although it may be a calamity to you"; he predicted that except for George Vanderbilt's Biltmore House in Asheville, North Carolina, designed by Hunt, there would be no other estate equal to Harbor Hill in the United States. The project promised to bring a realization of the architect's fantasies and dreams, if not of the wishes of the client's husband. White on occasion sent Katherine Mackay salmon he had caught at the Restigouche Club, which she interpreted as tokens of their friendship. While the house was undergoing its finishing touches, Stanford, friend as well as architect, was invited to stay with the Mackays, who promised to have "a special girl" there for him.[15]

Planning for the Mackay estate began in 1899; the mansion was completed by 1902, although interior decoration and furnishing and the construction of outbuildings went on until 1906. The opinionated Katherine Mackay insisted upon the mid-seventeenth-century château style for her house. White therefore modeled the exterior of Harbor Hill on Mansart's Château de Maisons near Paris, with an elaborated central entrance pavilion, projecting side wings, steeply pitched crested roof, and prominent chimney stacks. Set on terraces, the mansion had exterior walls of Indiana blue limestone with rough-textured stone quoins, emphasizing the corners. Here in the New York exurbs was a sumptuous French château that White deemed eminently fitting for leading figures of the American plutocracy.

The Mackay château reeked of luxury. From the front entrance hall guests might move directly ahead into the huge main hall of the house, 48 feet wide and 80 feet long, the walls of dark paneled oak, partly covered by large Gobelin tapestries. The 38-foot-high ceiling was of molded plaster, and a musicians' gallery projected from the floor above. The salon–drawing room to the left of the hall, decorated in Louis XV style, had cream-colored walls and a molded ceiling, and was dominated by a large portrait of Mrs. Mackay over the French fireplace. Extending beyond the salon was a glass-enclosed conservatory. The stone room, with a plethora of carved stone surfaces and an antique coffered ceiling, served as a second drawing room and for display of some of the Mackays' remarkable collection of Italian Renaissance paintings. On the opposite side of the main hall, the large English Renaissance-style dining room featured natural colored oak paneling and an antique mantel. At the front of the house, the billiard room and the great stair hall were arranged at the ends of the long transverse entrance hallway. Bedroom suites, a sitting room, a study, servants' rooms, a nursery and playroom, and service rooms were on the second and third floors of the mansion. On the extensive estate grounds, designed by Guy Lowell, farm buildings, stables, kennels, greenhouses, a small race track, a water tower, and tennis and squash courts were erected; most of the outbuildings were designed by the architectural firm of Warren & Wetmore.[16]

Here at Harbor Hill was "conspicuous consumption" on the truly outlandish scale that so amused the social critic Thorstein Veblen. Reporting on Harbor Hill and its mistress, *Town Topics,* the society gossip sheet, suggested that money had been poured on the Mackay estate "so thick and fast that you can almost see it lying on the ground." All in all, though, the journal found the place a "delightful extravagance" and decidedly in keeping with "one of the most delightfully extravagant young women of the day—Mrs. Clarence Mackay," who was well known as "a perfect specimen of wilful, wistful beauty." Her predilection for the color mauve was a subject for comment; she favored it in her clothing, her stationery, her boudoir, and even in her choice of postage stamps. "Without mauve, life would be a blank for her." Katherine Mackay would make a splash in person as well as with her home.[17]

Extravagant though she might be in creating her estate and crafting her life-style, Katherine Mackay, as lady of the manor, took on the benevolent duties traditionally associated with that role. One of her projects was to renovate and stock the Free Circulating Library at the village of Roslyn. In 1905 she commissioned White to design an Episcopal parish church in Roslyn as a memorial to her parents. She did not like White's first ideas for Trinity Church and Parish House, however, and demanded that he start over again, which he did. As completed in 1907, Trinity Episcopal was stylistically out of keeping with the architect's main body of later work. In a Norman Romanesque mode, like an ancient English country church, it had an intricately trussed roof, supported by buttresses, and was topped by a slablike open bell tower. The architect in this case accommodated his design to his rich and demanding client and friend.[18]

Two country house projects on which Stan worked intermittently at the same time as Harbor Hill developed, in contrast to the French-derived mansion, the American Georgian mode of the eighteenth century. Both

301

houses were reminiscent of George Washington's Mount Vernon beside the Potomac River. For Alfred Atmore Pope, a Cleveland ironmaster, Stan was asked to collaborate with Pope's only child, his daughter Theodate, an aspiring student of architecture, to create an elegant house in Farmington, Connecticut. Theodate Pope had graduated from Miss Porter's School in Farmington and later persuaded her father to retire there. In 1898 White supervised Miss Pope in designing the twenty-nine-room dwelling, named Hill-Stead, on an estate of 275 acres, and guided its construction in 1899–1901. A large two-story portico topped by a balustrade was designed to shelter the entire front of the main section of the Pope house, the bowed windows of the living room on the center right and of the office on the extreme left alone breaking the symmetry of the entrance front. Alfred Pope collected impressionist art, and his remarkable collection of paintings and drawings by Manet, Degas, Monet, Matisse, Cassatt, and Whistler was informally arranged in the comfortable, rambling house. Theodate Pope went on to become a licensed architect in 1912.[19]

The second of the Mount Vernon–style houses was for Stan's "spree" companion, the well-to-do real estate investor James Lawrence Breese, whose photography studio on West Sixteenth Street was so important to White as the scene of the Pie Girl Dinner and the place where many of his young women friends had their pictures taken. In 1898 the architect began designs for a large colonial revival country house for Breese and his wife to be built at Southampton, near the eastern end of Long Island; the work dragged on for eight years into 1906. A small old house, brought to the site, formed the nucleus of the far larger structure that White created. Like the Pope house, the Breese residence, known as The Orchard, was erected with a two-story columnar portico sheltering the entrance front. Although larger than the Pope house, with thirty-two rooms, The Orchard stood on a more modest property, some 16 acres, much of it planted with orchards. The central block and the side wings of the dwelling at the back embraced on three sides a courtyard with a formal garden. A trellised colonnade surrounded the rear garden.

Less formal and less ornate than most of the other White mansions, the Breese country house was simply a cozy, domestic large house, though it had many of the accoutrements of the other great houses. The most unusual feature of The Orchard was the 78-foot long high-ceilinged studio, later converted into a music room with a pipe organ. Breese also arranged for a billiard room, a bicycle room, and a squash court for his summer home. White acquired eighteenth-century doorways for the house, and Breese purchased for it more than fifteen hundred art objects that White had collected. The client's purpose here, in part at least, was to help out the architect as his financial situation deteriorated after the turn of the century. "The effect of the whole place," *House and Garden* reported, "is strikingly happy and suggestive of peaceful domesticity, and absolutely different from anything surrounding it."[20]

Meanwhile, as the great houses were commissioned, designed, and constructed by turns, White went on and on with yet another project, which, like Box Hill, was never finished and which occupied him for much of his working life. He had first become involved with the Cheney family, textile manufacturers of South Manchester, Connecticut, when he worked in Richardson's office on house designs for Rush and James Cheney and a business building in Hartford. Some years later White himself commissioned the Cheneys to create special new fabrics for his use in interior decorating, at one point experimenting, though unsuccessfully, with an antique velvet reproduced on modern looms.

The four children of Rush and Julie Ann Cheney never married, and about 1888 they set up housekeeping together in a large, rambling, Queen Anne–style house they had inherited from their father. They proceeded to remodel and redecorate their house almost continuously and eventually even had it rebuilt as a neoclassical dwelling. Both "the girls," Anne and Louise Cheney, and "the boys," Harry and Robert, frequently corresponded with Stan and came to depend on him for even the smallest decision relating to their house; he would be their "umpire" when they could not agree. Anne, the eldest and dominant sibling, wrote to White sometimes two or three times a week over a period of some seventeen years. White probably gave the Cheneys as much of his attention—often on trivial matters—as he did any of his clients. He selected wallpaper for them, chose rugs and paintings, posted off gifts of salmon, and even advised them about appropriate wedding presents to give. Tremendously loyal, he not only guided them in matters of taste but served as a sort of father confessor and social arbiter for them. Stan and Bessie occasionally came to visit, and the Whites entertained the Cheneys in New York. Years after White's death, his son Larry, as a professional architect, took over his father's role as the Cheneys' decorator-consultant.[21]

Large and sumptuous city residences, along with a few modest city dwellings, were also important in the body of work White did in the 1890s through the turn of the century. Most of the houses White created in New York were ones that he himself regularly visited and were thus a continuing part of his own life. With these houses, added to his gentlemen's clubhouses, Madison Square Garden, his own Gramercy Park and St. James residences, and several other works, White in effect designed the stage scenery on which the drama of his life was played.

While Stan was involved in his work on the Century Association clubhouse, he was closely associated with the club treasurer, J. Hampden Robb, the city parks commissioner, who at that time invited the architect to design a large residence for him. The Robb house, erected in 1889–91 at the northeast corner of Park Avenue and Thirty-fifth Street, was a boxy but imposing Renaissance classical structure, rising directly behind the sidewalk. The avenue front was dominated by a large double porch supported by twinned corner columns, topped by a balustrade. The upper-story walls of dark red-brown brick and trim, resting on a light-hued stone base, were richly decorated with rosettes, garlands, shields, and other devices. On the side street, a two-story oriel rose above the service entrance. White's Chicago house for the newspaperman Robert W. Patterson, erected in 1892–95, repeated the main motifs of the Robb house on a somewhat less expansive scale.[22]

While the Robb mansion was being completed, White, in a sharp departure from his usual modes, made his only New York City venture into low-cost housing. As a favor to his friend and frequent collaborator, the contractor David H. King, Jr., who was building the King Model Houses on a tract in Harlem, the architect provided plans and designs for small attached houses on the north side of One Hundred Thirty-ninth Street between Seventh and Eighth avenues. King's project was to offer, a promotional brochure indicated, "sunny, convenient, and commodious" housing for those "not millionaires." White's four-story townhouses, varying from 17 to 23 feet in width and set back from the street, had small front yards and small rear yards opening on alleyways. Modestly ornamented by small balconies and rosettes, which emphasized the principal floors, White's houses were faced in variegated Roman brick above a brownstone base. The "harmonious, well-proportioned, and tasteful" King Model Houses, many of them designed by other architects as well, were considered attractive, well built, and superior to most of the drab brownstone housing being erected for middle-income families at the end of the century.[23]

Close friendship with the client was characteristic not only of the model houses for King but also of most of the large city residences White created. For Henry W. Poor, one of his brokers and a man who came to share one of his hideaways, Stan designed a very large and elaborate townhouse, rebuilt from two older houses. After the Whites moved in 1898 to the large corner house on the west side of Lexington Avenue and Gramercy Park North, White desired to protect the property value by keeping up the tone of the neighborhood. In 1899 he therefore helped negotiate the sale of 125 and 127 East Twenty-first Street, the house on the east side of Lexington Avenue at Gramercy Park North and the one next to it, which had been turned into boarding houses, to Henry Poor, who originally intended to remove the two old houses and construct a large new dwelling for himself on the lots. The old houses were well built, however, and so he decided to have them remodeled into a single large house. He engaged White for the work and was said to have spent more than a quarter of a million dollars in the renovations.

Poor also delegated Stan to decorate and furnish the remodeled double-house mansion. White put his agents in Europe on the lookout for suitable things. From the island of Capri in the Bay of Naples, the artist Charles Coleman arranged to have a sidewall fountain from an old monastery sent for Poor's house, along with antique amphorae and oil jars. An account by William Partridge, a draftsman who worked under McKim and did not care for White, has it that Stan designed the library in Poor's house with the exact dimensions of a Venetian Renaissance ceiling he had already acquired and had in storage in New York. Subsequently, while in Venice, White cabled Poor concerning his find of a splendid antique ceiling, asking if he should purchase it. Poor eventually paid a price much higher than the ceiling already in White's warehouse had cost. That ceiling, according to Partridge, was sent to Poor's house as if it had just arrived from abroad. Whether Partridge's account was true or not, White was always insistent when it came to what he felt was most suitable for a house he decorated, and he frequently persuaded his clients to purchase things from his own large cache of goods brought from Europe. The profits from the sales of those goods, of course, constituted much of White's income. There is no evidence that his clients felt cheated.[24]

Certainly Poor did not feel cheated. Like White's clients almost without exception, Poor was delighted with his new house and appreciative of Stan's "personal interest and incessant attention to the work." Although the costs of the house had gone beyond what was first agreed upon, "any excess of cost over the original estimates amounts to nothing," Poor wrote, "in view of the result obtained, and to say that I am satisfied with it puts it mildly!" He and his wife were, in fact, "*enraptured*" by their house, "the most beautiful house in the world," which they saw as an embodiment of White's "own personality and charm" and a continuing reminder "of the many happy hours" their architect-friend had spent with them as it was being constructed. Poor's later financial speculations, unfortunately, brought him down in the panic of 1907, and he lost this "most beautiful house" to his creditors.[25]

Considerably smaller was the highly distinctive townhouse White created in 1901–2 on a narrow lot at 22 East Thirty-fifth Street for his friend Thomas B. Clarke, one of the foremost collectors of American paintings of the time. Stan did not charge Clarke a fee. The most conspicuous feature of the Clarke house was an eye-catching, delicately detailed two-level oriel on the second and third stories of the street front, put there to bring as much light as possible into the rooms where a portion of Clarke's large picture collection was displayed. Clarke and his wife both enthusiastically expressed appreciation of the personal attention White had given to their house and wrote him: "Your genius and taste is everywhere shown in [our] beautiful house. . . . We could never have had such a perfect residence without your head and heart." The happy associations with the architect seemed to be almost as important to many of the clients as the ultimate product itself.[26]

The East Seventy-third Street house in an American mode that Stan created in 1902–3 for another good friend, the artist-illustrator Charles Dana Gibson, was comparatively modest. Neo-Georgian–Federal in style, echoing American designs of the beginning of the nineteenth century, the elegantly composed Gibson house façade was more restrained than much of White's work at the turn of the century and foreshadowed the Lambs Club exterior, created soon after. Like the Clarkes, Gibson was delighted with his house: "The beauties of the front," he wrote before his residence was completed, "occupies [sic] my whole attention. . . . There is so much to be joyful for."[27]

Another friend for whom Stan undertook a major project about the same time was Charles T. Barney; he had already designed a substantial house for Barney at 10 East Fifty-fifth Street in the early 1880s. In 1887, the Barneys sold the Fifty-fifth Street house to Joseph Pulitzer, the newspaper publisher, and took a large house for themselves at 67 Park Avenue. As acting president and then president of the Knickerbocker Trust Company, Barney had seen his fortune advance considerably. He and his wife, the sister of the financier William C. Whitney, decided to enlarge their home to make it more suitable for large-scale entertaining. Barney had accumulated a collection of paintings for which appropriate display space was needed as well. Early in 1901 Stan began a large-scale program of renovation of the Park Avenue house, gutting the interior and almost completely rebuilding it as well as adding a new section, while the family took temporary quarters in the Holland House Hotel. Meanwhile, Stan sought out art objects for Barney. Among many other things, he sold him a Renaissance marble monument he had placed on loan earlier at the Metropolitan Museum of Art. White also did interior work on Barney's steam yacht, *The Invincible*.[28]

Work on the Park Avenue house dragged on for what seemed to the Barneys an interminable time. A destructive fire at their country home added to the Barneys' discomfort. By the end of November 1901, Mrs. Barney was very worried about her husband. In a confidential letter to White, Mrs. Barney wrote of her husband's "tendency to melancholia" and urged the architect to hurry along the rebuilding of their house so that they could move back in. "Charley is horribly depressed," she wrote. "He seems to have 'let go' entirely, & I dread to think of what the future may hold for him if I cannot get him out in his own home soon." She herself was "oppressed with anxiety" about her husband. "It is because you are such a magician that I ask the miracle of you." A few years later Barney himself would become "a magician" of sorts for Stan as his financial adviser. But Barney's melancholia at this time was a grim foreshadowing of what would happen to him even later.[29]

Most of the large city houses were in New York, but one of Stan's more striking urban residences was the dwelling for Elinor Medill and Robert W. Patterson in Washington, D.C. Following his earlier design for their Chicago mansion, completed in 1895, the new Patterson residence, erected in 1900–1903 on Dupont Circle, at one of the more important intersections in the national capital, was a handsome house molded to its irregular, V-shaped site and created especially for the cosmopolitan entertainments characteristic of the city. Stan worked closely with Mrs. Patterson to gather furniture, rugs, tapestries, and curtains for the residence, and made a good commission on the furnishings. He once suggested to her that he had given more "thought and study" to this project than to any he had done and boasted that "it would be one of the nicest houses in the whole country." The Patterson mansion, styled in a Renaissance Florentine mode and covered by white glazed terra cotta, was one of the earliest American houses with an inside garage for automobiles.[30]

A grander and more ornate residence was the thirty-five room Venetian-style Stuyvesant Fish house (1897–1900) in New York City, sometimes referred to as "the Palace of the Doges," at 25 East Seventy-eighth Street. While her husband headed a railroad and paid the bills, the tall, imperious, caustic Mrs. Fish vied with the Astors and the Vanderbilts in running New York society. Her social innovations, including vaudeville entertainments, sometimes shocked the staid elements of the upper crust but nonetheless brought refreshing variety into what many conceded were all too often repetitiously dull rituals. The five-story Fish house centered on a great hall of white marble and included an all-white ball-room, said to be the largest in New York. Crimson, gold, and dark brown were the principal colors that Stan and Mame Fish used for most of the rooms. Mrs. Fish once said that her house "would be an uncomfortable place for anyone without breeding." She was pleased that the mansion provided a fitting ambience for her life-style. As one close to her and often in her social circle, White showed discrimination in providing a luxuriant display that particularly suited her.[31]

For Joseph Pulitzer, the publisher of the *New York World*, the newspaper that Richard Grant White years earlier had helped to found, White created one of his most sumptuous New York townhouses in 1900–1903. A decade earlier the firm had undertaken renovations on Pulitzer's Fifty-fifth Street house, formerly the residence of Charles T. Barney, and for the publisher's summer place at Bar Harbor, Maine, Stan designed a tower addition, which Pulitzer greatly admired. After fire destroyed the Fifty-fifth Street house, Pulitzer commissioned White to provide an Upper East Side mansion for him, and early in 1901 he acquired property at 7 East Seventy-third Street. White found working with Pulitzer difficult, though, because of the client's many demands, which were sometimes at odds with the wishes of his wife, who was very much involved with the house design, and also because of Pulitzer's infirmities—he was nearly blind and acutely sensitive to noise—which had to be taken into account.[32]

Pulitzer was adamant regarding some of the things he did *not* want in his new house: "No ballroom, music room, or picture gallery under any disguise. . . . There must be no French rooms, designed or decorated to require French furniture—least of all old furniture. . . . I want an American home for comfort & use, not for show or entertainment." White gave careful study to Pulitzer's requirements and assured the publisher that his design would be for "a dignified, quiet, and at the same time, a rich house." When Mrs. Pulitzer was reported to have disliked some of the early studies, White wrote her husband that he was certain he was creating "as beautiful a house as I can make" but promised to do whatever the couple wanted.[33]

After several preliminary studies were rejected, Stanford eventually created a Venetian Renaissance palace for the Pulitzers, basing the façade on Baldassare Longhena's Rezzonico and Pesaro palaces along the Grand Canal. For the nearly blind journalist, the architect had plaster models built, which Pulitzer examined with his fingers. The final molded, plastic quality of the mansion's façade probably reflected Pulitzer's testing of various surface elements. Despite Pulitzer's original strictures, the publisher and his wife eventually agreed to a music room, a ballroom-salon, and French decorative touches for the house, no doubt influenced by

By the mid-1890s, White was one of the best-known figures in New York. Famous as architect, decorator, and designer of art objects, prominent as socialite and clubman, and well known as art entrepreneur and private collector, he attracted notice throughout the city.

Soon after their marriage, Stanford and Bessie White rented as a summer cottage a old farmhouse at St. James on the north shore of Long Island. After Bessie received large inheritance, they purchased the property and began to renovate the house Box Hill. On summer weekends, the family enjoyed boating, swimming, fishing sailing, and golfing. Stan and Bessie *(below)* pose in Roman togas with Bessie' brother Jim on the left and her sister Ella on the right on the beach near the house.

After the death of Stan's father, his mother Alexina made her home with Stan and Bessie. Lawrence Grant White, Stan and Bessie's son, who was born in 1887, was clothed in dresses for many years and was very close to his grandmother, who took charge of his education before he began formal schooling. About 1900, McKim and Mead visited White for an outing at Box Hill. Here Larry runs toward the men.

The Villard Houses *(above)*, on Madison Avenue in New York, marked the turning of McKim, Mead & White away from more informal modes of design to adaptation of stylistic elements from the classical Renaissance tradition of Europe. White did most of the interior decorating of the principal house south of the courtyard. The campus for New York University in the Bronx was White's most important large-scale endeavor. White designed the Gould Library *(below)* as the focal point of the campus, recalling the Pantheon of ancient Rome.

White also did important work at the U.S. Military Academy at West Point, New York, including the large and austere Cullum Memorial Hall, designed for ceremonies and social events. Battle Monument at the military academy marked White's early collaboration with Frederick William MacMonnies. The first version had a statue, Victory *(right)*, which White realized was awkward and immodest in pose, and like the first version of Diana on Madison Square Garden, it was soon replaced by a more modest and sedate figure, known as Fame.

In 1898, the Whites moved into a large rented house on the west corner of East Twenty-first Street and Lexington Avenue overlooking Gramercy Park. In this grandly impressive house, Stanny created the opulent surroundings he seemed to crave. The drawing room was filled with some of the architect's choicest treasures.

White purchased art goods on a substantial scale from European and New York dealers. Some of the best pieces remained in his own home. The dining room of the East Twenty-first Street house *(above)* looked toward the rear of the house and the music room. On the floor above, White created a picture gallery *(below)*, where he displayed part of his huge collection.

Delighting in fantasy, Stanford, dressed in a full coat of mail, and Bessie, as a Byzantine princess, were photographed before attending a ball.

A connoisseur of beauty, White for years carried on a secret life of philandering and assignations. In 1901, he arranged to meet a dancer and chorus girl, Evelyn Nesbit, whose beauty had been widely commented on in the New York press.

Although his private life seemed out of control—his health deteriorated and his lavish spending led to financial disaster—his artistic creativity was reaching new heights. The neoclassical Knickerbocker Trust Company *(above)*, on the northwest corner of Fifth Avenue and Thirty-fourth Street, was the most fashionable bank in New York. Rosecliff *(below)*, the French-chateau-style country home of Hermann and Tessie Oelrichs, in Newport, became one of the principal showplaces of the resort community.

Harbor Hill, the mansion White designed for Clarence and Katherine Mackay, in Roslyn, New York, was one of the architect's largest and most luxuriant residences. It impressed many at the time by the extent to which money had been lavished on its construction and decoration. The opulence of the great stair hall set the tone for the interior design of the great house.

In New York City, the Gorham Building *(above)* provided luxuriant showrooms and efficient workplaces for the Gorham silver manufactory on midtown Fifth Avenue. The entrance façade porch for St. Bartholomew's Church *(below)*, originally located on Madison Avenue at Forty-fourth Street, was the outcome of White's collaboration with several artist friends.

A short distance north of the Knickerbocker Trust Company and the Gorham Building, the Tiffany Building *(above)*, on Fifth Avenue at Thirty-seventh Street, was styled in the manner of a Venetian palazzo; large areas of glass flooded the interior showrooms with light. The Madison Square Presbyterian Church *(below)*, facing Madison Square on the east, was considered by many of White's contemporaries a perfect jewel and his most beautiful building.

Evelyn Nesbit was largely out of White's life by the time of her marriage in April 1905 to Harry Thaw, a wealthy, eccentric playboy from Pittsburgh. Yet Thaw's intense jealousy and openly expressed hatred of White were a grim foreboding of what would occur. Meanwhile, White's social whirl continued in the early years of the new century. Present at the spectacular James Hazen Hyde ball at Sherry's ballroom in February 1905, he stood at the rear of a group of friends.

The pace of work, play, and continuing self-indulgence in White's life took a very evident toll. Gertrude Käsebier, a talented photographer, shows White as he appeared to her in his early fifties, worn out, prematurely old.

On June 25, 1906, at the roof garden of Madison Square Garden, Harry Thaw approached the architect, sitting pensively at a table. Thaw fired three shots, killing White instantly. After two sensational trials, Thaw was declared not guilty by reason of insanity and confined for years in an institution for the criminally insane.

Although White's many surviving buildings provided a memorial to the immensely talented, central figure of New York's Gilded Age, some of his friends determined to have a more personal memorial. In 1921, the White Memorial Doors on the Gould Library at the New York University Bronx campus were dedicated. The doors, embellishing one of his most striking buildings, were a symbol of the many doors Stanford White himself had so often opened to help other artists during his lifetime.

the architect's suggestions as to what was most fitting for such a grand residence. The Pulitzers' changes in their ideas and "contrary orders" for the interior design, however, occurred so frequently that at one point White remonstrated that his firm had "certainly made twice as many studies, and done twice as much work on this [project] as we have ever done on any interior work before." Moreover, a struggle ensued to get some minor bills for decorating work finally settled.[34]

Pulitzer demanded absolute quiet in his sleeping quarters, but when he first used his bedroom he discovered that vibrations coming from a sump pump in the cellar and noise from an elevator door in the hallway prevented him from sleeping and drove him nearly frantic. He denounced White's house as a "wretched failure." An accoustical expert was called in and succeeded in improving matters so well that when firemen entered the cellar one night to put out a small fire, the owner of the house did not even wake up. The publisher still was not satisfied with his private quarters, however, and had another architectural firm erect a separate bedroom wing behind the mansion. An entrance passageway resting on ball bearings, with three doors, led to the annex, which was so well insulated from outside sounds that Pulitzer's secretaries dubbed it "the vault." Years later the Pulitzer mansion was converted into luxury apartments.[35]

For all the opulence of these several great-house commissions, Stan's most lucrative client relationship was with William C. Whitney. He designed additions and alterations for large houses for Whitney at 2 West Fifty-seventh Street in 1889–90, at 871 Fifth Avenue in 1897–1902, and at Westbury, Long Island, in 1900–1902. He also purchased a great many expensive tapestries, mantels, room ceilings and paneling, paintings, and art objects for Whitney's houses. On his trips to Europe from 1889 onward, White had access to substantial accounts to use for purchases at his discretion for the Whitney residences. For example, in the twelve months ending September 1893, he spent some $363,000 on furnishings and art works for Whitney. A total in excess of $450,000 went for the same purposes in the years 1897–99. On his own visits to Europe, Whitney himself searched for things for his houses and sometimes requested that White make a final decision for him. Stan mainly used his regular dealers in Paris, Rome, and Florence for his purchases, priding himself on what he chose, but he was sometimes irritated that he had to compete for many things with Mrs. Jack Gardner, who was spending lavishly on art objects for her museum home, Fenway Court, in Boston.

While White's architectural work on the Whitney houses was done as a member of the firm, his purchases for Whitney were his private business and provided him with substantial income, with a customary commission of 10 percent of the purchase price of the items. Although it is possible that on occasion White may have padded the bills or goods purchased for his clients, there is no evidence on that point. As a gesture of friendship and to cement their relationship, Stan also designed without charge a monument at Woodlawn Cemetery in the Bronx for Whitney and his family.[36]

By the 1890s William Collins Whitney was one of the richest and most powerful men in New York. Years before, as a student at Yale College, he had become a good friend of Oliver Payne from Cleveland, who later gained great wealth as a partner of John D. Rockefeller and treasurer of the Standard Oil Company. Whitney eventually courted and married Payne's sister Flora. Trained in the law at the Harvard Law School, Whitney set up a New York law practice after the Civil War, dealing mostly with corporate law. From 1875 to 1882 he was corporate counsel of the City of New York, involved with proceedings against the Tweed Ring. Subsequently he worked for Grover Cleveland in his successful bids for the presidency in 1884 and 1892 and served as Secretary of the Navy during Cleveland's first administration. Meanwhile, Whitney built up a large fortune in various endeavors, but especially in consolidating New York street railways. He purchased huge tracts of land in New York State and Massachusetts and was said at one time to own more land in those states than anyone except the state governments themselves.

In 1892 Whitney's old friend and brother-in-law, Colonel Oliver Payne, who was unmarried, moved to New York City and took a large house at 852 Fifth Avenue. Early in 1893 Flora Whitney died, leaving her husband $3 million from her estate. When William Whitney remarried in 1896, Colonel Payne, outraged that his brother-in-law was not being faithful to the memory of his first wife, broke off contact with him. Two of Whitney's children, Harry Payne and Dorothy, stood by their father in the dispute, while two others, Pauline and Payne, sided with their uncle, who promised most of his fortune to them. Stan distanced himself from the family quarrel and, affable and diplomatic, was able to keep on a good relationship with both William Whitney and Colonel Payne, for whom he also did a great deal of work.

In November 1896 Whitney purchased 871 Fifth Avenue, a massive brownstone on the northeast corner of Sixty-eighth Street, for his new wife, Edith, and turned it over to White for remodeling and expansion. A short time later, in February 1897, a tragic accident occurred on the Whitney plantation in Aiken, South Carolina. While horseback riding, Edith Whitney struck her head on a low bridge and sustained terrible injuries. She died a few months later. Whitney nonetheless went ahead with the work on his Fifth Avenue house. The architect retained only the shell of the original house and had the interior entirely reconstructed, adding a large, sumptuous ballroom wing and bringing to the mansion the spoils he had gathered in Europe for Whitney, "a veritable patchwork of European castles."[37]

For the Whitney mansion interior, White chose an Italian Renaissance mode, although it was reported that the owner later regretted having selected this style since so many architectural elements had to be taken from Italian palazzi, making the decoration difficult and expensive. From the entrance on Sixty-eighth Street, one entered a low, broad reception hallway, with a reception room and Whitney's office on the Fifth Avenue side. A broad marble staircase, its walls hung with rare Italian tapestries, rose to the main-floor grand hallway covered by a Florentine coffered ceiling. Overlooking the avenue on this floor were the library, with black oak bookcases and brocaded crimson hangings on the walls, and, to the rear, the drawing room, the walls covered by rich, figured red velvet. In the dining room, on the other side of the grand hallway, the ceiling was taken from the Barbarini Palace in Rome and the sides of the room were covered by sixteenth-century Italian wall paintings. Behind, a conservatory connected with the ballroom, its walls covered with paneling taken from a château near Bordeaux and with rare tapestries. The chimney pieces had all been removed from Italian palaces. Old master paintings were hung here and there, including works that Stan had acquired by Van Dyke and Reynolds. Although Whitney indicated he did not care for White's design of the railing for the great stairway, he was highly satisfied with the architect's work as a whole and with what he got for his expenditures on the alterations and decorations of the house, said to total $3.5 million. The mansion was widely praised. The *New York Times,* for example, judged that the house "in the beauty and costliness of its interior decorations is almost without a rival in this country."[38]

On January 4, 1901, the ground and main floors of the Whitney mansion were opened to some four hundred guests for a housewarming and "coming out" party honoring Whitney's niece, Helen Barney, the daughter of his sister Lilly and her husband Charles Barney. Stan and Bessie attended, the latter in a white satin gown. Policemen were on duty to hold back the crowds gathered on the sidewalk outside, and dancing went on until 3:00 A.M. A second party in December 1901 honoring Whitney's stepdaughter, his second wife's daughter, was again a notable social event. Work on the house interior continued well into 1902. John

311

La Farge provided large stained-glass windows, of which he was very proud, though he feared that one of them had cost him far more than he would ever get for it. In December 1903 Whitney honored another niece, Katherine Barney, at what was said to be the largest private ball ever held in New York City. Six hundred guests danced and dined in Whitney's mansion, "the scene, the most brilliant smart New Yorkers ever saw." The actress Ethel Barrymore was identified as "the belle of the ball" by *Town Topics*. In the Whitney mansion White had created the perfect ambience for these elaborate turn-of-the-century parties. Here, as one account had it, "Mr. Whitney has as near an approach to a Venetian or Florentine palace of the days of Leonardo da Vinci and Michel Angelo as is possible to obtain." Here was a palace for an American Renaissance prince.[39]

After Whitney's death in 1904, the mansion was sold to James Henry Smith, a Wall Street broker and bachelor, known as "Silent Smith" for his laconic manner, who had inherited a huge fortune from an uncle in London. Smith retained the Whitney staff, who were said to be able to serve a hundred guests on golden plates at an hour's notice. When Stan learned of the sale, he wrote to tell Smith how delighted he was that Smith had purchased the Whitney house. The letter rather obsequiously asserted that with the new owner "its splendors will keep on waxing" and suggested that an upstairs picture gallery might be built to enhance the splendor of the mansion even more. Smith was very friendly with William Rhinelander Stewart, who had worked with White on the Washington Memorial Arch, and traveled abroad with Stewart and his wife. When the Stewarts were divorced in 1906, Mrs. Stewart married Smith, but on their honeymoon trip in 1907, Smith suddenly died in Kyoto, Japan.[40]

Just a few days before the former Whitney mansion was to be sold at auction, it was acquired by Whitney's son, Harry Payne Whitney, and his wife, Gertrude Vanderbilt Whitney, the sculptor, who had been living at Harry's father's old Fifty-seventh Street residence. They then made the Fifth Avenue mansion their home. Stan surely would have been gratified that the house had returned to the Whitney family, for he had been close to Harry Whitney and his wife for many years. He had assisted Gertrude in getting instruction from Daniel Chester French in 1900 when she was starting on her career as a sculptor; he had advised the couple on the purchase of paintings and had frequently bid for them at auctions; and he had undertaken alterations of their Long Island home at Roslyn (Westbury), selecting furnishings for that residence.[41]

While Stan gave artistic advice to Harry and Gertrude Whitney, he now and then sought advice himself from Harry's uncle, Colonel Oliver Payne, about the stock market; Colonel Payne even came to White's rescue at times by putting up his own money to help the architect with a margin account. The older Payne, like "Mr. R." and "Dummy" Mead at times, was something of a father figure for White, and Stan's notes to him sometimes included expressions of embarrassment and apology for having bothered him. ("I made a vow that I would never trouble you again about by my stock affairs and really feel very much ashamed to have done so.") Like William Whitney, Colonel Payne provided White with substantial funds for the purchase of art objects for his own mansion at 852 Fifth Avenue, and White did some decorating work there in 1894, even selecting linens, china, and glassware for the house. Stan was the partner in charge of the large building (erected 1899–1901) for the Cornell Medical School, of which Payne was a primary benefactor. He designed a piano case for the colonel and large iron gates for Payne's Southern home, Greenwood Plantation, in Thomasville, Georgia. For Payne's yacht *Aphrodite* he designed the décor of some of the cabins, choosing wallpapers, curtains, linens, and statuary for the ship. Stan also created a figurehead for the yacht, which the sculptor Philip Martiny executed for him. The architect was so disappointed with the piece that, characteristically, he undertook to have it redone and replaced at his own expense.[42]

White's most important work for Colonel Payne, however, was the large house he created in 1902–6 for Payne's nephew, Payne Whitney, at 972 Fifth Avenue. On February 6, 1902, Payne Whitney married Helen Hay, the daughter of John Hay, Secretary of State under Presidents McKinley and Roosevelt. As a wedding present, White presented the couple with a small bronze copy of the Diana, while Colonel Payne bought them a lot on Fifth Avenue south of Seventy-ninth Street and had the house built as his gift to the newlyweds. Although the rebuilt house for Payne Whitney's father, William C. Whitney, had cost almost as much, and interior decoration and furnishings were very costly, the Payne Whitney mansion, costing about a million dollars for the building, was the most expensive private house that White designed. Colonel Payne shied away from acquiring things for the house, not wishing to impose his taste on the couple. Stan was, however, asked to make purchases by young "Paynie," and he bought many things for him and Helen.[43]

Designed in an Italian high Renaissance style, the five-story light gray granite structure, conjoined with another house to the north, contained about forty rooms. White created a delicately bowed front, rising through four stories and accentuated by entablatures between the stories. The rusticated ground floor was centered by an intricately carved, marble-enframed entryway. On the main floor the three front windows were tall and arched, the spaces above occupied by carved cherub figures while those higher up were surmounted by swags and masks on the third story and by panels on the fourth. The right side of the mansion open to the south, repeated the themes of the street façade. In the interior a treasure trove of things White had collected was installed—old coffered ceilings and chimney pieces, carved architectural fragments, embossed leather, and antique tapestries and wall coverings. The Payne Whitney house interior was one of the most sumptuous that White created.[44]

The pace of construction of the Payne Whitney house proceeded much too slowly for the new owners, however, and Helen Whitney persuaded Stan to have workmen on the job in the evening as well as during the day, much to the discomfort of neighbors, who threatened to complain to the Board of Health if work did not cease after ten o'clock. Helen finally became so annoyed with the delays that she wrote Stan she had lost all interest in the place and "felt like chucking the whole thing and getting a nice ready made house." But she moved furnishings into upper-floor rooms in January 1906 and kept at Stan to hurry the work along. Until early June 1906, White was very much involved with the house and ordered his assistants William Kendall and William Richardson to get all the help they needed in the office so that he could get off to Europe to purchase objects that summer with peace of mind about this important project.[45]

Another conspicuous Fifth Avenue commission was begun in 1904 for Virginia Fair Vanderbilt, Tessie Oelrich's sister, and her husband, William Kissam Vanderbilt, Jr. Immediately adjacent to the large François I-er mansion that Richard Morris Hunt had designed and built for William Kissam and Alva Smith Vanderbilt in 1878–83, White created a miniature French château for the younger Vanderbilts. William, Jr., had grown up in the Hunt mansion, for years the most admired house on Fifth Avenue, and White's emulation of the older architect's work reflected both young Vanderbilt's taste and White's great admiration for Hunt. Smaller than his parents' dwelling, the W. K. Vanderbilt, Jr., house clearly echoed the floor divisions, window arrangements, roof lines, elaborated dormers, and general treatment of the older building, and the sumptuous interiors were again characteristic of White's work for wealthy clients. The Vanderbilt house was completed in 1907.

Finally, an additional urban commission just around the corner from the Vanderbilt house provides further documentation concerning Stanford's relationship to his house clients. The marriage of Mrs. Rita Acosta Stokes to Philip Lydig, "considered the Adonis of Society in New York," took place in February 1902, and after an extended honeymoon trip the newlyweds temporarily settled in the former Stuyvesant Fish house on Gramercy Park. Within a few months, Rita Lydig was engaged with White in planning for a modest new house, somewhat comparable in size and appointments to the Charles Dana Gibson house. But in 1905, White undertook alterations on a large house at 32 West Fifty-second Street for the Lydigs.[46]

He worked closely with Mrs. Lydig, who relied on his taste and judgment almost completely. From Hot Springs, Virginia, in September 1903, Mrs. Lydig wrote that *he* should decide if the tapestry hung in the house was suitable and the stair rugs should be laid "according to your desires and suggestions." The stair rail should not be covered "unless you first approve of the velvet" chosen. The drawing room furniture should be arranged "as you suggest so it will be comfortable." Her husband wanted to hang his elk heads on the library wall between the Holbein pictures, but "not unless you think it correct." She was, she wrote, "so happy you like my house," but then, "how could you help it, when it is entirely yours."[47]

The great houses White created reflected their clients' personalities and tastes, some more than others, but in the end they were White's works, personal creations of this architect as artist. He was highly persuasive in bringing clients around to his way of thinking and in getting done what he wanted. Following Hunt, who died in 1895, White had the cachet of being the most fashionable designer of his time. His was a body of work of high quality that by and large realized his own deeply held artistic vision of adapting European forms, especially those of the Italian Renaissance, to contemporary needs and conditions.

White often persuaded his clients to go beyond what they had originally agreed to in the size, scale, ornamentation, and expenses of their great houses, confident of his own ability to create something appropriate for them and truly impressive. For an American plutocracy, often unsure of itself and attempting to mold an image rooted in the past, Stanford White was eminently appropriate as a creator of images. With discriminating taste, a penchant for the opulent, and a good deal of showmanship, he was perfectly suited for his times.

21

Evelyn

☙

By the beginning of the new century, White in his late forties had become decidedly middle-aged in appearance. He was portly, his red hair was now intermixed with gray, and his complexion was rather sallow, though his energetic, hyperactive manner and intense enthusiasms were still very much in evidence. At times he had to wear eyeglasses, but he never allowed himself to be photographed with them on. As a young man Stan's inattention to his dress had occasionally evoked comment, but over time he had become more concerned about his clothing and sought out the finest outfitters. He replenished his wardrobe on visits to London; with extravagant flair, he would select morning coats, dinner jackets, loose-fitting sack coats, waistcoats, trousers, and other items from his favored Old Bond Street tailors, and he often wrote from home to have alterations made and arrange for further purchases to be shipped from London. In New York he favored Brooks Brothers, whose store was close to his home and office on Broadway at Twenty-second Street. He would sometimes order something exotic from an outfitter, such as Siberian moose shoes or boots made from old porpoise hides, fitted for his size nine foot. Well aware that he was an object of observation and comment in public places, he wanted not only to get the best for himself but also to make an impression of refined elegance.[1]

The beginning of the twentieth century brought White, always a leader of fashion, into the age of motoring. The new automotive technology fascinated the architect, and motorcars provided him with a convenient means of getting about the city for both work and play. The motorcar quickly became an accustomed—and often irritating—part of his life. He learned to drive, tested cars, rented cars, purchased cars, hired drivers, and made use of cars daily. He also got into endless hassles over the mechanical failures of his vehicles. He became involved in a few minor accidents. He even joined the Automobile Club of America. In the spring of 1901, he rented a steam-powered Locomobile, with a driver furnished by the Locomobile Company, and later that year he rented an electric two-seater "runabout," although he soon turned it in for another because it could achieve a top speed of only 9 miles an hour on level ground, and a turtle, he said, "could pass it on a hill." In October 1902 he purchased an Oldsmobile, after a trial of two weeks, but he had constant trouble with it. On a trip to St. James, the car broke down and had to be ignominiously towed by a horse into Huntington Village, where it remained for several days until parts were delivered. He soon turned the Oldsmobile back, because every time he took it out something broke. His automobile troubles were common enough for the times.[2]

White then ordered, for January 1903 delivery, a Rainier electric hansom, for which he designed the interior, paying $3,500 for the machine. But this car also brought on constant headaches: The batteries died time and again after only slight use. The Rainier "groaned and ground in a way that was pretty unbearable . . . making me perfectly nervous to ride in it," and in February, the first time he took Bessie out for a ride in it, the batteries went dead after less than 5 miles and Stan found himself "very much chagrined." In March the steering gear suddenly broke and he was "flung out of the machine," and in December the car ran up on a sidewalk, broke through a railing, and "nearly killed" him. Since he wanted the Rainier available for business trips during the day and for his social life, "bumming around" the city, in the evening, he was cautioned by the Rainier Company to have his driver recharge the batteries in the early evening before he went out as well as overnight. "The batteries having been out all day do not have as much life as you require for your strenuous evening's work," he was advised. In July 1903 he leased another electric hansom and took a second driver into his employ, so that he had both day and night chauffeurs in full-time service. Early in 1904 White, always seeking the best available, contracted to purchase an elegant royal blue Panhard & Levassor limousine, at a "special" and "strictly confidential" price of $7,400, but a few months later, fearful about his mounting living expenses, he canceled the order. That summer he purchased instead a more modest Franklin electric car; by the spring of 1905 he had also bought a used Charron car from Whitelaw Reid and had employed one Otto Zemmerle as his principal driver. On one trip to Box Hill, Zemmerle was arrested for speeding in Roslyn, and Stan had to pay a $25 fine. Despite the annoying mechanical problems, the new cars delighted Stan. He bragged

318

o friends when things went well about the ease of getting to Box Hill, and he became intrigued with the idea of designing car bodies. With so few cars as yet on the streets of New York, White's cars were conspicuous and helped identify him as a well-to-do man about town.[3]

White's reputation both as a public figure in the city and as a prominent socialite was well established by the turn of the century. The press regularly noted his presence at the theater, at balls and receptions, and at athletic events. *Town Topics* mentioned White as a leading figure of the "ruling set," led by Mrs. Stuyvesant Fish, Mrs. O. H. P. Belmont, and Mrs. Hermann Oelrichs. The gossip sheet also characterized him as one of the "well-known *viveurs*" in the city, one of those who really made New York "a jolly place" and contributed a zest to social occasions. White had mixed feelings about such publicity. After the *New York World* included his silhouette, along with those of other well-known New Yorkers seen together at a ball at Madison Square Garden, White wrote an angry private letter to an executive of the newspaper. He complained of the "roasting" and of being grouped with such people as "Diamond Jim" Brady and the proprietor of the Haymarket dance hall, men he did not know and did not wish to be associated with publicly. Stan asked to be left out of this kind of publicity.[4]

The female-dominated "ruling set," in which White was an acknowledged leading figure, was the more lively component of fashionable New York society, a circle rivaling the rather staid and conventional component headed by Mrs. William Astor, whose husband had been heir to a huge fortune in real estate. From her large French Renaissance-style mansion on Fifth Avenue at Sixty-fifth Street, designed by Hunt, Mrs. Astor presided over "the Four Hundred," the inner set of New York society. She and a few others largely decided who would be acceptable at the great balls and the lavish formal dinner parties that characterized their entertainments. It was Mrs. Astor who somewhat earlier in the 1880s determined that the very wealthy Vanderbilts might be received in fashionable society. Some years later Mrs. William K. Vanderbilt, also the mistress of a Hunt-designed mansion on Fifth Avenue, was divorced from her husband and married shortly afterward to the wealthy Oliver Hazard Perry Belmont, a son of August Belmont, who represented the Rothschild banking interests in the United States. As Mrs. O. H. P. Belmont she became a recognized leader in the more lively and accessible set, along with "Mame" Fish, whose husband's fortune had come from railroads, and "Tessie" Oelrichs, heiress to a huge Western mining fortune. The press often chronicled and reveled in the sometimes unconventional entertainments of those socially powerful women, who, like

Mrs. Astor, could determine the social eligibility of newcomers. White designed houses, as we have seen, for Mrs. Fish in New York City and Mrs. Oelrichs in Newport and the recreation pavilion for Mrs. Astor's son in Rhineback.

At a great distance from the fashionable world of New York, Henry Adams, in his perceptive way, suggested that Stanford White had come to epitomize the ostentatious, materialistic essence of New York and, indeed, something of the character of the new century. Writing privately to his confidante Elizabeth Cameron, Adams asserted that New Yorkers are "busy smiling at our investments. We are grand. The new rich are impayable [priceless] here, and Stanford White is their Moses and Aaron and Mahomet." It was all very "amusing," according to Adams. Stanford had worked closely with Adams on the Memorial to Marian Adams, and the two men saw each other occasionally. In early 1901 *Town Topics* took brief note of the arrival of another figure on the New York social scene: Mr. Harry K. Thaw of Pittsburgh, very rich and very showy, "who has been knocking at society's portals," had "procured a card for Mrs. Astor's ball" and "has arrived."[5]

Although White was viewed in the press as a lively presence on the social scene, the early part of 1901 was filled with troubles and worry for him, arising in part from his huge stock market losses. In addition, Larry, now a student at St. Mark's School in Southborough, Massachusetts, fell ill with pneumonia. Stan and Bessie were called to his bedside. Just as Larry was at his worst, another boy at the school died of pneumonia, "and of course that set Bessie nearly crazy." When Larry was on the mend, his parents brought him back to the Gramercy Park house; they arranged for an express train to make a special stop so that Larry could be transported without having to change trains.[6]

At times White's professional workload seemed almost overwhelming. It was particularly heavy in the office in 1901, for McKim was often away that year, occupied with his duties as head of the American Academy in Rome, as a member of the Washington, D.C., Senate Park Commission, and as architect of several large projects. In June and July McKim visited Europe with Daniel Burnham, Frederick Law Olmsted, Jr., and Charles Moore of the Park Commission to study cityscapes in Paris, Rome, Venice, Vienna, and Budapest—and in England. Leaving "Dummy" in charge of the firm's ongoing projects, Stan managed to slip away, too, in June for his regular fishing trip to Canada. One or another of the partners was away from the office so often that McKim once suggested they ought to have a flagpole over the building "to raise an absent flag, so that people might know as they do in yachting, whether the owner is aboard or not!"[7]

To add to White's troubles, his longtime legal adviser, Prescott Hall Butler, whose counsel White had often sought, died on December 10, 1901, after a long and severe illness. Bessie went into mourning for her brother-in-law for a full year, removing herself from social life. She had been devoted to Butler, whose affection for her was always apparent, since childhood. Because of his closeness to Bessie and possibly because he had been so knowledgeable about Stanford's financial affairs, Butler left a modest bequest to Bessie of the annual income from a fund of $30,000, which would be paid to Larry White after he reached the age of twenty-five.[8]

A few months before Butler's death, in this period of very heavy work and stock market losses, White, then forty-seven years old, acquired a new friend, who would become the greatest passion of his life. On or about August 1, 1901, he arranged for a luncheon at his Twenty-fourth Street hideaway, inviting two young dancers from the musical *Florodora*, then playing at the Casino Theater, along with a friend named Reginald Ronalds. Stan had been acquainted with one of the girls, Edna Goodrich, for some time; he had arranged for Rudolf Eickemeyer to photograph her and had sent her to his dentist for work on her teeth. Edna, "a big girl, plump and voluptuous," had previously visited the apartment above F. A. O. Schwarz's store and seemed right "at home" there. The other guest, brought by Edna, was Florence Nesbit, "a very striking girl," then only sixteen years old. Her mother had given permission for Florence to accept White's invitation for lunch, and at her mother's insistence she had dressed like a schoolgirl of thirteen.[9]

A few months earlier photographs of Nesbit had appeared in a New York theatrical magazine, which characterized "the beautiful model" as "a slight, almost fragile girl, with a magnificent head of hair, fresh eyes, and a smile that is girlish winsomeness itself." She was pictured in other newspapers and in several clothing advertisements, and Stan's friend Charles Dana Gibson drew her portrait for a *Collier's* centerfold as "The Eternal Question." *The New York Standard* that fall, alluding to her posing career, called Florence "the freshest Broadway model," who was "making a hit in New York's Art World." Since June, while continuing to pose during the day, she had been appearing in the evenings as a Spanish dancer in the popular musical, the youngest member of the company. White was already collecting clippings about Nesbit for a scrapbook and had gone to see *Florodora* several times.[10]

When the two girls rang the bell at 22 West Twenty-fourth Street, the outer door was opened by an electrical lock, and there on the upper landing stood Stanford White, tall, imposing, smiling, with "hair all burnished copper" standing up "like velvet pile." He escorted the girls into the apartment. Florence was captivated by the sumptuous furnishings, the many paintings, the heavy red velvet curtains, and the artful indirect lighting. The luncheon table was set for four. The two men were exceptionally attentive to the girls, and Florence later recalled that she felt very grown up. At lunch she tasted champagne for the first time, but Stanford would let her have only one glass. After lunch, when White's friend left, the architect suggested that the girls go with him upstairs. There, in the middle of a high-ceilinged top-floor studio, on ropes covered with red velvet, hung a red velvet swing. Stan urged Florence to sit on the swing and then pushed her higher and higher until finally her feet pierced a large Japanese paper parasol hanging from the ceiling. It was great fun, and they all laughed a lot. No doubt Stan enjoyed the theatrics and spectacle of the swinging as much as the girls did. As the party broke up, White asked Florence to visit his dentist to have her teeth looked at, as he often did with his young women friends. He gave the girls a short ride around Central Park in his electric hansom, took Edna on to a dentist's office, and returned Florence to her hotel.[11]

A few days later White invited Florence to lunch again at Twenty-fourth Street. This time a plump blond chorus girl named Elsie Ferguson was also a guest, along with Thomas B. Clarke, the art collector and dealer, who, Nesbit thought, looked "as old as Methuselah." At that second lunch, her impression of White was very positive. As she later wrote: "He emerged as a splendid man, thoughtful, sweet and kind; a brilliant conversationalist and an altogether charming companion," with "a very fatherly manner." Stan, in turn, obviously was captivated by the beautiful young girl, whose lively intelligence was readily apparent. Again, after their meal they went upstairs to the room with the red velvet swing. Stan was surprised to learn that Nesbit had not had her teeth looked at by his dentist, as he had requested, and he then asked her to have her mother call at the McKim, Mead & White office so that he could make the necessary arrangements. An imperfection in a front tooth, he felt, slightly marred her striking beauty. Her mother did come to see White shortly at 160 Fifth Avenue. She was utterly charmed by the architect, seemed touched by his concern for her daughter, and agreed to have Florence visit the dentist, which the girl soon did.[12]

Florence Evelyn Nesbit had spent her early years in Tarentum, near Pittsburgh, where she had been born on December 25, 1884; for years she believed that she was a year younger. Her father, a lawyer, had died when she was very young, leaving his widow with two small children in difficult circumstances. For years Mrs. Nesbit struggled to support herself by taking in roomers in one rented house after another and by working as a dressmaker. Eventually the mother and daughter settled in Philadelphia. Mrs. Nesbit took a job as a sales clerk at Wanamaker's Department Store, and Florence worked in the stock room. Florence's younger brother, Howard, in poor health, was boarded with an aunt on a farm. In Philadelphia an elderly painter upon meeting Florence was so struck by the young girl's looks that he asked to paint her portrait. Soon she was asked to pose for other artists, including book illustrators and one who designed stained-glass windows. Mrs. Nesbit disliked her work at Wanamaker's and hoped to find work as a dress designer, so, after a year in Philadelphia, she and Florence moved to New York late in 1900.

Florence carried letters of introduction from Philadelphia artists to painters in New York. Her mother called on the painter Carroll Beckwith with a photograph of Florence, and he hired the girl to pose for him. Soon she was asked to model for other artists, including Charles Dana Gibson. The magazine story about the beautiful young model appeared, and a theatrical agent offered to get her a part on the stage. Florence had long dreamed of working in the theater, but her mother and Beckwith did not like the idea. After a brief time of rehearsing, she appeared as a Spanish dancer in the *Florodora* chorus, the "baby" of the company, very much pampered by others at the theater. She was delighted with her new career. Before long James A. Garland, a well-to-do New Yorker, was so taken by the youthful dancer that he invited her and her mother for excursions on his yacht. The yachting parties and a visit to Rector's restaurant, one of the Broadway lobster palaces, where she, her mother, and the man who later became her stepfather were seated in the section reserved for those who were well known, opened up new and exciting worlds for the girl.[13]

Following the luncheons at the Twenty-fourth Street apartment, White, who was decidedly infatuated, beseiged Florence with flowers and invited her, as he had Ruth Dennis and other young women, to after-performance supper parties at the Tower studio. Several times, she later revealed, she and White had supper alone at the Tower. Sometimes, in the wee hours of the morning, she and Stan took the elevator to the upper loggia and then climbed up the steep winding staircases to the very feet of Diana to look out over the silent city, standing there "for a long time, holding hands and softly talking." White told her about the Pie Girl Dinner of 1895 and its aftermath, and it was her opinion that the architect and his friends had been "saved" by the intervention of the authorities. Several times White took her for rides in his chauffeur-driven car. When her friend Garland warned her against White, whose reputation, he said, was that of a "voluptuary," she refused to see Garland any more. Stan arranged to have Eickemeyer photograph Evelyn, as she preferred to be called, in Japanese kimonos, and she later visited the McKim, Mead & White office to look over the photographs. White wrote to a Philadelphia photographer who earlier had taken pictures of Evelyn to order copies of all the pictures he had.[14]

Mrs. Nesbit was pleased with the attentions the famous architect was paying her young daughter. Blinding herself to the reality of the situation, she appeared to trust his intentions completely. Evelyn later wrote that her mother considered White "so kind, so thoughtful, and, above all things, so safe." When she found it necessary in late September to return to Pennsylvania for a few days, White assured her that he would look after her daughter while she was away. Evelyn visited 160 Fifth Avenue during that time and was introduced to McKim by White, who said: "This little girl's mother has gone to Pittsburgh and left her in my care." Well aware of his partner's proclivities, McKim could only respond with "My God!"[15]

One evening while her mother was away, White brought Evelyn to the Twenty-fourth Street apartment for a late supper. No one else was there. She came, she later wrote, innocent of the "big and stunning facts of life." This time Stanford did not limit her to a single glass of champagne. After the supper he led her to a small room, the walls and ceiling of which were covered with mirrors; on one side was a large couch covered in moss-green velvet. The "novelty and unreality," she later wrote, of the multiple reflections in this room of fantasies held her "spellbound." Here she drank more champagne. They returned to the supper room and then went into a tiny rear bedroom. Chintz draperies hung from the ceiling to the floor. A nude portrait by Robert Reid hung over the fireplace, in which a cozy log fire was burning. A large canopied four-poster bed dominated the small room. The dome of the canopy and the headboard of the bed, as well as the wall beside the bed, were mirrored, and tiny electric lights were lit all around the top of the bed; by pushing buttons different colors could be cast upon the overhead mirror. The lights, the mirror, the fabrics, the bed—all made for an atmosphere, which White had artfully contrived, of consummate sensuality. After Evelyn tried on "a ravishing yellow satin Japanese kimono embroidered in festoons of wisteria," yet another glass of champagne was handed to her. As she sipped, she felt a pounding in her ears and became dizzy. Suddenly she passed out.[16]

When she regained consciousness, according to Evelyn's compelling autobiographical account, she found herself naked except for an undergarment and lying on the bed beside White, who was unclothed. Frightened, dizzy, embarrassed to see blood on the sheets, confused, yet nonetheless aware that she was no longer a virgin, she let out "one suppressed scream." Stan tried to quiet her and soothe her, "petting and kissing" her, but he trembled as he touched her. He handed her the kimono and put on his robe. As they dressed he cautioned her to tell no one of the incident, not even her mother. A short while later he took her to her hotel.[17]

Early the next afternoon Stan came to see Evelyn, who had been sitting in a chair and staring out the window since her return to her hotel many hours earlier. When she refused to look directly at him, he knelt beside her, picked up the edge of her dress, and kissed it. He tried to sooth her with words to the effect that she must not be worried, that everything was all right. He told her that "she had the most beautiful head he had ever seen" and he would do many things for her. He assured her "everybody did these things" and "that that was all people were born for and lived for." "The great thing in this world was not be found out," he added. She was so pretty and slim, he told her, he could not help himself. He later said that "only very young girls were nice, and that the thinner they were the prettier they were. Nothing was so loathsome as a stout or fat woman." She must never get fat. He made her swear not to tell her mother about what had happened.[18]

From that time, for six months or so, she and White saw each other almost daily, sometimes at the Twenty-fourth Street apartment and at other times at private supper parties in the Tower apartment. Their sexual intimacy continued. Here was the beautiful woman/child White had always idealized, someone he could play with who gratified him sexually. Stanford, Evelyn later remembered, loved to push her "stark naked on the red swing and laugh aloud with delight as he sent me soaring toward the ceiling until my bare feet crashed through the Japanese parasol." He liked to march about the studio with Evelyn on his shoulder, a bunch of grapes in one hand and a glass of champagne in the other. In Evelyn's view, these were esthetic rather than sexual enjoyments for the architect. As she remembered, she fell "head over heels in love with him." He asked her to pose again for Eickemeyer at the Twenty-second Street studio behind Henry Poor's house. Here she was entranced by a life-size painting of a nude woman standing on a Persian rug, set on a wall unframed, with a rug of exactly the same design laid up against the painting so that the woman appeared to be stepping down into the room. Evelyn posed on a white bearskin rug before the fireplace in one of White's kimonos. Tired after an hour of posing, she lay back, and Eickemeyer photographed her as "The Little Butterfly." Once Henry Poor walked into the room where she was sitting naked before a fire, much to her embarrassment.[19]

At luncheons and late evening suppers in the Tower studio, Evelyn met many famous people, particularly artists and men and women from the theater. There was considerable backstage gossip about Stan's friendship with Nesbit, for his attentions were not especially disguised. He arranged for an apartment for her and her mother at the Wellington, on Seventh Avenue and Fifty-sixth Street, and took charge of the decoration of the rooms. He paid their bills and gave them a weekly allowance of $25. There is no evidence that her mother suspected anything. White hired a piano teacher for Evelyn. One day Josef Hofmann, the concert pianist, came to lunch at the Tower room and, on the old upright Steinway, played Beethoven's "Moonlight Sonata" and the Chopin Valse in D flat Major, the latter piece especially for Evelyn, who was studying it at the time. For Christmas, Stan gave Evelyn a large pearl on a platinum chain and a set of white fox furs. A draftsman in the McKim, Mead & White office later recalled Nesbit coming into the office "dripping with furs" and pestering White. Other men also showered her with flowers and jewelry, but she turned them down. "I loved Stanford White. I wanted only to be with him," she later wrote.[20]

Stan saw Evelyn often that winter, but he was increasingly concerned about her constancy. He once gloomily told a friend that "Evelyn plays with me as a kitten might. She doesn't really care for me." One wonders whether at this time memories ever came to mind of his father's gorilla story, with its warning that not every woman a man encountered really wanted to become intimately involved with him.[21]

For a brief time he was diverted from his affair by another civic endeavor. A visit to New York in February 1902 by Prince Henry of Prussia, the brother of Kaiser Wilhelm, was the occasion for a gala reception at the Metropolitan Opera House. The prince, an admiral of the German fleet, came to the United States for the christening (by Theodore Roosevelt's daughter, Alice) of a new imperial yacht being built in this country. He encountered a tumultuous reception wherever he went. The entire supervision of the decoration of the opera house was given over to White, whose reputation as an impresario of civic extravaganzas was well established.

A rigid constraint was placed on what could be done in the opera house because of performance schedules and a strict budgetary limitation of $7,500. Although the gala for Prince Henry was to take place on February 25, workmen could not begin decorating before midnight on

Evelyn

February 24, and everything had to be finished by midafternoon the
next day. On the exterior of the opera house, White had a representation
of the imperial yacht outlined in small electric lights, three German
eagles in lights, and flags and bunting. In the main lobby trellises were
erected and filled with the greenery of smilax vines and full-blossomed
American Beauty roses. In the auditorium the ceiling was covered by
streamers of greenery with electric lights, and a large movable curtain
of smilax and some 3,500 lights was installed on the stage. A royal
box was set up at the parterre level by combining the five central boxes;
a frame was built around the royal box, and under it an arch of American
Beauty roses was hung. Some three hundred flower boxes were fastened
on the other boxes, and the side walls were covered by masses of smilax.
Lobbies, hallways, and cloakrooms were also decorated, and Stanford
brought in some of his own rugs and tapestries to be used. The *New
York Commercial Advertiser* commented that the decorations would "establish a new record for grandeur in interior floral arrangement." It is
possible that Evelyn was present at the gala.[22]

By the end of February, after all his work at the opera house and
the emotional upheavals of his affair with Evelyn, Stan was, as McKim
put it, "terribly nervous and run down." His doctor ordered him to
take a trip to the South to break away for a time from his hectic, "driven"
life in New York. In early March he went to Washington, D.C., to
look over some work, then on to Richmond, Virginia, where Bessie
joined him. They traveled by train to St. Augustine and Miami in Florida,
and then by boat to Nassau in the Bahamas for a few days in the sun.
The Whites returned to New York directly by steamer from Nassau,
although they were forced to change ships after the first one they boarded
broke down. On the homeward voyage Stan amused himself by working
out plans and designs for ship staterooms and saloons "that would be
a great improvement on anything now afloat." McKim felt that his
partner had recovered nicely from his run-down condition with the three-
week holiday.[23]

In contrast to the romantic fling of the past several months with the
young dancer, Stan's relations with his wife were, as usual, matter-of-
fact and businesslike, though their notes were usually affectionate. A
check for $70 a week for Stan's share of household expenses was to
be sent from the office to her, but sometimes Stan forgot about it and
Bessie had to write the bookkeeper Martin to have it posted. There
were always matters at the Twenty-first Street house and at Box Hill
that needed White's attention: "Dear Stanny, Please remember about
the servants' bathroom at St. James & the leaks in the roof. Also please

begin to think about the work around the barnyard. . . . Affecly, Bessie.''
White's associations with Evelyn did not reverberate with admonitions
of servants' bathrooms, leaky roofs, and barnyards.[24]

When the immensely popular *Florodora* ended its run in January 1902,
George Lederer, a producer, invited Evelyn to join the cast of another
musical, *The Wild Rose,* which he named after her. Lederer had Evelyn
take singing lessons and paid her so much attention that his wife named
her in the divorce suit she later instituted. Lederer, who, the *New York
Herald* reported, was startled by "the Raphael-like vision of Miss Florence" when he first saw her, like half a dozen other men, proposed to
her and, like the others, was turned down. Although she flirted with
other men, she probably was not sexually involved with others at that
time. The new show, with Evelyn playing a gypsy girl, opened in Philadelphia. White attended the first performance and gave a party late in
the evening for some of the cast and managers. *The Wild Rose* came to
the Knickerbocker Theater in New York and turned out to be a hit. In
August the entire company of the popular musical was invited to Newport
to perform privately for Mrs. Cornelius Vanderbilt and her guests. Evelyn,
as the very young star, was becoming widely known even in the upper
social circles that White often frequented.[25]

In mid-June 1902 Stan went off to the Restigouche camp for a month
of fishing. Mead, who received an honorary degree from Amherst College
while White was away, wished him "good fishing," assured him that
nothing would go wrong in his absence, and advised him not to "hurry
back on business accounts." White returned to New York for a couple
of weeks in July, and then on August 1 went back to Quebec, this
time taking Bessie and Larry with him for eight days of fishing. All
three of them caught both young and spawning salmon and "had bully
sport." On the day he left for the second trip with his family, Stan
instructed a New York florist to deliver to Evelyn at the Wellington,
every morning at ten o'clock for nine days, three white roses with cards
he enclosed, and at the stage door of the Knickerbocker Theater, each
evening at seven o'clock for eight days, three red roses with enclosed
cards, except on Sunday evening, when the red roses were to be sent
to the Wellington instead of to the theater.[26]

Early in the summer of 1902, at a Tower party before he went off to
Canada, Stanny had introduced Evelyn to John Barrymore, then working
as a newspaper cartoonist. She found the young man "very amusing"
and "liked him very much." When Stan was called to the phone, Barrymore asked for her address and phone number, which she gave, and
that evening he sent her a cluster of violets with an American Beauty

rose, enclosing a sentimental inscription on a card. While Stan was away fishing in Canada, Barrymore began to court Evelyn openly and soon asked her to marry him. Barrymore later recalled that Evelyn was "the most maddening woman, the most utterly distracting woman I have ever known. She was the first woman I ever loved."[27]

One night Barrymore and Evelyn drank so much red wine that they could hardly stand up. Rather than face Evelyn's mother, they went to the future actor's hall bedroom to sleep off the effects. Mrs. Nesbit was furious the next day when she learned where Evelyn had been. White, by then back in New York, was just as angry, and took Evelyn to his physician, Dr. Nathaniel B. Potter, to have her questioned and examined to see if she had been seduced. Both Barrymore and Evelyn denied that anything had happened between them. White, Evelyn recalled much later, was afraid Mrs. Nesbit would accuse Barrymore of having violated the girl and as a result would learn about his own sexual intimacy with Evelyn. He informed Evelyn, not altogether truthfully, that she was "the only girl in the world who can point her finger at me."

That evening Stan asked Barrymore and Evelyn to come to the Tower room. Barrymore repeated his proposal to Evelyn in front of White. Evelyn, no doubt wanting to make Stanford jealous, appeared openly delighted with the idea. The architect, believing that the offer of marriage was not distasteful to her, stormed and raged and demanded to know what they would live on if they married. Barrymore impishly replied that they would live on "love." Beside himself with anger, Stan told Evelyn that the whole Barrymore family was "queer" and that John's father was in a sanatorium. Evelyn had a scene with her mother, too, who did not like the "little pup." The daughter stubbornly asserted that she would marry Barrymore if she wanted to and no one could stop her. Headstrong and perceptive, Evelyn had become very much aware of her considerable power over men and recognized that her mother was no match for her.

To get Evelyn away from Barrymore, White, with the support of her mother, who felt that Evelyn was too young for the stage, sent her in late October to a boarding school in Pompton Lakes, New Jersey, run by Mrs. Mathilda Beatrice De Mille, the mother of Cecil B. De Mille, the film producer. At the small Pamlico School for Girls, Evelyn studied music, literature, psychology, and even philosophy. She remained at the school about six months. Young Barrymore came to the school to see Evelyn, and when she refused to meet him he left "ardent notes" for her on the tennis court and elsewhere. White took care of the girl's expenses, just as he was continuing to provide for her brother Howard's schooling at the Chester Military Academy. The Philadelphia *Enquirer* some months later headlined a story, "America's Prettiest Girl Model Has Exchanged the Rose and the Gauze Draperies for the Student's Cap and Gown" and asked, "What will be the future of this young woman whose face is the most perfect ever seen?"[28]

While at the school in April 1903, Evelyn suddenly experienced sharp abdominal pains. Her condition was diagnosed as appendicitis. Dr. Potter and another physician were summoned from New York to operate. The other girls were sent away for the afternoon, while the operation was performed at the school. Although it was later rumored that the medical procedure was an abortion, no evidence has been found to substantiate that suggestion. Stan was at Evelyn's bedside when she recovered from the anesthetic, and he soon had her taken to a private New York sanatorium on East Thirty-third Street, directed by her surgeon, Dr. John B. Walker.[29]

Another visitor to Evelyn's bedside at the school and then at the sanatorium was Harry K. Thaw, who, like many other men, had been captivated by the beautiful girl. While she was dancing in *Florodora,* Evelyn had often received flowers and other gifts from a "Mr. Munroe," whom she had not met. Another girl in the cast at the same time repeatedly invited Evelyn to accompany her to Rector's some afternoon for tea. When Evelyn finally accepted the invitation, in December 1901, she first encountered Harry Thaw, who had sent her the presents as Mr. Munroe. Thaw was a man without occupation, apparently very well-to-do, obviously a playboy. His eccentric manner, rapid speech, and protruding wild eyes, however, repelled her, she later recalled, and his incessant questioning as to why her mother allowed her to see Stanford White disturbed her. She was surprised that Thaw knew she was seeing White. Thaw told her that he had once gone with others to a party at the Tower apartment. White later, he informed her, had blackballed him at the Knickerbocker Club. Thaw seemed to her obsessed by the architect, whom he referred to as "that beast." Evelyn soon learned that Thaw had previously pursued Frances Belmont, one of the Sextette leads in *Florodora,* but one evening he had snubbed her in front of his friends at Sherry's restaurant. Miss Belmont, furious at the slight, planned revenge. When Thaw set up a party for several girls at Sherry's, none of them showed up. Belmont had persuaded White to invite all of them to a supper at the Tower. Thaw was greatly embarrassed by having been stood up and blamed White for his humiliation. Even before Evelyn met him, Thaw had conceived an intense hatred of the successful and famous architect. When Stan learned of her encounter, he warned her to have nothing to do with Thaw.[30]

Evelyn

Harry K. Thaw, who was thirty years old in 1901, had come from Pittsburgh. The son of a man who had made a fortune in railroad speculations and mining leases, he was a partial beneficiary of his father's estate, estimated at some forty million dollars. One of his sisters married a nephew of Andrew Carnegie, and another an impecunious British aristocrat. As a youngster Harry had been beset by learning and behavioral problems and was frequently in trouble. Thaw's father, aware of the son's instability, had left him only a small allowance, but his widowed mother gave him substantial sums and supported him handsomely. Harry threw money around, spending lavishly on himself and on others, but his eccentric behavior gave him a decidedly unsavory reputation. When a salesperson angered him one day, he crashed his car into a shop window. He attempted to ride a horse into the Union Club after he was turned down for membership there. He badly thrashed a young male hotel employee for taking some money left out on a table and then stripped the boy, forced him into a bathtub, and rubbed salt into his bleeding back. The incident was hushed up, but word of it got about. Thaw was rumored to have scalded a girl in a bathtub and whipped girls in a New York brothel and at a hotel. In January 1902 he brought eighteen-year-old Ethel Thomas to his Fifth Avenue apartment and repeatedly lashed her with a dog whip. She at once instituted a suit for $20,000 against him but fell ill and died (probably of other causes) before the case was resolved. Stories of Harry's behavior, if not simply his staring eyes and his rapid speech, caused people to avoid him. Behind his back some called him "Mad Harry."[31]

As Evelyn recuperated from her operation in the spring of 1903, Thaw deluged her with flowers and came to see her regularly, though not when White was around. Evelyn was still resentful over the way White had treated her in the Barrymore "tangle" and felt that her former close relationship with the architect was at an end. Thaw, meanwhile, was on his best behavior; he seemed attentive and caring toward her and respectful toward her mother. He offered to send them both on a trip to Europe so that Evelyn could rest and continue her recuperation in new surroundings. White, unaware of Thaw's suggestion, also came to think that a European trip was a good idea for Evelyn. Mrs. Nesbit agreed. The architect gave Evelyn a Cook's letter of credit so that they could return home at any time, and in late May he saw the women off from New York. Unbeknownst to White, Thaw's valet accompanied the two women on the same ship.[32]

Meanwhile, Thaw made his way to France. Evelyn and her mother met him in Paris. The playboy rented a large apartment, where they

331

settled in, and treated the women to meals in the most expensive restaurants, bought them fashionable clothing, and took them to the races. It was evident to the Nesbits, however, that Thaw became "insanely jealous" if another man so much as looked at Evelyn, and he went into a rage if White's name was mentioned. Sometimes he disappeared without a word, leaving the women by themselves, ignorant of his whereabouts, for days at a time.

In Paris, Harry eventually proposed marriage to Evelyn, but she refused him on the grounds that she wanted a stage career. Thaw persisted, but also told her he could not marry her if she was not a virgin. Evelyn later wrote that what she then did was "the greatest, the most terrible, the costliest mistake of my life"—she told Harry about White's raping her and their subsequent intimacy. Thaw sobbed, raged, and kept interrogating her about the incident. He told Evelyn angrily that he already knew of her intimacy with White and had long had detectives following her in New York. By then she realized that his jealousy of White was a monomania. Thaw informed White's friend Elizabeth Marbury, who was in Paris, about what he had learned; she advised him to forget the past and to marry Evelyn, if the girl would have him. Soon after, on a visit to London, Evelyn and her mother, who disliked and distrusted Thaw intensely, quarreled about her relationship with him. Evelyn left her mother to return to Paris with Thaw, while her mother went back to New York.[33]

For some weeks, Thaw and Nesbit traveled about Europe, giving the impression they were married and living together in intimacy. Evelyn had discovered drug paraphernalia in a box in Thaw's bedroom in Paris but at the time had not been greatly concerned. Her feelings toward Thaw changed markedly, however, with an incident in the Austrian Tyrol. One night at the Schloss Katzenstein, a nearly deserted castle where they were staying, Thaw entered her room as she was sleeping, stripped her, and clapped his hand over her mouth. "Every bit of humanity had gone out of him; he was a monster, a fiend, a demon," she later wrote in her convincing account. Stark naked, his eyes glassy, Thaw took a cowhide whip to her and clawed at her, hurting her badly. She remained in bed for a week, and it took more weeks for "the telltale marks of abuse" to heal. He repeated the sadistic attack while still at the Austrian castle, once later in Switzerland, and yet again back in Paris. By now he made no secret of his use of cocaine and morphine. In calmer moments he begged her forgiveness and plied her with gifts. Often at night, though, he awakened her to talk about her relationship with White. Now Evelyn wanted only to get away from him, and in

October she returned to New York, accompanied by Elizabeth Marbury and Elsie de Wolfe, while Thaw stayed on in Paris. Evelyn's mother later disclosed that she had in her possession ten shirtwaists that Thaw had ripped in fits of sadism from Evelyn's body.[34]

White had had a difficult time since Evelyn's departure from New York in late May. His financial situation was a constant worry, he was often ill, and the workload in the office was heavy. That spring of 1903, the Royal Society of British Architects awarded its gold medal to McKim, who was completing his term as president of the American Institute of Architects. McKim was the second American to be so honored by the British architects, the only previous one being Richard Morris Hunt. Stan, who never showed any jealousy of others close to him, was pleased by the international honor given his partner, as he was two years later, when McKim and Saint-Gaudens were among the first Americans named to the newly formed Academy of Arts and Letters. On June 10 McKim sailed for Europe to accept the medal. He would be away for three months, his long absence increasing the pressures of work on White at the office.

Nevertheless, Stan slipped off to the Restigouche camp, a holiday he had long been looking forward to. In May he had written a Chicago friend: "I shall die if I don't get off to Canada salmon fishing on the 1st of June—I mean it is the only chance of health and Life I have." He had not been able to persuade anyone to accompany him, however, and the fishing turned out poor. Continuing to feel under the weather, he came back early. He did return to the Restigouche club in early August, this time accompanied by Bessie and Larry, both of whom loved the sport of fishing as much as he, and the three of them "had bully fishing, killing sixty in a week."[35]

After the London Royal Society awards ceremony McKim, whose health was increasingly fragile, traveled to the spa at Carlsbad, in Bohemia, for a water cure. From there he reported to his younger partner that the tedious water cure was "all rather depressing," though he suggested that the Carlsbad regimen "would be the salvation of Dummy." He added solicitously: "I hope you are cutting down on some things and really taking some care of yourself," and he sent his love to his partner and to Bessie. In response, Stanford complained to Charley about his own troubles: "At present I am having the hardest sort of work trying to go to the Yacht Races, attend to business, having my family in town to take care of every evening, and other things to take care of later in the evening. My health is really suffering under the strain." Bessie and Larry had gone with him on J. P. Morgan's *Corsair* for the yacht races. In another letter White wrote McKim that he "would give anything" if only he could take a three-week cure somewhere. Approaching the age of fifty, he was, he wrote, "getting very much disturbed over my growing corposity, and the fact that, although I can run up hill with a moderate amount of agility, my breath gives out in a way that makes me actually sick." His notes to Bessie when she was in the country that summer were affectionate, perhaps indicating his increasing awareness of age and its demons.[36]

When Evelyn returned from France in October, Stan welcomed her back warmly. Evelyn realized by this time, she later wrote, that the intense love she had once felt for the architect had come to an end, though she continued to appreciate his remarkable qualities and to feel an attachment to him. When she informed White about "the nightmare" at the Schloss Katzenstein, he took her at once to see Abe Hummel. Dwarflike, with a very large head, his face covered with warts, Hummel was a well-known wily criminal lawyer whom Stanford had previously employed. After sixteen interviews with White and Nesbit in his office in the New York Life Insurance Building, the "toadlike" Hummel drew up an affidavit, which he filed with the Supreme Court of the State of New York, setting forth what Evelyn said Thaw had done to her and stating also that Thaw had tried, though unsuccessfully, to get her to charge White with having betrayed her. The affidavit thus protected White. Hummel sent White a bill for $1,000.[37]

That fall Evelyn was hired as Florence Nesbit to appear in *A Girl from Dixie* at the Madison Square Theater. About that time she became friendly with the theatrical producer Sam Shubert, to whom she sometimes wrote in a flirtatious way. It appears that White, as he turned fifty, was still strongly attracted to her. On December 21 he instructed his secretary to continue clipping anything for his scrapbook found in the newspapers both concerning himself personally and concerning Evelyn. He saw Evelyn occasionally and repeatedly warned her to keep away from Thaw, who had returned to New York. Thaw soon discovered where Evelyn was living, however, and once more besieged her with flowers and other gifts. She gave in and agreed to see him again.[38]

On Christmas Eve, 1903, Thaw met Evelyn after her performance at the Madison Square Theater, and she went off with him to a supper party at Rector's restaurant and later to his hotel apartment. A few minutes after they had left the theater, according to the stage doorman, White arrived looking for Evelyn. He had been at the theater earlier in the evening and had invited Evelyn to a birthday party he was preparing for her.

Told by the doorman that she had just left with Thaw, Stan became "black in the face from anger." He hurried backstage to her dressing room to see for himself whether she had gone. A few moments later, returning to the stage door, White pulled a revolver from his coat pocket. He then stormed away, shouting loudly, "I will find and kill that bastard before daylight."[39]

"More like Hell than Anything Else"

The next morning, Christmas Day, after her reconciliation with Harry, Evelyn sent a note to Sam Shubert, the producer of *A Girl from Dixie:* "I'm not a bit well & really not able to go on. The doctor says 'c'est impossible.' Be good." From that time on, Evelyn saw Thaw regularly. Her presence at a dinner given by Thaw on January 6, 1904, was noted in the press. Her close relationship with White was at an end. Evelyn's mother remained very much opposed to her nineteen-year-old daughter's having anything more to do with Thaw, whose erratic behavior she had come to know only too well in Paris. When he sent a gift of furniture to them, the mother had it returned. Harry's persistence nonetheless won Evelyn over, and she soon moved into a hotel in which he had rooms. Eventually he persuaded her to go back to Europe with him. In June 1904 they sailed for Genoa, taking along with them a former college football player friend of Harry and a maid for Evelyn.[1]

Harry and Evelyn traveled together in Europe for several months. After a visit to Monte Carlo, where Thaw gambled heavily, they went on to Paris. Thaw's behavior, Evelyn recalled, was often eccentric: He was frequently drunk and appeared sometimes to be under the influence of drugs. If White's name came up in conversation, he always went into a terrible rage, and at one point he threatened to kill Evelyn if she even mentioned White again. He began to carry a gun in order to protect himself, he claimed, against the notorious Monk Eastman Gang, whom, he was convinced, White had employed to kill him. Thaw's paranoia about White and his obsession with the architect's sexual activities were evident in an incident at the village of Domremy, Joan of Arc's birthplace. While they were motoring through the village, Evelyn mentioned something about artists admiring Saint Joan. Thaw stopped the automobile and went to a visitors' book to write: "Joan of Arc would not have been a virgin long if Stanford White had been around." Evelyn's mother, remarried and known as Mrs. Holman, when she heard that "Florence" had gone to Paris again with Thaw, wrote White that she had hoped he would try to keep her daughter away from Thaw, whom she denounced as "a scoundrel, villain, and a man with murderous intent." "I hope and pray you won't give up trying," she wrote. White, meanwhile, continued to provide support for Howard Nesbit, Evelyn's brother, at a military academy in Chester, Pennsylvania. That generous act, while winning Mrs. Holman's support, certainly showed his continuing interest in the girl. Evelyn later recalled that White had occasionally written her that year.[2]

Although Evelyn was largely out of Stan's life by 1904, Dick White was a continuing worry. Stan still sent money regularly to his roving, irresolute brother, then living in Seattle. For a brief time Dick had involved himself in Alaskan real estate and mining ventures, but, unsuccessful as usual, he had returned to Seattle. Although ordinarily a loner, for a time he became something of a joiner, like his younger brother. In Seattle Dick served as president of the local chapter of the Fraternal Order of Eagles and was, he wrote Stan, a founder and president of the Alaska Club. He purchased a small boat for prospecting, but a steamship company somehow wrecked it. He obtained an interest in oil lands on the Olympic Peninsula in Washington and in some copper and gold mines near Ketchikan, Alaska, but neither venture came to anything. What he really wanted was to return to Alaska and prospect for gold. Time and again he begged his brother to send him more funds—if not enough to get him back to Alaska, then at least sufficient to allow him to leave the Northwest, where he was finding opportunities scarce, and move to San Francisco. At one point Dick asked his brother to use his influence with President Theodore Roosevelt to get him a federal position. Stan responded in no uncertain terms that the firm had only a professional acquaintance with the President through its remodeling of the White House, which had been McKim's project anyway. He himself had absolutely no political connections and, what was more, knew nothing about politics.[3]

While Dick was a persistent annoyance, Larry (or Larrie, as White usually wrote), though occasionally a worry, was a source of pride. Stan's feelings for his son seemed, at least on the surface, to be as affectionate as those his own father had had for him. Larry received a generous allowance of $60 a month, both when at St. Mark's School and at home, and was strongly advised by his father to make his money last: "The one thing you want to absolutely set your mind against is ever thinking of spending more money than you have," he preached, no doubt aware of the outstanding negative example he himself was setting. Stan asked his son always to remind him when he had a birthday coming up, for he himself was "getting old and getting a very poor memory" for such matters, which indicates that the boy was not foremost in his father's thoughts. By the summer of 1904, sixteen-year-old Larry had the use of a new Franklin car at St. James to drive about as he wished. Stan sometimes allowed Larry to use the Tower apartment for a party for his friends. One time, Larry asked his father to order a bunch of violets for the "date" he would be escorting to a dance. "Don't worry, I am not in love," he wrote. "She is ugly & not very attractive, but I had to ask her to the dance, as her mother sent me my invitation."[4]

Besides occasional favors for his son, White continued to help out new friends and old. When Bernard Berenson, the art historian, stopped in New York on a visit from Italy, Stan found him "quite an art authority" and altogether "a charming fellow." White asked his friend Charles Deering to arrange for privileges at the Chicago Club on Berenson's forthcoming visit to the Midwest. He seldom saw Saint-Gaudens, who was weakened by cancer and mostly remained in New Hampshire, but on the sculptor's infrequent visits to New York Stan arranged to meet him and sometimes tried, though without success, to get him out to Box Hill. Saint-Gaudens suffered a terrible blow when, on October 4, 1904, fire swept through his studio at Cornish, destroying much of his work of recent years. Gus continued to have Stan arrange to forward letters he did not want his wife to see, which had been addressed to him at The Players or the McKim, Mead & White office.[5]

Unlike most other years, White generally stuck close to New York in 1904. In February he and Bessie entertained 250 friends at a musical evening at their Gramercy Park home, catered by Sherry's. McKim and Mead were often out of town that year, and Stan lamented the pressures of work at the office. He did get away on a brief midwinter visit to Colonel Oliver Payne's plantation estate at Thomasville, Georgia, and made a few weekend country excursions. He also made short visits to the Restigouche Salmon Club in June, with Jim Breese as a fishing companion, and in August alone, and that time "the trip was a fiasco all around." But he did have the pleasure of a visit in November to the Louisiana Purchase Exposition at St. Louis. White had been named to the Advisory Committee for Applied Arts for the Exposition, but he attended in a private capacity with his client Clarence Mackay, who provided a private railway car for the trip. They had a really "bully time," White reported. The occasion no doubt brought back memories of his great enjoyment of the Chicago fair eleven years earlier.[6]

Despite some moments of social pleasure, however, Stan's deteriorating financial situation overshadowed everything else. Looking back to the turn of the century, he calculated that his regular living expenses, his substantial purchases of art goods, and his losses in stock market specula- tions had combined by the beginning of 1901 to put him into debt in the sum of $321,000. Then in the Northern Pacific panic, in May 1901, he had lost about $625,000, covered in part by a cash margin account with his brokers of slightly more than $235,000. His net loss in the panic thus added about $388,000 to his debt. By mid-May 1901, he estimated, he had a total debt of $709,000. For some years he had been using some of Bessie's money, with her consent, for stock purchases, and she too had lost heavily in the Northern Pacific panic. At that point he felt his case was "hopeless and desperate." One letter shows that he had even contemplated suicide: His financial plight gave him the greatest mental distress, "so much so that it [was] hard work at all to stick to my affairs & to stop myself ending the whole business." To pay the brokers and the most pressing of his other debts, he borrowed heavily from friends, family, and his partners and put out short-term notes with many merchants. In about two years, from his earned income, from commissions, and from sale of some goods, he had been able to pay off more than $100,000 of his indebtedness. At the same time he had kept up premium payments on his insurance, amounting at one point to $235,000 in regular life insurance and a $100,000 accidental death policy. Still, by early 1903 he had come to feel that he was "now more at the end of my tether than I ever have been."[7]

At the end of March 1903, therefore, White had asked his friend and client Charles T. Barney, president of the Knickerbocker Trust Com- pany, to take over supervision of his finances and help him get out from under the nearly $600,000 in debt he estimated he still owed, including pressing bills of $70,000 needing immediate payment and long- term notes and other obligations. McKim and Mead had loaned him $63,000, and the estate of his brother-in-law, Prescott Butler, had ad- vanced him some $60,000. He owed about $121,000 to Bessie. He was approximately $90,000 in debt to Henry Poor. He had loans of

$50,000 from the Knickerbocker Trust Company, and he owed substantial sums to William C. Whitney, Harry Payne Whitney, James Breese, Whitelaw Reid, Henry A. C. Taylor, Duveen, and Barney himself. Barney had agreed to assist him, first by consolidating some of the debts and paying off a few obligations, and then by arranging a new $100,000 bank loan. Stan figured that he owned antiques and other art objects worth from $300,000 to $350,000. He assigned art goods at 121 East Twenty-first Street, at Box Hill, and at the Tower apartment and insurance policies to Barney as collateral on the new loan, although some of his property was already tied up as collateral on earlier loans.[8]

By early June 1903, on Barney's advice, White and his partners had drawn up a new arrangement for the distribution of McKim, Mead & White profits. In a formal document, Stan acknowledged, as his partners were aware, that he had overdrawn his personal account in the firm at this point by $75,000, and therefore, under the equal division of profits in force since the early years of the firm, he was indebted to each of his partners in the sum of $25,000. The three men had agreed that on any share of profits from the firm thereafter owing to White the annual premiums due on the life insurance assigned to Barney should be considered a first lien; that yearly interest on the debts of $25,000 to McKim and to Mead should be considered a second lien; and that remaining profits up to the sum of $25,000 be paid to White as income, but anything over this amount would be applied to liquidating the indebtedness to McKim and Mead. To Bessie, Stan had then assigned all household property belonging to him, "exclusive of pictures and antiques otherwise assigned" in the house on Twenty-first Street and gave his share of "all furniture, improvements, or property contained in or on her place at St. James, Long Island" and paintings and tapestries at Twenty-first Street in return for checks totaling $84,000. At this point, then, in mid-1903, almost everything White owned, except for art goods stored in warehouses or placed at various studios, had been turned over to creditors or assigned as collateral for loans.[9]

In late 1903 and 1904, despite the huge indebtedness, White's customary lavish scale of expenditures went on, for the most part. He appeared unable to cut back, unwilling even to consider retrenchment, except in large-scale stock-market speculations, which he could not continue. He seemed completely caught up in the role of Stanford White, known publicly not only as famous architect, decorator, showman, and socialite, but as collector and connoisseur, party-giver extraordinaire, extravagant spender, cultivator of life's luxuries. The spending continued, mostly on credit.

He was constantly dunned by mail for payment of overdue bills and beseiged by creditors at the office seeking settlement of what was owed them. With many of the creditors he played an unending game of paying a small sum and putting the unpaid balance on a short-term, interest-bearing note. Every two or three months such debts would be rolled over into new notes. As one example, purchases in just seven months from Siebrecht & Sons, Florists & Nurserymen, including bouquets, corsages, bunches of violets, and the rental of plants and trees for Tower parties, amounted to $4,643; small payments with notes and the further purchases adding to the bills went on for years. By 1904–5, White owed large sums, some of them three and four years overdue, to at least four other New York florists as well. He owed thousands of dollars to jewelers, decorators, photographers, booksellers, art dealers, and caterers. On August 1, 1904, he owed Sherry's restaurant $4,495, most of it long overdue. There were blizzards of pleas for payment or at least for a note that might be sent out for discounting. Many creditors threatened legal action, especially after bill collectors had repeatedly called at 160 Fifth Avenue and were turned away each time without seeing the architect. Some creditors offered to let White pay whatever sum he might be willing, just to get a long overdue account settled. Even laborers on projects at Box Hill were not receiving wages owed them and, in effect, were helping support his lavish life-style at their expense. Edgar L. Smith, who early in the century supervised work on the estate, wrote to White on December 31, 1903: "In Reguard to Labor at your Place at St. James L.I., the men I hired to work are getting tired of wating for their money and are going to Take Legal action to get it if it does not come at once."[10]

The socialite banker Barney, whom White characterized as "the best friend I have and the best fellow in the world," by consolidating many of White's debts had relieved him of some pressure and embarrassment. Yet even the 5 percent interest charge was a challenge for White to meet, both on the large loan of $100,000 from the New York Loan & Improvement Company and on smaller notes he had with the Knickerbocker Bank. On his regular checking account with the Knickerbocker Bank, White overdrew as a matter of course, at one point to the amount of $22,293. The overdrafts were incorporated into additional bank loans. Interest on the several loans, along with life insurance premiums and storage and insurance charges on his art goods, were "enough to break my back," he lamented. The only way he saw to get out of the morass was by selling all the goods he had in storage and on loan to friends. Early in 1904 he began to plan for a sale in February 1905.[11]

The only large creditor who put a great deal of pressure on White for immediate payment was his landlord, Henry Taylor, who had been helping him out for years. Since moving into 121 East Twenty-first Street in 1898, Stan had actually paid neither rent nor taxes on the house. He estimated that he owed Taylor $53,000 for the six years ending May 1, 1904. He also estimated that as of a year earlier, he had put $80,000 in alterations and improvements into the dwelling, considerably more than the $15,000 in improvements originally agreed to. White asked Taylor, therefore, to accept $20,000 as the owner's share of the improvements, and after a cash payment of $13,450, including interest, to accept a note for $20,000 for the remainder of his debt.[12]

Taylor agreed to the proposition, but within a year he was demanding at least half payment on the note, or $10,000. By then White found it impossible to make the payment, and he asked Taylor's agent to stop pressing him until he could sell some of his effects to raise the cash. He explained that "*all* the property" he owned was assigned to Barney for the benefit of his creditors and that there were liens against his income with McKim, Mead & White. If Taylor pressed for payment of the note, Stanford warned, he would be forced into bankruptcy, and any settlement with the sale of his things would bring less than half payment for the face value of the debt. "I do not know but, on the whole, this might be the best thing to happen to me, as I am staggering under a load which I fear I really will not be able to carry; but, at the same time," he went on, perhaps deluding himself as to what he might be able to accomplish, "I have the intention, if I can, of paying my debts in full and of paying interest on them."[13]

In a small attempt to retrench, White decided to sublet the East Twenty-first Street house, fully furnished, to Frederick De Peyster Foster of Tuxedo, New York, as of early January 1905. Foster paid White $6,000 to have use of the house for four months. White moved personal belongings into McKim's apartment at 9 East Thirty-fifth Street, which his partner had made available to him. McKim's daughter Margaret was then living in the apartment, which White would share. As he began to shave his expenses, Stan contemplated giving up his "little eagle's nest way up in the top of the Tower." He retained the Tower apartment, however, for it meant more to him, it seemed, even than the richly furnished family house. Alexina White, still very much the loving mama solicitous of her son's needs—she sometimes wrote him that he needed to get new shirts—moved to an apartment at 56 West Fifty-seventh Street while the Gramercy Park house was sublet.[14]

In a brief respite from the turbulence of his finances, as a favor to

McKim, and to demonstrate his support for the American Academy in Rome, White joined McKim, Mead, and a number of other prominent architects, sculptors, painters, writers, educators, diplomats, business- men, government officials, and other leaders at the Arlington Hotel on the evening of January 11, 1905, for "the most distinguished dinner ever given in Washington." McKim had spent months organizing the dinner, sponsored by the American Institute of Architects, to celebrate the restoration of the White House, the founding of a substantial endow- ment for the American Academy, and the growing acceptance of the arts in American life. A special train carried guests from New York City. President Theodore Roosevelt and the Secretaries of State and War headed the roster of luminaries at the dinner. Henry James was there, and Saint-Gaudens, though not well, even agreed to say a few words to the assemblage. In McKim's view, "no such tribute to Art has ever before been paid in this country." White had a splendid time, though the evening provided only a temporary reprieve from worry over the problems that beset him.[15]

Added to White's financial troubles at this time was his health. Early in 1905 he admitted to being "very much discouraged" about his physical condition. For months he had been taking "treatments" from Dr. William West, an osteopathic physician, at his home, at the firm's office, and at Dr. West's sanatorium on East Twenty-fifth Street. For five or six years White had experienced bowel trouble, and in recent months he had begun to have painful attacks of sciatica. Although he had "good spells and bad spells and acute spells, which usually lasted for some three days," the bowel and leg conditions, he complained, had not really improved with the many treatments by Dr. West. But the fault, he admitted, was his own, since his physical problems were half "due to nervous troubles and half to my diet and drinking at night." For a short holiday and change of climate, he went off to Ormond, Florida, for a few days in the latter part of January, taking in an automobile race nearby at Daytona.[16]

Before Stan went south, Bessie sailed from New York on January 14 for a four-month holiday in Europe, accompanied by her widowed sister Nellie Butler, a lengthy separation perhaps indicative of how far apart they had moved. Although Bessie had lent a good sum of money to her husband, her own inherited fortune was sizable enough for her to travel abroad in a comfortable style. The women landed in Naples and went south for a trip through Sicily, followed by early spring visits to Rome and Venice and an April sojourn in Paris. While she was traveling, Bessie sent a cablegram almost daily to Stan in New York with the single word "Serene" to assure him that all was well. To "My darling Bess" in Paris, Stan wrote of his plans to go to Canada for fishing on the first of June and sailing for Europe the last week in June on a short buying trip, though he realized that his schedule would mean "it will be an awful little time that I have to see you."[17]

When he returned to New York's social whirl from Florida, White was conspicuously present on January 31 at one of the most elaborate and well-publicized social events of the first years of the twentieth century, the James Hazen Hyde costume ball, held at Sherry's restaurant. The host, twenty-eight years old, looking very French with a pointed black beard and mustache, greeted his six hundred guests in a costume of black silk knee britches, black silk stockings, white shirt, and bottle-green coat. Educated in France and at Harvard College, a bibliophile and a patron of the theater and the opera, Hyde was the very wealthy son of Henry Baldwin Hyde, founder and president of the Equitable Life Assurance Society. Since the death of his father in 1899, when he had inherited controlling interest in the large insurance firm, he had served as vice president of the company but—proud, aristocratic, and domineering—had often been at odds with the new president.

Hyde planned a spectacular party commensurate with what he saw as his elevated social position. He hired the architect Whitney Warren to transform Sherry's ballroom, which White had created some years before, into a French court ballroom at Versailles at the time of Louis XVI. The supper room on the floor below the ballroom was decorated as an eighteenth-century French garden, carpeted with grass and rose petals and brilliant with statuary and flowers set against vine-covered trellises and arbors. During the evening the Metropolitan Opera Company orchestra played in the ballroom, the ballet corps from the Metropolitan Opera danced, and the French actress Gabrielle Réjane with her company performed in a short comedy. Photographers hired to record the event had a temporary studio arranged just off the ballroom. Posing with seven friends, Stanford, who dressed as a diplomat in white tie and tails, displaying a "Star Order" on his chest, gazed soberly straight at the camera, his face puffy, looking tired and bored.[18]

Tired and bored though he may have been, Stan was greatly impressed by the lavish decorations and the ostentatious display that Hyde and Warren had contrived. The architect wrote the next day to Colonel Payne, at his winter home in Georgia, that the Hyde ball "was a great sight, and altogether the finest and most complete thing that has ever been done here." He was especially taken by his client Mrs. Clarence Mackay, "the sensation of the ball," who came as Theodora in a gown of spun silver and gold with a train 10 feet long "held up by two little Numidians," and wearing a towering silver and turquoise crown. To Bessie in Europe, Stan wrote simply: "The Hyde ball was the most gorgeous affair I ever saw."[19]

The lavish expenditure on the Hyde ball led to considerable negative publicity in the press for Hyde and demands for investigation of the insurance company, for it was rumored that large amounts of company money had been spent on the party. Equitable Life officials, at odds already with the imperious Hyde, demanded his resignation, and the insurance firm was reorganized to lessen his influence. Public outcry intensified as disclosures were published about questionable insurance company practices generally. A New York State investigative committee was set up to look into insurance companies and their policies and procedures. As counsel to the committee, Charles Evans Hughes emerged as the leading figure in the investigation, which greatly helped his subsequent political career. As a result, new laws were passed providing more stringent supervision and regulation of the insurance industry. At the end of 1905 James Hazen Hyde, now out of the company and condemned by the press, left the United States to live in self-imposed exile in France, where he remained until 1941.[20]

Anticipating the sale of those of his goods that were unencumbered, White had leased the sixth floor of 114–120 West Thirtieth Street on April 5, 1904, for an $1,800 annual rent. To make the space usable, he arranged to have the electrical system rewired, the floors cleaned, and the ceiling and closets whitewashed. Here, on the top floor, Stan had available some 5,000 square feet of floor space, to which he soon had furniture, tapestries, paintings, statuary, and other objects, mostly antiques that he had collected over a period of twenty years, brought for storage and cataloging prior to the sale. More than a thousand items were placed in the warehouse, taken from the Twenty-first Street house, from dealers' storage rooms, and from artists' studios where they had been on extended loan. The sale, to be conducted by the American Art Galleries, was scheduled for February 27, 1905, but was postponed until April 23.[21]

It was not to be. Tragically, on February 13, 1905, at 1:55 in the afternoon, fire was discovered on the fifth floor of the warehouse, apparently started by a short in the electrical wiring. The blaze spread rapidly and quickly engulfed the upper part of the structure; an hour and half later, the fifth and sixth floors collapsed in flames into the fourth story. Except for some stone statuary, some bronze pieces, and some ironwork, everything White had stored in the building was destroyed. The loss was staggering. For months he had been counting on the sale to relieve the pressure from his creditors. He estimated his loss from the fire at from $250,000 to $300,000. Insurance on most of the items had run out. As for the others, he had failed to transfer insurance on goods taken from his residence, expecting the objects to be in the warehouse only a short time. "Dame Fortune," he wrote a friend, "seems to wish the last drop of blood out of me, and she has practically done so this time."[22]

At McKim's place, where he was staying, White sat in "stony misery" for two days, McKim reported, and then "broke down completely and sobbed at the breakfast table like a child. Then he made his mind up to it and threw it off, so that one would think he had forgotten all about it." He had "behaved and borne up like a soldier in the loss of his things," McKim wrote Bessie ("Dear Lizakins") in Naples. Though White continued to give a stoic impression of bearing up after the disastrous fire, he must have been devastated by the loss. He immediately wrote Larry in Cambridge to caution him not to worry his mother or spoil her vacation and only to give the fire "the most casual and slight mention" in his letters. He also wrote Jim Breese, then in Naples, to "say nothing but to make light of it" if he saw Bessie there. He acknowledged, however, that it was "about as bad as it can be" and asked Breese for another loan of $15,000 to $25,000 to meet his most pressing debts.[23]

The sympathy of Stanford's friends, McKim said, was "universal." Many friends wrote to try to console him, not only for the shattering financial disaster but also for the sad loss of so many beautiful things he had collected over the years, which had given him so much pleasure. One New York art dealer suggested that "your consolation must be that these objects quickened the sense of beauty in your nature and that they now form part of your mental constitution." As frequently happened, strangers wrote White asking him to help *them*. Two carpenters who had lost their tools in the fire petitioned Stan "to bee so kynd & consider us a litle that we should bee able to obtain sum other tools. We are willing to work at anything if eu could give us a chance."[24]

White estimated after the fire that he still had goods worth $75,000 to $100,000 in storage elsewhere that might be sold, but there seemed little chance he could dig himself out of the hole he was in. He realized he was much worse off than he would have been if he had gone into bankruptcy after the Northern Pacific panic in 1901 and had started out anew. In April, two months after the fire, his landlord Henry Taylor once more pressed for payment on his $20,000 note, demanding at least

$5,000 by the first of May and threatening proceedings against him if payment was not forthcoming. Stan thereupon arranged with his lawyer to have all his available property assigned to Charles Barney for the benefit of *all* his creditors, so that Taylor might be forestalled. He assigned to Barney, as security for new loans from the New York Loan & Improvement Company, mantels, newels, columns, a fountain, tiles, doorways, and the parlor and dining room antique ceilings at the East Twenty-first Street house, to prevent Taylor from getting them. All those were fixed items in the house that White had counted as "improvements" in his earlier arrangement with Taylor. He turned over to Bessie his share in the Restigouche Salmon Club, his shares in the Nissequogue Trout Club, and his automobiles, and he reaffirmed the transfer to her of all his property at Box Hill. To protect his partners from his creditors, he assigned to them "all right, title, and interest in property belonging to McKim, Mead & White, now in the office building at 160 Fifth Avenue." As of April 29, 1905, he concluded that he owed $183,833 to his preferred creditors and $507,258 to his other creditors, or a total of $691,000. His largest creditor was Bessie, to whom he estimated that he owed $126,500. On May 23 he sold to Barney mantels, tapestries, paintings, and musical instruments both already at Barney's house and at the Gramercy Park residence to the value of $152,100.[25]

In order better to protect McKim, Mead & White from his creditors and to prevent his partners as individuals from being held liable for his debts, White, according to an unsigned document in the White Papers, on May 1, 1905, arranged a highly significant new agreement with his partners. Referring to the settlement of June 1903, whereby liens on his share of profits in the firm would provide payment for his life insurance premiums and interest on preferred notes, White agreed that since that settlement had been drawn up and the income had "proved inadequate to discharge these obligations," the equal-shares partnership of White, Mead, and McKim would be dissolved:

> I now and hereby release my partners from all obligations entered into in the partnership agreement made between Charles F. McKim, William R. Mead, and Stanford White; and release to the said Charles F. McKim and William R. Mead all right, title, and interest in the profits, for myself, my heirs or assigns, in any and all business done by the said firm of McKim, Mead & White, and I agree that the said firm shall continue business under the name of McKim, Mead & White, and whatever services I perform for the said firm shall be recompensed by a monthly payment of $1,000.00.

According to the new arrangement, White would continue working for the firm as a salaried employee. The long-standing formal partnership was at an end.

That drastic measure, however, appears to have been a form of insurance to be brought forward and put into effect only if necessary to ward off creditors. McKim, Mead & White journal entries indicate that a share of profits equal to those of McKim and Mead was allotted to White two months later on June 30, another at the end of the year, and one approximately the same at the end of the following fiscal year. Still, the firm's cash books tell another story: White was indeed put on a salary of $1,000 a month, and dividends paid to his partners on several occasions after the agreement were not paid to Stan. In addition to his monthly salary, White received cash payments for some "loans"; large premiums for his life insurance were paid by the company; and he was paid very large commissions on goods purchased through the company for Colonel Oliver Payne. The sum of the insurance premium payments, the monthly salary checks, and the additional loans about equal the cash dividend payments made to the two senior partners. It must be emphasized that the new formal paper arrangement, even if not fully implemented, sadly demonstrated how far White had fallen from his earlier position. Even to put such an arrangement on paper must have been tremendously humiliating for him, a senior partner in his own firm ignominiously demoted to employee status.[26]

Meanwhile, the situation respecting Evelyn had reached something of a resolution when, in the spring of 1905, she and Thaw were married. White reportedly said this was a good thing, since "she was foolish and headstrong and would thus be out of all temptation." Evelyn and Thaw had returned to the United States late in the fall of 1904 from their second visit together in Europe. At a New York hotel they had refused to register as man and wife and had been asked to leave. The volatile Thaw had made a scene, and the press had reported the incident. From then on the press covered their every move. In February 1905 Evelyn underwent another operation for what she later said were intestinal adhesions. While she was recuperating in a private sanatorium, Thaw was extremely attentive to her and had meals prepared in the Waldorf-Astoria kitchen and sent to her. He continued to ask her to marry him and even sent his own mother from Pittsburgh to Evelyn to plead in his behalf. Under this full-scale barrage, Evelyn finally surrendered, and they were married in Pittsburgh on April 4. Her mother, from whom she had been estranged for some time because of their differences over Thaw, and her stepfather attended the wedding.[27]

The newlyweds journeyed West for a honeymoon trip, stopping first in Chicago. There, Evelyn later revealed, Thaw (with his "virgin complex," as she called it) insisted that they stay at an old-fashioned hotel called "The Virginia," because that would "annoy your friend, Mr. White, who is so *different*." They visited the Grand Canyon and Yosemite Park, where, the press reported, Evelyn killed a 6-foot rattlesnake "after a hard fight with an umbrella." Later they went to the Pacific Northwest and to Banff in the Canadian Rockies. For some months after their return, Harry and Evelyn resided in Pittsburgh at the Thaw family mansion, where, according to Evelyn, Harry's mother dominated everyone. Evelyn felt stifled and bored in the Pittsburgh house, especially when Harry went off and left her alone with her mother-in-law. Later in the year there were rumors that the couple were separating. Early in the summer of 1906, prior to a projected trip to Europe, the Thaws came to New York City and stopped at the Lorraine Hotel. One afternoon on the way to her doctor, Evelyn saw White on the street, but they did not speak.[28]

The lives of the Thaws nonetheless continued to be intertwined with that of White in, for Stan, an ominous way. On February 14, 1905, the day after the warehouse fire, a man named P. L. Bergoff called at the 160 Fifth Avenue office and asked to speak to White concerning an important private matter. Ushered into White's room, he introduced himself as a private detective and said he had information that White was being shadowed about the city by persons unknown on bicycles and by car. White "became very nervous and bit his lips." He admitted that a few weeks earlier he himself had realized he was being followed in the street but thought that the surveillance had stopped. Bergoff, no doubt hoping to take on White as a client, suggested that they go out to the street right away to see if there were people trailing him. Bergoff left and stationed himself outside. White went out a few minutes later and walked north to the Fifth Avenue Hotel, through the hotel, and then on to the Continental Hotel. He could see that he was indeed being followed. "You are right, young man," he said to Bergoff. "There are two men on foot, one man on a bicycle, and a woman."[29]

White hired Bergoff to furnish two men a day to find out what was going on. Those operatives soon discovered that a whole crew of men and women in the hire of the Greater New York Detective Agency, headed by John E. McKenna, were following Stanford White wherever he went. White asked Bergoff to put more men on the job and to spare no expense to discover who was paying McKenna's agency. He rejected outright Bergoff's surmise that Bessie might be having him followed.

For the next fourteen months, Bergoff reported to White "almost daily" when he was in the city. At times the surveillance cost $100 a day, and White ultimately paid out several thousand dollars for detectives, an amount he could ill afford. When Bergoff sent one of his force to apply for a job at the Greater New York Detective Agency, and the man was hired to trail White, it was discovered that Harry K. Thaw was paying for the detectives.[30]

White was annoyed and greatly concerned. Actress friends of his, he learned, were also being trailed by the Greater New York detectives, probably to observe whether they were seeing him. He told Bergoff that Thaw was "crazy as a bedbug" and insanely jealous of his wife, whom White no longer saw. White disingenuously characterized his friendship with her earlier as "disinterested." He refused to have detectives put on Thaw or Nesbit or to have the detectives following him arrested, figuring that the publicity from such an arrest was just what Thaw wanted. A woman who knew White and who saw Thaw in New York about this time reported that the playboy had pulled out a revolver at her home and threatened to kill White when he saw him. Stan complained to his lawyer that he was being "persecuted by Thaw" and entertained the idea that he might be in danger, but, the lawyer recalled, White believed Thaw would never try to harm him: "That dude won't attack me with a pistol. He hasn't nerve enough. All he is trying to do is to scandalize me."[31]

In his obsession about White, Thaw had written to and had gone several times to see Anthony Comstock, the head of the New York Society for the Suppression of Vice, to demand that he do something to expose Stanford White and other prominent New Yorkers who were engaged, in Comstock's words, in "the most awful and disgusting proceedings that have ever been brought to my attention." Thaw denounced White and his friends as "moral perverts" who had ravished many young girls. Comstock investigated various charges, but no one would come forward to give evidence, so nothing was done. Comstock tried to rent a studio in the Madison Square Garden Tower to keep an eye on White, but there was such a long waiting list for these choice accommodations that he was unsuccessful.[32]

One detective employed by the Greater New York Detective Agency, which was spying on White, reported that White once took two young women to a studio in the West Twenties and had wine delivered there, but no other witnesses supported his statement. On the other hand, the head of the Greater New York Agency and several of the detectives employed there told reporters that from early 1905 onward they had found absolutely no instance whatsoever of improper conduct on the part of Stanford White.[33]

On May 9 Bessie returned to New York from Europe with her sister. McKim offered his third-floor rooms to Stan and Bessie, but they preferred to take possession once again of the Twenty-first Street house. At the end of May Stan left for his long-planned customary three weeks of fishing in Quebec, stopping on the way to have dinner in Boston with Larry, who was attending Harvard College. After the respite at the Restigouche camp, Stan had a very busy ten days in New York before sailing for Europe himself on June 29 on the *Lorraine,* his first trip abroad since 1900. He had quite a sendoff. A detective and a woman friend trailing White, it was later revealed, took passage on the same ship, and Stan's own detective reported that it seemed "every working member of the McKenna Agency was on hand and as [White] ascended the gangplank jeered at him," although Stanford pretended not to notice. Thaw was obviously still trying to pester White.[34]

The architect's 1905 visit to Europe was strictly a business trip, primarily to look for and purchase things for Payne and Helen Whitney, who were with him part of the time. Colonel Oliver Payne, as always, was paying for the things for his nephew's mansion. "In certain ways," Stan wrote on his return, "I had a bully time in Europe . . . but I worked too hard and did little else but work." He visited more than fifty dealers and galleries and complained of exhausting trips by train from Paris to Rome and back, though he made stops in Florence and elsewhere in northern Italy. Willie MacMonnies went with him from Paris to Italy, and the sculptor's company made the long trip more pleasant. Back in Paris, White arranged to meet with James Gordon Bennett to discuss the newspaperman's projected mausoleum. Also in Paris, Henry Adams, the historian and Stan's former client, reported that White had rushed in to see him and announced "with huge excitement" that the Whitneys had succeeded in buying a Clouet portrait of Henry II for their salon. The Whitneys spent more than $300,000 for purchases on the trip, so Stan's 10 percent commission made the European excursion financially worthwhile. Engrossed as always by the artistic traditions of the past, White was amazed in Paris, he wrote Gus, by "the utter rottenness of the present French Art," much of which was strikingly untraditional. He was unsure whether the entries in the Rome Prize competition, still tied to the past, were worse in painting or in architecture: "They simply were both sickening." He returned to New York at the end of August.[35]

He returned to more trouble. McKim had collapsed and was completely unable to work. According to Mead, McKim was "all right physically, but when he attempts to do any work he goes to pieces." McKim had hated "to give up and is very sensitive about his condition." Mead felt that his partner had "been overburdened all winter" with his attention to the American Academy in Rome, his responsibility for arranging the American Institute of Architects dinner in January, and his extensive work on the library for J. P. Morgan as well as many other projects. McKim himself admitted that he had not felt well for weeks: "I have had to carry more than one load this year," he wrote (probably referring not only to his architectural projects and the work for the American Academy but also to his daughter Margaret's ill health and, it would seem, to White's troubles), "and my nerves which have held out so well for so long have felt the strain, accompanied by disordered digestion and depression." McKim had left New York in early August, before White's return from Europe, to stay with his daughter at Narragansett Pier, Rhode Island. After a month at the seaside resort, he came to the Whites' place at St. James for a few days and then, accompanied by his physician, joined Daniel Burnham of Chicago for a fishing trip in northern Wisconsin. He returned east to stay for a short time at Hyde Park, New York, at that time giving Mead the power of attorney to manage his affairs and sending his opera tickets on to the Meads and the Whites. He offered his residence on Thirty-fifth Street to Stan and Bessie if they decided to rent out their town house again. In November McKim was back at Box Hill, "at the 'Court of Saint James' for an after-cure."[36]

The attraction of the White country house for McKim was not only the peace and quiet it offered but also the companionship there of Bessie. McKim had always been very fond of Bessie and was well aware of what she had to put up with from her husband. His affection for her permeates his letters. Bessie was often "Lisa" or "Cissie" to him, still something of the young girl whom he had first come to know at Smithtown through Prescott Hall Butler, even before she was courted by White. While Stan was in Europe, McKim had sent Bessie birthday greetings: "I love to think that when you receive this you will be—just nineteen years old, and that I shall be at Saint James with you, to wish you courage and Godspeed and many, many returns of the day." Trials and tribulations would come and go, he told her, but the love of "laughter and love of friends" would endure, making "life most worth living." Bessie, on her side, was always devoted to McKim. When he had recovered somewhat and left Box Hill, Bessie wrote to Stan: "We miss him awfully."[37]

By early January 1906 McKim felt well enough to come to the office for an hour or so a day. In December he had gone briefly to a friend's plantation in South Carolina for shooting and horseback riding and he returned there once again in late January. Three months later he felt strong enough for a few hours each day at the office. Massage treatments morning and evening and being out of doors, he believed, helped him most.[38]

The burden of McKim's work only added to Stan's difficulties, of which by now his own health was the most pressing. In November 1905 he thought he was nearly at his "wit's end." Since his return from the buying trip in Europe, his health problems, all his own work, the burden of McKim's collapse, and his financial troubles "have made the two months I have been here more like hell than anything else." His sciatica had become much worse and required prolonged medical attention: He took regular massage treatments as well as a course of treatments with a battery-powered electrical device. He started drinking bottled Contrexeville mineral water once again and tried a diet of Kefir Kumyss, a beverage made from fermented cow's milk. Still, with the pain in his hip joint and his leg and the stiffness of his knees, he at times felt "little better than a cripple." For a break from the New York winter, he took short trips in January and April 1906 to Colonel Payne's plantation at Thomasville, Georgia. Surprisingly, a "quack medicine," analyzed as iron and potassium iodide with liquorice, gave him some relief from the pain of the sciatica.[39]

A few months earlier Gertrude Käsebier, an immensely talented photographer, had touched up a likeness she had taken of White some time before. Käsebier labored carefully over the photograph and created a powerfully revealing likeness of the rapidly aging architect as he appeared to her. With a penetrating and steady look, the eyes dominate the sober portrait, catch our gaze, and demand that we try to understand him, accept him as he is. Shoulders hunched, flabby-faced, his gray hair thinning—prematurely old—he is someone who has lived fully and recklessly, who has seen it all, but at the same time a man tremendously proud of what he has accomplished. A master of visual expression and psychological insight, Käsebier achieved a deeply poignant biographical statement in this portrait.[40]

On April 18, 1906, a terrible earthquake shook northern California, devastating the region. The earth tremors and the severe fire that followed destroyed much of San Francisco and killed more than 450 people there. On his return from Georgia in April, White almost at once became immersed in the architectural implications of the natural disaster. He was asked for advice on how to rebuild the office buildings of the Bay City so as to protect them from future disasters. White suggested to Daniel Burnham, the Chicago architect who was working on a city plan for San Francisco, that systems of cross-bracing, the elimination of all extraneous elements—projecting string courses, balconies, and cornices— and absolute prohibition of brickwork that could loosen were essential in rebuilding. Above all, adequate and stringent building codes had to be enacted. William Richardson, now a partner in the firm, was sent to California to represent McKim, Mead & White.

Similar advice might have been given to White himself: to strengthen the essential elements, remove the extraneous, and adhere to regular codes of action. At a time of financial, professional, and personal crises, such advice might have helped him regain control of his own life. Probably, though, it was already too late. "The San Francisco disaster," White complained to a friend, "has added so much to my labors that I have hardly had time to think."[41]

The Sidewalks of New York

I n the half-century since the Exhibition of 1853, when Richard Grant
   White could look out over his city from the Latting Observatory
tower, the appearance and character of New York had changed markedly.
By the beginning of the twentieth century the city had become a world
metropolis, commercially and financially powerful, its populace highly
diverse and cosmopolitan, including many newly arrived immigrants.
It had become a place of vast and conspicuous disparities of wealth.
With the amalgamation of five boroughs in 1898, the population of
New York had increased to about 3,437,000 inhabitants in 1900, some
five times the number who lived in the physically smaller New York at
the time of Stanford White's birth. Elevated railways, erected on Third,
Sixth, and Ninth avenues in the 1870s, opened up new areas for residence
and increased the ease of moving about the city; movement was facilitated
even more by the opening of the first segment of the Interborough Rapid
Transport subway system in 1904. New York was fast becoming a new,
modern city, incorporating for its residents all the frustrations and the
gratifications characteristic of twentieth-century urban life. In its rapid
growth, increasing wealth, expanding transportation system, and imperial
dimensions, New York as a metropolitan city was a striking embodiment
of turn-of-the-century America as a whole.[1]

   The New York cityscape boasted countless new landmarks, although
much would still be familiar to someone who had known the city half
a century before. As earlier, the waterfront remained crowded with vessels, and the streets of lower Manhattan were cluttered and congested.

Among the most prominent additions were the Brooklyn Bridge (1883), majestically soaring over the East River, the 743 open acres of Central Park, between Fifth and Eighth avenues north of Fifty-ninth Street, and several newly erected skyscrapers, clustered especially in lower Manhattan. For a time after its completion in 1899, the Park Row Building, facing City Hall Park, was at thirty-two stories the tallest building in the world. The most widely admired of the very high new structures was Daniel Burnham's Flatiron Building, twenty-three stories tall, erected in 1903 just south of Madison Square at the intersection of Fifth Avenue and Broadway. White's Madison Square Garden, just to the northeast, and Washington Memorial Arch and the Judson Church and Tower at Washington Square, to the south, were, of all his many buildings, especially notable additions to the New York cityscape.

In the earliest years of the new century, White made additional significant contributions to the cityscape, creating along the sidewalks of New York some of his most powerful and impressive buildings. Despite the turmoil of his personal life, he was in those years at the height of his artistic powers. He was gifted with the capacity, it seemed, to seal off his worries and the turmoil of his private life when at the drafting board, so he could focus all his mind and energy on the creative process. The control he had lost in his own life returned to him as he dealt with his art. In those final commercial, religious, and civic buildings, along with simultaneous work on some of the great houses, he made bold statements about artistic values. Continuing to mine the past for inspiration but adapting the ideas he took with imagination, he paid careful attention to details and the needs of his own day. Working closely as usual with his clients, many of them personal friends, he created several outstanding showplaces for New Yorkers. Critics enthusiastically praised those works as, one by one, they were completed. Some of the final monuments to his creative talent are extant, though a few have been mutilated almost beyond recognition. As always, Stan complained he was so "driven" by the burdens of work that he scarcely had time to think, but it is apparent that the press of serious work was indispensable to him.

One of White's notable commercial designs at the time was for the midtown banking rooms of the Knickerbocker Trust & Safety Deposit Company at the important intersection of Fifth Avenue and Thirty-fourth Street, on the northwest corner, directly across from the Waldorf-Astoria. That was the site of the former Alexander T. Stewart mansion, which had been used as a clubhouse for some years after Mrs. Stewart's death. Charles Barney, the bank president, had long been a client, friend, and financial adviser, and it was perhaps not surprising that White was selected o replace the mansion with a building of his own design. Some of the white marble used on the bank was said to have come from the Stewart residence. The Knickerbocker Trust Company building was completed in 1904.

For the choice site, White created an elegant classical structure, which for years was a notable landmark on the avenue. Although only three stories plus an attic in height and measuring a fairly modest 75 feet frontage on the avenue and 125 feet on the side, the temple-like bank gave an impression of largeness and monumentality because of the scale of the colossal fluted Corinthian columns, the splendid elaborated entablature, and the richly embellished frieze. Between the columns and the pilasters the building wall was a screen of bronze grillwork and glass, providing considerable light to the interior and emphasizing, by the contrast of materials, the strength and solidity of the vertical members. A small pedimented doorway centering on the avenue front marked the principal entrance of the bank. Within the large street-level banking room, the rhythm established on the exterior was repeated in simpler columns of Cippolino marble and with large screens of bronze grillwork from the Tiffany Studios. In the basement, safety-deposit vaults were erected off a reception room embellished by white marble. Montgomery Schuyler, the influential architecture critic, called the colonnaded front 'one of the most impressive visual objects on Fifth Avenue, or indeed in the street architecture of New York.'' New Yorkers, Schuyler wrote, 'ought to feel very much obliged to the architect for giving us something so good to look at.'' The bank building, in the critic's view, was ''a modern classic.''[2]

A few blocks north and one block east, at the southwest corner of Forty-fourth Street and Madison Avenue, another of White's most admired designs was completed late in 1902. The porch for St. Bartholomew's Church was a gift of the widowed Alice Gwynne Vanderbilt and her children in memory of Cornelius Vanderbilt II, who had died in 1899. The fashionable church building, dominated by a tower soaring some 200 feet, had been built in 1872 in a northern Italian Renaissance style by James Renwick, the architect of St. Patrick's Cathedral. In the summer of 1893 White had supervised interior alterations of the church, and six years later, when Mrs. Vanderbilt wanted a memorial to her husband, she consulted White. At first she decided on doors for the church, but White, unsurprisingly, persuaded her to provide a full entrance porch. He suggested a front modeled after the porch of the Church of St. Gilles near Arles, which he had visited on his short tour of southern France with McKim and Saint-Gaudens in 1878. The Vanderbilts had already

359

used the scheme of the St. Gilles porch at the huge family mausoleum designed by Richard Morris Hunt on Staten Island, so they were familiar with the general scheme.

White created "every detail of the minutest character" of the St. Bartholomew's Church porch and gathered a team of sculptor friends to work together under his direction in making a harmonious composition. Corinthian columns of Cippolino marble were erected to enframe the three portals of Indiana limestone and support a frieze with Biblical scenes flanking the central entrance. The sculptor Andrew O'Connor carved the frieze and assisted Daniel Chester French with the Apotheosis of Christ in the tympanum, or round-arched space, above the central doorway. The right tympanum, with adoring angels before the infant Jesus and the child John the Baptist, was sculpted by Philip Martiny, while that on the left, a madonna with the infant Christ, was by Herbert Adams. O'Connor and French decorated the central doorway with cast bronze panels illustrating stories of the Apostles. Martiny also carved four large statues placed in niches of the portico. In 1902 White also worked on the church proper, removing the spire from the tower, making alterations on the rectory, and providing a new mosaic floor in the aisles of the nave. Some years later, in 1914, a new St. Bartholomew's Church was commissioned for a Park Avenue site. The architect Bertram G. Goodhue was asked at that time to create a structure that would harmonize with White's work on the porch of the old church building. As Goodhue's church neared completion, the White portal was rebuilt onto the new church. Today it provides a distinctive, highly decorative block front amid the glass-fronted skyscrapers of Park Avenue.[3]

Saint-Gaudens thought the church front as a whole was "really bully," in fact "one of the finest things" that Stan had done ("and that's saying a good deal, old man"), though he was critical of Martiny's niche statues, which looked to him "like shop work such as is rushed through at $3.00 a day in a marble yard." Cass Gilbert, who had returned from Minnesota to practice his profession in New York, was equally enthusiastic about the St. Bartholomew's porch. He wrote White that he even felt a sense of obligation to his former employer for providing "a thing of such charm and beauty" to New Yorkers: "Your skillful use of color, your disposition of sculpture and of decorative ornament, and the harmony of the scheme you have in its relation to the older parts of the building, have all excited my keenest interest and appreciation." The sculpture on the porch, he declared, was "an epochmaking work in American art." Mrs. Vanderbilt, the donor, was "very much pleased with the work," also confident "that it will mark an era in American art." Although he church portal was highly acclaimed, Stan regretted that the porch had been rushed to completion in only six months, so that marble of a fully uniform color could not be found.[4]

Just north of the Knickerbocker Trust on Fifth Avenue, two of White's most striking and widely noticed commercial structures went up about the same time. The Gorham Building was built on the southwest corner of Thirty-sixth Street between 1904 and 1906, while the Tiffany Building, on the southeast corner at Thirty-seventh Street, was built between 1903 and 1906. Both were outstanding additions to what was, at the turn of the century, the most luxurious shopping district of the city, and they still stand forth today, despite unfortunate alterations and defacing, as two of the most elegant buildings of the midtown New York cityscape.

The Gorham Building was commissioned by the silver company both as a showcase for the display of its many products to retail and wholesale customers and as a workshop in which goods were crafted. Edward Holbrook, the president of the company, was very much taken by the modest size of the Knickerbocker Trust building and so decided to limit his own to eight stories. With that proviso, White undertook to create "a pure Florentine type of building," characterized by an arcaded base of two stories, a simple shaft of four stories, and a high, loggia-like two-story attic, surmounted by a broadly spreading cornice. To get the effect of the Florentine prototype for his commercial structure, he made "dozens and dozens of studies," working closely with the president of the company. White was proud of the Gorham Building and felt that he had "succeeded fairly well in accomplishing what [he] was after"— a striking adaptation of a historic style to modern-day utilitarian commercial needs.[5]

It was said of White that as he designed and supervised the construction of the Gorham Building, "no detail throughout all the building escaped his vigilant eye." Polished gray granite columns were placed at the base to form a colonnade. Large areas of glass opened to show-window displays and provided considerable light for the two main exhibition and sales floors. The two uppermost stories, devoted to design studios and workshop rooms, were also characterized by large areas of glass, here covered by metallic grills. The underside of the projecting copper cornice, visible from the street below, was gilded and richly polychromed. For the spandrels, or spaces above the large arches in the colonnade, the sculptor Andrew O'Connor, "who did such splendid work on St. Bartholomew's Church," created a series of allegorical figures of art and industry relating to the silversmith's trade. Small balconies were centered on the street and avenue façades of the building, and a large decorative ornamental panel with animal figures was placed just below the loggia attic on the main front. Bronzework, crafted in the Gorham Company foundry, was fashioned into a frieze above the base as well as elsewhere on and within the building. The interior was richly appointed. Great care was taken in designing and selecting the appointments: The mahogany and glass showcases in the main-floor showroom were designed, it was said, to be "in the very simplest and highest style of the art." For both exterior and interior, White strove above all for a "feeling of elegance and simplicity." The Gorham Building immediately became one of the most admired buildings in New York. To one critic, the Gorham was "the best piece of work that Mr. White ever did," and to another it was "perhaps the most beautiful store building in America."[6]

Also Italian Renaissance in inspiration, but in this case Venetian rather than Florentine, White's Tiffany Building provided another showplace on Fifth Avenue. For the jewelry company headquarters, store, and light manufactory, White took his inspiration from Sanmicheli's mid-sixteenth-century Palazzo Grimani along the Grand Canal in Venice. Enlarging his adaptation from the original and simplifying many elements, the architect created another of the most remarkable and elegant buildings of the city, a Venetian palace for New York shoppers. The exterior of the Tiffany Building was clothed in white Italian marble and divided into three horizontal divisions, with almost all the space between the forceful paired columns and pilasters given over to glass, making for great openness and lightness within the structure. The Tiffany Company itself boasted that the new building "unquestionably reaches the highest mark of artistic excellence up to the present time."[7]

Opulence, richness, and refinement characterized not only the exterior but also the interior of the seven-story Tiffany Building. The street-level showrooms were distinguished by a high, elaborately coffered ceiling, supported by polished purplish-gray marble columns, teak woodwork and floor, and ornately inlaid teak showcases in which jewelry and other costly items were displayed. Especially noteworthy on the main floor were the bronze screens surrounding the principal elevators. The exhibition rooms at this level and above were flooded with light. Tiffany-manufactured bronzes were shown on the second floor, and pottery and glassware on the third level. Photography and engraving were carried on at the fourth floor, while goldsmiths and diamond cutters and polishers worked on the fifth floor. Clocks and leatherworks were found on the sixth floor. The top floor was a large vaulted hall used for exhibitions. Below the basement-level shipping rooms were storage vaults at the sub-basement level. Delivery vans were kept at the Tiffany garage, contructed simultaneously nearby on Forty-first Street. To one critic, the Tiffany store was a remarkable adornment to the city, a harbinger of progress for commercial buildings, and, considering its fireproof construction, a building that made for "the health, happiness and safety of individuals."[8]

A few blocks away in the James Building, on the southwest corner of Broadway and Twenty-sixth Street, White installed a small showroom for the Havana Tobacco Company. The showroom was envisioned as an advertisement for the company and its products, representing "a cool, clean, sweet, spacious tropical apartment as might give something of the illusion of Cuba." The walls, floor, ceiling, and columns of the room were of polished white marble. Pierced marble screens and old marble seats were set about the showroom, interspersed with potted palms and tropical plants. Rugs and tapestries added a colorful touch here and there. On two walls, Willard Metcalf painted a mural frieze of Cuban landscapes. The Havana Tobacco Company store was, according to one visitor, all in all "a fine show" and "assuredly the best-looking store in the world."[9]

White's final major project was erected from 1904 into 1906, just off Fifth Avenue facing the east side of Madison Square, at the northeast corner of Twenty-fourth Street. The Madison Square Presbyterian Church was an important building for an important congregation. It stood close to Madison Square Garden and the Farragut Monument, which had been so significant in White's early career. Although Stan for years had disliked the crusading, moralistic minister of the church, Dr. Charles H. Parkhurst, whose earlier church stood on the opposite corner to the south, he worked in harmony with the building committee and created a widely admired jewel. One friend wrote White that the Madison Square Church was "quite as much a monument of your taste as anything else you have put your hand to on the same scale." Many critics have judged the church White's most beautiful building, indeed, "his masterpiece." One commentator said it was "like a Byzantine jewel," a work to bring the passer-by "to a full stop of admiration." In 1907 the church won a medal of honor awarded by the New York Chapter of the American Institute of Architects.[10]

Classical-Byzantine in inspiration, the polychrome Madison Square Presbyterian Church was cruciform in plan, topped by a dome covered with green and yellow tiles and a lantern, and fronted by an elegant portico of six 36-foot columns of pale green granite. The sculptor Adolph Weinman, a pupil of Saint-Gaudens, executed the figures in the portico pediment. The exterior of the church was faced in buff yellow brick and glazed terra cotta above a white marble base. White worked closely with craftsmen at the Atlantic Terra Cotta Company in Perth Amboy, New Jersey, designing the terra cotta for the church. Even though the church was soon wedged between tall buildings on the north and the east and had to compete with Napoleon Le Brun's lofty Metropolitan Life Insurance Company tower across Twenty-fourth Street, it held its own with its neighbors, its scale firmly established by the great columns of the portico and by the massive entablature. Inside, a vestibule led from the porch to the high-ceilinged church sanctuary, lighted principally by small windows in the drum below the dome and by three large stained-glass windows facing south. Behind the church but attached to it stood the parish house, with an entrance on Twenty-fourth Street.

At the dedication ceremonies on October 14, 1906, four months after White's death, a huge crowd milled about the Madison Square Presbyterian Church, attempting to get inside. In his dedicatory address, the Reverend Parkhurst "lament[ed] the absence" of the architect, who had made this church "the idol of his thought and effort." White, the minister said, had deeply impressed himself "upon the regards of those of us with whom, in the work, he has been most closely associated." The occasion of the dedication was "less bright" because he could not be there "to contemplate the final outcome of his splendid genius."[11]

Despite all this acclaim, a few years later Madison Square Presbyterian would be demolished to make way for a huge insurance company building. The columns and many of the architectural elements were incorporated in a newspaper office building in Hartford, Connecticut, while other architectural pieces were sent to the Brooklyn Museum and to the Metropolitan Museum of Art. Replicas of the widely admired church were later erected in West Virginia and in California.[12]

In those early years of the new century, Stanford was also occupied with other New York commissions somewhat removed from midtown Fifth Avenue. One project, in which he was involved more than just as architect, was a hotel for Garden City, Long Island, a town established in 1869 by the merchant Alexander T. Stewart as a model residential suburb. After the death of Stewart's widow, Cornelia, in 1886, and protracted legal battles, her heirs, of whom Bessie White was one, resolved to manage the Garden City property from Cornelia's estate jointly. The Garden City Company was set up, and White was named one of the directors. The architect undertook to renovate and enlarge a small hotel that stood on the property, giving it a neo-Georgian look, and to build a small casino and clubhouse. The renovated Garden City Hotel was opened in 1895. Four years later a fire destroyed the building. Soon after, White rebuilt the hotel in the same neo-Georgian mode with a large new central tower modeled on that of Independence Hall in Philadelphia. Stan and McKim often went to Garden City to play golf, and McKim sometimes stayed in the hotel as a summer retreat.

An unusual project that White undertook about the same time was a power station for the Interborough Rapid Transit Company, the first subway company in New York City. Erected at Eleventh Avenue and Fifty-ninth Street, the long, massive building, topped by five tall smokestacks, was provided with a dignified and almost monumental front through the repetition of a standard unit, a lofty arched window framed in banded brick pilasters. An entablature above and an elaborated cornice provided additional artistic detail. After the power station was finished in 1904, one critic deemed it "simple, dignified, and beautiful," a work that "cannot fail to have an uplifting influence on the neighborhood." This temple to power still stands today, immensely impressive.[13]

Simultaneously in 1903, White was caught up in a large-scale project to replace the old 1870s Grand Central Terminal on Forty-second Street with a new office building and station. White's lifelong interest in new building technology—even though he was largely committed to the past stylistically—had finally led to his involvement with the skyscraper form. His competition entry for the project envisioned a huge steel-skeleton building, most of it fourteen stories above street level, standing over the below-ground tracks. Rising from this elevated base was a skyscraper tower sixty stories high, projected as the tallest building in the world, with a fanciful steam jet shooting upward from its top and lighted red at night. The upper part of the tower recalled the tower of Madison Square Garden. White's proposal for the New York Central station project, however, was considered too grandiose and impractical for the needs of the railroad, and the commission was awarded to another entry.[14]

Finally, bringing the architect back to the category of his first professional design experiences in New York City were two sculptural projects of 1905 and 1906. In collaboration with Willie MacMonnies, White designed a base for an equestrian statue of General Henry W. Slocum for a central Brooklyn location on Eastern Parkway. MacMonnies worked on the statue in Paris, but the sculptor and architect coordinated their artistic endeavors closely, and the composition was completed in 1905. MacMonnies was highly pleased with White's pedestal for his statue, which he said justified his "absolute confidence" in the architect's judgment. Indeed, Stan's pedestals, the sculptor modestly affirmed, always seemed "infinitely better than the statues on them."[15]

As early as 1898 White had started working on plans for a monument to be erected in Brooklyn to memorialize the more than 15,000 colonial soldiers and sailors who were believed to have perished in English prison ships anchored in New York harbor during the Revolutionary War. A Prison Ship Martyrs' Monument Association of Brooklyn was set up, and its president invited White and MacMonnies to provide a sketch to be used in raising money for a monument on an elevated site in Fort Greene Park. Stan made use of the Detroit Bicentennial Memorial column idea for the project. Congress appropriated $100,000 in matching funds in 1902, and soon a like sum was contributed by the State of New York, the city, and the association. A limited competition was held, and White's close friends Saint-Gaudens, Henry Bacon, and Whitney Warren as the jury not surprisingly chose Stan's design for the monument. On a large terrace platform what was said to be the world's tallest Greek Doric column (148 feet, 8 inches) was erected. Adolph Weinman, brought in as sculptor, designed a tall brazier of bronze for the summit of the column. Bones of the eighteenth-century prisoners, which had been put in an old crypt long before, were transferred to a vault on the site. The cornerstone of the Martyrs' Monument was laid on October 28, 1907, and the monument was dedicated a little over a year later. The Martyrs' Monument remains today one of the most striking civic memorials in New York City.[16]

White's 1905 trip to Europe included a short visit in Paris with his longtime client James Gordon Bennett to discuss plans for a Bennett family burial vault and monument that the newspaperman had some time before commissioned. Stan had begun work on the project as early as 1896 and had turned out many different designs for it over the intervening years. Bennett owned a large plot of land in Washington Heights, in upper Manhattan, overlooking the Hudson River, and for a burial vault and monument to his family he turned once again to his favorite device, the figure of an owl, which had been used on the roof edge of the Herald Building.

The publisher commissioned White to design a huge bronze owl monument, a bizarre and grandiose project that would rival the Statue of Liberty in New York harbor. For the site, Bennett proposed a viewing platform placed inside the head of the bird large enough to accommodate a dozen people, with outlooks over the Hudson through the owl's eyes. A vault was to be built underneath the creature, although at times the idea of suspending a sarcophagus for Bennett's remains inside the great hollow statue was considered. Stan's earliest studies were for a bronze owl 60 feet high placed on a 55-foot-high pedestal and, later, an owl 80 to 100 feet high on a similar pedestal. White preferred the former scheme as more in keeping with the site and the buildings there. Bennett contemplated donating a large tract of land at Fort Washington to the city for a park, provided the monument might be erected there and the city would agree not to run streets through the property. Later on Bennett, in a burst of megalomania, called for the projected owl statue to be 151 feet high. At one point Bennett considered a large statue of Minerva instead of an owl, but by the summer of 1905, when Stanford saw him in Paris, the client had gone back to favoring the owl design.[17]

With the fantastic Bennett Mausoleum and owl project, White had come back to the client with whom he had worked on the Newport Casino at the very start of his professional career with the new firm. Had the bizarre project for Bennett actually materialized, White would have created a truly striking icon that would surely have become one of the best-known images associated with New York. No doubt it was fortunate for his later reputation as an architect that the outlandish project was not realized. The Bennett commission was abandoned at the time of White's death.

The several major projects in and around New York that White did complete during the first years of the twentieth century provide compelling evidence of his great talent as a designer and his ability to utilize stylistic elements derived from the past for contemporary purposes. The Gorham and Tiffany buildings, the Madison Square Presbyterian Church, and the Knickerbocker Bank were among the best buildings he ever did. Despite ill health, financial troubles, and the diversion of his energies in so many different directions, despite the Nesbit–Thaw imbroglio, his principal works of the first years of the twentieth century were among his greatest achievements.

24

"I Could Love a Thousand Girls"

☙

Since his cancer operations in 1900, Gus Saint-Gaudens had stayed close to his home and studio in Cornish, New Hampshire. He seldom made the trip to New York and saw little of White. Soon after Gus had first begun to spend summers in Cornish, Stan had visited him there briefly in August 1888, but after that he never returned. Gus occasionally invited his friend to come for another stay, but he did not press the matter, obviously aware of White's aversion to Augusta and of the architect's ever crowded schedule, which made such a trip difficult to fit in. Gus once explained to Stanny that he realized Cornish was a long way from New York and added, cryptically, that if White were to come "you would be twenty-four hours without KIFE (if you know what that means), unless you brought a Houri along with you." Gus was obviously well aware of his friend's liking for beautiful young women, but what he meant by "KIFE" we can only imagine. At any rate, even a short visit to the upper Connecticut Valley could mean a jarring interruption of White's professional, social, and sex life.[1]

In the winter of 1905–6 Gus's condition deteriorated and he returned to Boston in March for another major operation. Directly after the surgery he began writing his reminiscences—focusing in part, of course, on his long friendship with White—which were later edited and published by his son, Homer. In the spring, however, Saint-Gaudens and White were once again in collaboration, as they exchanged notes about two projects and tested ideas on each other. One project was a fountain for a site in Pittsburgh. Stan sent his friend a perspective incorporating his suggestions for the piece. They also began work on a small carved stone slab, like

369

a Greek stela, with a full-length figure of "Beauty" to honor the artist James A. McNeill Whistler, for the military academy at West Point.

By early May, Stan, anxious to see "Gusty" once more, was proposing that he and Charley come up to Cornish, but the sculptor tried to discourage a visit at that time because of continuing terrible weather and the condition of the roads. With mock seriousness, Stan sent Gus some religious tracts along with the suggestion that they might do him some good since he had been so long "amongst the trees, frost, icicles, and mud" of New England that his soul had no doubt been "cleansed of lechery and evil thoughts." Gus wrote back that he thought the real reason Stan had chosen that particular time for a visit, after Gus had been trying in vain for twenty years or so to get him there, was that White had heard the young actress Ethel Barrymore was going to be there. White did not make the trip north; however, in June Gus came to New York to undergo X-ray treatments, and the two old friends saw each other then.[3]

By late spring McKim, whose health remained precarious, was spending weekends at a small cottage on the White property at St. James, which he dubbed "The Hermitage." He had leased a car and hired a chauffeur for the trip to Long Island. Charley asked Stan, to whom he often deferred on such matters, to see if the insurance that had been arranged for the car was appropriate: "I would not bother you if I were not groggy and nervous today or knew of anybody in the automobile business but yourself who could settle the matter for me," he wrote his partner. Charley regarded his younger colleague as a man of the world who could deal effectively with the practical, routine demands of life, as Charley, even at his best, believed he himself could not.[4]

McKim was usually feeling well enough to come to the office in the mornings, when in the city, and attempted to keep up with all that was going on. In a mid-May letter to Mead, who was in Europe, Charley commented that Stan "is alternately in the seventh heaven and the other way round, but is blooming and looking forward to the Restigouche," after which he was planning a trip to Europe with Clarence Mackay, White's client for Harbor Hill, "for the purchase of certain objects of bigotry and virtue." In another note a fortnight later, Charley assured Mead: "The office is moving along as usual. I do not think you are coming back to anything disturbing."[5]

Shortly before leaving for the Canadian fishing camp, White visited Agnes Palmer, a young actress he knew who was a friend of Evelyn and was then convalescing in a hospital. He told her, she later recalled, that Thaw always carried a pistol and that he was aware Thaw had threatened to kill him. The actress advised White to have Thaw arrested, but Stan scoffed: "Oh, Thaw is crazy. He is a 'dope' fiend. He lives on the stuff. He won't hurt anybody. I don't fear him." When Evelyn's friend May MacKenzie called on White, he reportedly told her that he intended to get Evelyn back. May passed that information on to Evelyn, who seemed to enjoy arousing her husband's jealousy and informed him about the remark. Later newspaper accounts indicated that Thaw had recently been spotted on several nights near the White residence on Twenty-first Street and that Stan had been observed talking earnestly with Evelyn Thaw on a street corner one day.[6]

White left New York on June 2, 1906, for his cherished fishing vacation in Canada, but this time he took only a brief holiday and was back in New York by June 15. On his return, the architect met with Bergoff, his hired detective. He was highly agitated at constantly being shadowed by Thaw's detectives. He told Bergoff that he had become "a nervous wreck" and planned to take the matter to the courts to stop being hounded.[7]

On Friday, June 22, White put in a full day at his office. He checked on the progress of current projects, dictated some letters, and took care of legal matters regarding Bessie's Park Avenue Hotel property. It is most likely that he spent that evening "on the town," probably with a visit to The Players, where Gus was staying. The next day he was driven out to Box Hill for the weekend.[8]

Two guests at St. James that weekend were Leroy King, a Harvard College friend of Larry White, and Laura Chanler, the daughter of Winthrop Astor Chanler, Stan's longtime friend, and Margaret Terry Chanler, who became well known as an author. Larry and Laura, who were almost exactly the same age, had met at a dancing class in New York City. Stan enjoyed having the young people around, though he and eighteen-year-old Larry usually had little to say to each other. On Sunday White offered Laura an amber necklace as a present. Bessie had previously refused it in the belief that amber meant bad luck. Laura, aware of Bessie's refusal, did not accept the gift either. Stan slipped the "bad luck" necklace into a pocket of his jacket. At Sunday dinner, in the tiled dining room, Laura sat between Larry and his father. All that day, especially at the dinner table, Larry was highly critical of everything and everybody. When Stan apparently could bear his son's carping no longer, he pointed at Laura and said to Larry: "You like this, don't you?" Larry, obviously embarrassed at his father's boorish behavior, fell silent for the rest of the meal.[9]

On Monday morning, June 25, Stan and his chauffeur left Box Hill before seven o'clock to return to the city. At his office during the day, he conferred with Saint-Gaudens about the West Point Whistler project.

Larry, Leroy, and Laura returned to New York about 4:30 P.M. so that Laura could catch a late afternoon train up the Hudson Valley. King accompanied Laura to the station, while Larry went to the house on Twenty-first Street. King then went to the Whites' house, where the two youths dressed for a planned dinner with Stanford White. Toward evening, when the architect returned from his office to dress for dinner, four of Thaw's detectives followed him home and stayed on his trail for several hours.[10]

Stan dressed for the evening and took Larry and Leroy with him in his electric car to Martin's restaurant on Twenty-sixth Street between Broadway and Fifth Avenue, just across from Madison Square. Long considered a Bohemian rendezvous, Martin's had moved to this location in 1899, when Delmonico's had vacated the premises for its large new quarters on Fifth Avenue at Forty-fourth Street. Martin's, with its French cuisine and French atmosphere, was frequented by many artists and writers. A large café with cushioned wall seats occupied the Broadway side, while the main restaurant faced on Fifth Avenue. A terraced balcony overlooked the main dining room. As White and the two young men entered and passed through the dining room on their way to the terrace, Evelyn Thaw, dining there at a table with her husband and two male friends, noticed him.

The Thaws, who were planning to leave for Europe in a few days, were staying at the Lorraine Hotel on Fifth Avenue, near Sherry's. Earlier that evening, while Evelyn was bathing and getting dressed, Harry Thaw, in evening clothes and muffled in a long black topcoat, despite the mild June temperature, had gone to Sherry's bar to wait for his wife. There he had drunk three whiskies and had paid, in a characteristic gesture, with a hundred-dollar bill. Evelyn, wearing a white dinner dress and a black picture hat, came by for him, and they went out to their electric car to be driven by their chauffeur south on Fifth Avenue to Martin's. They were joined for drinks and dinner at the restaurant by two acquaintances, Thomas McCaleb and Truxton Beale.

Harry seemed more agitated than usual that evening. When Evelyn saw White walk across the restaurant, she passed her husband a note saying, ''The B. was here a minute ago, but went out again.'' Evelyn's note piqued Thaw's jealousy, as she knew it would, and his agitation grew more intense. About nine o'clock, after dinner, Evelyn and her three companions walked the short distance from Martin's to Madison Square Garden, where they took the elevator to the Roof Garden to take in the opening-night performance of a new musical, *Mamzelle Champagne*. While Evelyn sat at a table watching the performance with McCaleb and Beale, joined there by another acquaintance, a man named Wharton, Harry moved restlessly about the Roof Garden. He sat down briefly at a rear table with James Clinch Smith, Bessie White's brother, whom he knew slightly. Thaw asked Smith if he would like to meet "a buxom brunette who was not very pretty but who was interesting." Smith answered that he was not interested.[11]

Following their dinner at Martin's, White took Larry and Leroy by car to the New Amsterdam Theatre, where they attended a revue on the roof garden. White then went on to the Manhattan Club, leaving his car and driver close to Madison Square Garden. At the club he wrote a note with a simple message of greeting to Paula Marr, a young actress playing in Atlantic City. The note was posted at 9:15 P.M. About 10:50 P.M. he left the club, walked to the Garden, and took the elevator to the Roof Garden, which he reached at five minutes to eleven.[12]

Stan took a seat at a table reserved for him to watch the closing moments of the show. He had helped to back the musical, but the opening-night performance, he soon saw, was lackluster, and it was apparent that the show would not be a hit. As the tenor Harry Short on stage was singing "I Could Love a Thousand Girls," Harry Stevens, the caterer for the Roof Garden, stopped briefly to talk with the architect at his table. Stan asked to be introduced to Maude Fulton, one of the singers on the stage. As Stevens left White to go backstage, Stan remained sitting pensively, his right elbow on the table, chin in hand, listening to the music.

Meanwhile, the Thaws and their friends rose to leave. As they neared the elevators, Harry suddenly turned and walked forward toward the side of the stage. For a few moments he stood behind some shrubbery, still wearing his overcoat, the collar turned up. Several spectators noticed the curiously garbed pale man with an "almost haunted look" on his "deadly white" face lingering beside the stage. Then, to their horror, they saw him pull out a small automatic revolver from under his coat as he walked directly to White's table.

Thaw stopped squarely in front of White, 2 or 3 feet away. He lifted his arm and fired three shots in quick succession. White uttered no sound, slid sidewise from his chair, and crashed to the floor, his right arm pulling the table partly over on top of him. His head and neck were black from gunpowder. A pool of blood appeared on the floor.

For a brief moment the music went on, but then it stopped. The Roof Garden erupted with screaming and shouting. Men and women at nearby tables stood up, pushed aside their chairs, and scrambled to get away.

After firing the gun, Thaw raised the weapon above his head, the barrel pointed downward, and emptied the remaining bullets from the chamber. They clattered to the floor. Starting toward the elevators, he was heard to mutter, "You'll never go out with that woman again."

On stage, the singers stood transfixed by the horrible sight before them. The conductor motioned the singers and musicians to go on, but the show came to a halt. Two of the chorus girls fell to the stage in a faint. The Roof Garden manager climbed on a table and pleaded with the audience to leave the premises. A doctor approached White, knelt down beside him, and pronounced him dead.

An engineer employed at the Roof Garden, who was standing near the elevator, saw what had happened and ran forward to grab Thaw by the shoulder. A policeman came up. Thaw calmly handed over his revolver. At that point Evelyn rushed up to her husband and cried, "My God, Harry. What have you done? What have you done?"

"It's all right, dear," Thaw responded, "I have probably saved your life."

Crowded around them, men and women were pushing toward the stairs and elevators and trying to get out. James Clinch Smith walked over to the body. The face was "burned beyond recognition," and he did not even realize that his brother-in-law was the victim. Someone brought a white sheet or tablecloth from backstage and placed it over White's body. An undertaker, summoned to the Roof Garden, soon had the body removed.[13]

Thaw and his party were taken into the elevator and down to the street, where Harry was handed over to another policeman. The officer grasped Thaw's arm and told him he was under arrest. He then asked Thaw why he had shot White. "He deserved it," Thaw replied. "I can prove it. He ruined my wife and then deserted the girl." Unnoticed, Evelyn slipped away and was driven to the boarding house of her close friend May MacKenzie, where she went into hiding. Harry appeared composed. He handed the policeman a bill and asked him to telephone Andrew Carnegie and tell him that he was in trouble. The officer, ignoring the request and holding Thaw's arm tightly, walked with Thaw to Fifth Avenue and then north to Thirtieth Street and west across Broadway and Sixth Avenue to the Tenderloin District police station. There, as Thaw was booked, he unaccountably gave his name as "John Smith" and identified himself as a student, thirty-three years old, from Washington, D.C. Hundreds of people soon congregated in the streets around Madison Square Garden, and a large crowd gathered in front of the police station.

One witness to the murder was Albert Payson Terhune, later famous as an author of dog stories, who was at the Roof Garden that evening to pinch-hit as drama critic for the *Evening World*. He immediately rushed to the nearest telephone he could find, only to discover a man using it for "a smirking conversation with one Tessie." The man refused to give up the telephone, so Terhune, who had considerable experience as a boxer, proceeded to yank it away from him and to telephone in his story to his news desk, all the while fending off the irate man he had displaced.[14]

Newspaper reporters quickly converged on the Whites' Gramercy Park house, where they roused Lizzie Hanlon, the housekeeper. Summoned to the front door, she was horrified at what she was told. A short time later Larry White returned home, having made a post-theater visit to the Harvard Club and accompanied Leroy King to the train station. Stunned by the news the reporters had given him, he said he had never heard Harry Thaw's name before. Larry at once rushed to Madison Square Garden to look for his father's car and driver. When he found the chauffeur, they started out immediately for Long Island. They reached Box Hill about 3:30 in the morning. Larry camped outside his mother's bedroom door and waited until daylight to awaken her and tell her what had happened. Bessie, the press reported, received the news calmly. Stan's mother was prostrated with grief when informed of her son's death, though the full circumstances were not revealed to her. Early in the morning Bessie and Larry returned to their Manhattan residence, where two of Bessie's sisters awaited her. Alexina White came to the city later.[15]

Meanwhile, newspaper reporters telephoned news of the murder to McKim, who was staying with his daughter at his home on Thirty-fifth Street. Although frail and nervous, Charley set about the next morning to direct arrangements with Mead, who had returned to New York. Very early in the morning of June 26, only a few hours after the murder, three of the McKim, Mead & White draftsmen who had worked under White, including J. Frank Stimson, went to Stan's private office hideaway on the sixth floor of 160 Fifth Avenue, where they gathered up and burned a number of photographs, which they considered pornographic, lest they be used against White. The McKim, Mead & White office was closed that morning and remained closed until after White's funeral.[16]

A short time later Harry Lynke, one of White's private secretaries, sent some 160 books of erotica and various photographs, paintings, and letters from White's office to Jim Breese. This collection of books curiously included at least a dozen volumes on flagellation, including

375

such works as *The Romance of Chastisement, Memoirs of Private Flagellation,* and *The Pleasures of Cruelty.* Thaw's own sexual obsession, which Evelyn had experienced at the Schloss Katzenstein and afterward, had been of interest to Stan as well, it appeared. Some of the books may have come from the library of Richard Grant White, who had collected erotica, but others, no doubt, had been purchased by Stan himself.[17]

The day after the murder an autopsy of White's body was conducted at the undertaker's establishment. It was discovered that one bullet had entered White's left eye and lodged at the base of the brain, another had gone into his left nasal cavity and mouth and into his brain, and the third had pierced the inner side of his right arm. The two examining doctors declared in their report that White's physical condition was so poor that he probably would have died a natural death in a year or so. They discovered that the dead man had suffered from Bright's disease of the kidneys, incipient tuberculosis, and fatty degeneration of the liver, probably the result of years of heavy drinking. Personal effects found on White were turned over to his widow, including what was described as "a heavy gold ring of peculiar design," with figures of two naked females and one male. A full cast White's head was made, and a few sandy hairs and reddish whiskers lodged in the plaster.[18]

On Thursday, June 28, Harry Thaw was arraigned before a grand jury and remanded without bail to the Tombs prison, charged with the murder of Stanford White. That same morning White's coffin, which had been brought to the Twenty-first Street house, was opened for a final viewing and then removed shortly after eight o'clock to the Thirty-fourth Street ferry and taken across the East River to Long Island City. A private train composed of a funeral car and two carriages with passengers from New York left Long Island City at 9:15 A.M. for the north shore of Long Island. McKim, Peter Cooper Hewitt, and William A. Evarts had made the funeral arrangements. Mrs. Richard Grant White remained at the Gramercy Park house.

The funeral service at the St. James Episcopal Church, a simple country church that the Smith family had had built, was "in very good taste," according to A. W. Drake, who represented the Century Company, but he could "not remember a sadder one." About two hundred people attended, including McKim, Mead, Thomas B. Clarke, Peter Cooper Hewitt, Nicola Tesla, James Breese, William Astor Chanler, several employees of the firm, and family servants. Saint-Gaudens did not feel well enough to go. A choir from St. Bartholomew's Church in New York sang. The altar was banked with orchids, lilies, and roses. Afterward,

376

the mourners "followed the pall-bearers who carried the coffin through the long avenue to the grave, the choir chanting and singing hymns." McKim later designed the stone for his partner's grave in the St. James churchyard.[19]

After White's death, business for *Mamzelle Champagne* became brisk. Many patrons requested seating at the table where White had been shot. The murder and its aftermath generated a vast outpouring of newspaper copy and probably became the most fully reported American scandal of the early years of the century. Almost at once, in many press accounts, the victim became the villain.

Here was a highly sensational story about one of the best-known figures of the city. The press was determined to make the most of it. James Gordon Bennett, with whom Stan had had a long association, cabled the *New York Herald:* "Give him Hell!" That was just what the *Herald* and other newspapers and magazines did. A few people quoted in the press praised White's artistry and his acts of charity, but the negative comments were far more numerous in early accounts. Stories about Stan's private life, his Tower apartment and other hideaways, and his involvement with showgirls flooded the newspaper columns. The press demolished White's reputation. *Vanity Fair* headlined one story about the murder of this " 'gay' man about town": "Stanford White, Voluptary and Pervert, Dies the Death of a Dog." Even the relatively staid *New-York Tribune* reported, two days after the murder, that "along Broadway last night there were but few expressions of regret for White's death. In the vernacular of Broadway, 'Stanford White got only what was coming to him.' . . . Tenderloin cabmen spoke harshly of his reputation. One of them said to a Tribune reporter: 'I knew that fellow would be killed sooner or later, but I thought that it would be a father that would do it—not a husband.' " Many people on the city's streets appeared to be well aware of aspects of White's secret life, especially his penchant for underage girls. The *Tribune* reported that White "was described by those . . . who had known him for years as a man whose friendship was an insult."[20]

The highly respectable *New York Times* printed a letter about White purporting to have been sent to Evelyn Thaw from a Brooklyn mother who lamented the unknown fate of her daughter, now lost to her: "She was pure and good until she met that moral leper. She had just turned sixteen. She pleased his fancy for a moment." The gossipy *Town Topics* let it be known that "some such deplorable incident has been anticipated." Even some people who had known White claimed to be unsurprised at what had happened: The diplomat Henry White wrote McKim from

Rome: "I have long feared as you know that he would come to an untimely end, but I must say that I did not expect such a tragedy as the incident which has befallen him." Henry White went on to express sympathy for Bessie, "who has had so much to bear from him."[21]

McKim did his utmost to comfort Bessie, who remained secluded at Box Hill. Dick White came from Seattle to be with his mother and his sister-in-law. He was quoted in the press as saying he had not seen his brother for eight years and had a family of his own "to look out for." Alexina White was placed under the care of a trained nurse and for some time was not allowed to see newspapers. Bessie and Larry devoted themselves to acknowledging as many of the thousands of letters, cables, and telegrams as they could. Larry became "the mainstay and support, as well as constant companion, of his mother." Charley McKim's devotion to Bessie was constant as ever. After Stan's death, he wrote her that she had "for years made life more worth living" for him and would always be "the dearest Friend I have on Earth—because the one who has taught me the most and to whom I owe the most." Charley assured Bessie that he would forever admire "the great nature that was born in you to cheer and brighten the lives of your friends and all those who come in contact with you." Bessie's "fortitude in these days of her distress," McKim wrote a friend, "has been an example to those about her." With his poor health, McKim himself was the object of concern for many friends. Yet he managed to keep up his spirits; in a reference to the company logo, he affirmed that "the ship" had not been "dismasted nor demoralized" and pledged that "we shall go on to the end together, whatever happens."[22]

Unlike the press at large, numerous artist friends and others sent condolences to McKim, expressing their sympathy for him and their own sense of loss. The architect Cass Gilbert said White "was one of the great artists of his time and the world loses by his death." The sculptor Janet Scudder always considered White "the acme of the artistic in America," and his death was "a most deplorable blow to the Fine Arts," in truth, "a national calamity." "The captain of the ship of the fine arts had been taken from us," Scudder wrote, "and we knew that there was no one to take his place." The critic Roger Fry wrote McKim from London that White's death was "a loss that America can ill afford." Glenn Brown, on a business trip to New York about a week after the murder, was tremendously impressed by the "universal sorrow among art workers at his loss."[23]

Some of White's fellow professionals in the American Institute of Architects, the Architectural League, and the Society of Beaux-Arts

Architects expressed their great sense of loss to the profession; White's remarkable eye for "quick and generous appreciation of all that is beautiful" and "the love and enthusiasm with which he devoted himself to Art" were noted. To these fellow professionals and friends, "whatever he produced had the touch of genius," and his influence, they believed, would continue as "a stimulus to the artistic development of this country." In their estimation, Stan had been "a commanding personality."[24]

Some of the young actresses White had known were questioned by the district attorney's office and interviewed by the press. Edna McClure said Evelyn had often teased Harry about White and dared him to do something. She also said that she herself had frequently attended parties in White's Tower apartment and that they were always respectable. Mazie Follette, who had also been at many of White's parties, denounced "the outrageous expressions which have been cast upon the memory of Mr. White" and said that there was always lots of fun at his parties but nothing to be ashamed of. "The women of the stage regarded Mr. White as a big brother," she went on. "He was a good friend and a jolly good fellow who liked girls, and loved to have youth and beauty around him."[25]

Yet few among White's closest friends spoke out in public about the architect. In fact, several left the city and hid from reporters. Some men in the White circle suggested to McKim that something should be done to counteract the vilification and mud-slinging. From Paris, Charles Dana Gibson, like several others, expressed outrage and anger at the newspaper accounts and urged a memorial gathering at which Stan's friends could express their admiration and affection publicly. "It's hard to realize," Gibson lamented, "that Stanford (so full of life) is dead." A fortnight after the murder, the journalist Richard Harding Davis suggested that a "Standford [sic] White Scholarship" be set up by friends and admirers to provide funds for study in Europe. He wanted "to say, or do, or write something in behalf of the memory of a man who was very kind to me, and who is, or, for a few days, was, being damnably misrepresented." McKim told Davis that the time was "most opportune" for an appreciation of White in print: "I hasten to ask you to write something in behalf of the memory of the man as we knew him—to whom the world owes so much. . . . We all hope that you will write some expression of your feelings and estimate of Stanford as soon as possible." McKim then called upon Saint-Gaudens to provide an estimate of White for publication and told him that Davis had "asked permission to write" something about White. Gus agreed to prepare a statement.[26]

Davis's spirited defense of White was published in *Collier's Magazine* on August 4, 1906, and reached a large number of readers. The article confronted head-on the hostility in the press toward White and denounced the "hideous misshapen image" that had been broadcast so widely. In his years as a newspaperman, Davis wrote, he had never before encountered "an attack made upon any one as undeserved, as unfair, as false as the one" made upon White. The stories about White's hideaways were false, he asserted, and even the young woman the architect was accused of debauching had spoken out with indignation against the abusive press attacks. White was "a most kind-hearted, most considerate, gentle and manly man . . . as incapable of little meannesses as of great crimes," a man brimming over with enthusiasms who greatly admired beauty in women as he admired beauty in all things. "He loved life and got much more out of it in more intelligent and more different ways than any other man of his day in New York City." The architect was always generous, Davis pointed out. He encouraged fellow artists, assisted students and beginners, and helped countless people who had no claims on him whatsoever. "When a man or woman was in trouble, Stanford White was the first man in New York to whom he or she could turn, knowing that, asking no questions, preaching no sermon, it would give him pleasure to serve them." As artist and architect, he had "left his mark upon New York City as few other men have done," contributing to the success of civic functions and public celebrations and creating some of the most important buildings in the city. No one could walk about New York "without being indebted to Stanford White for something that is good and uplifting." Davis found it unthinkable that such a person could have been "degraded and contemptible." So great was the hostility engendered toward White, however, that one public library removed Davis's books from its shelves in reaction to the article, and the author himself was accused of being "a depraved romancer."[27]

Saint-Gaudens agonized for weeks over the wording of a public statement about his fellow artist and close friend but found that whatever words he put down were inadequate to express what he wished to say. Nonetheless, following Davis's article Gus sent *Collier's* a letter praising what the novelist had written as truly "the living portrait of the man, his character, and his life." Above all, Saint-Gaudens wrote, Stan's "almost feminine tenderness to his friends in suffering and his generosity to those in trouble or want, stood out most prominently." To Gus it was "unbelievable" that White, "with his astonishing vitality, enthusiasm and force" was gone.[28]

Richard Watson Gilder, editor of the *Century*, with whom White had worked often, also paid a public tribute to the murdered man. Gilder recounted their long friendship and expressed the opinion that White "had the swiftest perception of beauty of any man I ever knew. His apprehension was lightning-like, and so was his execution." Gilder praised not only White's architectural achievement but also his picture frames, magazine covers, pedestals, and temporary decorations. White was invariably kind and generous, Gilder wrote. "To meet Stanford White in the street and be greeted with a burst of commendation meant to many an art-worker weeks of cheerful plugging away; for everyone knew that his appreciation was as discriminating as it was hearty."[29]

Other extended tributes to White appeared in American journals in the weeks that followed. *American Art News* called White's death a "veritable loss to the cause of art in America." A man "of unusual art taste, knowledge and judgment, and of rare force and energy," White had done "much through his work and influence in architecture and decoration, to improve the art taste of New Yorkers, and indirectly of Americans." His was indeed "a rare and forceful personality that did much for the good of the cause of art in America." In *The Critic,* a New York art journal, White was described as "our first architect of real genius," and his death was termed "a distinct loss to this country and particularly to the city." His name "stood for beauty, and the buildings that he has built will live as noble monuments to his name and keep his memory green from the Atlantic to the Pacific coast." *The Architectural Review* lamented that with White's death the world had lost "an eminent architect, who, by his extraordinary creative power and his innate sense of beauty, has made it a better place in which to live."[30]

A *New York Evening Post* article, reprinted in the *Nation* and in the *American Architect and Building News,* was less charitable, however. It suggested that the artist in White had been to a large extent undone by both "the follies of the times and his own frailties." White had "indominable" force and an architectural creativity equaled only by that of Richardson in America, yet his output of important work was small considering his creative power and the impression he made on others. Surely, "his was genius of a high order," and yet his artistic energies were somehow "unutilized or even perverted." White "seems to have been in a large degree the victim of the society which he sought above all else to please, to which he was the titular arbiter of taste." Far too often, he had lowered his standards to the "ignorance and vanity" of a wealthy but half-educated clientele. Time and energy that might have been given to creative designing were spent on despoiling the palaces of Europe of mediocre things for his patrons. Though "he was immensely the superior of his world, he was content to be its purveyor," wasting himself "in such brokerage." The anonymous *Post* writer concluded that White's fate was the fate of the artist in America generally: He so often meets indifference to his best endeavors and encourages a "positively demoralizing vanity" by catering to half-trained tastes. The age, it would seem, had "tended to debase the artist to its own standards or to shut him up in the murky atmosphere of adoring cliques." In sum, "the frittering away of genius, as illustrated by the apparently successful career of Stanford White, is an exhortation to all true artists to master that most difficult art of being in the world, but not of it." Tastemaker for his age, he all too willingly became the servant of his times, succumbing to the flashy standards of the day.[31]

White's will, filed for probate on July 11, was a relatively simple, straightforward document. It left $1,000 and mining interests in New Mexico to his brother Dick, $2,000 and copyright income from his father's books to his mother, and the residue of the estate to Bessie, who was named executrix. Larry White was not mentioned in the will. All claims to property in the partnership of McKim, Mead & White had already been assigned to the surviving partners, who after a fair appraisal would pay his widow whatever might be due her. His personal property was encumbered by large debts. He left no real estate in New York.[32]

After the shock of the murder and the scandalous accounts in the press, Bessie felt she had to get away from the heated atmosphere of New York. For some months McKim had been planning a trip to Europe in the late summer of 1906, hoping to leave about the time that White was originally scheduled to get back from his projected short midsummer buying trip. In July Charley arranged for Bessie and Larry to accompany him on the *Baltic*, departing on August 1. He took a double cabin for Larry and himself and an adjoining cabin for Bessie. Dick White stayed with his mother at St. James.

The rest and quiet of the voyage, with the routine of shuffleboard and bridge, did wonders for Bessie, who had recovered considerably from her prevoyage exhaustion by the time they debarked at Liverpool. The three traveled together to Edinburgh, where they went to see Gus and Stan's Stevenson memorial in the Cathedral of St. Giles. McKim left the Whites in Scotland. Bessie and Larry visited the Trossachs, north of Glasgow. For a time McKim was ill in bed in London, but he caught up with Bessie and Larry in Paris, where they hired a car and made excursions out from the city. The Whites and McKim took a motor trip of several days in Normandy and Touraine. Bessie was delighted to have Charley along: "He preaches architecture to Larry by the hour," she wrote Saint-Gaudens. In Paris they spent time with Charles Dana Gibson and his wife Irene, and all spoke most affectionately of Saint-Gaudens, whose letter to *Collier's* they had recently seen. Bessie and Larry returned from Europe with McKim on the *Provence,* arriving back in New York in late October.[33]

Larry went at once to Cambridge for his final year at Harvard College, while Bessie closed up the house at Saint James. She then joined her son in Cambridge, renting a small house on Kirkland Street, close to Harvard Yard. She planned to remain there, away from New York, near Larry for the winter months. The trial of Harry K. Thaw for the murder of Stanford White was scheduled to begin shortly.

25

Aftermath

O n January 23, 1907, the case of the People against Harry K. Thaw, accused of the murder of Stanford White, opened in the Supreme Court of the State of New York. Judge James Fitzgerald presided in a courtroom in the Criminal Court Building, New York City. The prosecution team was led by District Attorney William Travers Jerome, then in his mid-forties. Jerome had long been acquainted with White and had shared membership with him in several gentlemen's clubs. At the time of the trial Jerome was involved in a secret liaison with a young woman half his age, a relationship that if revealed might have ruined his career. Besides his professional obligations, Jerome was thus drawn to White's defense and the prosecution of his killer by social ties and by bonds of sympathy and understanding.[1]

Since the murder, the Thaw family had been arranging for Harry's defense and involving themselves in activities they felt might help his case. Harry's widowed mother, on her way to Europe at the time of the murder, had hastily returned to the United States. She hired a publicist named Benjamin Atwell, who attempted to gain sympathy for his client by conducting a campaign of slander against White. The Thaws financed three plays based on the case, with the names of the characters only slightly disguised. Newspaper articles were planted. Atwell later published a book-length defense of the murderer in *The Great Harry Thaw Case*. The family spared no expense in hiring the best lawyers they could find to defend Harry.

Named to lead the Thaw team was Judge William M. K. Olcott, who believed a plea of insanity would provide the best chance to save his client, a defense favored as well by George Carnegie, Harry's brother-in-law. "What the family should do," Carnegie advised, "is lock Harry up in the bughouse where he belongs.'' From his jail cell, Harry Thaw refused to plead insanity, however, and his mother supported his decision. A new defense team was organized, with John B. Gleason serving as Thaw's personal counsel and Delphin Michael Delmas, a nationally known advocate from California, acting as primary defense spokesman in the courtroom. The short, plump Delmas, blessed with a sonorous voice and rumored to be the illegitimate son of Napoleon III, was engaged for a fee rumored to be $50,000, or by one account $100,000. At Harry's urging, the defense stressed an appeal to ''the unwritten law''—that a husband may do whatever is necessary to protect the honor of his wife.[2]

Evelyn cooperated fully with the Thaw family, doing what she could to help her husband's case. She regularly visited him in his cell at the Tombs prison and remained loyal to him even though horrified at his murderous act. She agreed to appear on the witness stand. One lawyer warned her that by going on the stand and giving full and explicit revelations about her past and her relationships with White and with Thaw, she would in effect put herself on trial and, he feared, destroy herself. He advised her not to testify. But Evelyn felt certain that the Thaws would take care of her financially, no matter what happened. She attended the trial each day, accompanied by her friend May MacKenzie, and sat with her mother-in-law and two sisters-in-law. Evelyn dressed demurely in a jacket with a large white flat collar and a bow tie. Many thought she looked like an innocent young schoolgirl. Irvin S. Cobb, who covered the trial for Pulitzer's *Evening World,* was struck, like many others, by Evelyn's beauty. She was, he wrote, ''the most exquisitely lovely human being I ever looked at.'' When she was called to the witness stand, her simple and unaffected manner and her detailed accounts of her relationships with White and with Thaw no doubt gained some sympathy for her husband.[3]

Each day of the trial, huge crowds of people gathered in the street outside the court building, but few could get inside. More than a hundred reporters were assigned to the case. The courtroom was always jammed. The selection of jurors went on for eight days; 336 possible jurors were examined before twelve men were ultimately chosen. When the trial proper began, after a summary by the assistant district attorney of the evidence to be presented, Larry White was called to the witness stand to give his account of the events on the evening of June 25 the previous year. In all, nine persons testified in the half-day presentation by the prosecution, some of them eyewitnesses to the actual murder.

Following this testimony, Attorney John B. Gleason opened the defense with an argument of temporary insanity for his client. Thaw had shot

White, he said, "under the delusion . . . that he was the agent of Providence." There was, Gleason asserted, insanity in the Thaw family, and Harry Thaw had "a psychopathic temperament": Under the stress of the events of the time, he had suffered temporary insanity. A physician from Pittsburgh, a specialist in nervous diseases, was brought to the stand as the first defense witness. He testified that he believed that Thaw suffered from a delusion. Jerome in cross examination succeeded, however, in destroying the doctor's credibility by getting him to admit he could not name a single book on mental or nervous diseases or anything found in such books. Other witnesses were also called to testify on the point of Thaw's nervous temperament.[4]

After the first witnesses, Attorney Delmas felt that the opening defense testimony had gone very badly and succeeded in convincing the Thaws that he must have complete charge of the case himself. Thomas McCaleb, who had been with Evelyn and Harry on the Madison Square Garden roof, then testified about his impressions of what had taken place that evening. The doorkeeper of the Madison Square Theater, who on Christmas Eve, 1903, had heard White threaten to kill Thaw after Evelyn had gone off with him, gave his account of that incident. Then, on February 7, Evelyn Thaw, dressed like a schoolgirl and speaking with a "childish lisp," was put on the witness stand, under oath, to begin her extended testimony about her long relationships with White and with the man who became her husband.

Evelyn astonished spectators in the courtroom with the calm way she recounted events. At the heart of her testimony was a highly graphic account of her seduction in the Twenty-fourth Street apartment, including her belief that she had been drugged, along with her statements as to what she later told Thaw about White and how Thaw had reacted. She testified that when she went with White to Abe Hummel's office, after her return from Europe in 1903, to provide an affadavit about Thaw, she had told the lawyer "a lot of stuff that wasn't true." She also testified that White had told her friend May MacKenzie only a month before the murder that he would get her (Evelyn) back.[5]

Evelyn's widely reported testimony about her relations with White and Thaw was so shocking to many readers that a public outcry arose over the propriety of publishing stenographic accounts of the trial testimony. Throughout the country mass meetings were held, countless letters to editors appeared in newspapers, and sermons were preached decrying the publication of the testimony. Moreover, "tons of letters and telegrams from all over the country" arrived at the White House, demanding that the President take action to stop newspapers from publishing what was being said at the trial. President Roosevelt asked Postmaster General G. B. Cortelyou whether it might be feasible to have newspapers carrying details of the Thaw case barred from the mails. The same action was reportedly contemplated by the government of Canada. Indictments were returned by a Marion County, Kentucky, grand jury against Louisville newspapers that had printed Evelyn's testimony. The U.S. Post Office decided against any action.[6]

The Union League Club in New York passed a resolution condemning the publication of "the disgusting testimony" of the Thaw trial "as a national calamity." A bill to restrict the press was introduced into the legislature of the State of Washington. In the nation's capital, a resolution in condemnation of White and the Thaw trial proceedings was introduced in the House of Representatives. It denounced "the loathsome and licentious acts of the said Stanford White" as having "a demoralizing influence on the youth of the land" and authorized the President to exclude all publications from the U.S. mails "containing the revolting details of this case." A store in Memphis, Tennessee, put up a sign forbidding discussion of the Thaw trial on the premises after a fight had erupted from an argument about the case. A man in Illinois, another in Wisconsin, a woman in Ohio, and a girl in Pennsylvania were taken into custody in demented states said to have been caused by reports of the Thaw trial proceedings. The courtroom disclosures, moreover, brought such notoriety to Mrs. De Mille's school, which Evelyn had attended in New Jersey, and so many families withdrew their daughters, that the school was closed and the owner went into bankruptcy.[7]

In the midst of the proceedings, the trial was adjourned for a few days after the wife of a juror became very ill and died. When the trial resumed, Harry Thaw's will was put in evidence. The will included a provision that if Thaw died in any suspicious way, $50,000 was to be used from his estate to investigate the circumstances of his death. A codicil of the will, dated April 4, 1905, the day of his marriage, provided that money be used to secure redress and damages for young women, specified by name, said to be victims of "White and other inhuman scoundrels." Money was also provided in trust for Dr. Charles H. Parkhurst, Anthony Comstock, and other respectable men to prosecute suits on behalf of "American girls, victims of the said Stanford White."[8]

Cross-examination of Evelyn Thaw was delayed, and other witnesses were heard in the interim. More medical doctors were brought to the stand to testify as to Thaw's deranged condition. His mother, too, told of his erratic behavior since childhood. When Evelyn returned to the stand, Jerome handled her roughly. He got her to admit that White had supported her with $25 a week regularly for long periods when she did not have a stage engagement. She admitted that White corresponded with her when she was abroad and at other times. She admitted going on Garland's yacht and being named a corespondent in the Lederer divorce case. She admitted to having had operations; when asked "were not some of them of a nature not countenanced by all surgeons?" she responded that "I know that one was not," a possible admission to having had an abortion. She said that White sent her to the Pompton School in New Jersey in order to get her away from John Barrymore. She admitted traveling in Europe with Thaw as his wife but denied the allegations of beatings she had made to Abe Hummel in 1903. She told of discovering the syringes and her realization that Thaw was addicted to cocaine.[9]

Evelyn also clearly stated her opinion of White: "As a friend there was nobody that I could think of nicer than Stanford White, outside of the one act of his. He was as nice as he could possibly be; he was very kind, very considerate, especially to my family. He did a good many things for my family outside of the one awful thing." White, she emphasized, "was kind and considerate and exceedingly thoughtful, much more thoughtful than most people." In Evelyn's view, "he had a very peculiar personality and a very strong personality—people liked him very much; he made a great many friends and always kept them; they were always unwilling to believe these things about him until they actually found out. And then they could not understand." To Evelyn, except for his sexual propensities and actions, White was an admirable person.[10]

Abe Hummel, who had recently been brought to justice by District Attorney Jerome and disbarred for conspiring to have a client commit perjury, was summoned from prison to discuss on the witness stand the affidavit he had drawn up in November 1903. Hummel testified that in 1903 Evelyn had denied that White had drugged and wronged her. He said Evelyn had told him that Thaw had prepared documents for her to sign to the effect that White had drugged and wronged her and that when she had refused to sign them he had beaten her. By now Jerome, who had been trying to build his entire case on the fact that Thaw was sane, had become convinced by the medical experts and by Thaw's demeanor at the defense table that the defendant actually was incurably insane. Believing Thaw was incapable of conducting his own defense and unfit for trial, Jerome for a time reversed his stance.[11]

As the testimony was drawing to a close, Judge Fitzgerald appointed a "lunacy commission" of three men, who took testimony and deliberated for several days. Medical experts were summoned, and Harry Thaw testified privately before the panel. He answered questions lucidly. On April 4 the commission unanimously concluded that Thaw was a sane man, that he understood the charges against him, and that he was fully capable of participating in his own defense.[12]

For the better part of April 8 and 9 Delmas delivered his summation for the defense in resonant tones to a packed courtroom. He justified Thaw's act on the grounds of "the unwritten law." He vilified White for his criminal act against the young girl: "O better for Stanford White that he never had been born than he had lived to see that day. Rather his ears should never have been opened than to have heard the shriek of anguish of his victim! He, the strong, the powerful, had lured a child to her ruin." Then, more impassioned yet: "O, Stanford White, did you imagine that the cry of the fatherless child in the city of millions would not be heard of God?" At the moment of the shooting, Delmas stated, Thaw was driven by momentary insanity, a brainstorm in defense of the honor of his wife. But immediately after shooting White, Delmas declared with a rhetorical flourish, "Thaw spread out his arms making of his body the sign of the cross, a circumstance which denoted the character of the act. His arms were spread out like the arms of a priest after the sacrifice of the mass has been consummated and he has turned to the worshippers to bid them depart." Harry K. Thaw, his attorney asserted, had "struck for the purity of the home, for the purity of American womanhood, for the purity of American wives and daughters, and if he believed on that occasion that he was an instrument of Divine Providence, who shall say he was in error?" Delmas labeled such insanity "*dementia Americana,*" a truly American characteristic.[13]

Prosecutor Jerome summed up his case against Thaw on April 10. Once again he stressed Thaw's sanity, and then he ridiculed Delmas's bombastic summation. "Nothing in this case," Jerome told the jury, "shows anything but deliberate, cold-blooded, premeditated murder." Then, with a rhetorical flourish of his own: "It seems to me that the voice of Stanford White is crying out from the grave: 'Can't you say a word for me against this thick blackening that the defense has put upon my memory? Must I be consigned to the everlasting fires of hell unheard and undefended?' " Jerome emphasized that Evelyn had continued to see White for months after she was supposedly "drugged" and "wronged" by the architect. She had testified at length as to her kind treatment by him. Thaw, Jerome emphasized, had been aware of exactly what he was doing. Judge Fitzgerald then instructed the jury and discussed possible verdicts.[14]

After forty-seven hours of intermittent deliberation, as crowds of up to 13,000 people milled about the Criminal Court Building, the jury announced on April 12 that following eight ballots it was deadlocked. Seven members of the jury had voted for a verdict of guilty of murder in the first degree, while five had voted for acquittal on the grounds of insanity. The jury was discharged. The trial had gone on for almost twelve weeks.[15]

Day after day, the sensational trial had exposed the lives of the three principal figures to public view, providing entertaining newspaper reading, topics of general conversation, and subjects for moral commentary. Well known as a celebrity in life, Stanford White was becoming even better known in death. And the scalding exposure went on.

A year after the start of the first trial, a second trial of Harry K. Thaw opened on January 6, 1908. Judge Victor J. Dowling of the New York Supreme Court presided. Once again, William Travers Jerome conducted the prosecution. The defense team of lawyers this time was led by Martin W. Littleton, who two years earlier had faced District Attorney Jerome in court in the successful defense of Colonel William Mann against a perjury charge. A. Russell Peabody served as Thaw's personal counsel. As in the first trial, Evelyn Thaw attracted a great deal of public attention. As in the first trial also, the selection of jurors was time-consuming; 372 men were examined over a period of five days and two night sessions before twelve were chosen for the panel.[16]

The defense in the second trial focused unsparingly on Thaw's erratic behavior since early childhood to reinforce the claim that Thaw was insane at the time of the shooting. Insanity in the families of both Thaw's father and his mother was shown. It was pointed out that Harry had been expelled from two colleges because of his conduct; at least once he had tried to commit suicide; he had experienced several manic episodes. Evelyn, dressed once again as a young schoolgirl but always remarkably self-possessed, testified at length. She revealed that she had turned over White's letters to her to Thaw and had turned over Thaw's letters to her to Abe Hummel. Anthony Comstock testified that Thaw had come to him and made serious accusations about White, which he had been unable to investigate fully.

Unlike the first trial, the second proceeded rapidly. Littleton summed up the case for the defense on January 29. He recounted the testimony relating to Thaw's insanity and stressed Thaw's long history of irrational behavior. In his summary, District Attorney Jerome emphasized Thaw's rational condition on June 25, 1906, when he played cards with friends that afternoon, carried on a sensible conversation at dinner at Martin's restaurant, and spoke lucidly and rationally with James Clinch Smith at the Roof Garden only a few moments before he fired the bullets at White. On February 1, 1908, after twenty-five hours of deliberation, the jury, rejecting the prosecutor's case, reached the verdict that Thaw was not guilty on the grounds of insanity at the time of the shooting.[17]

A little over a week later, the twenty-four jurors from the two Thaw trials met together for a banquet at the Broadway Central Hotel. The first trial jurors had already held a reunion to reminisce about the proceedings and to read each other the crank letters they had received. An "Association of Thaw Jurors" was organized.[18]

Harry was taken to Matteawan Asylum for the Criminal Insane in Fishkill, New York. His trip there seemed almost like a triumphal procession, for Evelyn's testimony and the effective public relations campaign the Thaw family had financed had gained him considerable public sympathy. Friends and acquaintances toasted his escape from execution, and crowds followed him about. At the asylum, diagnosed as a paranoiac, Thaw was eventually placed in comfortable accommodations and allowed a great deal of freedom, even the opportunity on occasion to leave the grounds.

In May 1908 Thaw sought full release through official channels, but his petition for a writ of habeas corpus was denied, and the decision was upheld on appeal. District Attorney Jerome now had to take the position, contrary to his consistent stance in the second trial, that Thaw was incurably insane in order to keep him incarcerated. The following year, in July, Thaw once again sought to be freed, and another hearing on his sanity was held. This time a New York brothel keeper testified that Thaw had been a regular patron of her establishment some years earlier and had been wont to take a whip to young girls there for his pleasure. Evelyn Thaw testified that her husband had threatened to kill her when he was released. The court decided that Thaw was still insane, a decision reaffirmed on appeal, and he was recommitted. Evelyn occasionally saw her husband on visits he made outside the asylum. On October 25, 1910, in Berlin, Germany, she gave birth to a son, whom she named Russell William Thaw, affirming that Harry Thaw was the father of the child.[19]

In July 1912 Thaw sought release from the asylum a third time, but once again he was declared insane and remanded into custody. A fourth attempt at release also failed in March 1913. Then on August 17, 1913 Thaw walked out of the asylum and by prearrangement was spirited away by car to Canada, where there appeared to be considerable public sympathy for him. Jerome instituted extradition proceedings. Canadian authorities eventually decided that Thaw was an undesirable alien and informally and forcibly moved him across the border into Vermont. Thaw got to New Hampshire, but he was extradited to New York and brought back to the Tombs prison in New York City. Finally, in June 1915, a hearing before a jury was accorded to him, and this time he was found sane. He was released on July 15, 1915, acquitted of all charges against him. Soon afterward he sued Evelyn for divorce on grounds of adultery. He denied parentage of Russell Thaw.

Even as the first trial was in progress, the world of beauty that White had assembled around himself was being taken apart. White's obligations to dealers at the time of his death were substantial, and it was reported in the press that he was overdrawn by about $600,000 at the firm of McKim, Mead & White; considering the amount he owed his partners a few years earlier, that figure seems far too high. Many dealers had sent goods on consignment, and some of his things were scattered about in studios, in warehouses, and in the firm's office, as well as in his houses and Tower studio, so that it was a large undertaking just to inventory the items. There was a suggestion that friends of White get together and purchase the house at 121 East Twenty-first Street and its contents to preserve as a museum of art honoring White. But White's heavy indebtedness and the climate of opinion during the trial precluded implementation of anything of the sort.[20]

White's possessions began to be dispersed. An auction sale of furnishings from the Gramercy Park residence was conducted on April 4–6, 1907, in the picture gallery of the house, by Thomas Kirby of the American Art Galleries, a longtime friend. The catalogue for the sale listed more than four hundred items, including musical instruments, tapestries, vases, mantels, and the elaborate old Italian Renaissance drawing room and dining room ceilings. The Princeton Club, which had leased the White townhouse from Henry Taylor, acquired many things at the sale for its new premises. David Belasco, the producer, bought several pieces for his collection, and Gifford Pinchot, the conservationist, was a spirited bidder. William Randolph Hearst purchased the dining room ceiling for $3,000. The Metropolitan Museum of Art acquired an elaborate baroque doorway with an ironwork gate from the picture gallery. White's superb tapestries brought some of the highest prices at that first sale.[21]

A week later, on April 11–12, 123 of White's paintings were put up for sale at Mendelssohn Hall, including works by Ryder, Chase, Inness, Brush, Dewing, and Hassam, among the Americans. A fine Reynolds portrait, two works by Godfrey Kneller, and one attributed to Holbein were auctioned. White's collection of sirens, nymphs, bacchantes, women bathers, and female nudes was largely sold off at this time. A third sale of 549 items was conducted at the American Art Galleries on November 25–26, 1907, including furniture, rugs and carpets, chests, shields, swords, screens, statues, and even thirty-three stained-glass window panels. The three sales brought more than $260,000 for the White estate. On December 10, 110 pieces, including antique marbles, stone mantels, fountains, and sarcophagi, were auctioned at a warehouse on Eleventh Avenue and Twenty-seventh Street. Some years later, in March 1934, Bessie White was to place for auction a large collection of furniture, rugs and carpets, statuary, and tapestries. One critic at the depression-year sale was struck by how many buyers were acquiring things in order, she said, "to make real again moments that had gone into tender memories" of " 'those wonderful days' of Stanford White's prominence in the social and artistic world."[22]

While a good part of White's treasure was being dispersed, his social world, too, was breaking up. Ravaged by the cancer he had so long been battling, Gus Saint-Gaudens remained at his Cornish studio, directing his assistants when he was able, in his final months. He fell into a deep coma in late July 1907 and died in the early evening of August 3. The sculptor's body was taken to Boston for cremation, and the ashes were returned to Cornish, where a memorial service was held in the studio. Eventually the ashes were placed in a sepulcher monument in the lower garden of the estate.

Another major support of Stanford White's world was removed about three months later. On October 22, the suspension of the Knickerbocker Trust Company, after a run by depositors, coming on rumors of insolvency, brought shock and great consternation in the city. Stan had designed the striking Thirty-fourth Street headquarters for the bank and had worked on the downtown branch at 60 Broadway as well, and he had done much of his banking with the Knickerbocker Trust. Charles T. Barney, the president, long Stan's close friend and financial adviser, resigned. The brother-in-law of William C. Whitney and director of about sixty corporations, Barney had been prominent for years in New York society. The Knickerbocker Trust Company was "distinctly and distinctively the Society bank of New York," where a great many New Yorkers prominent in fashionable life did their banking. The suspension of the Knickerbocker Bank was a primary factor in the financial Panic of 1907. A few days after the bank closed its doors, it was rumored in the press that Mrs. Barney was instituting divorce proceedings because of her husband's infatuation with another woman. Barney, after resigning as head of the bank, had fallen into a severe depression. On November

14, 1907, at his home, he put a revolver to his head and committed suicide. It was reported that he had recently tried once before to take his life. Upton Sinclair, the muckraking author, made the collapse of the Fifth Avenue bank, housed in a building of "overwhelming magnificence," and the suicide of its president, clearly based on Barney, the subject of his 1908 novel, *The Moneychangers*. In the story, the machinations of a character resembling J. P. Morgan ultimately determines the fate of the bank and of the American economy.[23]

McKim had pulled himself together to help Bessie and Larry in the summer and fall of 1906, and he assisted Mead with the worrisome work of settling White's affairs. By the next year his nervousness and exhaustion had worsened, however. Saint-Gaudens's death, the failure of the Knickerbocker Trust Company, and Barney's suicide were further jarring blows to McKim. His absences from the office became more frequent and longer, and by 1908 it was evident to some of those close to him that his mind was slipping. At the office he was said to be away on an "extended vacation," and the senior men covered for him. At times he stayed at a cottage at Narragansett Pier, Rhode Island, where he had vacationed in the past, and his daughter Margaret often joined him there. In the summer of 1908 he invited Mead to come there for a visit, and in a characteristic gesture wrote his partner: "But whether you come or not, all I can say with all my heart is how much I wish the ship of the office (of which you really always were & now are & long may you remain the *helmsman*) may plough on: 'Vogue la Galère.'" By 1909 his depression was so deep and his health so frail that he had an attendant at his side continuously. For a time he stayed in a private sanatorium. His heart gradually weakened. McKim died at the St. James cottage on September 14, 1909, at the age of sixty-two.[24]

Memorial meetings for McKim were held in New York City in November and in Washington, D.C., in December 1909, the latter in conjunction with the annual meeting of the American Institute of Architects, of which McKim had been president some years earlier. Cass Gilbert, the retiring president of the Institute and a "graduate" of the McKim, Mead & White office, conducted the memorial service. President William Howard Taft spoke at the ceremony as a gesture of respect for the man who had done so much to beautify the national capital. The AIA gold medal, which had been awarded to McKim the previous year, was presented to Mead on behalf of Margaret McKim. Among the many tributes, the most touching came from Joseph H. Choate, former Ambassador to the Court of St. James's, who spoke of McKim's great loyalty in friendship, his charm, his love of beauty, and his "sweet reasonableness."

For Choate, as for so many others, "To know him was to love him."[25]

Mead, the helmsman, kept the firm on course for several years longer, active in the profession and devoted to the welfare of McKim's American Academy in Rome. In 1913 Mead received the gold medal of the American Academy of Arts and Letters for his "distinguished services in the creation of original work in architecture." That same year the firm of McKim, Mead & White moved to new offices on the sixteenth floor of 101 Park Avenue. Mead retired from active participation in the firm in 1920, and other partners carried on. The last surviving founding partner died on June 20, 1928, in a Paris hotel room. He was buried in the Protestant Cemetery in Florence, Italy, beside his brother, Larkin Mead, the sculptor.

Lawrence Grant White, who completed his course of study at Harvard College in 1907, after three years there, and took his degree with the class of 1908, enrolled subsequently at the Ecole des Beaux-Arts in Paris, from which he received a diploma in 1913. He joined his father's firm in 1914 and became a partner of McKim, Mead & White in 1920, the year of Mead's retirement. For years, he was a leading figure of the art world of New York, not only as a prominent architect but also as a trustee of the Metropolitan Museum of Art and as president of the National Academy of Design. He and Laura Chanler were married in 1916, and with their three sons and five daughters the family filled to overflowing the house at St. James. Larry always remained reticent about his father, whose work he greatly admired. That admiration was evident in *Sketches and Designs by Stanford White,* which he published in 1920. Alexina White, Stanford's mother, a figure from the distant past, lived until January 6, 1921. Bessie White spent her latter years in a small cottage on the St. James property, where she died on July 4, 1950. Larry, who served in the United States Navy during both world wars, died at Box Hill on September 8, 1956, at the age of sixty-eight. Laura Chanler White, his widow, who had been with Stanford the day before his murder, died in 1984.

Harry Thaw was in the news now and then in the years following his release. In 1917 he was arrested and charged with the kidnapping of a nineteen-year-old youth. Thaw had taken the young man to a hotel and there had beaten him unconscious with a whip. To forestall Harry's imprisonment, Thaw's mother arranged for a lunacy commission in Pennsylvania to declare him insane; he was committed to a psychiatric hospital near Philadelphia. After a sanity hearing in 1924, however, Thaw was adjudged sane and released. The youth's family settled out of court with the Thaws. Nightclub disturbances and a suit for beating up a nightclub hostess brought him more attention. He was banned as an undesirable from entering England. Thaw died on February 22, 1947, of a heart attack in Miami Beach, Florida, at the age of seventy-six, leaving an estate of more than a million dollars, including a $10,000 bequest to his former wife Evelyn.

As with Harry Thaw, the notoriety Evelyn acquired from the murder and its aftermath remained with her for the rest of her days. She always regretted that she had tried to save her husband: "I paid in self-respect as well as in reputation for Thaw's eventual escape from the 'chair.'" She once commented that "Stanny White was killed, but my fate was worse. I lived." The substantial financial support she had been led to expect from the Thaw family for her testimony at the trials was not forthcoming. Mrs. Thaw discovered that Evelyn had become involved in an affair with one of Thaw's lawyers and refused to do more than provide her with $1,000 a month for the two and one-half years following Harry's arrest. By 1909, Evelyn Thaw had to make her own way as best she could. After the birth of her son, her situation became even more difficult. For a few years she supported herself by appearing in musical comedies, on the vaudeville circuit, and in motion pictures. At the time of the outbreak of World War I she was dancing in Europe, and she returned to New York from France on the same ship as Bessie White, probably unbeknownst to Bessie. In 1915 Evelyn was married to Virgil Montani, known as Jack Clifford, her dancing partner. They were later divorced.[26]

As her dancing and acting career wound down in the early 1920s, Evelyn became involved in several unsuccessful ventures, including speakeasies and cabarets in New York, Atlantic City, New Orleans, and Biloxi, Mississippi. Heavy drinking and drug addiction, beginning long after she learned of Thaw's proclivities, plagued her life for many years, and more than once she attempted suicide. Her autobiography, published in a second version in 1934 (the first appeared in 1914), gained her considerable public sympathy. She wondered, in the book, why she, "of all the thousands of girls on Broadway at the time" was "doomed to play such a part on the stage of life," when she was so "immature, untrained," and could not "withstand or oppose the forces of evil which Thaw especially represented." Yet that was her destiny, she believed, and she ultimately had no regrets. In 1937 she made an unsuccessful attempt at a Broadway comeback as a torch singer. Later she received $50,000 for the use of her story and as a technical consultant for the motion picture *The Girl in the Red Velvet Swing*, starring Ray Milland as White, Joan Collins as Evelyn, and Farley Granger as Harry, released in 1955. In an interview at that time, she revealingly admitted her regrets and bitterness about what she had done at the trials and her continuing respect and love for Stanford White: "The world didn't see what I remember best, myself on the stand trying to save a husband I didn't love from going to the chair for killing the man I did love." In her later years Evelyn lived quietly in California, a student of theosophy, teaching ceramics and enjoying sculpting, which she had taken up years before. She died in a nursing home on January 17, 1967, at the age of eighty-two.[27]

Friends of White, mindful of the public portrait that had been painted of him right after his murder, wished to honor the loyal friend and talented artist they had known. An exhibit at the Century Association in March 1909 of watercolors, oil paintings, and sketches by well-known American architects gave "the place of honor" to a group of watercolor views of Greece and Italy by White. A decade later, in 1919, a group of Century Club friends got together to plan a gift of memorial doors honoring White for the library at New York University in the Bronx. Thomas Hastings headed the executive committee, assisted by Thomas Dewing, Frederick MacMonnies, and several others among White's close friends. Lawrence Grant White was invited to design the pair of bronze doors; eight panels were created by Herbert Adams, Philip Martiny, Andrew O'Connor, and Adolph Weinman, and the inscription was modeled by Janet Scudder, taking her inspiration from the lettering on the Farragut Monument. All those artists had worked with Stanford White. "The whole undertaking was a labor of love to perpetuate the memory of one whose influence on American architecture was great, and who endeared himself to many by his kindness and generosity." Before the installation of the doors, they were exhibited in the Fifth Avenue windows of the Gorham Company Building, which White had designed.

At the dedication on December 10, 1921, Royal Cortissoz, who had worked at 57 Broadway many years before, gave the principal address, and Thomas Hastings, another "graduate" of the firm, presented the doors to Chancellor Elmer Brown of the university. Brown later wrote Larry White that he and his collaborators had "given to the world of art and to New York University a work of great lasting value." It was suggested that the doors were an especially appropriate memorial, since Stanford White himself had always been opening doors for others during his lifetime. Bessie was highly pleased with the doors and appreciative of the memorial.[28]

For some two decades, Stanford White was a commanding force in New York life. He helped to shape the city, contributed to its pleasures, and played a leading role on its public stage. His effect on the physical setting of the city and the nation was substantial. As a central figure in American art life and an arbiter of taste for the world of wealth, he helped to set fashions in architecture, interior design, and decoration, while providing support for many artists. His vitality, enthusiasm, and encouragement were widely recognized as powerful stimulants to others to bring more beauty into the American scene. He was, as well, a leading figure in New York upper-class social life and club life. Turn-of-the-century New York would have been different without the strong personality and influence of White at the center of so many events.[29]

As an architect, he maintained high standards for comfort and design, and some of his buildings became among the most notable of his times. Madison Square Garden, the best known of his works while it stood, provided a remarkable recreational center for the populace of the city, the design itself strongly reinforcing the pleasurable uses of the building. His Washington Memorial Arch became one of the principal icons of the New York landscape. The Judson Church, Tower, and Hotel, like the arch, contributed importantly to the face of Greenwich Village, just as the Garden and the Presbyterian Church helped shape the environs of Madison Square. The Knickerbocker Bank, the Gorham Building, the Tiffany Building, the Herald Building, the Century and Metropolitan clubhouses, and the porch for St. Bartholomew's Church stood out in the midtown area. And farther uptown, some of the mansions he created were outstanding contributions to the streetscape. To an often drab, monotonous, and colorless city, White brought a brilliant touch. His several great country houses too were among the most spectacular of the times. Many of his buildings are extant and even today give pleasure as things of beauty.

With his partners, White dominated his profession in the United States for some years. The firm of McKim, Mead & White was highly influential in establishing modes for public and private design. White, with his partners, looked to the past, especially Italy of the Renaissance, for artistic inspiration, but he was in no sense a slavish copier. Rather, he reinterpreted elements of that past he so much admired for his own day and its needs. His art contributed to the exuberant, materialistic surge of the times and helped reinforce dominant social patterns of lavish consumption and conspicuous display. Unlike his discontented, supercritical father, who denounced the rush for riches and the flashy display of America, while always yearning for wealth himself, Stanford White reveled in the opportunities for and the pleasures of luxuriant consumption that his city and his America could offer. He joyfully rode the crest of the wave of his age's materialism.

White's murder on the rooftop of Madison Square Garden by Harry Thaw and the disclosures about the architect's earlier involvement with Evelyn Nesbit have become embedded in American popular lore. Like Teddy Roosevelt, White is remembered not only for his achievements but even more for the more colorful aspects of his life, and because he represented the times in which he lived.

The popular portrait has considerable truth in its lineaments, for White was obviously colorful as an individual and did embody significant currents of American life during his times. His commitment to hard work, his large body of important commissions, and the fame he gained, through his works, his life-style, and his talent for self-promotion, were characteristically American. His passion for beauty and aesthetic enjoyment was within a current of American life increasingly important since the mid-nineteenth century. His extravagance, his self-indulgence, his compulsive pleasure-seeking were characteristic of segments of American society at the turn of the century and after. With those traits and his artistic talents he was well suited to be the interpretor of his age.

With his talents as a decorator and designer as well as an architect, White could lay out the materials for a whole way of life for his clientele. Architect, designer, decorator, impresario, showman, tastemaker, he more than anyone else orchestrated the conditions of living for the rich and powerful of the times.

White was honored by the press, sought out for commissions, and rewarded handsomely. His creative life was full, and he achieved a great deal that remains memorable. Yet he always wanted more—more wealth to acquire more beautiful things, fuller experiences and sensations, more joy and pleasure, and, no doubt, even more recognition. He gratified himself to the fullest, often without restraint. Savoring the luxuries of life to the fullest and driven as a sensualist of both aesthetic and sexual pleasures brought him ultimately to a life out of control and, from the web of circumstances in which he became enmeshed, to tragedy and destruction. Tastemaker for his times, he became a casualty of the way of life he so brilliantly served.

A Note on the Sources

The richest source of materials for this book has been the collection of Stanford White Papers, located in the Prints and Drawings Room of the Avery Architectural and Fine Arts Library at Columbia University, including thirty-five press books of approximately five hundred pages each, with copies of letters sent out from White's private office, and two other press books including miscellaneous letters and Lawrence Grant White correspondence; and fifty boxes of letters, bills, receipts, advertisements, and ephemera written and received by Stanford White. The Avery Library collection includes as well drawings, sketches, photographs, miscellaneous correspondence, and recollections relating to White useful for this study.

The second large and important collection is that in the New-York Historical Society, where a substantial part of the McKim, Mead & White office materials was deposited some years ago. From the Map and Print Collection, scrapbooks, project files, photographs, newspaper and journal clippings, cash books, bill books, journals, and drawings have been used for this book. From the Manuscript Collection of the Society, equally relevant are the Stanford White Collection and the Richard Grant White Collection, as well as letters and papers, diaries, interviews, and files relating to other persons.

Other collections highly valuable for this study are in the Manuscript Division of the Library of Congress; the Theater Collection and the Manuscript Division of the New York Public Library; the Archives of American Art; the New York University Archives; the Newport Historical Society; the United States Military Academy Archives; the Shubert Theater Archives; The Players Archives; the American Institute of Architects Archives; the American Academy and Institute of Arts and Letters Library; the Columbia University Oral History Project; the Century Association

401

A Note on the Sources

Archives; the Dartmouth College Manuscript Division; and the Franklin D. Roosevelt Presidential Library.

Unpublished materials privately held by the White family have been essential for this study. Some twenty dissertations, theses, and essays have been important for the preparation of the work, as well.

Charles C. Baldwin, *Stanford White* (New York, 1931), the only previous biography of White, though fragmentary, has been useful. The fullest and best study of the firm of McKim, Mead & White is Leland M. Roth, *McKim, Mead & White, Architects* (New York, 1983), which, along with Roth's introductory essay in the reprint of the *Monograph of the Works of McKim, Mead & White, 1879–1915* (New York, 1973; orig. ed., 1915) and his *Architecture of McKim, Mead & White, 1870–1920: A Building List* (New York, 1978), is highly important for the study of Stanford White. Richard Guy Wilson, *McKim, Mead & White, Architects* (New York, 1983) sets forth an important interpretation of the stages of design in the work of McKim, Mead & White and includes splendid illustrations of some of the works of the firm. Lawrence Wodehouse, *White of McKim, Mead & White* (New York, 1988), provides a stylistic analysis of White's oeuvre and includes the most complete list of his designs on pages 261–74. Among the hundreds of other books and articles dealing with or touching on Stanford White, Charles Moore, *The Life and Times of Charles Follen McKim* (Boston, 1929), is very useful, as is Homer Saint-Gaudens, ed., *The Reminiscences of Augustus Saint-Gaudens,* 2 vols. (New York, 1919). The major works dealing with the murder of White and the subsequent trials of Harry Thaw are discussed in note 2, Chapter 25. Books, articles, or manuscript materials relevant to particular subjects are cited in the notes.

I. Principal Manuscript Collections

SW Papers Stanford White Papers, Avery Architectural and Fine Arts Library. Columbia University in the City of New York

PB Press Book

Box Letter Box

SW Coll Stanford White Collection, Manuscript Division, New-York Historical Society

MMW Coll McKim, Mead & White Collection, Map and Print Collection, New-York Historical Society

RGW Coll Richard Grant White Collection, Manuscript Division, New-York Historical Society

NYHS New-York Historical Society

AAA Archives of American Art

LC Manuscript Division, Library of Congress

NYPL   New York Public Library
SG Papers   Saint-Gaudens Papers (microfilm), Dartmouth College Library

II. Other Manuscript Collections
    Freer Papers, AAA
    Cass Gilbert Papers, LC
    MacCracken Papers, New York University
    McKim-Maloney Papers, NYPL
    Moore Papers, LC
    Reid Family Papers, LC
    Richardson Papers, AAA
    Robinson Locke Collection, Theater Division, NYPL
    Rutan Papers, AAA
    Saarinen Papers, AAA
    Saint-Gaudens Papers, LC
    Richard Grant White Papers, Columbia University

III. Name Abbreviations in Notes
    ASG   Augustus Saint-Gaudens
    AW   Alexina (Nina) Black Mease White
    BW   Bessie Springs Smith White
    CFM   Charles F. McKim
    EN   Evelyn Nesbit
    LGW   Lawrence Grant White
    MMW   McKim, Mead & White
    RGW   Richard Grant White
    SW   Stanford White
    WRM   William Rutherford Mead

Notes

⌖

1. The New York Exhibition continued in 1854. Four years later, in 1858, the Crystal Palace was destroyed by fire. Among the most popular exhibits were the Singer sewing machine, the Morse telegraph, daguerreotypes by Matthew Brady, Otis elevator safety devices, and steam and hydraulic engines. Paintings by William Sidney Mount and statuary by Hiram Powers were among the American art works exhibited.

2. *Town Topics,* 56 (July 5, 1906): 11.

3. Reprinted in George C. Foster, *New York in Slices* (New York, 1849), pp. 73–74.

4. *American Whig Review,* 3 (June 1846): 641 ff., and Alden A. Freeman, "Richard Grant White," *New York University Quarterly,* 4 (May 1881): 89.

5. Richard Grant White (RGW) to James Russell Lowell, July 25, 1880, Richard Grant White Collection, New-York Historical Society (hereafter RGW Coll).

6. Allyn Stanley Kellogg, *Memorials of Elder John White . . . and of His Descendants* (Hartford, 1860), pp. 145–46; RGW to Lowell, July 25, 1880, RGW Coll.

7. Obituaries in the *New York Times,* April 9, 1885, p. 5, and the *New-York Tribune,* April 9, 1885, p. 2, gave May 23, 1822, as R. G. White's birth date. In a letter, May 11, 1857, to his wife (RGW Coll), White indicated that he was born in 1822. His tombstone in Rosedale Cemetery, East Orange, N.J., carries his birth date as May 23, 1820. Kellogg, *Memorials of Elder John White,* p. 220, gives May 23, 1821, as RGW's birth date.

8. *New York Times,* December 19, 1880, p. 5, and December 26, 1880, p. 7.

9. Fred E. H. Schroeder, "Nothing if Not Critical: A Biography of Richard Grant White," Ph.D. dissertation, University of Minnesota, March 1968, pp. 28–30.

10. Alexina White's birth date is taken from her tombstone in Rosedale Cemetery, East Orange, N.J. Charles C. Baldwin, *Stanford White* (New York, 1931), p. 31, gives July 4, 1830.

11. Schroeder, "Nothing if Not Critical," p. 48; RGW to Augusta White, August 7, 1849, RGW Coll. Augusta White died in 1878.

12. RGW to Alexina White (AW), July 21, 1852, RGW Coll.

13. RGW to AW, July 9, 1852, RGW Coll.

14. RGW to AW, February 4, 1856, RGW Coll.

15. RGW to Little, Brown & Co., October 5 and 21, 1858, RGW Coll; Schroeder, "Nothing if Not Critical," p. 80.

16. RGW to AW, May 8 and 11, 1857, and June 13, 1858, RGW Coll.

17. RGW to editors of *The Spectator,* July 30, 1863, RGW Coll; Freeman, "Richard Grant White" (note 4 above), p. 92; RGW to AW, March 17 [1861], RGW Coll.

18. RGW to Little, Brown & Co., October 5, 1858, and October 21, 1867; to General Webb, November 23, 1859; and to Edmund D. Stedman, June 24, 1861, RGW Coll. Schroeder, "Nothing if Not Critical," p. 80; Maxwell F. Marcuse, *This Was New York,* 2d ed., rev. (New York, 1969), p. 254.

19. James Wynne, *Private Libraries of New York* (New York, 1860), pp. 411–32; Richard Grant White, *Catalogue of a Private Collection of Books* (New York, 1861); RGW to AW, March 17 [1861], RGW Coll.

20. RGW to Abraham Lincoln, July 6, 1862, copy, RGW Coll; George Templeton Strong, *Diary,* ed. Allan Nevins and Milton Halsey Thomas (New York, 1952), vol. 3, pp. 147, 163, 425. See Richard Grant White, *National Hymns* (New York, 1861), p. 79 and *passim,* for a Civil War hymn contest that RGW supervised.

21. RGW to AW, October 26, 1863, and March 17 [1861], RGW Coll.

22. Francis P. Church, "Richard Grant White," *Atlantic Monthly,* 67 (March 1891): 305.

23. Richard Grant White, *Chronicles of Gotham,* Book First (New York, 1871), p. 40.

24. *New York Times,* May 20, 1871, p. 5.

25. Schroeder, "Nothing if Not Critical," pp. 241, 245, 265; RGW

2. "Mr. R."

to T. B. Aldrich, October 5, 1884, and RGW to AW, July 26, 1869, RGW Coll.

26. Alexina B. White, *Little-Folk Songs* (Boston, 1879), pp. 36–37, 75–76.

27. RGW to AW, October 11, 1858, RGW Coll.

28. Press Book (PB) 18:370, PB 24:473, and Box 38:25, Stanford White Papers, Avery Library, Columbia University (hereafter SW Papers); *New York Times*, September 19, 1880, p. 5.

29. Stanford White (SW) to AW, September 27 [1867], in "Early Letters and Sketches" (1931), Robert White Collection; Richard Grant White Papers, Columbia University; Aline Saarinen, Introduction to Davis Galleries Exhibition, 1963, Cain Coll, Avery Library; Julian Hawthorne, *Shapes That Pass* (Boston, 1928), p. 101; see SW sketch of a house, pictured in Leland M. Roth, *McKim, Mead & White, Architects* (New York, 1983), p. 27, dated 1864, and his sketch of a riverbank dated 1866 at the Davis and Langdale Gallery, New York City.

30. RGW to AW [1867] and September 10, 1868, RGW Coll; Otto Heinigke to SW, May 13, 1892, Box 33:1, SW Papers.

31. RGW to AW, September 10, 1868, RGW Coll.

32. Richard Grant White, *Catalogue of a Collection of Books in the Library of Mr. Richard Grant White* (New York, 1870); *New York Times*, October 21, 1870, pp. 4, 5, and October 25, 1870, p. 1.

33. Church, "Richard Grant White" (note 22 above), p. 309; *New York Times*, July 19, 1869, p. 5; RGW to AW, October 23, 1863, and n.d., RGW Coll.

34. Hawthorne, *Shapes That Pass*, p. 92; Schroeder, "Nothing if Not Critical," p. 215.

35. Richard Grant White, *The Fall of Man* (New York, 1871), pp. 8, 27, 46.

36. White, *Fall of Man*, pp. 47–48.

37. RGW to AW, Wednesday [1870], RGW Coll.

CHAPTER 2
"Mr. R."

1. Royal Cortissoz, *John La Farge: A Memoir and a Study* (New York, 1911; reprint, New York, 1971), pp. 117–18; Royal Cortissoz, "Some Leaders of Our Architectural Renaissance," *Scribner's Magazine*, 86 (July 1929): 100; F. L. Olmsted to SW, April 9, 1885, Frame 407, Stanford White Collection, New-York Historical Society (hereafter SW Coll).

Notes

2. Although it is commonly believed that White entered Richardson's office as a draftsman in training beginning in 1872, to assist with the Trinity Church project, there is persuasive evidence that he came there two years earlier, by the summer of 1870, at the age of sixteen. Looking back on his preparation, White himself in 1890 stated explicitly: "I entered Mr. H. H. Richardson's office in 1870." SW to Charles F. Tabor, February 25, 1890, PB 2:482, SW Papers. White, who left Richardson's employ in 1878, also later indicated that he had "studied Romanesque architecture with Richardson for eight years." SW to H. C. Fahnestock, September 7, 1905, Box 33:302, SW Papers. As further evidence, a letter dated August 2, 1870, from Richardson's partner, Charles D. Gambrill, to Charles Rutan, then a young office assistant and draftsman in the firm, asks Rutan to return to the office "to look after the shop on Saturday, because Mr. White is laid up with a bad felon on the fore-finger of his right hand" and could not be there. Charles D. Gambrill to Charles H. Rutan, August 2, 1870, Rutan Papers, 1260:1, Archives of American Art (AAA). Moreover, White must have had substantial architectural training before venturing on the difficult and responsible work he undertook in 1872, which implicitly indicates an early association with Richardson. Ann Jenson Adams, "The Birth of a Style: Henry Hobson Richardson and the Competition Drawings for Trinity Church, Boston," *Art Bulletin,* 62 (September 1890): 414, does not mention White among the staff of four in Richardson's office in the spring of 1872. Charles Moore, *The Life and Times of Charles Follen McKim* (Boston, 1929), quoting an account by W. R. Mead, indicates that White entered Richardson's office "as a very young man" (p. 41).

3. Charles A. Coolidge, "H. H. Richardson and His Works," Reel 643:484, Richardson Papers, AAA.

4. SW to Charles T. Barney, September 18, 1901, Architects' Education, M-15, McKim, Mead & White Collection, New-York Historical Society (hereafter MMW).

5. Moore, *McKim,* p. 38 and *passim;* passport, McKim-Maloney Papers, New York Public Library (NYPL).

6. Coolidge, "H. H. Richardson and His Works," Reel 643:486–87, Richardson Papers; W. A. Langton, "The Method of H. H. Richardson," *The Architect and Contract Reporter,* 63 (March 9, 1900): 156–58; Mariana Griswold Van Rensselaer, *Henry Hobson Richardson and His Work* (Boston, 1882), pp. 124, 128–29. See also James F. O'Gorman, *H. H. Richardson and His Office: Selected Drawings* (Cambridge, Mass., 1974), and *H. H. Richardson: Architectural Forms for an American Society* (Chicago, 1987).

7. Paul R. Baker, *Richard Morris Hunt* (Cambridge, Mass., 1980),

408

2. "Mr. R."

p. 167; J. J. Glessner, "Recollections of Richardson," Reel 643:477–78, Richardson Papers.

8. Henry-Russell Hitchcock, *The Architecture of H. H. Richardson and His Times*, rev. ed. (Cambridge, Mass., 1961), pp. 110–16; Jeffrey Karl Ochsner, *H. H. Richardson: Complete Architectural Works* (Cambridge, Mass., 1982), pp. 24–27, 68–70, 73–77.

9. Ochsner, *Richardson*, pp. 78–81, 90–93, 96–98.

10. Hitchcock, *Architecture of H. H. Richardson*, pp. 133–36; Ochsner, *Richardson*, pp. 111–13; Jeffrey Karl Ochsner, "H. H. Richardson's Frank Williams Andrews House," *Journal of the Society of Architectural Historians*, 43 (March 1984): 20–32.

11. Ochsner, *Richardson*, p. 114.

12. Moore, *McKim*, p. 39; C. F. McKim to E. Winchester Donald, March 21, 1893, McKim Papers, Library of Congress (LC); Box 33:302, SW Papers.

13. SW to AW, "Sunday noon, 1873," Frame 724, SW Coll; SW to AW, October 29, 1872, February 23, 1873, and n.d., "Early Letters and Sketches," Robert White Coll; "Original Sketches by Stanford White," Robert White Coll.

14. "H. H. Richardson's Men," Reel 643:473–74, Richardson Papers, AAA. See also SW to Charles H. Rutan, August 17, 1872, Rutan Papers, AAA.

15. SW to AW [1874], "Early Letters and Sketches," Robert White Coll.

16. Julia Richardson Shepley to SW, September 6, 1894, Box 31:3, SW Papers; Reel 643:511, Richardson Papers.

17. "H. H. Richardson's Men," Reel 543:475, Richardson Papers, AAA; Charles Price, "Henry Hobson Richardson: Some Unpublished Drawings," *Perspecta*, 9–10 (1965): 203; Mariana Griswold Van Rensselaer, "Recent Architecture: IV. Churches," *Century Magazine*, 29 (January 1885): 331; Hitchcock, *Richardson*, pp. 139–40. Adams, "The Birth of a Style" (note 2 above), 428, finds the source of Trinity tower in an illustration of the Salamanca tower in George Edmund Street, *Gothic Architecture in Spain* (1865), a book that Richardson owned. SW prepared a sketch of Richardson's tower design for the *New York Sketch Book of Architecture*, March 1874.

18. "The Ten Best Buildings," *American Architect and Building News*, 17 (June 13, 1885): 282–83; *Preservation News*, May 1982, p. 2.

19. Ochsner, *Richardson*, pp. 133–39; see also Historic American Building Survey, RI-342, p. 11, on the Sherman house. In 1920, the architect Dudley Newton considerably enlarged the house through the addition of a service wing.

20. Glenn Brown, *Memories 1860–1930* (Washington, D.C., 1931),

pp. 28–29. See also Glenn Brown, "Stanford White," *American Institute of Architects Quarterly Bulletin*, 7 (July 1906): 107.

21. Ochsner, *Richardson*, pp. 172, 190–91.

22. H. H. Richardson to F. L. Olmsted, cited in O'Gorman, *Richardson, Selected Drawings*, p. 122; Ochsner, *Richardson*, pp. 157–59; Henry-Russell Hitchcock and William Seale, *Temples of Democracy: the State Capitols of the U.S.A.* (New York and London, 1976), pp. 200–202.

23. Larry Homolka, "Richardson's North Easton," *Architectural Forum*, 124 (May 1966): 72–77.

CHAPTER 3
A Web of Friendships

1. RGW to AW, August 27, 1878, RGW Coll; SW to Maggie White, January 22, 1876, in "Early Letters and Sketches," Robert White Coll.

2. RGW to AW, August 22 and 27, 1874, RGW Coll. After RGW's death, the quartet continued, with newcomers replacing those who dropped out. More than half a century after its founding the musicians were still playing regularly, and in later years the publisher Henry Holt, who played the cello, was a member of the group that RGW had originally organized. Chloe Arnold, "The Fellowship of the Fiddle," *American Mercury*, 11 (June 1927): 220–26; Henry Holt, *Garrulities of an Octogenarian Editor* (Boston, 1923), p. 19.

3. RGW to President of the Pennsylvania Railway, October 11, 1876; RGW to AW, August 25 and 27, 1878; and E. P. Loiseau to RGW, June 1, 1878, RGW Coll. Fred E. H. Schroeder, "Nothing if Not Critical: A Biography of Richard Grant White," Ph.D. dissertation, University of Minnesota, March 1968, p. 212.

4. Julian Hawthorne, *Shapes That Pass* (Boston, 1928), p. 91; Winifred Skolnikoff, "Richard Grant White," M.A. thesis, Columbia University, 1959, p. 45.

5. RGW to AW, May 23 [1877], RGW Coll; Skolnikoff, "Richard Grant White," p. 45.

6. RGW to SW, October 8, 1876, RGW Coll; Hawthorne, *Shapes That Pass*, p. 92; quoted in Francis P. Church, "Richard Grant White," *Atlantic Monthly*, 67 (March 1891): 304.

7. RGW to Julian Hawthorne, October 19, 1876, and RGW to Richard Mansfield White, October 11, 1876, Richard Grant White Papers, Columbia University, microfilm.

8. RGW to AW, August 27, 1878, RGW Coll; E. P. Whipple, "Richard Grant White," *Atlantic Monthly*, 49 (February 1882): 219.

9. 2073:311–12, Saarinen Papers, AAA; SW to Maggie White, March 31, 1877, "Early Letters and Sketches," Robert White Coll.

10. Algonac Diary (October 1875–January 1879): August 6, 1876, September 16, 1877, and *passim*, Frederic Delano Papers, Franklin D. Roosevelt Library, Hyde Park, N.Y.; quoted in Rita Kleeman, *Gracious Lady: The Life of Sara Delano Roosevelt* (New York, 1935), p. 83; Geoffrey Ward, *Before the Trumpet* (New York, 1985), p. 104 f. Aline Saarinen in her fragment, unpublished biography of SW suggested a romantic involvement of SW with Anais Casey but provided no documentation, 2073:311, Saarinen Papers.

11. H. Van Buren Magonigle, "A Half Century of Architecture," *Pencil Points*, 15 (March 1934): 116.

12. Richard Guy Wilson, "The Early Work of Charles F. McKim," *Winterthur Portfolio*, 14 (Autumn 1979): 235–67.

13. James H. Morse, diary, September 8, 1880, vol. 5, pp. 124–25, and September 17, 1874, vol. 2, p. 45, Manuscript Division, NYHS.

14. Homer Saint-Gaudens, ed., *The Reminiscences of Augustus Saint-Gaudens* (New York, 1913), vol. 1, pp. 159–60.

15. Homer Saint-Gaudens, *Augustus Saint-Gaudens* (Concord, N.H., 1927), p. 7; Mrs. Daniel Chester French, *Memories of a Sculptor's Wife* (Boston, 1928), pp. 185–87; C. Lewis Hinds, *Augustus Saint-Gaudens* (New York, 1908), p. xxvii.

16. Daniel H. Burnham to Homer Saint-Gaudens, February 11, 1908, Saint-Gaudens Papers, LC.

17. Rosamond Gilder, ed., *Letters of Richard Watson Gilder* (Boston, 1916), p. 82; Will H. Low, *A Chronicle of Friendships, 1873–1900* (New York, 1908), pp. 234–37; Arthur John, *The Best Years of the Century* (Urbana, Ill., 1981), p. 81. White did decorative work on the façade of the East Fifteenth Street house and in the Gilders' later residence on Clinton Place (East Eighth Street), and he remodeled an old stone oil refinery into a summer cottage for the Gilders at Marion, Massachusetts.

18. Charles Moore, *The Life and Times of Charles Follen McKim* (Boston, 1928), p. 41.

19. *American Architect and Building News*, 2 (December 29, 1877): 419.

20. Wilson, "Early Work of C. F. McKim," 259; Montgomery Schuyler, "Charles F. McKim," *Architectural Record*, 26 (November 1909): 381; *American Architect and Building News*, 2 (December 8, 1877): 394. The Tuckerman Building now serves as a dormitory for New York University.

21. 2073:318, 319, 328, and 342, Saarinen Papers.
22. Morse, diary, 8: 106–7.
23. Ronnie Rubin, "The Tile Club, 1877–1887," M.A. thesis, New York University, 1967, p. 10 and *passim*; E. V. Lucas, *Edwin Austin Abbey* (New York, 1921), vol. 1, pp. 52–54; William M. Laffan, "The Tile Club at Work," *Scribner's Monthly,* 17 (January 1879): 408; William H. Sheldon, "Autobiography," Manuscript Division, NYHS.
24. H. H. Richardson to SW, February 22, 1878, Robert White Coll.
25. Reel 13:895 and Reel 14:238, Saint-Gaudens Papers, microfilm, Dartmouth College Library (hereafter SG Papers).
26. Reel 14:227, 228, 230, 233, SG Papers.
27. Homer Saint-Gaudens, "Intimate Letters," *Architectural Record,* 30 (August 1911): 110; Reel 14:235, SG Papers.
28. Box 14:10, SW Papers; Reel 14:176–77, SG Papers.

CHAPTER 4

The Discovery of Europe

1. Charles Baldwin, *Stanford White* (New York, 1931), pp. 70 ff., for this and the following paragraphs. Typescripts of the original letters are found in "Stanford White's Letters from Europe, 1878, Typed by his son, Lawrence Grant White, 1936," Robert White Coll.
2. Augusta Saint-Gaudens to her mother, July 19, 1878, Reel 19:741–42, SG Papers; Maitland Armstrong, *Day Before Yesterday* (New York, 1920), p. 266.
3. Baldwin, *White,* p. 75.
4. Reel 19:743–44, SG Papers.
5. This and the following paragraphs are based on SW to RGW and AW, August 30–September 1, 1878, Frames 740–57, SW Coll.
6. Reel 19:753, SG Papers.
7. "St.-Gaudens–McKim Bronzes," *Bulletin of the New York Public Library,* 43 (September 1939): 642–45; Margaret Bouton, "The Early Works of Augustus Saint-Gaudens," Ph.D. dissertation, Radcliffe College, 1948, pp. 320, 323, 324–29.
8. Bouton, "Early Works," pp. 327, 469. Lawrence White's interpretations of the phrases may have been told him by his father or, more likely, by McKim. No evidence for such incidents occurring on the excursion has been found. Other interpretations of the phrases may be valid. See "St.-Gaudens–McKim Bronzes," 644.
9. See sketches, drawings, and watercolors in the Davis & Langdale Gallery, New York City. Exhibits of White's European sketches and watercolors were held by the Davis Gallery in 1963 and 1965.

10. SW to RGW, October 17, 1878, in "Letters from Europe," and in Baldwin, *White*, p. 86.

11. SW to RGW, October 17, 1878, and SW to AW, November 6, 21, 1878, Frames 734, 731–32, SW Coll.

12. SW to AW, November 21, 1878, "Letters from Europe."

13. SW to AW, November 21 and December 1 and 12, 1878, in "Letters from Europe"; Baldwin, *White*, pp. 92–94; Homer Saint-Gaudens, ed., *The Reminiscences of Augustus Saint-Gaudens* (New York, 1913), vol. 1, p. 261.

14. SW to AW, November 21 and December 12, 1878, in "Letters from Europe."

15. Homer Saint-Gaudens, ed., *Reminiscences*, vol. 1, pp. 259, 262.

16. Homer Saint-Gaudens, ed., *Reminiscences*, vol. 1, p. 214; ASG to John Dix, February 12, 1879, Reel 6:96–98, and Augusta Saint-Gaudens to her mother, February 12, 28, 1879, Reel 19:718, 787, SG Papers; SW to AW, January 12, 1879, "Letters from Europe."

17. Augusta Saint-Gaudens to her mother, January 31 and February 28, 1879, Reel 19:774, 777, 783, 854, SG Papers; SW to AW, n.d., "Letters from Europe."

18. Augusta Saint-Gaudens to her mother, March 13 and 31, April 4 and 16, and May 2, 4, and 8, 1879, Reel 19:802, 812, 817–20, 827, 845, 854, 859, SG Papers; SW to William Rutherford Mead (WRM), March 27, 1879, "Holographs of Famous Architects," *American Architect*, 143 (March 1933): 11; ASG to Richard Watson Gilder, April 8, 1879, Reel 7:494, SG Papers.

19. Augustus Saint-Gaudens, "Sketchbook with Notes and Drawings," July–August 1879, American Academy and Institute of Arts and Letters Coll; SW to AW, June 11, July 7, 1879, "Letters from Europe."

20. SW to AW, August 15, 1879, "Letters from Europe"; ASG to J. J. Cisco, August 23, 1879, Reel 6:107–8, SG Papers.

21. SW to ASG, August 1879, Reel 14:323, SG Papers; Baldwin, *White*, pp. 99–100.

22. Reel 14:320–30, 253–54, 261, SG Papers; Baldwin, *White*, pp. 99–101.

23. Reel 14:261, SG Papers.

CHAPTER 5

A New Beginning

1. SW to ASG, September 9, 1878, Reel 14:261, 283, SG Papers; Charles Moore, *The Life and Times of Charles Follen McKim* (Boston, 1929), quotes on pp. 41, 46.

2. Articles of Co-partnership, reproduced in Leland M. Roth, *The Architecture of McKim, Mead & White, 1870–1920: A Building List* (New York, 1978), p. xiii; Box 38:25, SW Papers. Other partnership agreements were signed later: see PB 33:251, Box 18:11, and PB 28:f. 499, SW Papers, and McKim, M-3, MMW.

3. SW to ASG, October 17, and September and October 1879, Reel 14:265, 341, 324–25, SG Papers.

4. ASG to Maitland Armstrong, September 24, 1879, in Maitland Armstrong, *Day Before Yesterday* (New York, 1920), p. 285; SW to ASG, October 17, 1879, Reel 14:264–65, SG Papers.

5. SW to J. J. Cisco, October 4, 1879, and SW to ASG, October 7, 1879, Reel 14:257–58, 278, SG Papers.

6. PB 15:338, SW Papers; Homer Saint-Gaudens, ed., "Intimate Letters of Stanford White," *Architectural Review*, 30 (September 1911): 290; SW to ASG, December 17, 1879, Reel 14:292, SG Papers.

7. ASG to SW, March 14–15, 1880, Reel 13:916, SG Papers.

8. SW to ASG, April 1, 1880, in Homer Saint-Gaudens, ed., "Intimate Letters," 116; Reel 14:220, SG Papers; William Webster Ellsworth, *A Golden Age of Authors* (New York, 1919), p. 157.

9. Farragut Pedestal Articles of Agreement, December 13, 1879, Frame 477, SW Coll; ASG to SW, November 6, 1879, and March 14–15, 1880, and SW to ASG, December 17, 1879, Reel 14:190–91, Reel 13:916, Reel 14:292, SG Papers.

10. James Edward Kelly Papers, Box 8, Ms. Div., NYHS; James Grant Wilson, *Memorial History of the City of New York*, 4 (New York, 1893): 214; Ellsworth, *Golden Age*, p. 160; *New York Times*, May 25, 1881, p. 4, and May 26, 1881, p. 5.

11. The sinuous lines of the pedestal decoration provided a forerunner of American Art Nouveau work, which came to fruition many years later.

12. Ellsworth, *Golden Age*, p. 160; Mariana Griswold Van Rensselaer, "Mr. St.-Gaudens's Statue of Admiral Farragut," *American Architect and Building News*, 10 (September 10, 1881): 119; Richard Watson Gilder, "The Farragut Monument," *Scribner's Monthly*, 22 (June 1881): 166–67; anon., "The Farragut Monument," *American Architect and Building News*, 10 (September 10, 1881): 120. The Farragut Monument deteriorated badly during the subsequent half-century. In the 1930s, because of the work's condition, it was decided to replace the pedestal-exedra completely. In place of the original bluestone, the base and exedra were recarved in black granite, under the supervision of the sculptor Karl Gruppe. The recarved monument—the statue figure having been given a new patina—was re-erected a short distance to the east of the original site in Madison

5. A New Beginning

Square. The original Farragut pedestal was taken to the Saint-Gaudens Historic Site in Cornish, N.H. Farragut File, M-19, MMW.

13. SW to ASG [1880], Reel 14:222, SG Papers; Homer Saint-Gaudens, ed., "Intimate Letters," pp. 114–15; Homer Saint-Gaudens, ed., *The Reminiscences of Augustus Saint-Gaudens* (New York, 1913), vol. 1, p. 273. The two artists also collaborated in 1883 on a small mausoleum for David Stewart, a wealthy ironworks owner, in Green-Wood Cemetery, Brooklyn. With the sculptor Launt Thompson, White in 1880 created a small monument honoring Llewellyn Haskell in West Orange, N.J.

14. SW to ASG, May 8, 1880, in Homer Saint-Gaudens, ed., "Intimate Letters," p. 285; Homer Saint-Gaudens, ed., *Reminiscences,* vol. 1, pp. 225–26, 272.

15. Maud Howe Elliott, *This Was My Newport* (Cambridge, Mass., 1944), pp. 153–54.

16. *Newport Mercury,* October 25, 1879, p. 2, and December 6, 1879, p. 2.

17. Mariana Griswold Van Rensselaer, "Recent Architecture in America: II Public Buildings," *Century,* 28 (July 1884): 330–31; 2073:244–45, Saarinen Papers. See also Alan T. Schumacher, "The Newport Casino: Its History," unpublished manuscript, 1986.

18. *Harper's Weekly,* 31 (August 27, 1887): 611; *Preservation News,* 17 (October 1977): 6. In 1900 a fire destroyed all of the casino except for the towers and arch, which were subsequently used for a tearoom, an ice cream parlor, a dance hall, offices of the Chamber of Commerce, and a cultural center.

19. *New-York Tribune,* May 13, 1893, in Scrapbook, 1892–94, p. 138, MMW. The Short Hills Casino was destroyed by fire in the early 1980s. Other McKim, Mead & White casinos were erected in Kansas City, Missouri; Stockbridge, Massachusetts; and Garden City and Babylon, Long Island, New York.

20. J. Walter Ferguson, *Kingscote: Newport Cottage Orné* (Newport, 1977). The summer after David King's death in 1894, the house served as the British "Summer Embassy," the residence of Julian Pauncefote, British Ambassador to the United States. In 1972 Kingscote was deeded to the Preservation Society of Newport County, and it is now open to the public.

21. Ferguson, *Kingscote,* pp. 33–34; *Historical American Building Survey, Rhode Island,* p. 307; see also John A. Cherol, "Kingscote in Newport, Rhode Island," *Antiques,* 118 (September 1980): 476–85.

22. See Vincent Scully, *The Shingle Style and the Stick Style,* rev. ed.

415

(New Haven, 1971), pp. 26–29; William B. Rhoades, *The Colonial Revival* (New York, 1977), vol. 1, pp. 376 ff. The firm also created several shingle-style houses on the eastern end of Long Island in the 1880s and early 1890s. White designed the small shingle-style Shinnecock Hills Golf Clubhouse in 1892. See the excellent study by Mosette Glaser Broderick, "A Place Where Nobody Goes," in Helen Searing, ed., *In Search of Modern Architecture: A Tribute to Henry-Russell Hitchcock* (Cambridge, Mass., 1982), pp. 185–205.

23. *Newport Mercury,* September 3, 1881. Somewhat similar Oriental-like porch posts were found on White's Cyrus Hall McCormick house in Richfield Springs, New York, erected about the same time.

24. The Osborn house was later incorporated into the Mamaroneck Beach and Tennis Club.

25. From 1899 to 1903, Choate served as Ambassador to the Court of St. James's. After his death in 1917, his widow kept the house, and upon her death it devolved upon the Choates' daughter Mabel, who had the gardens considerably enlarged. In 1948, Mabel Choate bequeathed Naumkeag to the Trustees of Preservation, a Massachusetts charitable trust, which opened the property to the public. See "The Choates at Naumkeag," pamphlet (Stockbridge, Mass., 1968).

26. Searles Castle is now the home of the John Dewey Academy.

27. *New York Sun,* January 14, 1883, p. 3.

28. *New York World,* March 29, 1885, in Scrapbook no. 1, p. 22, MMW; 2073:356, Saarinen Papers.

29. Edmund Gosse, "Notes on America," *The Critic,* 6 (January 24, 1885): 38; Mariana Griswold Van Rensselaer, "Recent Architecture in America: City Dwellings," *Century,* 31 (February 1886): 557. The Tiffany house was razed in 1936.

30. SW to ASG, Reel 14:245, SG Papers, quoted in Charles Baldwin, *Stanford White* (New York, 1931), p. 151.

CHAPTER 6
57 Broadway

1. Philip Sawyer, *Edward Palmer York: Personal Reminiscences* (Stonington, Conn., 1951), p. 17; Inventory, December 31, 1885, Journal, 1882–88, MMW.

2. Sawyer, *York,* p. 21; H. Van Buren Magonigle, "A Half-Century of Architecture: A Biographical Review," *Pencil Points,* 15 (March 1934): 115–16; Albert Randolph Ross, "Stanford White as Those Trained in His Office Knew Him," *Brickbuilder,* 15 (December 1906): 246.

3. Magonigle, "Half-Century," p. 115.

4. September 7, 1927, Box 12, Cass Gilbert Papers, LC; Magonigle, "Half Century," p. 116; Glenn Brown, *Memories 1860–1930* (Washington, D.C., 1931), pp. 487–89; Charles Baldwin, *Stanford White* (New York, 1931), p. 116; Sawyer, *York,* p. 18; Lawrence Grant White, *Sketches and Designs by Stanford White* (New York, 1920), p. 17; 2073:464–65, Saarinen Papers, AAA.

5. Royal Cortissoz, *The Painter's Craft* (New York, 1930), p. 429; Brown, *Memories,* pp. 334, 340.

6. Egerton Swartwout interview, Reel 3:841, D. M. Lockman Papers, Ms. Div., NYHS.

7. Magonigle, "Half-Century," p. 116; Henry Bacon, "Charles Follen McKim: A Character Sketch," *Brickbuilder,* 19 (February 1910): 44; William T. Partridge to William A. Delano, May 22, 1940, Ware Coll, Avery Library.

8. Scrapbook, 1906–11, p. 320, MMW.

9. W. T. Partridge, "Recollections of Charles F. McKim," Ware Coll.

10. Magonigle, "Half-Century," p. 116; Monroe Hewlett, "Stanford White as Those Trained in His Office Knew Him," *Brickbuilder,* 15 (December 1906): 245; William A. Boring, Statement, McKim Papers, LC.

11. Francis S. Swales, "Master Draftsmen: Pt. I, Stanford White," *Pencil Points,* 5 (April 1924): 61.

12. Partridge, "Recollections."

13. Royal Cortissoz, "Some Critical Reflections on the Architectural Genius of Charles F. McKim," *Brickbuilder,* 19 (February 1910): 23; SW in *Art Age,* 3 (January 1886): 100; SW to Moses King, October 22, 1889, PB 21:18, SW Papers.

14. Mead recalled that Wells came to work three or four months before White joined the firm. Baldwin, *White,* pp. 114, 357; also Charles Moore, *The Life and Times of Charles Follen McKim* (New York, 1929), p. 327. Magonigle, "Half-Century," p. 223, and some other sources indicate Wells entered the firm shortly after White.

15. Royal Cortissoz, "The Artistic Genius and Lovable Traits of Stanford White," *New-York Tribune,* November 7, 1920, sec. VII, p. 2; C. Howard Walker, "Joseph Wells, Architect, 1853–1890," *Architectural Record,* 66 (July 1929): 14–18; J. M. Wells to Cass Gilbert, February 4, 1883, Gilbert Papers.

16. Royal Cortissoz, "Auspicious Omens in the New Year: The Cancelleria," *New York Herald Tribune,* January 7, 1940, sec. VI, p. 8.

17. Lawrence Grant White, oral history, Columbia University, pp. 108–9. Cass Gilbert also related this incident: see Swales, "Master Draftsman," p. 62, and Moore, *McKim,* p. 49 f.

18. Joseph M. Wells to SW, August 1 and October 10, 1880, and

January 18 and 24, 1881, Frames 676–77, 678–83, 684–89, 668–69, SW Coll.

19. Homer Saint-Gaudens, ed., *The Reminiscences of Augustus Saint-Gaudens* (New York, 1913), vol. 1, pp. 306, 307, 311; James R. Morse, diary, March 2, 1884, Ms. Div., NYHS.

20. W. R. Mead to Cass Gilbert, March 28, April 6 and 8 and July 18, 1882, and September 7, 1927, Gilbert Papers; see also tribute of Gilbert to SW, *AIA Quarterly Bulletin,* 7 (July 1906): 106.

21. Cass Gilbert to Clarence Johnston, August 24, 1882, quoted in Robert A. Jones, *Cass Gilbert, Midwestern Architect in New York* (New York, 1982), pp. 50, 52.

22. SW to Cass Gilbert, November 1, 1882, Gilbert Papers.

23. Cortissoz, "Artistic Genius," 2; Royal Cortissoz, "Some Leaders of Our Architectural Renaissance," *Scribner's Magazine,* 86 (July 1929): 105; Royal Cortissoz, *American Artists* (New York, 1923), p. 298.

CHAPTER 7
Bessie

1. RGW to AW [June 1880], RGW Coll. The Whites lived at 29 Waverly Place, 22 Washington Place, and 330 East Seventeenth Street in the early 1880s.

2. RGW to AW [June 1880], RGW Coll.

3. RGW to AW, March 29, May 23, and n.d. [1880], RGW Coll.

4. Howard Crosby to RGW, April 12, 1881, RGW Coll; *Catalogue of the University of the City of New York, 1881–1882* (New York, 1882), pp. 54, 74.

5. Bessie Smith White, "Memories," 2073:685, Saarinen Papers; CFM to Bessie Smith, August 15, 1880, copy McKim Papers, LC.

6. 2073:679–82, Saarinen Papers.

7. 2073:683–86, Saarinen Papers. Butler eventually had the valentine poems privately printed in a volume for Bessie.

8. 2073:686–87, 198–99, Saarinen Papers.

9. 2073:366, Saarinen Papers.

10. SW to "Miss Bessie," September 21, 1880, and Bessie Smith to SW, [September 1880], "Letters from Stanford White's Wedding Tour, 1883–1884," compiled by Lawrence Grant White, Robert White Coll; 2073:367, Saarinen Papers.

11. 2073:372–73, Saarinen Papers.

12. John Higham sees the cult of masculinity as a rebellion against the dull routines and frustrations of American urban-industrial culture

beginning in the 1890s. See "The Reorientation of American Culture in the 1890s," in John Higham, ed., *Writing American History* (Bloomington, Ind., 1970), p. 79.

13. SW to AW, March 2, 1882, and SW to RGW, March 27, 1882, "Stanford White's Letters to His Mother Written During His Mexican Trip," Robert White Coll.

14. SW to AW, March 28 and April 14, 1882; SW to Cornelia Butler, April 12, 1882; and SW to RGW, April 26, 1882, all in "White's Letters . . . During His Mexican Trip."

15. SW to Bessie Smith [August] 31, 1883, "Letters from Stanford White's Wedding Tour, 1883–1884"; Homer Saint-Gaudens, ed., *Reminiscences of Augustus Saint-Gaudens* (New York, 1913), vol. 1, pp. 294–303.

16. ASG to his wife, September 3, 1883, Reel 13:869, SG Papers; 2073:383, Saarinen Papers; SW to Bessie Smith [September] 1883, "Letters from Stanford White's Wedding Tour, 1883–1884."

17. SW to Bessie Smith, August 1883 and [1883]. "Letters from Stanford White's Wedding Tour, 1883–1884."

18. 2073:380, 676–78, 663–64, Saarinen Papers.

19. Journal, 1882–88, MMW Coll.

20. Dorothy Weir Young, *The Life and Letters of J. Alden Weir* (New Haven, 1960), p. 158.

21. 2073:690, Saarinen Papers; Charles Baldwin, *Stanford White* (New York, 1931), pp. 163–65; Maitland Armstrong, *Day Before Yesterday* (New York, 1920), p. 286.

22. Louise Hall Tharp, *Saint-Gaudens and the Gilded Age* (Boston, 1969), p. 173; 2073:667, 391, Saarinen Papers. The plaque of Bessie White is now in the Metropolitan Museum of Art.

23. 2073:670, 659, Saarinen Papers; Baldwin, *White*, p. 166.

24. SW to George C. Mason, March 12, 1884, Box 3:5, American Institute of Architects Archives, Washington, D.C.

25. SW to AW, April 23, 1884, "Letters from Stanford White's Wedding Tour, 1883–1884."

26. SW to AW, April 23, 1884, and SW to Cornelia Butler, May 3, 1884, "Letters from Stanford White's Wedding Tour, 1883–1884"; SW to AW, May 6, 1884, quoted in Baldwin, *White*, p. 167.

27. SW to RGW, May 18, 1884, "Letters from Stanford White's Wedding Tour, 1883–1884"; Earl Shinn, *A Book of the Tile Club* (Boston, 1886), p. 100.

28. SW to ASG, October 25, 1905, PB 33:423, SW Papers; SW to AW, May 31, 1884, "Letters from Stanford White's Wedding Tour,

1883–1884''; Bessie White to Prescott Hall Butler, June 5, 1884, Frames 697–700, SW Coll.

29. Bessie White to her sister, July 9, 1884, Frames 713–15, 717, SW Coll.

30. SW to AW, July 14 and August 22, 1884, "Letters from Stanford White's Wedding Tour, 1883–1884."

31. Tharp, *Saint-Gaudens*, p. 183.

32. J. M. Wells to Cass Gilbert, July 30, 1884, Gilbert Papers.

33. *Ibid.*

CHAPTER 8
"Simpler and More Classic Forms"

1. On the idea and artistic manifestations of the American Renaissance, see Richard Guy Wilson, Dianne Pilgrim, and Richard Murray, *The American Renaissance 1876–1917* (New York, 1979).

2. See William C. Shopsin, Mosette Broderick, *et al.*, *The Villard Houses: Life Story of a Landmark* (New York, 1980), the definitive study; Royal Cortissoz, "Some Leaders of Our Architectural Renaissance," *Scribner's Magazine*, 86 (July 1929): 107; Charles S. Baldwin, *Stanford White* (New York, 1931), pp. 357–58.

3. Henry Villard, *Memoirs of Henry Villard, Journalist and Financier, 1835–1900* (Boston, 1904), vol. 2, pp. 316–17, 321. White did additions to Villard's Dobbs Ferry house in 1891–92.

4. Mariana Griswold Van Rensselaer, "Recent Architecture in America: City Dwellings," *Century Magazine*, 31 (February 1886): 557. The Commodore William Edgar house (1886) and the H. A. C. Taylor house (1886), both in Newport and both designed by McKim, also reflected the new emphasis on balance, formality, and historical reference.

5. Anon., "Mr. Villard's Italian Palace," *Building*, 2 (December 1883): 38; Shopsin, Broderick, *et al.*, *Villard Houses*, pp. 63–85; Channing Blake, "Stanford White's New York Interiors," *Antiques*, 102 (December 1972): 1060–61; Joseph M. Wells to Cass Gilbert, July 30, 1884, Gilbert Papers.

6. When in 1910 the Reids had a large tower addition built, they chose William Kendall of McKim, Mead & White to do the work. At that time the dining room was considerably enlarged.

7. SW to Whitelaw Reid, January 26, 1888, Reid Papers, LC; Whitelaw Reid to SW, February 15, 1892, August 24 and 27, September 7 1894, and May 4, 1895, 2073:1013, 1106–1107, 1021, Saarinen Papers.

8. SW to Whitelaw Reid, April 5, 1888, Reid Papers.

9. SW to E. A. Abbey, September 19, 1895, PB 14:48, SW Papers

Whitelaw Reid to SW, December 14 and 23, 1895, March 31 and May 8, 1897, 2073:1142–44, 1159, 1163, Saarinen Papers; E. V. Lucas, *Edwin Austin Abbey* (New York, 1921), vol. 2, pp. 306, 402; SW to E. A. Abbey, August 15, 1904, PB 31:298, SW Papers.

10. SW to Mrs. Harrison, March 19, 1896, PB 15:338–39, SW Papers. In recent years, the south wing and the central section façade of the Villard houses have been incorporated into the lofty Palace Hotel, erected adjacent to the east. For the stylistic changes in the work of McKim, Mead & White, see Richard Guy Wilson, *McKim, Mead & White, Architects* (New York, 1983), pp. 20–25, 58–59, and *passim*, and Leland M. Roth, *McKim, Mead & White, Architects* (New York, 1983), pp. 115 ff.

11. Mariana Griswold Van Rensselaer, "Recent Architecture in America: Commercial Buildings," *Century*, 28 (August 1884): 521; Baldwin, *White*, p. 123. On West Forty-second Street, the firm also constructed in 1882–83 "The Percival," an apartment house for bachelors: see *The Graphic*, January 15, 1883, Scrapbook no. 1, p. 25, MMW.

12. Maitland Armstrong, *Day Before Yesterday: Reminiscences of a Varied Life* (New York, 1920), p. 307; Susan Hobbs, "John La Farge and the Genteel Tradition in American Art, 1875–1910," unpublished Ph.D. dissertation, Cornell University, 1974; PB 2:282, SW Papers.

13. Charles H. Dorr, "A Study in Church Decoration," *Architectural Record*, 33 (March 1913): 187.

14. Scrapbook, 1870–88, p. 64, MMW.

15. Lucas, *Abbey*, vol. 1, p. 216; George G. De Witt to SW, May 26, 1898, Box 13:18, SW Papers.

16. Scrapbook, 1887–1901, p. 160, MMW; CFM to SW, September 21, 1889, Box 45:24, SW Papers.

17. *Town Topics*, 17 (June 2, 1887): 2.

18. CFM to Charles Rutan, December 26, 1885, 1260:071–075, Rutan Papers.

19. CFM to Charles Rutan, January 8, 1887, 1260:078–079, Rutan Papers.

20. WRM to CFM, December 19, 1887, McKim Papers, LC; Scrapbook, 1887–1901, p. 313, MMW; see also Walter Muir Whitehill, "The Making of an Architectural Masterpiece: The Boston Public Library," *The American Art Journal*, 2 (Fall 1970): 13–35.

CHAPTER 9
Family Ties

1. 2073:668, Saarinen Papers.

2. RGW to T. B. Aldrich, October 5, 1884, RGW Coll; James H.

Notes

Morse, diary, January 30, 1883, and February 22, 1893, vol. 6, p. 89, and vol. 10, p. 40, Ms. Div., NYHS; *The Critic and Good Literature,* April 12, 1884, pp. 169–70.

3. *New York Times,* January 16, 1881, p. 10; *Century,* 27 (April 1884): 948.
4. 2073:429, Saarinen Papers; *New-York Tribune,* April 9, 1885, p. 2; *New York Times,* April 9, 1885, p. 5.
5. Fred E. H. Schroeder, "Nothing if Not Critical: A Biography of Richard Grant White," Ph.D. dissertation, University of Minnesota, 1968, p. 363.
6. "Memorandum on Estate of Richard Grant White," RGW Coll; *Catalogue of the Library, Engravings, Oil Paintings and Musical Instruments Belonging to the Estate of the Late Richard Grant White, Esq. of New York* (New York, 1885).
7. 2073:685, Saarinen Papers; Laura Chanler White interview, November 19, 1983.
8. 2073:685, Saarinen Papers.
9. SW to AW, 1886, quoted in Charles C. Baldwin, *Stanford White* (New York, 1931), p. 172.
10. *New York Times,* October 26, 1886, p. 1; October 27, 1886, p. 5; October 28, 1885, p. 5; October 29, 1886, p. 3.
11. Richard M. White to SW, October 14 [1887], Box 48:9, SW Papers.
12. Aline Saarinen, "The Splendid World of Stanford White," *Life,* vol. 61 (September 16, 1966): 87–108.
13. PB 6:164, PB 9:148–49, PB 13:491, SW Papers; Van Wyck Brooks to Aline Saarinen, June 30, 1959, 2072:713, Saarinen Papers; Edward Simmons, *From Seven to Seventy* (New York, 1922), p. 239.
14. PB 1:19 and Box 34:17, SW Papers; Frame 426, SW Coll; *Harper's Weekly,* June 28, 1890, Scrapbook, 1887–1901, p. 152, MMW. The fishing club was spelled "Ristigouche" in some documents.
15. PB 2:216, PB 18:282, 289, and PB 35:233, SW Papers; Lawrence G. White, oral history, unpublished ms., pp. 9–10, Columbia University.
16. SW to ASG, April 6, 1889, PB 2:18; SW to DeForest, April 10, 1889, PB 2:27; and PB 2:64, 65, 73, SW Papers.
17. Dorothy Weir Young, *The Life and Letters of J. Alden Weir* (New Haven, 1960), pp. 170–71; SW to WRM, August 23, 1889, and CFM to SW, September 21, 1889, Box 45:24, SW Papers; Charles Merrill Mount, *John Singer Sargent* (London, 1957), p. 134.
18. SW to R. M. White, April 25, 1890, PB 3:101, SW Papers.
19. The correspondence in the SW Papers on management of the proper-

422

ties coming from the Stewart Estate is vast. See, for example, PB 5:98, 54, 142; PB 18:13, 248, 250, 296, 316, 422; Box 11:1, 2, 4; Box 34:6; Box 44:1–5.

20. PB 5:355, PB 20:331, and PB 25:477, SW Papers; L. B. Atterbury to SW, March 11, 1891, and January 8, 1892, SW Coll.

21. Frames 719–21, SW Coll.

22. Lionel Moses, "The Stanford White House at St. James, L.I.," *Art World*, 3 (1917): 351–55; Box 11:1, SW Papers.

23. PB 13:420 and PB 18:294, SW Papers.

24. Box 29:1, and PB 5:80, 262, 274, 374, SW Papers.

25. PB 5:428, PB 6:314, PB 14:265, PB 17:12, SW Papers; Frame 958, SW Coll.

26. Box 48:1, 9, 11, 13, 15; PB 1:282–83, 372, 464; and PB 2:341, SW Papers.

27. SW to R. M. White, February 2, 1889, PB 1:412–13; PB 1:288, SW Papers.

28. SW to C. T. Barney, November 18, 1893, PB 8:257; Box 28:8; and PB 16:311, 312, 313, SW Papers.

29. PB 2:318, SW Papers; Scrapbook, 1887–1901, pp. 187, 175, 173, MMW.

30. PB 3:29, 31, 62; PB 5:102, 126, 129, 322, 407, 455, SW Papers.

31. PB 2:315; PB 1:372a; PB 3:412, 412a, 413, 424; PB 4:135; PB 5:260, SW Papers.

32. PB 18:298, SW Papers.

CHAPTER 10
The Consummate Clubman

1. SW to Charles de Kay, PB 19:367, SW Papers. A 1901 listing of clubmen of New York enumerated White's clubs and associations as follows: Union, Knickerbocker, Metropolitan, City, University, Turf and Field, Meadow Brook Hunt, Racquet and Tennis, Kismet, Riding, Players, Adirondack League, Century, Manhattan, New York Yacht, American Institute of Architects, American Fine Arts Society, and Ardsley Casino. In addition he had been, was then, or would become a member of the Tile, Brook, Lambs, Harmonie, Grolier, Somerset of Boston, Vaudeville, National Arts, Strollers, Nissequogue Gun, Nissequogue Trout, Restigouche Salmon, Pallachucola, Jereboam, Saint Nicholas Ice Skating, Tuesday Night, St. Andrew's Golf, Smithtown Outing, Garden City Golf, Metropolitan Opera, Riding, and Edenia clubs, as well as the National Steeplechase Association, the Manhattan Municipal League, the Municipal Art Society,

the National Sculpture Society, the New York Zoological Society, the New York Society of Archaeology, the American Social Science Association, the Brooklyn Institute of Arts and Sciences, and the Charity Organization Society of the City of New York. He joined the New York chapter of the Automobile Club of America. In 1891 he was named an honorary member of the Trinity Historical Society of Dallas, Texas.

2. E. V. Lucas, *Edwin Austin Abbey* (New York, 1921), vol. 1, pp. 115–16; Charles Baldwin, *Stanford White* (New York, 1931), p. 228; Earl Shinn, *A Book of the Tile Club* (Boston, 1886), pp. 27 and *passim*; Mahonri Sharp Young, "The Tile Club Revisited," *American Art Journal,* 2 (Fall 1970): 91.

3. Richardson Wright, "The New Tenants at No. 16," *The Players Bulletin,* Winter 1958, pp. 13–21.

4. William Winter, "The Players," *Harper's Weekly,* 33 (January 19, 1889): 51.

5. 2072:992, Saarinen Papers.

6. Maurice F. Egan, *Recollections of a Happy Life* (New York, 1924), p. 151; PB 3:305–7, PB 1:463, 477, Box 9:10, 100, and PB 4:14, all SW Papers; SW to Lawrence Hutton, January 18, 1889, and May 16, 1891, and SW to Sypher & Co., June 19, 1889, Archives, The Players.

7. *New York Times,* January 1, 1893, in Scrapbook, 1892–94, p. 123, MMW.

8. PB 4:11; PB 12:18; and PB 2:60, SW Papers; Homer Saint-Gaudens, ed., *The Reminiscences of Augustus Saint-Gaudens* (New York, 1913), vol. 2, pp. 118–19.

9. Scrapbook, 1892–94, pp. 140–42, MMW.

10. Scrapbook, 1870–88, p. 110, and Scrapbook, 1887–1901, n.p., MMW; PB 1:394, SW Papers.

11. James H. Morse, diary, January 10, 1891, Ms. Div., NYHS; Century Club, 37, MMW.

12. CFM to SW, August 2 and September 21, 1889, Box 45:24, SW Papers.

13. Norcross Brothers to MMW, October 15 and December 11, 1889, and Francis Lathrop to MMW, January 2 1891, Archives, Century Association; H. F. Spaulding to SW, October 14, 1890, and other files, Century Club, 37, MMW.

14. Russell Sturgis, "The Works of McKim, Mead & White," *Architectural Record,* Great American Architects Series, May 1895, p. 6.

15. Morse, diary, January 10, 1891, Ms. Div., NYHS; Century Club 37, MMW.

16. Henry Holt, *Garrulities of an Octogenarian Editor* (Boston, 1923), pp. 111–12; Century Association, *The Century, 1847–1946* (New York, 1947), p. 7; PB 26:432, PB 30:315, SW Papers.

17. Scrapbook, 1894–1904, p. 42, MMW.

18. Paul Porzelt, *Metropolitan Club of New York* (New York, 1982), pp. vii, 9, and *passim*.

19. Metropolitan Club, M-79 (I) and (III), MMW.

20. Egerton Swartwout, "An Architectural Decade," unpublished ms., p. 29, Walker O. Cain; R. M. Hunt to SW and MMW, June 18 and September 16, 1892, and November 14, 1893, Metropolitan Club, M-79 (V), MMW.

21. SW to Lockwood De Forest, January 17, 1894, PB 8:474, and SW to Mrs. Alexander, February 24, 1894, PB 9:80, SW Papers; H. A. C. Taylor to SW, February 14, 1894, Metropolitan Club M81 (I), MMW; Edward Simmons, *From Seven to Seventy* (New York, 1922), p. 243.

22. Scrapbook, 1894–1904, p. 43, MMW.

23. Scrapbook, 1892–94, pp. 42–51, MMW; Metropolitan Club M80 (I) and M81 (II), MMW.

24. H. Van Buren Magonigle, "A Half-Century of Architecture: A Biographical Review," *Pencil Points*, 15 (September 1934): 465; SW to T. B. Clarke, December 15 and 22, 1897, PB 19:190, 221, and Box 34:3, SW Papers.

25. Scrapbook, 1894–1904, p. 299, MMW.

26. Thomas B. Clarke, *The Brook* (New York, 1930); *Town Topics*, 50 (October 29, 1903): 6.

27. PB 30:298, SW Papers; Reel 14:67, SG Papers.

28. Herbert D. Croly, "The Harmonie Club House," *Architectural Record*, 19 (April 1906): 236–43.

29. Florence F. Kelly, "A Club-Women's Palatial Home," *Indoors and Out*, 4 (May 1907): 77.

30. Mrs. J. Borden Harriman, "The Colony Club," *Century*, 107 (November 1923): 107–11; Landmarks Preservation Commission, May 16, 1966, no. 8, Lp0236.

31. Ishbel Ross, *Taste in America; an Illustrated History* (New York, 1967), p. 140. Elsie de Wolfe's work on the Colony clubhouse gave her her start as a professional decorator. SW had known her for some years and had assisted her in purchases and sales of art objects. See Box 37:8, SW Papers. In 1964 the former Colony Club became the home of the American Academy of Dramatic Arts.

32. PB 23:68 and PB 25:210, SW Papers.

Notes

CHAPTER 11

"A Permanent Ornament to the City"

1. Richard M. White to SW, June 14, 1887, Box 48:10, SW Papers; Mariana Griswold Van Rensselaer, "The Madison Square Garden," *Century,* 47 (March 1894): 732.

2. For this and the following paragraphs, see Andy Logan, "That Was New York, The Palace of Delight," *New Yorker,* 41 (February 27, 1965): 41 ff., and Van Rensselaer, "Madison Square Garden."

3. Journal, 1888–94, MMW.

4. SW to WRM, July 31, August 7, 1889, and WRM to SW, July 27, 1889, all Box 45:24, SW Papers.

5. SW to WRM, August 13 and 15, 1889, Box 45:22, and WRM to SW, September 7, 1889, Box 45:24, SW Papers.

6. CFM to SW, December 7, 1889, quoted in Charles C. Baldwin, *Stanford White* (New York, 1931), pp. 358–59.

7. SW to Webster Wells, January 31, 1890, Wells, M-3, MMW; Cass Gilbert to SW, February 11, 1890, Frames 335–36, SW Coll; H. Van Buren Magonigle, "A Half-Century of Architecture: A Biographical Review," *Pencil Points,* 15 (May 1934): 223; Royal Cortissoz, *Augustus Saint-Gaudens* (Boston, 1907), p. 85; Box 29:8 and PB 15:338, SW Papers.

8. SW to ASG, April 2, 1890, PB 3:60, SW Papers.

9. *Truth,* June 19, 1890; *Chicago Tribune,* June 29, 1890; and *New York Herald,* June 17, 1890, Scrapbook, 1887–1901, pp. 22, 42, and 20, MMW.

10. *New York World,* June 17, 1890, Scrapbook, 1887–1901, p. 19, MMW.

11. *New York Daily Graphic,* June 17, 1890, Scrapbook, 1887–1901, p. 19, MMW; undated clipping, 2072:1013, Saarinen Papers.

12. Van Rensselaer, "Madison Square Garden," 732, 741.

13. 2073:453, Saarinen Papers.

14. Van Rensselaer, "Madison Square Garden," 741.

15. Charles Baldwin, *Stanford White* (New York, 1931), p. 202.

16. Homer Saint-Gaudens, ed., *The Reminiscences of Augustus Saint Gaudens* (New York, 1913), vol. 1, p. 393; "The Madison Square Garden Weather Vane, The Huntress Diana," *Scientific American,* 65 (December 26, 1891): 407. White recalled the first Diana as 1 feet tall rather than 18 feet.

17. SW to ASG, October 3, 1891, PB 4:263, and J. B. Knight to T J. Vanderbent [1892] and to SW, February 9, 1892, Box 33:8 SW Papers.

18. Quoted in 2072:1002, Saarinen Papers; *New York Mercury*, November 22, 1891, Scrapbook, 1887–1901, p. 77, MMW.

19. *New York Times*, November 2, 1891, Scrapbook, 1887–1901, p. 69, MMW.

20. Edward H. Bowen to SW, April 26, 1892, Box 9:14, SW Papers; *Frank Leslie's*, March 31, 1892, and *New York Home Journal*, November 11, 1891, quoting the *New York Sun*, Scrapbook, 1887–1901, p. 73, MMW; *New-York Tribune*, November 8, 1891, p. 6.

21. E. H. Johnson to SW, August 29, 1892, Box 33:7, SW Papers.

22. SW to Homer Bradley, November 9, 1893, PB 33:4, SW Papers; Frederick P. Hill, *Charles F. McKim, the Man* (Francestown, N.H., 1950), pp. 27–28.

23. *New York Sun*, September 13, 1892; *Rochester Union and Advertiser*, n.d.; and *New York Recorder*, November 22, 1892, in Scrapbook, 1892–94, pp. 3 and 46, MMW. The first Diana was damaged in a fire that swept the exposition grounds in 1894; the upper part was later exhibited at the Chicago Art Institute.

24. When Madison Square Garden was razed in 1925, the second Diana was offered to New York University in anticipation that the Tower might be rebuilt on the Bronx Heights campus, which White had designed. Funds were not available, however, and the second Diana was installed permanently in the Philadelphia Museum of Art. Several small casts of it were made. PB LGW:127, 128, 156, SW Papers.

25. *Collected Stories of O. Henry* (New York, 1979), p. 504. The sitter for Diana was a prominent New York artists' model named Julia (Dudie) Baird. For the first Diana, Saint-Gaudens prepared an 18-inch figure, which was enlarged to 18 feet at the foundry. For the second Diana, Miss Baird was propped up on two ladders and plaster was applied directly to sections of her body. From the casts a 5-foot, 6-inch figure was made, which Saint-Gaudens enlarged to 13 feet. See *New York Herald*, November 21, 1897, 5th sec., p. 9, and December 5, 1897, p. 1.

26. *New York World*, May 10, 1893, and *Providence Journal*, June 9, 1893, Scrapbook, 1892–94, pp. 8 and 23, MMW. For the year ending April 30, 1903, the Garden made a profit of $54,500. Box 6:6, SW Papers. The Garden was put up for sale in 1908 and purchased by a real estate syndicate in 1911. The New York Life Insurance Company held a first mortgage, and when the syndicate went bankrupt in 1916, the insurance company took over the building. It was razed in 1925 to make way for the New York Life Insurance headquarters building.

27. Frank W. Langer to SW, October 13, 1894, Box 10:17, and Frank Sturgis to SW, n.d., Box 9:5, SW Papers.

28. *New York Evening Telegram,* April 30, 1892, and other miscellaneous clippings, Scrapbook, 1887–1901, pp. 175, 178, MMW.

29. *New York Morning Journal,* November 2 and 3, 1892, and *New York World,* April 15, 1894, Scrapbook, 1892–94, pp. 8 and 10, 261, MMW; Box 10:8, SW Papers.

30. Henry C. Brown, *Fifth Avenue Old and New, 1824–1924* (New York, 1924), pp. 70–71; Van Rensselaer, "Madison Square Garden," p. 746; Scrapbook, 1892–94, p. 8, MMW.

31. *New York Sun,* March 24, 1892, Scrapbook, 1887–1901, pp. 190–91, MMW; PB 5:170, 145, and Hermann Oelrichs to SW, March 19, 1892, Box 9:10, SW Papers; *Buffalo-Commercial,* August 8, 1896, Scrapbook, 1894–1904, p. 162, MMW.

32. PB 5:215, 272, 442, 499; PB 12:145; PB 21:370; Box 6:10, 20; Box 9:8; Box 29:9; and Box 38:7, SW Papers; Goldwin Goldsmith, "I Remember McKim, Mead and White," *AIA Journal,* 13 (April 1950): 170; Edward R. Hewitt, *Those Were The Days: Tales of a Long Life* (New York, 1943), pp. 229–34.

33. PB 23:124, PB 30:398, Box 15:5, Box 6:4, Box 14:2, and Box 22:10, all SW Papers; Evelyn Nesbit, *Prodigal Days: The Untold Story* (New York, 1934), pp. 33–34.

34. SW to J. A. Chanler, May 31, 1892, PB 5:451, SW Papers.

CHAPTER 12
"Municipal Commissioner of Public Beauty"

1. Gunther Barth, *City People* (New York, 1980), discusses communal factors bringing a sense of urban identification.

2. *New York Times,* April 28, 1889, p. 16, and July 19, 1896, p. 25; I. N. Phelps Stokes, *The Iconography of Manhattan Island* (New York, 1895–1928), vol. 5, p. 1999; PB 1:449, SW Papers.

3. Scrapbook, 1887–1901, p. 230, MMW; *American Architect and Building News,* 25 (May 18, 1889): 238.

4. PB 2:60, 134, 144, SW Papers; Washington Memorial Arch Committee Records, minutes, May 6, 1891, Scrapbook I, Mss. Coll, American Academy and Institute of Arts and Letters; see also Washington Memorial Arch materials, Old Mixed File 205, MMW.

5. *New York Times,* May 1, 1890, p. 8, and May 13, 1890, p. 9.

6. *New York Times,* May 31, 1890, p. 1.

7. PB 5:307, SW Papers; Washington Memorial Arch Committee Records, Scrapbook III and minutes, March 28, 1892, in Scrapbook I, Mss. Coll, American Academy and Institute of Arts and Letters.

8. Rosamond Gilder, ed., *The Letters of Richard Watson Gilder* (Boston, 1916), p. 189; *New York Times,* April 6, 1892, p. 10.

9. Washington Memorial Arch, Old Mixed File 205, folder 2, MMW; PB 8:469 and Box 33:13, SW Papers.

10. *New York Times,* May 5, 1895, p. 3. The large statues of Washington against the north faces of the arch piers were delayed for many years. Herman A. McNeil's statue of Washington as Commander-in-Chief was completed in 1916, and A. Stirling Calder's statue of Washington as President in 1918.

11. Charles C. Baldwin, *Stanford White* (New York, 1931), pp. 197–98.

12. Henry James, *The American Scene* (New York, 1907), p. 90; Misc., M-3, January 18, 1895, MMW.

13. "The Judson Memorial," *The Illustrated Christian Weekly,* 21 (February 21, 1891): 120–22; *Christian Union,* March 21, 1889, and *New York Daily News,* January 25, 1891, in Scrapbook, 1887–1901, pp. 153, 178, MMW.

14. In 1933, the Judson Hotel was acquired by New York University for student and faculty housing; it later became an undergraduate residence hall.

15. *New York World,* March 14, 1891, Scrapbook, 1887–1901, pp. 187–88, MMW; SW to Carrère & Hastings, November 23, 1899, PB 23:315, also PB 23:17, 154, 166, SW Papers.

16. Walter Hines Page to SW, October 25, 1892, Box 9:15; SW to Bobbie, January 28, 1904, PB 30:137; and SW to William Rideing, April 6, 1896, PB 15:417, all SW Papers.

17. PB 3:272; PB 4:291; PB 6:59, 103, 111, 142, all SW Papers.

18. PB 6:54, 81, 94, 141, SW Papers; *New York Times,* October 13, 1892, p. 1.

19. Scrapbook, 1892–94, pp. 55–59, 63, MMW; PB 6:191, SW Papers.

20. *Boston Home Journal,* October 8, 1892, Scrapbook, 1892–94, p. 66, MMW; Andy Logan, "That Was New York: Town Topics," *New Yorker,* 41 (August 14, 1965): 66.

21. SW to Robert Goelet, October 14, 1892, PB 6:227, and December 23, 1892, PB 7:40; SW to D. H. Burnham, October 14, 1892, PB 6:223; SW to John S. Sargent, November 14, 1892, PB 6:362; SW to A. D. Weekes, December 6, 1892, PB 6:438; PB 6:432, 453, all SW Papers.

22. Abbott Thayer to SW, December 28, 1892, Box 29:4; William J. Matheson to SW, November 23, 1892, Box 33:15; and Dr. T. S. Robertson to SW, n.d., Box 9:14–15, all SW Papers.

23. Gerald Langford, *The Richard Harding Davis Years* (New York, 1961), p. 137; Lawrence Grant White, oral history, pp. 12–13, Columbia University; SW to J. S. Kennedy, December 5, 1893, PB 8:319–20; SW to T. Dewing, June 3, 1893, PB 7:241.

24. SW to Mavrogeni Bey, November 17, 1893, PB 8:259–60; SW to Joseph Haik, November 29, 1893, PB 8:318, SW Papers.

25. Langford, *Davis Years,* p. 141; Hotel Victoria manager to SW, May 13, 1893, Box 29:3, SW Papers; CFM to W. S. Richardson, May 13, 1893, Box 1:2:116, McKim Papers, LC.

26. Box 1:2:116, McKim Papers, LC; Edward D. Adams to SW, March 28, 1893, SW, M-3, MMW.

27. *New York Press,* May 1, 1893, Scrapbook, 1892–94, p. 175, MMW.

28. Lawrence Grant White, oral history, p. 13, Columbia University; SW to McDonald and Charles Deering, June 10, 1893, PB 7:274; SW to Thomas Dewing, June 3, 1893, PB 7:241; PB 8:101, 389; PB 9:49, 71; PB 10:261, all SW Papers.

29. Governor W. T. Thornton to Grover Cleveland, May 23, 1893, Box 29:11; SW to Grover Cleveland, June 9, 1893, PB 7:255; SW to R. M. White, June 9, 19, 1893, PB 7:256–57, 312–13, 327; Box 29:12, all SW Papers.

30. SW to Russell Sturgis, May 12, 1897, PB 18:55; also PB 6:270, SW Papers.

CHAPTER 13
With Gus and Willie

1. Frames 454, 476, 492, 503, SW Coll; Reel 10:22, 27 and Reel 14:7, SG Papers.

2. M. G. Van Rensselaer, "Saint-Gaudens's Lincoln," *Century,* 35 (November 1887): 39. Leonard W. Volk had made the Lincoln cast in 1860. The two artists also collaborated on a nearby fountain in Lincoln Park and on a seated figure of Lincoln, cast in 1906 and unveiled in 1926 in Grant Park, Chicago, after Lawrence Grant White completed the architectural setting.

3. Homer Saint-Gaudens, ed., *The Reminiscences of Augustus Saint-Gaudens* (New York, 1913), vol. 1, pp. 353–54. The Springfield park was located in a deteriorating neighborhood, and in 1899, after acts of vandalism, *The Puritan* was removed to a new site close to the Springfield Public Library. A slightly altered version of this statue, known as *The Pilgrim,* was installed in 1905 in City Hall Plaza, Philadelphia. White's Battell Memorial Fountain (1899) in Norfolk, Connecticut, was also designed as an ensemble of a fountain court, and benches.

4. Ernest Samuels, *Henry Adams: The Middle Years* (Cambridge, Mass., 1958), pp. 298–99; SW to Henry Adams, January 9, August 9, and August 13, 1888, PB 1:91, 218, 228, SW Papers; Henry Adams, diary, September 30 and December 10, 1888, Adams Papers.

Reel 600, Mass. Hist. Soc. About this time, in 1887–88, Saint-Gaudens modeled a relief portrait of the writer Robert Louis Stevenson reclining on a couch, at work on a manuscript; SW provided frames for three versions of the Stevenson relief, and the third and largest was unveiled in June 1904 as a memorial to Stevenson in the Church of St. Giles, Edinburgh.

5. SW to Henry Adams, May 31 and October 26, 1889, PB 2:114–15, 245, SW Papers; John Flanagan to Richard Watson Gilder [March 1908], Gilder Papers, NYPL.

6. Henry Adams to R. W. Gilder, October 14, 1896, Reel 1:28, SG Papers; ASG to John A. Braeman, March 4, 1900, SG Papers, LC. SG's 1874 figure *Silence* also presaged the Adams Memorial figure.

7. Henry Adams to Elizabeth Cameron, February 6, 1891, and Henry Adams to John Hay, June 21, 1891, in J. C. Levenson, ed., *The Letters of Henry Adams*, vol. 3 (Cambridge, Mass., 1982), pp. 406, 494; Henry Adams, *The Education of Henry Adams* (New York, 1918), p. 329.

8. Frames 505–6, SW Coll; Box 9:5, SW Papers.

9. Burke Wilkinson, *Uncommon Clay: The Life and Works of Augustus Saint-Gaudens* (New York, 1985), pp. 140, 219–20; Box 36:11, SW Papers.

10. SW to Col. Higginson, March 9, 1896, PB 15:298, and SW to ASG, December 4, 1895, PB 14:432–33, SW Papers.

11. SW to Judge R. S. Tuthill, May 31, 1895, PB 13:416, and, on Logan as a private work, MMW to C. G. Blake, June 9, 1897, PB 18:269, SW Papers.

12. Reel 13:925, SG Papers; PB 16:420, SW Papers; Homer Saint-Gaudens, ed., *Reminiscences,* vol. 2, p. 109.

13. CFM to SW, December 27, 1893, McKim Papers, LC; SW to ASG, May 22, 1894, February 18 and May 27, 1895, and April 24, 1896, PB 9:483, PB 12:390, PB 13:372–73, and PB 16:8, and SW to F. W. MacMonnies, May 28, 1895, PB 13:386, SW Papers.

4. ASG to Col. Higginson, August 13, 1904, Reel 2:216, SG Papers. William Kendall of McKim, Mead & White did the final work on the architectural setting.

5. SW to ASG, February 24, 1900, PB 24:89; SW to T. Dewing, February 26, 1900, PB 24:76; and SW to F. J. Hecker, September 24, 1900, PB 24:371, all SW Papers; *Town Topics,* 43 (April 12, 1900): 9; Frank J. Hecker to SW, July 18, 1900, 2073:818–19, Saarinen Papers.

6. Lockman Papers, Reel 2, two interviews, Ms. Div., NYHS; Edward

J. Foote, "An Interview with Frederick W. MacMonnies, American Sculptor of the Beaux-Arts Era," *New-York Historical Society Quarterly,* 41 (July–October 1977): 102–23.

17. SW to W. G. Hamilton, October 13, 1889, PB 2:223, SW Papers.

18. *Leslie's Weekly,* June 3, 1897, Scrapbook, 1894–1904, p. 167, MMW; SW to ASG, November 6, 1890, PB 3:356, and SW to George F. Babb, November 21, 1890, PB 3:376–77, SW Papers.

19. F. W. MacMonnies to SW, January 6, 1892, and n.d., Misc., M-7, MMW.

20. MacMonnies interview, Lockman Papers, Reel 2, Ms. Div., NYHS; SW to F. W. MacMonnies, October 9, 1894, PB 11:199; Annual Report of the Superintendent, USMA, p. 7, 1897, Archives USMA. In 1903 the statue turned in a high wind and had to be secured; in 1972 the granite sphere cracked and was replaced.

21. Wilkinson, *Uncommon Clay,* p. 244.

22. F. W. MacMonnies to SW, n.d., Box 33:12, and SW to F. W. MacMonnies, May 28 and November 16, 1895, PB 13:386 and 14:307, SW Papers; SW to Frank Squier, May 25, 1895, Squier Papers, NYHS.

23. CFM to F. W. MacMonnies, October 27, 1897, MacMonnies, M-9, MMW; SW to F. W. MacMonnies, March 6, 1896, PB 15:279–80.

24. PB 26:223, SW Papers.

CHAPTER 14

160 Fifth Avenue

1. J. S. Kennedy to MMW, December 4, 1893, M-3, Misc., MMW; PB 10:341 and Box 10:2, SW Papers; Egerton Swartwout, "An Architectural Decade," unpublished ms., p. 72, Office of Cain, Ferrell, & Bell.

2. C. H. Reilly, "The Modern Renaissance in American Architecture," *Journal of the Royal Institute of British Architects,* 17 (June 25, 1910): 634; Swartwout, "Architectural Decade," pp. 74–77; Leland M. Roth, *McKim, Mead & White, Architects* (New York, 1983), p. 5.

3. Office petition, n.d., Prints and Drawings Coll, Avery Library, Columbia University; Reilly, "Modern Renaissance," 634; Box 32:1, SW Papers; CFM to WRM, July 6, 1894, McKim Papers, LC.

4. 2073:471, Saarinen Papers; SW to U. N. Bethell, April 13, 1901, PB 25:308, and Kennedy & Marks to SW, June 27, 1904, Box 41:3, SW Papers; Swartwout, "Architectural Decade," p. 111.

5. H. Van Buren Magonigle, "A Half-Century of Architecture," *Pencil Points,* 15 (March 1934): 118.

6. CFM to SW, September 18, 1902, Box 21:4, SW Papers.

7. Memorandum, January 28, 1903, Box 7:18; SW to T. D. Wadelton, February 9, 1903, PB 28:82; SW to H. O. Watson, March 1, 1906, PB 34:269, all SW Papers.

8. Goldwin Goldsmith, "I Remember McKim, Mead & White," *Journal of the American Institute of Architects,* 12 (April 1950): 169–70; C. A. Johnson to SW, January 31 and March 5, 1900, Box 36:1, SW Papers. Charles Moore, *The Life and Times of Charles Follen McKim* (Boston, 1929), p. 330, placed Goldsmith at the Twentieth Street office in July 1891.

9. Box 47:8, SW Papers; *New York Times,* July 7, 1906, p. 2; 2073:470–71, Saarinen Papers.

10. D. Everett Waid, "The Business Side of an Architect's Office: The Office of Messrs. McKim, Mead & White," *Brickbuilder,* 22 (December 1913); 267–70; Swartwout, "Architectural Decade," p. 115; WRM to SW, February 16, 1905, Box 41:11, SW Papers.

11. Swartwout, "Architectural Decade," p. 113.

12. *Ibid.,* pp. 119–20; WRM to CFM, December 19, 1887, McKim-Maloney Papers, NYPL; CFM to L. Dunham, February 29 and March 2, 1892, McKim Papers, LC.

13. Philip Sawyer, "Stanford White as Those Trained in his Office Knew Him," *Brickbuilder,* 15 (December 1906): 247; PB 15:426, PB 12:175, and PB 35:274, SW Papers.

14. Magonigle, "Half-Century," 117; Swartwout, "Architectural Decade," pp. 111–12; Reel 3:815, D. M. Lockman Papers, Ms. Div., NYHS.

15. P. Whitney 508, IV, MMW; quoted in 2072:1056, Saarinen Papers.

16. SW to C. T. Barney, M-15, Arch. Educ., MMW; PB 8:228 and PB 11:288, SW Papers.

17. Frederick Platt, *America's Gilded Age: Its Architecture and Decoration* (Cranbury, N.J., 1976), p. 228; Lionel Moses to WRM, January 16, 1899, Box 38:8, SW Papers.

18. Box 10:448, 270, PB 15:331, and Christina Darrow to SW, September 4, 1903, with note by WRM, Box 37:8, SW Papers; Moore, *McKim,* pp. 329–30.

19. Bernardo Guadagni to SW, December 27, 1904, Box 22:14, SW Papers; 2073:474–75, Saarinen Papers; Swartwout, "Architectural Decade," p. 126.

20. Frederick P. Hill, *Charles F. McKim, the Man* (Francistown, N.H., 1950), pp. 28–29; Philip Sawyer file, photographs, Prints and Drawings Coll, Avery Library, Columbia University.

21. SW to ASG, September 27, 1894, PB 10:356, and SW to T. W.

Dewing, October 9, 1894, Box 10:406, SW Papers; Swartwout, "Architectural Decade," pp. 113–14.

22. PB 5:306, SW Papers.

23. Reel 3:817, D. M. Lockman Papers; Swartwout, "Architectural Decade," pp. 80–88; MMW to Thomas Hastings, November 11, 1897, 2073:738, Saarinen Papers; SW to ASG, December 6, 1897, Reel 10:19–20, SG Papers.

24. SW to D. H. Burnham, May 13, 1905, PB 33:158, SW Papers.

25. MMW to Joseph Pulitzer, April 27, 1901, Pulitzer, M-15, MMW; Leland M. Roth, *The Architecture of McKim, Mead & White, 1870–1910: A Building List* (New York, 1978), p. 178; MMW Journals, 1888–94 and 1894–1901, MMW.

26. Lionel Moses, "McKim, Mead and White: A History," *American Architect*, 121 (May 24, 1922): 414; William T. Partridge, "Recollections Concerning Charles Follen McKim and Stanford White," ms., Ware Coll, Avery Library, Columbia University; PB 31:385, SW Papers.

CHAPTER 15
"The Finest and Most Harmonious Effect"

1. SW, "Work in Progress," May 28, 1894, Misc., M-3, MMW.

2. S. G. W. Benjamin, "Steam Yachting in America," *Century*, 24 (August 1882): 603, 607.

3. Scrapbook, 1887–1901, p. 169, MMW; PB 4:65, 161, SW Papers.

4. Quoted in Charles Baldwin, *Stanford White* (New York, 1931), p. 219 f.; telegram, SW to "Larkspur" (Paris), Herald, M-20, MMW.

5. *New York Herald*, August 4, 1892, Scrapbook, 1892–94, p. 92, MMW.

6. The statuary was the work of Antonin Jean Carles of Paris.

7. *Scientific American*, May 4, 1895, and *Commercial Gazette*, May 28, 1893, Scrapbook, 1892–94, pp. 320, 88, MMW; CFM to W. R. Richards, May 13, 1893, McKim Papers, LC; Richard O'Connor, *Courtroom Warrior* (Boston, 1963), p. 182. In 1928 the north portion of the Herald Building was razed for a skyscraper. The remaining south half was demolished in 1940 for another structure. The bell figures were donated to New York University and re-erected in Herald Square, directly across Broadway from Macy's department store.

8. Minutes, Plans and Building Committee, 1892, Archives, Bowery Savings Bank.

9. "Description of the New Bowery Savings Bank Building," February 7, 1893, pp. 1, 4, Archives, Bowery Savings Bank.

10. Scrapbook, 1892–94, p. 100, MMW.

11. SW to George E. Waring, August 22, 1893, PB 8:2; PB 8:189, SW Papers; CFM to Wendell Garrison, November 24, 1893, McKim–Maloney Papers, NYPL; CFM to Montgomery Pickett, September 28, 1893, McKim Papers, LC.

12. Henry M. MacCracken to SW, January 22, 1892, NYU, 129, MMW.

13. SW to H. M. MacCracken, January 25, 1892, and H. M. MacCracken to SW, September 2, 1892, NYU, 129, also White, Misc. M-3, MMW; 22:2,4, MacCracken Papers, Archives, NYU.

14. NYU, 129, MMW; H. M. MacCracken to SW, September 3, 1896, NYU Library, Misc. M-10, MMW; H. M. MacCracken to MMW, October 17, 1901, Old Mixed File, 246, MMW.

15. H. M. MacCracken to SW, July 24 and October 24, 1896, NYU Library, Misc. M-10, MMW.

16. SW to H. M. MacCracken, April 1, 1897, 24:2, MacCracken Papers, Archives, NYU; H. M. MacCracken to MMW, October 17, 1901, Old Mixed File, 246, MMW.

17. Montgomery Schuyler, "The Architecture of American Colleges, IV," *Architectural Record,* 27 (June 1910): 456–57.

18. SW to H. M. MacCracken, January 11, 1898, 24:3, MacCracken Papers, Archives, NYU; quoted in Andrew S. Dolkart, "Gould Memorial Library," Landmarks Preservation Commission, Designation List 146-LP1087 (August 11, 1981), p. 10.

19. SW to Prof. Lieut. Col. E. W. Bass, March 14, 1892, PB 5:223, SW Papers; Superintendent's Letter Book (SLB), 9:108, Archives, USMA.

20. Stanley P. Tozeski, "Records Relating to Cullum Memorial Hall," 1974, and SLB, 9:270, Archives, USMA.

21. CFM to SW, June 28, 1894, and CFM to WRM, July 6, 1894, McKim Papers, LC; SLB, 9:270, 361–62, Archives, USMA.

22. C. W. Larned to SW, March 27, 1900, and C. W. Larned to WRM, May 26, 1899, Cullum Memorial, C-200 (3,4), MMW.

23. SLB, 11:343–44, Archives, USMA; West Point, Old Mixed File, 548, MMW; SW to D. H. Burnham, May 8, 1903, Charles Moore Papers, LC.

24. MMW to Col. A. L. Mills, May 14, 1903, West Point, Old Mixed File, 544, MMW; SW to D. H. Burnham, November 24, 1902, and May 8, 1903, Charles Moore Papers, LC.

25. SW to D. H. Burnham, September 23, 1903, PB 29:262, SW Papers.

26. Scrapbook, 1894–1904, p. 235, MMW. SW also worked with Sherry on a restaurant for the Narragansett Pier Casino and for a projected hotel-restaurant in London.

27. George Humphrey Yetter, "Stanford White at the University of Virginia: The New Buildings on the South Lawn and the Reconstruction of the Rotunda in 1896," unpublished M.A. thesis, 1980, School of Architecture, University of Virginia, pp. 10, 14, and *passim*. See also *idem*, "Stanford White at the University of Virginia: Some New Light on an Old Question," *Journal of the Society of Architectural Historians*, 40 (December 1981): 320–25.

28. Yetter, "New Buildings," pp. 16–19.

29. *Ibid.*, pp. 24, 65–66; University of Virginia, V-172 (I, III), and Misc., M-4, MMW.

30. University of Virginia, V-171 (II), MMW.

31. Edward Simmons, *From Seven to Seventy* (New York, 1922), p. 241.

32. SW to Ethelred, March 19, 1896, PB 15:334, SW Papers; Yetter, "New Buildings," pp. 67–68.

33. SW to J. M. Page, October 22, 1903, PB 29:383, SW Papers.

34. SW to R. M. White, October 28, 29, 1896, PB 17:38, 44, and July 28, 1897, PB 18:367–68, SW Papers.

35. R. M. White to SW, Misc. letters, University of Virginia, V-172 (IV), MMW; Box 34:18, PB 18:367–68, PB 19:380, and PB 20:377, SW Papers.

36. W. J. Thornton to SW, May 2, 1906, University of Virginia, V-172 (I), and SW to E. A. Alderman, May 31, 1906, University of Virginia, Misc., M-4, MMW.

37. Stanford White, "The Buildings of the University of Virginia," *Corks and Curls*, 2 (1898): 127–30. In a program of reconstruction, 1972–85, the interior of the Rotunda was returned to its condition before the fire of 1895.

38. White was also involved in industrial village design for the Niagara Power Company at Echota, near Niagara Falls, N.Y., where he supervised the creation of a powerhouse, offices, an assembly hall, and workers' houses, and, on a smaller scale, at Roanoke Rapids, N.C., where for the Roanoke Rapids Power Company he designed a spinning mill, a small church, and workers' houses. See Leland Roth, "Three Industrial Towns, By McKim, Mead & White," *Journal of the Society of Architectural Historians*, 38 (December 1979): 317–47.

39. For SW's "philosophy" of architecture in this and the following paragraph, see PB 13:372–73; PB 18:297; PB 15:337 and 431, SW Papers.

40. See references in note 39 and H. Van Buren Magonigle, "A Half-Century of Architecture," *Pencil Points*, 15 (January 1934): 12.

CHAPTER 16

The Business of Art

1. Edith Wharton, *A Backward Glance* (New York, 1939), p. 149; September 23, 1890, Frames 228–29, SW Coll.

2. Glenn Brown, *Memories 1860–1930* (Washington, D.C., 1931), p. 29.

3. Architectural League of New York, *Proceedings* (New York, 1889), p. 6.

4. PB 2:128, 407, 429, 452, 453, 472; PB 3:13; PB 12:458; Box 12:13; Box 13:11; Box 16:14; Box 31:7, 9; Box 39:5, SW Papers.

5. PB 3:433; PB 4:461; PB 5:52; Box 1:2; Box 29:14, SW Papers; SW to E. Vedder, December 18, 1891, 2323:226, Vedder Papers, AAA.

6. PB 4:7, 8, SW Papers.

7. *New York World*, June 1, 1893, Scrapbook, 1892–94, p. 139, MMW; Wayne Craven, *Sculpture in America* (New York, 1968), pp. 478–79.

8. Clippings, May 18, 1892, Scrapbook, 1887–1901, p. 200, MMW.

9. PB 9:9; PB 10:4, 10, 458; and Box 39:2, 5, SW Papers.

10. Gordon S. Parker, "The Work of Three Great Architects," *World's Work,* 12 (October 1906): 8058; Lawrence Grant White, *Sketches and Designs by Stanford White* (New York, 1920), pp. 24–25.

11. SW to Mrs. J. J. Astor, December 26, 1899, PB 23:405–10; SW to Mrs. Potter Palmer, April 21, 1903, PB 28:361–62; and PB 21:24 and PB 22:41, 42, SW Papers.

12. PB 28:361, SW Papers. See Box 5, SW Papers, for extensive Acton correspondence.

13. See Wesley Towner, *The Elegant Auctioneers* (London, 1971). In 1923 the Kirby gallery would become the Parke-Bernet Gallery.

14. Box 49:8, SW Papers.

15. Twombly, Misc., M-15, MMW.

16. Box 35:9, 12, SW Papers.

17. L. G. White, *Sketches and Designs* p. 24. SW to Henry Prellwitz, January 12, 1897, PB 17:256; SW to Robert Chanler, March 11, 1903, PB 28:199; SW to C. C. Coleman, October 23, 1889, PB 2:234, SW Papers.

18. See Channing Blake, "Stanford White's New York Interiors," *Antiques,* 102 (December 1972): 1060–67; J. Monroe Hewlett, "Stanford White, Decorator," *Good Furniture,* 9 (September 1917): 160–79; Susan J. H. Harris, "McKim, Mead and White's Domestic Interiors, 1890–1909: A Catalogue of Decorative Treatment," un-

published M.S. thesis, Historic Pres., Avery Library, Columbia University, 1981. See also Edith Wharton and Ogden Codman, Jr., *The Decoration of Houses* (New York, 1897), expounding principles of interior design generally like those White was simultaneously putting into practice.

19. Sadakichi Hartmann to SW, December 9, 1903, Box 37:15, SW Papers; Chicago *Times*, February 1, 1895, Scrapbook, 1894–1904, p. 148, MMW.

20. Childe Hassam to SW, September 21, 1904, Box 14:1, and SW to Alexander G. Cabus, September 28, 1894, PB 10:360, SW Papers.

21. SW to Walter Rowlands, March 28, 1898, Rowlands Papers, LC; William Ellsworth, *A Golden Age of Authors* (New York, 1919), pp. 158, 162; Frames 87, 88, 228, and 324, SW Coll; Box 45:4, 5; Box 39:1; Box 22:8, 9; PB 2:23, 24; PB 15:244, SW Papers.

22. Box 13:10; PB 26:223, 52, 150; PB 33:196; PB 23:299, SW Papers.

23. SW to H. P. Whitney, December 10, 1890, PB 24:35; SW to D. C. French, December 13, 1900, PB 25:49; Gertrude Vanderbilt Whitney to SW, n.d., Box 36:18, SW Papers.

24. Julia Brewster to SW, April 14, May 27, 31, 1906, Box 35:2; SW to Sadakichi Hartmann, July 15, 1897, PB 18:324; SW to Alfred Brennan, August 26, 1901, PB 26:26, SW Papers.

25. E. A. Abbey to SW [1895], Box 39:1, and Lloyd Warren to SW, February 14, 1902, Box 21:22, SW Papers; C. A. Platt to SW, August 21, 1890, Avery Library Misc. Coll.

26. PB 3:420, 427, 248, and PB 4:20, SW Papers.

27. Edward Simmons, *From Seven to Seventy* (New York, 1922), pp. 250–51, 239; also in Charles Baldwin, *Stanford White* (New York, 1931), pp. 278, 273.

28. Box 21:3, SW Papers; Janet Scudder, *Modeling My Life* (New York, 1925), pp. 186–88; Baldwin, *White*, pp. 180–81.

29. Scudder, *Modeling*, pp. 196–97; Baldwin, *White*, pp. 282–83.

30. SW to H. W. Poor, December 10, 1901, PB 26:190; SW to J. P. Morgan, February 5, 1903, PB 28:60–61; and SW to Dowdeswell, March 26, 1903, PB 28:253, SW Papers.

31. PB 12:124, 142; PB 14:489; PB 19:335, 336; PB 20:494, SW Papers.

32. SW to S. P. Avery, November 21, 1892, PB 6:350; SW to H. S. Mowbray, January 4, 1893, PB 7:135; SW to F. D. Millett, January 24, 1894, PB 8:497; SW to H. Bolton, December 16, 1892, PB 6:481–82, SW Papers.

33. Annie A. Beebe to SW, Nov. 20, December 13, 1894, and January 30, 1895, Box 39:4, 5; SW to A. A. Beebe, November 22 and December 27, 1894, PB 12:71, 181; SW to ASG, March 2, 1898,

PB 19:348; SW to Henry Prellwitz, May 11, 1906, PB: 35:140; SW to E. A. Abbey, August 15, 1904, PB 31:298, SW Papers.

CHAPTER 17
The Social Whirl

1. SW, "Work in Progress," May 28, 1894, Misc., M-3, MMW; CFM to SW, June 28, 1894, McKim Papers, LC; SW to W. E. Stewart, December 11, 1894, Old Mixed File, 205, MMW; SW to Devereux Emmet, January 4, 1895, PB 12:201, SW Papers.

2. Lillian Nordica to SW, January 14 [1895], Box 30:11; Edmund Stanton to SW, November 18 and 24, 1890, Box 9:5; Box 10:16; Box 22:4; Box 33:13; PB 8:183; PB 12:41; and PB 30:29, all SW Papers.

3. "Vaudeville Club," *Harper's Weekly,* 36 (December 1892): 1243; PB 6:173; PB 7:30, 33, 41; PB 8:168B, 168D, 169, 447, 453, 460, 490, 497; PB 9:143; PB 12:380, 392, SW Papers.

4. SW to D. Emmet, January 4, 1895, PB 12:201; Gerald Langford, *The Richard Harding Davis Years* (New York, 1961), p. 167.

5. Box 30:4 and PB 13:59, SW Papers; Frame 364, SW Coll.; CFM to G. v. L. Meyer, April 24, 1895, McKim Papers, LC.

6. SW to C. D. Gibson, May 13, 1895, PB 13:284; H. W. Poor to SW [May 19, 1895], Box 30:15; see also Edward Simmons, *From Seven to Seventy* (New York, 1922), pp. 247–48, excerpted in Charles Baldwin, *Stanford White* (New York, 1931), pp. 277–78.

7. *New York World,* October 13, 1895, p. 29; C. B. Macdonald to SW, October 9, 1895, Box 30:7, SW Papers; *New York Evening Journal,* July 2, 1906, p. 2; Allen Churchill, *Park Row* (New York, 1958), p. 73. James Gibbons Huneker, *Painted Veils* (New York, 1928), describes the Pie Girl Dinner, pp. 147–54.

8. Box 39:7 and PB 13:332, SW Papers; SW to Frank Squier, July 31 [1895], Squier Papers, NYHS.

9. PB 13:385, SW Papers; SW to Mrs. Hewitt, November 21, 1905, PB 33:485, SW papers.

10. SW to J. M. Whistler, September 20, 1895, PB 14:54; SW to R. M. White, October 5, 1895, PB 14:105; also PB 14:4, 30, and Box 30:7, all SW Papers.

11. SW to BW, November 26, 1895, PB 14:385, 397, SW Papers.

12. PB 16:14; PB 21:20; PB 32:233, SW Papers.

13. PB 15:253, SW Papers; *New York Sun,* February 5, 1897, Scrapbook, 1894–1904, p. 166, MMW; Langford, *Davis,* p. 185.

14. *Vanity Fair,* April 11, 1896, White, Misc., M-3, MMW; PB 14:216;

PB 15:7, 9, 253, 379; PB 21:19, 37; PB 23:12; PB 25:359; PB 27:77, 83; Box 6:1; Box 10:10, all SW Papers.

15. PB 15:469; PB 16:141; PB 17:23, 24, 26, SW Papers.

16. SW to C. D. Gibson, August 8, 12, 1896, PB 16:316, 327, SW Papers.

17. SW to James Breese, November 2, 1896, PB 17:53, 55, 56; SW to J. A. Chanler, September 24, 1896, PB 16:430–40, SW Papers.

18. Lately Thomas, *A Pride of Lions* (New York, 1971), pp. 195–96.

19. *Ibid., passim.*

20. *Ibid.*, pp. 191 ff.; PB 18:181 and PB 27:299, SW Papers; Reel 4:168 and Reel 145:82, SG Papers.

21. Thomas, *Pride,* pp. 274–75; Book of Deeds, 297:485, August 22, 1898, Dutchess County Clerk's Office, Poughkeepsie, N.Y.; PB 22:210; PB 28:237; PB 32:177–78; PB 33:173, 174, 300; PB 37:9; Box 24:10, 11; Box 42:6, all SW Papers; *New York Times,* June 13, 1899, p. 12; December 5, 1900, p. 2; August 17, 1904, p. 1; September 21, 1905, p. 5; October 30, 1906, p. 6; October 16, 1908, p. 12; and October 17, 1908, p. 9.

22. CFM to Charles Hitchcock, July 19, 1897, McKim Papers, LC.; Leland M. Roth, *The Architecture of McKim, Mead & White, 1870–1920: A Building List* (New York, 1978), p. 178.

23. PB 18:396, 424–27, SW Papers. Commission income was $180,289 in 1897 and $397,342 in 1898, the highest firm income until 1906, when it reached $399,572. See "Cost of Drawings, Commissions, 1880–1919," Walker Cain Bequest, Avery Library, Columbia University.

CHAPTER 18
"In a Hole All the Time"

1. Edward Simmons, *From Seven to Seventy* (New York, 1922), p. 237.

2. Box 19:2, SW Papers.

3. PB 19:31, 32, 35, 60; PB 24:16; Box 13:13; Box 34:1, SW Papers.

4. PB 14:330; PB 19:307, 412; PB 20:19–20; PB 23:40, 406–7, SW Papers; Frames 121, 135, SW Coll.

5. PB 19:501, 505; PB 20:3, 90, 157, 302, SW Papers; CFM to E. A. Darling, May 24, 1898, McKim Papers, LC.

6. Box 10:13; Box 34:18; Box 12:21; PB 13:408, 439; PB 14:63; and PB 17:325, SW Papers; Journal, 1894–1901, MMW.

7. PB 17:325; PB 19:444; PB 20:21; PB 21:57, 63, 65, 67, 209, 252; Box 34:18, SW Papers.

8. PB 22:8, 98, 258, 392; PB 23:202; Box 12:5, 11, 15, SW Papers.

9. PB 23:38, 269; PB 25:88; Box 40:12, SW Papers.

10. PB 24:91; PB 23:78, 202, 262, 269, 379, 383; PB 38:7; Box 36:10, SW Papers.

11. PB 13:428; PB 17:457, SW Papers.

12. *Commercial Advertiser*, February 25, 1898, 2072:990, 2073:202, Saarinen Papers; PB 19:385, 399, SW Papers.

13. PB 20:3, 129, 326, 378, 429; PB 22:306, 418; PB 28:117, 417; Box 20:14; Box 37:9, SW Papers.

14. PB 21:98, 145, SW Papers.

15. PB 21:147, 175, 286; PB 22:394–95; Box 13:1; PB 24:324, SW Papers.

16. PB 22:395 and "Inventory," Box 18:15, SW Papers; Survey of E. 21st. St., 35:1.95, Prints and Drawings Coll, Avery Library, Columbia University.

17. For this and the following paragraph, see Plan, 35.1.149, Prints and Drawings Coll, Avery Library; "Inventory," Box 18:15, SW Papers; and Lawrence Grant White, *Sketches and Designs by Stanford White* (New York, 1920), p. 25.

18. Box 46:5, 7, 10, 14, 15, 19; Box 42:4, SW Papers.

19. Box Hill, Drawer 34:131, 396; Drawer 35:200, 204, Prints and Drawings Coll, Avery Library; F. W. Kelsey to SW, April 22, 1903, Box 20:3; also Box 15:3; Box 18:15; and PB 26:117, SW Papers.

20. Barr Ferree, *American Estates and Gardens* (New York, 1904), pp. 141–46.

21. PB 28:292–94, 330, 349; Box 7:13, SW Papers.

22. Bessie White, Scrapbooks, in the possession of Cynthia Jay.

23. Lawrence Grant White, oral history, p. 10, Columbia University; AW to SW, October 11 and August 9, 1899, Box 38:22, SW Papers.

24. SW to Charles Deering, October 8, 1900, PB 24:410; PB 24:310, 321, and 328, SW Papers; Lawrence G. White, Sketchbook, in the possession of Cynthia Jay.

25. CFM to WRM, July 2, 1900, McKim Papers, LC; CFM to SW, July 30, 1900, Saint-Gaudens, Misc., M-11, MMW; CFM to Glenn Brown, July 31, 1900, Archives, AIA.

26. SW to E. O. Wolcott, September 24, 1900, PB 24:375; SW to ASG, October 25, 1900, PB 24:447; also PB 24:361, 363, 366; PB:25:30, 60, 483, SW Papers; Charles Coleman to SW, August 30, 1900, Frames 154–56, SW Coll.

27. SW to E. O. Wolcott, September 24, 1900, PB 24:375, and SW to ASG, October 25, 1900, PB 24:447, SW Papers.

28. PB 22:444; PB 23:345; PB 24:252, SW Papers.

29. SW to W. A. Chanler, October 3, 1900, PB 24:403, SW Papers.
30. PB 29:61; PB 25:378, 425–26, 344; Box 40:9, SW Papers.

CHAPTER 19
"Bachelors for the Evening"

1. R. L. Patterson to SW, September 14, 1904, Box 14:19; SW to
   C. B. Macdonald, September 14, 1894, PB 10:307; PB 10:366,
   369, 370; PB 6:276–78, 300, SW Papers.

2. Patricia J. Pierce, *The Ten* (Concord, N.H., 1976), pp. 77, 70,
   81; T. Dewing to C. Freer, August 28, 1894, Reel 77, Freer Papers,
   AAA; PB 2:90 and PB 12:350, 420–21, SW Papers.

3. Frames 299–300, SW Coll; SW to T. Dewing, February 5, 1895,
   PB 12:350; F. MacMonnies to SW [1895], Box 30:8; T. W. Dewing
   to SW, September 16 [1895], Box 39:9; SW to C. Freer, March
   5, 1900, PB 24:108, SW Papers; T. Dewing to C. Freer, July 22,
   1898, Reel 77, Freer Papers, AAA.

4. J. M. Wells to C. Gilbert, December 12, 1886, Cass Gilbert Papers,
   LC; Cass Gilbert to SW, February 11, 1890, frames 335–36, SW
   Coll; Royal Cortissoz, "The Artistic Genius and Lovable Traits of
   Stanford White," *New-York Tribune*, November 7, 1920, sec. VII,
   p. 2; ASG to J. M. Wells, n.d., Frame 508, SW Coll.

5. T. Hastings to ASG, November 15, 1905, Reel 11:82, SG Papers;
   T. Hastings to J. H. Hyde, May 23, 1906, Hyde Papers, NYHS;
   T. Hastings to SW, February 13, n.y., frame 344, SW Coll; T.
   Hastings to SW, January 18 and 23, 1900, Box 42:13; February
   23, 1898, Box 13:20; August 14, 1893, Box 33:5; and October 8,
   1903, Box 37:13, SW Papers.

6. David Gray, *Thomas Hastings, Architect* (Boston, 1933); anon.,
   "The Work of Messrs. Carrère and Hastings," *Architectural Record,*
   vol. 27, January 1910.

7. Gray, *Hastings*, pp. 4, 5, 9, *passim*; H. Van Buren Magonigle,
   "A Half-Century of Architecture—A Biographical Review," *Pencil
   Points,* 15 (November 1934): 564.

8. *Town Topics,* 43 (March 22, 1900): 1; 43 (May 3, 1900): 4; and
   43 (May 10, 1900): 4–5; PB 24:193, PB 42:13, SW Papers; Curtis
   Channing Blake, "The Architecture of Carrère and Hastings," unpublished Ph.D. dissertation, Columbia University, 1976, vol. 1,
   p. 19, *passim*.

9. Charlotte Warren to SW [1895], Box 31:9 and [1900], Box 36:17;
   Whitney Warren to SW [1895], Box 31:10, 11; also Box 38:23
   and Box 36:18; SW to G. von L. Meyer, July 25, 1899, PB 23:105,
   SW Papers; Lawrence Grant White, oral history, p. 110, Columbia
   University.

10. Helen M. Tomlinson, "Charles Lang Freer, Pioneer Collector of Oriental Art," unpublished Ph.D. dissertation, Case Western Reserve University, 1979, pp. ix, 94, 200; Meryle Secrest, *Between Me and Life: Biography of Romaine Brooks* (Garden City, N.Y., 1979), p. 131; *New York Times,* September 26, 1919, p. 13; Keith N. Morgan, "The Patronage Mix: Charles A. Platt, Architect, and Charles L. Freer, Client," *Winterthur Portfolio,* 17 (1982): 128–29.

11. Box 40:13, SW Papers; C. Freer to ASG, February 26, 1906, Reel 7:71, SG Papers.

12. SW to The Players, March 1, 1894, PB 9:100, and SW to Nicola Tesla, March 2, 1895, PB 12:436, SW Papers; Lawrence Grant White, oral history, pp. 35–36, Columbia University; Margaret Cheney, *Tesla: Man Out of Time* (Englewood Cliffs, N.J., 1981), pp. 84–86.

13. *Town Topics,* 43 (January 11, 1900): p. 4; J. Breese to SW, September 11, 1895, Box 39:3; SW to J. Breese, May 13, 1895, PB 13:282, and August 20, 1894, PB 10:229; also Box 13:8, Box 42:3, PB 9:279, PB 12:335, PB 17:307, PB 19:125, PB 13:301, SW Papers.

14. Frames 459–60 and 505–6, SW Coll; SW to ASG, July 15, 1904, PB 31:233, SW Papers.

15. 2073:207, Saarinen Papers; T. W. Dewing to SW, February 14 [1895], Box 39:9, SW Papers.

16. Arthur Weekes to SW, July 18 and August 10, 1892, Box 29:9; Henry Poor to SW, March 5, 1894, Box 10:24; also Box 8:13; Box 42: 3, 4, 7; Box 34:14; Box 30:8, 10; Box 42:3, 4, 7; PB 13:477; and PB 4:152, SW Papers.

17. Box 39:7 and Box 12:6; SW to Charles Deering, July 7, 1897, PB 18:292; SW to C. B. Macdonald, September 14, 1894, PB 10:307, SW Papers.

18. Ruth St. Denis, *An Unfinished Life: 'An Autobiography'* (New York, 1939), pp. 23, 24; *New York Times,* February 10, 1895, p. 23, and February 12, 1895, p. 2.

19. St. Denis, *Unfinished Life,* p. 24; PB 13:151, 166, 273, and Box 39:9, 10, SW Papers.

20. St. Denis, *Unfinished Life,* p. 25; Box 39:10, SW Papers.

21. St. Denis, *Unfinished Life,* p. 28; PB 10:345, SW Papers.

22. St. Denis, *Unfinished Life,* pp. 38, 39; Journals, 1900–1928, Box 1, Ruth St. Denis Coll, UCLA Res. Library, Special Coll; Suzanne Shelton, *Divine Dancer: A Biography of Ruth St. Denis,* (New York, 1981), pp. 39, 48.

23. St. Denis, *Unfinished Life,* p. 34; Shelton, *Divine Dancer,* p. 58; PB 35:139, SW Papers.

24. St. Denis, *Unfinished Life*, p. 24; 2073:207, Saarinen Papers.

25. PB 30:129, SW Papers; quoted in Burke Wilkinson, *Uncommon Clay: The Life and Works of Augustus Saint Gaudens* (New York, 1985), p. 219.

26. Allen Churchill, *Park Row* (New York, 1958), p. 217; T. Dewing to C. Freer, n.d., reel 77, Freer Papers, AAA.

27. Frame 332, SW Coll; Lois Banner, *American Beauty* (New York, 1982), p. 175; Box 37:10 and Box 38:23, SW Papers.

28. Box 4:6; Box 23:2; Box 37:9, 91, 127; PB 26:9; PB 30:97, 143, 379; PB 31:451, SW Papers.

29. Box 35:17; Box 36:4; Box 21:4, 5; Box 4:6, 17; Box 30:346, SW Papers.

30. *Town Topics*, 55 (April 12, 1906): 13; Andy Logan, "That Was New York," *New Yorker*, August 14, 1965, pp. 37 ff.; Robert R. Rowe, "Mann of Town Topics," *American Mercury*, 8 (1926): 271–80; Box 13:7; Box 21:17; PB 30:135, SW Papers; William d'Alton Mann, *Fads and Fancies of Representative Americans* (New York, 1905), pp. 56–57. Amélie Rives, the former wife of J. A. Chanler, wrote a play, *The Fear Market*, based on Colonel Mann, which was produced in 1916.

31. PB 3:412, 412a, 413, 424; PB 4:135; PB 13:397, 399; PB 21:403; PB 24:407; SW to D. H. King, Jr., October 13, 1899, PB 23:247; Box 39:9; Box 23:1, SW Papers; Frames 289–90, 302–3, SW Coll.

32. Box 4:7; Box 34:1; Box 12:9; Box 37:6; Box 40:10; Box 42:4, 5; PB 26:413; PB 23:99, 135; PB 24:453; PB 27:217; PB 28:354, SW Papers.

33. PB 25:215; PB 26:105; Box 40:6; Box 28:9; PB 31:71, 94, 460; PB 34:420; Box 38:2; PB 24:402, 384; Box 36:20; PB 21:324; PB 29:68, 148; PB 28:282, 382; Box 6:5; Box 8:7, 9; Box 7:6; Box 41:18; Box 49:8, SW Papers. For his art objects, White also rented covered storage space on the roof of the Mohawk Building and in various warehouses—in 1899 at 525 West Twenty-third Street, in 1903 on the ground floor at 542 West Twenty-second Street, and in 1903–4 on the top floor of 530 West Twenty-second Street. He also kept things at Eugene Glaenzer's at 540 West Twenty-first Street, for which he had designed a building extension. His largest storage area, however, was at 114–120 West Thirteenth Street.

34. SW to ASG, January 29, 1899, PB 21:418.

CHAPTER 20
The Great Houses

1. See Paul R. Baker, *Richard Morris Hunt* (Cambridge, Mass., 1980), pp. 334–35 and *passim*.

20. The Great Houses

2. See Richard Guy Wilson, *et al.*, *The American Renaissance, 1876–1917* (New York, 1979), esp. Part I.

3. Among the several large houses that White designed but are not discussed in this chapter were those for Robert Garrett, Baltimore (1884–87, 1892–93); Pierre Lorillard, Jr., Tuxedo Park, N.Y. (1887–91); Prescott Hall Butler and William D. Guthrie, New York (1895–97); George L. Williams, Buffalo (1895–99); Thomas Nelson Page, Washington, D.C. (1896–97); Levi P. Morton, New York (1896–98); Henry B. Hollins, New York (1899–1901); William C. Whitney, Westbury, N.Y. (1900–1902); and Benjamin W. Arnold, Albany (1901–5).

4. *Newport Mercury*, August 12, 1893, p. 1; Leland M. Roth, *The Architecture of McKim, Mead & White, 1870–1920: A Building List* (New York, 1978), p. 97.

5. *Chicago Tribune*, February 2, 1896, Scrapbook, 1894–1904, p. 151, MMW; Barr Ferree, *American Estates and Gardens* (New York, 1904), p. 362.

6. Scrapbook, 1892–94, p. 95, MMW.

7. H. Van Buren Magonigle, "A Half-Century of Architecture: A Biographical Review," *Pencil Points*, 15 (March 1934): 117.

8. Ophir Hall, Misc., M-7, MMW; Box 17:4, SW Papers; 2073:1095, 1098, 1099, 1129, 1136, 1052–53, Saarinen Papers; Merrill Folsom, *Great American Mansions and Their Stories* (New York, 1963), p. 222. In 1949 Manhattanville College of the Sacred Heart purchased the mansion and surrounding acreage, converting the library into a chapel and erecting new academic buildings on the grounds. Corporation offices were later built on other parts of the former Reid property.

9. In the late 1930s the Mills mansion was donated to New York State and became a historic site open to the public.

10. PB 19:395 and PB 32:22, SW Papers; *Town Topics*, 20 (July 5, 1888): 8; *New York Herald Tribune*, February 21, 1941, p. 29.

11. See J. Walton Ferguson, *Rosecliff* (Newport, 1977), *passim*; Rosecliff is now owned by the Preservation Society of Newport County and is open to the public. The movie "The Great Gatsby" was filmed in part at Rosecliff.

12. Ferguson, *Rosecliff;* Barr Ferree, "Rosecliff," *American Homes & Gardens*, 2 (March 1906): 155–60.

13. PB 24:59–61 and Box 42:1, SW Papers.

14. "Court and Pool Building at 'Ferncliff,'" *Architectural Record*, 18 (July 1905): 20–26; PB 33:438, SW Papers.

15. Lawrence Wodehouse, "Stanford White and the Mackays: A Case Study in Architect–Client Relationships," *Winterthur Portfolio*, 11 (1976): 287–88; Mackay, 263, MMW; Box 41:9 and Box 14:14,

445

SW Papers; Lawrence Wodehouse, *White of McKim, Mead & White* (New York, 1988), pp. 33–42.

16. P. de W., "The Founding of an American Estate: Harbor Hill," *Town and Country*, 57 (August 16, 1902): 10–14.

17. "Saunterings," *Town Topics*, 46 (November 21, 1901): 5, and 53 (January 19, 1905): 5.

18. During World War II Harbor Hill was used as a radar station. In 1947 the palatial dwelling was demolished, and a few years later the estate was sold and divided up. Of White's works, only the gatehouse and water tower survive. White also worked on a hunting lodge for the Mackays at High Point, North Carolina. 2073:807, Saarinen Papers. The Mackays' daughter Ellin, born at Harbor Hill in 1903, became the wife of Irving Berlin, the songwriter, in 1926.

19. *New York Times*, travel section, September 14, 1975, pp. 1, 16. Theodate Pope married John W. Riddle, but the couple had no children. After their deaths the Pope house was left to a private trust, to be maintained as the Hill-Stead Museum.

20. John A. Gade, "Long Island Country Places, Designed by McKim, Mead & White: II. 'The Orchard' at Southampton," *House and Garden*, 3 (March 1903): 117–26; *New York Times*, May 6, 1962, real estate section, p. 1. The Orchard for some years was owned by Charles E. Merrill, a broker, who willed it to Amherst College. It was later used as a boys school. In the mid-1980s it was converted into twenty-nine condominium units.

21. PB 11:169; PB 35:75, 146; Box 22:8; PB LGW:15, 20, SW Papers; 2072:850, 948, and 2073:499, 505–7, Saarinen Papers; Cheney, Old Mixed Files 34 and 596, MMW.

22. In the early 1920s the Robb house was transformed into the Advertising Club of New York. In the late 1970s the building was converted into cooperative apartments.

23. "The King Model Dwellings" (New York, 1891), Reel 50, no. 677, *American Architectural Books*, Avery Library, Columbia University. SW designed low-cost workers' houses for power companies at Niagara Falls, N.Y., and at Roanoke Rapids, N.C. See Leland M. Roth, *McKim, Mead & White, Architects* (New York, 1983), pp. 140–43, 206–8.

24. PB 22:257 and PB 30:311, SW Papers; *New-York Tribune*, April 15, 1900, Scrapbook, 1894–1904, p. 118, MMW; Charles Coleman to SW, September 27, 1900, Frames 140–41, SW Coll; William T. Partridge, "Recollections Concerning Charles Follen McKim," unpublished ms., Ware Coll, Avery Library, Columbia University.

25. H. W. Poor to SW, March 15, 1901, Frame 421, SW Coll; quoted in Charles Baldwin, *Stanford White* (New York, 1931), p. 271.

26. Fanny M. Clarke to SW, Easter Sunday [1902], Box 40:10, SW Papers; T. B. Clarke to SW, April 11, 1902, M-3, Misc., MMW.

27. C. D. Gibson to CFM, September 10, 1892, Gibson, Misc., M-9, MMW.

28. SW to C. T. Barney, November 16, 1901, Scrapbook XIII, Cain Coll, Avery Library, Columbia University; PB 24:123–24, 207, SW Papers.

29. Box 40:5, SW Papers.

30. Albert Stevens Crockett, *Peacocks on Parade* (New York, 1931; reprinted, 1975), p. 152; SW to R. W. Patterson, February 16, 1901, Cain Scrapbook, 13:18, Rare Books Coll, Avery Library, Columbia University; Roth, *McKim, Mead & White*, p. 261.

31. Quoted in Allen Churchill, *The Upper Crust* (New York, 1970), p. 199.

32. Joseph Pulitzer to SW, July 25, 1896, SW, Misc., M-3, MMW; Roth, *McKim, Mead & White*, pp. 259–61; PB 12:201, SW Papers.

33. J. Pulitzer to SW, April 11 [1900], quoted in W. A. Swanberg, *Pulitzer* (New York, 1967), p. 280; SW to J. Pulitzer, November 27 and December 28, 1900, Pulitzer, Misc. 15, MMW.

34. SW to Mrs. Pulitzer, February 13, 1902, Pulitzer, Misc. 15, MMW.

35. WRM to W. C. Sabine, April 14 and November 16, 1903, Pulitzer, Misc. 15, MMW; Swanberg, *Pulitzer*, pp. 313–14; Allen Churchill, *Park Row* (New York, 1958), pp. 177–78.

36. Box 28:2, 3, 4, 8; Box 49:6, 11, SW Papers; Frames 693–94, 779 ff., 782–83, SW Coll.

37. W. A. Swanberg, *Whitney Father, Whitney Heiress* (New York, 1980); Wesley Towner, *The Elegant Auctioneers* (London, 1971), p. 178.

38. Scrapbook, 1887–1901, p. 219, MMW; *New York Times,* February 18, 1900, Scrapbook, 1894–1904, p. 258, MMW; *New York Herald,* May 22, 1904, Frame 719, Florence Levy Coll, NYHS; W. C. Whitney, Misc., M-9, MMW.

39. W. C. Whitney, Misc., M-9, MMW; *New York Times,* January 5, 1901, p. 3; *Town Topics,* 45 (January 10, 1901): 2, and 50 (December 24, 1903): 1; Scrapbook, 1894–1904, p. 250, MMW.

40. SW to J. H. Smith, May 30, 1904, PB 31:126, SW Papers.

41. PB 18:184, 186, and PB 19:332, 334, SW Papers; Frame 696, SW Coll; H. P. Whitney, Misc. M-9, and Old Mixed File 566, MMW.

42. PB 11:429, 479; PB 22:334; PB 23:21, 28, 156, 243, 346; PB 19:243; and PB 21:10, 233, SW Papers.

43. Box 14:19, SW Papers; P. Whitney, W-504 (I), MMW.

44. *New York Times*, May 1, 1949, real estate section, p. 1.

45. P. Whitney, W-505 (I) and 506 (IV), MMW.

46. *Town Topics*, 49 (January 30, 1902): 4 and 49 (February 13, 1902): 1.

47. PB 28:37–38, 56, SW Papers; Rita Lydig to SW, September 21, 1905, 2073:797, Saarinen Papers.

CHAPTER 21
Evelyn

1. Glenn Brown, *Memories 1860–1930* (Washington, D.C., 1931), p. 29; Elizabeth D. Lehr, *"King Lehr" and the Gilded Age* (Philadelphia, 1935), p. 202; Box 27:20; Box 23:1, 4; Box 38:16; PB 32:254; PB 20:270, SW Papers.

2. Box 6:1; PB 25:311; PB 26:233; PB 27:271, 280, 295, 305; Box 21:12, 17, SW Papers.

3. PB 35:281; PB 32:175; PB 28:83, 120, 172, 207, 232, 239, 307; PB 30: 49, 118; PB 33: 135, 90; Box 20:8, 9, 14; Box 14:16, 19; Box 41:6, 12; Box 22:13; Box 32:2; Box 23:10, SW Papers.

4. *Town Topics*, 43 (January 11, 1900): 1 and 46 (September 5, 1901): 4; *New York World*, February 8, 1903, Met. sec., p. 1; PB 28:78, SW Papers.

5. Worthington C. Ford, ed., *The Letters of Henry Adams*, vol. 2 (Boston, 1930), p. 312; *Town Topics*, 45 (March 7, 1901): 5.

6. PB 25:224, 229, 247, 249, SW Papers.

7. CFM to WRM, August 23, 1901, McKim Papers, LC. For the many important turn-of-the-century projects directed by CFM, see Leland Roth, *McKim, Mead & White, Architects* (New York, 1983), pp. 245–334.

8. SW to BW, July 25, 1901, PB 26:2–5, and PB 26:63, 65, SW Papers; CFM to WRM, August 23, 1901, McKim Papers, LC; *Town Topics*, 48 (November 27, 1902): 5; *New York Times*, January 19, 1902, p. 2.

9. Evelyn Nesbit, *Prodigal Days: The Untold Story* (New York, 1934) pp. 3, 17. The following paragraphs are in part based on *Prodigal Days*, the second version of Nesbit's autobiography. Her earlier autobiography, written under the name Evelyn Thaw, *The Story of My Life* (London, 1914), is more critical of SW than the second version. The two autobiographies and newspaper-reported trial testimony differ on some minor details.

10. *Broadway Magazine*, March 16, 1901, and *New York Standard*, September 7, 1901, in Robinson Locke Scrapbook, 358, Theater Coll, NYPL; Nesbit, *Prodigal Days*, p. 17.

11. Nesbit, *Prodigal Days*, pp. 25–28; Thaw, *Story*, p. 52.

12. Nesbit, *Prodigal Days*, pp. 28–30; *New York Times*, February 8, 1907, p. 2, and February 22, 1907, p. 2; Thaw, *Story*, p. 66.

13. Nesbit, *Prodigal Days*, pp. 8–25.

14. PB 26:84, 136, SW Papers; Nesbit, *Prodigal Days*, pp. 31–34.

15. Nesbit, *Prodigal Days*, pp. 37–38; Thaw, *Story*, p. 66.

16. Nesbit, *Prodigal Days*, pp. 40, 41; Thaw, *Story*, p. 71; *New York Times*, February 8, 1907, pp. 2–3.

17. Nesbit, *Prodigal Days*, pp. 41–42, 206.

18. William Travers Jerome and Francis P. Garvan, *The Famous Hypothetical Question in the Trial of Harry K. Thaw for the Murder of Stanford White* (New York, 1907), p. 6.

19. Nesbit, *Prodigal Days*, pp. 43–46; *New York Times*, February 22, 1907, p. 2, and February 23, 1907, pp. 1–2; Box 18:14 and PB 27:31, 221, SW Papers.

20. 2072:918–19, 934–38, Saarinen Papers; PB 26:83, SW Papers; Nesbit, *Prodigal Days*, pp. 47, 50–51, 200.

21. *New York World*, April 14, 1907, p. 18, in Robinson Locke Scrapbook, 359, Theater Coll, NYPL.

22. M. Grau to SW, February 11, 1902, Prince Henry, Misc., M-10, and *New York Commercial Advertiser*, February 19, 1902, Scrapbook, 1887–1901, p. 293, MMW; PB 26:292A; SW Papers; 2073:236, Saarinen Papers.

23. PB 26:338, 341, 342, 353, 393, and Box 21:20, SW Papers; CFM to WRM, April 2, 1902, McKim Papers, LC.

24. Box 21:20, 22, SW Papers.

25. Nesbit, *Prodigal Days*, pp. 57–58, 61; *New York Herald*, May 4, 1902, Robinson Locke Scrapbook, 358, Theater Coll, NYPL.

26. PB 27:4, 15, 112, 120; WRM to SW, June 27, 1902, Box 20:5; and SW to Siebrecht & Son, August 1, 1902, PB 27:91, SW Papers.

27. For this paragraph and the next two, see Nesbit, *Prodigal Days*, pp. 60–67; *New York Times*, February 9, 1907, p. 2; John Kobler, *Damned in Paradise: The Life of John Barrymore* (New York, 1977), pp. 72–73.

28. Nesbit, *Prodigal Days*, pp. 68, 73–74; *New York Times*, February 26, 1907, p. 2; *Enquirer*, November 27, 1903, Robinson Locke Scrapbook, 358, p. 16, Theater Coll, NYPL; Donald Hayne, ed.,

The Autobiography of Cecil De Mille (Englewood Cliffs, N.J., 1959), p. 34.

29. Box 20:11 and PB 28:449, SW Papers; Nesbit, *Prodigal Days*, pp. 68, 73–74.

30. Nesbit, *Prodigal Days*, pp. 6–7, 52; *New York Times*, February 8, 1907, p. 3.

31. *New-York Tribune*, July 14, 1906, p. 1; *New York Times*, July 14, 1906, p. 3, and August 4, 1906, p. 12; Nesbit, *Prodigal Days*, p. 193.

32. Nesbit, *Prodigal Days*, pp. 76, 78, 81; *New York Times*, February 9, 1907, p. 2.

33. Nesbit, *Prodigal Days*, pp. 81 ff., 96, 100–105.

34. Nesbit, *Prodigal Days*, pp. 106, 108, 109–13, 117, 286, and *passim*; Richard O'Connor, *Courtroom Warrior* (Boston, 1963), p. 228; *New York Times*, January 25, 1907, p. 2, and February 26, 1907, pp. 1–2.

35. SW to J. B. McDonald, May 21, 1903, PB 28:477, and PB 29:162, 164, 203, SW Papers.

36. CFM to SW, June 30 [1903], Box 20:5; SW to CFM, August 28, 1903, PB 29:230, and SW to CFM, August 19, 1903, PB 29:203; 29:191, 296, 259, SW Papers.

37. Nesbit, *Prodigal Days*, pp. 121, 122–25; Howe & Hummel Statement of Account, Box 37:15, SW Papers; *New York Times*, February 26, 1907, p. 1, and March 19, 1907, p. 2. For some years, White had known Abe Hummel, who, in partnership with William F. Howe, was one of the most famous criminal lawyers of the day. It is probable that in early 1902 White used Hummel's services to pay off one of the girls—possibly Edna Goodrich—who claimed that he had taken advantage of her. See Richard H. Rovere, *Howe & Hummel: Their True and Scandalous History* (New York, 1947), and Nesbit, *Prodigal Days*, p. 50.

38. Nesbit, *Prodigal Days*, p. 128; Box 18:14, SW Papers.

39. *New York Times*, February 7, 1907, pp. 1–2, February 22, 1907, p. 2, and February 23, 1907, p. 2; Jerome and Garvan, *Famous Hypothetical Question*, p. 12.

CHAPTER 22

"More like Hell than Anything Else"

1. Evelyn Nesbit to Sam Shubert, December 25, 1903, Shubert Archives; *New York Times*, February 22, 1907, p. 1; Robinson Locke Scrapbook, 358, Theater Coll, NYPL.

2. *New York Times*, July 9, 1906, p. 1, July 23, 1906, p. 14, and

February 27, 1907, p. 1; Evelyn Nesbit, *Prodigal Days; the Untold Story* (New York, 1934), pp. xii, 89, 131, 135, 138, 143; PB 32:119, SW Papers.

3. Box 38:22, 23; Box 7:11, 12, 13; PB 24:261, 374; Box 21:20, 21; and SW to R. M. White, May 8, 1905, PB 33:132, SW Papers.

4. SW to LGW, October 6, 1903, PB 29:317–18; PB 28:303; PB 31:264, 271; LGW to SW, April 27 [1905], Box 14:21, SW Papers.

5. SW to Charles Deering, December 31, 1903, PB 30:78; PB 32:8, 34; PB 30:164, SW Papers; Saint-Gaudens, Misc., M-11, MMW; 2073:799, Saarinen Papers; *American Art News,* November 5, 1904, p. 2.

6. PB 30:133, 160, 161–164; Box 22:6; PB 31:116, 159, 186, 278, 296; Box 14:8; PB 32:35, SW Papers.

7. SW to C. T. Barney, March 30, 1903, Box 21:20; PB 29:53, SW Papers.

8. Box 21:20; PB 28:456–67, 459, 465–68, 488; Box 49:4, SW Papers.

9. Box 18:16; PB 28:295–96, 499; PB 33:251; Box 20:7; Box 21:20; Box 32:7, SW Papers. From the surviving records it is impossible to establish full particulars of White's finances, assignments, and property settlements. Some documents indicate that the same items were assigned as collateral for different loans.

10. Box 3:5, 6, 9; Box 18:4, 5, 12; Box 23:4, 5, 12, 13, 15; Box 27:19; Box 49:3; E. L. Smith to SW, December 31, 1903, Box 7:3, also 4, 5, 6, SW Papers.

11. Box 14:3, 7, 16; Box 6:10; PB 30:170; Box 41:3, 11, 12, 13; Box 35:18; PB 31:74–75, SW Papers.

12. SW to H. A. C. Taylor, May 30, 1903, Box 15:6; PB 29:46–47; PB 28:428, SW Papers.

13. PB 31:85–86, 98–99; Box 32:7; Box 18:6; PB 32:351–53, SW Papers.

14. PB 32:219, 283, 329, 505; Box 22:10; Box 6:4; Box 14:13, 21; Box 32:2, 219; Box 14:27, SW Papers.

15. Charles Moore, *The Life and Times of Charles Follen McKim* (Boston, 1929), pp. 242–46; CFM to R. W. Gilder, January 11, 1905, Gilder Papers, NYPL.

16. Box 6:20; Box 32:7; SW to Dr. W. West, January 5, 1905, PB 32:256, 318, SW Papers.

17. PB 32:207, 257; PB 33:132; SW to BSW, April 24, 1905, PB 33:85, SW Papers.

18. *Town Topics,* 53 (February 2, 1905): 2, and 54 (September 14, 1905): 1; *New York Times,* February 1, 1905, p. 9.

19. SW to Col. O. H. Payne, February 1, 1905, PB 32:318–19, SW Papers; SW to BSW, February 7, 1905, Robert White Coll.

20. *New York Times,* July 27, 1959, p. 25.

21. Box 18:1, 11, 13; PB 30:409, 421; PB 31:75; Box 6:4, 10; Box 14:11, 12; Box 22: 8, 11, SW Papers.

22. PB 32:7; Box 15:4; and SW to A. Cheney, February 17, 1905, PB 32:406, SW Papers; *New York Times,* February 14, 1905, p. 10.

23. CFM to BW, March 17, 1905, in Moore, *McKim,* pp. 295–96; SW to LGW, February 14, 1905, PB 32:381, and SW to J. Breese, February 14, 1905, PB 32:387–88, SW Papers.

24. Louis Ehrich to SW, February 19, 1905, Box 32:1, and Arnold Gluck and Hyman Rand to SW, n.d., Box 32:4, SW Papers.

25. SW to Lewis Cass Ledyard, April 29, 1905, PB 33:105–7; Assignments, April 29, 1905, PB 28: inserts following 499; PB 28:487; Box 15:9; Box 18:16, SW Papers.

26. Partnership Dissolution, May 1, 1905, PB 28: following 499. Note profit and salary allocations, MMW Journal, 1901–6, and Cash Book, 1904–9, MMW. William N. Kendall, Burt L. Fenner, and William S. Richardson were admitted as partners in the firm as of January 1, 1906. The partnership dissolution obviously seemed necessary to White as well as to his partners.

27. *New-York Tribune,* July 10, 1906, p. 2.

28. Nesbit, *Prodigal Days,* pp. xi, 142, 146, 147, 151, 154, 166, 170 Robinson Locke Scrapbook, 358, p. 39, Theater Coll, NYPL.

29. *New York Times,* July 1, 1906, pp. 1–2.

30. Ibid.

31. *New York Times,* July 1, 1906, p. 2, and June 30, 1906, p. 1 *New-York Tribune,* July 1, 1906, p. 4, and July 10, 1906, p. 2.

32. New York *Evening Mail,* June 28, 1906, p. 31; Heywood C. Brou and Margaret Leech, *Anthony Comstock: Roundsman of the Lor* (New York, 1927), pp. 247–48; *New York Times,* July 1, 1906, p 2.

33. *New York Times,* July 3, 1906, p. 3, and July 4, 1906, p. 1.

34. *Town Topics,* 53 (June 1, 1905): 1; *New York Times,* July 1, 190€ p. 2; PB 33:138, 294, and Box 41:9, SW Papers. White indicate that this was his first trip abroad in four years, but no evidenc has been located for a 1901 trip.

35. PB 33:252, 253, 287, 294, 478, SW Papers; Worthington C. For ed., *The Letters of Henry Adams,* vol. 2 (Boston, 1938), p. 46(Payne Whitney, 503 (II), MMW; MacMonnies 2d interview,

19, D. M. Lockman Papers, Ms. Div., NYHS; SW to ASG, September 5, 1905, PB 33:294, SW Papers.

36. WRM to Bernard Green September 25, 1905; WRM to W. P. Garrison, September 5, 1905; CFM to W. P. Garrison, August 14, 1905; CFM to BW, October 25, 1905, McKim Papers, LC; Box 41:7, 9, and PB 33:484, SW Papers.

37. CFM to BW, June 15, 1905, McKim Papers, LC; Box 14:21, SW Papers.

38. CFM to Margaret McKim, January 4, 1906, and April 13, 1906, McKim Papers, LC.

39. PB 33:479, 404, 485; Box 35:15; PB 34:149, 156, 328, 361, 493; PB 35:111, 122, SW Papers.

40. The original photograph was published in *World's Work,* 9 (November 1904): 5439, and probably was taken in 1902 or 1903. The later version, reproduced herein, may have been done in 1904. I am indebted to Barbara L. Michaels for this information.

41. PB 34:494–95 and PB 35:30, SW Papers.

CHAPTER 23
The Sidewalks of New York

1. See Robert A. M. Stern, Gregory Gilmartin, and John Massengate, *New York 1900: Metropolitan Architecture and Urbanism, 1890– 1915* (New York, 1983), pp. 11–25 and *passim.*

2. Montgomery Schuyler, "A 'Modern Classic,' " *Architectural Record,* 15 (May 1904): 431–44; Lawrence Grant White, *Sketches and Designs by Stanford White* (New York, 1920), p. 27; Knickerbocker Trust Co., Misc. M-16, MMW. Ten additional stories were added to the structure in 1919–20; in 1962 the building was remodeled, and all traces of the original exterior were removed. See Edward B. Watson, *New York Then and Now* (New York, 1976), p. 57.

3. David Lowe, *Three St. Bartholomew's: An Architectural History of a Church* (New York, 1983), pp. 6–10; Russell Sturgis, "A Fine Work of American Architectural Sculpture," *Architectural Record,* 15 (April 1904): 292–311; PB 30:178–79, SW Papers; SW to Cass Gilbert, October 29, 1902, Gilbert Papers, LC.

4. St. Bartholomew's Church, S 596 (II, IV), MMW.

5. SW to J. Gade, April 19, 1904, PB 30:423–25, SW Papers.

6. SW to J. Gade, April 19, 1904, PB 30:423–25, SW Papers; John S. Holbrook, "The Gorham Building," *New York Architect,* vol. 2, November 1908; Gordon S. Parker, "The Work of Three Great Architects," *World's Work,* 12 (October 1906): 8058; Alfred H.

Granger, *Charles Follen McKim: A Study of His Life and Work* (Boston, 1913), p. 38; Box 41:3, SW Papers.

7. *The New Home of Tiffany & Company* (New York, 1905), p. 14.

8. *New Home of Tiffany & Company;* Henry Olmsted, Jr., "Essentials and Costs of a Modern Jewelry Store: The Tiffany Building," *Architecture*, 12 (August 15, 1905): 126.

9. A. C. David, " 'The Finest Store in the World,' " *Architectural Record*, 17 (January 1950): 45, 48, 43.

10. PB 9:14, SW Papers; Robert W. de Forest to SW, January 8, 1904, Madison Square Presbyterian Church, Misc., M-20, MMW; Aline Saarinen, "The Splendid World of Stanford White, *Life*, 61 (September 16, 1966): 108; Charles Baldwin, *Stanford White* (New York, 1931), p. 234; John Jay Chapman, "McKim, Mead and White," *Vanity Fair*, 13 (September 1919): 37.

11. *Dedicatory Service of the Madison Square Presbyterian Church*, October 14, 1906 (New York, 1906), p. 29.

12. Madison Square Presbyterian Church, Misc. M-20, MMW.

13. J. M. Bowles, "Business Buildings Made Beautiful," *World's Work*, 9 (November 1904): 5507.

14. Leland M. Roth, *McKim, Mead & White, Architects* (New York, 1983), pp. 316–17.

15. F. W. MacMonnies to SW, December 8, 1902, Slocum, Misc. M-8, MMW.

16. SW to F. W. MacMonnies, November 22, 1898, PB 21:106, SW Papers; Prison Ship Martyrs Monument Misc., M-12, MMW.

17. J. G. Bennett to SW, May 27, 1905, and misc. corres., Bennett Park, Misc. M-7, MMW; SW to Epernay, September 4, 1896, PB 16:393, SW Papers.

CHAPTER 24
"I Could Love a Thousand Girls"

1. ASG to SW, Sept. 8, 1905, Frame 486, SW Coll.

2. ASG to C. L. Freer, Reel 7:54, 62, 79, SG Papers; ASG to SW May 7, 1906, Frame 428, SW Coll.

3. ASG to SW, May 5 and 7, 1906, Frames 492 and 428, SW Coll. SW to ASG, May 12, 1906, PB 35:58, SW Papers.

4. Box 35:16, 63, SW Papers.

5. 5:15:126, 128, 144, McKim Papers, LC.

6. *New York Evening Mail*, June 26, 1906, p. 13; *New York Times*, August 6, 1906, p. 2.

7. *New-York Tribune*, July 1, 1906, p. 4; PB 33:130, 171, SW Papers.

8. PB 35:180–81, SW Papers.

9. Claire White interview, June 2, 1983, and Laura Chanler White interview, November 19, 1983.

10. ASG to C. L. Freer, July 21, 1906, Reel 7:54, 79, SG Papers; *New-York Tribune*, July 1, 1906, p. 4. Laura Chanler White recalled years later that Larry White and Leroy King had been with her all that evening and that Larry and his friend had not dined with SW at Martin's, as the newspapers reported (e.g., *New York Times*, June 26, 1906, p. 1) and as Larry White testified at the first trial. She recalled that Larry and Leroy had gone with her and a sister for sandwiches to a friend's house in New York and that later they put her on the train at Hoboken for Geneseo, N.Y. (Note in the Edward Albee ms. now in possession of Mrs. Cynthia Jay). If Laura's account is true, Larry testified inaccurately in order to keep Laura Chanler's name out of the newspapers and to protect her reputation.

11. Evelyn Nesbit, *Prodigal Days: the Untold Story* (New York, 1934), pp. 172–73; *New York Times*, February 12, 1907, p. 1, and March 13, 1907, p. 2; *Town Topics*, 55 (June 28, 1906): 10.

12. *New-York Tribune* and *New York Times*, June 26, 1906, p. 1, for this and the following paragraphs; *Town Topics*, 56 (August 2, 1906): 12; Nesbit, *Prodigal Days*, pp. 174–76; *New York Herald*, July 10, 1906, p. 4.

13. *New York Times*, March 13, 1907, p. 2.

14. Albert Payson Terhune, *To the Best of My Memory* (New York, 1930), pp. 216–17.

15. *New York Times*, June 26, 1906, p. 1, and June 27, 1906, p. 3.

16. 2072:712, Saarinen Papers.

17. Box 8:13, SW Papers.

18. *New-York Tribune*, June 27, 1906, p. 2, and June 29, 1906, p. 2; *New York Times*, June 29, 1906, p. 2; 2072:694, Saarinen Papers. The death mask is now in the Prints and Drawings Collection of the Avery Library, Columbia University.

19. A. W. Drake to R. W. Gilder, June 29, 1906, Gilder Papers, NYPL; *New-York Tribune*, June 29, 1906, p. 2; *New York Times*, June 29, 1906, p. 2.

20. Andy Logan, "That Was New York; The Palace of Delight," *New Yorker*, 41 (February 27, 1965): 41; *Vanity Fair*, July 13, 1906, in Robinson Locke Scrapbook, 358, p. 67; *New-York Tribune*, June 27, 1906, p. 2, and June 28, 1906, p. 1.

21. *New York Times*, July 1, 1906, p. 2; *Town Topics*, 55 (June 28, 1906), p. 1; Henry White to CFM, July 6, 1906, McKim Papers, LC.

22. 5:15:203–4, 206, 238, McKim Papers, LC; *New York Times*, July 4, 1906, p. 1; *New York Herald*, July 2, 1906, p. 5. The McKim,

Mead & White logo pictured a ship under sail with the motto *Vogue la Galère* ("Let the Ship Sail on").

23. C. Gilbert to CFM, June 26, 1906, McKim–Maloney Papers, NYPL; Janet Scudder to CFM, June 1906, McKim Papers, LC; quoted in Charles Baldwin, *Stanford White* (New York, 1931), p. 306; Roger E. Fry to CFM, June 30, 1906, McKim–Maloney Papers, NYPL; Glenn Brown, *Memories 1860–1903* (Washington, D.C., 1931), p. 30.

24. Resolution, July 24, 1906, *American Institute of Architects Quarterly Bulletin,* 7 (July 1916): 108.

25. *New-York Tribune,* July 9, 1906, p. 1, and July 10, 1906, p. 2; *New York Times,* July 8, 1906, p. 2., and July 14, 1906, p. 3.

26. C. D. Gibson to CFM, July 14, 1906, McKim Papers, LC; R. H. Davis to CFM, July 9, 1906, McKim–Maloney Papers, NYPL; CFM to R. H. Davis and CFM to ASG, July 11, 1906, McKim Papers, LC.

27. Richard Harding Davis, "Stanford White," *Collier's Magazine,* 37 (August 4, 1906): 17; Gerald Langford, *The Richard Harding Davis Years* (New York, 1961), p. 255.

28. ASG to Glenn Brown, July 30, 1906, in Brown, *Memories,* p. 31; Homer Saint-Gaudens, ed., *The Reminiscences of Augustus Saint-Gaudens* (New York, 1913), vol. 2, p. 252.

29. Richard Watson Gilder, "Stanford White," *American Institute of Architects Quarterly Bulletin,* 7 (July 1906): 104.

30. "The Death of Stanford White," *American Art News,* 4 (July 14, 1906): 2; "The Lounger," *The Critic,* 49 (August 1906): 104; "Stanford White, 1853–1906," *Architectural Review,* 13 (July 1906): 101.

31. "The Artist in Our World," *Nation,* 83 (July 1906): 5–6, and *American Architect and Building News,* 90 (July 7, 1906): 6.

32. *New York Times,* July 12, 1906, p. 2.

33. CFM to Margaret McKim, August 4, 1906, McKim Papers, LC BW to "Sister," September 13, 1906, Frames 702–5, SW Coll CFM to ASG, August 10, August 24, and November 8, 1906, Reel 10:45–50, 76–77; C. D. Gibson to ASG, October 8, 1906, Reel 7:372; BW to ASG, September 25, 1906, Reel 13:861 ff., SG Papers

CHAPTER 25
Aftermath

1. Richard O'Connor, *Courtroom Warrior: The Combative Career c William Travers Jerome* (Boston, 1963), pp. 113, 196–97.

2. Evelyn Nesbit, *Prodigal Days; the Untold Story* (New York, 1934)

p. 188. The literature on the SW murder and the trial of Harry Thaw includes Frederick A. Mackenzie, ed., *The Trial of Harry Thaw* (London, 1928), a summary of trial testimony, with backgrounds of the case; Benjamin H. Atwell, *The Great Harry Thaw Case; or, A Woman's Sacrifice* (Chicago, 1907), the Thaws' family-sponsored work; Frederick Lewis Collins, *Glamorous Sinners* (New York, 1932); Charles Samuels, *The Girl in the Red Velvet Swing* (New York, 1953); Gerald Langford, *The Murder of Stanford White* (Indianapolis, 1962); O'Connor, *Courtroom Warrior*, pp. 171–242; and Michael Macdonald Mooney, *Evelyn Nesbit and Stanford White: Love and Death in the Gilded Age* (New York, 1976). See also the first autobiography by Evelyn Nesbit Thaw, *The Story of My Life* (London, 1914), and the fuller second version by Evelyn Nesbit, *Prodigal Days*, and also the curious publications, Mary Copley Thaw, *The Secret Unveiled* (White Plains, 1909), and Harry K. Thaw, *The Traitor: Being the Untampered With, Unrevised Account of the Trial and All That Led to It* (Philadelphia, 1926), the latter an often incoherent diatribe, providing good evidence of Thaw's mental condition two decades after the crime. Concerning the three Thaw plays, see the Robinson Locke Scrapbook, 359, p. 21, Theater Coll, NYPL. At least two early films, *The Thaw–White Tragedy* (American Mutoscope and Biograph Co., 1906) and *The Unwritten Law: A Thrilling Drama Based on the Thaw-White Case* (Sigmund Lubin, 1907, and probably commissioned by the Thaw family), relate to the White murder.

3. Irvin S. Cobb, *Exit Laughing* (Indianapolis, 1941), pp. 199, 227; Nesbit, *Prodigal Days*, pp. 189–91. Nesbit stressed in her second autobiography that Thaw's act on June 25, 1906, was premeditated (p. xi), and she felt that District Attorney Jerome did not use all the evidence he could have used. She thought he was trying to get "a conviction and an insanity verdict at the same time" (p. 205) and could get neither.

4. *New York Times*, February 5, 1907, p. 2, and February 6, 1907, pp. 1–3.

5. *New York Times*, February 8, 1907, p. 2, and February 9, 1907, p. 2.

6. *New York Times*, February 12, 1907, pp. 1–2, February 15, 1907, p. 3, and March 3, 1907, p. 2.

7. *New York Times*, February 15, 1907, p. 2, February 16, 1907, p. 2, February 19, 1907, p. 2, and March 27, 1907, p. 2; Philadelphia *Telegraph*, December 28, 1907, Robinson Locke Scrapbook, 359, p. 28, Theater Coll, NYPL.

8. *New York Times*, February 19, 1907, pp. 1–2; New York Attorney

General's Office, People of the State of New York on the Relation of Mary C. Thaw against John W. Russell [1912], pp. 37–43.

9. *New York Times,* February 20, 1907, pp. 1–2, February 21, 1907, p. 2, and February 22, 1907, p. 2; Mackenzie, ed., *Trial,* p. 133.

10. *New York Times,* February 22, 1907, p. 2.

11. *New York Times,* March 20, 1907, pp. 1–2.

12. *New York Times,* April 5, 1907, pp. 1–2.

13. *New York Times,* April 9, 1907, pp. 1–2, and April 10, 1907, pp. 1–2; quoted in Mackenzie, ed., *Trial,* p. 19.

14. *New York Times,* April 11, 1907, pp. 1–2.

15. *New York Times,* April 13, 1907, p. 1.

16. *New York Times,* January 7, 1908, p. 1, and January 11, 1908, p. 5.

17. *New York Times,* February 2, 1908, p. 1.

18. *New York Times,* April 21, 1907, pt. 2, p. 15, and February 9, 1908, pt. 2, p. 7.

19. Mackenzie, ed., *Trial,* p. 257.

20. *New York Times,* March 29, 1907, p. 1; *Town Topics,* 57 (March 28, 1907): 6.

21. *Illustrated Catalogue of the Artistic Furnishings and Interior Decorations of the Residence No. 121 East Twenty-first Street* (New York, 1907); *New York Herald,* April 7, 1907, and *New York Times,* April 7, 1907, in Florence Levy Papers, D45:716, AAA.

22. *Old and Modern Paintings Belonging to the Estate of the Late Stanford White* (New York, 1907); *Illustrated Catalogue of Valuable Artistic Property Belonging to the Late Stanford White* (New York, 1907); *Catalogue of Antique Marbles and Stone Mantels* (New York, 1907); *Art News,* 32 (March 17, 1934): 14; Mary F. Roberts, "A Sentimental Approach to Antiques: Stanford White Collection," *Arts and Decoration,* 41 (May 1934); 60.

23. *New York Times,* October 23, 1907, pp. 1–2, November 15, 1907 pp. 1–2, and November 16, 1906, pp. 1–2; *Town Topics,* 58 (October 31, 1907): 4, (November 7, 1907): 1, and (November 21, 1907) 6, 11.

24. 2073:217–18, Saarinen Papers; CFM to WRM, June 18 [1908] McKim, Misc. M-3, MMW; *New York Times,* September 15, 1909 p. 1.

25. *American Architect and Building News,* 96 (December 29, 1909) 281. McKim's net estate was valued at $268,666, including a $6,00(note from the estate of Stanford White, *New York Times,* May 10 1910, p. 9.

26. Nesbit, *Prodigal Days*, pp. 206, 216, and *passim*; *New York Times*, January 19, 1967, pp. 1, 31; *Boston Post*, August 9, 1914, Robinson Locke Scrapbook, 360, p. 22, Theater Coll, NYPL.

27. Nesbit, *Prodigal Days*, pp. 307, 314–15; *New York Journal American*, September 14, 1955, p. 28.

28. Scrapbook, 1906–11, p. 315, MMW; *Memorial Meeting in Honor of the Late Stanford White* (New York, n.d.); E. E. Brown to L. G. White, December 21, 1921, Memorial Doors, Misc. M-18, MMW; PB LGW:42, SW Papers.

29. See the brilliant, impressionistic estimates of SW by John Jay Chapman, "McKim, Mead and White; Especially Concerning the Influence of Stanford White on American Architecture," *Vanity Fair*, 13 (September 1919): 37, 102, 104, and Aline Saarinen, "The Splendid World of Stanford White," *Life*, 61 (September 16, 1966): 87–108.

Acknowledgments

For assistance with the preparation of this book, over many years, I am particularly indebted to members of the White family, especially Robert and Claire White, Cynthia White Jay, Frederick Lawrence Peter White, Ann White Buttrick, and the late Laura Chanler White. As with previous work, I am indebted to the staff of the Avery Architectural and Fine Arts Library at Columbia University, including, in particular, Janet Parks, Angela Giral, Herbert Mitchell, Harriet Stratis, Janet Baldwin, Ruri Yampolsky, William O'Malley, Katherine Martinez, Kitty Chibnik, and Bela Baron. At the New-York Historical Society, always courteous, efficient, and helpful were Wendy Shadwell, Thomas Jennings, Helena Zinkham, Steve Novak, and Catherine Schmidt, whom I wish to thank. Of great help at the Archives of American Art were Garnett McCoy, Karin Weiss, and Sheila Hoban, and, at the Library of Congress, Charles Kelly and William Dorman. John Dryfhout, Curator of the Saint-Gaudens National Historic Site, has been most cooperative and helpful. For their criticisms, I am indebted to the several readers, including Ormonde de Kay, Elizabeth Kemp Baker, Sarah Bradford Landau, and Mosette Broderick. The crafting of the work was greatly aided by my editor, Joyce Seltzer, whose comments, criticisms, and complaints forced me to rethink and rework many parts of the manuscript.

I should also like to express my gratitude for their assistance to the following persons: Kenneth Ames, Terry Ariano, Sherry Birk, Gladys Bolhouse, Sara Holmes Boutelle, Tom Brennan, the late Alan Burnham, Ann M. Burton, Arlene Carmen, Mary Ann Chach, Richard Champlin, Ken Cobb, Lynne Davuono, Willard R. Espy, Thomas Frusciano, the late Rosamonde Gilder, Brendan Gill, Christopher Gray, Ronald J. Grele, Barbara Haws, Nancy Johnson, Pamela D. Lehrer, William Long, Peter

461

Acknowledgments

J. McGurk III, Brooks McNamara, Pat Mercer, Barbara L. Michaels, James E. Mooney, Monique Panaggio, Louis Rachow, Kenneth Rapp, Robert Schnare, Marianne Stolp, Daniel Syndacker, Edward Teitelman, Neville Thompson, Father Webster, Tony P. Wrenn, Bonnie Yockelson, and Andrew Zaremba.

For permission to quote from manuscript materials I wish to thank the following: Robert White and the White family: Stanford White Papers, Richard Grant White Collection, Lawrence Grant White Oral History, and White family manuscripts; Walker O. Cain: Egerton Swartwout, "An Architectural Decade"; Donald Harry Louchheim: Aline Saarinen Papers; American Institute of Architects Archives; Archives of the American Academy & Institute of Arts & Letters: Richard Watson Gilder Papers; The Archives of American Art; Avery Architectural and Fine Arts Library. Columbia University in the City of New York: Stanford White Papers, Ware Collection materials, Philip Sawyer Papers, Miscellaneous Collection materials, Cain Scrapbooks; Century Association Archives; Dartmouth College Library: The Papers of Augustus Saint-Gaudens; Library of Congress Manuscript Collection: Charles F. McKim Papers, Charles Moore Papers, Whitelaw Reid Papers, Augustus Saint-Gaudens Papers; The New-York Historical Society: Stanford White Collection, Richard Grant White Collection, James H. Morse Diary, D. M. Lockman Papers; Richard Watson Gilder Papers, Rare Books and Manuscripts Division, The New York Public Library, Astor and Tilden Foundation; Malony Collection of McKim-Garrison Family Papers, Rare Books and Manuscripts Division, The New York Public Library, Astor, Lenox and Tilden Foundation; New York University Archives: Henry M. MacCracken Papers; Oral History Collection, Columbia University in the City of New York: Lawrence Grant White Oral History; Shubert Archives: Sam Shubert Papers; United States Military Academy Archives: Cullum Memorial Hall Records.

Illustration Credits

Richard Grant White; Alexina Mease White: Saarinen Papers, Archives of American Art, Smithsonian Institution

Stanford White, ca. 1875: Saarinen Papers, Archives of American Art, Smithsonian Institution

H. H. Richardson's office: Houghton Library, Harvard University, on deposit from Shepley Bulfinch Richardson and Abbott

Stanford White on rooftop: Saarinen Papers, Archives of American Art, Smithsonian Institution

57 Broadway Building: Museum of the City of New York

Newport (R.I.) Casino: Courtesy of the Preservation Society of Newport County

Narragansett Pier (R.I.) Casino: Harper's Weekly, August 27, 1887

Naumkeag: Courtesy of Naumkeag Museum, Prospect Hill, Stockbridge, MA. Property of the Trustees of Reservations

Tiffany House: Monograph of the Works of McKim, Mead & White, 1879–1915

Augustus Saint-Gaudens (1878): Courtesy of Saint-Gaudens National Historic Site, Cornish, NH

Farragut Monument: Monograph

Watts Sherman House library; Kingscote dining room: Courtesy of the Preservation Society of Newport County

Stanford White before marriage; Bessie White in wedding dress: Courtesy of Cynthia Jay

Temporary Washington arch: Courtesy of The New-York Historical Society, New York

Washington Memorial Arch: New York University Archives

Madison Square Garden: Monograph

Garden arena, Venetian scene: Harper's Weekly, April 11, 1903, courtesy of the New York Life Insurance Company

Diana: Courtesy of the New York Life Insurance Company

Madison Square Garden decoration: Monograph

Illustration Credits

Saturday night at The Players Club: Harper's Weekly, February 12, 1890. Courtesy of The New-York Historical Society, New York

Century Association: Monograph

Metropolitan Club; Colony Club: Monograph

New York Herald Building: Courtesy of The New-York Historical Society, New York

Bowery Savings Bank: The McKim, Mead, & White Collection. Museum of the City of New York.

Sherry's Hotel; Sherry's ballroom: Monograph

Fifth Avenue at Twenty-second Street in 1892, Columbian arch: Courtesy of The New-York Historical Society, New York

Metropolitan Opera House ball: Harper's Weekly, January 18, 1890. Courtesy of The New-York Historical Society, New York

Stanford White in formal dress: Culver Pictures

Box Hill, early alteration: The McKim, Mead & White Collection. Museum of the City of New York

On the beach: Courtesy of Cynthia Jay

Alexina White and Lawrence Grant White: Avery Architectural and Fine Arts Library. Columbia University in the City of New York

McKim, Mead, White, and Larry White: Saarinen Papers, Archives of American Art, Smithsonian Institution

Villard Houses: Museum of the City of New York

New York University Gould Library: New York University Archives

Cullum Memorial Hall, USMA; Battle Monument with Victory, USMA: U.S. Military Academy Archives

The Whites' townhouse; drawing room: The McKim, Mead & White Collection. Museum of the City of New York

Dining room and music room; picture gallery: The McKim, Mead & White Collection. Museum of the City of New York

Stanford and Bessie in costume: Courtesy of Cynthia Jay

Stanford White in 1901: Courtesy of The New-York Historical Society, New York

Evelyn Nesbit with pitcher: Photo by Gertrude Käsebier. Saarinen Papers, Archives of American Art, Smithsonian Institution

Knickerbocker Trust Company: Monograph

Rosecliff: Courtesy of the Preservation Society of Newport County

Harbor Hill; stairhall, Harbor Hill: Monograph

Gorham Building: Monograph

St. Bartholomew's Church porch: Courtesy of The New-York Historical Society, New York

Tiffany Building: Monograph

Madison Square Presbyterian Church: Courtesy Metropolitan Insurance Companies

Evelyn Nesbit: Courtesy Shubert Archive

Harry Thaw: AP/Wide World Photos

Illustration Credits

James Hazen Hyde ball: The Byron Collection. Museum of the City of New York

White portrait by Gertrude Käsebier: The McKim, Mead & White Collection. Museum of the City of New York

Sketch of the murder: New York Herald, June 26, 1906

Memorial doors: New York University Archives

Index

467

Index

Index

Breese, James Lawrence, 249, 250, 254, 271, 273, 279–80, 283, 287, 290, 302–303, 339, 341, 347, 375, 376
  house of ("The Orchard," Southampton, N.Y.), 302–303
Brennan, Alfred, 241
Brewster, Julia, 240
Broadway & Seventh Avenue Railroad Company, 216
Brook, The (N.Y.C.), 145–46
Brookline, Mass., 24, 25
Brooklyn Bridge, 358
Brooklyn Museum (Institute of Arts and Sciences), 196, 216, 230, 364
Brooks, Rev. Phillips, 22, 191
  monument to (Boston), 191–92, 196
Brooks Brothers, 317
Brown, Elmer, 398
Brown, Glenn, 27, 81, 82, 232, 378
Bruges, Belgium, 52, 53
Brunswick Hotel (N.Y.C.), 150
Brush, George de Forest, 266, 273, 393
Brussels, Belgium, 53
Bryan, Thomas Jefferson, Collection, 3
Bryan, William Jennings, 254
Bryant Park Studio Building (N.Y.C.), 290
Buffalo State Hospital, 22, 23
Bunce, Gedney, 54, 55, 102
Bunker, Dennis, 241
Burnham, Daniel, 190, 209, 233, 320, 353, 355, 358
Butler, Cornelia Smith, 92–93, 121, 175, 248, 269, 344
Butler, Prescott Hall, 92, 93, 94, 98, 102, 103, 129, 137, 175, 248, 257, 261, 269, 270, 320, 340, 353
  houses of (N.Y.C.), 445n.3; (St. James, N.Y.), 93

Cabell Hall (Univ. of Va.), 227
Cable Building (N.Y.C.), 216
Cabus, Alexander G., 239
Cady, J. Cleveland, 248
Cairo, Egypt, 177–78
Calder, A. Stirling, 429n.10
Cambridge, Mass., 8
Cameron, Elizabeth, 130, 188, 320
Cancelleria, Palazzo (Rome), 106, 107

Candy, Capt. Henry Augustus, 66
Carbon Studio (N.Y.C.), 279, 283, 287
Carmencita, 130, 249
Carnegie, Andrew, 171, 331, 374
Carnegie, George, 331, 385
Carrère, John M., 80, 276
Casey, Anais, 34, 411n.10
Casey, Henry, 34, 55
Castle Garden (N.Y.C.), 2
Central Park (N.Y.C.), 176, 358
Century Association (N.Y.C.), 10, 123, 126, 134, 139–41, 142, 144, 145, 146, 152, 215, 279, 282, 304, 398, 399
Century Company, 239, 376
Cesnola, Louis de, 233
Chamberlain, Julia, 178
Chanler, Alida, 255
Chanler, Amélie Rives (Princess Troubetzkoy), 255, 256, 257
Chanler, Elizabeth, 251
Chanler, John Armstrong (Archie), 251, 255–57, 270, 273
Chanler, John Winthrop, 255
Chanler, Laura (Mrs. Lawrence Grant White), 371, 372, 396, 455n.10
Chanler, Lewis, 257
Chanler, Margaret, 251
Chanler, Margaret Terry, 371
Chanler, Robert Winthrop, 178
Chanler, William Astor, 270, 376
Chanler, Winthrop Astor, 256, 257, 371
Charleston, S.C., 121–22
Chartres, France, 55–56
Chapin, Chester W., 185
Chapin, Deacon Samuel, 185–86
Chase, William Merritt, 39, 98, 99, 134, 163, 175, 241, 393
Chavannes, Puvis de, 125
Cheever, J. D., 289
Cheney, Anne, 303
Cheney, Harry, 303
Cheney, James, 27, 303
Cheney, Julie Ann, 303
Cheney, Louise, 303
Cheney, Robert, 303
Cheney, Rush, 27, 303
Cheney Building (Hartford, Conn.), 27, 232, 303

469

Index

Chicago, Ill., 179–80, 185, 189–90, 282
Chicago fair: see World's Columbian Exposition
Chihuahua, Mexico, 96
Choate, Joseph H., 64, 73, 81, 193, 395–96
   house of (Stockbridge, Mass.), 73–74, 76
Choate, Mabel, 416*n*.25
Chronicles of Gotham, 11
Cisco, John J., 62
City College of New York, 208
Civil War, 10, 291
Clark, Davida, 189
Clarke, Thomas B., 176, 236, 290, 306, 322, 376
   house of (N.Y.C.), 306
Clemens, Samuel: see Twain, Mark
Cleveland, Grover, 137, 169, 180, 310
Clifford, Jack, 397
Cobb, Irvin S., 386
Coleman, Caryl, 137
Coleman, Charles C., 235, 269, 270, 278, 305
Collins, Alfred Q., 240
Collins, Joan, 397
Colman, Samuel, 72
Colonial revival style, 36, 39–40, 70, 219
Colony Club (N.Y.C.), 146, 147–48
Columbia University, 205, 218, 219
Columbian Fountain (Chicago fair), 195
Columbian Quadricentennial, 175–76, 180, 204
Comstock, Alexander, 165
Comstock, Anthony, 351, 388, 391
Connecticut State Capitol (Hartford), 25
Consiglio, Palazzo del (Verona, Italy), 213
Constantinople, 101
Contrexeville Spa, France, 251, 252
Cooper, James Fenimore, 11
Cooper, Peter, 165, 190
   memorial to (N.Y.C.), 190, 191, 196
Cooper Union (N.Y.C.), 190, 193
Corbett, James J., 175
Cornell Medical School (N.Y.C.), 313
Cornell University, 18
Cornish, N.H., 188–89, 274, 339, 369, 370, 394

Cortelyou, G. B., 388
Cortissoz, Royal, 85, 89, 231, 275, 398
Cowdin, John Elliot, 250
Cox, Kenyon, 25, 179
Cram, Goodhue & Ferguson, 222
Croton Distributing Reservoir (N.Y.C.), 1, 174
Crystal Palace (N.Y.C.), 1, 2, 405*n*.1
Cullum, George W., 220
Cullum Memorial Hall (West Point), 220–21, 222
Custom House (N.Y.C.), 9, 15, 16

Daly, Augustin, 136
Darwin, Charles, 15
Daumet, Pierre-Gérôme-Honoré, 20
Davis, Richard Harding, 177–78, 253, 379–80
De Koven, Reginald, 137, 248
De Mille, Cecil B., 329
De Mille, Mathilda Beatrice, 329, 388
De Wolfe, Elsie, 148, 249, 333
Deering, Charles, 339
Delano, Sara, 34–35
Delmas, Delphin Michael, 386, 387, 390
Delmonico's
   ballroom, 131
   restaurant, 3, 65, 138, 156, 223, 372
Dennis, Ruth: see St. Denis, Ruth
Depression of 1893, 143, 216
Detroit Bicentennial Memorial, 192, 278, 366
Dewey, George, 233
   memorial arch to (N.Y.C.), 192
Dewing, Thomas, 86, 87, 99, 113, 132, 138, 179, 192, 239, 244–45, 265, 266, 273, 274–75, 278, 289, 393, 398
Diana, statue of (Madison Square Garden), 158–59, 160–61, 179, 186, 195, 244, 251, 266, 313, 323, 427*nn*.23, 24, 25
Dijon, France, 49
Donald, Rev. E. Winchester, 110, 111
Douai, France, 52
Dowling, Judge Victor J., 390
Drake, A. W., 376
Drayton, J. Coleman, house (N.Y.C.), 74
Drew, John, 137

470

Index

471

Index

Gilbert, Cass, 80, 88–89, 103, 104, 108, 153, 275, 378, 395

Gilded Age, xi, 11, 105, 112, 154, 183, 231, 252, 253, 291–92, 315, 381–82, 398–400

Gilder, Helena de Kay, 38, 43–44, 55, 171

Gilder, Richard Watson, 38–39, 55, 65, 87, 98, 99, 137, 169, 170, 171, 239, 380–81, 411n.17

Gilmore, Patrick, 150

Giralda (Seville, Spain), 157

Girl from Dixie, 334, 337

Girl in the Red Velvet Swing, 397

Glaenzer, Eugene, 236–37, 444n.33

Gleason, John B., 386–87

Goelet, Ogden, 112

Goelet, Robert, 72, 112, 113, 123, 142, 164, 262, 273, 277

house of ("Southside," Newport, R.I.), 72, 107, 112

mausoleum for (Bronx, N.Y.), 113

schooner cup for, 113

Goelet, Mrs. Robert, 165

Goelet Brothers Office Building (N.Y.C.), 112–13

Goelet Building (N.Y.C.), 112, 113, 216

Goldsmith, Goldwin, 201–202

Goodhue, Bertram G., 360

Goodrich, Edna, 321, 450n.37

Gorham Building (N.Y.C.), 361–62, 367, 398, 399

Gosse, Edmund, 76

Gothic revival style, 71, 216, 222

Gould, Jay, 218

Gould, Joseph, 267

Gould Memorial Library (N.Y.C.), 218, 219, 226

Grace Church (N.Y.C.), 2

Gramercy Park (N.Y.C.), 129, 135, 136, 137, 265, 266

Grand Army Plaza (Brooklyn, N.Y.), 195

Grand Central Terminal (N.Y.C.), 150, 365

Granger, Farley, 397

Grant, Hugh, 171

Greater New York Detective Agency, 350–52, 372

Guthrie, William D., house (N.Y.C.), 445n.3

Haik, Joseph, 178

Hale, Nathan, statue (N.Y.C.), 194

Hall of Fame (N.Y.C.), 218, 219

Halladay, Ben, 294

Hampden County Courthouse (Springfield, Mass.), 22, 23

Hampton Court, 33

Hanlon, Lizzie, 375

Harbor Hill: see Mackay, Clarence, house of

Harlem River Drive (N.Y.C.), 232–33

Harmonie Club (N.Y.C.), 146–47

Harnett, Charles, 202

Harriman, Edward H., 271

Harriman, J. Borden, 147

Harrison, Benjamin, 168

Hartmann, Sadakichi, 239, 240–41

Hartshorn, Stewart, 68

Harvard Club (N.Y.C.), 134

Harvard University, 19, 20, 92, 269, 352, 383

Haskell, Llewellyn, monument (West Orange, N.J.), 415n.13

Hassam, Childe, 239, 393

Hastings, Helen Benedict, 147, 277

Hastings, Thomas, 80, 141, 175, 208, 275–77, 280, 398

Havana Tobacco Co., showroom (N.Y.C.), 363

Hawthorne, Julian, 13, 15, 33

Hawthorne, Nathaniel, 13

Hay, John, 109, 313

Haymarket dance hall (N.Y.C.), 319

Hearst, William Randolph, 393

Hecker, Frank, 278

Henry, Prince, of Prussia, 326–27

Henry Poor & Company, 271, 289

Hernandez, Figueroa, 235

Herter Brothers, 276

Herter mansion (N.Y.C.), 199, 211

Hewitt, Peter Cooper, 165, 250, 376

Hewlett, Monroe, 84

Higginson, Henry Lee, 171

Hill, James J., 271

Hoffman House (N.Y.C.), 150

Index

Index

McKenna, John E., 350, 352
McKim, Annie Bigelow, 36, 39, 40, 41, 44, 60
McKim, Charles Follen
  and American Academy in Rome, 212, 252, 320, 344, 353, 396
  and American Institute of Architects, 232, 333, 334, 395
  childhood of, 20
  death of, 395
  designs of, 40, 67, 68, 82, 106, 114, 115, 129, 134, 142, 161, 175, 179, 184, 196, 212, 216, 218, 230, 244, 251, 263, 293, 338, 353
  editorial work by, 36
  education of, 20, 153
  estate of, 458n.25
  health of, 76–77, 114, 203, 252, 260, 333, 353, 354, 370, 395
  marriages of, 36, 40–41, 76–77, 114–15
  memorial service for, 395–96
  as partner, ix, 35, 57, 60–62, 65, 85, 94, 140, 152, 160, 177, 200, 201, 203, 211, 215, 226, 269, 324, 327, 334, 340, 347, 348, 349, 370, 375, 376
  personality and character of, 81–83, 202, 203, 204, 215, 378, 379
  residences of, 260, 343, 352
  in Richardson's office, 19–23
  social life of, 87, 89, 92, 93, 98, 99, 103, 128, 207, 233, 249, 250, 258, 273, 277, 365, 377–78
  travels of, 39, 44, 45–52, 70, 252, 262, 320, 339, 359, 382–83
McKim, Julia Amory Appleton, 114–15
McKim, Lucy, 106
McKim, Margaret, 40, 260, 343, 353, 375, 395
McKim, Mead & Bigelow, 40, 60
McKim, Mead & White, 57, 60–61, 65, 66, 69, 74, 76, 79–89, 105, 110, 112, 114, 115, 116, 117, 125, 138, 139, 141, 142, 145, 149, 151, 152, 165, 171, 176, 199–210, 211, 213, 215, 216, 220, 221, 222, 223, 229, 239, 258, 276, 292, 295, 296, 322, 324,

McKim, Mead & White cont.
  326, 339, 341, 342, 343, 348–49, 355, 375, 382, 393, 395, 396, 399, 440n.23
McKinley, William, 254, 255
McNeil, Herman A., 429n.10
Mead, Larkin G., 35, 240, 396
Mead, William Rutherford, ix, 35, 39, 40, 41, 60, 61, 70, 80–81, 83, 85, 86, 89, 91, 99, 114, 115, 151, 152, 175, 200, 201, 202, 206, 207, 212, 213, 223, 225, 229, 250, 258, 269, 273, 293, 296, 313, 320, 328, 333, 339, 340, 344, 348, 353, 370, 376, 395, 396
Mease, Charles Bruton, 6
Mease, Charles Graham, 120
Mease, Sarah Graham, 6
Mechanics Laboratory Building (Univ. of Va.), 227
Melba, Nellie, 248, 283
Merchants Exchange (N.Y.C.), 2
Metcalf, Willard, 250, 266, 363
Metropolitan Club (N.Y.C.), 134, 142–44, 146, 211, 243, 249, 399
Metropolitan Fair (N.Y.C.), 10
Metropolitan Life Insurance Company Building (N.Y.C.), 364
Metropolitan Museum of Art (N.Y.C.), 125, 196, 233, 241, 243, 244, 306, 364, 393, 396
Metropolitan Opera Company, 345
Metropolitan Opera House (N.Y.C.), 112, 138, 171, 248–49, 282, 326–27
Milland, Ray, 397
Millet, Francis (Frank), 25, 75, 134
Mills, Darius Ogden, 108, 294, 296
Mills, Ogden, 296, 297
  house of (Staatsburg, N.Y.), 296
Mills, Robert, 224
Mills, Ruth Livingston, 296
Mitchell, Dr. S. Weir, 256
Mohawk Building (N.Y.C.), 199ff., 208, 211, 290, 444n.33
Moore, Charles, 320
Moret, France, 49
Morgan, Anne, 147
Morgan, Commodore E. D., house ("Beacon Rock," Newport, R.I.), 293

Index

Index

Index

Index

479

Index

Index

Index

White, Stanford *cont.*
as partner, 57, 60–61, 76, 79–80, 83–84, 85, 88–89, 100, 115, 116, 199–210, 211, 254–55, 341, 348–49
personality of, 14, 16, 18, 27, 29, 33, 83, 84, 85, 88, 92, 98, 99, 113, 167–68, 201, 202, 203, 204, 205, 240, 243, 259, 274, 280, 281, 282, 283, 285, 288, 322, 380, 381, 389, 399
portraits of, 51, 354
religious interests of, 23–24, 111
residences of, 31, 91–92, 117, 121, 126–28, 128–29, 263–67, 286, 289, 303–304, 327–28, 341, 343, 348, 352, 375, 393; *see also* Box Hill; White, Stanford, hideaways of
signature of, 185
social life of, 31, 34–37, 39–42, 73, 85, 87, 91, 94–95, 96, 128, 130–31, 133–48, 164, 175, 179–80, 184, 195, 207, 247–58, 259, 263, 273–90, 311, 319–35, 339–40, 343–44, 345–46, 365, 369–73, 379
surveillance of, 350–52, 372
training and apprenticeship of, 18–29, 42–43, 408*n*.2
travels of, 23, 39, 45–57, 59, 70, 95–97, 100–103, 121–22, 124–25, 131, 177–80, 259–60, 269–70, 327, 344, 345, 352–53
trial (Thaw) testimony about, 385–92
wedding of, 99–100
women, relationships with and attitudes toward, 53, 57, 77, 125, 244–45, 254, 273, 274, 278, 279–81, 282–85, 286–87, 288–90, 292–93, 300–301, 321–35, 337–38, 350, 351, 377, 379, 398
writings of, 174, 228
hite Collection, 126, 348, 401

White House (Washington, D.C.), 344, 387
White Star Lines pavilion (Chicago fair), 179
Whitman, Walt, 118
Whitney, Dorothy, 310
Whitney, Edith, 310, 311
Whitney, Flora Payne, 310
Whitney, Gertrude Vanderbilt, 240, 312
Whitney, Harry Payne, 310, 312, 313, 341
Whitney, Helen Hay, 313, 314, 352
Whitney, Pauline, 310
Whitney, Payne, 310, 313, 352
house of (N.Y.C.), 313–14
Whitney, William C., 124, 235, 269, 306, 309–12, 313, 341, 394
houses of (N.Y.C.), 309–12; (Westbury, N.Y.), 445*n*.3
monument for (Bronx, N.Y.), 310
Whittemore, John Howard, 228–29
Wild Rose, 328
Williams, George L., house (Buffalo, N.Y.), 445*n*.3
Winans, Ross, 75
house of (Baltimore), 75, 88
Women's Christian Temperance Union, 160
Words and Their Uses, 12, 118
World's Columbian Exposition, Chicago, 160–61, 175, 179–80, 212, 340
Worthington, H. P., 32
Wyandank, 93
Wright, Frank Lloyd, x
Wynne, James, 10

Yacht Club, New York, 277–78, 293
York, Edward P., 80

Zemmerle, Otto, 318
Zucker, Alfred, 218